1916

THE LONG REVOLUTION

- Edited by -

Gabriel Doherty and Dermot Keogh

MERCIER PRESS

WHAT YOU NEED TO READ

Mercier Press
Douglas Village, Cork
www.mercierpress.ie

Trade enquiries to Columba Mercier Distribution,
55a Spruce Avenue, Stillorgan Industrial Park, Blackrock, Dublin

ISBN: 978 1 85635 545 2

10 9 8 7 6 5 4 3 2 1

Mercier Press receives financial assistance from
the Arts Council/An Chomhairle Ealaíon

Printed and bound in Ireland by Colour Books

1916

THE LONG REVOLUTION

To Gillian

CONTENTS

ACKNOWLEDGEMENTS

The editors wish to thank the following individuals for their unstinting assistance in the preparations for the original conference, and during the preparation of this volume:

First, and foremost, the speakers at the original conference and other contributors to this volume: President Mary McAleese, Dr Garret FitzGerald, Professor Keith Jeffery, Dr Jérôme aan de Wiel, Mr. Gerry White, Dr Brendan O'Shea, Rosemary Cullen Owens, the Hon. Mr Justice Adrian Hardiman, Dr Owen McGee, Dr Brian P. Murphy, Professor D.G. Boyce, Professor Francis Carroll, Dr Séamus Murphy, Rory O'Dwyer and Dr Michael Wheatley. Thanks are also due to Dr Margaret MacCurtain who acted as a sessional chair at the conference.

From University College Cork: President Gerry Wrixon and Vice President Michael O'Sullivan; Catherine Fairtlough (President's office); Brian Dunnion, Dara O'Shea and Marie McSweeney (Marketing office); Tony Perrott (Audio-Visual services); Martin Hayes (Computer centre); Sheila Maguire and the General service operatives (General services); Alanah Carey Bates and staff (Glucksman gallery); Geraldine O'Sullivan and staff (Campbells catering); Professor David Cox, Marian Dineen (College of Arts, Celtic Studies and Social Sciences); Professor Matthew MacNamara (Department of French).

From the library, University College Cork: the Librarian, John Fitz-Gerald, and his staff, particularly those members who have worked in the 'Special Collections' section over the years, notably Helen Davis, Peadar Cranitch, Anne Cronin, Teresina Flynn, Catherine Horgan, Cronán Ó Doibhlín, and Mary Lombard.

From the Department of History, University College Cork: the secretaries, Charlotte Holland, Deirdre O'Sullivan, Geraldine McAllister, Norma Buckley, Veronica Fraser, Margaret Clayton, and Sheila Cunneen; postgraduate assistants, John Dennehy, Nicholas Harrington, Sarah Fahy, Tim O'Regan, John O'Donovan, David Coleman; staff members, Dr Andrew McCarthy, Dr Mike Cosgrave, Dr Larry Geary, Dr Donal Ó Drisceoil, Dr Diarmuid Scully, Dr Damian Bracken, and Professor Donnchadh Ó Corráin.

From the archives of the Irish College in Rome: the Rector, Monsignor Liam Bergin; the Vice Rector, Fr Albert McDonnell; the archivist, Vera Orschel; secretarial staff, Andy Devane and Alison Mills.

From Military Archives, Cathal Brugha Barracks, Dublin: Commandant Victor Laing.

From the National Archives, Dublin: the Director, David Craig, and all his staff, most notably Catriona Crowe and Tom Quinlan.

From Áras an Uachtaráin: Maura Grant, Emer Grenville, and Pamela McDermott.

From the Department of the Taoiseach: John Kennedy, Cathal Hunter, Jerry Kelleher, and Colette Tuite Gallagher.

From the office of the lord mayor of Cork: Susan O'Flynn; from the office of Dr FitzGerald: Sharon Kelly; from the Courts Service: Jean Coyle; from Oxford University: Dr Kinch Hoekstra; from SIPTU: Manus O'Riordan.

From Mercier press: Brian Ronan, Clodagh Feehan, and – as always – Mary Feehan, for her outstanding professionalism.

We also wish to record our thanks to our families for their constant support – from the Keogh household, Anne, Aoife, Clare, Eoin and Niall; and from the Doherty household, Gillian and Méabh.

The conference was organised with financial assistance from the Conference Fund of the College of Arts, Celtic Studies and Social Sciences, University College Cork.

This volume has been produced with financial assistance from the Commemorations Initiatives Fund of the Department of the Taoiseach.

NOTE ON SPELLING

Given the important role played by the cultural nationalist movement in Ireland during the period covered by this volume, there are a number of individuals and institutions mentioned in it whose names have both Irish and English forms. In order to avoid confusion an attempt has been made in the text both to standardise spelling where more than one variation exists, and to utilise the most commonly used form in preference to any alternatives. To take but a few examples involving significant individuals, Pádraig Pearse was alternatively known as P.H. Pearse, Patrick Pearse, Pádraic Pearse, and Pádraig MacPiarais; Seán MacDermott was often referred to as Seán MacDiarmada; Éamonn Ceannt as Edward, or Ned, Kent; and Thomas MacDonagh as Tomás MacDonagh. Where possible, one form (sometimes Irish, sometimes English, sometimes a mixture of both, depending on usage) has been used – save, of course, in citations, where the original form has invariably been provided.

ABBREVIATIONS

AOH	Ancient Order of Hibernians
BBC	British Broadcasting Corporation
CC	Catholic Curate
CIÉ	Córas Iompair Éireann
CMA	Competent Military Authority
DAA	Drapers Assistants Association
DBC	Dublin Bakery Company
DMP	Dublin Metropolitan Police
DORA	Defence of the Realm Act
DORR	Defence of the Realm Regulations
FOIF	Friends of Irish Freedom
GAA	Gaelic Athletic Association
GPO	General Post Office
ILPTUC	Irish Labour Party and Trade Union Congress
INTO	Irish National Teachers' Organisation
IPP	Irish Parliamentary Party
IRA	Irish Republican Army
IRB	Irish Republican Brotherhood
ITGWU	Irish Transport and General Workers Union
ITUC	Irish Trades Union Congress
IWCA	Irish Women's Citizen's Association
IWFL	Irish Women's Franchise League
IWRL	Irish Women's Reform League
IWSF	Irish Women's Suffrage Federation
IWSLGA	Irish Women's Suffrage and Local Government Association
IWWU	Irish Women Workers Union
JCWSSW	Joint Committee of Women's Societies and Social Workers
KC	King's Counsel
MGR	Midland Great Railway
MP	Member of Parliament
MRIA	Member of the Royal Irish Academy
MWFL	Munster Women's Franchise League

NCR	North Circular Road
NUWGA	National University Women Graduates Association
PP	Parish Priest
RDS	Royal Dublin Society
RIC	Royal Irish Constabulary
RTÉ	Radio Teilifís Éireann
SIPTU	Services, Industrial, Professional and Technical Union
SMA	Special Military Area
TCD	Trinity College Dublin
UCD	University College Dublin
UIL	United Irish League
USA	United States of America
UVF	Ulster Volunteer Force
UWUC	Ulster Women's Unionist Council
WSPU	Women's Social and Political Union
YMCA	Young Men's Christian Association

LIST OF CONTRIBUTORS

D.G. Boyce is Professor Emeritus in the Department of Politics and International Relations, University of Wales Swansea.

Francis Carroll is Professor Emeritus of History at the University of Manitoba

Rosemary Cullen Owens lectures in Irish history in the Women's Education, Research and Resource Centre, School of Social Justice, University College Dublin.

Gabriel Doherty lectures in the Department of History, University College Cork.

Garret FitzGerald is Chancellor of the National University of Ireland.

Adrian Hardiman, MRIA, a history graduate of UCD, is a judge of the Supreme Court.

Keith Jeffery is Professor of British History at Queen's University Belfast.

Dermot Keogh is Professor of History, and head of the Department of History, University College Cork.

Mary McAleese is President of Ireland.

Owen McGee is the author of *The IRB: the Irish Republican Brotherhood, from the Land League to Sinn Féin*, Four Courts, Dublin, 2005, and is currently working on a biography of Arthur Griffith.

Brian P. Murphy OSB is a member of the Benedictine community at Glenstal abbey, Co. Limerick.

Séamus Murphy lectures in philosophy at the Milltown Institute, Dublin. He is a Jesuit.

Rory O'Dwyer lectures in the Department of History, University College Cork.

Brendan O'Shea is an author and historian whose specialised areas of interest include Irish history, the Balkans and the Middle East.

Michael Wheatley is a visiting research fellow at the Institute of Irish Studies, Queen's University Belfast.

Gerry White is an author and historian whose specialised areas of interest include the military history of Co. Cork, the War of Independence and the Civil War.

Jérôme aan de Wiel is Visiting Professor in the Department of History, University College Cork.

PREFACE

Garret FitzGerald

During the ninety years since the 1916 Rising so much has been written about that seminal event that a potential reader might be tempted to react sceptically to yet a further work on the subject. 'Is there any more to be said at this stage about the Rising?' he or she might be tempted to exclaim.

This book of historical essays triumphantly rebuts any such presumption – and indeed leaves enough issues for further research, analysis and debate to show that in history there is never a last word.

In the brief space permitted to me here I cannot attempt to review all of these essays, many of which deal with issues that, so far as I am aware, have not previously been addressed.

Amongst these is Adrian Hardiman's cogent exposé of the illegality of the post-Rising court martials which were established, he points out, under the Defence of the Realm Act, and thus were subject to law – rather than operating under martial law, which he quotes the Duke of Wellington as having said 'was neither more nor less than the will of the general who commands the army ... [which] means no law at all.'

Another such piece is that by Séamus Murphy on 'Easter ethics', which seeks to apply just war theory to the Rising. It is difficult to refute his basic thesis that the Rising failed to meet several key criteria of just war theory. But he goes on to give six grounds for believing that the Rising was ethically wrong, and several of these depend upon an assertion that the War of Independence that followed from the Rising was 'extraordinarily unnecessary, given that what the Treaty achieved was not that different from what the home rule legislation had achieved'. This is a remarkable statement upon which to base an argument about what he sees as the futility of the Irish struggle for independence. For home rule as enacted left Britain in control of peace and war for Ireland, with the British army remaining on Irish territory, and the levying of customs duties retained in British hands. Moreover, any Irish home rule government would have had very limited taxation powers, which would have precluded Ireland from setting its own corporate tax rate, as Northern Ireland is still precluded from doing, to the visible distress today of its business and political leaders.

Given the strategic importance of Ireland for Britain until the end of the Cold War, there is no reason to believe that Britain would have allowed a home rule Ireland to move peacefully to independence much before the end of the twentieth century – whereas the independent state won by the War of Independence, with its own Irish army replacing British forces on its territory, had secured unfettered sovereignty by 1931, and was free thereafter to evolve at its own pace, and without British opposition, into a republic outside the Commonwealth. Independence, moreover, gave the Irish state the power to develop its economy, in part at Britain's expense, by devising a competitive corporate tax system which played a key role in generating economic growth, eventually at three times Britain's own growth rate.

Séamus Murphy can legitimately argue a case against the morality of 1916 in 'just war' terms, and he can make a case that the price paid for independence, in terms of a seventy year legacy of sporadic violence, was a high one – but he weakens these arguments by attempting to minimise the huge difference between the independence secured in 1921 and what home rule would have offered.[1]

Owen McGee attempts to sort out the roles played in the organisation of the Rising on the one hand by key members of what became known as the 'Military Committee' – initially Pearse, Plunkett and Ceannt, later joined by Seán MacDermott, and later still by Connolly – and on the other by the IRB leaders Clarke and, once again, MacDermott. The evidence supports his thesis that a key role in preparing the Rising was in fact played by MacDermott, and that Pearse's emergence as the hero of the affair was largely fortuitous, reflecting his oratorical and PR skills – skills which, it appears, led Clarke to invite him first to speak at the O'Donovan Rossa funeral and then to read the Proclamation outside the GPO.

Both of these points would have been given even more weight had Dr McGee cited Denis McCullough's account of the circumstances in which he became president of the IRB; a significant event, no reference to which, curiously, is included in his contribution to this book.[2] This appointment appears to have been motivated by a desire by Clarke and MacDermott, respectively treasurer and secretary of that secret organisation, to have the IRB presidential role exercised a good physical distance away from Dublin, where they were preparing the Rising. In this connection it is important to understand that, together with the president, these two constituted the executive of the IRB – and that under its constitution the decision of any two of these three officials was binding on its members!

When in late 1915 McCullough told MacDermott that he intended to propose Pádraig Pearse as president of the IRB, to replace John Mulholland who had resigned, MacDermott dismissed the idea, saying: 'For the love of God, don't be stupid, don't be foolish!' 'Why? Isn't he an excellent man?' asked McCullough. 'We never could control that bloody fellow,' MacDermott replied – adding, in relation to the presidency of their organisation, that he and Clarke would 'get all that fixed'. Later he told McCullough that they had chosen him for the job, which he accepted under protest.

The fact that ultimately MacDermott rather than Clarke was responsible for the decision to ignore MacNeill's countermanding order also emerges from McCullough's account. For, having been given reason to believe that the Rising was imminent despite his not having been given the agreed fortnight's warning, McCullough hurried to Dublin, and finally tracked down a deliberately elusive MacDermott at Clarke's house two days later, on Easter Sunday night. On arrival there he asked Clarke what was going to happen. 'I declare to God,' Clarke replied, 'I know nothing more than you do. All I know is that I have orders to report to Daly on Sunday morning and have my arms and equipment ready.'

Owen McGee also brings out the very contingent nature of the declaration of a republic in the GPO – a declaration that later played such a key role in the Treaty 'split' and subsequent civil war. He explains that when 'Clarke announced in the GPO that a republic was going to be proclaimed, [he thought it necessary in order to impress world opinion] many Irish Volunteers were apparently surprised, presumably because, as members of the Irish-Ireland generation, most had never expressed any interest in republicanism, an ideology generally associated with the supposedly "priest-eating" republic of France' – which, apart from the anomalous case of Switzerland, was, of course, the only non-monarchy in Europe at that time.

The unfamiliarity, and indeed improbability, of the idea of a republic to most people at that time was reflected a day or two later in the easy assumption by Pearse and Plunkett – when discussing with my father, Desmond FitzGerald, the possible future of Ireland if Germany won the war – that our new state too would be a monarchy, perhaps under such a figure as the Kaiser's sixth son, Joachim, whom they believed to be unmarried, and thus available to marry a Catholic and bring his children up as Irish-speaking

Catholics.[3] (Understandably, perhaps, they were unaware that Joachim had in fact married a Protestant princess just six weeks earlier).

In his paper on 'The Catholic church, the Holy See and the 1916 Rising' Dermot Keogh, despite some reservations about Owen McGee's account in his recent book as to who was and was not an IRB member, believes that 'Dr McGee's general thesis has validity'.[4] In that contribution to this book Professor Keogh has deployed to good effect his familiarity with the historical relationship between the Holy See and Ireland, and with the role played by members of the Irish hierarchy, especially in the aftermath of the Rising, giving what must be the definitive account of these matters.

Another important paper challenges conventional wisdom on an important issue. Rory O'Dwyer, in his 'The golden jubilee of the 1916 Easter Rising', rejects the view promoted by Conor Cruise O'Brien in 1981 that the 1966 commemorations witnessed an 'explosion of nationalist sentiment' that produced 'the greatest orgy ever of the cult of the Rising'.[5] O'Dwyer notes that this opinion was echoed in 1994 in less dramatic terms by Dermot Keogh: 'What the celebrations did was to sensitise the Irish public and allow for greater uncritical receptivity to the message of physical force nationalism.'[6]

O'Dwyer concludes his comprehensive, and I think convincing, review of the events of that golden jubilee year with these words:

> The scale of the commemoration in 1966 is unlikely ever to be equalled, nor the level and quality of historical scholarship produced at the time to be exceeded. The high level of nationalist feeling in the period was generally harnessed in a very positive fashion, whereas republican militant sentiment was effectively curtailed. With much state ceremony the 'ghost' of 1916 was laid to rest in a dignified and respectful tribute. It was now time to move on.

Conor Cruise O'Brien, then at the peak of his radical period, used that occasion to accuse all Irish governments of betraying what he described as the revolutionary tradition of Tone, Pearse and Connolly, and he concluded correctly, and with apparent regret, that 'Connolly's Republic is as far off as ever'.[7]

For my part, at that time I was certainly very alive to the negative consequences of 1916. I wrote in the quarterly *Studies* about the subsequent death by violence of so many people: policemen, jurymen doing their duty, landlords, and a cabinet minister, Kevin O'Higgins, as well as many members of the IRA – not to speak of the demoralisation that followed these political divisions of the Civil War, the perpetuation of out-worn hatreds, as well as the inferiority complex, the destructive xenophobia and the inverted snobbery that had derived from the period of British rule – all of which under different and less violent circumstances might have gradually faded away in the decades after independence.

Consequently, I felt in 1966 that it was not too surprising that as the years had passed a reaction against 1916 had set in. Public attitudes to the Rising had become more critical, particularly as the propagandists for extreme nationalism had alienated the sympathies of many young people and had contributed to growing cynicism about the national movement of 1916 and the years that had followed. The case *for* 1916 had, I felt, been allowed to go by default, and so I went on to make what seemed to me, forty years ago, to be an already neglected case *in favour* of the Rising.

I argued that nothing that had happened over the fifty years since that event had proved – or even given strong grounds for believing – that the men of 1916 had been wrong in their conviction that in the years leading up to the Rising a sense of Irish national identity had been ebbing away, and needed a powerful catalyst to revive it. If they were right in this, I concluded, then anyone who believed that Ireland as an independent national entity had something to offer the world, and that the Irish people could do more for themselves and for their neighbours by self-reliant control of their own affairs, within whatever international framework might emerge in the increasingly inter-dependent world of the second half of the twentieth century, must acknowledged a debt to the leaders of 1916.

Recognising, of course, that others may legitimately take a different view of the balance of good and evil consequences of the Rising, I recall these views here because they demonstrate that at least to one observer in 1966 the situation we seemed to be facing at that time was not that the commemoration of the Rising risked reviving extreme nationalism but rather that already at that time there was a need to be reminded of the case to be made in favour of 1916.

Of course some may feel that the violence that broke out in Northern Ireland soon after that commemoration, and which lasted for almost thirty years thereafter, gave a measure of retrospective validation to Conor Cruise O'Brien's 1981 view of the golden jubilee. But retrospective views – being wise after the event – is not history; and on the facts of what happened during the golden jubilee that year I believe Rory O'Dwyer's analysis of those events stands up to scrutiny better than Conor Cruise O'Brien's.

A particular strength of this book is the inclusion of three papers on the neglected issue of 1916-related events external to Ireland. One of these – the paper by Keith Jeffery on 'The First World War and the Rising: mode, moment and memory' – does the very useful historical job of putting Pearse's militarism into its contemporary context, showing how much he was a man of his time in his 'sanguine vision', one that to us, several generations away from that Europe, seems so strange and off-putting. Jérôme aan de Wiel's 'Europe and the Irish crisis, 1900–17' sets 1916 in its wider European context, and raises the little discussed question of whether the concluding stages of the home rule crisis in July 1914 may, perhaps, have encouraged Germany to engage militarily with France as well as Russia in the belief that, at that moment, Britain was too racked by internal conflict to come to France's aid. Finally, Francis M. Carroll's 'America and the 1916 Rising' throws new light on the role that the Irish in the United States played in the preparations for that event.

The other essays throw new light upon such issues as the deep pre-Rising antipathy between the Irish party and those who were preparing that event, as well as upon the evolution of Irish party attitudes to that event during the rest of the year 1916; the role of the Ulster Volunteers in stimulating the foundation of the Volunteers in the south; that of censorship and propaganda in the run-up to and aftermath of the Rising; Constance Markievicz's triple feminist, labour and republican roles; the Easter mobilisation of the Volunteers in Cork; and an overview of the recent commemorations of the ninetieth anniversary of the Rising. The book also publishes for the first time the contemporary account written by Monsignor Michael Curran (the representative of Archbishop Walsh who was ill at the time) of his experiences and contacts during and just after the Rising.

Finally, President McAleese's remarks in Cork at the conference that gave rise to this book – an address that, somewhat surprisingly I felt as a member of the audience on that occasion, led to some controversy at the time – provides a fitting opening to this rich historical feast.

INTRODUCTION

Gabriel Doherty, Dermot Keogh

It is no coincidence that commemorations of major historical events usually incorporate both popular and academic elements. The process of reflection to which such anniversaries give rise provide a valuable public service, in that they stimulate open debate. In the popular sphere the forms in which such debates are conducted include public addresses, newspaper supplements, television and radio documentaries, symposia, and, in some cases, feature films that reach a mass, sometimes global, audience. At an academic level, too, such events are also a stimulus to activity. It is often the case that commemorations are the spur to the publication of invaluable collections of original source material, full scale biographies, or minutely researched monographs.

Commemorations also stimulate the production of edited volumes of scholarly essays, which subject the events or individuals under review to the findings of the latest historiography. Such publications serve as a convenient forum for the dissemination of academic debates, producing considered, competing and, at times, conflicting assessments by historians and others.[1] Ireland has been no exception to this rule, and over the last decade – which has seen, amongst many other events, commemorations of the Great Famine, the 1798 rebellion, and the Act of Union – worthy edited volumes on these and other topics have appeared on public bookshelves.[2]

Given that previous anniversaries of the Easter Rising have also been marked in this way it might reasonably be asked whether any useful purpose will be served by the addition of another tome to this small but highly distinguished corpus.[3]

Not surprisingly the editors of this volume believe the answer to this question is a resounding yes, the reasons for which relate to the circumstances of its origin. Its genesis is to be found in the conference 'The long revolution: the 1916 Rising in context', hosted by the Department of History, University College Cork, on 27–8 January 2006, to mark the ninetieth anniversary of the 1916 Easter Rising. The conference was generously supported by the Commemorations Initiatives Fund of the Department of the Taoiseach, the Conference Fund of the College of Arts, Celtic Studies and Social Sciences, University College Cork, and by the Department of History, University College Cork.

The event attracted a great deal of media attention, largely in response to the opening address, '1916 – a view from 2006', which was delivered by President McAleese. It is clear, such was the vigorous nature of this response, that the speech ranks among the most important to have been delivered on the subject of the state's origins by a sitting President in recent decades. For that reason the editors are delighted to be able to reproduce the text in full herein.

The conference, however, encompassed far more than the President's speech, central and significant though it undoubtedly was. The range of topics addressed by the other speakers – covering international, national and local dimensions of the Rising, and aspects of its intellectual, legal and symbolic legacy – and the informed question-and-answer sessions that followed each paper, ensured that the event was both an instructive and enjoyable affair. That certainly seems to have been the consensus of the 200-plus members of the public who were in attendance.

In answer, therefore, to the question as to the justification for the volume, there is an on-going, manifest public demand for the supply of reliable, informed opinion on the Rising. There is no doubt that the event continues to interest, fascinate, in some cases inspire and in others repel, large numbers of Irish people – witness the extraordinary degree of public engagement with, and involvement in, the various events held throughout the year to mark its ninetieth anniversary.

Given both the public level of interest in the Rising manifested over the past twelve months and its signal importance for the Irish polity, it is incumbent on those with a professional interest in the field to offer informed opinion in a timely, and appropriate, fashion. It is the view of the editors that the volume does just that.

Spanning the worlds of academia, politics, and the law; drawing on the expertise of both established scholars and their younger counterparts; building on previous research on the subject and utilising newly-available archival material, and revisiting old controversies and (perhaps) generating new ones, the volume will, we feel sure, make a worthy contribution to this much-discussed, and oft-misunderstood, event.

The work is made up of three intermingled elements, which vary greatly in length. The first comprises the eight papers delivered at the original conference, suitably revised to render them appropriate for publication. The second contains the seven papers that have been commissioned by the editors for inclusion in the volume. The third element is a single text. It contains relevant extracts from the Witness Statement given by Fr Michael Curran (secretary to William Walsh, archbishop of Dublin at the time of the Rising) to the Bureau of Military History, whose recently opened files have been one of the most welcome additions to the Irish historical scene in many years. It is included here as an exemplar of the new, previously under-utilised, or unreleased material upon which much of the analysis in the rest of the volume is based.

A word or two is in order regarding the title of the volume. It is the considered view of the editors that the events of 1916 can best be understood, neither as a starting point (though it clearly gave the republican cause a momentum that it had previously lacked) nor as a terminus (crucial though it undoubtedly was, for example in the subsequent collapse of the Irish party), but rather as a decisive turning point in the history of Ireland over the *longue durée*. Quite clearly the roots of the Rising went as deep as its harvest was abundant, and both the build-up to, and legacy of, the event are covered here.

The volume does not aspire to being a comprehensive history of the Rising, and there are obvious omissions. Of these the cause of Labour is the most significant (a consequence of the speed with which the volume has been produced, and the demands upon the prospective contributor's time, rather than wilful exclusion). Rather it seeks to identify and probe key interpretative issues associated with the event, with a view to stimulating debate in these (and other) areas in the build-up to the centenary of the Rising. As such the editors are confident that it will appeal to both popular and academic audiences.

1916 – A VIEW FROM 2006

Mary McAleese

How glad I am that I was not the mother of adult children in January 1916. Would my twenty year old son and his friends be among the tens of thousands in British uniform heading for the Somme, or would they be among the few, training in secret with the Irish Republican Brotherhood, or with the Irish Volunteers? Would I, like so many mothers, bury my son this fateful year in some army's uniform, in a formidably unequal country where I have no vote or voice, where many young men are destined to be cannon fodder, and women, widows? How many times did those men and women wonder what the world would be like in the longer-run as a result of the outworking of the chaos around them, this context we struggle to comprehend these years later? I am grateful that I, and my children, live in the longer-run; for while we could speculate endlessly about what life might be like if the Rising had not happened, or if the Great War had not been fought, we who live in these times know and inhabit the world that revealed itself because they happened.

April 1916 and the world is as big a mess as it is possible to imagine. The ancient monarchies, Austria, Russia and Germany, which plunged Europe into war, are on the brink of violent destruction. China is slipping into civil war. On the western front, Verdun is taking a dreadful toll and, in the east, Britain is only weeks away from its worst defeat in history. It's a fighting world where war is glorified and death in uniform seen as the ultimate act of nobility, at least for one's own side.

And on 24 April 1916, it was Easter Monday in Dublin, the second city of the extensive British empire which long included, among its captured dominions, the four provinces of Ireland. At four minutes past noon, from the steps of Dublin's General Post Office, the President of the Provisional Government, Pádraig Pearse, read the Proclamation of independence.

The bald facts are well known and reasonably non-contentious. Their analysis and interpretation has been both continuous and controversial ever since. Even after ninety years a discussion, such as we are embarked upon here, is likely to provoke someone. But in a free and peaceful democracy, where complex things get figured out through public debate, that is as it should be.

With each passing year, post-Rising Ireland reveals itself and we who are of this strong independent and high-achieving Ireland would do well to ponder the extent to which today's freedoms, values, ambitions and success rest on that perilous and militarily-doomed undertaking of nine decades ago, and on the words of that Proclamation. Clearly its fundamental idea was freedom, or in the words of the Proclamation 'the right of the people of Ireland to the ownership of Ireland' but it was also a very radical assertion of the kind of republic a liberated Ireland should become. 'The Republic guarantees religious and civil liberty, equal rights and equal opportunities to all its citizens and declares its resolve to pursue the happiness and prosperity of the whole nation and all of its parts cherishing all of the children of the nation equally.' It spoke of a parliament 'representative of the whole people of Ireland and elected by the suffrages of all her men and women' – this at a time when Westminster was still refusing to concede the vote to women on the basis that to do so would be to give in to terrorism. To our twenty first century ears these words seem a good fit for our modern democracy. Yet ninety years ago, even forty years ago, they seemed hopelessly naïve, and their long-term intellectual power was destined to be overlooked, as interest was focussed on the emotionally-charged political power of the Rising and the renewed nationalist fervour it evoked.

In the longer-term the apparent naïveté of the words of the Proclamation has filled out into a widely-shared political philosophy of equality and social inclusion in tune with the contemporary spirit of democracy, human rights, equality and anti-confessionalism. Read now in the light of the liberation of women, the development of social partnership, the focus on rights and equality, and the ending of the special position of the Catholic church to mention but a few, we see a much more coherent, and wider-reaching, intellectual event than may have previously been noted.

The kind of Ireland the heroes of the Rising aspired to was based on an inclusivity that, famously, would cherish 'all the children of the nation equally ... oblivious of the differences which have divided a minority from the majority in the past'. That culture of inclusion is manifestly a strong contemporary impulse working its way today through relationships with the north, with unionists, with the newcomers to our shores, with our marginalised, and with our own increasing diversity.

For many years the social agenda of the Rising represented an unrealisable aspiration; until now that is, when our prosperity has created a real opportunity for ending poverty and promoting true equality of opportunity for our people and when those idealistic words have started to become a lived reality and a determined ambition.

There is a tendency for powerful and pitiless elites to dismiss with damning labels those who oppose them. That was probably the source of the accusation that 1916 was an exclusive and sectarian enterprise. It was never that, though ironically it was an accurate description of what the Rising opposed.

In 1916 Ireland was a small nation attempting to gain its independence from one of Europe's many powerful empires. In the nineteenth century an English radical described the occupation of India as a system of 'outdoor relief' for the younger sons of the upper classes. The administration of Ireland was not very different, being carried on as a process of continuous conversation around the fire in the Kildare Street Club by past pupils of minor public schools. It was no way to run a country, even without the glass ceiling for Catholics.

Internationally, in 1916, planet earth was a world of violent conflicts and armies. It was a world where countries operated on the principle that the strong would do what they wished and the weak would endure what they must. There were few, if any, sophisticated mechanisms for resolving territorial conflicts. Diplomacy existed to regulate conflict, not to resolve it.

It was in that context that the leaders of the Rising saw their investment in the assertion of Ireland's nationhood. They were not attempting to establish an isolated and segregated territory of 'ourselves alone' as the phrase 'sinn féin' is so often mistranslated, but a free country in which we ourselves could take responsibility for our own destiny, a country that could stand up for itself, have its own distinct perspective, pull itself up by its bootstraps, and be counted with respect among the free nations of Europe and the world.

A Google search for the phrase 'narrow nationalism' produces about 28,000 results. It is almost as though some people cannot use the word 'nationalism' without qualifying it by the word 'narrow'. But that does not make it correct.

I have a strong impression that, to its enemies, both in Ireland and abroad, Irish nationalism looked like a version of the imperialism it opposed, a sort of 'imperialism lite' through which Ireland would attempt to be what the great European powers were – the domination of one cultural and ethnic tradition over others. It is easy to see how they might have fallen into that mistaken view, but mistaken they were. Irish nationalism, from the start, was a multilateral enterprise, attempting to escape the dominance of a single class and, in our case a largely foreign class, into a wider world. Those who think of Irish nationalists as narrow miss, for example, the membership many of them had of a universal church which brought them into contact with a vastly wider segment of the world than that open to even the most travelled imperial English gentleman. Many of the leaders had experience of the Americas, and in particular of North America with its vibrant attachment to liberty and democracy. Others of them were active participants in the international working class movements of their day. Whatever you might think of those involvements, they were universalist and global rather than constricted and blinkered.

To the revolutionaries, the Rising looked as if it represented a commitment to membership of the wider world. For too long they had chafed at the narrow focus of a unilateral empire which acted as it saw fit and resented having to pay any attention to the needs of others. In 1973 a free Irish republic would show by joining the European Economic Community that membership of a union was never our problem but, rather, involuntary membership of a union in which we had no say.

Those who are surprised by Ireland's enthusiasm for the European Union, and think of it as a repudiation of our struggle for independence, fail to see Ireland's historic engagement with the European continent and the Americas. Arguably Ireland's involvement in the British Commonwealth up to the dominion conference of 1929 represents an attempt to promote Ireland's involvement with the wider world even as it negotiated further independence from Britain. Éamon de Valera's support for the League of Nations, our later commitment to the United Nations and our long pursuit of membership of the Common Market are all of a piece with our earlier engagements with Europe and the world which were so often frustrated by our proximity to a strong imperial power – a power which feared our autonomy, and whose global imperialism ironically was experienced as narrowing and restrictive to those who lived under it. We now can see that promoting the European ideal dovetails perfectly with the ideals of the men and women of 1916.

Paradoxically in the longer-run, 1916 arguably set in motion a calming of old conflicts with new concepts and confidence which, as they mature and take shape, stand us is in good stead today.

Our relationship with Britain, despite the huge toll of the Troubles, has changed utterly. In this, the year of the ninetieth anniversary of the Rising, the Irish and British governments, co-equal sovereign colleagues in Europe, are now working side-by-side as mutually respectful partners, helping to develop a stable and peaceful future in Northern Ireland based on the Good Friday Agreement. That agreement asserts equal rights and equal opportunities for all Northern Ireland's citizens. It ends forever one of the Rising's most difficult legacies, the question of how the people of this island look at partition. The constitutional position of Northern Ireland within the United Kingdom is accepted overwhelmingly by the electorate north and south. That position can only be changed by the electorate of Northern Ireland expressing its view exclusively through the ballot box. The future could not be clearer. Both unionists and nationalists have everything to gain from treating each other with exemplary courtesy and generosity, for each has a vision for the future to sell, and a coming generation, more educated than any before, freer from conflict than any before, more democratised and globalised than any before, will have choices to make and those choices will be theirs.

This year, the ninetieth anniversary of the 1916 Rising, and of the Somme, has the potential to be a pivotal year for peace and reconciliation, to be a time of shared pride for the divided grandchildren of those who died, whether at Messines or in Kilmainham.

The climate has changed dramatically since last September's historic announcement of IRA decommissioning. As that new reality sinks in, the people of Northern Ireland will see the massive potential for their future, and that of their children, that is theirs for the taking. Casting my mind forward to ninety years from now I have no way of knowing what the longer-term may hold but I do know the past we are determined to escape from and I know the ambitions we have for that longer-term. To paraphrase the Proclamation, we are resolved to 'pursue the happiness and prosperity of the whole island'. We want to consign inequality and poverty to history. We want to live in peace. We want to be comfortable with, and accommodating of, diversity. We want to become the best friends, neighbours and partners we can be to the citizens of Northern Ireland.

In the hearts of those who took part in the Rising, in what was then an undivided Ireland, was an unshakeable belief that, whatever our personal political or religious perspectives, there was huge potential for an Ireland in which loyalist, republican, unionist, nationalist, Catholic, Protestant, atheist and agnostic pulled together to build a shared future, owned by one and all. That's a longer-term to conjure with but, for now, reflecting back on the sacrifices of the heroes of 1916 and the gallingly unjust world that was their context, I look at my own context and its threads of connection to theirs. I am humbled, excited and grateful to live in one of the world's most respected, admired and successful democracies, a country with an identifiably distinctive voice in Europe and in the world, an Irish republic, a 'sovereign independent state' to use the words of the Proclamation. We are where freedom has brought us. A tough journey, but more than vindicated by our contemporary context. Like every nation that had to wrench its freedom from the reluctant grip of empire, we have our idealistic and heroic founding fathers and mothers – our Davids to their Goliaths. That small band who proclaimed the Rising inhabited a sea of death, an unspeakable time of the most profligate world-wide waste of human life. Yet their deaths rise far above the clamour – their voices, insistent still.

Enjoy the conference and the rows it will surely rise.

EUROPE AND THE IRISH CRISIS,
1900–17

Jérôme aan de Wiel

In 1988 Professor Dermot Keogh wrote: 'The theme of Ireland and twentieth century Europe has not been tackled in any systematic way.'[1] Sixteen
years later, in 2004, Professor Joseph Lee emphasised this fact again: 'The
subject of Ireland's relations with continental European countries in the
twentieth century is a grossly neglected one.'[2] Yet, as various diplomatic
and military archives located in Berlin, Brussels, Freiburg, Paris, Rome and
Vienna reveal, continental Europe was much interested in Ireland between
the turn of the century and the end of the First World War. For a long
time, Ireland was of interest to foreign powers opposed to England and then
Britain. By occupying her they believed that the British would have to surrender. Spain tried first, followed by France, but all in vain.[3] Even imperial
Russia seemed to have had some interest, as a document in the French military archives shows that 'a Franco-Russian landing in Ireland' might have
been contemplated in the summer of 1902 just after the Boer War, which
had exposed serious weaknesses in the British army.[4] When the Great War
broke out in 1914, Germany's turn to play the Irish card had come.

The aims of this paper are to shed new light on Germany's involvement
in Ireland and also to analyse France's reaction to the events in Dublin in
1916. Austria-Hungary had been interested in Ireland before the beginning
of the hostilities in Europe. It would seem that Vienna bore in mind the
home rule crisis in the summer of 1914 in the formulation of her disastrous
policy towards Serbia that would ultimately lead to war. How was the news
of the Easter Rising received in Vienna and Budapest? Also, the Vatican
knew about two weeks beforehand the date of the Rising. What was Eoin
MacNeill's role in the events? The paper will also confirm that some British officials at the highest level took the decision to let the Rising happen
intentionally in order to decapitate the republican movement. This is proven
by the existence in the German archives of a document entitled *Aufgabe P.*

The years between 1890 and 1907 saw some major realignments in the system of European alliances. Briefly, in 1892 a military alliance was signed between France and Russia. Owing to naval tensions between Britain and Germany, the *Entente Cordiale* between Britain and France saw the light in 1904. Eventually, the Anglo-Russian Agreement became a reality in 1907. The latter led to the formation of the so-called Triple Entente countries – Britain, France and Russia. It must be pointed out that the Entente and the Agreement the British signed were not military alliances, but from Germany and Austria's perspective this constituted a strategic encirclement.[5] From that moment onwards, the German leaders would try to drive a wedge between their rivals but their efforts were not successful. In a future war, which many statesmen and militaries expected sooner or later, the German general staff relied on the famous 'Schlieffen Plan', which consisted in first knocking out France before rapidly transferring all divisions to the east front to deal with the advancing Russian army.[6] But the Germans were most preoccupied with the United Kingdom and its vast empire, which they considered to be their most dangerous enemy. Would the British interfere if Germany entered a war against France and Russia? This question bordered on the obsessive in Berlin. But did Britain not have a weak western flank, Ireland, which might be exploited or which might prevent her from entering a continental war? Germany was well aware that Ireland was rife with political tensions due to the nationalists' struggle for home rule, which was opposed by unionists.

Kaiser Wilhelm II of Germany was closely following the Irish crisis. He was personally informed by Dr Theodor Schiemann, a historian, who was corresponding with George Freeman.[7] Freeman was a journalist who specialised in foreign affairs and was then working for the *Gaelic American* in New York, the newspaper owned by the Irish republican and Clan na Gael leader, John Devoy. Freeman and Schiemann had begun their correspondence in 1906 and had been put in touch with each other by a German editor working in Japan. Freeman had offered to work 'against England' [sic].[8] Most of their correspondence concerned anti-British propaganda and occasionally work of a cloak-and-dagger nature. Once, Schiemann asked how many Irishmen were serving in the royal navy, the answer to which Freeman was not able to ascertain.[9] Obviously the idea was to figure out whether Irishmen could be relied upon to disrupt the organisation of the royal navy.

As for the Kaiser, he became more and more frustrated by Britain's attitude towards Germany and more and more aggressive in his comments regarding Ireland. He was being kept up to date about the latest developments in the Irish crisis by reports from his embassy in London. When, on 14 September 1912, Richard von Kühlmann, the *chargé d'affaires* of the embassy, suggested that the crisis would weaken England as a world power because of the influence the Irish exercise in America, the Kaiser wrote in the margin: 'That would be a great boon.'[10] There was also some interaction between Germany and Austria-Hungary about Ireland. In August 1907 Chancellor Bernhard von Bülow sent a letter to Aloys von Aehrenthal, the powerful Minister of Foreign Affairs in Vienna, in which he explained that the British would probably not be involved in a European war lest uprisings should happen in Ireland and India. Bülow explained that this might be useful to know for Emperor Franz Josef before his scheduled meeting with King Edward VII.[11] There was even more. In November 1908 the Irish nationalist Frank Hugh O'Donnell met the Austro-Hungarian ambassador, Count Albert von Mensdorff, in London. He had come to offer a plan of alliance between nationalist Ireland and Austria-Hungary designed to break the strategic encirclement imposed by the Triple Entente. Mensdorff thought that O'Donnell was 'a little … eccentric' but was sufficiently impressed to send a full report to Aehrenthal in Vienna. Interestingly, although the report was marked 'secret', the Austro-Hungarians passed it on to their German allies.[12] The matter was entrusted to Dr Schiemann, who lost no time in contacting George Freeman in New York. Freeman, however, advised the Germans to have nothing to do with O'Donnell as he was not reliable.[13]

It must be emphasised here that these early contacts between the Irish republicans and the Germans did not result in concrete measures. After all, when the war broke out in 1914 there were no risings in Ireland nor anywhere else in the British empire, except a short rebellion led by Christiaan de Wet in South Africa. Not even contingency plans had been thought out, something bitterly regretted by Freeman in 1915.[14] The explanation of this lies probably in the fact that deep down the Germans still believed they could reach an agreement with the British and make sure that they would not interfere in a general war on the continent.

The home rule crisis intensified when, in 1913, the unionists set up the Ulster Volunteer Force (UVF) and the nationalists retorted by establishing the Irish Volunteers. It now looked as if a large scale civil war was only a matter of time. The Ulster crisis attracted the foreign press, but not only journalists arrived in Ireland. Baron Georg von Franckenstein, from the Austro-Hungarian embassy in London, was among them, and his stay in the country became controversial.[15] It should not be forgotten that the 25,000 rifles delivered to the UVF on the night of 24–5 April 1914 came from the Steyr armament factory in Upper Austria.[16] The archives in Vienna reveal that Franckenstein wrote a report precisely on 24 April.[17] This was a most striking coincidence to say the least and prompts the question as to what he was really doing in Ireland all the more since the report has since gone missing. It is unlikely to be ever recovered as vast amounts of secret files were destroyed in Vienna after the war.[18] In 1939 Franckenstein published his memoirs in which he categorically denied any wrong-doing. The problem is that he seemed to have contradicted himself. In February 1913 he had been in India, and as he himself stated in his memoirs: 'The purpose of my travels and stay in India was to study the general political situation and to ascertain what attitude the natives would adopt in a world war.'[19] This was exactly what people accused Francken-stein of having done in Ireland. Similar accusations were levelled at Rich-ard von Kühlmann of the German embassy, who was suspected of having gone on a secret mission to Ulster in the summer of 1914. Like Franck-enstein, Kühlmann denied everything. The plot thickens here, however, as Margot Asquith, wife of the British Prime Minister, Herbert Asquith, clearly remembered Kühlmann telling her that he had gone to Ulster.[20] Both men's roles remain cloaked in mystery.

When the Austro-Hungarian Archduke Franz Ferdinand was assas-sinated in Sarajevo on 28 June 1914 by a young Serbian nationalist, seri-ous tensions developed between Austria-Hungary and Serbia, involving the major European powers. Historians have named this the 'July crisis' during which politicians, diplomats and militaries were wondering who was going to do what. What was Ireland's role in the unfolding events that would lead to the outbreak of the First World War? As seen, Germany was essentially obsessed by the position of the United Kingdom. As Professor A.T.Q. Stewart wrote in 1967: 'The influence of the Irish crisis on Ger-man policy has generally been underestimated.'[21] This continues to be the case today as the many books dealing with the outbreak of the war rarely take into account the Irish crisis. And yet there can be little doubt about the veracity of Professor Stewart's assertion. Indeed, on 26 July 1914 the Belgian ambassador in Berlin, Baron Henri Beyens, wrote that Germany could now wage war 'in extremely favourable circumstances'. Among the reasons he mentioned was the situation in the United Kingdom: 'England … is paralysed by her internal dissensions and her Irish quarrels'.[22] Beyens could not have known how right he was for on the very same day a British regiment opened fire on a nationalist crowd in Dublin after a gun-running operation for the Irish Volunteers at Howth. Four people died and forty were wounded. The incident became known as the Bachelor's Walk massacre. The long-awaited civil war looked to be on its way. The next day Albert Ballin, the German ship owner and personal friend of the Kaiser, reported from London, where he had been sent to ascertain the political situation, that Britain's reaction to Austria-Hungary's ultimatum to Serbia had been very 'mild'. He related it to the 'present situation'.[23] Undoubtedly, Ballin had the Irish crisis in mind.

Still on 27 July Germany rejected a British offer of mediation emanating from Foreign Secretary Sir Edward Grey, and advised the Austro-Hungarians to also reject it.[24] They took this piece of advice.[25] Indeed, why should they accept the offer of a disunited United Kingdom? Besides, on 12 July, twelve days before the Austro-Hungarians' fateful ultimatum to the Serbians, their ambassador in Berlin, Count Ladislaus Szögyény, had already informed them that the Germans thought that 'above all, England is anything but bellicose at the moment'.[26] In Britain politicians at the highest level and of all shades of opinion began to suspect that the Central Powers were taking into account the Irish crisis in the formulation of their policy. On 30 July Prime Minister Herbert Asquith secretly met his political opponents, Andrew Bonar Law (leader of the Conservative party) and Sir Edward Carson (leader of the Unionist party), somewhere in the suburbs of London. Bonar Law and Carson wanted the prime minister 'to postpone for the time being the second reading of the Amending bill [which provided for the possible exclusion from home rule of certain Ulster counties] … in the interest of the international situation'. Asquith replied: 'I agreed and read to them the latest telegrams from Berlin which, in my judgement, assume that the German government are calculating upon our internal weakness to affect our foreign policy.' A short time later he met John Redmond, the leader of the Irish party, to whom he related his rather extraordinary meeting. Redmond 'thought it an excellent chance of putting off the Amending bill'.[27]

On 3 August 1914, when Germany declared war on France, Field Marshal Franz Conrad von Hötzendorf, the Austro-Hungarian commander in chief, wrote: 'England's attitude proves to be unfriendly and doubtful. To [our] military attaché [in London], it seems, however, that there is no desire for war for the time being, taking into account the Ulster crisis and the civil war.'[28] To point out that Conrad and his military attaché were wrong, as there was no civil war, is to miss the point. What matters here is their interpretation, and this interpretation must have encouraged

Conrad and others in persevering in their offensive against Serbia. That there was no civil war in Ireland was largely due to Redmond's intervention in the House of Commons on 3 August when he put forward that the UVF and the Irish Volunteers would defend Ireland against a foreign (i.e. German) invasion. It can be safely said that Redmond spoiled Berlin and Vienna's expectations. It also helps to explain why the British cabinet was so hesitant in committing itself to help France and Russia. On 1 and 2 August Grey had told the dismayed Russian and French ambassadors that it would be difficult to send a force of 100,000 British soldiers to the continent because of possible inner troubles in the United Kingdom.[29] On 4 August, a genuinely United Kingdom declared war on Germany and, on 12 August, on Austria-Hungary. Ambassador Mensdorff had already warned Vienna on 3 August: 'Navy and army are mobilised but there are still no decisions as to how they will be used. Enthusiastic adoption in parliament; approval of the opposition, including the two Irish parties.'[30] As for Redmond, he later exhorted the Irish Volunteers to fight abroad. This provoked a division within the Volunteer movement and the expulsion of the pro-Redmond members from the Executive Committee. But only a few thousand rank and file members remained faithful to their leader and founder, Professor Eoin MacNeill. Within the ranks of these Irish Volunteers, secret members of the IRB were determined to rise against the British while they were fighting against the Germans; among them were Pádraig Pearse and Joseph Mary Plunkett.

During the first months of the war in Europe, the Irish nationalist Roger Casement was busy negotiating an alliance with the German ambassador to the United States, Count Johann Heinrich von Bernstorff. Later Casement and Franz von Papen, the military attaché of the embassy, worked out the idea of setting up an Irish brigade composed of Irish prisoners of war detained in German camps.[31] Bernstorff informed Berlin that Casement would arrive in Germany soon.[32] What Bernstorff did not know, however, was that his messages were being intercepted by the British. On 5 August 1914 a team of British secret servicemen disguised as fishermen had cut the transatlantic cables between Germany and the United States. This forced the Germans to use other cables or use wireless that the British could either tap or intercept. It now became a question of being able to decode German messages. The British were blessed with extraordinary luck. On 11 August the Australian navy confiscated a codebook from a German ship, the crew of which had ignored the fact that war had been declared. On 6 September the Russians found a second codebook on a German battleship and sent it to London. Eventually, on 30 November, an English trawler found in its nets a third codebook! By that time the British had already cracked one of the German codes. A room in the admiralty in London became specialised in deciphering. It was the soon-to-be legendary room 40 under the command of Captain Reginald Hall.[33] All this meant that communications between New York and Berlin would be intercepted, including the ones of the future Easter Rising.

Roger Casement arrived in Berlin on 31 October 1914 after an eventful journey. He was introduced to several people in the ministry of Foreign Affairs. Dr Schiemann described to the Kaiser his meeting with Casement in most flattering terms: 'The impression I got from Casement is extremely favourable. He is a real strength for our interests and is motivated by the hatred of English policy.'[34] Casement then travelled to Charleville in occupied north east France where the German high command had its headquarters. There he exposed his plans regarding the formation of an Irish brigade the purpose of which was to participate in the liberation of Ireland. The commander in chief, General Erich von Falkenhayn, agreed to separate Irish prisoners of war from English and Scottish ones.[35] This was hardly surprising as Falkenhayn believed that Britain was Germany's main enemy; everything, therefore, should be undertaken to destabilise the British. A special camp was set up near Limburg an der Lahn, not too far away from Frankfurt am Main. As is well known, the whole operation was a fiasco. At the most fifty five men volunteered and they were not quality soldiers. Even Casement feared them and refused to let them attend mass in the local cathedral.[36] As early as 25 January 1915 the military authorities in Frankfurt informed Berlin that the Irishmen in Limburg were mainly 'urban working class scum who were physically and mentally most inferior'.[37] Casement rapidly began to have doubts about the project and the sincerity of his German allies. In the words of his biographer, Angus Mitchell, 'Hints of paranoia started to permeate his journal as his recruitment efforts floundered and his despondency with the war deepened.'[38]

This failure was a let-down for Casement but not really for the Germans. Indeed, Ireland played no part at all in their overall strategy during 1914 and 1915. Before the war, in May 1914, Captain Blum of the submarine section had submitted a plan to turn Ireland into a submarine base, from where a trade war against Britain could be waged. Admiral von Tirpitz had been informed about the proposal.[39] But in October 1914 Captain Schlubach questioned the strategic value of the Irish coast as he believed that all submarines needed to do was to block the entries of the harbours of Dublin and Belfast.[40] Under these circumstances there was no need to set up bases. In fact the setting up of such bases made little sense as it would have necessitated the opening of supply lines between Germany and Ireland. This implied that the German navy would already have beaten the royal navy. If this was the case all the Germans had to do was to blockade Britain. The British would then have had to sue for peace with their army cut off from them in France. On 23 August Admiral Karl von Truppel pointed out: 'A conclusive victory of our fleet, risings in Egypt, the Suez Canal, India and Africa are possibilities but no certain factors.'[41] The fact that he had not mentioned Ireland was very relevant. It was little wonder that Casement became impatient and depressed.

Back in Ireland, the small group within the IRB known as the Military Council became aware that the Germans had to be convinced of their intentions. By way of Spain, Italy and Switzerland, they sent Joseph Mary Plunkett to Berlin where he met Casement in April 1915.[42] The two men produced an impressive thirty two page report, outlining the history of the Irish Volunteers, the strength of the British army in Ireland and the country's strategic value.[43] Not surprisingly, the Germans were not convinced by their arguments. The meetings between both men and the Germans appear to have been tense.[44] Plunkett returned to Ireland without any specific German promises. Casement warned him that the Irish Volunteers should not attempt a rising without the support of the German army.[45] It must be stressed that both men did their best to persuade their allies, but that they largely overestimated the abilities of the German navy.

But at the beginning of 1916 events suddenly gathered momentum. In Dublin the secret Military Council decided to launch a rising on Easter Sunday, 23 April, for which German arms would be urgently required. On 5 February John Devoy received a message containing the Military Council's decision. He lost no time in contacting Ambassador Bernstorff who in turn sent a coded message to Berlin on 16 February.[46] The German general staff immediately offered to help. Why this sudden change of attitude towards Ireland? On 21 December 1915 General Erich von Falkenhayn had met the Kaiser to outline his new plan for a decisive offensive. He explained that Britain was the 'archenemy' and that France was 'England's tool on the continent'. He believed that the British would finance the war until Germany was beaten. According to him the best way to eliminate Britain was 'to knock her best sword out of her hands', in other words the French army. A major offensive would be directed against the French at Verdun. Simultaneously a new unrestricted submarine warfare campaign would be directed against British shipping even if this could provoke the United States into declaring war. The offensive would begin in February 1916.[47] There was another major reason to deliver the knock-out blow to Britain. The first food riots had occurred in Berlin in October 1915 and had been caused by what the German population called the 'hunger blockade' imposed by the royal navy.[48] In Falkenhayn's mind, however strange this might sound, the offensive against Verdun was in fact part of a general offensive against Britain. If, besides this offensive and the new submarine campaign, a rising could also be fomented in Ireland, so much the better. So it was that the future Easter Rising became part of a wider offensive against Britain. This explains why the Germans suddenly agreed to help the Irish republicans after one and a half years of inactivity.

The preparations for the Easter Rising in Germany are well known and do not need to be detailed here. Briefly, Casement was totally opposed to the gun-running project that consisted of sending only 20,000 old Russian rifles, 10 machine guns and 4,000,000 rounds of ammunition to the republicans in Ireland.[49] Without the participation of German soldiers Casement believed that a rising would be a futile bloodbath. It is striking that German support for the proposed action was, to say the least, limited. It should be noted that by 1916 German industry was producing 250,000 quality rifles and 2,300 quality machine guns a month![50] It looked as if the general staff wanted to organise a low-cost expedition to Ireland. The reason for this was probably that it was still not totally convinced of the seriousness of the republicans' intentions. On 21 March 1916 Captain Karl Spindler of the German navy was ordered to transport the arms to Tralee Bay, arriving between 20 and 23 April, where he would be met by an Irish pilot boat. Spindler left Lübeck on 9 April aboard the *Aud*, pretending to be a Norwegian fishing boat.[51] As for Casement, he was finally allowed to leave Germany for Ireland aboard a submarine.[52] The Germans' decision remains most curious as they knew that he was against the Rising and that there was an obvious risk that he might try to prevent it.

In London on 12 February 1916, Lord French, the commander in chief of the home forces, had a conversation with Augustine Birrell, the Irish chief secretary. Birrell told him that the Irish Volunteers were not much of a danger but that he would like to see them 'get a real good "knock"'.[53] Birrell's remark might well have appealed to French, a man who favoured strong-arm tactics. In April 1918 he would advocate the bombing of Ireland by the royal air force in order to make her accept conscription.[54]

Two months later, around 8 April, a most intriguing meeting took place in the Vatican. Count George Plunkett, a papal knight, had an audience with Pope Benedict XV. He had come to ask his blessing for the future rising. Indeed, some time before, Eoin MacNeill had explained that a rising was morally not justifiable. Pearse had then agreed but now knew that MacNeill had to be neutralised lest he should prevent the Rising. Therefore, MacNeill was not informed of its preparations until the very last moment.[55] This is, at least, the official version. Because the republicans feared the possible negative reaction of the Irish Catholic church, it seems that it had been decided to send Plunkett to the Vatican to ask the pope for his opinion on the matter. Plunkett gave Benedict a long letter written in French, justifying the Rising and giving the date of its beginning. His audience lasted nearly two hours and nobody else was present. According to Plunkett, he was 'deeply moved' and, although he refused to bless the Rising, he did bless the republicans. Plunkett was also struck 'with the Pope's familiarity with the Irish cause, and the arguments put forward by England'. This was hardly surprising, as the nationalist-minded Monsignor Michael O'Riordan, the rector of the Irish College in Rome, regularly informed the pope of the latest developments in Ireland. It must also be borne in mind that the Vatican was not on friendly terms with Britain. The British had excluded the pope and the curia from the future peace negotiations in a secret treaty with Italy signed in 1915, the details of which the Vatican had soon obtained. But there was more. Plunkett said that he had been sent by Eoin MacNeill, which was also clearly stated in the letter. This would mean that, contrary to the commonly-held belief that MacNeill had been deceived by Pearse and others until the very last moment, he in fact knew about the future uprising. In 1933 a public controversy broke out between Plunkett and MacNeill, who totally denied having had anything to do with Plunkett's mission in Rome. The whole episode remains a mystery. But it would beggar belief that a papal knight and a devout Catholic as Plunkett would have lied or deliberately misled the pope.[56]

In the meantime Captain Spindler and the *Aud* were approaching the Irish coast. Spindler had been spotted a few times by the royal navy but, to his greatest surprise, the British let him pass. In his memoirs he wrote: 'Our luck in this respect began to seem a little uncanny. Could there be something behind it? Did the British know about our coming?'[57] The answers to Spindler's questions are 'yes'. Captain Hall and room 40 had decoded the messages between New York and Berlin and deliberately chose not to inform the British authorities lest they should betray to the Germans that they had cracked their codes. Hall also believed that, if a rising occurred, it would be a golden opportunity for the British army to get rid once and for all of the Irish republicans who were badly equipped in arms.[58] In other words, the security risk would be minimal. It is known that Hall did warn Admiral Bayly in Queenstown, who patiently waited for the *Aud* to show up.[59] If Bayly had been warned it is most unlikely that somebody like Lord French had not been. It would have been totally irresponsible of Hall not to have warned the commander in chief of the home forces. As noted above, French would have welcomed the opportunity to give the Irish Volunteers 'a real good "knock"'. But there is no evidence to substantiate this theory and some people had a rather poor opinion of French after his handling of the British Expeditionary Force in France.[60] Furthermore, Hall tended to act as a maverick.[61] Spindler arrived in Tralee Bay on Thursday 20 April, but as Volunteer planning had gone awfully wrong, nobody came to collect the arms. He decided to leave the next day lest he should be spotted by the British. The royal navy, however, caught him on Saturday. Casement arrived on Friday by submarine, but was caught almost on arrival. He was immediately transferred to London, where, on Sunday 23 April, he was interrogated by Hall in person.[62] Casement pleaded to be allowed to contact some people in Dublin to cancel the Rising, but Hall refused. According to Casement, he even said: 'It is better that a cankering sore like this should be cut out.'[63]

There is no reason not to believe Casement as it all makes perfect sense. As is well known, due to MacNeill's last minute intervention, the Rising eventually began on Monday 24 April. On that day also, the German supreme army command called off its submarine campaign against Britain as the Americans had protested.[64] There was no need to upset the Americans, all the more since, theoretically, the Irish republicans should be fighting by now. The Irish phase of Verdun had begun. The Easter Rising lasted until Saturday 29 April when Pearse and the republican soldiers surrendered to the British forces. It caused about 450 deaths, 2,600 wounded, and the destruction of Dublin city centre.[65] In May General Sir John Maxwell and his courts martial had the republican leaders shot; Casement would be hanged in August. This upset the population but also shocked Prime Minister Herbert Asquith who informed French that he was 'a little surprised and perturbed by the drastic action of shooting so many of the rebel leaders'. French warned Maxwell about Asquith's reservations but added that he personally would not interfere with his freedom of action.[66] Again, French's remark makes perfect sense if he had been informed by Hall or simply if he saw the execution of republican leaders as a perfect way to rid Ireland of disloyal elements.

But how had the French and the Austro-Hungarians reacted to the Rising in Dublin? Colonel Artus de la Panouse, the French military attaché in London, reported that it was obvious that Germany's plan was to divert more British troops to Ireland, troops that would be better used on the front line. He also wrote that Sir Edward Carson had to bear some of the responsibility as it was he who had introduced the fashion of smuggling German arms into the country.[67] On 19 June 1916 he sent a report to General Joseph Joffre, the commander in chief of the French army. About the republican leaders, de la Panouse wrote: 'All those who took part in the [Rising] ... showed real courage during their court martial and also when about to die.' After this military tribute, he said that the British 59th division was now occupying Ireland whereas it should have been sent to France. This was bad news for Joffre who was planning, with General Douglas Haig, an offensive on the Somme, due to begin shortly, in order to relieve Verdun.[68]

In Austria-Hungary the news of the Rising was greeted with satisfaction and glee by the press. This was no surprise as the 'hunger blockade' imposed by the royal navy in the north and the Italians in the south was having dreadful effects.[69] In Vienna the conservative *Reichspost* wrote that the Irish people had ceased to support John Redmond's policy of reconciliation between the Irish and the British. It also made a comparison between the present British 'hunger blockade' and the Great Famine in Ireland: 'England's war of starvation plan ... has not been invented for the first time by British rulers. It was already used by [English royal] dynasties with cold calculation against the Irish.'[70] In Budapest the liberal *Pester Lloyd* opined: 'In this war, liberal England has had the dubious honour to have had to put down a long and well-prepared rising ... Not in fermenting Russia, not in the polyglot Austro-Hungarian monarchy did the revolution flare up, but in liberal England who lets herself be called the defender of small nations.'[71]

It was, of course, in Germany that news of the Rising was most eagerly awaited. Once the seriousness of the fighting in Dublin became known in Berlin, mainly through the reports of an agent codenamed W.29d (which were forwarded to spymaster Walter Nicolai), the German secret service conceived a disinformation and scaremongering campaign directed against the Allies.[72] The operation took place in Berne in Switzerland on 29 April. A double agent, pretending to work for France, contacted the French embassy and handed over a bogus report containing information he had gathered in Germany. The report was a clever mixture of true facts and lies.

Among other things, it described the preparations for the Rising and stated that 'Casement was assured by the German government that he would get twenty million shillings if it succeeded'. The impression the report wanted to give was Germany's total commitment to the Irish cause and that her navy was able to reach the Irish coast whenever it wanted. Although this cannot be substantiated, Nicolai was probably behind the operation. But French military intelligence knew that the spy was, in fact, working for Germany and was not duped. It is not known whether the French informed the British about this German operation, but General Joffre's headquarters were kept up to date.[73]

As early as 6 May 1916 Ambassador Bernstorff sent a coded message to Berlin, explaining that he had been approached by Irish-American leaders who wanted support for a new rising. On 11 June the general staff answered: 'Fundamentally willing to give further support to the Irish by all means. Request for speedy information concerning nature, timeframe and size of needed help.'[74] It was not surprising that the Germans showed so much eagerness. The Rising had failed but it had shown that the Irish republicans meant business. During the following months the admiralty and the general staff put together a plan codenamed *Aufgabe P.* The support envisaged was three times more important than the one for the Easter Rising: 60,000 rifles, 20 machine guns and 12,000,000 rounds of ammunition. The sending of soldiers was initially planned but was eventually abandoned. Two steamers would deliver the arms in Galway and Tralee harbours. They would be accompanied by submarines to prevent the royal navy from approaching. The date set for the landing was 21 February 1917. Despite the naval battle of Jutland, which had taken place on 31 May 1916 and which had shown that the German navy would not be able to break the blockade of the royal navy in the North Sea, the German admiralty was convinced that the steamers could reach Ireland undetected during the long winter nights, under cover of fog and with the help of storms.[75] Of course Captain Spindler's *Aud* had shown that such a voyage was feasible after all. The Germans, moreover, still did not know that room 40 was busy decoding their messages.

On 24 December 1916 Ambassador Bernstorff and John Devoy were informed of *Aufgabe P.*[76] Interestingly, this new German departure was once again associated with a renewal of unrestricted submarine warfare, which was to begin on 1 February 1917.[77] The Germans were ready to go when, on 16 January 1917, Bernstorff sent a message cancelling the whole operation.[78] What had happened? After the Easter Rising, John Devoy was corresponding with an Irish Volunteer called Liam Clarke, who was trying to re-organise the Volunteer movement. In one of his messages Clarke emphatically stated that, if a second rising was to take place, the Germans had to send not only arms but also men. Clarke also wrote that some republicans had been dissatisfied with the German help during the Easter Rising.[79] Since the general staff had decided not to send soldiers, Devoy sent a coded message to Berlin outlining the reasons why *Aufgabe P* had to be cancelled.[80]

But it was not the end of the story yet. As the archives in the Public Record Office in London show, room 40 had intercepted and decoded the messages regarding *Aufgabe P*, including the one that cancelled the operation. Once again, this was a golden opportunity to get rid of disloyal elements in Ireland and keep the republican movement decapitated. On 17 February 1917 Dublin Castle was warned and a list of about thirty republicans and republican sympathisers was drawn up. These men were arrested on 21 February, the night the Germans were supposed to come. Among them were Terence MacSwiney, Dr Patrick McCartan, Darrel Figgis, Seán T. O'Kelly and J.J. O'Kelly. There was nothing that proved their involvement in *Aufgabe P* and Liam Clarke was not on the list.[81] As Dr Brian Murphy has written: '[The men] … were given a sharp reminder that ultimate power lay with the British government.'[82] But, above all, what the *Aufgabe P* episode does prove, beyond any doubt, is the truth of the theory put forward by Professor Eunan O'Halpin in 1984, namely that Captain Reginald Hall intentionally let the Easter Rising happen.[83] Indeed, the British approach to the Easter Rising and to *Aufgabe P* is essentially the same.

The saga had a last, somehow amusing, twist. On 21 March, in the House of Commons in London, the independent nationalist parliamentarian Laurence Ginnell asked the home secretary under what conditions the arrested Irishmen were detained. What Ginnell ignored, however, was that General Bryan Mahon wanted him, together with Count Plunkett and Father Michael Flanagan, to be arrested too! But, fearing adverse political repercussions, Ginnell, Plunkett and Flanagan had been let off the hook.[84]

Finally, Professor Stewart's assertion that the Irish home rule crisis played a role in the events leading to the outbreak of the First World War is totally founded. The Irish factor in German and Austro-Hungarian decision-making was an important one as both Germans and Austro-Hungarians deemed that it would in all likelihood prevent the British from entering a wide-scale conflict in Europe. Their mistake was dreadful. The combination of the Serbian crisis in central Europe and the Irish crisis in western Europe was lethal. Also, there can be no longer any doubt that some British officials at the highest level let the Easter Rising deliberately happen. We know the name of at least one man involved, Captain Reginald Hall, and the name of another man who was warned, Admiral Bayly. But they cannot have been the only ones. It would seem rather obvious that some people in the army were also involved. These facts ultimately lead to the question: who was responsible for the outbreak of the Easter Rising? It might well be argued that Hall had little choice in the matter as he wanted to protect his extremely valuable source of information. Arresting Pádraig Pearse and others before the Rising took place might have revealed to the Germans that something was wrong with their codes. But could those 450 deaths, 2,600 wounded and the destruction of Dublin city centre not have been avoided? Did Reginald Hall and Foreign Office Secretary Arthur Balfour not work out a clever way of keeping from the Germans the fact that they had intercepted and decoded the famous Zimmermann telegram in February 1917, in which the Germans promised their help to Mexico if she went to war against the United States?[85] On that occasion nobody was either killed or wounded. If the Military Council initiated the Easter Rising and therefore bore a great responsibility, can it not be argued that some British officials bore a greater responsibility still for letting it happen?

THE ULSTER CRISIS: PRELUDE TO 1916?

D.G. Boyce

Two images dominate historical memory of the Ulster crisis of 1912–14, as seen in the grainy, black and white film of the time: the Ulster Volunteer Force (UVF) marching and drilling; and the Irish Volunteers looking equally resolute. They seem to bear witness to the militarisation of Ireland and the readiness to resort to armed force by unionists and then nationalists; and thus point towards the Easter Rising because, as Eoin MacNeill wrote in his memoirs, Sir Edward Carson exercised one of the most influential effects on the Irish revolution when he exploited British laws in Ireland through the creation of the UVF. Now the British army could not be used to prevent the enrolment and drilling of Volunteers in any part of the twenty eight [sic] counties. Yet there are more important issues to be explored which arise from the pre-war Ulster crisis. MacNeill went on to declare that the Irish Volunteers represented citizen forces which would rival the UVF claim to hold Ireland 'for the empire'.[1] Pádraig Pearse, at the Rotunda meeting where the Irish Volunteers were founded, would go no further than to claim that 'Ireland armed would at any rate make a better bargain with the empire than Ireland unarmed'.[2] And there was a significant interlude, between the outbreak of the great European war in August 1914 and the Easter Rising of April 1916, when history seemed about to move in a different direction, with nationalist Volunteers and Ulster Volunteers serving in the same army and in the same uniform, though mutual suspicions remained.

MacNeill's claim that Carson was unwittingly the originator of the Easter Rising and the revolution that followed must be explored. The passing of the Parliament Act of 1911 meant that the British House of Commons could override the House of Lords by passing identical legislation in three successive sessions, provided that two years elapsed between the second and third readings; thus, in the ordinary run of things and parliamentary opposition notwithstanding, the 1912 home rule bill would have become law in any event by 1914. This constitutional change meant that the controversy – and possibly crisis – over the bill would be a prolonged one.

Moreover, the Parliament Act specified that bills must be introduced in the last two circuits in precisely the same form as they left the Commons the first time. Committee and report stages were dispensed with, since Commons' amendments were not allowed. The Parliament Act authorised the Commons to 'suggest' amendments to the House of Lords, but the Liberal Prime Minister, H.H. Asquith, insisted that any such 'suggestions' must not destroy the identity of the bill. As the Conservative leader, Andrew Bonar Law, pointed out, the opposition could debate the bill, but were not allowed to alter a single line.[3]

Two further complications were embedded in the bill's passage through parliament. The general election of November 1910 resulted in the Liberal government being returned to power, but with 272 seats, exactly the same number as the unionists. Labour won forty two seats and the Irish party eighty four. Thus the Liberals depended heavily on the Irish nationalist vote in the House of Commons, though they knew that the nationalists likewise depended on them, since the Irish party was unlikely to want to vote out a Liberal government and replace it with a unionist one. The second dilemma was a peculiarly Liberal one. The government was not unaware of the Ulster unionist difficulty, and as early as February 1912, two months before the bill was introduced in the Commons, Lloyd George and Winston Churchill formally proposed in cabinet that Ulster, or those counties in which Protestants were in a clear majority, should be given an option to contract out of the home rule bill as introduced. The question for the government was: if such a concession were offered, at what stage should the offer be made? Would it be tactically most opportune to make it at the outset; withheld as a concession to be made later; inserted as an amendment to the bill; or indeed made at all? The Gladstonian tradition was that Ireland should be treated as a unit for the purpose of self-government – as Asquith re-affirmed in the first reading, 'Mr Gladstone's position is strongly fortified by our later experience.'[4] Ulster unionists, however, were adamant that this would place them under the heels of their traditional enemies and that they ought not be coerced into living under a system of government that they feared and detested.

Victorian Liberal thinking was primarily concerned with protecting the rights of individuals rather than distinct communities, and the 1912 bill specifically denied the right of the proposed devolved legislature to 'establish or endow any religion or prohibit the free exercise, or to give a preference, privilege, or advantage, or impose any disability or disadvantage, on account of religious belief'.[5] But this was of no comfort to Ulster unionists, who saw themselves as a distinct people, loyal men and women, holding their province for Britain and the empire. The unionist opposition accused the government of turning the House of Commons into a 'market-place where everything is bought and sold'. This very unparliamentary language – what Asquith called the 'new style' – branded the unionist opposition as both irresponsible and dangerous.[6] It also seemed to confirm that the whole Ulster crisis was one manufactured by the unionists for their own selfish political ends: thus, once again, nationalists could claim that the divisions in Ireland between unionist and nationalist were the fault of obdurate British politicians, and need not be addressed within Ireland itself.

Later generations of nationalists – and some contemporary nationalist thinkers such as Sinn Féin's founder, Arthur Griffith – professed astonishment that a modest measure of devolution should occasion such a fervent protest from unionists in Britain and Ireland. But apart from the belief (propagated by nationalists themselves since 1886) that home rule offered 'freedom' and 'independence', the 1912 bill was a serious measure of self-rule. It was true that the Westminster parliament was to remain sovereign, and that it retained unimpaired authority over questions of peace and war, treaties, the levying of customs duties, coinage, postal services and, for six years, the Royal Irish Constabulary. The Irish parliament could not endow religion or impose religious disabilities. It had limited taxation powers, and could not add more than 10 per cent to the rate of income tax or death duties. Irish membership of the House of Commons was to be reduced from 103 to 42, though the 42 could speak on all subjects, and were not confined to contributing to debates on subjects affecting Ireland alone.[7] But the key point in the bill was not its definition of the powers of the Irish parliament, but its lack of definition: for the new parliament could make laws for the 'peace, order and good government of Ireland'. This left a large and unlimited scope for the parliament to enhance its powers, in an age when states across Europe were embarking on social policies that would significantly increase their legislative output and executive control.

There can be no doubt that the crisis over the 1912 home rule bill did mark a significant change in the Irish political climate. This was the third such bill to be placed before the British parliament. Those of 1886 and 1893 occasioned heated opposition from British and Irish unionists alike, but the grave threats to Irish Protestants, and especially to Ulster Protestants, were not met by any serious armed opposition. There was plenty of fighting talk, but that was all. In June 1892 at a great unionist convention in Belfast, one speaker proclaimed 'firm and unchangeable determination of the people of Ulster to resist by constitutional means and, if need be, by force the passing of the home rule bill into law'. Another, neatly adopting Gladstone's phrase when he declared his determination to resist agrarian violence in Ireland in the early 1880s, warned that the resources of civilisation were not yet exhausted; but when they were, 'it remained for them, as loyal sons of sires agone, to find out how they might resist the resolution of the imperial parliament to hand them neck and heel to a tyranny that was beyond the conception of the English elsewhere'.[8] But the *Irish Times* noted that the speeches at the convention contained 'no threat, no boast, no bluster. The purpose was that more than a million of the people of Ireland should say simply no.'[9] Alvin Jackson has explained that, because unionism had only a generally narrow and inadequate constituency base, with few pressure groups beyond the Orange Order able to claim a mass membership (and virtually none long surviving the defeat of the second home rule bill), unionism was for all practical purposes a parliamentary movement, and it was to MPs in the House of Commons that northern Protestants looked for political redress or personal advancement.[10]

Yet twenty years later words were replaced, or perhaps reinforced, by deeds; and the proceedings of the British parliament became increasingly irrelevant to the clash of ideologies in Ireland itself. What was described as potentially a matter of life and death in 1892 was now indeed a matter of life and death in 1912, since the home rule bill must pass into law. Moreover, the Ulster unionists had, by 1912, provided themselves with their own organisation, the Ulster Unionist Council, which held its first meeting in March 1905, and which offered a more representative and permanent body for Ulster Protestants, as well as a more narrowly focused political perspective.[11] The Irish unionist parliamentary party was now looking more like a first – or, in due course, a second – amongst equals, rather than the representative of general unionist opinion. The increasingly particularist outlook of Ulster unionists was reflected in their decision in September 1911 to set up a provisional government for Ulster should the home rule bill become law. Ulster unionists were glad to have British unionist support for their stand against home rule, but it was not their only, nor indeed their main, pillar of resistance.

This resistance took a more ominous shape when, as early as 1910 and on local initiative on the part of Orange Order lodges, volunteers offered themselves as defenders of the Union. Although Sir Edward Carson and Sir James Craig welcomed the UVF, they played no part in the organisation's day-to-day running; this was indeed a new departure in unionism.[12] Institutions, however, expressed but did not create the Ulster unionist mood of 1912. A new generation of political leaders had emerged, new men, Edwardians like James Craig and Fred Crawford, who found a militant stand more congenial than had their forebears. The importance of the South African war of 1899–1902, which introduced a spirit of militant patriotism in Great Britain and worked the same spell in Ireland, should not be underestimated. It occasioned the formation of Volunteer forces, comprising civilian soldiers who had not engaged in warfare before 1899. One such force was the City of London Imperial Volunteers, in which the later Irish republican Erskine Childers enlisted 'to do something for one's country'.[13] And the early debacles in the campaign against the Boers gave new impetus to the idea of military conscription in the United Kingdom, which was almost unheard of before then. Tunes of glory were being played all over the British Isles. Irish nationalists, for their part, insisted that they held common cause with the Afrikaaners, and would indeed themselves resort to arms if such an option were likely to succeed, which they conceded it was not, at least for the foreseeable future.[14]

The crisis over the third home rule bill raised political, constitutional and even moral issues which, the Ulster unionists claimed, justified a resort to force of arms. These were stated in 'Ulster's Solemn League and Covenant' which thousands of Protestants signed in September 1912. 'Being convinced in our consciences', the signatories pledged themselves to use all means necessary to defeat a conspiracy which, they believed, would be disastrous to Ulster's and Ireland's material well-being, destructive of Protestants' civil and religious liberty, and perilous to the unity of the empire. Bonar Law declared in the House of Commons in June 1912 that the Liberal government 'are putting themselves in a position from which they cannot recede ... That means that they know that if Ulster is in earnest, if Ulster does resist, there are things stronger than parliamentary majorities. They know that in that case no government would dare to use British troops to drive them out.'[15] It was equally true, however, that if Ulster unionists were in earnest, they too might put themselves in a position from which they could not recede; and the use of troops, and their willingness to be employed as an instrument of force, was not – as yet – in any doubt.

Ulster and southern Irish unionist fears about the real character of Irish nationalism were perhaps reinforced by new forces that were stirring at the turn of the century. The Gaelic League, founded in 1893 with the aim of 'de-anglicising Ireland', and bringing to a point earlier nationalist ideas that there was a distinct gaelic nation, or even race, suggested that those who did not belong to that race or nation might be treated as foreigners, uncomfortable interlopers in a country to which they did not 'really' belong. This, it must be stressed, was not the purpose of the league's founder, Douglas Hyde, himself a Protestant, who sought to use language to overcome Irish religious divisions. But this noble idea was diluted by those who saw the league as a means of furthering the separatist cause, or as a way of excluding those who did not 'belong'. The determined efforts by the Catholic church to infiltrate and guide the league, as it did other kinds of pressure groups and organisations, was likewise an uncomfortable sight. Paul Bew has demonstrated that unionists had fears about the Irish language under home rule; for example, at the committee stage of the home rule bill in October 1912 unionists moved an amendment with the aim of preventing an Irish parliament making Irish a qualification for holding public appointments,[16] though the first occupant of the chair of Irish in Queen's University Belfast in 1909 was an Anglican clergyman, the Reverend F.W. O'Connell.[17]

Religious divisions remained the bedrock of Irish politics. For Ulster Protestants the enemy was, as it had been since 1886 (and indeed since the 1830s and 1840s, when 'the Liberator', Daniel O'Connell, roamed the Ulster border area), the Catholic majority in Ireland, which carried its own potent ideological mixture of religion, grievance, and desire to reverse history's verdict that Protestants would be up, and they, the Catholics, would be down. This ideology accommodated the home rule movement as comfortably as more radical nationalism: the men of '98 were as much the property of Redmond and his followers (especially his followers) as they had been of Parnell and his, and the new Sinn Féin party and its. The Irish party did not, in principle, rule out the use of force to achieve freedom.[18]

Ulster unionists did not need new foes, gaelic or otherwise, in the period 1912–14; they felt they had enemies enough. On Ulster Covenant day Dr William McKeon, former moderator of the Presbyterian church, claimed that:

> We are plain, blunt men who love peace and industry. The Irish Question is
> at bottom a war against Protestantism; it is an attempt to establish a Roman
> Catholic ascendancy in Ireland to begin the disintegration of the empire by
> securing a second [sic] parliament in Dublin.[19]

Between 1898 and 1902 there appeared ominous signs of Roman Catholic 'triumphalism'. The Ancient Order of Hibernians, a kind of Catholic mirror image of the Protestant Orange Order, was founded in 1898; a 'Catholic Association' in 1902. Then in 1908 the papacy promulgated the *Ne temere* decree which laid down regulations for bringing up children in marriages in which one of the partners was a non-Catholic. This soon made its impact on Ulster life, when, in 1910, a Mrs McCann, a Presbyterian married to a Roman Catholic, in a union in which each attended their own church, found herself the centre of controversy. It was claimed that Mr McCann's priest visited their home to tell the couple that their marriage was invalid according to the *Ne Temere* decree, and that they must remarry in a Roman Catholic ceremony. It was alleged that Mrs McCann's husband began to ill-treat her, and that he made off with the children (and the furniture), leaving her destitute. Her minister, a Mr Corkey, claimed that the incident demonstrated the 'cruel punishment' which the Roman Catholic church was ready to inflict on any member of the Protestant faith 'over whom she gets any power'.[20] There were some doubts about the details of the case, but in the febrile atmosphere of Ulster's religion and politics, it provided a rallying cry for Protestants, and pushed the Protestant churches (not always well-disposed towards each other) together, in a way that foreshadowed the solidarity with which they confronted home rule. The Presbyterians, repositories of Ulster radicalism in days gone by, were the first to mobilise, warning in a convention on 1 February 1912 that 'our civil and religious liberties would be gravely imperiled'. On Ulster day, when the covenant was signed, St John Ervine (unionist in politics but a leading light in the Irish literary revival) wrote that 'Belfast suspended all its labours and became a place of prayer.'[21]

Out of this political/religious atmosphere came the rational and moral argument that a body of British citizens, utterly opposed to a measure which threatened to deprive them of their citizenship, had the right to resist an unjust law by force. When Lord Milner was canvassing for signatures to a British covenant on the lines of Ulster's Solemn League and Covenant, he asked: 'When before, in our lifetime, have thousands upon thousands of sober steady-going citizens deliberately contemplated resistance to an Act of Parliament, because they were sincerely convinced that it was devoid of all moral sanction?' There were a great many people who still entirely failed to realise 'what the strength of our feeling is on this subject. They think it is just an ordinary case of opposition to a political measure, a move in the party-game.' This might be true of many unionists, 'but there is certainly a large body, who feel that the crisis altogether transcends anything in their previous experience, and calls for action, which is different, not only in degree, but in kind, from what is appropriate to ordinary political controversies.'[22]

This line of argument offered a more palatable reason for resistance than the narrow ground of Catholic/Protestant enmity. It attracted the support, though conditional support, of the eminent Vinerian Professor of English Law in Oxford university, A.V. Dicey. Dicey, a most forceful opponent of Irish home rule since 1886, cited the example of Lord Hartington, who asked: did not Ulster unionists have the right to resist home rule as James II had been resisted by England and Protestant Ireland in 1688–90, especially if home rule was to be imposed by force? Dicey described this as an 'old Whig doctrine' that oppression and especially resistance to the will of the nation 'might justify what was technically conspiracy or rebellion'. But he insisted that the Ulster unionists should offer only moral resistance, which might endure for a year or a year and a half after home rule became law; this would be 'fully justified'. Unionist resistance should be 'conducted with extreme attention to the preservation of order'. In July 1912 he reiterated his concern that Ulster's resistance must be passive; but he feared that Ulster unionists would not have the 'self-control necessary for carrying out the very difficult policy of passive resistance within the limits of the law, tho' I believe it would be successful'. Even in the case of oppression with which Ulster was menaced, 'no loyal citizen should, until all possibilities of legal resistance is exhausted, have recourse to the use of arms'.[23]

Ulster unionists gave notice of their determination to by-pass this suggested era of passive resistance on 24–5 April 1914, when they carried out a daring gun-running adventure at the port of Larne, landing 25,000 rifles and 3,000,000 rounds of ammunition. The possibility of moral resistance was further endangered by the character of the UVF, which began as a 'bottom up rather than top down' unit in many areas; their activities might, especially in time of increased tension, be hard to control.[24] Thus the commanding officer of the 2nd battalion, South Down regiment, Roger Hall, issued orders that Volunteers were 'not to mix themselves up in riots or street fights unless to protect themselves or other Protestants, who may be assaulted, or when called upon by the police to assist them'. The police were to deal with 'ordinary rowdyism, and Volunteers were not to interfere' unless the police found themselves 'unable to cope with the disturbance and call for help'. No rifles or revolvers were to be used 'until the last extremity' and indiscriminate revolver firing was 'strictly forbidden'. Revolvers were not authorised in the UVF and any Volunteer carrying one 'does so on his own responsibility, and must take the consequences if arrested'.[25]

Hall was harking back to the Volunteer movement of the late eighteenth century, when the Irish Volunteers (almost exclusively Protestant) were deployed on law and order tasks, as well as defying the British government. But the question was what would happen if the Liberal government of 1914 sought to assert its authority by deploying the British army against the UVF (which the British government of the 1770s had not done). The unionist peer, the Earl of Selborne, who enjoyed cordial relations with several senior Liberals, warned that if the government attempted to 'crush Ulster with the army and fleet', then Ulster's resistance 'would take all the forms, with which we are familiar in the history of such cases, some heroic and some hideous'. 'Russian methods' must fail.[26] Dicey took the ominous, and probably accurate, view that if the shooting began, 'British soldiers will, in any case, do their duty, and not forget that the primary duty of the soldier is obedience to lawful orders.'[27]

It was hard for any British government, not least a Liberal government, to weigh up the consequences of using force to crush Ulster unionist resistance. There was, as so often in politics, a balance of evils to be assessed. What confounded the Liberals was their bungled attempt, not to crush, but perhaps overawe the UVF in March 1914, when it was still a poorly armed organisation. On 14 March 1914 Winston Churchill warned in a speech in Bradford that it was time 'to go forward and put these grave matters to the proof'.[28] On the same day the war office wrote to Lieutenant General Sir Arthur Paget (commander in chief in Ireland) that 'evil-disposed persons' may try 'to obtain possession of arms, ammunition and other government stores'. Steps must be taken to safeguard depots in the north, but also in the south of Ireland.[29] At a meeting on 19 March at which Winston Churchill and Augustine Birrell, the chief secretary for Ireland, were present, Paget was told that the third battle squadron of the royal navy was to be sent to Lamlash in Scotland 'in order to be available if required'.[30] Paget was concerned about the impact of sudden troop movements in the middle of a political crisis and on 20 March gave the impression to his senior officers that the army might soon engage the UVF, in which case Ireland might be 'ablaze by Saturday, and would lead to something more serious than quelling of local disturbances'. He said that the war office had authorised him to inform officers domiciled in Ulster that they might be excused duties, and permitted to 'disappear' from Ireland, but others would not be thus permitted to choose whether or not they would obey orders. Brigadier General Sir Hubert Gough admitted that he could not claim exemption as a resident of Ulster, but added that 'on account of birth and upbringing, and many friendships, he did not see how he could bear arms against the Ulster loyalists, and that, if he did take up arms against them, he could never face his friends again.'

Fifty seven out of seventy officers of the third cavalry brigade at the Curragh camp responded that, if their duty involved the initiation of active military operations against Ulster, they would chose dismissal.[31] When Gough and three senior commanders went to London to meet Seely (the secretary for war) the following Sunday, the minister acknowledged in writing that the government had no intention of using the armed forces to 'coerce Ulster'.[32] This concession was withdrawn by the government and Seely resigned on 25 March, but the episode cost the government its credibility, and opened it to Law's censure that there had been a 'plot against Ulster'.[33] There is no evidence for this, but it is hard to explain the sudden lurch towards 'precautionary' movements on 14 March, since the Ulster crisis was no worse then than it had been before that date; perhaps government ministers did not so much plot against Ulster as bluff against Ulster.

Whatever the official motives, Ulster unionists rejoiced at the failure of the 'plot'. Paramilitary organisations could act, it seemed, with impunity. But nationalist suspicions at the partiality of the official and military response to the UVF was shown when, on 26 July 1914, the Irish Volunteers emulated the UVF and landed guns and ammunition at Howth, near Dublin, but this time openly and in daylight. Clumsy efforts by the police and then the army to intercept and disarm the Volunteers resulted in soldiers opening fire on civilians who were goading them, resulting in the death of three people and the wounding of thirty eight.

While these dramatic events unfolded, efforts were being made between government and opposition to reach some kind of compromise that would save John Redmond's face and prove acceptable to the unionists, British, Ulster and Irish. Given that so many parties had to be satisfied, it is hardly surprising that the prospects were not good. Law, for his part, was not hankering after civil war; his belief was that, as he wrote to Dicey in June 1913, 'the best chance of avoiding civil war, or something like it, is to convince ministers that we are in earnest.'[34] But this desire to show earnestness drove him into dangerous waters, including the idea of amending the annual Army Act, which was passed to legalise the existence of the armed forces for the next twelve months (this again was a legacy of the seventeenth century 'Glorious Revolution' and King James II's determination to use the army to fight for his throne). The unionist leadership discussed this in 1912, and again in 1913, with the intention of amending it to prevent the use of troops to coerce Ulster, but finally abandoned the plan in March 1914 when, indeed, the Curragh episode made it redundant.[35] Carson spoke the language of rebellion, but feared the outcome if matters were put to the proof.[36] Sir James Craig, for the Ulster unionists, went on with his preparations for such an event. Southern Irish unionists looked with alarm on the efforts being made by all sides to find a compromise, for these became more focused on the expedient of finding some special treatment for Ulster, or part of it, and abandoning the rest of Ireland to home rule. Not all British unionists were satisfied with seeking a compromise of the Union in the form of special treatment for Ulster unionists. Irish home rulers were uneasy about what concessions might be demanded of them in order to disarm Ulster unionist resistance. They had also the substantial Catholic population in Ulster to consider.

The Liberal government, seeking to find a compromise, was obliged to put pressure on John Redmond on the Ulster issue, for where else was compromise to come from? A survey of the attempts made to offer special treatment for Ulster, with some form of exclusion from the home rule bill for some period of time, and for some area of the province, shows how the Liberals were retreating from the Gladstonian tradition of seeing Ireland as the unit of devolution, with safeguards for individuals, to one that saw Ulster or perhaps four or six counties of it, as a bloc to be excluded. On 9 March 1914 Asquith proposed an amendment to the home rule bill that would allow the electorate of each Ulster county, with Belfast and Londonderry, to vote whether it wished to opt out of home rule for six years. The time limit was fixed so that before it expired the electors of the United Kingdom would have been twice consulted (i.e. not later than December 1915 and not later than December 1920); and if it ratified the inclusion of the excluded counties, then Ulster should have no cause for resistance. In June 1914 an amending bill offering 'county option' for six years was introduced in the House of Lords by Lord Crewe, but the peers rejected it and voted instead for the permanent exclusion of the whole of Ulster. On July 21–4 a conference held at Buckingham palace between the party leaders failed to find a way out of the dilemma: Redmond would go no further than county option, which meant the exclusion of four Ulster counties; Law wanted six; Carson demanded the 'clean cut' of the whole province of Ulster. Asquith was prepared to give way on the time limit for exclusion, but suggested leaving out of the bill south Tyrone, north Fermanagh and the four north eastern counties, except for south Armagh. This was unacceptable to both unionists and nationalists.[37]

United Kingdom participation in the European war on 4 August forced the issue. John Redmond used all his influence, such as it was, with the government to oblige it to pass the home rule bill.[38] In any event Asquith could hardly take the country into war with the Irish and Ulster questions utterly unresolved. His compromise was that the home rule bill be placed on the statute book, but accompanied by a suspensory Act 'for twelve months or such later date (not being later than the end of the present war) as may be fixed by His Majesty by Order in Council.' He promised an amending bill dealing with the Ulster question, and when the bill was given formal assent on 18 September Asquith conceded that the coercion of unionist Ulster was an 'absolutely unthinkable thing'.[39]

The war worked immediate changes on the Irish political scene. In a sense it marked a closure of the Ulster crisis, for within a short time Carson and Redmond respectively pledged the Ulster and the Irish Volunteers to the British war effort. In so doing both made concessions. Carson had hoped in August 1914 to pledge the UVF to the British side, with two battalions to be sent abroad, but only if the home rule bill were postponed.[40] But when the government pressed on with its bill (much to the disgust of British unionists) Carson, a thorough-going imperial patriot, could hardly stand over his demand. Redmond came best out of the last stages of the bill, because he had after all gained what not even the great Parnell sought – a home rule measure on the statute book. Furthermore, by urging the Irish Volunteers to 'take their place in the firing line in this contest' he had (as one of his severest critics William O'Brien acknowledged) made the best possible use of the Volunteers: 'in fighting England's battle in the particular circumstances of [the] war … they were fighting the most effective battle for Ireland's liberty.'[41]

Yet Redmond did not yet have his parliament; and if Irish nationalist disillusionment with the war were to surface, then he might be in an awkward position. But this is not to say that any such disillusionment would have seriously undermined Redmond's position, though his very success in getting the home rule bill passed into law further reduced his room for manoeuvre. He could hardly refuse to help the war effort, especially as Ireland's friends in the British empire (and Redmond had and valued such friends) were enthusiastic supporters of the British war effort. On the Ulster unionist side there is evidence that some at least believed that the UVF as the sharp edge of resistance was a spent force. Lord Dunleath of Co. Down, describing himself as 'one of the Pioneers of the Volunteer Movement', wrote to Carson on 9 March 1915 that the general idea in the minds of the men who promoted and organised this movement was to give as strong an expression as possible of their resolve to resist the policy of home rule. Speeches in and out of parliament, and monster demonstrations in Ulster, had apparently failed to interest the English and Scotch electors, or to concentrate their attention on the passionate abhorrence of home rule on the part of the Protestant population of Ireland and of the industrial inhabitants of Ulster.

Thus it was the 'plain duty of those of us who were possessed of influence to take some step, which would convince the government of the reality of our determination to resist this policy by every means in our power'. They had organised the Volunteers, gradually equipped and trained them into a fairly efficient force of volunteer infantry, and finally provided them with arms and ammunition. This had the desired effect of turning English and Scottish attention towards Ulster and had assisted, and would assist, her political leaders in the future. Until a few months ago 'we found ourselves on the brink of a conflict with the armed forces of the Crown'. Now the war offered a favourable opportunity to reconsider 'our position and future policy'. Dunleath claimed that 'many of us are undoubtedly willing, if necessary, to risk our lives in defence of what we believe to be our rights and liberties, but I venture to think that an encounter with the armed forces of the Crown would inflict a serious injury upon our cause, and that every possible effort should be made to avoid the possibility of any calamity of this character.'

He did not think 'that our men are prepared to go into action against any part of His Majesty's forces, and we [their leaders] should not consider ourselves justified in calling upon them to do so'.

Dunleath understood that unionist politicians would like very much to be able to assert in their speeches that the Volunteers would undoubtedly come out and fight at the first attempt to administer the home rule Act, 'but I venture to suggest a strong hope that this assertion will not be made or encouraged by the leaders of the unionist party'. He now fell back upon Dicey's belief that the best way for unionists was to offer passive resistance, at least in the first instance (especially against paying taxes to the home rule parliament); if payment were enforced, the Volunteers would always be available to resist and 'our men would like nothing better than to go out against the nationalists'. He concluded that 'our political position as passive resisters, supported by a large body of armed Volunteers, should be a strong one – whereas if even a single British soldier or sailor was killed or wounded in Ulster, I am afraid that our future prospects would be extremely gloomy.'[42]

This was to some extent put to the test in 1919 when, as the British government again took up the home rule burden, Carson threatened that he would 'call out the Ulster Volunteers' if there were any attempt to take away the rights of Ulstermen – a threat which prompted an angry response in the British press and in parliament. Government spokesmen defended Carson uneasily, with one Conservative MP dismissing Carson's loyalty as 'the loyalty of Shylock'.[43]

It is unlikely that even the common experience of war would have overcome the ideological divide between Ulster unionist and Irish nationalist, though there were signs of a mutual acknowledgement of each other's bravery in combat, and respect for each other in this momentous enterprise. Nevertheless, few would have predicted that at the war's end the home rulers would be dismissed from the political landscape, and Ulster unionists left as the sole occupiers of the patriotic ground. Fewer still would have expected the separatist rebellion of Easter 1916. Contemporaries could not of course foresee that the Ulster unionist protest against home rule would in any way contribute to the Easter Rising; and for the historian this remains an intriguing question. The debate had an early start. Bulmer Hobson complained that 'it seemed to the Irish people that the English desired to have it both ways and when they [the Irish] sought to enforce their national rights by the methods of Fenianism they were told to agitate constitutionally, and when they acted constitutionally they were met by methods of Fenianism.'[44] Ronald McNeill, Lord Cushendun, acknowledged that the methods adopted by unionists might be said to contribute a 'bad example', though he thought them justifiable as the 'lesser of two evils'. He added archly that 'there was something humorous in the pretence put forward in 1923 and afterwards that the violence to which the adherents of Sinn Féin had recourse was merely copying Ulster. As if Irish nationalism in its extreme form required precedent for insurrection from Ulster.'[45]

Some modern historians tend to agree with Bulmer Hobson. Jeremy Smith writes that:

> In organising themselves against home rule and exposing British governmental weakness, they [the UVF] encouraged nationalists to emulate their example … 'The Orangeman who can fire a gun,' Patrick Pearse wrote in 1913, 'will

certainly count for more in the end than the nationalist who can do nothing cleverer than make a pun.' The seeds of events in Ireland over the following decade were clearly planted in the pre-war period.[46]

Michael Laffan acknowledges that Bonar Law and Carson 'were to be deeply shocked and repelled by much that happened in Ireland during the decade which followed their defiance of parliamentary government, but without their example the Irish revolution would not have come about', and he quotes General Maxwell in June 1916: 'The law was broken, and others broke the law with more or less success.'[47]

This brings the historian into the fascinating but dubious realm of virtual history. We cannot know what would have happened had the Ulster and southern Irish unionists meekly accepted the home rule parliament which they believed threatened their lives and liberties in 1912–14; likewise we cannot know what would have happened had John Redmond meekly accepted that the Ulster unionist opposition was in earnest in its desire to resist Dublin rule, and abandoned his belief that Ireland, a nation pure and indivisible, must not be denied her birthright. What we do know is that Redmond's leadership, indeed the whole character of the nationalism of his day, was regarded with increasing distaste by separatists, who from the early summer of 1915 planned their riposte – a rising, with German help, during the war. Michael Laffan remarks perceptively that 'the Irish Volunteers' popularity did not mean that Irish nationalists had been converted en masse to the idea of revolution', which implies, to say the least, that a free choice lay in the hands of the separatists of 1916, and they resolved to take it.[48]

But there is the question of the guns that were taken into Ireland in 1912–14. Ben Novick calculates that there were more than 66,000 rifles in Ireland in the hands of paramilitary organisations by March 1915, and if Ireland was not a country of guns in the nineteenth century, she quickly made up for that in the early twentieth. [49] Guns are important; but so is the will and the opportunity to use them. Michael Wheatly's analysis of provincial nationalist opinion reveals 'a mass political mobilisation, militarism and a bellicosity of language unseen in recent times'.[50] It is true that the overwhelming majority of the Irish Volunteers who declared they would use guns in 1913–14 did in the end do so: but in British army uniforms, against the Germans and the Turks. Paradoxically, the minority of Irish Volunteers who used them in Ireland in 1916 shouldered, not the best available weapons of the day, but a 'grab-bag assortment of outdated weapons'.[51] The key point was not the condition of the weapons they employed but the belief that the gun was indeed a keystone of liberty; and that belief, though never lost by separatists, and praised even by home rulers, was thrust to the forefront of Irish politics by the Ulster rebellion.

If Ulster's stand for union reinforced the 1916 rebels' conviction that the rifle was the instrument of freedom, then it failed to direct their attention to what, in retrospect, seems like another, rather more obvious, conclusion. They completely ignored the implications of the Ulster crisis, and simplified Irish politics into an age-old confrontation between 'England' and 'Ireland'. Their Proclamation insisted that all Irishmen and Irishwomen owed allegiance to the Republic, now actually in being. It failed to recognise the existence, let alone the beliefs, of the Ulster unionists whose armed defiance of home rule Pearse professed to admire. Nearly five years after the Rising, on 21 September 1920, Lord Grey (who on 3 August 1914 described Ireland as 'the one bright spot on the map of Europe') set out a grim, but realistic, choice for Irish nationalists and Ulster unionists. 'At present,' he wrote, 'Ulster wrecks anything that nationalist Ireland will accept: Sinn Fein clamours for a united Ireland and either willfully ignores the Ulster difficulty or says it is our business to see that the difficulty is overcome.' Grey proposed to apply what he called the 'coercion of facts, which both sides have hitherto declined to face'. Irishmen, he concluded, must choose between: '(1) compromise and agreement with each other; or (2) a divided Ireland; or (3) civil war'. Grey believed that when they understood the logic of the situation he had no doubt that they would choose the first of these courses.[52] He was mistaken. And it seems not unreasonable to say that the partition of Ireland, unthinkable in the home rule episodes of 1886 and 1893, but emerging, painfully, as the possible base of some sort of compromise in 1913–14 was, after the Easter Rising, hard to avoid.

'IRRECONCILABLE ENEMIES' OR 'FLESH AND BLOOD'? THE IRISH PARTY AND THE EASTER REBELS, 1914–16

Michael Wheatley

I

The response of the Irish party to the Easter Rising was in one key respect unambiguous – the Rising was condemned and deplored. It was variously described as criminal, insane, politically stupid, a direct threat to home rule, hopelessly impractical, foolish or, using one of the most heavily-used words of the time, 'misguided'. Criticism was still commonplace months after the Rising, expressed by speakers and writers right across the party, whether pledge-bound MPs in the parliamentary party or the large body of councillors, officers and activists who remained at the heart of the party's mass affiliates, the United Irish League (UIL) and Ancient Order of Hibernians (AOH).

Nevertheless, attitudes towards the rebels themselves were ambivalent. Certainly, the party's leader, John Redmond, described them as 'irreconcilable enemies' who had made an 'attempt to torpedo home rule and the Irish party', but the dilemma faced by his party was acute.[1] The rebels, for all the damage they had done, were nationalist Irishmen. According to the *Longford Leader* (owned by the party MP, J.P. Farrell), they were the constitutional movement's 'own flesh and blood'.[2] Moreover, the Irish party remained proud of its Fenian antecedents and had for decades praised a long succession of rebels and martyrs to the cause. John Fitzgibbon MP (who had himself, like Farrell, been an imprisoned agitator) could well understand the 'mental agonies' of those arrested after the Rising: 'These men can be consoled by the fact that they had in the past history of Ireland many comrades who suffered the same treatment, so that it is not to be wondered at.'[3]

These varied attitudes were reflected in the differing tone of public statements made by the party's two most prominent figures, Redmond and his chief parliamentary colleague, John Dillon. Their statements and speeches were widely publicised at the time and the differences between the two men have been well analysed by subsequent historians.[4] However, the attitudes of their followers in Ireland remain relatively unstudied. It is simply not known how far the bulk of the Irish party endorsed Redmond's outright condemnation of the rebels, Dillon's seething defiance of British stupidity and brutality, or both. Study at the local level may also shed some light on the more fundamental issue of just how much Irish party activists identified with the rebels and, ultimately, of how much they were tuned to the same militant, nationalist, anglophobe wavelength as the movement which would very soon displace them, Sinn Féin.

As in my previous work on pre-Rising nationalist public opinion, this study is based primarily on an analysis of weekly, provincial newspapers published in five politically-linked counties in the Irish midlands and east Connacht – Leitrim, Longford, Roscommon, Sligo and Westmeath.[5] The political affiliations of these papers were clearly flagged – twelve were nationalist, two independent and two unionist.[6] At the time of the Rising, eight of the nationalist papers were consistent supporters of the Irish party and four were opponents. Competition between these local titles remained intense, which meant that while owners and editors still saw themselves as the vanguard of opinion, they could never move so far ahead of their readers as to risk losing circulation, printing contracts and advertisers. The provincial press remained just as much the mirror as the leader of local opinion.

Admittedly, the provincial press was past its pre-war prime. Local newspapers were severely constrained in size by the wartime scarcity of newsprint. Their reporting after the Rising was curtailed by military censorship, albeit a censorship that was distinctly patchy and inconsistent in its effect. They also faced intensifying competition from the daily *Irish Independent,* which had sustained an increase in circulation of some 60 per cent, to well over 90,000 copies, since the outbreak of war. Nevertheless, they remained the most important forum for the dissemination of the views of the intertwined commercial, professional and political elites of 'small town' Ireland and, in particular, for the expression of local Irish party opinion.

II

The immediate responses of the provincial press to the Easter Rising were formed in a climate of profound shock and confusion. Information was sparse and rumours were abundant. Train and postal services to Dublin were disconnected for over a week and nearly all of the Dublin press was temporarily out of action. However, certain elements of hard news did feature consistently across the provincial press as it went to print ahead of the first weekend of the Rising. There had been an armed 'Sinn Féin' rebellion in Dublin in which numerous prominent buildings had been occupied, but which had been contained by substantial troop reinforcements. There had been heavy shooting, looting and many deaths. Both the Irish Citizen Army and Irish Volunteers had taken part. There had not been a general uprising across Ireland and most other major towns and cities in Ireland were 'quiet'. There had been German involvement – the arrest of Sir Roger Casement, having landed in Ireland from a 'German ship', was reported across the local press.

The local nationalist press was swift to condemn. This applied to both pro- and anti-party papers. In Roscommon town, the anti-party *Roscommon Journal* pronounced the Rising to be 'an outrage and a crime against the teachings of the Church'. In Boyle, the pro-party *Western Nationalist* wrote of 'revolution, desolation and horror' stating that untold calamity would bring infamy on the instigators and drive the country back a generation. The *Sligo Nationalist* declared that whoever hoped for intervention by a foreign despot was not a patriotic Irishman. 'He must be marked as an enemy of his country, and the brand of criminality will sear his soul.' For the *Westmeath Examiner*, owned by Redmond's friend, John Hayden MP, it was a dark and bitter chapter in Irish history, a well-organised plan originating in Berlin, and not in any circumstances justified. No doubt, it said, some of those in Dublin were not badly motivated, 'but the fool is often as bad as the criminal'.[7]

A week later, condemnations of the blind folly of the rebels, their manipulation by Germany and the criminality of the Rising still pervaded the local press. For the Athlone-based *Westmeath Independent*, the Rising was a crime against the government of the country and against Ireland, causing 'the bitterest resentment against the mad fanaticism' which had occasioned it. 'Poor dreamers' had been deluded by German intrigue.[8] News coverage was now far more extensive, with eyewitness reports from local people trapped in Dublin, detailed reports of events across Ireland

and, right across the press, news of martial law and the first arrests and executions.

What also appeared in Irish party papers, though, was a distinctive, party-political narrative. The Rising had endangered home rule – by alienating British opinion it placed the post-war implementation of home rule in jeopardy. The *Westmeath Independent* had stated, as early as 29 April, that the blackest element of the crisis would be that the 'ridiculously designated' rebellion would be seen in England as Irish ingratitude towards English democracy.[9] By 6 May several others took up the theme. To avoid the poisoning of Anglo-Irish relations, to preserve home rule, it was vital that Irishmen rallied to their natural political leaders, the Irish party, and isolated the minority. Moreover, the blow to home rule had been deliberate, struck by rebels who were long-standing enemies of the Irish party. Party papers now pointed the finger at 'men here and there throughout Ireland' who did not rebel in Dublin, but who gave countenance and support to the Rising's organisers. The *Sligo Nationalist* pledged to 'meet them and fight them foot by foot on this issue'. The *Westmeath Examiner* and *Roscommon Messenger* (both owned by John Hayden) attacked those who had always been opposed to the chosen leaders of the Irish people. 'We have such all around us, though they are not numerous … They pose as idealists and a quite superior sort of Irishman.' Before God they were equally responsible for the Rising with those who actually rebelled.[10]

This political theme was entirely in accord with the personal manifesto issued by the party's leader on 3 May. Although he was in no doubt that 'Germany plotted it, organised and paid for it', Redmond also denounced his Irish political enemies, the 'insane movement' which risked dashing the cup of liberty from Ireland's lips. For years, the Irish party had been 'thwarted and opposed by the same section'. Their rebellion 'was not half as much treason to the cause of the Allies as treason to the cause of home rule'.[11] Redmond amplified these remarks just over a week later, in his cable addressing American opinion via the New York paper, *Ireland*. It was not so much hatred of England as hatred of home rule and the Irish party that was at the bottom of the movement, which was run by 'Sinn Féin cranks', German agents and remnants of Larkinite discontent. 'It was even more an attempt to hit us than to hit England … I beg our people in America not to be unduly disturbed by this futile and miserable attempt to destroy Ireland. It has failed – definitely, finally failed.'[12]

That a significant element of the Irish party, and above all its leader, should immediately go for the political jugular of its nationalist opponents is not surprising. 'Constitutional' and 'advanced' nationalists had been in bitter opposition to each other since the autumn of 1914 and had attacked each other with all the vigour and invective of nationalist splits since the days of Parnell. The primary cause of this division was the war, and in particular the Irish party's open encouragement of wartime recruiting into the British army to serve in 'the firing line'. As J.J. Lee has summarised, Ireland's participation in the war was intended to secure the operation of home rule, woo British opinion, unite nationalists and unionists in shared wartime comradeship and secure better arms and training for the Volunteers. By contrast, Irish 'neutrality' in the war would play into the hands of unionists, make partition certain, and forfeit British support.[13] The party's commitment to support England and her allies in the war was essential to avoid outraging British opinion in the midst of what was already seen as the most terrible war in history. Home rule may have been on the statute book, but both the date of its implementation and the degree of Ulster's exclusion were unknown. Both remained within England's gift. The Roscommon MP John Hayden, speaking in May 1916, summarised the choice faced by the party in 1914:

> Suppose, at such a moment, Mr Redmond had said 'Ireland will hold aloof from the war unless you put the Home Rule Act into operation and defy the Ulster Volunteers,' what would have happened? Not only would the Home Rule Act not be in force but it would not now be on the statute book. It would have been dead for their generation anyhow.[14]

According to the Longford MP J.P. Farrell, speaking in November 1916, 'he [Redmond] had to decide in a moment whether to antagonise the British people in a fashion that could never be forgiven or forgotten, or endeavour to retain their friendship and goodwill.' Farrell continued: 'We can always revert to the policy that will revive the rule of Cromwell. Any fool can do that.'[15]

As for the minority of nationalists in 1914 who could not accept a wartime alliance with 'England', they were, indeed, dismissed by the Irish party as fools, cranks and factionists, as mischief-makers, utterly inexperienced, impractical intellectuals, socialists or people of no standing. Above all, they were pilloried as 'Sinn Féiners'. This was partly because several of their leaders had in recent years been members of Arthur Griffith's Sinn Féin party. By 1914, as Matthew Kelly has written, Griffith's incessant journalism had succeeded in establishing 'an almost exclusive association between Sinn Féin and advanced nationalism'.[16] However, the Irish party also sought to link all of its nationalist opponents to a small movement that many believed to be a cranky failure. Moreover, the 'Sinn Féiners' were now branded, again and again, as 'pro-German' or, as the propaganda sheet the *National Volunteer* described them, 'the Sinn Féin–Larkinite combination who have suddenly become convinced of the ineffable beauties of German militarism'.[17] The headlines for the first article in the first edition of the *National Volunteer*, in October 1914, summed up the Irish party line:

The German empire
Mushroom power
Facts about Kaiser's land
Prussian home rule
The workers disfranchised
What the Sinn Féiners would impose on Ireland.[18]

In November, the paper published *The Sinn Féin Voght*, parodying the separatist, nationalist verse of the *Shan Van Vocht*:

We are patriots so bold
Says the Sinn Féin Voght
From a German–Gaelic mould
Says the Sinn Féin Voght
With dissension as our tool
Used by every crank and fool
We'll try and smash home rule
Says the Sinn Féin Voght.[19]

For much of 1915, the party believed that it had won its struggle with its opponents. In July, speaking to the *New York World*, Redmond dismissed them as 'what is called the Sinn Féin movement ... simply a temporary cohesion of isolated cranks in various parts of the country', which did not 'count for a row of pins so far as I am concerned'.[20] By the end of the year, however, it was clear to many press and police observers that constitutional nationalism was weakening, relative to what almost all called its 'Sinn Féiner' opponents. The response of the Irish party was to try to boost its flagging organisation on the ground, and to increase the volume of its verbal attacks. In late 1915 and early 1916, organisers such as John Keaveny, a Connacht director of the Hibernians, toured counties such as

Leitrim, Roscommon and Sligo trying to revive UIL branches. To the Breedogue, Roscommon UIL, Keaveny denounced 'the Sinn Féin element … malcontents, carpers, with penny-pistol ideas for emancipating Ireland'. Addressing the Kilmayral UIL branch, he spoke of 'hot-headed and irresponsible boys', who would 'play into the hands of Carsonites after the war and nothing will get up English backs quicker than all the sneering'. It was Sinn Féiners who were doing this and they were 'openly pro-German'. To the Frenchpark UIL, again in Roscommon, Keaveny declaimed that there was never a more meaningless party than 'the Sinn Féin movement' but he then slightly spoiled the effect by stating that its object was to overthrow the Irish party.[21] At the beginning of April 1916, J.P Farrell told the Edgeworthstown, Longford UIL, that the Sinn Féiners were malcontents who had never done any constructive work for Ireland. To cheers, he declared his belief that there was Dublin Castle or German money behind them. On 15 April, the *Sligo Champion* carried a signed article, 'Irishmen, Beware of Sinn Féinism', by the local Protestant home ruler R.G. Bradshaw. Irishmen would lose all if German militarism gained the ascendant. Those who claimed that Ireland was sacred to the Germans were 'disciples of Judas' and 'traitors'. 'Sinn Féinism', he concluded, 'is pro-Germanism' and its followers 'are marked out to be shunned'.[22]

This strain of invective was, therefore, sustained by the party right up to the eve of the Rising. When that uprising materialised out of the blue, it was immediately labelled as both 'Sinn Féin' and 'pro-German', using language honed over the previous eighteen months. That the rebels were Sinn Féiners was, for party speakers, axiomatic. That they were pro-German was corroborated by the reference to 'gallant allies in Europe' in the Proclamation of the Republic and by events on the Kerry coast – the arrest of Casement and the sinking of the *Aud*. The rebels struck at the heart of the party's 'pro-England' wartime political strategy. As John Dillon put it in his famous parliamentary speech of 11 May:

> I say that these men, misguided as they were, have been our bitterest enemies. They have held us up to public odium as traitors to our country because we have supported you at this moment and have stood by you in this great war.[23]

III

There was, however, another party attitude towards the Sinn Féiners, which was apparent in the months before the Rising. For all that they were political opponents, individual Sinn Féiners did receive sympathy and support from many constitutional nationalists if their actions led to their being prosecuted by the authorities. As an example of this, in the second half of 1915 a succession of resolutions was put up at council meetings, protesting against the arrest and deportation to Britain of Irish Volunteer organisers. Though many of these resolutions were blocked or amended by Irish party stalwarts as Sinn Féin-inspired, they often produced heated debate and expressions of sympathy from individuals who were still clearly constitutional nationalists. In a few cases, including Sligo corporation, the Longford guardians and the Roscommon town commission, the resolutions passed. The pro-party newspaper the *Western Nationalist* (set up in Boyle as recently as 1908 to counter Jasper Tully's vitriolic, anti-party *Roscommon Herald*) criticised what it saw as injustice. Under the Defence of the Realm Act (DORA), military officers could order people out of the country if they were thought to be hindering recruiting. It was unjust that any man could be deported simply because he preached politics with which the military disagreed.[24]

More widespread, within the five counties studied here, was sympathy for local men who suffered at the hands of the authorities. In Westmeath, at the beginning of September 1915, a young man named Edward Moraghan was at Mullingar railway station when he got into a row with a group of soldiers. He called them cowards to enlist, said that England should fight her own battles and was promptly arrested. He was subsequently sentenced by magistrates to three months' hard labour. The sentence triggered considerable criticism. In particular, the treatment of a young man seen as hot-tempered but respectable (with two brothers away in the army and the only remaining support for his farmer father) was contrasted with the impunity with which English strikers and 'conscriptionist' critics of the war were allowed to operate. Patrick McKenna, the UIL national director for south Westmeath and a protégé of John Hayden, briefly resigned in protest from Westmeath County Council until the lord lieutenant remitted Moraghan's sentence.[25]

More seriously, two local Volunteer leaders were arrested in Co. Sligo in November. In Tobercurry, Patrick Dyar was charged with speaking against recruiting and possessing anti-recruiting documents. Dyar, a book-keeper, had persuaded thirty two local men to sign a document pledging that they would resist conscription even at the cost of their lives. He received one month in prison. On his release in December he was greeted with the traditional torch-light procession and band parade. As the *Western Nationalist* put it, 'poor hot-headed Irishmen are safer prey' than English labour leaders.[26] Rather more dramatic was the case of Alex McCabe, one of Dyar's few fellow Irish Republican Brotherhood (IRB) men in Co. Sligo. McCabe was charged with possessing explosives on railway premises. When arrested, he was in possession of forty two gelignite cartridges, twenty detonators, five coils of fuse wire, an automatic pistol and a list of arms purchases.[27] This was, as the local press reported it, a 'sensation', and McCabe was taken to Dublin, under heavy escort, where he was eventually tried in February 1916. McCabe's case epitomised the confusion of local opinion about Sinn Féiners. As an anti-war activist and Volunteer, he had been an irksome rival to the Irish party – in July 1915 he had been suspended from his teaching post by the local parish priest, Rev. O'Grady of Keash, because of his 'objectionable political activity'.[28] When he became a prisoner, however, he became a nationalist victim in British hands. A 'McCabe Indemnity Fund' was set up and the *Sligo Champion* printed a brief appeal for contributions.[29] The Sligo MP John O'Dowd asked parliamentary questions about his constituent's conditions of imprisonment and terms of trial; J.P. Farrell even visited him in prison, on the pretext that he was the nephew of one of his own Longford constituents.[30] Such gestures of support, however, were as nothing to that of the Dublin jury, which accepted McCabe's defence that the explosives were for fishing, ignored the judge's direction and after twenty minutes' deliberation acquitted him.[31]

The main cause célèbre just before the Rising was not local, however, but was in nearby King's County (Offaly), in Tullamore. On 20 March 1916, Sinn Féiners in the town were trapped in their Volunteer Hall by a hostile crowd. Stones were thrown and shots were then fired from the hall. The crowd dispersed, but the police tried to enter the hall to disarm the Sinn Féiners. One police sergeant was shot and seriously wounded and thirteen men were subsequently charged with attempted murder.[32] Ten of these were still untried and under arrest at the time of the Rising. The anti-party *Midland Reporter*, controlled by the inveterate conspiracy-theorist Tully brothers, demanded to know who had supplied Union Jacks to the mob and had started them on their mission to attack the Volunteer Hall. However, it was the pro-war, pro-party *Westmeath Independent* that most strongly defended the Sinn Féiners.[33] The scuffle should never have taken place: both the police and Sinn Féiners had acted foolishly. Patience and not coercion was needed to win over young men and if England had not been able to win over all the elements of Irish life, was it to be wondered at? The lever moving Sinn Féin was not pro-Germanism but love of country, 'for, above all the wrangling in connection with the Sinn Féin movement, we must not lose sight of the fact that it is the product of patriotic inspiration'.[34]

The cases of Moraghan, Dyar, McCabe and the Tullamore men all triggered sympathy for individuals, if not for the Sinn Féin movement as a whole, but only once they had become prisoners of the police and 'Dublin Castle'. Many of the constitutional nationalists who followed these cases had themselves clashed repeatedly with the authorities over the years; a significant number had been imprisoned and some were still highly-regarded former Fenians. Moreover, such arrests occurred during a period in which repeated calls for active Irish participation in the war did not generate popular enthusiasm. The local refrain in late 1915 and early 1916 was that the war was not one of 'sentiment'. The majority of Irishmen were indifferent. As the *Longford Leader* put it at the beginning of 1916, it was 'never a peoples' war' and 'we see no prospect for an immediate end to our cruel period of suspense'.[35] The war itself was perceived to be going badly. Nothing occurred to change the general view that it would be long and its cost enormous. Recruiting in provincial Ireland, outside of its larger towns, remained slow. Politically, the perception was reinforced that nationalists were 'mere puppets in a continuously losing game':[36] the operation of home rule was stalled indefinitely; taxes were raised; public services cut; and bitter, unionist enemies admitted into the coalition government formed in May 1915. Throughout 1915 the fear of military conscription was pervasive, as was the belief that its imposition would end nationalist Ireland's support for the war.

In this period before the Easter Rising, the sense of victimhood and anglophobia that had long permeated nationalist political language was given full expression, not just in the 'mosquito press' of the anti-war opposition, but throughout the party-supporting press. This took the form of incessant complaints and denunciations of Tories, 'conscriptionists', the congested districts board, Dublin Castle, orangemen, the war office and the Ulster division. Consistently, such complaints were suffused with the belief that nationalist Ireland was treated unfairly relative to Ulster and to 'England'. Such a state of anglophobic hostility was at variance with the hopes and outlook of John Redmond.[37] His party might still pledge its loyalty to the 'leader of the Irish race', but the tone of much of the comment from its leading figures, both national and local, was distinctly sour. At the beginning of 1916, for example, the *Western Nationalist* wrote of John Dillon that 'there was a touch of the old, rebel spirit' in a parliamentary speech that Dillon made against conscription. Dillon declaimed that if England had treated Ireland decently in the past she would now have far more Irishmen fighting her battles. Incompetent officers had sacrificed Irish regiments at Gallipoli. 'I tell you that before this [Military Service] bill is passed we will demand their blood at the hands of the government.'[38]

At the local level, the mood was captured in a letter to the press at the end of 1915 from Patrick McKenna, the UIL national director who had so angrily protested about Moraghan's gaol term (and who would, in 1917, be the party's unsuccessful candidate in the South Longford by-election). McKenna was incensed because an official order had been made to control the sale of shotgun cartridges. The whole attitude behind this order was one of 'we cannot trust the Irish'. While, he wrote, 250,000 Irishmen could fight for the empire, in Ireland they could not be trusted to shoot snipe. Ireland was just as entitled to be an armed nation as any of the small nations fighting in the war. McKenna thanked God for being 'what they call an agitator … Whatever we gained was by agitation while we uniformly lost by moderation.' Referring to the arrested and deported Volunteers, he stated that there was no fair play for Ireland under DORA – an Irish anti-war dissident would get three to six months in jail while his Scottish equivalent got only five days. McKenna concluded, re-affirming his own political loyalties: 'I may mention that I am not in any sense a pro-German or a Sinn Féiner.'[39]

IV

Over the winter of 1915–16, political hostility to Sinn Féiners, therefore, co-existed with disillusionment with the war, outbursts of antipathy to England and sympathy for fellow nationalists in trouble. As a result, the subsequent response of the Irish party to the Easter Rising was anything but homogeneous. This is not to say that the rebellion was approved of: as already seen, it was condemned across the local nationalist press. Never-theless, party comment on the Rising, even before the succession of execu-tions and mass provincial arrests, made it clear that there were different levels of culpability among the rebels. It also sought to assign blame away from them and emphasised Ireland's victimhood. Calls for mercy and attacks on Ulster (particularly on Sir Edward Carson and the UVF) were both commonplace.

Such an emphasis was prominent in the *Westmeath Independent* as early as 29 April, before any of the executions and when the Dublin nationalist press was still unobtainable. This paper's condemnation of the Rising has already been noted, as has its immediate analysis of the threat posed to home rule. Its owner, Thomas Chapman, was a Protestant home ruler and Westmeath County Councillor who had two sons serving in the army. Its editor, Michael MacDermott-Hayes, was secretary of the south Westmeath UIL. Its leading article made it clear that the Rising was the action of 'a section of irresponsibles', but then went on to state that the Rising would almost certainly not have happened if home rule had been in operation (if it had happened, it would have been suppressed by Ireland alone, just as de Wet's 1915 rebellion in South Africa was suppressed without any need for imperial forces). The key people to blame for the uprising were Sir Edward Carson, for legitimising and justifying physical force, and James Larkin, the wild Dublin socialist. The paper contrasted the 'mistaken ideas of patriotism' of the Irish Volunteers with the 'pure scoundrelism' of the socialist Citizen Army – only the latter were looting in Dublin. 'A lot of regret must be for the young men who have been unfortunately led into this business.'[40]

A week later, the paper developed these themes. It still lamented what it called 'an outbreak of Larkinism' and an epidemic of madness in Dublin (it was not an Irish rebellion), but it now linked the rebels with the tradition of Irish 'valour'. 'These young men are Irishmen. They are the class from whom has been drawn the Irish soldier, who has made the world ring with his valour.' It also made an explicit plea for mercy and for there to be no more executions. 'Notwithstanding their crime, and it cannot be minimized, it is the duty of Ireland to plead for mercy for the misguided fellows dragged into this movement.' The crime of all the rebels was no worse than that of de Wet in South Africa. 'Mercy for the men; punishment, if it must be, for the leaders – but not the punishment of death!'[41]

The other major Irish party newspaper in the five counties was the *Sligo Champion*, mouthpiece for the shopkeepers, merchants and professional men who led nationalist politics in Sligo town, Co. Sligo and north Leitrim. The *Champion* produced no leading article on 29 April, but on 6 May the paper extensively quoted the opinions of an 'imperial contemporary' and was able to blame just about everybody except the rebels for the

Rising. Both the government and those classes who represented 'the government of Ireland by England' were culpable. The seeds of rebellion were sown by Carson, the UVF and unionism, and were bearing bitter fruit. The government had withheld the benefits of the home rule Act from Ireland. The war office had given no help to Redmond's efforts to retain the Volunteers as a constitutional force. Would the government now settle old scores against 'those fellow Irishmen who had apparently been led into a tragic cul-de-sac'? It was a tragedy that Irishmen had raised their hands in anger against other Irishmen.[42]

The tone of both of these prominent, establishment papers was not one of lambasting Sinn Féiners and pro-Germans. It was very much in tune with the Dublin *Freeman's Journal* which, when it re-appeared after the Rising, immediately blamed Carson, cited the South African precedent for leniency, and called for mercy. Its tone was one of sorrow for the misguided actions of fellow-Irishmen and anger at the malice and/or folly of those who were really to blame for the Rising – whether Carson, Larkin, Kitchener, Asquith, unionists, the UVF, the government or all of them. Such views effectively pre-dated the bulk of the official repression that followed the Rising. By 6 May (and the provincial papers went to print the day before that) only the first few executions of the Rising's leaders had taken place. Arrests outside Dublin were still limited. The papers' comments, therefore, reflected pre-Rising sentiments as much as post-Rising repression. When officials and the military embarked on an almost panicky coercion after the Rising, they were pouring petrol on the flames.

Military repression, and the nationalist response to it, now took hold. For weeks, the press would catalogue the workings of martial law (censorship, the ban on public meetings – initially including sports meetings – disarmament, house searches) and long lists of executions, prison sentences, arrests and deportations. As the inspector general of the RIC dryly put it in his monthly report for May 1916:

> As time passed, however, a reaction of feeling became noticeable. Resentment was aroused by the number of persons punished by courts martial and by the great number of those arrested and deported. It is reported that, as a result of the arrests in counties which remained quiet a belief is springing up in some quarters it is sought to brand the Sinn Féin rebellion as a Catholic and nationalist Rising.[43]

In the five counties, the impact of coercion was dramatic and brought home to small provincial towns the realities of the Rising. Under martial law powers, flying columns of soldiers and police toured the counties, formally disarming the Volunteers but also rounding up suspected rebel supporters using police lists of local, pre-Rising Sinn Féiners. In towns that had not had a military presence for some years, the effect of this military visitation was more marked and the scale of the official over-reaction even more apparent. On 7 May, Roscommon town (population in the 1911 census 1,858) saw no less than 700 soldiers arrive and take over the market square, post office, Harrison Hall and courthouse. The town was sealed off, pickets posted and houses and shops searched. All vehicles were stopped and inspected, including a hearse on its way to a funeral. Twenty seven men were then arrested in a town which had seen no incidents in the Rising, other than the hoisting of the tricolour over the old castle (for one day – it was taken down by boy scouts on Easter Monday).[44] The arrested men were detained and interviewed over two days and twenty were then released. The remaining seven were marched under military escort to the railway station. On their way they were given chocolates and cigarettes by local ladies.[45] Similar events unfolded in Longford, Athlone, Boyle, Strokestown, Cliffoney, Carrick-on-Shannon and Manorhamilton (but not in Mullingar or Sligo town, where, presumably, the local police did not generate lists of suspects). In Strokestown, Co. Roscommon, an armoured car and 150 mounted soldiers arrested just one man; a teacher who was 'quite a juvenile'.[46] In Longford, the town was sealed off on 5 May and arrests took place on the following day. Parties of soldiers then fanned out from the town to make arrests elsewhere. On 14 May 400 soldiers arrived back in Longford escorting seven Leitrim prisoners from Manorhamilton. The prisoners were surrounded by troops with fixed bayonets as they were marched through the town.[47] In total 133 men were interned and deported from the five counties, not counting a significant number picked up in the first few days but released before deportation.[48]

Many of the arrested men were undoubtedly Sinn Féiners, but in every town the immediate response was not to take pleasure at the discomfort of the Irish party's 'pro-German' enemies, but to protest at the arbitrary arrest of innocent men. J.P. Farrell denounced 'peripatetic bands of military … intensifying the bitterness' and sending 'misled young men' to England, 'many of them young men wholly innocent of any evil intent whatsoever'. Thomas Scanlan, MP for Sligo North, designated the Cliffoney deportees 'prisoners of war' and the *Sligo Nationalist* noted that 'they were merely members of the Volunteer force and had not seen any prohibition regarding arms.' They were aged from fifteen to twenty three years and their leader was only nineteen years old. Some, the paper reported, were the only support for their widowed mothers. Writing on the Athlone arrests, the *Westmeath Independent*'s leading article was entitled 'Our twelve'. It wrote that they were Irish Volunteers 'openly and above board', had complied with the law and were just as legal as Carson's Ulster Volunteers. Their arrest risked creating feelings of disgust and repugnance. They were 'almost all young men, all upright, of respectable character, sober, and the making of good citizens in any well-governed country in the world'.[49] The immediate release of all the internees was added to the growing list of nationalist demands – the end of martial law, no more executions, political status for the convicted men. Unlicensed protest meetings having been banned under martial law, a wave of council resolutions, parliamentary questions and appeals for funds duly followed.

It was in this environment, in which 'an extraordinary revulsion of feeling has taken place', that John Dillon's parliamentary condemnation of British stupidity, on 11 May, had such an impact in Ireland.[50] As noted above, Dillon freely admitted that the rebels had been 'our bitterest enemies', but he emphasised that 'the executions, house-searching throughout the country, wholesale arrests … have exasperated feeling to a terrible extent.' The elements of his speech which had the greatest impact were his defiance of Britain and his praise for the conduct and character of the rebels. British MPs were told that they were 'washing out our whole life work in a sea of blood', and were informed by Dillon that: 'It is the insurgents who have fought a clean fight, a brave fight, however misguided, and it would have been a damned good thing if your soldiers were able to put up as good a fight as did these men in Dublin.'[51]

The local nationalist press without exception reported Dillon's speech. It was described as 'great', 'a sensation' and 'thrilling'. Interestingly, the speech was immediately contrasted with the more restrained utterances of the party's leader, Redmond. The veteran factionist Jasper Tully (who for the last thirteen years had been an incessant critic of Dillon) now ironically praised Dillon more than Redmond: 'While we are all thankful to Mr Redmond for what he has done, there is hardly a man who has read Mr Dillon's speech who is not proud of it.'[52] As the *Sligo Champion* put it in a leading article, until Dillon spoke the response of the Irish party to the rebellion seemed mild and half-hearted.[53]

Local party rhetoric from the time of the arrests and Dillon's speech hardened appreciably. For example, the north Roscommon executive of the UIL met on 4 June under T.J Devine, who at the end of 1916 would be the Irish party's candidate in the Roscommon North by-election. Its demands were clearly expressed, and showed just how much local party sentiment towards the Rising had developed in just five weeks. It demanded:

- a full public inquiry into all 'executions without trial' and the murder of innocent civilians;
- the immediate removal of martial law;
- the immediate establishment of a home rule parliament 'for an undivided Ireland';
- an amnesty for 'all prisoners connected with the recent struggle for Ireland's freedom'.[54]

From early June onwards, almost every town in the five counties witnessed the launch of appeal funds; typically for the Irish National Aid Association (INAA), but sometimes for the more radical Volunteer Dependants' Fund (VDF). The former, ostensibly a relief fund for all who had suffered in the Rising, was undoubtedly more popular than the latter, which was specifically for the dependants of those who had actually taken part. Across Ireland up to 30 June, the INAA collected over £4,480 outside Dublin: the VDF some £1,131.[55] Irish party MPs, council leaders and town bosses initially maintained their political distinctiveness from Sinn Féiners by acting as prominent organisers and collectors for the INAA rather than the VDF. However, the merger of the two funds in August, which, according to the police, placed both under Sinn Féin control, made little or no difference to levels of activity, nor to the local participation of Irish party figures.[56]

Sometimes the sympathy of Irish party figures for the rebels was clear from the outset of the relief effort. One such figure was John Jinks, the mayor of Sligo. Jinks was by far the most prominent Irish party supporter in Sligo town and had a son serving in the army. At the beginning of June, he chaired the meeting held to launch the INAA in the town. He did state, like so many contemporaries, that the rebellion had been 'disastrous', but went on to say that there was a clear need to relieve the appalling distress of the rebels' dependants. He continued:

We, as Irishmen, are taking a great part in fighting the common enemy [i.e. Germany] at the present time, and treatment of this kind [the executions], in my humble opinion, is not at all justifiable, and the court martial proceedings in Dublin have taken away some of the best blood that Irishmen could produce (loud applause).

Jinks stated that he had known these men, and had heard them 'voice the cause of Ireland'. They were 'as true to Ireland as any man can be'. He called on his audience to show their appreciation for the rebels and their dependants by backing the fund, for 'these dear and tried friends of Ireland'. When a letter was read out at the meeting from one of the town's leading Protestants, Alexander Lyons, asking whether the fund would also support the families of soldiers and policemen 'murdered' in Dublin, the question was denounced by a Sligo corporation member, Charles Connolly, as 'diabolical and impertinent'.[57]

The resolutions and speeches of men like Devine in Boyle and Jinks in Sligo are highly significant. Both men were party 'bosses', who fitted the caricature of bourgeois party hacks with limited political horizons and an instinctive drive to control their party machines. Both stayed loyal to the Irish party during its subsequent collapse. Both, by the beginning of June, associated the rebellion not with the party's enemies but with the 'recent struggle for Ireland's freedom' and 'the cause of Ireland'. Their remarks were matched by numerous other party loyalists. For the party organiser John Keaveny in June, 'whatever the Sinn Féiners might or might not have been, one thing is certain – they were not satisfied with Dublin Castle and they sacrificed their lives for a cause which they believed to be right.' For John 'Foxy Jack' Fitzgibbon in May, 'these men were prompted by the purest motives and according to their lights they thought they were serving their country.' A few days later Fitzgibbon noted that 'the vast majority of them are admitted to be as fine a type of young fellows as any country ever produced.'[58] The party leadership's great political fear, that the rebellion would come to be seen as a general, nationalist, Irish uprising against Britain, alienating British opinion and damning home rule, was being realised. The new conventional wisdom was expressed with startling over-simplicity by the *Sligo Champion* in August:

> The Act that received the King's signature was indefinitely set aside. The Irish became impatient. The insurrection followed. Then came the heartless executions and an indefinite period of martial law.[59]

Public expressions of sympathy for the leaders of the rebellion, not just for their 'misguided' followers, now appeared regularly in the nationalist press. Early on, it had carried syndicated news stories about the 'pathetic' marriage of Joseph Plunkett on the eve of his execution, about how the green-clad Countess Markiewicz had kissed her revolver when she surrendered, or of how Thomas MacDonagh was 'glad to die for Ireland'.[60] In mid-May three papers, the *Westmeath Independent, Sligo Nationalist* and *Western Nationalist*, published an eye-witness account of the rebellion by an Athlone army officer, R.K. Brereton, who had been held captive in the Four Courts. The rebel officers, according to Brereton, were 'out for war, observing all the rules of civilised warfare and fighting clean. So far as I saw they fought like gentlemen.' They were 'men of education, incapable of acts of brutality'. The *Westmeath Independent* contrasted Brereton's treatment by Volunteer officers at the Four Courts (noting 'the soldierly and civilised actions of these insurgent officers') with the treatment of those same Volunteer officers by the army. At least one of these, Ned Daly, had been put up against a wall and shot.[61]

During June and July, the *Sligo Champion, Sligo Nationalist, Strokestown Democrat, Western Nationalist, Westmeath Examiner* and *Westmeath Independent* demonstrated the ineffectiveness of the military censorship. Between them, they published Pádraig Pearse's last letter to his mother, his poems *The Wayfarer* and *A Mother Speaks*, accounts of the heroic deaths of John MacBride and Con Colbert and complimentary assessments of the lives and characters of Pearse, Connolly, MacDermott, and Clarke.[62] The *Longford Leader* was an exception, but at the beginning of August made up by carrying an extensive interview with the Sinn Féin and IRB man John Cawley. The interview, published over two weeks, was conducted after Cawley's return home from his deportation to England. For years a critic and political enemy of J.P. Farrell, Cawley was given a platform by Farrell's newspaper to state:

> I think I can safely say that the Irish Volunteers are the finest and cleanest young fellows of any army in the world, and for deep religious convictions and ardent enthusiasm they would hold their own with any lay community in the world.

The interview concluded with Farrell's newspaper publishing *A Soldier's Song*.[63]

V

The response of the Irish party to the Rising, in this part of Ireland at least, had far more in common with Dillon's bitter anger against English repression than with Redmond's almost immediate attack on the party's Sinn Féin foes. Redmond, however, maintained his stance throughout 1916. In early October he spoke at Waterford. He did announce to loud cheers that the Irish party was going into parliamentary opposition, but he also re-iterated his belief that the Rising had been engineered by men who were the enemies of the constitutional movement for home rule. A few weeks later in Sligo, he would declare that 'the country has been suffering from what the Americans call a brain storm ... a gust of passion'.[64] During this period, though, his views were not widely expressed in his party, which instead evidenced more sympathy for 'the cause' and its martyrs. Redmond's followers also faced the challenge of deciding whether, as constitutional home rulers, they now had any credible role in Irish politics. It was all very well for Redmond to declare at Waterford that 'the constitutional movement shall go on', but with British and Irish opinion increasingly convinced that the Rising was indeed a Catholic, nationalist 'struggle for freedom', the justification for the party's wartime strategy – that if the Irish alienated British opinion they would lose home rule – was in tatters.

The party's first public defence of its continuing existence appeared as early as 9 May, in a formal manifesto issued by the parliamentary party. This tried to strike a balance between condemning the 'mad attempt at revolution' and expressing shock and horror at the executions and martial law, but far and away its longest section was a repetition of all the achievements of constitutional nationalism concerning land, housing, education and self-government. The Rising was a dangerous blow to the heart and hopes of Ireland, which faced the choice of being given over to hopeless, fruitless anarchy or giving its full support to the constitutional movement. As the *Longford Leader* wrote in commenting on the manifesto, either the Irish people stuck by the movement until its programme was achieved, or they faced 'anarchy, confusion and bloodshed'. If the people rejected the Irish party for 'a more exciting but definitely much more dangerous policy, then it is on their own shoulders'.[65] Presenting the Irish people with this choice was entirely consistent with Redmond's support for the war effort and his undiminished intention not to alienate British and unionist opinion. Home rule had to be secured and could only be so with the assent of British democracy. The use of force was therefore not only futile but also entirely counter-productive. Ireland's rights could be won only through constitutional action.

Locally, Redmond's strongest cheerleader was John Hayden MP, writing leading articles week after week that were published, almost identically, in both the *Roscommon Messenger* and *Westmeath Examiner*. Hayden, who for years had fought factional disputes in both Roscommon and Westmeath (notably against the Tully family and the independent MP Laurence Ginnell) remained the most bitter critic of the rebels and of the post-Rising, nationalist enemies of Redmond's party. The party, he declared in May, could be replaced only by secret societies, anarchy and socialism. In June he wrote that 'floodgates of claptrap' had been opened in an attempt to destroy the party. In August Ireland had to make proper use of the weapon forged by Parnell, but the party could do its work only if it had whole-hearted support. In September Hayden attacked 'the policy of a small section of the race, which culminated in the rebellion which Irish soldiers suppressed in five days' and which 'had nothing about it of a constructive character'. The Irish party in parliament could not be overcome – provided that they had the backing of the people. Hayden's papers backed every attempt of the party leadership to secure agreement with or concessions from the British. He hailed any parliamentary or oratorical success of Redmond, who had again donned 'the mantle of Parnell'. Redmond's speeches were 'marvels of fearless and merciless criticism'. Hayden lauded the party's efforts to obtain tangible benefits for Ireland, whether relating to teachers' pay, old age pensions, pensions for wounded soldiers, government control of the railways or the export of potatoes. The party was also given the sole credit for stopping the executions, freeing 1,400 detainees, blocking conscription and, at the top of the list, saving the constitutional movement from destruction. Only through the constitutional movement could wrongs be righted and reforms won.[66]

The difficulty with this approach was that it looked more and more barren and ineffective as the year progressed. The ability of the Irish party to deliver any amelioration of local conditions appeared small at best. Martial law was not lifted. Press censorship and the ban on unlicensed political meetings continued. Some deportees were released, but only in dribs and drabs. New wartime controls and regulations were announced almost every week. The use of non-jury, 'coercion' trials by stipendiary magistrates was extended. Ireland was subjected to what the *Longford Leader* called 'pinprick coercion', though the paper also went on to say that all Ireland was now branded as disloyal and untrustworthy; every week the life-long haters of Ireland called out for more coercion and for conscription. 'Ireland is to be crucified in this war and her sacrifices spurned.'[67]

Above all, the circumstances of the aborted 'Lloyd George settlement' (for the immediate implementation of home rule and the partition of six Ulster counties – a saga that ran from mid-May to the end of July) undermined the case that constitutional action could achieve anything. First in this sequence of events came the announcement by Asquith in mid-May that the Castle system of government had failed and that David Lloyd George would attempt to negotiate an alternative. This announcement raised exaggerated hopes of a settlement. However, it also inculcated a belief that physical force had achieved results denied to constitutional methods. John Fitzgibbon observed that the Rising had certainly brought home to England that there must be something wrong in Ireland when men would be willing to make such a sacrifice.[68] By August, the *Sligo Nationalist* could state that Easter Week demonstrated what could be achieved by the methods of Carson, 'carried out in real sincerity and with real ardour and courage'. Farrell's *Longford Leader* was more trenchant. The 'smug hypocrites' who oppressed Ireland 'move along lines of such smug self-confidence that it requires an earthquake like the Dublin Rebellion to get them to waken up'. English uppishness precipitated the rebellion and 'gave to young, hot-blooded Irishmen the notion that nothing could ever be got from England except by force'.[69] By September, the Royal Irish Constabulary (RIC) inspector general reported the widespread belief across Ireland that one week of fighting had achieved more than twenty five years of constitutional agitation.[70]

Secondly, the negotiation of the deal, and the rapid realisation that it did entail a 'clean cut' partition of six Ulster counties, triggered a wave of protest across the south and west of Ireland, as well as in Ulster. Repeated charges of weakness and surrender were made against the parliamentary politicians. Locally, protests against partition were voiced not just by individuals but also by party bosses, UIL branches, AOH divisions and county political executives. It was specifically on this issue that two further nationalist papers, the *Strokestown Democrat* and *Westmeath Independent,* broke with Redmond's leadership. For the *Westmeath Independent,* so long a bastion of Irish party propaganda, the game was clearly up at the beginning of June, when the headline of its leading article was 'Home Rule, Moyrah!' Cutting off a piece of Ulster would not be a settlement, but instead 'an outrage that would cry to heaven for vengeance'.[71] These defections meant that locally there were now as many nationalist papers (six) opposing Redmond as supporting him.

Thirdly, the collapse of the deal in late July was portrayed by the party as the result of unionist and English betrayal. In the party's eyes, they had tried honourably to complete the deal, and had faced what Hayden's papers called 'the wrecker conspiracy' of factionist and unionist opposition. The *Westmeath Examiner* denounced the utter inability of British statesmen to understand Ireland and 'mean and contemptible' conduct within the government. Now that there was deliberate betrayal and bad faith, it was impossible for Redmond to deal further with the government. Thomas Scanlan MP would later announce that Ireland was governed by 'despotism'. Britain would not get Irish cooperation in the war until Ireland achieved self-government. There was an 'almost incurable' atmosphere of distrust. 'Ireland will never again accept a promise from a British minister.'[72] If that was indeed the case, though, what was the point of seeking constitutional concessions from a British government or in parliament?

Finally, the news that the deal had collapsed was combined with the reinstatement of Castle government and the extension of coercion measures. For the *Longford Leader*, the government was 'building up the wall of hate'. Ireland now had a unionist chief secretary, DORA, martial law, the Crimes Act and '40,000 English troops ... No doubt we shall have to submit to such degrading and insulting conditions. Ireland cannot do otherwise. She is unarmed – undrilled and defenceless'. This was a view of Ireland depicted not by Sinn Féiners but by staunch party loyalists. The *Western Nationalist* lamented that 'the best of Irish blood is being shed for the treaty-breaker' and called on its readers to prepare: 'There are new Prussians at our doors.'[73]

In this environment, the ability of the constitutional party to achieve reforms and right wrongs was rendered, in the earlier phrase of Gladstone, 'almost a nullity'. The process of peacefully seeking concessions from the British government appeared exhausted. The response of the party leadership was to make it clear that they would go into parliamentary opposition, call for unity, and plead with their followers not to give up. The *Western Nationalist*, a week after calling on its readers to prepare for 'new Prussians' at their doors, now called on its readers not to despair. Ireland's tide would turn, and her 'impregnable line of defence' was that home rule was on the statute book. The *Roscommon Messenger* and *Westmeath Examiner* praised the 'sagacity and foresight' of the party's leaders and claimed that black was white in a leader headed 'The constitutional movement vindicated'. The *Longford Leader* welcomed the party's return to opposition, to 'the days of Biggar and Parnell'. However, it also highlighted the party's continuing dilemma, that it dared not abandon its support for the war. The paper wrote that if the party were to attack the government for its conduct of the war, 'and so bring comfort to the enemies of the country, they will be accused of playing a traitorous part which will tell very badly against them in England'. Home rule would be 'very seriously affected'.[74]

The position of the Irish party by the end of the summer was, therefore, dire. Its declared constitutional, parliamentary role was discredited. Its key wartime policy, of participating in the war to retain British popular support for Ireland's demands, appeared lost, but could not be changed. Its Sinn Féiner, pro-German foes were now Irish heroes, while it appeared to be both weak and futile. The *Westmeath Independent* wrote that if no better alternative were found, the Irish cause would descend into ignominy.[75] The Leitrim county inspector of the RIC put it simply: 'Mr. Redmond and his party are not now much thought of.'[76]

VI

In at least five counties of provincial Ireland, local opinion saw the Easter rebels as fellow nationalist Irishmen much more than as inveterate enemies of John Redmond's Irish party. They were certainly seen as foolish and misguided and their actions as destructive, but they were more the 'flesh and blood' of the Irish party than its 'irreconcilable enemies'. Following the Rising, after only two to three weeks in which party spokesmen and newspaper editors hurled well-developed, pre-Rising invective against 'Sinn Féiners' and 'pro-Germans', those who maintained a stance of clear hostility to the rebels, including Redmond himself, found themselves increasingly in the minority. Having initially been traduced as criminals and traitors, the rebels were now mistaken but brave, misguided but patriotic. In essence, they may have been fools, but they were 'our' fools.

This shift of language and opinion was undoubtedly accelerated, massively, by events. What Redmond would describe as 'gross and panicky violence' by the authorities, the sheer scale of military repression, could not have been better calculated to transform criminals into martyrs and political enemies into friends of Ireland.[77] This was then followed by the announcement, negotiation and abandonment of the Lloyd George settlement, a process of confusion and incompetence that both validated the use of revolutionary force and discredited its constitutional alternative.

Redmond believed that it was such events that resulted in 'all the ordinary factors of our national life' being 'violently wrenched away from the normal'.[78] For him, rebellion, repression and governmental betrayal had overturned an Irish political scene in which Ireland loyally supported the war effort, the goodwill of the British democracy had been won and home rule was assured.

The problem with Redmond's interpretation of events was that his party's view of the rebels, before the bulk of the executions and before the mass arrests in the provinces, was already ambivalent. The rebels were not universally damned as criminals. Instead, distinctions were made between the mass of the rebels in Dublin and their leaders, and between the Irish Volunteers and the socialist Citizen Army. Moreover, those who were to blame for the Rising were not Irish nationalists, but more traditional enemies – Carson, the UVF, the war office, Dublin Castle, the British government – together with the new bogeymen, Larkinite socialists. The rebellion was condemned not as a crime, but on the pragmatic grounds that it was bound to be defeated. The risk that it would be seen as a general Irish uprising, alienating English opinion and jeopardising home rule, was immediately identified, but in creating this danger the rebels were seen as foolish, not malicious. This latent sympathy for the rebels was quickly expressed by nationalists who, before the Rising, had already been disenchanted with the war, fearful of conscription, resentful of Ireland's unfavourable treatment relative to 'England' and supportive of local 'political prisoners'.

Before the Rising, the bulk of provincial nationalist opinion lagged well behind John Redmond in his enthusiasm for Ireland's participation in the war, even though the vast majority of nationalists still pledged loyalty to Redmond as their leader. After the Rising, Redmond's view of the world came even more adrift from those of his now-diminishing body of followers. Redmond was mistaken in his interpretation of the events of 1916. Ireland was not 'violently wrenched away from the normal' by the Rising; instead 'the normal', of angry, anglophobic nationalism, had been confirmed.

On 6 May, the *Sligo Champion* published a detailed eye-witness account of events in Dublin by local man and commercial traveller Matthew Flanagan, who was interviewed by the paper's editor, James Flynn. Flynn (secretary of the north Sligo UIL executive) would remain loyal to the Irish party throughout the war and, like so many local editors, was never slow to suppress news and views that were politically inconvenient to him.

What is remarkable is that the *Champion* on this occasion devoted several columns to an account, Flanagan's, which was clearly sympathetic to the rebels. Those rebels seen by Flanagan 'did all their work with amazingly systematic method'. They paid properly for any premises that they occupied. Damage was considerable, as might be expected when the military began to shell the Volunteers. 'A great many people who had no connection with the matter were detained.' Asked by Flynn whether he knew any of the men killed, Flanagan replied: 'Yes, they were a splendid class of men ... they appeared to be respectable citizens.' Flanagan continued:

> Even though these unfortunate men have been errant and foolish, they still claim our earnest consideration and protection. You know, Mr Flynn, blood will ever flow thicker than water.[79]

THE FIRST WORLD WAR AND THE RISING: MODE, MOMENT AND MEMORY

Keith Jeffery

The aim of this paper is to sketch out – to use a fancy word – a 'holistic' exploration of what might be termed the 'parallel narratives' of the 1916 Rising and the First World War, what I described in *Ireland and the Great War* as 'parallel texts', in which the similarities of experience might be more significant than the differences, great though they were in political (and other) terms.[1] But, to be sure, these are unusual parallels, for, unlike the parallel lines we learned about at school, which never meet (that is the point – or lack of it – I suppose) these parallel lines or parallel narratives, intersect, mingle, intertwine, and insinuate themselves in each other.

My contention is that the Rising *cannot* be understood outwith, or separated from, the broader context of the First World War, that European (and, indeed, global) catastrophe, whose shadow falls across the history of the first quarter of the twentieth century. This is not to say that the Easter Rising is not itself a unique, specifically Irish event, in its conception, implementation and legacy. Of course it is. *All* historical events are unique and specific, and there is much to be learned from a close exploration of the detail and specifically 'Irish' dimension of the Rising.[2] Most accounts of 1916 understandably have a primarily local perspective, and there will be much of this, and rightly so, over the anniversary year of 2006. But the issue raises a general problem for all historians, of whatever subject or period, which is how to balance the specific and the general. Too much of the former may provide fascinating 'micro-history', and no doubt there is interest in studying the pin-points of paint in a Pointillist picture, but one also needs to stand back to get a sense of the whole picture, the wider perspective, if you like. On the other hand, the danger of being too broad and too general is the loss of the particular, unique character of any historical event, its specificity and its essence. So, a balance must be struck between the general and the particular, the broad and the narrow (perhaps 'focused' would be a better word), till we get a complete (or something approaching it) picture of the matter under discussion.

With this in mind, I want to examine the events of 1916 and thereabouts, and their legacy, in the broader context of the First World War. This war, asserted one reluctant participant in Ireland, 'broke, like a blaze of light' and all was 'suddenly turned vital, and invested with reality'.[3] Thus we will investigate the 'vitality' and 'reality' of the time, exploring in turn the themes of mode, moment and memory.

MODE

War, as Karl von Clausewitz famously observed, is 'nothing but the continuation of policy with the admixture of other means'.[4] This oft-quoted (usually wrongly as 'war is the continuation of politics by other means') aphorism suggests that there is a 'seamless robe' of political activity, that war does not spring from nowhere, from some political vacuum, and that the resort to arms can be understood as just one point along a spectrum of possible political activity. For individuals and groups to contemplate political violence, and to accept both the possibility and the potential legitimacy of war, moreover, an environment needs to exist within which violence is an acceptable policy option. This is as much a social matter as it is political, or even philosophical, and some writers have pointed to the progressive militarisation of Europe and European society in the nineteenth and early twentieth centuries as powerfully contributing to the likelihood of war.

By the beginning of the twentieth century every significant power in Europe, apart from the United Kingdom, had embraced compulsory military service, and was able to mobilise mass, conscript armies in defence of perceived national interests. The rise of mass society, underpinned by the staggering changes resulting from industrialisation, urbanisation and steady economic development, and the relentless advance of nationalist ideologies, through which the 'nation-state' had come to be seen as the highest form of human political organisation, produced a situation where nationality and democracy had come closely to be identified, with the obligations of one balanced by the rights of the other. Military conscription, thus, became the corollary of universal manhood suffrage. For the ruling classes, moreover, military service appeared to offer a way of controlling and disciplining the turbulent, threatening urban masses of the industrial age.[5]

But many people willingly embraced military, and militaristic, ideals. Political groups on both the left and right asserted the benefits of military organisation and discipline, and, all across Europe, men were increasingly to be seen in uniform. Even Britain, with its longstanding distrust of standing armies and military power, was affected by the lure of military service, which might help resist the challenges of industrial mass society. Much of this was 'muscular christianity', with the Salvation Army and Boys' Brigade in the vanguard. Sabine Baring-Gould's stirring hymn hit the spot precisely: 'Onward Christian Soldiers, marching as to war ... Like a mighty army, moves the Church of God'.[6] Robert Baden Powell's more secular Boy Scout movement was specifically designed to harness and direct the energies of modern (and potentially decadent) British youth into constructive and patriotic military activities.[7]

Ireland, of course, was not at all immune from this tendency, as David Fitzpatrick has demonstrated with his customary eye for telling detail.[8] To the British paramilitary organisations may be added specifically Irish ones, such as Fianna Éireann (founded in Belfast by Bulmer Hobson in 1902), all sustained by the rising tide of militarism in Europe. The apotheosis of militarism (or should that be paramilitarism?) in Ireland came with the unionist Ulster Volunteer Force (UVF) of 1913 and its nationalist shadow, the Irish Volunteers, established eleven months later. In the early twenty first century it is often asserted that the Irish are 'good Europeans', reflecting and embracing the manners and mores of our continental colleagues. So, too, was the case in the early twentieth century. The UVF and the Irish Volunteers were not just sturdy Irish associations, with indigenous origins and embodying purely local political aspirations, but they were part of a European-wide phenomenon, in which many men (and some women) opted to bear arms in proud support of their national political aspirations.

In Ireland and Britain enlistment to such paramilitary organisations was massively outstripped by the 'rush to the colours' after the outbreak of the First World War. One of the great conundrums of the history of this period is how to explain the apparently inexplicable situation when extraordinarily large numbers of men across Ireland and Britain volunteered to serve in the armed forces of the United Kingdom. Although recent scholarship has shown that, across Europe, the 'spirit of 1914' was not so unwaveringly warlike as has been supposed, the numbers of recruits are extremely impressive and need explanation.[9] Over 140,000 Irishmen volunteered to join the armed services during the First World War.[10] Of these some 50,000 joined in the first six months, from August 1914 to

February 1915, clearly reflecting the greatest intensity of 'war enthusiasm'. But 90,000 men enlisted in the succeeding forty five months – 10,000 in July to November 1918 alone – and any explanatory model for the extraordinary resilience of Irish recruitment in the context of changing Irish political circumstances will have to come up with something better than an explanation which ascribes it to a kind of patriotic social tsunami which swept men willy-nilly away to the war.

The discussion of recruitment offered in *Ireland and the Great War* challenges the simplistic assumption that everyone joined up in August 1914 and that they did so in a sort of Pavlovian response to the political bugle-call of deluded and war-inflamed leaders. It seeks to demonstrate that this phenomenon was not at all simple, and that there were multiple motivations for enlistment: social, economic, fraternal, personal, psychological, idiosyncratic, as well as 'patriotic'. A good Cork example of how an individual might explain why he joined up is Tom Barry, the later IRA commander, who claimed that a simple desire for adventure was a powerful motive. For many at home the war offered excitement and the chance of glorious opportunity. Barry enlisted in June 1915. Seventeen years old, he said he 'had decided to see what this Great War was like ... I went to the war for no other reason than that I wanted to see what war was like, to get a gun, to see new countries and to feel like a grown man'.[11] This was nearly a year after the war had started, and, among other things, provides some evidence that the recruiting rush of the early days does not tell the whole story.

Nor does enlistment in the forces of the Crown tell the whole story of Irish military recruitment during the First World War. For if the very many (mostly) young men of 1914 and 1915 rallied to the military call and marched off to war, like Gadarene swine, or lemmings (or whatever suitably dismissive simile you may choose), so too, surely, did the young men of 1916. As the men of Ulster – and the rest – marched towards the Somme – and Gallipoli – to an apocalyptic soldier glory, so too did those Volunteers who seized the GPO on Easter Monday in 1916. And both groups, we may hazard, were swallowed up by the violence they embraced, whatever their motivation.

In *Ireland and the Great War* it is, moreover, suggested that the reasons for enlisting on the rebel side might be just as multi-faceted as for those who went away to war; that the forces which propelled men like Garrett FitzGerald's father into the Volunteers and the GPO might not be so very different as those which propelled other young men into the 16th

(Irish) division and the trenches of the western front. There has sometimes been an easy assumption that while the latter were simply afflicted by a 'surge of naïve patriotism', the former were seized of a much higher calling, a 'surge of sophisticated patriotism' (certainly not any sort of 'narrow nationalism'), one might suppose, responding to a legitimate appeal for 'national' service.[12] It seems to me, however, that there are secular and even venal motivations for enlistment on both sides; that, for example, adventure, comradeship, political ambition, and so on, might plausibly be advanced as factors for joining the Volunteers as much as, say, the Munster Fusiliers.

This is not to say that patriotic and political motives did not matter. Of course they did, but they do not alone, or in every case, provide a complete explanation for enlistment. The explanation for such a complex phenomenon as joining up lies in combinations of motives, with varying intensity in individual cases. It may also be observed that the reasons offered, both at the time and afterwards, may also vary. Looking back to 1914–18 and 1916, modern commentators have tended (outside Ulster) to downplay the political motivations of those who joined the British army. The prevailing orthodoxy in nationalist Ireland is that no true Irishman could possibly have joined the British army for patriotic and legitimate Irish reasons, or even (horrible thought) for a species of *British* loyalty. The favoured, 'secular', explanation is economic. 'Taking the King's shilling' was just that. It was, as James Connolly asserted at the time, merely 'economic conscription'.[13] On the other hand, the political dimension of enlistment in the rebel cause has generally been amplified. Inevitably this reflected the changing political situation in Ireland where, naturally enough, 'lower' reasons were asserted for joining the British side, and 'higher' for the Irish.

The historian of enlistment also has to beware of too ready an acceptance of veterans' explanations for their actions. Their stories about why they joined up – on whatever side – may also be inflected by subsequent, and changing, political circumstance. Tom Barry's explanation, cited above, was published some thirty years after the event. His story *may* be true, and very probably is, but let us for a moment speculate that in 1915 an *additional* reason might have been a faith in John Redmond's assurance that joining up was a patriotic duty and would be good for Ireland. It seems improbable that, whatever might have been the case in 1915, a distinguished IRA veteran would admit to any such thing a generation later in an utterly changed Ireland. Barry's explanation makes very good sense for the late 1940s, whether or not it is also true for the actual time of enlistment.

MOMENT

If the prevailing militarism of Europe and Ireland provided the context and mode for mobilisation of all sorts, the actual events of the war, too, powerfully accelerated the possibility of 'physical force' action in Ireland. The First World War provided both the opportunity for the Irish republican rising of Easter 1916, as well as a suitably violent model for political action. The split in the Irish Volunteers of September 1914, following Redmond's commitment in his famous speech at Woodenbridge, Co. Wicklow, of 'Young Ireland' (as he put it) to the cause of Britain and 'gallant little Belgium', moreover, released the militants from the tedious necessity of having to argue their case with moderate, constitutional nationalists.[14]

Declaring that since the anti-Redmond Volunteers 'may be depended upon to act vigorously, courageously, promptly, and unitedly if the opportunity comes', Pearse believed that 'we are at the moment in an immensely stronger position than ever before'. Calculating in a characteristically airy fashion that the support of 10–15,000 men might be forthcoming, he asserted with superb confidence that 'this small, compact, perfectly disciplined, determined *separatist* force is infinitely more valuable than the unwieldy, loosely-held-together mixum-gatherum force we had before the split.'[15] Pearse, too, was increasingly refreshed and invigorated by the dramatic and heroic events of the western front. 'The last sixteen months,' he wrote in December 1915, 'have been the most glorious in the history of Europe. Heroism has come back to the earth.' The crucial motivating factor – and one, of course, which could transform Ireland – was patriotism:

> It is patriotism that stirs the people. Belgium defending her soil is heroic, and so is Turkey fighting with her back to Constantinople. It is good for the world that such things should be done. The old heart of the earth needed to be warmed with the red wine of the battlefields. Such august homage was never before offered to God as this, the homage of millions of lives given gladly for love of country.[16]

Although James Connolly scornfully rejected this specific sanguine vision, he thought that Irish working class rebellion, especially against so great an imperial power as England, might precipitate the general toppling of capitalism.[17] He had his own battle in mind. 'Starting thus,' he wrote at the beginning of the war, 'Ireland may yet set the torch to a European conflagration that will not burn out until the last throne and the last capitalist bond and debenture will be shrivelled on the funeral pyre of the last war lord.'[18]

Pearse's apparently bloodthirsty remarks, and the way he appeared to embrace the slaughter of the war, might be criticised – at the very least – for simply being in terribly bad taste. These days, moreover, outside the armed services (and there usually only in private), or perhaps on some sporting occasions, it is felt inappropriate to celebrate, or commend, or luxuriate in the inspiration, excitement, exhilaration, or even joy, of conflict. But this may well be at a loss to our historical understanding. As I have already tried to demonstrate, Pearse was not speaking in some social or political vacuum. Lots of his contemporaries (in Ireland and elsewhere) were similarly touched by the insane intoxification of violence, and many welcomed the war, from the usual suspects like Rupert Brooke and Laurence Binyon to the Italian radical artists of the Vorticist movement, along with English fellow-travellers like Wyndham Lewis, to folk much nearer home.[19] 'War,' declared a Belfast Methodist early in the conflict, 'is a kind of purgatory. It is a painful but salutary remedy for softness, slackness and sensuality.'[20] Just a month after the war had started the Church of Ireland primate, Archbishop Crozier of Armagh, affirmed 'from all seeming ill God will work out good'. 'Religion,' he asserted, 'will become a great factor in human life, and the breaking up of German aggressive militarism will bring a long and lasting peace.'[21] Towards the end of 1914 Crozier's colleague, James Keene, the bishop of Meath, while deploring the human cost of the war, echoed the theme of purification: 'We believe that this fiery trial will prove to be a purifying discipline. If it leads to a moral and spiritual renewal of our nation the loss will end in gain.'[22] In April 1915 the Catholic Bishop Sheehan of Waterford and Lismore affirmed the patriotic necessity of taking part in the conflict. 'The war,' he wrote, 'is not an English war alone or a French or a Belgian war. It is an Irish war to save our country and our people from ruin and misery.'[23] In September 1916, while appealing for more priests to come forward to serve as military chaplains, Cardinal Logue, the Catholic primate, wrote of 'the imperishable glory which Irish Catholic soldiers have won for their country'.[24]

Pearse, thus, was not the only person to perceive some positive benefits from the blood-letting of the battlefields. For him and his ilk, moreover, the fighting at Gallipoli and on the western front made violence more likely at home, not just by the example set, but also through the handy belief that 'England's extremity is Ireland's opportunity'. It followed, too, that England's enemy might be Ireland's friend. Sir Roger Casement, among others, sought to secure practical German assistance for Irish republican endeavours, and the planning for the Rising assumed that there would be such help. The Proclamation which Pearse himself read at the start of the Rising recorded the support of 'gallant allies in Europe'. But, as we know, although a German ship, the *Aud*, indeed arrived off the west coast of Ireland with a cargo of arms, it was intercepted by the Royal Navy and scuttled on Good Friday. The same day Sir Roger Casement was landed in Co. Kerry from a German submarine – his mission ironically was to try to prevent the planned rising on the grounds that insufficient German assistance was being provided – but he was quickly captured and later executed for treason.

Yet the failure of Berlin to help out was not at all apparent to the authorities (or the general public) at the time, and the Rising was, quite understandably, widely seen as a mainly German-inspired affair. John Redmond denounced the Rising as a 'German invasion of Ireland, as brutal, as selfish, as cynical as Germany's invasion of Belgium'.[25] The fighting in Dublin was seen as just another part of the Europe-wide battle front. As one soldier, who had seen a comrade die by his side during the attack on the City Hall, said: 'The only thing which made it possible to bear was the certainty they were fighting Germany as truly as if they were in France.'[26] Some soldiers, it is said, even thought they were in France. There is the (possibly apocryphal) story of the British reinforcements landing at Kingstown (Dún Laoghaire) and discovering to their surprise that the natives spoke English.[27] The parallel with the western front extended into the aftermath of the Rising, when the destruction in Dublin was commonly compared to that in Flanders: 'Ypres on the Liffey' was a caption in one illustrated souvenir pamphlet.[28]

The assumption, moreover, that the Rising was part of the wider conflict well suited the self-perceptions of the rebels themselves. They saw themselves (and *had* to see themselves) as soldiers in a real army, fighting a real war, rather than the subversive criminal gunmen the government would have them be. After the surrender the rebels asserted, but did not receive, the status of prisoners of war, hence (in part) the shock of the executions. So it is that the war, and prevailing assumptions about the war, inevitably suffused the events of Easter 1916 and the attitudes of all the participants concerned. It could not have been otherwise, but it is a point about which we still need to be reminded, since narratives of the Rising too often neglect the essential, wider context. Confining the story to the island of Ireland alone results in limited, *insular* history, restricted in scope and deficient in its explanatory power.

One further point might be made about the 'moment' of Easter 1916, its relation to the 'mode' of action, and the way in which the events of that week echo down through the Irish experience of conflict throughout the twentieth century. On the first day of the Easter Rising the following Irishmen (there may well have been more) were killed at the South Dublin Union (a comparatively neglected zone of operations in the historiography of the Rising): John Traynor, William McDowell, James Quinn, John Brennan, Michael Carr, James Duffy and Thomas Treacy – the first three were rebels, the others were serving in the Royal Irish Regiment.[29] It was not only men who perished. Nurse Margaret Keogh was also killed that day, caught, perhaps, in crossfire. We could go on matching death for death in each Irish domestic campaign of the century: 1919–21, 1922–3, 1956–62, 1969–97. But the majority of casualties on whatever side they were aligned (and not forgetting the 'innocent bystanders') were Irish people. It might be argued that these successive bursts of violence of Irish against Irish – violence certainly exacerbated by that of 1916 – begin to look like successive bouts of *civil* war, with all the complexity, intransigence and bitter division so characteristic of that mode of conflict. Terence Denman, writing in his excellent study of the 16th (Irish) division, remarks – and this is a not uncommon assertion – that the First World War 'prevented the outbreak of a bloody civil war in Ireland'.[30] I wonder. Perhaps it did nothing of the sort. Perhaps what it prevented was only the particular type of civil war anticipated and feared in the summer of 1914. It may in fact be that the First World War actually precipitated an Irish civil war which began in earnest in 1916 and which has continued with varying intensity and shifting location for eighty years.[31]

MEMORY

The study of 'memory' and 'commemoration' has become quite a growth industry in recent years. This has not by any means just been restricted to Ireland, but it has a peculiar relevance on this island, where 'history' and the commemoration of historical events have an applied political dimension, which frequently stimulates lively debate and often robust disagreement.[32] This is certainly true of the 1916 Rising and the First World War, not just in this particular anniversary year of 2006, but from the very start.

In the centre of the Irish midlands town of Birr there is a fifty foot-high mid-eighteenth century Doric column, which used to be surmounted with a statue of the duke of Cumberland. It was erected to mark his victory over Catholic Jacobite forces at Culloden in Scotland in 1746, a victory that secured the Protestant monarchy in Britain. Sometime in the late nineteenth century the statue was removed, ostensibly because it was in a dangerous condition, but reputedly after having been damaged by men from a Scottish regiment barracked locally.[33] In the early autumn of 1919 this unusual and unexpected memorial – no other monument to Culloden exists beyond the battlefield itself – came under discussion in the town. Looking to put up a war memorial, the Birr 'Comrades of the Great War' (an ex-servicemen's association later subsumed within the British Legion) applied to the Urban Council to use the site for this purpose. Simultane-ously, and evidently as a response, the local branch of the Transport Union applied 'for the site for the erection of a statue to the late James Connolly', who had been executed as one of the leaders of the 1916 Rising.[34] Neither application succeeded, nor has either a Great War memorial or a statue of James Connolly ever been erected in the town.

The vacant space at the top of the Birr column illustrates one theme that emerged in the years after 1918: the mutually challenging commem-oration of what might collectively be called Irish war dead. The empty column, which survives to this day, epitomises another Irish response to the painful legacy of 1914–18: a willing, perhaps even a wilful, suppres-sion of the public 'memory' of those years. This national 'amnesia', however, contrasts sharply with the fervent celebration of the war effort by Irish unionists, especially those in the north of Ireland, for whom the losses sustained by the 36th (Ulster) division at the battle of the Somme in 1916 represented a sealing with blood of the political union with Great Britain, a kind of parallel 'blood-sacrifice' (if that is what it was) to that of Easter 1916.[35]

In Ireland the 'memory' and commemoration of the Great War has been inextricably bound up with that of the conflicts at home. This is above all exemplified by the strikingly different place of 1916 in the unionist and nationalist traditions. But even here there are ambiguities. While the Easter Rising serves as an iconic event for Irish republicans, and the first day of the Somme, 1 July, has become a sacred point of reference for Ulster unionists, 1916 also saw the first engagement on the western front of the Redmondite 16th (Irish) division, also in the battle of the Somme, though not until September. The service of the two divisions – one the 'child' of the UVF and the other John Redmond's 'pets'[36] – alongside each other in June 1917 at Messines ridge, in what for that stage of the war was a notably successful attack, has provided another evidently fruitful possibility for commemoration (though the two divisions' participation at Langemarck two months later in a more conventionally catastrophic battle has *not*).[37]

To those Irish people who served abroad in the Great War, we must add those who rallied to the revolutionary side between 1916 and, say, 1923. Some, indeed, like Tom Barry, fought in different armies (though rarely at the same time) in 1914–18, 1916, 1919–21 and 1922–3. The varying ways in which the service and sacrifice of these different groups of Irish soldiers has been marked and commemorated reflect broader political and social circumstances in Ireland, north and south. To the 'parallel narratives' of enlistment explored already, therefore, we can add parallel (and sometimes conflicting) patterns of commemoration.[38]

The Irish landscape is littered with war memorials of one sort or another.[39] Many of these are monuments of a familiar sculptural type, but some are not. Who would have thought, for example, that there is in Cork a public commemoration of Field Marshal Sir Douglas Haig, the commander in chief of the British Expeditionary Force from 1915 to 1919? It exists in Haig Gardens, a small 'colony' of soldiers' cottages off the Boreenmanna Road, built in the 1920s by the Irish Sailors' and Soldiers' Land Trust.[40] In independent Ireland many of the more traditional Irish war memorials are celtic crosses – a quintessentially Irish design, fully in keeping with the gaelic patriotic dynamic of the 1916 rebels, or at least most of them.[41] The First World War memorials in Bray and Nenagh can be compared with, for example, similar celtic crosses in Oldcastle and Murroe (Co. Limerick), though the latter commemorate the struggle for national independence. Yet at a distance they look rather the same, appropriately enough since it can be argued that each one of them was put up to commemorate men who died for a high patriotic cause. But the nature of the patriotism involved is not always so clear-cut. Among the inscriptions on the Belfast war memorial unveiled in 1929 are the words 'Pro Deo et Patria' ('For God and Nation'). The same words appear on the statue of Archbishop Croke erected by the Gaelic Athletic Association in Thurles in 1922. While it is just possible that the same god may have been referred to, it is less certain that the 'nation' was the same in each case. So it is with the rituals surrounding the memorials. Outside Northern Ireland, for at least thirty years after independence, celebrations of *Irish* military endeavour were frequently accompanied by manifestations of *British* identity. The

Great War celtic cross in Longford was shrouded with a Union Jack just before its unveiling on 27 August 1925, and in the mid-1950s 'God Save the Queen' continued to be sung at ceremonies at the Irish National War Memorial in Islandbridge by the river Liffey.[42]

If we return to Cork, there is another celtic cross close to the university campus: the Royal Munster Fusiliers Boer War memorial sited on Gilabbey rock in Connaught avenue, which was used as the Great War memorial from 1919 until 1925. But this memorial is dedicated to those 'who lost their lives in the service of the empire', and it seems very likely that Cork nationalists wishing to commemorate their war dead may have felt uncomfortable doing so at this specific monument. Perhaps reflecting its 'imperial' character (as well as its rather isolated location in a residential neighbourhood), the Boer War memorial was also prone to attack. One of several incidents occurred in November 1925 when 'a very loud explosion' resulted in 'only slight damage'.[43] Thus a new memorial was erected, closer to the city centre, which significantly eschews any 'patriotic' trope, but was dedicated (on St Patrick's day 1925) by the 'Cork Independent Ex-Servicemen's Association' in 'memory of their comrades who fell in the Great War fighting for the freedom of small nations'. The location of this monument on the South Mall further illustrates some ambiguities of Irish war memorials generally. Next to the First World War memorial (which now has 1939–45 added), in what has been designated a 'Peace park', is a small stone dedicated to those who died in the atomic bomb attacks on Hiroshima and Nagasaki in 1945. Fifty yards away is a massive gothic-style monument erected in 1906 'through the efforts of the Cork Young Ireland Society to perpetuate the memory of the gallant men of 1798, 1803, 48 and 67 who fought and died in the wars of Ireland to recover her sovereign independence'. It might be asserted that the scale of these three memorials is in inverse proportion to the cataclysmic nature of the international events commemorated, but their size and location no doubt aptly represent the relative political salience of those events to the majority of Irish people (or, at least, to the people of Cork, which may not be the same thing at all).

There are elements in the erection of the new Great War memorial on the South Mall which emphasised the common experience of nationalist and unionist, Protestant and Catholic, and this reflects the emergence of a belief that shared military experience, and the shared human costs of that experience, might transcend local Irish political and sectarian differences. This theme has strongly emerged in recent years, and in the way Ireland's involvement with the First World War has been 'remembered' and com-memorated. But if we look at our more domestic Irish conflicts, the situa-tion has been, and in some cases remains, rather different. In sharp contrast to any notion of common suffering and common experience across the whole community, the northern 'Troubles' which flared up from the late 1960s produced an intensified polarisation of society which has helped entrench (a handy military metaphor) political attitudes. One thing largely absent (to our great cost) from what we might call the 'civil war' of the past thirty years is any sustained sense that shared military experience on each side of the conflict might have any sort of reconciling potential. And the same can be said of 1916. If we are serious about trying to extract some good from common suffering in 1914–18, then we must also seriously contemplate the possibility that some good might be extracted from an understanding of the common suffering and loss, not just on the battle-fields of continental Europe, but also here at home.

Commemoration in Ireland in 2006 seems to be set in a pattern which matches Easter 1916 with the First World War, and specifically the battle of the Somme, as if these are 'equal and opposite'. They are not. Setting aside the grotesque imbalance of casualties suffered in each set of events – a comparative handful (though no single fatality is casually to be dis-missed) on one side as opposed to tens of thousands on the other – the balancing of the Easter Rising and the Somme deftly lets us duck the issue of how to commemorate those Irish soldiers who died during Easter week 1916 fighting *against* the rebels. Without coming to terms with the experience of Irish fighting Irish in 1916, we can scarcely contemplate any resolution (is that too optimistic a term?) of our more recent conflict.

It has to be admitted, however, that the impulse to enlist Ireland's First World War experience in a kind of benign military mobilisation, occu-pying a moral high ground where all sections of the community might find a place, has indeed helped undermine the barriers of mutual com-munal ignorance that sustain much of the continuing social antagonisms on our island. In *Ireland and the Great War* I celebrated the achievement, for example, of the 'Island of Ireland peace tower', dedicated at Mesen/ Messines in Belgium on 11 November 1998.[44] Although criticisms can be made of the whole scheme, its imaginative harnessing of shared memory and shared experience, and the drawing together of the now fairly distant past with the altogether more contentious and hazardous present, provides an opportunity (to paraphrase General Sir Oliver Nugent's words at the unveiling of the Virginia, Co. Cavan, war memorial) for differing interpretations of what we may *believe* to be our duty to be accommodated in a creative rather than destructive fashion.[45] Ireland's domestic (and not just recent) past is perhaps so painful that we may require the more remote experience of, for example, the First World War to help us come to terms with it.

While the growing public interest in Ireland's experience during 1914–18 is illustrated by the official acknowledgement of First World War anniversaries (and the sense that if Easter 1916 is to be commemorated so too should 1 July), it has also stimulated wider cultural developments. Another component of our 'memory' of historical events stems from the imaginative transmission and modulation of those events by creative writers and artists. One recent example, which tellingly explores the history of what we might call 'Rising-cum-war', is Sebastian Barry's Booker prize short-listed novel, *A long, long way*, which tells the story of Willie Dunne, son of a Dublin policeman, who enlists in the British army in August 1914.[46]

For the most part, the majority Irish wartime experience, of Catholic, usually nationalist, soldiers, has been ignored, in historical studies as much as in literary works. This, however, has changed significantly over the past ten years or so, during which some historians have shifted their focus on to the war, and begun to recover the 'forgotten' history of nationalist Ireland's engagement with the conflict. But perhaps we have to go one step further. Even categorising the Irish experience of the war as *either* 'nationalist' *or* 'unionist' misses the point that *most* people *most* of the time do not act or think in self-consciously political terms. And these are the very people Barry so vividly (and so illuminatingly) treats in his novel.

Willie Dunne is essentially apolitical, at the start of the book following (insofar as he thinks about it at all) his father's loyalty to crown (King George V) and country (Ireland). Here Barry marvellously recreates an early twentieth century environment where, despite the increasingly urgent political conflict between nationalist home rulers and predominantly Ulster unionists, the majority of people were not bothered by politics one way or the other. That the 1916 rebels were themselves aware of this is reinforced by Garrett FitzGerald's observation that the men of 1916 acted in part in an effort to 'save nationalism from extinction'.[47] Yet Dunne himself cannot remain unaffected by the seismic wartime shifts in the Irish political landscape. He happens to be in Dublin on leave at the start of the Rising, when what he witnesses unsettles him, and leads to a falling-out with his father.

During Easter week Dunne travels from Dublin back to Flanders. In actuality this would have been an improbable feat, but in context it is a rewarding literary manoeuvre which allows Barry to counterpoint the similarities, and the differences, of Irish soldiering at home and abroad, as well as the challenge which the Rising offered in 1916 to notions of patriotism and national allegiance. One fellow infantryman, a nationalist who is later executed for disobeying orders, tells him: 'I came out to fight for a country that doesn't exist, and now, Willie, mark my words, it never will.'[48] So it is for Willie, too. He observes the widening distance 'between the site of war and the site of home',[49] a phrase which in Barry's text irresistibly reminds us not only of Pierre Nora's *lieux de mémoire* but Jay Winter's contemplative exploration of the cultural history of the Great War in *Sites of memory; sites of mourning*.[50] In 1918, after another leave in Dublin, Willie Dunne finds himself happy to be going back to the war. The front line, among his friends, is the only place for him: 'He knew he had no country now.'[51]

This may well have been the case in 1918 – Willie Dunne had no country *then* – but it seems to me self-evidently the case that, in the early twenty first century, Willie Dunne *does* have 'a country' now, a country which is mature enough and 'grown up' enough to accommodate and accept a plurality of experiences, allegiances, and even identities, within what Garret FitzGerald has called 'our Irish Pantheon'. Writing in the aftermath of the unveiling of the Island of Ireland peace tower in 1998 he wrote: 'nationalist Ireland now has the capacity to understand and accept the points of view of both the majority and the minority of nationalists in August 1914.' There is no longer any need, he continued, to take sides, 'to identify with either Redmond or Pearse. Both played valid roles and can now be accepted side by side in our Irish Pantheon.' The Irish state, he concluded, has 'reached maturity'.[52] This is a worthy conclusion, but perhaps FitzGerald over-anticipated full maturity a little, for surely there should be room in 'our Irish Pantheon' for more than just Redmond and Pearse, exemplars of but two of Ireland's plural political traditions.

It might be that the 'long revolution' (as it is sometimes characterised) which we might contemplate in this anniversary year of 2006 is not some narrowly political matter, but a revolution in *comprehension*, bringing us to an understanding of Ireland's past which comprehends (and I use that term in its plural meanings) and legitimately accepts the Ireland of nationalists (of whatever stripe), the Ireland of unionists, and the Ireland of those with no particular political commitment at all.

Perhaps now is the time to look sceptically at the militarised and militaristic *mode* of 1914–18, which provided the *moment* for the corrosive violence of 1916, both in Ireland and on the continent. If we must sustain a *memory* of that time, it should be one that counts the considerable costs, both political and human. The political costs were decidedly long-lasting in an Ireland where the violence of the wartime years and immediately following polarised opinions and embedded lethal animosities across the island. But, above all, there were the human costs, the lives of Irish people cut short by this violence. So it should be that those who lie in Arbour Hill, or in the 'silent cities' maintained by the Commonwealth War Graves Commission along the western front, or Glasnevin, or even Grangegorman military cemetery in Dublin, where some of the Irish soldiers of 1916 rest, might be remembered and commemorated, not as representatives of separate and antagonistic groups (which they may well have been), but together, as Irish, pure and simple.

WHO WERE THE 'FENIAN DEAD'?
THE IRB AND THE BACKGROUND
TO THE 1916 RISING

Owen McGee

The Irish Republican Brotherhood (IRB) was known during the Irish revolution mostly by repute and it died amidst great controversy. Unlike the
Sinn Féin party or the Irish Volunteers, it was a secret and revolutionary
movement that had a long history. Today it is usually remembered for two
reasons only: organising the 1916 Rising and producing the charismatic
revolutionary leader Michael Collins. The IRB and its political traditions
did not begin in 1916 or in 1919, however, but rather during the mid-
nineteenth century. Indeed, at no stage during the early twentieth century
did the IRB's membership reach even a tenth of what it had been during
the earlier period. It is hardly surprising, therefore, that one of the IRB's
veteran figures maintained that, although its motives were the subject of
wild speculation by many people during 1922, 'none of these people know
anything about it, about its organisation or its aims or its work':

> None of these people know anything about the way in which the movement
> they have ruined was made, about the hard, unpaid, untrumpeted work of com-
> mon unpretentious men of all ages in the years between the rise of Parnell
> and the election of 1918. Revolutionary movements do not rise up from the
> ground in a night, or in a year, or in ten years. The seed has to be sown over a
> long series of years.[1]

Historians have traditionally seen the nineteenth century IRB (popularly known as 'the Fenians') as having been important only during the
era of strained Anglo-American relations between 1862 and 1872.[2]
Most famously, the (British infiltrated) 'Fenian Brotherhood' in America
attempted to take control of the IRB in Ireland, ultimately forcing a two
day abortive struggle to take place in March 1867 between the police and
unarmed IRB followers in Dublin and Cork.[3] This led to mass arrests and
sensational trials, thereby causing what was termed 'Fenianism' to capture
the public imagination. However, throughout the mid- to late-nineteenth

century, the IRB was usually able to maintain a following of about 40,000 men, a figure equal to the membership of those confederate clubs which had provided most IRB founders with their baptism of fire in 1848.[4] This continuing relevance of the IRB after 1872 was reflected by the fact that various Irish politicians, who were eager to capture the middle ground of Irish public opinion, looked for the IRB's assistance in asserting their political influence during the 1870s and 1880s.

The IRB remained in a peak organisational condition up until the spring of 1884. At that time, however, having succeeded in infiltrating and heavily compromising Clan na Gael (the IRB's Irish-American supporting body), British intelligence was able to pounce on the IRB, seize its documentation (including its account books) and arrest or imprison several of its leaders.[5] Over the next six months, while Dublin Castle held the IRB's chief organiser, P.N. Fitzgerald, in custody, Parnell negotiated with the Catholic bishops, giving them an effective right of veto over the Irish party's policies and choice of candidates, while the Catholic hierarchy in turn formally declared in October 1884 that they recognised the Irish party as the church's mouthpiece in British politics.[6] Simultaneously, aristocratic Ulster tories revived the moribund Orange Order, created an 'Ulster party' in opposition to the 'Irish party' at Westminster, and were able to persuade the powerless, lower middle or working class Presbyterian community in Ulster (which had in the past been inclined towards republicanism) to join the Orange Order *en masse* as a means of expressing their distaste for the clerically-controlled Irish party.[7] This polarised Irish society and political representation on both religious and north-south grounds, giving birth to what would later be described as the 'two Irelands'. Indeed, while the home rule episode of 1886 would be often presented as a triumph of Irish nationalism, there is much evidence to support a directly contrary view. Michael Davitt argued that the suppression of the democratically governed Land League and the rise of a National League controlled by an unaccountable committee led by Parnell and the Catholic bishops was actually a counter-revolution, causing the *demise* of Irish nationalism.[8] While Parnellite historiography dismissed this claim of Davitt as a personal prejudice, it reflected a much broader school of thought.

Unlike the rest of Europe, nineteenth century Ireland did not experience its greatest democratic upheaval in 1848 but rather during the Land League revolution of 1879–81, in which the IRB played a leading role. Indeed, the IRB reached its peak overall strength, in a numerical, financial and military sense, at this time, with nearly 40,000 members, much funding and almost 10,000 firearms. The Home Rule League of the parliamentary classes, by contrast, had only a few hundred members, little funding and very limited popular support.[9] Furthermore, in so far as Parnell or the British government attempted to contain the situation in Ireland after 1881 or 1884 through agreement with the church, the counter-revolution identified by Davitt certainly followed a comparable pattern to similar counter-revolutions which historians have identified as having taken place across Europe in the wake of the democratic upheavals of 1848 – many of which helped to maintain the political institutions of the *ancien régime* in Europe right up until 1918.[10] Indeed, not without reason, one historian has typified the post-1886 high political consensus established regarding Ireland as a concordat-like arrangement, designed to make the Catholic community the future bedrock of the Union in Ireland.[11] Certainly, it was at the British government's request that the bishops formally declared their total support for the undefined concept of home rule in February 1886 after Prime Minister Gladstone promised that his traditionally anti-Catholic Liberal party would begin working with Parnell's party in advancing the educational programme of the church. This ensured that Catholic Ireland, although obviously not nationalist Ireland, could henceforth rely on both of the leading British political parties to champion its interests.[12] Like the bills his Liberal party would later introduce in 1893 and 1912, Gladstone's home rule bill of 1886 would not have lessened the sovereignty of Westminster over Ireland in any way.[13] The Catholic church and Parnell's party needed to sell the home rule idea to the Irish public thereafter, however, so that the Liberal party would keep to its promise to support Catholic interests.

An underlying aim of the 'new departure' programme of 1878, and a perpetual hope of the IRB, had been that Irish MPs in Westminster would withdraw from the British imperial parliament and make a stand for Irish independence. The IRB would back up such an action in the form of a citizens' defence force, akin to the Irish Volunteers of 1780–2, the first supposed champions of civic virtue in Ireland.[14] This did not, however, occur until 1918. Indeed, up until that time, very many Catholics evidently desired nothing more than the creation of an Irish society that would be structured according to Catholic social doctrine, with the church in greater control of education matters – something that was perfectly possible to achieve under British rule.[15] This is essentially why Irish Catholic MPs, from the days of Daniel O'Connell to those of John Redmond, joined the church in denouncing Irish nationalist revolutionaries as men who were advocating a sinful creed of 'forceful' (or actual and physical) resistance to a just political order, which was based on the moral force of the British constitution, as well as the principle of 'a brighter and better future for Ireland, and for England', guided by 'thrice-blessed signs of peace and hope. The future is with God'.[16]

Under the Union, the church and Catholic MPs in Westminster encouraged the Irish public to view itself as belonging to a 'Catholic country' or a 'Catholic nation'. Their actual motive in doing so, however, was to ensure that a primary sense of identification by Catholics with their religion could make them *immune* to the revolutionary or secular ideology of political nationalism, which was considered by the church to be a godless mammon, born out of the French Revolution. It was also naturally opposed by Irish MPs at Westminster since the rise of sedition in Ireland would cut the ground out from under their feet. The claim of Thomas Meagher, the creator of the Irish republican tricolour in 1848, and thereafter the IRB, that an Irish nationalist politics could never come into being until the Irish political community began to assert its complete independence from the Catholic church was based upon just such a reading of the situation.[17] Indeed, it was a condition of continued existence of Maynooth College after 1795 that all entrants had to take an oath to suppress sedition in Ireland.

The IRB slowly but surely disintegrated after 1884 for various reasons. The most important of these were the activities of British intelligence (which virtually controlled Clan na Gael's treasury), the great risk in remaining a member of the IRB after the amount of evidence produced against it by the Irish party and the British government at the *Times* commission, and the effects of the Catholic church's perpetual proscription of the IRB. Indeed, many who left the IRB at this time evidently did so to avoid the fate of most Fenian figures of the nineteenth century who had been baptised Catholics but never abandoned the republican movement or its seditious Irish nationalist goals. This was to be excommunicated, socially blacklisted (often leading to unemployment or emigration) and, ultimately, denied the last rites and buried in an unmarked grave – this practice being the primary reason why the IRB felt it necessary to launch a tradition of looking after their deceased comrades' graves, as well as the well-being of the widows and children of the Fenian dead. As a result of all these setbacks, by the time Tom Clarke (who first joined the IRB in 1878) was sent to Ireland by John Devoy in the wake of P.N. Fitzgerald's death and burial in an unmarked grave in October 1907, the IRB had been reduced to a tiny organisation of little more than 1,000 members.[18]

Traditionally, historians have seen Tom Clarke's arrival in Ireland in late 1907 as initiating a chain of events which led directly to the 1916 Rising and a revival of the IRB. This, however, was only partly true. In fact, the IRB continued to suffer from an organisational decline. The major reason for this was that the rise of the Irish-Ireland movement after 1898 dealt a *coup de grace* to the already decimated IRB by giving birth to two movements, both opposed to the political traditions of the IRB, that became the most popular in Ireland alongside the Orange Order. These were the Ancient Order of Hibernians (AOH), which being a strictly Catholic society was dogmatically opposed to republicanism, and the Gaelic League, whose members invariably boycotted all secret societies. Previously, the IRB had much in common with European revolutionary movements of its day. This was reflected in its adoption of the ethos of a secret, freemason-like, revolutionary 'brotherhood',[19] its anti-clericalism, its advocacy of democratic citizens' defence forces (an egalitarian, or 'republican', political culture often maintained in France by familial connections, or radical local elites)[20] and its equation of republicanism with the (then) revolutionary notion of democratic liberty and a challenge to the coercive power of unaccountable monarchical states.[21]

The new 'Irish-Ireland' generation, however, professed contempt for the whole of Ireland's nineteenth century past on the grounds that Irish society had fallen under the influence of secret freemason-like interest groups and anti-clerical elements, and that the Irish language and Irish history had not been generally taught in schools. True, the Christian Brothers did teach the Irish language and Irish history, but their version of Irish history made no distinction between the history of the Catholic community and the history of the United Irishmen, the Young Ireland movement and the Fenians. In their day, all these movements had been denounced and opposed by the church but, after 1900, youths were taught to view them as having been part of 'the unbroken continuity and permanence of the Gaelic tradition', symbolised by the Irish language and the Catholic religion.[22] As they sought to overcome religious differences in Ireland, Irish nationalist revolutionaries were perpetually denounced by Catholic elites up until the 1890s as advocates of the views of 'immoral', meaning non-Catholic, newspapers. From the 1900s onwards, however, it was an article of faith for all advocates of 'the philosophy of Irish-Ireland' that the only means of safeguarding Ireland's future was to protect it from the influence of non-Catholic reading material. Indeed, by the time Sinn Féin and the Ulster Unionist Council were formed in 1905, Irish public opinion was fully accustomed to the existence of a north-south, politico-religious polarisation in the country, which was seen to be akin to a conflict between a British and an Irish nationalism. It could well be said, however, that what this polarisation really reflected was the equal fear of Irish Protestants and Catholics (according to their own respective definitions or prejudices) of the prospect of living in a 'godless' state or society.

Central to the formation of Sinn Féin was Arthur Griffith's abandonment of his long-standing republican opposition to the Catholic church's stance on education matters, after he realised that the predominantly Catholic population of Ireland was never going to accept republicans' secular nationalist ideology. Indeed, it was precisely by encouraging *greater* Catholic control over the primary (national school) education system that Griffith was able to prompt many to consider his proposal that Sinn Féin could potentially become an ideal replacement for the Irish party.[23] In turn, like the Irish party's press, the *Sinn Féin* newspaper refused to publish any material that was critical of the role of the Catholic church in Irish politics. After Whitehall had granted state recognition to the Catholic University/UCD and following Rome's promulgation of the *Ne Temere* decree in 1908, some Catholic bishops, being satisfied that the future well-being of Catholic Ireland had been safeguarded, encouraged Joseph Devlin's AOH (heretofore the backbone of support for the long-faltering Irish party) to begin supporting Sinn Féin,[24] which was already popular among young ecclesiastical students in Maynooth College.[25] Meanwhile, following in Maud Gonne's footsteps, Countess Markievicz, an aristocrat and former debutante, joined Sinn Féin and helped turn the semi-militaristic boy scouts unit, Fianna Éireann (a separate body to the IRB), into a fairly popular youth movement.[26] Significantly, Markievicz felt it necessary to become a Catholic if her nationalism was to be taken seriously.[27]

These developments were crucial to the creation of the so-called 'revolutionary generation' in early twentieth century Ireland, but it should be stressed that Tom Clarke's impact on the IRB from 1907–16 rested upon a very different and far more localised dynamic. Central to his rise in the IRB was the removal from authority of P.T. Daly, a Dublin labour activist, committed Irish speaker and printer with *An Cló Cumann*. Having become the secretary of a (nominally) reunited IRB in 1904, Daly marginalised all IRB veterans and directed all young members to work only in the public Irish-Ireland social movements, thereby causing the revolutionary underground to dwindle away through the lack of an organisational nucleus.[28] In time he also misappropriated IRB funds while, in one way or another, reports of some IRB meetings he chaired were received by Dublin Castle.[29] During the early to mid 1900s, P.N. Fitzgerald, the old IRB chief organiser, was critical of Daly's mismanagement of the IRB,[30] while Daly in turn worked to counteract Fitzgerald.[31] Soon after Clarke arrived in Ireland, he discovered that IRB veterans were correct in claiming that Daly was acting against the IRB's best interests and had misappropriated their funds. With the support of P.S. O'Hegarty, the leader of the Wolfe Tone clubs, John O'Hanlon (a veteran IRB figure from the 1880s) was soon able to co-opt Clarke onto the IRB Supreme Council along with three other veteran figures, Fred Allan, John MacBride and M.F. Crowe.[32] Daly was thereafter expelled, causing Allan (the IRB leader of the 1890s) to resume his old position as IRB secretary, while Clarke became the new IRB treasurer.[33] Allan soon discovered to his horror that the IRB had been reduced from the organisation of about 10,000 members that he had led a decade before to one containing little over 1,000 men, confined mostly to the Wolfe Tone clubs in Dublin, and that little or no communications existed between its followers countrywide.[34] This situation was not about to change, however.

Clarke's next significant impact on the IRB revolved around the attempt of two young republican journalists, P.S. O'Hegarty and Bulmer Hobson, to form a rival journal to *Sinn Féin*. Previous efforts, *The Republic* and the *Irish Nation and Peasant*, had been boycotted by Catholic opinion and were short-lived, but Hobson persuaded Allan and Clarke to take up the idea by forming *Irish Freedom (Saoirse na hÉireann)* in November 1910.[35] However, after Patrick McCartan (a recent American envoy sent by the somewhat controversial figure of Joseph McGarrity)[36] sent Fr Eugene Sheehy to Philadelphia to forward an IRB progress report, Allan was incapacitated in his role as IRB secretary, while both Markievicz and Gonne began supporting McCartan's efforts to wrest control of *Irish Freedom* out of Allan's hands.McCartan appealed to Clarke, as IRB treasurer, to support him, but Clarke, feeling divided loyalties, first hesitated and then refused. McGarrity, the Clan treasurer since the autumn of 1904, then gave McCartan the necessary funds. Thereafter, Allan, MacBride, O'Hanlon, Crowe and other IRB veterans offered their resignations when they learned that McGarrity was financially supporting his envoy McCartan, and deliberately not funding the IRB Supreme Council. Many members of the Wolfe Tone clubs resigned with them, but Clarke and a majority of the younger members of the clubs (who were also Gaelic League members) opted not to resign and so the veterans were not reinstated and a new Supreme Council had to be created.[37] McCartan and Hobson thereafter encouraged many of their non-IRB associates to become lead writers for *Irish Freedom*, a fact that played a significant role in making this a more popular journal. It should be stressed, however, that neither revival nor decline of the IRB occurred as a consequence.

During the first thirty years or so of its existence, the IRB had been a nationwide organisation with tens of thousands of members, a central force in Irish popular politics, a quite effective underground party, and a would-be revolutionary citizens' defence force. Before and after 1912, however, it was little more than a tiny committee, struggling to stay alive. Hence Major Nicholas Gosselin, the head of special branch since the mid-1880s, had retired happily in December 1904, satisfied that an Irish nationalist threat no longer existed. It was not until 1919 that special branch funding would again equal the level reached during the mid 1880s.[38] The youths who joined the IRB during the 1900s via the Gaelic League or Dungannon clubs (a group of short-lived literary and debating societies operated by Bulmer Hobson and Denis McCullough) had no experience of being part of a disciplined revolutionary movement. Instead of being a priority, the IRB was to them little more than an interesting, American-funded subset of the new Irish-Ireland and Sinn Féin movements that existed in the light of day and were built around the Gaelic League. It was the latter movement that was most important to them, for which they acted as propagandists, decided their loyalties and which, indeed, had a significant power over Irish public attitudes.

Tom Clarke was virtually the only member of the IRB's post-1912 leadership who knew that the organisation was but a shadow of its former self. Considered by some former IRB leaders of the 1880s as a 'republican through and through', Clarke was nevertheless very conscious of the fact that he had never before played a role in directing the organisation.[39] From 1909 onwards, therefore, he constantly sought the counsel of John Daly, his wife's uncle and former boss in the IRB (having been chief organiser from 1872 to 1880), who had extensive experience both in politics and as a revolutionary leader. Like Clarke himself, Daly had spent over a decade in prison after being framed by spies and *agent provocateurs* during the spring of 1884.[40] Most recently, he had been a pro-labour mayor of his hometown of Limerick (1899–1902) where, since the 1870s, he and all republicans had been denounced by the local Catholic bishop, Dr

O'Dwyer.[41] Nevertheless, during the late 1890s Daly was able to become a prosperous baker. At Clarke's request, he funded various IRB ventures after 1909. Notwithstanding his illness and old age, Daly also advised Seán MacDermott – the man Clarke appointed to replace the veteran figure of Fred Allan as IRB secretary – about the reorganisation of the IRB. Indeed, alone of all the younger men, MacDermott was brought into very close counsel with the Daly-Clarke family, who were hypersensitive about maintaining security in the IRB.[42] While Clarke admired the young propagandists who wrote for *Irish Freedom* (particularly Hobson),[43] he evidently had a much greater sense of respect for his old revolutionary cohorts.[44] His tendency to trust in IRB veterans was perhaps best demonstrated by his choosing Clontarf Town Hall (an establishment run by another old revolutionary comrade, Michael McGinn)[45] for most Supreme Council meetings right up until January 1916.[46]

Not until after the formation of the Ulster Volunteer Force was Clarke able to persuade the young *Irish Freedom* propagandists to consider the idea of bearing arms, or to follow the lead of James Stritch, an IRB veteran who had built a drilling hall behind the site of the republican movement's former headquarters during the mid 1880s.[47] Meanwhile, after the lockout of all Dublin transport workers in the summer of 1913, the socialist-republican James Connolly and the IRB man Seán O'Casey formed the Irish Citizen Army to defend the workers' rights. Bulmer Hobson, however, tried to popularise the idea of forming a volunteer force specifically by targeting the editorial staff of the Gaelic League organ, *An Claidheamh Soluis*, namely Pádraig Pearse, The O'Rahilly and Eoin MacNeill, who was also a leading UCD academic. The fact that the Catholic press was now generally critical of the home rule proposals for granting Ireland no legislative or fiscal autonomy (no such criticisms had been made in 1886 or 1893), allied with Hobson's close friendship with Countess Markievicz (with whom he was co-leader of Fianna Éireann), no doubt played a significant part in encouraging MacNeill to support the idea. This led to the formation of the Irish Volunteers in November 1913. Its executive included several leaders of the stridently Catholic AOH, who were then wavering between the Irish party and Sinn Féin in their sympathies.[48]

London IRB men like O'Hegarty and Collins (both of whom came from old Cork IRB families)[49] would later claim that the Irish Volunteer movement was virtually the IRB's invention.[50] So it might have seemed to them from a distance. However, the volunteer movement was led by what might be best described as the 'Gaelic League party'. Men like MacNeill,

The O'Rahilly and Pearse were neither republicans nor revolutionaries, but Catholic intellectuals who, like the Catholic bishops, were sympathisers with both the Irish party and Sinn Féin. Like the former, they also felt aggrieved by the British government's handling of the home rule crisis. At the time, the Irish party was accusing the British government of betraying its trust by allowing the formation of the Ulster Volunteers. Some Irish party supporters attempted to portray this as a 'betrayal of democracy' but the reality was that the Ulster and Irish parties were nothing more than marginal constituencies, representing collectively less than one tenth of the total electorate of the United Kingdom; democracy, thus, had nothing to do with the matter. The only 'betrayal' involved was the British government's reneging on the unofficial, and far from democratic, concordat-like arrangement established in 1886, whereby the Irish party understood that they were to become *the* future mediators of the Union in Ireland.

Over the previous thirty years, establishing the political and educational basis of a Catholic governing class for the Union in Ireland was central to the Irish party's purpose. However, if it and the Catholic church formerly had a strong common cause due to their mutual concern for providing for Catholic education, unlike the Irish party, the church's primary concern with education had always been religious, not political, and stemmed not least from its desire for missionaries. Indeed, as Ireland had the only predominantly Catholic population in the English-speaking world, the Irish population was central to Roman Catholic missionary work in North America, Australia and all British territories. The church's role in inspiring D.P. Moran's generation to advocate a 'philosophy of Irish-Ireland', whereby Irish people were encouraged to view themselves as a special race destined to become a spiritual beacon for the rest of the world, and as morally superior to all secular or Protestant societies, was rooted in this same missionary concern. To some extent this concern had become even more acute with the passage of time because of the ever-growing secularisation of European and British society – a development from which the church was naturally determined to protect Irish society at all costs.

Within a few months, the Irish Volunteers acquired tens of thousands of members, generally through the AOH, the largest social organisation among Irish Catholics. Unlike the IRB, however, the Irish Volunteers was neither a revolutionary nor a republican movement. Rather it was a public body that identified with the mainstream of Irish Catholic society and, as such, was to receive support from some of the Catholic bishops.[51] Recognition of this fact is important to understand the role the IRB played in the organisation of the 1916 Rising and events thereafter, as well as the history of the Irish Volunteer movement and the conflicting attitudes that emerged between various IRB and Volunteer (later 'IRA') figures. Meanwhile, it should not be forgotten that owing to their very status as volunteers, the members of the Irish Volunteers were not only almost entirely unarmed but also unsalaried. Consequently, a large proportion, having little opportunity to earn good money (or to bear arms), were prepared to enlist in the British army, via John Redmond's 'National' Volunteers, once the call arose not long after the outbreak of the First World War in August 1914. The 'Gaelic League party' generally opposed Redmond's initiative, however. Their supporters included G.N. Plunkett, a papal count, and his son, Joseph Mary Plunkett, both of whom attempted to contact Rome and the German government after they realised that the outbreak of the First World War had brought about a completely new situation in Europe.[52] The first instigators of the latter initiative, however, were two men who were formerly prominent British civil servants, namely Erskine Childers and Roger Casement. Both men opposed the British war effort (they had long foreseen a war with Germany) and supported the Irish Volunteers' efforts to import arms. (They arranged the Howth gun-running in July 1914 once Whitehall renewed the special coercive arms acts for Ireland that it had dropped temporarily in 1912 to facilitate the formation of the Ulster Volunteers.)[53]

As Clan na Gael had begun raising funds for the Irish Volunteers that spring,[54] and as the IRB hoped to use the Volunteers as a recruiting ground to revive its organisation, Clarke, MacDermott, John Daly and Devoy were very angry with Hobson for not using his influence in the Volunteers to prevent its members from enlisting in the British army.[55] This decision on Hobson's part was interpreted by them as a political surrender to Redmond's party – an attitude that demonstrated the importance of the 'generation-gap' in Irish nationalist circles at this time. Hobson and many leaders of the Irish Volunteers did not consider Redmond's success in persuading men to enlist in 1914 as being of great importance. This was because they knew perfectly well that the influence of the Irish Volunteers and Gaelic League, the movements upon which they intended to base their future careers in Irish public life, had not been significantly lessened as a consequence.

Meanwhile, Redmond's only real political power since 1910 stemmed from his personal status as an accepted and senior figure of the British political establishment (like Carson, he was viewed by many as a potential cabinet member); the Irish party itself was moribund. Its unpopularity at this time was reflected by the fact that numerous Catholic writers championed the Irish Volunteers and denounced the Irish party for supporting Britain's war effort against the last great Catholic power in Europe, Austria-Hungary. 'Sceilg's' *Catholic Bulletin*, an enthusiastic supporter of the Irish Volunteers and fierce critic of the National Volunteers, likewise opposed the war by expressing fears regarding what effect it might have on the future of the papal states.[56] Such concerns were shared by several devout Volunteer officers whom Hobson provided with Irish-American contact details during 1914. These included Pearse, who went to America to collect funds for his dying Irish language school, and Thomas Ashe (at that point considering entering a monastery), who went on a Gaelic League fund-raising tour.[57]

Veteran revolutionaries viewed the course of events in Ireland in a very different light. Being an old anti-clerical republican, Devoy was no more in favour of Ireland's future being determined by a Catholic party than were the Ulster Presbyterians.[58] Meanwhile, Clarke evidently entertained a hope that the Ulster and Irish Volunteers (he supported both) might join together in Ireland, since they were both seemingly opposed to Whitehall's politics of home rule, as upheld by Redmond.[59] To such men, as well as John Daly and even Griffith (whose basic politics were formed long before the arrival of the Irish-Ireland generation), the Irish party still appeared powerful because they had been fighting against its politics and machinations for decades. Indeed, nothing would make Devoy happier during the 1910s than to see all the old Irish party candidates defeated, given that he viewed them as having betrayed the Irish nationalist movement of the later nineteenth century.[60] Veteran figures like Devoy, Daly and Clarke felt a very strong need for a revolutionary gesture to destroy the Irish party and desired to make the IRB the instrument for this. By contrast, individuals such as McCartan and Hobson, both of whom followed Casement's lead, tended to view such old revolutionaries as 'narrow partisans' and desired instead to go with the general flow of opinion with the public Volunteer and Gaelic League movements.[61] Neither of these movements was in favour of revolution or rebellion in the country, but they were clearly in a very strong position to take over from the Irish party as the political leaders of the Irish Catholic community.

It was Roger Casement, not the IRB, who initiated diplomatic contacts with Germany during 1914. Casement offered to raise an Irish brigade to fight for Germany and represented himself as an official political representative of MacNeill, Hobson and the Irish Volunteer executive. Clarke and the IRB did not like Casement's involvement in revolutionary affairs and were wholly opposed to this idea of working with Germany. Devoy, the Clan's secretary, did not like it either,[62] but J.T. Keating, the Clan chairman, and McGarrity, its treasurer, supported Casement's initiative, and so Devoy had to follow suit, meeting Casement and a German emissary in New York. From October 1914 until April 1915, the Clan's funds were sent to Casement in Germany instead of the IRB in Ireland, though Casement accomplished, and generally did, nothing with this money.[63]

Following the outbreak of the First World War, *Irish Freedom* was suppressed under the new censorship regime and several members of the post-1912 Supreme Council simply resigned once Clarke argued that the IRB needed to use the war as an opportunity to launch a revolution. In turn, having been deprived of all Clan funding, the IRB was in no position to revive its organisation. Indeed, the IRB would probably have completely collapsed at this time were it not for the fact that, at the bidding of Clarke, John Daly funded MacDermott when he travelled the entire country during late 1914 and early 1915 in an attempt to swear several Irish Volunteer officers into the IRB, thereby nominally recreating a Supreme Council.[64] In May 1915, however, MacDermott was arrested after making a seditious speech, thereby bringing this push to re-establish the IRB to a sudden halt.[65] Clarke responded by appointing in his place as IRB secretary Diarmuid Lynch, a New York Gaelic Leaguer who had worked occasionally for Devoy as a Clan-IRB envoy since 1911, until such time as MacDermott was released from prison. Thereafter, in June 1915, Lynch invented a strange three man 'Military Committee', consisting of Pearse (the 'director of organisation' of the Irish Volunteers), Joseph Mary Plunkett and Éamonn Ceannt. This committee technically did not belong to the IRB and only Clarke and Lynch knew of its existence.[66]

Since 1913, Clarke's Wolfe Tone clubs had some success in attracting volunteers to large Manchester martyr demonstrations in Dublin, alongside the Transport Workers Union, Irish Citizen Army and the 'Old Guard Union' (the IRB veterans' association).[67] Partly as a result, it was possible during July 1915 to bring the Irish Volunteers into concert with Devoy and Clarke's plan to organise a large public funeral in Dublin for Jeremiah O'Donovan Rossa (1831–1915), a man with a long, troubled career, who had been a bedridden invalid for the last five years of his life.[68] Indeed, although the 'O'Donovan Rossa Funeral Committee' included a dozen retired (or semi-retired) veterans of the IRB organisation of the period 1878–95,[69] as well as several Dublin Trades Council figures, the Rossa funeral was primarily an Irish Volunteer demonstration (the *Catholic Bulletin* played a significant role in advertising it).[70] In the souvenir booklet for the event, Rossa was made a symbol of all sorts of causes, although the only living people who had ever been politically associated with him were Devoy, Daly and Clarke. Recognising his great power as an orator, Clarke persuaded Pearse to deliver a graveside speech at the event on behalf of the Wolfe Tone clubs, of which Clarke himself was president, MacDermott vice president and James Stritch the treasurer. Fearing that, like MacDermott, he would be arrested Pearse initially declined, but Clarke persuaded him to go ahead with the plan. As a result, Pearse delivered a famous speech that concluded pointedly with lines that *seem* to have referred specifically to the defeats which the IRB had suffered during the mid-1880s and the very negative consequences which Clarke knew these had had for the organisation:

> The defenders of this realm have worked well [against the IRB], in secret, and in the open … They think they have pacified half of us and intimidating the other half [into giving up]. They think that they have foreseen everything; they think they have provided against everything; but the fools, the fools, the fools! They have left us our Fenian dead, and while Ireland holds these graves, Ireland unfree shall never be at peace.[71]

The following month, upon his release from prison, MacDermott joined the 'Military Committee' all of whose members were then sworn into the IRB.[72] This body then became known as the (semi-official) 'Military Council', although it was still technically subordinate to the IRB Supreme Council, of which McCullough, Clarke and MacDermott were the leaders. No revolutionary force yet existed in the country but fears were growing in the Irish Volunteers that their organisation might soon be suppressed because of its seditious, anti-war stance.

It was not until January 1916, at a secret meeting in Clontarf Town Hall, that the earliest plans for a rebellion were actually made. In early February, a Supreme Council cipher reached Devoy in New York, declaring that a rebellion would occur in April regardless of circumstances, and requesting that the Clan purchase and import arms for the IRB.[73] In the meantime, the Citizen Army leader James Connolly (who was very eager for a rebellion) was co-opted onto the Military Council by Clarke, while MacDermott played a significant role in persuading Pearse that a rebellion would be morally justifiable. Owing to American neutrality laws, the Clan could not send arms from America. Taking advantage of names learned from Casement eighteen months earlier, however, Devoy contacted German officials himself, although he made clear to the Germans that no military assistance for Ireland was being requested, only an opportunity to purchase firearms.[74] A shipment of arms was duly purchased by the Clan and was supposed to be sent to Limerick, although British intelligence succeeded in counteracting the plan, owing to its intelligence agents in the Clan treasury. Casement himself, upon learning that the Clan had attempted to purchase German arms on Devoy's initiative, warned MacNeill that plans for rebellion must be afoot and ordered him not to countenance the idea under any circumstances.[75] This helped to scotch whatever slight hope may have existed that the Irish Volunteers *en bloc* could be made to join an effort at rebellion, to assist in which plan MacDonagh had been co-opted onto the Military Council in early April.[76] In the days before the planned date for a rebellion, MacDermott and Pearse were secretly ordered by Clarke to issue instructions to various volunteer units or IRB circles outside Dublin to be ready to rise. As no formal plans for insurrection existed, however, most figures outside Dublin had no idea why they had received such orders.

Clarke had no option left but to rely entirely on the ranks of the Dublin IRB and Wolfe Tone clubs to create some kind of rebel force. By kidnapping Hobson, he attempted to ensure that, through his own presidency of the Wolfe Tone clubs, he could order the whole of the Dublin IRB's ranks to take part. Meanwhile the leader of the Dublin Gaelic Athletic Association, Harry Boland (whose father had been an IRB-Parnellite figure during the early 1890s),[77] also persuaded some men to take part,[78] as did James Connolly within Irish Citizen Army circles. In London, Seán MacDermott approached Mark Ryan, a seventy two year old former IRB leader, and apparently informed him of the plans for a Dublin revolt.[79] Several London IRB men, including Michael Collins, did indeed take part. Fred Allan seems to have known about the Rising plans but decided not to take part and tried, in vain, to dissuade his best friend John MacBride (who had lived with Allan's family since 1905) from engaging in what he knew would be a suicidal act.[80] According to G.A. Lyons, who had hoped to bring the Dublin IRB and Belfast Protestants together in a volunteer force in 1911 and who was stationed at Westland Row during the Rising,[81] the simple and hastily drawn up plan for a rebellion in Dublin – namely seizing various public buildings, proclaiming a republic and hoping the public would then rally to the rebels' side – followed virtually the same parameters as a plan that James Connolly had suggested to the IRB seventeen years earlier.[82] This might indicate that Connolly was responsible for inspiring the conduct of the Dublin Rising, which was really nothing more than an 1848-style citizens' revolt (effectively the last such episode in European history), when would-be 'free citizens' manned various public buildings (or 'barricades') in defence of a cause of national liberty in the face of an unaccountable monarchical government and virtually waited to be shot to pieces. As Michael Collins would note, the 1916 Rising was intended by the IRB to be 'a wonderful gesture – throwing down the gauntlet of defiance to the enemy, expressing to ourselves the complete freedom we aimed at'.[83]

The Daly-Clarke family had the Proclamation of the Republic drafted and signed in the home of J.W. Power, a republican of the Land League days.[84] Tom Clarke, as the first signatory, was appointed president of the provisional republican government, while Pearse was appointed the 'commander in chief' of the government's forces and Connolly the commander of the Dublin forces (which, in practice, was much the same thing).[85] The other four signatories had no designated rank as members of the so-called Provisional Government.[86] However, the first two signatories of the Proclamation, Clarke and MacDermott, as treasurer and secretary respectively of the three man executive of the IRB, could theoretically claim to have done so on behalf of the whole IRB organisation, as per its constitutional rules, thereby making the rebellion officially an act of the IRB.[87] This was no doubt Clarke's desire, so as to attempt to vindicate his old comrades, the IRB's 'Fenian dead'. Reputedly, Pearse was again persuaded by Clarke to act as an orator, reading the rebels' Proclamation outside the GPO, before two flags were raised: first a plain green flag bearing the words 'Irish Republic' and then Meagher's old 1848 tricolour,[88] which had not been publicly displayed in Ireland for fifteen years.[89]

When Clarke announced in the GPO that a republic was going to be proclaimed, many Irish Volunteers were apparently surprised, presumably because, as members of the Irish-Ireland generation, most had never expressed any interest in republicanism, an ideology generally associated with the supposedly 'priest-eating' republic of France. Realising that he was effectively rebelling on behalf of an organisation (the IRB) that no longer existed, Clarke justified his action by stating that if some such action was not taken in Ireland at that particular moment in time, it would never occur.[90] He also stated that if the attention of the international community was ever to be attracted to Ireland's desire for independence, only a republic could 'appeal to the imagination of the world'.[91] This reflected the fact that the revolutionary ideal of the IRB had always been, in John MacBride's words, to 'add another republic to the republics of the world', alongside the two pioneers of modern democratic governments in the western world, namely the republics of America and France.[92] The insular separatism of the Irish-Ireland movement, which desired to protect Ireland from secular currents of thought or the influence of the outside world, was not something that had been shared by the old republicans who, in the words of Clarke's old mentor John Daly, desired to 'demolish the Bastille of history'.[93] Not surprisingly, familiar as it was with the Daly-Clarke connection going back to the 1880s, one of the very first actions taken by Dublin Castle, after suppressing the small revolt in Dublin and executing its leaders, was to raid Daly's Limerick home.[94]

The 1916 Rising (not unlike Ulster Presbyterians' 'solemn' protest in 1912) not only took the form of a citizens' revolt, it was evidently intended to be one. MacDermott noted that, ultimately, he was relieved that most Irish Volunteers had not been brought into the conspiracy, because there would have been an unnecessary degree of death and destruction as a result.[95] Another illustration of this side to the Dublin revolt was the diverse motives of those who took part. Apart from greying IRB republicans, the rebels included young socialist members of the Citizen Army, Catholic intellectuals who were leaders of the Volunteers and various individuals who probably simply felt a need to do *something* since it was feared that they all were about to be arrested anyway and the Volunteer movement suppressed. Furthermore, if some people within the GPO did not know that a republic was going to be proclaimed, it may be presumed that many of the rebels who gathered elsewhere in Dublin, at the request of various (non-IRB) Volunteer officers, also had no such thoughts on their minds. Indeed, were it not for the printing of the Proclamation, no one would probably have known afterwards that the Rising was nominally a republican affair, since a republican demand had not been made in Ireland for very many years.

The Rising did not go to plan. The rebels in the GPO, armed only with rifles, believed they were going to be engaged in a gun battle with British soldiers, but instead were shelled by artillery or gunboats on the Liffey, with the inevitable result that most properties and businesses on O'Connell Street and the surrounding areas were indiscriminately destroyed. This helped create resentment against the rebels for instigating such destruction in the city centre. As Clarke had hoped, however, public opinion altered dramatically once he and the rebel leaders were executed, for this ensured that they became martyrs, of one kind or another.[96]

As the Catholic press was already very sympathetic to the Irish Volunteers, it was naturally resentful that the British government not only executed various Volunteer leaders but embarked on widespread arrests thereafter. This prompted John Dillon, the *Catholic Bulletin*, numerous Dublin priests and the IRB's old enemy, Bishop O'Dwyer of Limerick, to express sympathy for the executed rebels, the latter proclaiming that the rebellion should wake the British government up to its need for home rule.[97] As the Gaelic League party was already antagonistic to the Irish party, a swing to Sinn Féin was to be expected in the wake of the executions. From New York, however, John Devoy was amazed by priests' expressions of sympathy with the deceased rebels, as he interpreted events in Ireland in a very different light to the much younger Irish-Ireland generation.[98] Meanwhile, much to the chagrin of the IRB in Dublin, once sympathy for the executed rebels and all political prisoners reached a height during the winter of 1916, the Catholic press latched onto the singular personality of Pearse, who was falsely presented as the leader and organiser of the Rising.[99] Shortly thereafter, Pearse was even cited by some priests as a role model for Irish Catholic youths:

> Everything is overshadowed by the Christian concept, and the religion that is found here [in Pearse] centres in Christ and Mary. The effect of fifteen centuries of Christianity is not ignored or despised ... Ancient, medieval and modern Gaelic currents meet in him ... He will appeal to the imagination of the times to come more than any of the rebels of the last one hundred and thirty years ... His name and deeds will be taught by mothers to their children long before the time when they will be learned in school histories ... They will think of him forever ... as a martyr who bore witness with his blood to the truth of his faith, as a hero, a second Cuchulainn, who battled with divine frenzy to stem the waves of the invading tide.[100]

Such propaganda helped to turn the 1916 Rising into a Catholic event in the mind of the general Irish public and retrospectively gave it great popularity. The ideal of 'adding another republic to the republics of the world' clearly did not have the same appeal to the Irish-Ireland generation as much as the refrain of the hunger striker Thomas Ashe, 'let me carry your cross for Ireland, Lord', a motto more suited to an Irish Christian missionary than an Irish nationalist or republican. The mood of this time was perhaps best reflected by the fact that, in late 1915, James Connolly felt that he was going totally against the grain of Irish public opinion by suggesting that the needs of the body could sometimes be placed before the needs of the spirit.[101]

During 1916–17, Fred Allan, Joseph McGrath and others raised funds for the families of executed 1916 rebels, most of which was then handed over to Kathleen Clarke (Tom's widow). Mrs Clarke then chose Michael Collins to be the new IRB secretary, Harry Boland to be the new treasurer, and Seán McGarry (ex-manager of *The Republic* and formerly a close friend of Tom Clarke) as president.[102] Thereafter, these men, most notably Collins, attempted to turn the IRB into a directing revolutionary committee within both the Irish Volunteers and Sinn Féin, to ensure that both organisations would take up the IRB's republican ideals. Only two of the commanders of the haphazard 1916 forces were not executed, namely Countess Markievicz and Éamon de Valera, both of whom were made icons of the Rising as soon as public opinion began to be swayed in its favour by the Catholic press. As is well known, the latter went on to become the new leader of Sinn Féin. Like Parnell, de Valera proved able to appeal to both revolutionary and conservative constituencies, while the Sinn Féin party of 1917–22, like the Irish party of 1880–5, was a conglomerate of nationalist revolutionary and conservative political elements. In the revolution that followed, however, one must be cautious not to overemphasise the importance of the IRB owing to the small size of its membership. Furthermore, recent studies have convincingly suggested that this 'revolution' for very many volunteers was simply an opportunity to revive the land war of the 1880s, and had little or nothing to do with ideological considerations.[103] In turn, debate on the revolution has become more realistic and begun to resemble some of the historical debates on the republican upheavals that took place in France between 1789 and 1871, and the motives of the various volunteer forces that took part in those struggles.[104]

To some extent one could say that *two* different risings took place in Dublin at Easter 1916. First, there was a republican rising, to vindicate the 'Fenian dead' of the nineteenth century, launch an independence struggle in Ireland, and revive the IRB. Second, there was an 'Irish-Ireland' rising, designed to champion the cultural separatism of the Irish-Ireland movement and, more specifically, the anti-First World War stance adopted by the Irish Volunteers. The 1916 Rising would not have happened were it not for Tom Clarke's IRB circle. However, it was the Irish-Ireland separatist ideal, which was already well-established by 1914, that the Rising was destined to symbolise in the mind of the general Irish public. This was the dual heritage of the 1916 Rising.

AMERICA AND THE 1916 RISING

Francis M. Carroll

When Pádraig H. Pearse walked out from the General Post Office in Dublin on Easter Monday 1916 to read the Proclamation of the Provisional Government of the Irish Republic it declared, among other things, that the rebellion that was just starting was 'supported by her exiled children in America'. As news of the Rising spread across the city the rumour grew, according to the poet and novelist James Stephens, that 'many Irish-Americans with German officers had arrived also with full military equipment'.[1] The recognition of this connection between America and Ireland should have come as no surprise. Historical circumstances had brought them together over the past centuries. America had been the refuge, the haven, to which the Irish could flee hunger and distress, social and religious discrimination, and political and economic constraints. The result was a huge population in the United States with Irish roots and many with a bitterness toward the British regime and a determination to assist any Irish movement to achieve independence. All of this gave Ireland and the United States a very interwoven history. While the actual Rising may have been a total surprise to the spectators along O'Connell Street that April morning, it should be no surprise that there was an American dimension to these monumental events.

For over 200 years North America had been the destination for Irish people struggling with economic, social, religious, and political disabilities at home. Extensive migration from Ulster in the seventeenth and eighteenth centuries meant that a high proportion of people with Irish connections in colonial America and in the early republic. The figures vary greatly, but it is estimated that by 1790 there were over 300,000 people in the United States of Irish descent, and the two decades prior to the war of 1812, including refugees from the troubled rebellions of 1798 and 1803, may have accounted for another 100,000.[2] 'Emigration is the great fact of Irish social history from the early nineteenth century,' Roy Foster has observed, and this was borne out following the War of 1812 when even larger numbers began to move from Ireland to the United States.[3]

Perhaps as many as 1,000,000 emigrated between 1815 and 1845, and at least 3,000,000 in the Famine years between 1845 and 1870. David Fitzpatrick has pointed out that in 1890 some 39 per cent of those born in Ireland were living abroad, the largest portion of them in the United States.[4] By the early twentieth century there were almost 5,000,000 people in the United States either born in Ireland or with Irish parents. By taking third and forth generation Irish-Americans into account, there may have been as many as 20,000,000 or about 21 per cent of the population.[5] As the Great War broke out in 1914 the United States had, therefore, an enormous population that had some kind of Irish connection. If even a fraction of their number supported an Irish cause a vast amount of money could be raised and great pressure could be brought to bear in the United States or in Ireland. The Irish-American community was a tool of great potential in the hands of any Irish political movement.

Linkage between Irish nationalist activity and the Irish-American community can be traced to Wolfe Tone's sojourn in the United States in 1795 and to the organising of the Friends of Ireland Society in 1840 in support of Daniel O'Connell's Repeal movement. The most serious of these connections was the creation by the Young Ireland rebel James Stephens of the Irish Republican Brotherhood (IRB) in 1858, to some extent at the prompting and with the financial support of John O'Mahony and Michael Doheny in New York. These men and many of their early followers had been part of the unsuccessful Young Ireland rebellion of 1848. The IRB, and its counterpart in the United States, jointly became known as the Fenian movement. During the course of the early 1860s they both grew into formidable organisations. The IRB may have had as many as 40,000 members, some of whom had been, or still were, soldiers in the British army, while in the United States of the 100,000 to 175,000 men of Irish descent who served in the union army in the Civil War, some 50,000, now with military training, joined the Fenian Brotherhood. Despite these large and, in the American instance, well-financed organisations, personal rivalries between the leaders, divided counsel, and a certain amount of bad luck resulted in neither the Irish nor the American Fenians actually carrying out successful military operations. The British suppression of the Fenian uprising in 1867 led to the arrest and imprisonment of many of the leading figures and the reversion of the organisation to a steadily diminishing secret society. In the United States the fiasco of the several attempted invasions of Canada and the divisions within the leadership led to Clan na Gael superseding the Fenians in the late 1860s. Unlike the American Fenians, the Clan was a secret society, led largely by former Fenians. However, within twenty years the Clan was also racked by a bitter split and murder scandal that lasted until 1900, considerably reducing its effectiveness.

While the physical force movement was struggling to re-organise itself in the 1870s and 1880s the Irish party came gradually under the control of Charles Stewart Parnell. The leadership that Parnell brought to the party at Westminster seemed to promise the implementation of home rule in Ireland through constitutional politics, and Irish-Americans rallied behind Parnell and the prospect of self-government in the form of the American Land League and the American National League. Parnell and various of his lieutenants, including his sister Fanny, travelled to the United States to rouse support for home rule and to raise funds for the party. However, Parnell's downfall in 1890, his death in 1891, and the failure of the home rule bill in 1893, led to a split in the Irish party and the collapse of the home rule movement. Not until 1900 were the differences patched up and the party reunited under John Redmond. While the more sympathetic Liberals in England were able to form a new government at Westminster in late 1905, it was not until the two general elections in 1910, the second of which (in December) left the Liberals and Conservatives with 272 seats each, that home rule again became a serious political prospect, with the Irish party holding the balance of power with 84 seats. Supported by the United Irish League of America, Redmond and leading members of his party, such as John Dillon and T.P. O'Connor, visited the United States repeatedly, raising thousands of dollars (perhaps as much as $100,000 in 1910 alone, leading to Redmond being labelled the 'dollar dictator' by his opponents) with which to fight elections and subsidise members of parliament. As the prospects for home rule rose, so did enthusiasm in America.[6]

It is difficult to imagine today the degree of support that existed for home rule across the United States. In 1910 President William Howard Taft, and several other American dignitaries, travelled by train to Chicago to attend the St Patrick's day dinner organised by the Irish Fellowship Club, as a gesture of support for home rule.[7] Former President Theodore Roosevelt was the guest of Redmond, T.P. O'Connor, and others in the House of Commons dining room at a reception and lunch in June 1910.[8] Judge Martin J. Keogh from New York wrote to Redmond in November of 1910 to assure him that: 'I have never felt more keenly interested in your work nor have I ever had more genuine admiration for the way you are conducting it than I have at the present time.'[9] When the home rule bill was introduced in April of 1912 some fifteen Irish-American community leaders sent a cable congratulating Redmond on this achievement.[10] As the home rule legislation worked its way through parliament, congratulations and praise poured in to Redmond. 'You have achieved more than I believed it possible to be done in the lifetime of an Irish Leader in our day, and more than all, you have the race at home and abroad solidly, sincerely, and almost unanimously with you,' Judge Keogh told Redmond when the bill passed its second reading in 1912.[11] When the third reading of the bill was passed, Congressman Goodwin of Arkansas introduced a resolution congratulating 'the people of Ireland' on its passage. Having been defeated in the House of Lords the home rule bill was introduced again and passed in the Commons on 9 June 1913. The following day Redmond read to the Commons a letter from Theodore Roosevelt that said that home rule 'bids fair to establish good will amongst the English-speaking people'.[12] If the passage of the home rule bill under the new rules of the reformed House of Lords seemed to imply the inevitable implementation of the measure, the emergence of militant unionism, particularly in Ulster, supported by the Conservative party in Britain, threatened otherwise and began to change the whole political picture.

Clan na Gael was reunited in 1900 under the leadership of John Devoy. Devoy was described as 'the greatest of the Fenians' by Pádraig Pearse, an admirer, and as 'a sleepless demon' by Patrick Egan, a critic. Although in his seventies, Devoy was the pivotal figure in the physical force movement before 1916. A former member of the French Foreign Legion, a Fenian recruiter, a supporter of Parnell, and a newspaper reporter and editor, Devoy devoted his whole life to Ireland. However, overshadowed by the likely success of home rule and unsuccessful in mounting any recent physical force operations, the Clan and the IRB faced serious difficulties in the early years of the century. By 1910 membership of the IRB in Ireland and Britain was down to between 1,500 and 2,000 from its high point of about 40,000 members. To make matters worse, these members were largely elderly men who saw the IRB as something of a social club rather than a revolutionary organisation. 'Nearly ten years J.[ohn] D.[evoy] of struggle and we are reaching what seems to be the end,' wrote John T. Keating, a Chicago member of the Clan's revolutionary directory, and he acquiesced in Devoy's conclusion that 'another period of mere negative policy ... will kill us if too much prolonged'.[13]

But what to do? Resistance to the Boer War had been ineffectual, opposition to the Anglo-American arbitration treaties had helped to defeat them but had not moved the Irish cause forward, and criticising home rule as a betrayal of Ireland's right to full independence seemed futile.[14] Throughout 1910 and 1911 Devoy and his colleagues speculated on the possibility of an Anglo-German war, but Anglo-German naval tensions had temporarily eased. One practical thing that the Clan leadership in the United States could do was help reinvigorate the IRB by introducing new people to the Irish organisation. A key figure was Thomas J. Clarke, who had been imprisoned in 1883 for revolutionary activities, migrated to the United States where he had worked for Devoy at the *Gaelic American*, and returned to Ireland in 1907 to serve on the Supreme Council of the IRB. Clarke is often regarded as the man who revitalised the IRB, and after a period of some struggle became the main link between the IRB and the Clan. Dr Patrick McCartan of Co. Tyrone, a friend and protégé of Joseph McGarrity, and Diarmuid Lynch, who had taught Irish language and dancing in New York, were recommended to the IRB by the Clan leaders. Young Irishmen and IRB members, such as Bulmer Hobson, Denis McCullough, Seán Mac Diarmada, Thomas MacDonagh, and Pádraig Pearse, were encouraged and supported by Clarke as well as by the Clan when they visited the United States.

Indeed IRB representatives were brought over from Ireland regularly to attend the annual meeting of Clan na Gael, during which time they learned about the American organisations and were strengthened in their desire to make the IRB more active. The Clan also provided funds for the Supreme Council of the IRB, between £600 and £1,000 per year although sometimes more.[15] James Connolly also spent eight years in the United States where, among other things, he edited an Irish-American labour paper called *The Harp*. Connolly was not a member of the Clan nor did he become a member of the IRB until January 1916, after he had founded the Irish Citizen Army, but while in the United States he did form an important friendship with John Devoy, which was to stand him in good stead with IRB figures like Tom Clarke.[16]

Less officially, the Clan, and particularly Clan leaders such as John Devoy and Judge Daniel F. Cohalan in New York and Joseph McGarrity in Philadelphia, gave support to the Irish-Ireland organisations that sent representatives to the United States to raise money. The Gaelic League, the Gaelic Athletic Association, Sinn Féin, the Abbey theatre, Pearse's school, St Enda's, and several other organisations all sought to create an Ireland that was culturally distinct from that of England. In the early years of the twentieth century these groups were largely overshadowed by the Irish party and the mainstream of Dublin culture. To the degree to which they represented an alternative they had the support of Clan members in the United States. The list of these counter-culture people from Ireland who toured the United States is impressive, and included Douglas Hyde, William Butler Yeats, Lady Gregory, Maud Gonne, John MacBride, Francis Sheehy Skeffington, Thomas Ashe, Bulmer Hobson, Pearse, and Roger Casement amongst others. Most of these people corresponded with Devoy at some time, and many had their arrangements facilitated by Joseph McGarrity, Judge Cohalan or Cohalan's friend, the Standard Oil lawyer and patron of the arts, John Quinn. In fact, Devoy grumbled to Cohalan that: 'The time of our men is constantly taken up with raising money for the [Gaelic] League, to the neglect of our own work,' but the complaint could also be made about other Irish-Ireland organisations.[17]

Although support and enthusiasm for home rule would continue for several years more, the beginnings of serious unionist resistance, and ultimately the outbreak of the Great War, fundamentally changed the Irish situation, in America as well as at home. The defiance of the unionists had two immediate results. The first was the formation of the Ulster Volunteer Force (UVF), which inspired the subsequent creation of the Irish Volunteers. The second was the opening of talks about the exclusion of Ulster from a self-governing southern Ireland, which provoked violent anger from extreme nationalists and growing disaffection among the home rulers in America.

The signing of the Ulster Covenant in 1912, together with the assurance of support from Andrew Bonar Law, the leader of the Tories, signalled the refusal of unionists to accept home rule for Ireland, then working its way through parliament. More dramatic defiance came in January 1913, when the unionist leader, Sir Edward Carson, organised the UVF. While many questioned the seriousness of this threat, the rhetoric of defiance, if not rebellion, remained very strong. The illegal importation of German guns into the port of Larne in April of 1914, together with the apparent refusal of elements of the British army in the Curragh camp a month earlier to obey any possible orders to undertake operations in Ulster, demonstrated that the British government was prepared to countenance private armies within the realm. At the instigation of Professor Eoin MacNeill, of University College Dublin, the idea was mooted, and a meeting was held in the Dublin Rotunda on 23 November 1914, to organise the Irish Volunteers. Although MacNeill became the commander in chief of the

Volunteers, members of the IRB held dominant positions in the organisation. Even so, the Clan was unsure how to react. Devoy's *Gaelic American* came out in favour of the Volunteers on 3 January 1914, but by spring, while the Volunteers were organising throughout the country, there had still not been much material response from America. The O'Rahilly wrote to Devoy from Dublin on 6 April and lamented: 'If the sincere Irish in America will not help us in this situation they will have neglected the greatest opportunity in a century.'[18] By May Clan leaders were urging Devoy that the Volunteers should be supported, and a disgruntled member from Philadelphia wrote to Devoy's assistant, James Reidy, reporting that the Clan members at a recent meeting agreed that, in view of the inaction thus far, the Irish-American Club should be sold and the proceeds sent 'to the men who are willing to do something that will redound to the credit of Irish nationalists throughout the universe'.[19] In early June the Clan sent out a circular to camps across the United States reporting that a meeting of Clan leaders in New York had endorsed the Irish Volunteers and created the Irish National Volunteer Fund committee, headed by Joseph McGarrity, Denis A. Spellessy, and Patrick J. Griffin, 'to aid the people of Ireland to organise, arm, and equip a permanent National Army of Defence for the protection of their rights and liberties and to maintain the Territorial Integrity of Ireland'.[20] They urged that Clan members give their support, and by mid-June McGarrity was able to send £1,000 to MacNeill to buy weapons and thousands more were promised.

This support from the Clan was almost immediately threatened by John Redmond's claim, as the elected leader of the Irish people, to control a majority of the representatives on the governing body of the Volunteers. Redmond and his followers were so hated and distrusted by the people in the Clan and the IRB that the matter of support for the Volunteers was seriously questioned (and the integrity of those IRB members of the board who had acquiesced seriously challenged). The physical force movements in both Ireland and the United States were in danger of splitting over this issue. Devoy and McGarrity consulted throughout June as to what to do. Judge O'Neill Ryan, a Clan member from St Louis, Missouri, summed up the dilemma:

> I do not know where 'we are at' on this Volunteer question. If the reports in the *Gaelic American* of last week are correct … we have lost control of the situation in Ireland, and it has passed into the hands of Redmond, *et al.*, which would mean that moneys raised here would be under their control. In other words,

we will be co-operating with the UIL [United Irish League] in this country to raise funds for an organisation which they will control and emasculate.[21]

It seemed to be an irresolvable problem. Devoy was in touch with Tom Clarke in Dublin and concluded that Hobson had been the key to the surrender to Redmond. McGarrity heard from MacNeill who made a strong appeal for support from America. He thanked McGarrity for the money that had been sent and said that, more than money, what were needed were arms and ammunition, that the British government's proclamation forbidding the importation of arms was illegal, and that the unionists in Ulster and Britain had forced Irishmen to take precautions to defend their rights. He concluded with a strong appeal to friends of Ireland in the United States:

> It is surely plain to the minds of every friend of Ireland and of Liberty that a unique and supreme call has gone forth, and that the one great opportunity of an age has arisen for the service of a sacred cause. We in Ireland do not hesitate to ask you our kinfolk in a land where freedom was won in no small measure by Irish valour and Irish devotion to liberty and by the outpouring of Irish lifeblood – rather we entreat and beseech you to join with us, making the grand effort of our lives and shrinking from no sacrifice that the peril and the hope of so great a crisis may demand.[22]

It was an appeal that was hard to resist, despite the mistrust and sense of betrayal. In these circumstances it was fortuitous that Sir Roger Casement, the distinguished humanitarian and retired member of the British consular service, arrived in the United States to represent the Provisional Committee to raise funds for the Irish Volunteers. Casement had sailed on the *Cassandra* to Montreal and was in New York by 18 July. Startled by the animosity toward Hobson and those members of the Provisional Committee who had voted to accept the Redmond members, Casement worked hard to convince Devoy, McGarrity, and other Clan leaders that, given Redmond's prestige and political domination in Ireland, there had been no alternative but to accept the participation of his nominees on the Provisional Committee – no choice, short of a destructive public fight. Casement assured Devoy and the Clan leadership that the loyal and reliable IRB members of the Provisional Committee would still hold the key positions and that when guns were obtained they would be placed in the hands of reliable elements. 'As it is we have kept the Volunteer body intact

– and if we can get guns into the hands of, say, a dozen chosen corps it will revolutionise the mind of the whole country' he told Devoy.[23] Although wary, Devoy was convinced of Casement's sincerity and good intentions.

Whatever lingering misgivings the Clan leaders had about the intervention of Redmond and his followers into the Volunteer organisation, in the end they continued to support it. Casement travelled along the eastern seaboard and as far west as Chicago, meeting Irish leaders and speaking to Irish groups, even meeting Theodore Roosevelt. He was a particularly effective publicist for the Volunteers. Devoy recorded that $50,000 was raised specifically for the Volunteers by the Clan and that roughly another $50,000 was sent to the IRB in the years before the 1916 Rising.[24]

Many of the anxieties that people had about the Volunteers were overshadowed by the momentous events that occurred at the end of July and early August of 1914. First of all, 1,500 rifles and ammunition that had been purchased in Germany were run into Howth harbour by Erskine Childers on 26 July and Kilcoole, in Co. Wicklow, by Conor O'Brien several days later. These were organised by Casement's circle of friends in Dublin and London, although the £1,000 sent in June helped to finance the purchase. The gun-running had an electrifying effect among the Irish in the United States, and as Bulmer Hobson wrote in his history of the Volunteers, the organisation never again lacked funds. Casement quoted Devoy as saying that the gun-running was 'the greatest deed done in Ireland in 100 years'.[25] Secondly, the attempt by the police and British army troops to seize the weapons as the Volunteers marched back into Dublin and the subsequent shooting by the soldiers at jeering crowds on Batchelor's Walk in Dublin seemed to many to signal the beginning of hostilities in Ireland over home rule and Ulster's separation. Even the *New York Times* came to this conclusion and ran the headline: 'British troops shed first blood in Ulster war'.[26] Finally, these dramatic events were themselves overshadowed by the outbreak of the Great War on 3 and 4 August 1914. The war, of course, created a whole new set of circumstances.

Quite apart from the matter of Redmond's control of the Irish Volunteers, which preoccupied the leaders of Clan na Gael in the United States, was the growing discussion about Ulster's exclusion from home rule for an undefined period of time. These talks, and Redmond's agreement, caused growing alarm among the supporters of the Irish party in the United States. While many non Irish-Americans saw nothing untoward in this proposition, it was anathema to the Irish-American community. Senator Henry Cabot Lodge wrote to a friend that he had always supported home rule for Ireland, but he saw nothing wrong with home rule for Ulster, using as an example the determination of Maine to separate from Massachusetts in the early nineteenth century. 'If you are going to have home rule and local self-government it must be applied fairly to all,' he concluded.[27] But W. Bourke Cockran, a congressman from New York and a moderate nationalist and long-time supporter of the Irish party, wrote in March of 1914, following a protest meeting at Carnegie Hall, that 'Irishmen here have been shocked beyond expression to learn that partition of the Island has become not merely a proposal that might be considered, but a proposal that has been actually accepted.' In a statement that was incredibly prescient Cockran concluded that if 'a revolt [against Redmond] were started in Ireland, I think the Irish in America would support it to a man'.[28]

The signing of the home rule bill into law by the king on 18 September, with the provision that implementation be suspended until the end of the war, met with a mixed response in the United States. Many now accepted home rule as an accomplished fact, but not all. Redmond's public statement just two days later, at Woodenbridge, Co. Wicklow, urging the Volunteers to join the British army, together with his speech in support of Britain in the war on 3 August, had the powerful effect of alienating large numbers of the Irish in America who had not aligned themselves with the Clan. In Ireland his appeal led to the separation of the original Irish Volunteers from Redmond's National Volunteers. In the United States, the leading home rule newspaper, the *Irish World*, came out in opposition to him, and Michael J. Ryan, president of the United Irish League of America (who had a German-American wife) was also opposed.[29] With the national leadership divided, the activities of the UIL were virtually suspended, and even the maintenance of a national office was in doubt. Redmond sent Alderman Daniel Boyle MP on a tour of the United States in 1915, but without much success. Early in the following year Boyle made another trip to raise money for a new publication, a monthly called *Ireland*, to be edited by J.C. Walsh and Shane Leslie. But even with lead articles by distinguished figures such as Cardinal Gibbons of Baltimore, the publication failed to find a readership or rally much support.[30] The passage and suspension of home rule for a divided Ireland, the urging of enlistment in British forces, the split in the Volunteer movement, and the reality of a major war between Britain and Germany placed in doubt the continued loyalty of many Irish-Americans to Redmond.

The outbreak of the Great War profoundly changed the direction of events for the Clan leadership in the United States and for Sir

Roger Casement as well. When war was declared, Casement told Joseph McGarrity: 'Perhaps Ireland's chance has come.'[31] Irish-Americans had worked together with German-Americans in years past to obstruct efforts to improve Anglo-American relations, so it was to be expected that as soon as war broke out they would again show solidarity. In large public meetings in New York, Newark, Atlantic City, Philadelphia, Washington DC, Chicago and St Louis, Britain's role in the war was condemned and John Redmond criticised for encouraging Irish involvement. As early as 9 August as many as 10,000 Irish-Americans gathered at Celtic Park in New York to denounce Redmond and home rule and to cheer the Kaiser. Prominent Irish leaders, such as John Devoy, Jeremiah A. O'Leary, and Shaemus O'Sheel, were conspicuous at these events and at German-American rallies as well.[32]

Devoy also arranged for a meeting between Casement and Georg von Skal, a journalist who worked as a propagandist for the German embassy. The same day the German military attaché, Franz von Papen, reported to the Foreign Office on the Celtic Park rally, saying that he had met Casement, from whom he learned that the Irish were 'ready to free themselves' if supported by Germany and supplied with arms for 50,000.[33] Casement drafted a long letter for the Irish-American community to the Kaiser on 25 August in which he outlined Irish-American support for Germany in the war, pointed out that while Britain held Ireland, Britain was able to maintain mastery of the seas, and petitioned that when Germany won the war the Kaiser would 'impose a lasting peace upon the seas by effecting the independence of Ireland and securing its recognition'. This was signed by the Clan executive, Devoy's name first, and sent to Germany through the embassy. There appear to have been several meetings with Ambassador Count Johann Heinrich von Bernsdorff, Captain von Papen, assistant attaché Wolf von Igel, von Skal, and other members of the embassy. On the basis of these contacts von Bernsdorff advised the Foreign Office on 27 September that if the war were expected to be a prolonged one, he recommended Germany's 'falling in with Irish wishes, provided that there are really Irishmen who are prepared to help'.[34] On 10 October Devoy, McGarrity, Judge Cohalan and Casement met with Ambassador von Bernsdorff, Captain von Papen, and Dr Bernhard Dernburg for an hour and a half at the German Club in New York. The ambassador was told that the war presented an opportunity for Ireland 'to overthrow English rule in Ireland and set up an independent government', that both weapons and officers were needed, but not money. Von Bernsdorff reported to the

Foreign Office that it was being urged upon him that the German government make a statement in favour of Irish independence and that Casement be permitted to travel to Germany.[35]

Casement's original trip to the United States did not encompass any mission in Germany. The precise origins are unclear. Joseph McGarrity sent Tom Clarke an undated letter, probably in August 1914, in which, in guarded language, he wrote: 'A friend whom you trust will be soon on his way to Germany,' which would seem to refer to Casement. William Irwin Thompson has argued that the German philologist, Kuno Meyer, in the United States in the autumn of 1914, suggested that an Irish brigade be formed by Irish prisoners of war from the British army, and Ambassador von Bernsdorff mentioned such a possibility in a dispatch to his Foreign Office on 27 September.[36] In any case, Casement was talking about a mission to Germany in letters to McGarrity on 23 September and the commitment was made at a meeting with Devoy, McGarrity, and Judge Cohalan on 5 October. The Clan, which had already been looking after Casement's expenses in the United States, provided $3,000 to get him started. Von Bernsdorff provided a letter of introduction to the imperial Chancellor, Theobald von Bethman Hollweg, and the Austrian consulate in New York booked the tickets to Norway on the Oscar II. Casement shaved his beard to become less recognisable and travelled with the passport of an Irish-American businessman, James E. Landy. Devoy and Judge Cohalan had some doubts about Casement's ability to carry out this enterprise, but McGarrity said: 'I will trust him with my life.'[37] Casement sailed on 15 October and arrived in Germany on the 31st. British attempts to intercept him in Christiania (Oslo), Norway, failed, and he was escorted from Norway to Germany by Richard Meyer of the German Foreign Office. Once in Germany, Casement had several objectives: to obtain a statement of German commitment to Irish independence; to enlist German support for an insurrection in Ireland; to publicise the Irish cause in Germany; and to create an Irish brigade from among the Irish prisoners of war. He was successful in obtaining a statement supporting Irish independence; had mixed results, at least to his own satisfaction, in enlisting support for and publicising the Irish cause; and was very discouraged with his attempts to organise an Irish brigade.[38]

The IRB also saw the outbreak of war as an opportunity to exploit Britain's difficulty. Bulmer Hobson later recounted: 'In the autumn of 1914, under the influence of [Seán] MacDermott, the Supreme Council of the IRB decided they would embark on an insurrection against the

British government before the European war came to an end.'[39] Although there were some objections, MacDermott and Tom Clarke were delegated to pursue the matter, which they did without much further consultation with the rest of the Supreme Council. They did work with a similarly small group from within the General Council of the Irish Volunteers, thus secretly committing that organisation to a rebellion also. All of this needed money, and the Clan and the Irish-American community began sending funds to both the IRB and the Volunteers. In September and November £2,000 was sent to the IRB when Thomas Ashe and Diarmuid Lynch returned to Ireland.[40] It was recognised that when the Irish Volunteers and the National Volunteers split in the autumn of 1914 a good portion of the money was seized by Redmond's forces. Funds had to be sent to the Irish Volunteers right away. The Cohalan papers show that $10,000 was withdrawn from the Irving National Bank on 20 October by the treasurer of the Irish National Volunteer Fund (and also taken to Ireland by Lynch), followed by another $15,000 on 12 November (taken to Ireland by John Kenney). More monies followed and in 1915 the Clan created an 'arms fund' to raise new money. Much of this was couriered to Ireland by an IRB messenger, Tommy O'Connor, who worked on a White Star passenger liner making regular transatlantic crossings.[41] The Clan also continued to subsidise Casement in Germany, although not the expenses of the Irish brigade. Funds for Casement were sent through the German embassy and by couriers, such as John Kenney, Seán T. O'Kelly, Joseph Mary Plunkett, Plunkett's sister Philomena, and the Philadelphia lawyer, Michael Francis Doyle.[42] Indeed, as plans for the Rising developed, quite apart from providing funds, Devoy, McGarrity, and Judge Cohalan became the main link between the IRB in Ireland and the German embassy and government.

It is fair to say that the Irish-American community was not unanimous in their support for Germany in the war. This should not be surprising; even people who did not favour the Allies and did not want the United States involved in the war found German objectives and practices to be deplorable. However, there was a significant portion of the Irish-American community who consistently saw all British actions as ruthless and selfish and regarded Germany as a possible saviour of Irish fortunes. In the aftermath of the sinking of the *Lusitania*, a turning point in the war, a large public meeting was held on 24 June 1915 in Madison Square Garden in New York. An enormous crowd of 75,000 people, largely Irish-Americans and German-Americans, came to hear the key speaker, William Jennings Bryan, President Wilson's former secretary of state, who had just resigned over the strength of Wilson's *Lusitania* note to the Germans. Georg von Skal chaired the meeting and Devoy and Jeremiah O'Leary were among the speakers. O'Leary, who ran the American Truth Society and published an anti-British journal called *Bull*, became so outspoken in his criticism of Britain and the United States, as it edged closer to war in 1916 and 1917, that he was eventually tried for treason.[43] Devoy, although he was regarded as a 'confidential agent' by the German embassy and his newspaper was barred from the mails when the United States entered the war, managed to avoid treason charges. James K. McGuire, the former mayor of Syracuse, New York, fully embraced an Irish-German alliance and wrote two books promoting the idea: *The King, the Kaiser and Irish freedom* in 1915, and *What could Germany do for Ireland?* in 1916. Years later all of these people would be accused of being in the employ of the German embassy.[44]

There were Irish-Americans employed by the German embassy, largely to sabotage the sale and shipment of munitions to the Allies in the war. Captains von Papen, von Igel, and Karl Boy-Ed hired Irish-American dock workers on both coasts to go on strike in order to slow down and disrupt the shipments, and to place incendiary devices on munitions ships to disable or sink them at sea. To expand this programme Captain Franz Rintelen von Kleist, of German naval intelligence, was sent to the United States in 1915, rather separate from the embassy. Because of his prestige and his good relationship with Devoy and other Clan leaders, James Larkin was actively recruited to serve as an intermediary between the Germans and the workers. Larkin had numerous meetings with the Germans, to the extent of being shown explosive facilities in Hoboken, New Jersey, and seems to have taken their money from time to time, but refused to become an active participant in their sabotage.[45] These activities linked the Irish and the Germans in the public mind in the United States and also served to demonstrate to the Germans the reliable anti-British sentiment of the Irish. These activities also came to the attention of the American government. On 18 April 1916, in an effort to stop the sabotage in the munitions industry, secret service agents raided the offices of Captain von Igel in New York. When the files and paper in the office were seized, much of the correspondence between Devoy and Judge Cohalan and the German embassy fell into the hands of the American government. There was immediate alarm that information about the Rising and its date would become public knowledge, or at least be conveyed to the British. Devoy, however, sent a reassuring note to McGarrity in a thinly disguised code:

I know you will be anxious after hearing of the fire in the house to learn if we all came off safe. I am glad to be able to inform you that all the papers relating to the property were saved except one little scrap, and that will not be much of a loss. The sale will come off on time and everything looks all right. We were very anxious for the whole day, but when the firemen got through with their work of salvage we found we had no cause for worry.[46]

Nine days later, and six days after the Rising, the British asked the State Department for any relevant information but were turned down by Secretary of State Robert Lansing.[47] Devoy, who despised the Wilson administration, publicly maintained that the Rising had been betrayed by the United States government. In fact, British intelligence had by this time broken the German code and was reading German transatlantic messages and had most of the material the American government had seized.

As the war unfolded there was a growing feeling among the Clan leaders that something had to be done to shape public opinion within the Irish-American community. By the autumn of 1915 Devoy became the centre of a discussion about the need for a national meeting to create a platform for opponents of Redmond and the current home rule measures. In December the idea of an Irish race convention was settled and on 15 January 1916 invitations were sent to Clan members; on 9 February the 'call' went out to the Irish-American community for a meeting in New York on 4 and 5 March.[48] The invitations were sent to Irish-American organisations all over the United States to send delegates. Well over 2,000 people attended, making it the largest Irish-American meeting ever held, and it was a perfect venue for strong speeches in favour of Irish self-government. The most important accomplishment of the Race Convention was the creation of a new public organisation, the Friends of Irish Freedom (FOIF). The president was Victor Herbert, famous composer and grandson of Samuel Lover; the treasurer was Thomas Hughes Kelly; and the secretary was John D. Moore – all blue ribbon figures, although the Executive Committee was dominated by Clan members. One of the first acts of the Friends was to create a bureau in Stockholm, Sweden, staffed by the former US diplomat, T. St John Gaffney, who was to serve as a link to Germany. The FOIF drew thousands of people across the United States, particularly from the moribund UIL, and specific provisions were made for associate membership for existing local Irish-American societies.[49] Of course no mention was made of the coming Rising in Ireland, although in retrospect it is clear that the organisation was intending to provide American support for the Rising and the subsequent Irish struggle. Indeed, the FOIF became the most important Irish-American nationalist organisation in the country over the next five years.

Although the plans for the Rising were worked out in 1915 and early 1916, under the leadership of Tom Clarke, the number of people involved remained a handful of the IRB and Volunteer leadership. The Americans had facilitated the movement of messengers in and out of Germany, but John Devoy was not informed of the actual Rising until 5 February 1916. He recounted receiving a coded message through Tommy O'Connor from the Supreme Council of the IRB. O'Connor began to decipher the message, but when the first sentence read 'Nobody but the Revolutionary Directory and the chief German representative must know the contents of this,' Devoy took the message home and decoded the rest of it himself. The key passage informed him that the Rising would take place on Easter Sunday, 23 April 1916 and that the Germans were to 'send a shipload of arms to Limerick quay' between 20 and 23 April.[50] Devoy immediately took these instructions to Captain von Papen, and the Germans provided a ship, the *Libau*, sailing by the name *Aud*, a similar Norwegian vessel. The ship was loaded with captured Russian rifles and ammunition, and the key element for an effective military effort in the Rising was set in motion. On 14 April, another courier, Philomena Plunkett, the daughter of Count Plunkett, delivered a note with instructions that the weapons be delivered on Saturday 22 April. Devoy duly conveyed this change of date to von Papen and the message was sent to Germany. However, the *Aud* had already sailed and, without a radio, was beyond reach.[51]

When the ship arrived off Tralee on the 20th, as arranged, there were no Volunteers to meet it – a result, perhaps, of the extreme secrecy surrounding the whole enterprise. The vessel was eventually hailed by a royal navy ship and escorted to Cobh (Queenstown) where its crew scuttled the ship. This misadventure deprived the Rising of a substantial supply of weapons and had the additional consequence of upsetting the timing by one day. In a second misadventure, Casement, by this time disillusioned with the Germans and disappointed in his effort to recruit a substantial Irish brigade from among Irish prisoners of war, was brought by submarine to Tralee Bay where he, Captain Robert Monteith and Sergeant Julian Beverley (Daniel J. Bailey) were landed on Banna Strand. Although Casement and Beverley were soon arrested, Monteith avoided detection in 1916 and eventually made his way to the United States. Casement may have hoped to cancel the Rising, but his capture, together with that of the *Aud*, certainly contributed to Eoin MacNeill's decision to do so. Thus when the Rising started on Easter Monday morning, on the orders of Pearse, Clarke, Connolly, and the others, the chance for surprise, for new weapons from Germany, and for a full complement of the Volunteers, had been lost.

The circumstances of the Rising in Dublin on Easter Monday 24 April 1916 are examined elsewhere in this volume. When the General Post Office was captured a coded message was sent to John Devoy in New York, 'Tom successfully operated today', which alerted him and his Clan colleagues to the fact that the insurrection had started.[52] For the next few weeks Devoy and others had to rely on the garbled newspaper reports from Ireland and Britain. Devoy's *Gaelic American* printed brave stories that were largely conjecture.[53] The reaction across the United States, among both the general public and most of the Irish-American community, was largely disapproval of the Rising as a mad escapade, probably rather cynically prompted by the Germans. However, with the executions of the signatories to the Proclamation and several others, opinion shifted to increasing criticism of the British authorities. Within the Irish-American community, the newly organised FOIF became a driving force in arranging for public meetings and passionate speakers denouncing Britain's ruthlessness and its hypocrisy in purporting to wage a war in Europe in defence of small nations. Even people outside the Irish community could see the irony in the situation. Theodore Roosevelt wrote to a friend in England:

> I wish your people had not shot the leaders of the Irish rebels after they surrendered. It was a prime necessity that the rebellion should be stamped out at once, and that the men should be ruthlessly dealt with while the fighting went on; but [Sir Edward] Carson himself had just been in the cabinet, and he and the Ulstermen about two years previously had been so uncomfortably near doing the same thing, and yet had been so unconditionally pardoned, that I think it would have been the better part of wisdom not to extract the death penalty ... [54]

The political dimension of these protests focused in the summer of 1916 on several congressional resolutions asking the British government to spare the life of Roger Casement, tried and convicted of treason in London in June. After extensive discussion the Senate passed a modified resolution seeking clemency for 'Irish political prisoners' on Saturday 29 July. The document was delivered to the White House, sent to the State Department, and then on 2 August encoded and cabled to the embassy in London and decoded there. The result was that although the resolution was delivered to the Foreign Secretary on the morning of 3 August, Casement had been hanged earlier that day. The British government had been kept fully informed of this whole procedure by their ambassador in the United States, Sir Cecil Spring-Rice, who told the Foreign Secretary privately: 'You will of course be prepared for a great explosion of anti-British sentiment to take place in case of Casement's execution.'[55] This refusal of the British government to be moved by this appeal from the United States provided plenty of ammunition to the Clan and the FOIF in their subsequent campaigns on behalf of Irish independence.

A more practical response to the Easter Rising in the United States was the creation of the Irish Relief Fund, which raised between $100,000 and $150,000. Despite letters of introduction from the American secretary of state, when Thomas Hughes Kelly and Joseph Smith attempted to distribute the relief money in Ireland they were denied entry, although surprisingly their two more politically extreme assistants, John A. Murphy and John Gill, were allowed to enter unmolested. Murphy and Gill worked with the Irish National Aid Association and the Irish Volunteer Dependents' Fund to distribute the funds.[56] Murphy reported that over 1,300 families had been assisted and about $25,000 a month expended.[57] Difficulties over the Irish Relief Fund, together with the unsuccessful Senate resolution on behalf of Casement, along with other matters more specifically related to the war, contributed to the steady decline in Anglo-American relations throughout 1916.

After the United States itself entered the war in April 1917, President Wilson, in the hope of eliminating a conspicuous source of British-American animosity, asked his ambassador in London to urge the British Prime Minister, David Lloyd George, to make an effort to implement some form of self-government in Ireland. In response Lloyd George, who had his own experience with this intractable problem, created the Irish Convention. The chairman of the convention was Sir Horace Plunkett, a man particularly well known and respected in the United States. The Convention did ease Anglo-American relations during the war, but it failed to devise an acceptable form of Irish self-government. Wilson was also troubled by those Irish-Americans who had identified so completely with Germany in the war that they could not accept the entry of the United States on the same side as Great Britain. John Devoy, Judge Cohalan, Joseph McGarrity, Jeremiah A. O'Leary, James K. McGuire, John T. Ryan, and others came under some degree of persecution by the American government for their actions.[58]

Once the war was over, and the newly re-organised Sinn Féin party successfully replaced the Irish party in the 1918 general election, Irish-Americans returned to a very public campaign for Irish independence. Another Irish race convention was held in Philadelphia on 22 and 23 February 1919. In addition to endorsing the outcome of the 1918 election in Ireland, the convention set in motion arrangements for the meeting of a delegation with President Wilson to urge that he work for Irish independence at the Paris peace conference. The convention also created the American Commission on Irish Independence that went to Paris and Ireland to try to obtain admittance for an Irish delegation to the peace conference. Although unsuccessful, the commission did keep the Irish question before the leading figures at the peace conference and it generated a great deal of publicity for the Irish cause.[59] The FOIF also launched the Irish Victory Fund which raised $1,000,000, which was used to finance the American Commission on Irish Independence, the early stages of the Irish bond certificate campaign, and numerous other Irish.publicity activities in the United States.[60] The Irish-American community helped to support the government of Dáil Éireann by purchasing $5,746,360 of bond certificates in a campaign launched in 1920 by Éamon de Valera during his trip to the United States. As the War for Independence ran on from 1919 to 1921, the destruction and misery caused stirred the humanitarian sympathies of Irish-Americans, who in turn contributed $5,069,194 to the American Committee for Relief in Ireland, which distributed these funds to the Irish White Cross in Ireland.[61] The nature of the conflict also stimulated the creation of the American Commission on Conditions in Ireland, a public body that held hearings in the United States on the nature of the war in Ireland. All of these efforts kept the Irish cause before the American public while many in the Irish-American nationalist movement clashed with de Valera during his trip to the United States. This clash resulted in a split in the movement and the creation in 1920 of a pro-de Valera organisation called the American Association for the Recognition of the Irish Republic.

Throughout all of this, from the election of the Irish party candidates in 1910 to the creation of the Irish Free State in 1921, the Irish-American community had a vital and dynamic role in the nationalist struggle in Ireland. Clan na Gael had helped revive the IRB, supported the Irish Volunteers, facilitated Casement's mission to Germany, provided the link to Germany during the war, and gave assistance after the Rising. Irish-Americans gave generously to every nationalist cause. Even the American government, albeit cautiously, attempted to nudge the British forward in dealing with Ireland. When the 1916 Proclamation called on Ireland's 'exiled children in America' it was not an idle gesture. The 'exiled children' were ready and they answered the call.

THE EASTER RISING IN THE CONTEXT OF CENSORSHIP AND PROPAGANDA WITH SPECIAL REFERENCE TO MAJOR IVON PRICE

Brian P. Murphy

'Ireland is like an exam paper: all questions, no answers.'[1] That was the observation of Arthur Clery and his dictum applies to many events in Irish history. It certainly is applicable to any telling of the story of the Easter Rising of 1916. This paper attempts to examine the events surrounding the Rising, both its causes and consequences, in the light of the censorship and propaganda that were taking place at that time.

Special reference is paid to Major Ivon Price (1866–1931), for several reasons. Firstly, he was appointed chief intelligence officer at the Irish military command at the outbreak of war in August 1914. In this capacity Price had a leading role in the application of the Defence of the Realm Act (DORA) of August 1914 in such areas as the press, the post and the surveillance of persons. This paper attempts to give not only some idea of the dissemination of the 'Sinn Féin propaganda' (especially the views of Pearse and Casement), to which Price objected in his evidence to the royal commission appointed to investigate the causes of the Rising, but also some outline of the methods that he used to counter it.

Secondly, Price's evidence to the commission was used extensively in its final report, possibly more than any other witness, and influenced its conclusion. This paper attempts to evaluate the worth of that evidence.

Thirdly, Price's role during the Rising and afterwards was significant, notably his attempt to bribe Eoin MacNeill to give false evidence against John Dillon and his comment on the murder of Francis Sheehy Skeffington by Captain Bowen Colthurst that 'some of us think that it was a good thing Sheehy Skeffington was put out of the way, anyhow.' This paper addresses these two issues and suggests some reasons why the ideals of the Easter Rising became acceptable, despite the continued efforts of Major Price and the British authorities to silence the growth of Irish republicanism.

Introduction

The evidence of Major Price to the royal commission on the rebellion in Ireland, which began its inquiry on 18 May 1916 at Westminster and published its findings on 3 July, may serve as an introduction to this study on the theme of censorship, propaganda and the Easter Rising. His evidence may also serve as a warning to the uncritical acceptance of original sources: his christian name was Ivon, not Ivor, as named in the royal commission.[2]

Ivon Price occupied a central position in the British administration in Ireland from the start of the war until the Easter Rising and after. A former member of the Royal Irish Constabulary (RIC), he had been seconded to the army in August 1914 where he was given the rank of major and, as indicated above, served in the intelligence section of army headquarters. Price brought to his task considerable skills: he had a law degree from Trinity College Dublin, and he had experience in the crime special branch department, which specialised in political work.[3] As chief intelligence officer, Price acted as an intermediary not only between the army and the civil authority at Dublin Castle but also between the army and the police authorities, both the RIC and the Dublin Metropolitan Police (DMP).[4]

When the first shots of the Easter Rising were fired outside the walls of Dublin Castle, on Easter Monday, 24 April 1916, Price was discussing Irish affairs with Sir Matthew Nathan, under secretary, and Arthur Norway, secretary to the Irish Post Office, inside the grounds of the castle. On the same day he made an armed intervention against rebels in the City Hall adjoining Dublin Castle. The physical proximity of Price to the events of the Rising and the centrality of his role in the Irish administration prior to the Rising makes his testimony to the royal commission extremely valuable. On a personal level it should be noted that his evidence was given in the context of the recent death of his son, Lieutenant Ernest Dickinson Price, who was killed in action on 19 March 1916 at La Targette in France.[5]

When asked by the commissioners concerning the state of propaganda in Ireland, Price replied frankly that 'his information was that the army lost 50,000 men as the result of the Sinn Féin propaganda in Ireland.'[6] Propaganda was, and is, a servant of policy and Price's observation of the effect of Sinn Féin propaganda on recruiting illustrated perfectly the two priorities of British government policy in Ireland after the outbreak of war on 4 August 1914: recruiting, and, on the world stage, the general conduct of the war. British propaganda reflected these two aims. However, in Ireland the introduction of a home rule bill by Asquith's Liberal government in April 1912 had created another political issue which generated its own propaganda and which remained an important issue during the war years.

For example, the Curragh 'mutiny' of 20 March 1914 provoked Eoin MacNeill and Roger Casement to write a joint letter to the *Irish Independent* on 27 March 1914. Adverting to the power of the press, they claimed: 'we can trace in the English unionist press for months past the anticipation of, and preparation for the great military *coup d'état*,' and they concluded that 'the thing that speaks to the world is the whole hearted and unanimous endorsement of the Curragh *pronunciamento* by the leaders and spokesmen of the English governing classes, the owners of Ireland who, as the "constitutional party", are ready and eager for the opportunity of again undertaking the government of Ireland by the army.'[7]

The private papers of H.A. Gwynne, editor of the *Morning Post*, lend substance to the allegations of Casement and MacNeill. In a letter, dated 23 March 1914, to Sir John French, chief of the imperial general staff, Gwynne informed him that 'it is therefore your clear duty to declare to the politicians that no settlement or agreement or statement will do the slightest good unless the government say in plain language that they have no intention of allowing the army to coerce Ulster.'[8] When no statement was forthcoming Gwynne informed French that 'the best thing he could do was to authorise me practically to announce his resignation, which I did in the *MP* [*Morning Post*] on Monday last 30 March.'[9]

The influence of the English unionist press could hardly be better illustrated: it could dictate the conduct of a general who, in 1918, was to be appointed lord lieutenant of Ireland. Commenting upon the incident, the historian Patricia Jalland observed that 'the Liberal government's home rule policy was undermined far more effectively by the Curragh crisis than by the intervention of the First World War.'[10] While the finer points of Jalland's conclusion may be debated, her linking of the home rule crisis and the Great War as jointly shaping the destiny of Ireland in these years can hardly be denied. Both of these issues dominated the process of propaganda and of censorship and had a direct impact upon the press, the postal service and personal liberty. Central to the implementation of this system was the Defence of the Realm Act that was passed on 8 August 1914.

The Defence of the Realm Act and the press

The introduction of a Defence of the Realm Act in August 1914, with its attendant Defence of the Realm Regulations (DORR), was the principal legal measure designed to silence political dissent not only in Ireland but also in England. It was used to control freedom of the press, freedom of speech, and the conduct of public meetings.[11] In effect the Act permitted the Dublin Castle authorities to use court martial procedures rather than the civil law of the land. The first suppression of advanced nationalist newspapers, that is newspapers that rejected participation in the war and the home rule policy as espoused by John Redmond, took place in December 1914. The royal commission noted that, although members of the Irish party were 'strongly against newspapers suppression', 'a flood of seditious literature was disseminated by the leaders of the Irish Volunteer party early in the war, and certain newspapers were suppressed'.[12]

It was not immediately apparent that DORA was the appropriate instrument to use against the press. Indeed, the call to ban the papers was first heard in the House of Commons and then publicised in the *Times* of London on 31 October 1914. Lord Northcliffe, the owner of the *Times*, although born in Dublin, manifested little sympathy for Ireland's position during the war years.[13] An editorial in the *Times* on 31 October 1914, under the heading 'Recruiting in Ireland', brought the issue of the Sinn Féin press to public attention. The editorial blamed the Sinn Féin journals for the lack of recruits, claming that they 'openly preach that for an Irishman to join Lord Kitchener's army is a crime comparable only with that of Judas'. On 24 November 1914 another editorial, on 'Sedition in Ireland', lamented the fact that 'the anti-British, anti-recruiting, and pro-German campaign in Ireland, to which we recently drew attention, still pursues its course of favoured impunity.' The Dublin correspondent confirmed that the 'anti-recruiting propaganda' of the Sinn Féin press was doing 'definite mischief' and the parliamentary correspondent provided supporting extracts from the *Irish Volunteer*, *Sinn Féin*, *Irish Freedom* and the *Irish Worker* to illustrate the claim. These papers, the editorial claimed, were engaged in the 'business of treason'. Debates on the issue immediately took place in parliament. Although Augustine Birrell, the chief secretary, stated that he did not regard the newspapers as threatening, he came under pressure during a debate on the issue to use the legislation of DORA against them.[14]

The debate was conducted in both the House of Commons and the House of Lords. On 25 November Walter Long, former chief secretary and former head of the Ulster Unionist Council, asked Birrell, 'what steps he proposed to take in order to render a repetition of this treasonable practice impossible'.[15] Birrell's reply did not please everyone. He stated that he, personally, did not regard the newspapers 'as a danger'. The following exchange then took place:

> Joynson-Hicks: When was this matter first brought officially to the notice of the right hon. gentleman, and what steps did he take?
>
> Birrell: I have been reading these papers for the last six weeks.
>
> Joynson-Hicks: And did nothing![16]

Birrell's benign opinion of the threat posed to recruiting by the advanced nationalist press was clearly not in accord with those of his colleagues. Following the debate it was resolved, on the advice of Lord Robert Cecil, to use the Defence of the Realm Act against the papers.[17] The papers suppressed under the powers of DORA on 2–3 December 1914 were *Sinn Féin*, *Irish Freedom*, *Ireland* and the *Irish Worker*. At the same time the circulation of the American weeklies, the *Gaelic American* and the *Irish World*, was prohibited in Ireland. The precedent of using DORA against the press had been established and was to be used again in the years ahead.[18]

ADVANCED NATIONALIST PROPAGANDA

From the British point of view the pages of these banned journals were seen primarily as a threat to recruiting. They questioned the validity of speeches in favour of recruitment, made by leading figures such as John Redmond and Tom Kettle, and they rejected the values that inspired the nationwide poster campaign urging Irishmen to fight at the front. This campaign, which was, in origin, centrally controlled from England, evolved into a Dublin-based Department of Recruiting, which was created in October 1915 under the direction of Lord Wimborne. It was supported by the leading Irish newspapers and by the *National Volunteer*, an Irish party journal.[19]

From the Irish point of view these journals offered a distinctive critique of the current political debate. For example, *Irish Freedom*, the journal associated with the Irish Republican Brotherhood (IRB), made its own particular views on home rule clear in April 1912, when it declared that: 'Nationalists of Ireland stand for the complete independence of Ireland, and they stand for nothing less. In the English empire they have no lot or part.' This rejection of John Redmond's policy on home rule was matched by a critical analysis of England's policy in regard to Germany, an analysis, significantly, that had been framed well before the war began. For example, in its issue of January 1913, having assessed the relative strengths of the English navy and that of Germany and her allies combined, the journal concluded that 'war between England and Germany is practically inevitable and its issue is uncertain.' This remarkably early perception of a coming world conflict gathered further impetus in August 1913 when an article by Roger Casement on 'Ireland, Germany and the next war' (originally published in the *Irish Review*, the journal associated with Thomas MacDonagh, Joseph Plunkett and Pádraig Pearse) was re-published in *Irish Freedom*. The voice and views of Casement against British world policy, based on his personal awareness of the workings of the British Foreign Office, provided the informed inspiration for much of the criticism of the war. 'It is evident,' Casement argued, 'that, Great Britain once defeated, Germany would carry the Irish question to a European solution in harmony with her maritime interests ... nothing advanced on behalf of England could meet the case for a free Ireland as stated by Germany.'[20]

The views of Casement on the war had also featured prominently in the *Irish Volunteer*. The very first issue of the journal, on 7 February 1914, contained an essay by him entitled 'From Clontarf to Berlin', which called for an expression of Irishness that was distinct from British imperial interests.[21] In another article on 28 February 1914, written before the Curragh mutiny, Casement called upon the Irish Volunteers to mobilise: 'Let all the recruiting in Ireland be for the Irish Volunteers alone,' he declared. He was also critical of 'John Bull' (Seán Buidhe), whom he called 'a coward and a bully'.[22]

At that time the Irish Volunteers spoke with one voice, with Casement and Tom Kettle sharing a Volunteer recruiting platform at Tullamore in April 1914.[23] Both men stressed the Volunteer ideal of religious toleration, Casement maintaining that they 'did not stand for any sect or sectional interest', Kettle speaking of the harmony of 'all creeds and classes'. That harmony among the ranks of the Volunteers was shattered by the outbreak of war and was effectively symbolised by the parting of the ways of Casement and Kettle.

Immediately war was declared, the issue of *Irish Freedom* for September 1914 had the banner headline 'Germany is not Ireland's Enemy', and the front page of notes had further extracts from Casement's essays in the *Irish Review* on the dangers of war. The editorial was uncompromising in its condemnation of the war. It asserted that 'Britain's interests and Ireland's interests never have been identical. They are not so now. The union of the shark with its prey is the only bond between us.' Shortly afterwards, on 19 September, the *Gaelic American*, John Devoy's American-based weekly, gave front page prominence to an article, dated 5 September, by Casement, who was in New York prior to his departure to Germany. The headline declared: 'Germany to win must cripple or destroy England'. The article examined how Germany might best win the war and it proposed that the most effective way of weakening England was to strike a blow through Ireland. There, Casement suggested, you assail 'the inviolable sanctuary of your chief enemy. You impair his prestige. You assail his self-confidence. You injure his self-esteem. You bring fear to his heart. You shake his empire.' A further letter of Casement's, dated 16 September, appeared in the *Irish Independent* on 5 October. It made the point that statistically Ireland was already contributing more troops to the war than England, even without counting the number of Irish who had enlisted in England, where, he remarked, the Berkshire regiment might more properly be called the 'Corkshire' regiment.

The views of Casement also motivated James Connolly and the *Irish Worker*. Following the departure of James Larkin to America in October 1914, the voice of Connolly became even more influential in Labour party circles. His main reason for opposing the war derived from his concern for the Irish working class and the solidarity of the cause of European workers. However, writing in the *Irish Worker* on 14 November 1914 under the banner headline 'We serve neither King nor Kaiser', Connolly contributed a full page article on 'Belgium rubber and Belgium neutrality'. Relying on consular reports of Casement and of other authorities, Connolly concurred with their verdict that

Belgium was given the alternative. Either to accept the terms of the Allies and enter the conspiracy against Germany – in which case no more publicity will be given to the Congo atrocities – or refuse to do so, and then England and France will proceed to annex the Congo in the interest of humanity.[24]

This association of 'red rubber' from the Congo with Belgium's role in the war sought to undermine the recruiting appeal that Irishmen should fight for gallant, little, Catholic Belgium. It was an association that Connolly and others were to highlight throughout the war.

While these feature articles on Britain, Germany and the war were appearing regularly in several journals, a series of articles by Terence MacSwiney and Pearse in *Irish Freedom* examined some of the principles that inspired the Volunteers. Those by MacSwiney ran from March 1911 until December 1912 and were published by Talbot press in 1921 as *Principles of Freedom*; those by Pearse ran from June 1913 to January 1914 and were published in book form by *Irish Freedom* in 1915 as *From a Hermitage*. The articles by Pearse offered a coherent expression of his changing ideology as he moved to join the Volunteers and the IRB. In these pages he expressed his concern that all should have the 'readiness and ability to shoot'; his regard for, and desire to co-operate with, the orangemen of north east Ulster; and his preference for 'the landless man against the master of millions'.[25]

However, it was not the positive ideology sustaining the Irish Volunteers that was the main worry of the Dublin Castle authorities. It was the constant attack on British war policy not only in the pages of *Irish Freedom* and the *Irish Volunteer* but also in the *Irish Worker, Sinn Féin, Ireland* and other journals. These journals were identified as responsible for the lack of recruiting and described by the royal commission as the 'small but venomous group of papers, representing the Sinn Féin movement and Larkinism and the original anti-British spirit, in which the volunteers [*sic*] were founded'.[26] While these journals were suppressed the monthly *Notes from Ireland* of the Irish Unionist Alliance continued publication until 1918.[27]

The December ban had grave implications for the printers of these journals. Sir Matthew Nathan stated that the *Irish Worker* had failed to observe all the requirements of DORA and, in consequence, 'the type and removable parts of the printing machinery were removed'. The same action was taken against Patrick Mahon, 3 Yarnhall Street, Dublin, the printer of *Irish Freedom*.[28] A reply to a question by Laurence Ginnell in the House of Commons on Mahon's case revealed that the competent military authority (CMA) was the person empowered to implement DORA. The office of the competent military authority, and the term CMA, became part of Irish life, as did DORA, in dealing not only with the press but also with dissident individuals and issues of postal censorship. Major Price was associated with many of these cases and they merit consideration.[29]

In a few short months after the commencement of the war, therefore, the context in which the propaganda contest between the British government and advanced nationalists was fought had been radically changed. No longer was it a matter of civil law but rather, with the introduction of the CMA and the creation of a special military area (SMA), the war was fought out under the terms of martial law defined by DORA and the associated regulations. Although the royal commission noted that the Defence of the Realm Amendment Act of 18 March 1915 had drawn 'the teeth' of DORA by permitting any subject to claim 'to be tried by a jury in a civil court', the application of the amendment to Ireland was not always observed. Indeed, the judicial process as applied to Ireland reflected the views of a Dublin committee, mainly composed of unionists, which had proposed that Lord Parmoor's clause, which permitted recourse to a jury trial, 'should be suspended by proclamation, so that charges under DORA might be dealt with by the military'.[30]

A case study shows that trial by jury was not a regular feature of DORA as applied in Ireland, and illustrates the role of the army and the police in the administration of the new Act. It also illustrates some of the functions of Major Price. On 29 July 1915 Herbert Pim, a convert to Catholicism and nationalism and a prominent writer under the pen-name of A. Newman, was charged, before a resident magistrate in Belfast, with failing to comply with section 14 of the DORA. In particular it was alleged that he had failed to comply 'with the terms of a notice served upon him at the instance of a competent military authority for Ireland requiring him to leave the area stated in the notice, namely Ireland'. That the whole of Ireland, as well as expulsion from particular counties, might be defined as a designated area from which one might be expelled illustrates the draconian powers of the Act.[31]

In the course of Pim's appearance before the resident magistrate, Major Price was asked by Mr Hanna, Pim's solicitor, to clarify the role of Major General Friend as the CMA. The following exchange took place:

> Mr Hanna: Who was it brought the names of Pim and two others before Major Friend?
>
> Major Price: I decline to give any information as to what guided Major General Friend in making the order.
>
> Mr Hanna: Did you bring the case before Major General Friend?

Major Price: No.

Mr Hanna: Then it was not the intelligence officer of the army in Ireland who brought it before him?

Major Price: I am not going to answer any questions of that kind ... my attitude is this: General Friend has made the order. I am not entitled to give any reason for the order.

Mr Hanna concluded with the declaration that 'if he [Mr Hanna] was not entitled to investigate the grounds of the suspicions on which the order was made ... what was the use of him appearing there at all. Why did not the military authorities court martial the accused?'[32]

The case study of Pim illustrates the manner in which the court martial characteristics of DORA were retained in Irish law, despite the March 1915 amendment allowing trial by jury. The case also illustrates the evolving character of the Irish police forces. The RIC and DMP had always monitored the political activities of suspect individuals – the police files on individuals with their weekly and monthly assessment bear testimony to that fact – but, with the introduction of DORA, these files were made available to the military authorities. In this way the police forces became an indispensable adjunct to the army and the court martial system.

Although the royal commission claimed that the crimes branch of the police forces was 'not specially qualified to deal with political crime', the history and record of the forces themselves tell a different story.[33] So too did Joseph Brennan, an official in Dublin Castle, who noted in his text of the commission's report that: 'Crime Special attend more to politics than to crime, and are less affected by boundaries than English police.'[34] The personal opinion of Brennan as to the political character of the police forces, and to their efficiency, was confirmed by the official record at the end of the War of Independence, which described the crimes branch of the RIC as highly organised with 'two special men stationed at Glasgow, Liverpool and Holyhead'.[35]

In the context of police efficiency and the careful surveillance of political suspects, it was inevitable that charges against other individuals would be brought under the terms of DORA. By October 1915 charges and barring orders had been imposed on twenty one individuals. Among them were Liam Mellows, Denis McCullough, Ernest Blythe, Seán MacDermott, Seán Milroy, Francis Sheehy Skeffington, Desmond FitzGerald, Terence MacSwiney, Thomas Kent, J.J. Walsh and P.S. O'Hegarty.[36] Many of the sentences were imposed for anti-recruiting speeches: for example, the arrest of MacDermott on 16 May 1915 in Tuam, Co. Galway was made under the terms of DORA, for making a 'seditious speech' that was 'calculated to discourage those present from joining the British Army'.[37]

The case of Francis Sheehy Skeffington was of particular interest and, in its denouement, of the utmost significance. He was arrested under the terms of DORA on 31 May 1915, shortly after he had published an open letter to Thomas MacDonagh in the *Irish Citizen* calling upon him to end the 'militarism' associated with the Irish Volunteers.[38] The British authorities, however, were not concerned with Skeffington's appeals for peace to the Irish Volunteers. Rather they were concerned to silence his calls for peace in the war. From the first issue of the *Irish Citizen* after the outbreak of war, which issue was accompanied by a poster declaring 'Stop the War', he had campaigned strenuously for peace.[39]

Sheehy Skeffington was arrested on the charge that a speech he had made was 'likely to be prejudicial to recruiting'. He was subsequently refused trial by jury and, on conviction, sentenced to six months' hard labour. He was, however, released ten days later, after a hunger strike.[40] In a speech from the dock he maintained that he was acting no more illegally than Sir Edward Carson. 'To say that "if conscription comes, we will not have it,"' he said, 'is no more a breach of the law than it was treasonable for Sir Edward Carson to say "if home rule comes, we will not have it".' Then, having condemned the military and despotic characteristics of DORA, he concluded that 'any sentence you may pass on me is a sentence upon British rule in Ireland.'[41] The same sentiments were expressed by George Bernard Shaw in a sympathetic letter to Sheehy Skeffington's wife, Hanna. 'The Defence of the Realm Act,' Shaw affirmed, 'abolishes all liberty in Great Britain and Ireland, except such as the authorities choose to leave us.'[42]

This loss of civil liberties was challenged by a gathering of thousands in the Phoenix Park, Dublin, on 12 September 1915. A pamphlet entitled *Defence of the Realm Act in Ireland* was published by a committee of public safety and a collection of rallying songs also appeared. One song was called 'Dora' and contained the lines: 'Her blue eyes are beaming like two bayonets gleaming / and she brought a supply of the same.'

These efforts to publicise the effects of DORA in Ireland were complemented by the virtually single-handed campaign of Laurence Ginnell to raise issues relating to the Act in the House of Commons. On 21 December 1915 he asked Birrell on what grounds action had been taken against the men who had been imprisoned under DORA: 'If they are not political,' he asked, 'surely they are not criminal?' To which Birrell replied: 'No Sir, they are grounds affecting the public safety.'[43] This was but one of hundreds of parliamentary questions asked by Ginnell at that time. Despite these questions, demonstrations and publications, DORA continued to be applied rigorously against the person.

DORA AND POSTAL CENSORSHIP

The censorship of the post to and from Ireland came to form part of the postal censorship organisation MI9, which was established at the outbreak of war. Under this structure mail coming into England and Ireland from European countries and the United States was censored. By the end of the war almost 5,000 civil servants were employed in this work. From small beginnings a vast edifice of surveillance was constructed: on 3 August 1914 one man was employed; by 31 December, 170 men and women were at work; by 31 December 1915, the total had risen to 1,453; by 30 June 1916, to 2,559; and by 4 November 1918, 4,861. A similar comprehensive system of cable censorship was also put in place under the control of Colonel A.G. Churchill.[44] Despite protests from the Foreign Office that it was not desirable to force America into the censorship net, the chief postal censor, Lieutenant Colonel G.S. Pearson, defended the system, maintaining that it was 'one of the most powerful weapons against the enemy' that the government possessed.[45]

This broad organisation of postal censorship was supported in Ireland by a specific system of surveillance in which Major Price had a central role. For example, an order dated 23 November 1914 by Lord Aberdeen, the lord lieutenant, empowered officials:

> to delay, detain, and transmit to Major I.H. Price, intelligence officer, who has been duly appointed censor at Irish command, Parkgate, Dublin, for examination by him, for our information, all postal packets addressed to any of the following persons at the addresses named or to any other addresses.

All telegrams and telegraphic communications were also to be sent to Price. This order was subsequently issued by Sir Matthew Nathan, under secretary at Dublin Castle, to the postmaster general and A.H. Norway, secretary to the Post Office.[46] When Lord Wimborne succeeded Aberdeen in early 1915, similar orders were issued. Another intelligence officer,

Colonel Hill Trevor, was appointed censor at Belfast garrison in order to organise surveillance in that part of Ireland.[47]

The staff at Price's disposal numbered only five and the system of censorship applied in Ireland differed somewhat from that employed in England. Whereas in England the aim of censorship was to detect German agents and the activities of pacifists, in Ireland political considerations were paramount. Ben Novik has found, in a detailed study of some sixty three censorship warants issued between August and December 1914, that 'more than two thirds (forty two in all) were for political reasons'. The censorship files themselves provide further testimony to the efficacy of the Irish police forces.[48]

Before a warrant could be issued there had to be clear evidence that censorship of the suspect's post was merited. This required information and this was provided by police reports. Not only were they detailed but also they contained a surprising awareness of IRB activity. For example, a report on IRB funding was submitted by the superintendent of the detective ('G') division of the DMP, on 30 November 1914; therein Sergeant Edwards of Belfast, after closely monitoring MacDermott's movements in the city on 21–2 December 1914, stated that 'as I have been informed that McDermott [sic] was here on very important IRB business I will make a further report when I get the necessary information from my informants.'[49]

The problem, from Major Price's point of view, was that the information provided by this form of censorship was not always acted on. One letter, written on 24 March 1916 (i.e. shortly before the Rising) from a member of staff at St Mary's College, Rathmines to a friend in America, was of particular concern to Price. It reported that a lot of people had been imprisoned under DORA on St Patrick's day; it praised the Volunteers who were 'getting stronger every day'; and it encouraged the correspondent to return to Ireland where 'we want the like of you to strike a blow at John Bull'.[50] Price read extracts from this letter, 'an extremely bad letter' he called it, in his evidence to the royal commission. He then recounted what had happened to the letter after it had been sent to the chief secretary, the under secretary and the lord lieutenant. Price reported that 'the under secretary [Nathan] wrote: "the outbreak in the summer – look upon as vague talk". Mr Birrell wrote: "the whole letter is rubbish"; and Lord Wimborne initialled it.' On hearing this account, the members of the commission laughed, and when Price added that 'this is only typical' more laughter ensued.[51]

Other incidents of this kind occurred before the Easter Rising. On the one hand they illustrate the close scrutiny under which the Irish Volunteers operated; on the other they reveal the confusion and the lack of resolve that existed at the heart of the Dublin Castle administration.[52] In the meantime advanced nationalists continued to publicise their views through the press and Major Price was again personally involved in some of the measures taken against them.

ADVANCED NATIONALIST PROPAGANDA – PHASE TWO

Despite the suppression of four newspapers in December 1914 the advanced nationalist press and, indeed, the advanced nationalist movement, continued to make its case in favour of an independent Ireland and against a British imperial war. This reality was recognised by the royal commission, which reported that:

> throughout the whole of the remainder of the year 1915 the Irish Volunteer party were active in their efforts to encourage sedition. Seditious papers were published, pamphlets of a violent tone issued and circulated, paid organisers were sent throughout the country to enrol and drill volunteer recruits, and the leaders themselves were active in attending anti-recruiting meetings at which disloyal speeches were openly made.[53]

In the light of these developments some people, such as Lord Midleton, Arthur Hamilton Norway and Major Price, blamed Under Secretary Nathan for bowing to the advice of John Dillon, deputy leader to Redmond in the Irish party. Price informed the commission that:

> one unfortunate thing which hindered us a good deal was the attitude of the official nationalist party and their press. Whenever General Friend did anything strong in the way of suppressing or deporting these men [the organisers] from Ireland, they at once deprecated it, and said it was a monstrous thing to turn a man out of Ireland.[54]

While Nathan admitted in his evidence that 'the suppression of seditious newspapers' was carried out 'against the advice of the Irish parliamentary party', he did not reveal the closeness of his ties with Dillon.[55]

Nathan and Dillon were on amicable terms, Nathan often visiting Dillon's Dublin home, and both men were concerned to preserve good order in Ireland. Dillon's objectives were to prevent the imposition of conscription during the war and to secure the enforcement of the home rule Act at the end of the war. The Dillon papers reveal that Nathan and Dillon conferred in some detail about the advanced nationalist press. A letter from Nathan to Dillon in November 1915, in which Nathan enclosed some current newspapers, provides a precise picture of the workings of that press.[56] Nathan declared: 'Here are all the Sinn Féin papers except one called the *Spark*, of which I have not been able to obtain a copy today. I also send you a statement shewing [sic] the approximate weekly circulation of these publications as it stood in the early part of last September.' Nathan concluded by observing, somewhat wryly, that 'I do not envy your Sunday's reading.'[57]

The approximate circulation of each paper in every county of Ireland was recorded and the total for the area under the control of the RIC was then added to the total under the control of the DMP to give the following results as the weekly circulation of each individual paper for the week ending 7 September 1915: *Irish Volunteer*, 3,746; *Nationality*, 3,860; *Hibernian*, 2,512; *Spark*, 1,618; *Worker's Republic*, 838. Further detail was provided of the publication of papers in Belfast.

These papers provided the same diverse type of propaganda as the four journals that had been suppressed in December 1914. While the *Irish Volunteer* presented a unique type of propaganda, combining both an expression of the ideals of Irish nationalism and military plans for the eventuality of action, the other journals sent by Nathan to Dillon publicised their own distinct vision for Ireland's future. For example, the voice of the Labour party and the Irish Citizen Army, lost with the suppression of the *Irish Worker*, secured representation again on 29 May 1915 with the publication of the *Workers' Republic*.[58] It was edited by James Connolly and published at Liberty Hall. A striking leader by Connolly on 5 February 1916 encapsulated his thinking in the months before the Rising. He wrote that:

> recently we have been pondering over the ties that bind this country to England. It is not a new theme for our thoughts; for long years we have carried on propaganda in Ireland, pointing out how the strings of self-interest bound the capitalist and landlord classes to the Empire.

These ties, Connolly lamented, had corrupted all classes of Irish life like 'a foul disease' and he felt that the degradation was so humiliating that 'no agency less potent than the red tide of war on Irish soil will ever be able to enable the Irish race to recover its self-respect.'[59] The advanced nationalist press, therefore, retained a socialist as well as a separatist republican dimension.

The socialist and the separatist press were united in their continued efforts to oppose recruiting. The *Irish Volunteer* of 22 May 1915, for example, contained an article by Pearse entitled: 'Why we want recruits'. He wanted them for the Irish Volunteers! The very title was a direct challenge to British recruiting policy and struck at the heart of British propaganda. Pearse concluded the article thus:

> we want recruits because we have absolutely determined to take action the moment action becomes a duty … We do not anticipate such a moment in the very near future; but we live at a time when it may come swiftly and terribly. What if conscription be forced upon Ireland? What if a unionist or coalition British ministry repudiated the Home Rule Act? What if it be determined to dismember Ireland? What if it be attempted to disarm Ireland? The future is big with these and other possibilities. And these are among the reasons why we want recruits.

Pearse's observation on the possible actions of the coalition ministry in England, formed only a few days earlier, on 19 May, was not only significant but also politically astute.[60]

Reflecting on these events Pearse discerned that a unique phase of Irish history was being acted out by all participants. On 1 June 1915, in a preface to the series of his articles that had appeared earlier in *Irish Freedom* between June 1913 and January 1914, he wrote of that time as 'a period which, when things assume their proper perspective, will probably be regarded as the most important in recent Irish history'.[61] He ended his brief preface to the book with the observation that 'the rest is history', without any apparent awareness that 'the most important' phase of Irish history was yet to come.

In fact, shortly having written these words, Pearse had a leading role in the greatest demonstration of advanced nationalism in Ireland for many years. The public funeral of O'Donovan Rossa, which took place on 1 August 1915, not only provided a platform for Pearse and the Irish Volunteer movement but also served as a dramatic exercise in propaganda. This did not happen by chance: it was carefully stage-managed. Significantly, the first sub-committee to be listed in the funeral arrangements was the publicity sub-committee. Among its members were Arthur Griffith, Éamonn Ceannt, Seán T. O'Kelly, J.J. O'Kelly (Sceilg) and Brian O'Higgins (Brian na Banban). The souvenir brochure, which itself had a propaganda purpose, was printed by Patrick Mahon, whose printing works had been demolished under the terms of DORA in December 1914.[62]

The names of all the leading figures who were to participate in the Easter Rising are to be found among the names of those who made up the thirteen sub-committees that managed the funeral arrangements, including some eighteen members of Cumann na mBan. The military ranks of the Volunteers were united with the ranks of the Irish Citizen Army, resembling a trial run for the Rising. In the listing of the guards for the procession, the ranks of the participating officers were given. For example, Commandant General Thomas MacDonagh, was designated the chief marshal, while Commandant James Connolly of the Citizen Army and Captain Pádraig O'Riain of Fianna Éireann were also listed. Beside the name of Seán MacDermott was written: 'in Mountjoy prison under the Defence of the Realm Act'. In apparent defiance of the authorities, there was no attempt to conceal the names of the participants.[63]

James Connolly and Arthur Griffith joined with Pearse in paying written tributes to O'Donovan Rossa. The words of Pearse at Rossa's graveside are well-known. Less adverted to is the reference to DORA that preceded his valediction. 'The defenders of this realm,' Pearse declared, 'have worked well in secret and in the open. They think that they have pacified half of us and intimidated the other half. They think that they have foreseen everything, think that they have provided against everything; but the fools, the fools! They have left us our Fenian dead, and while Ireland holds these graves, Ireland unfree shall never be at peace.'[64]

Advanced nationalist propaganda
– phase three

Pearse, and others, not only provided ideological and emotional support for the course that had been taken, but also, in his capacity as director of organisation, provided detailed plans of military organisation. Other military articles were provided by J.J. O'Connell, chief of inspection, and Eimar Duffy.[65] Giving evidence before the royal commission in 1916, Colonel Edgeworth-Johnstone, chief commissioner of the DMP, testified to the worth of these articles, showing clearly that he had read them, and stating that 'very clear and very good military articles were written every week in the *Irish Volunteer*, giving instruction as to hedge fighting, taking trenches, and all that sort of thing'.[66] Taken in conjunction with Pearse's earlier recommendation, in *Irish Freedom* of December 1913, that the Volunteers should be trained in the 'readiness and ability to shoot' and his private correspondence with Joe McGarrity, the evidence indicates that the Volunteers were not merely indulging in the gesture of a blood-sacrifice.[67]

While the military organisation and the morale of the Volunteers and the Irish Citizen Army were being built up, criticism of the war continued. Moved, however, by the huge number of Irish deaths on the western front and at Gallipoli, there was a marked change of attitude by the advanced nationalist press towards fellow Irishmen who had joined the ranks of the British forces. The cursing of recruits to the British forces gave way, as Novick remarked in James Connolly's case, to 'guarded respect and pity'.[68] This change was expressed most succinctly and sincerely by Eoin MacNeill in the *Irish Volunteer* of February 1916. 'Let me say plainly,' he wrote, 'that if any Irishman is convinced that he will serve Ireland by becoming a British soldier, and if he acts on that conviction, he is a patriotic and brave man.'[69]

The criticism that was made of the war still focussed on British war aims but a new dimension was added to the criticism: the British claims of atrocities by the Germans against the people of Belgium. As in the period prior to the war, Roger Casement was the most perceptive critic of British actions. Writing in the *Continental Times*, a self-styled 'cosmopolitan newspaper published for Americans in Europe', of 3 November 1915 and subsequently in the *Gaelic American*, Casement exposed the weaknesses in the Bryce report into German atrocities that had been published in late May 1915. Casement, who had spent some time in Belgium after the war had started, pointed out that Bryce had conducted his commission of inquiry in England and had relied, in the main, on the evidence of British soldiers. He rejected Bryce's findings as an exercise in propaganda. While admitting that Germany had committed wrongs in Belgium, he concluded that:

> it is not German barbarity which distinguishes this war from all others that preceded it. It is not the colossal numbers of men engaged; the vast holocausts of slain … it is that, above all other contests between nations and men, this war has revealed the baleful power of the Lie. That has been the chief weapon, the chief power displayed by the foremost of the belligerents.[70]

Casement also noted that within two months his majesty's stationery office had circulated 1,000,000 copies of the Bryce report throughout the world.[71] This propaganda campaign was conducted from Wellington house, London, which became the centre of British propaganda at the start of the war. The head of the centre was Charles Masterman, who operated in unison with the news department of the Foreign Office. Sir Gilbert Parker was appointed to head the section responsible for America and Sir William Wiseman, as intelligence officer, was sent to New York as director of the British Library of Information.[72] The structure and scope of the propaganda operation was so vast that the million copies of the Bryce report, as noted by Casement, were but a drop in the ocean of propaganda publications that flooded America and Europe.

The weekly *Gaelic American*, the circulation of which had been banned in Ireland in December 1914, continued to promote the writings of Casement about the war. The editor, John Devoy, was one of the three man *Clan na Gael* executive involved in planning the Rising in Ireland, and the journal reflected his well known militancy; a list of 'contributions to arm men of Ireland' was, for example, a regular feature of the paper. Advertisements were carried for Casement's book *The Crime Against Ireland*, and articles appeared in the autumn of 1915 defending the ideals of Casement and the Irish brigade, accompanied by photographs of members of the brigade.[73] In the issue of 27 November 1915 Casement wrote a detailed critique of Sir Edward Grey's foreign policy. In particular he described the process of 'secret armed conventions', 'secret military compacts', and 'conversations of naval and military experts', which, Casement claimed, were pledging England 'to the certainty of war' with Germany.

Another journal to publish a unique criticism of British war policy, and of Redmond's participation in it, was the *Catholic Bulletin*. Under the editorship of J.J. O'Kelly (Sceilg), it had evolved from a monthly journal of mainly Catholic interest into a paper of largely political comment. Founded in 1911, the transformation took place almost immediately with the beginning of the home rule debate. It regularly gave prominence to the statements of Bishop O'Dwyer of Limerick against Redmond's policy and, in particular, it contrasted Redmond's appeals for support for the war with those of Pope Benedict XV calling for peace. The issue of September 1915 listed all of the pope's appeals for peace and the October issue blamed Redmond for ignoring them. The close association of the *Catholic Bulletin* with its correspondents in Rome, Monsignor Michael O'Riordain and Father John Hagan of the Irish College, ensured that it was extremely well informed on papal affairs.[74] These two men were not only shaping opinion with their written articles but also they were shaping policy by their access to the pope and other cardinals. For example, in January 1916, Monsignor O'Riordain privately informed Bishop O'Dwyer that he had translated an article that the bishop had written attacking the Bryce report into Italian and had made the pope aware of its contents. In March 1916 the *Bulletin* contrasted Redmond's call to Irishmen to respond to the Bryce report into German atrocities with Bishop O'Dwyer's opinion that the report was 'a fraud upon simple people'.[75] Both men were also aware of Count Plunkett's private audience with the pope during his visit to Rome, 8–21 April 1916, in which the blessing of Pope Benedict XV was conferred on the Volunteers. Plunkett conveyed this news to members of the IRB who had constituted themselves as the Provisional Government of Ireland shortly before the Rising.[76]

The practical planning for the Rising, therefore, marched in tandem with written expositions that not only justified the rejection of Redmond's policy on home rule and the war but also offered a positive vision of an independent Ireland. In the months before the Rising, Pearse perfected his views on the character of Irish freedom and of Irish nationality. They appeared, in pamphlet form, in the 'Tracts for the times' series, between December 1915 and March 1916. The four pamphlets, *Ghosts*, *The separatist idea*, *The spiritual nation* and *The sovereign people*, provided ideological justification for a future Ireland as an independent nation and as sovereign people. They also offered the final confirmation that Pearse's own private conversion from constitutional home ruler to a physical force separatist had been completed.[77]

Pearse not only condemned the policy of Redmond as a betrayal of Parnell but also articulated a vision of a future Irish nation that incorporated, to a high degree, the socialist ideals of James Fintan Lalor. With obvious approval, Pearse declared that Lalor held 'that separation from England would be valueless unless it put the people – the actual people and not merely certain rich men – of Ireland in effectual ownership and possession of the soil of Ireland'. The ideals of Lalor, taken together with the writings of Tone, Davis and Mitchel, formed, in Pearse's opinion, the four gospels of Irish nationality. In that expression of nationality women were to enjoy the same franchise rights as men.[78]

The last words of *The sovereign people* were: 'And we are young. And God has given us strength and courage and counsel. May He give us victory.'[79] In his preface to this pamphlet, written at St Enda's on 31 March

1916, Pearse declared that 'this pamphlet concludes the examination of the Irish definition of freedom which I promised in *Ghosts*. For my part I have no more to say.'[80] Pearse knew that the time had come for action. He did, however, find time to contribute to the Proclamation of the Irish Republic and the *Irish War News*. Evidence of these writings were placed before the royal commission by Major Price, which concluded that 'a number of seditious books called "Tracts for the times" were circulated' at that time.[81]

While unaware of the significant role of the IRB in the planning of the Rising, it was evident that the Dublin Castle authorities were well aware of the strength of the Volunteers and of the tone of advanced nationalist propaganda in the months prior to the Rising. Not only had Nathan enclosed copies of many of the journals to Dillon on 13 November 1915, but also he had reported to Birrell on 18 December 1915, after consultations with Redmond and Dillon, that 'the present situation in Ireland is most serious and menacing'. Nathan added that Redmond:

> knows or should know that the enrolled strength of the Sinn Féin Volunteers has increased by a couple of thousand active members in the last two months to a total of some 13,500 and each group of these is a centre of revolutionary propaganda. He knows, or should know, that efforts are being made to get arms for the support of this propaganda.[82]

It was in this context that Major Price, who was supplying Nathan with information about advanced nationalist propaganda, became involved in the firm measures to suppress it.

Acting under the powers conferred by DORA, Price played an important part in the seizure of thousands of copies of *Spark*, *Honesty* and *The Gael* on 24 March 1916. He was also responsible for removing vital parts of the printing machinery of the Gaelic Press, 30 Upper Liffey Street, where the journals were published. All of these actions were conducted under orders issued by General Friend acting as the CMA. Joseph Stanley, the proprietor of the Gaelic Press, recorded that the military and the DMP had smashed his printing presses and rendered them useless. Major Price, he added, had offered no redress. Stanley himself was in the IRB and a close friend of Clarke and MacDermott. Under the pen-name of 'Gilbert Galbraith' Stanley edited *Honesty*, which had a circulation of c.10,000 in 1916. Other journals were seized during the raid, among them *An Claidheamh Soluis*, New Ireland, *Nationality* and the *Catholic Bulletin*.[83] Despite the damage to his printing press, Stanley provided assistance to the three men, Christopher Brady, Michael Molloy and Bill O'Brien, who, based in Liberty Hall, printed the original copies of the Proclamation of Irish independence.[84]

Major Price and the Easter Rising

Following the Rising, 24–9 April 1916, and the executions, 3–12 May, a 'Royal Commission on the Rebellion in Ireland' was immediately appointed. It worked swiftly and had concluded its work by July, when its report appeared. Granted his involvement in the early armed activity on the first day of the Rising, and his role as chief intelligence officer, it was inevitable that Major Price should be summoned to appear before the commission. His evidence, stressing the failings of the Dublin Castle civil authorities, had a significant bearing on its findings. Some of his criticisms of these authorities over their lack of response to his warnings about the contents of the post and of the advanced nationalist press have already been mentioned. Price's feelings and frustrations about the inadequacies of Dublin Castle were summed up in his reply to a question by the commission about the 'Tracts for the times'. Faced by this question concerning Pearse's final statement of his political beliefs, Price bluntly declared: 'I liken myself to John the Baptist preaching in the wilderness as to taking steps on the subject. The civil authorities did not think it desirable to take steps.'[85]

The judgement of the commission reflected this final critical observation of Price in regard to Birrell and Nathan. It stated that we are 'of the opinion that the chief secretary [Birrell] as the administrative head of Your Majesty's Government in Ireland is primarily responsible for the situation that was allowed to arise and the outbreak that occurred'.[86] It concluded that Nathan, although only taking up office in September 1914, 'did not sufficiently impress upon the chief secretary during the latter's prolonged absence from Dublin the necessity for more active measures to remedy the situation in Ireland which on 18 December last in a letter to the chief secretary he described as "most serious and threatening."'[87]

The report's damning indictment of the Dublin Castle civil administration, however, should not take away from the fact that it found that the authorities responsible for the implementation of DORA had conducted themselves admirably. The report stated that 'we do not attach any responsibility to the military authorities in Ireland for the rebellion or its results'.[88] Sir Neville Chamberlain, the inspector general of the RIC, and Colonel Edgeworth-Johnstone, the chief commissioner of the DMP, were commended and the report declared that 'for the conduct, zeal and loyalty of the RIC and DMP we have nothing but praise'.[89]

In other words the message from the royal commission was that, although the British civil administration had failed, the army and the police forces were beyond reproach. This finding is endorsed by reflection on the actions of Major Price. Consideration of his role, moreover, places DORA and the associated regulations at the centre of the British military strategy in Ireland. DORA was the weapon chosen to confront dissident protest against recruiting in 1914; to crush Irish rebels in 1916 (they were actually charged with engaging in action 'prejudicial to the Defence of the Realm'); and to wage the war against Irish independence from 1919–21. Major Price retained his position as chief intelligence officer in the immediate aftermath of the Rising and continued to play a central role in the application of DORA. Indeed, the system of surveillance of individual persons, the post and of the press continued with a heightened severity. A brief consideration of some of the actions associated with Major Price serves to illustrate the manner in which DORA, like a seamless thread, fashioned the character of the British presence in Ireland until 1921.

The first incident involving Price related to his dealings with Eoin MacNeill. MacNeill, who had been arrested on 2 May 1916, made a statement claiming that Major Price, who visited him in his cell at Arbour Hill prison on 5 May:

> began a conversation about my getting a death sentence. He then said my life would be spared if I made a statement implicating persons 'higher up than myself'. He said it would be enough to make a statement. I was not expected to support it by giving evidence. I asked what persons higher than myself he meant, and he said Mr Dillon and Mr Devlin. I said I could not connect them with the matter in any way. He then told me of Mr Birrell's resignation, speaking of it with great satisfaction.

Although Price denied the allegation, his known hostility to Dillon and his critical opinion of Birrell lends credibility to MacNeill's statement. Dillon himself became aware of MacNeill's statement at the end of May.[90]

The second incident concerning Price related to his dealings with Francis Sheehy Skeffington, who was shot by a firing squad on the morning of 26 April while a prisoner in Portobello Barracks, Dublin. Captain Bowen

Colthurst had ordered his shooting and that of two other prisoners without any form of judicial process. The two other men shot were both journalists: Thomas Dickson and Patrick McIntyre, editor of *The Searchlight*. When Major Fletcher Vane, second in command at Portobello Barracks, requested Major Price to establish a process of inquiry, he was informed by him that 'some of us think it was a good thing Sheehy Skeffington was put out of the way anyway'. Following his protest, Vane was demoted from his command and replaced by Colthurst.[91]

The comment of Price could only have been based on the well known pacificism of Sheehy Skeffington and his previous arrest under the terms of DORA. Significantly, there was no reference made to his death in the royal commission on the rebellion, even though there was mention of an article by him that had appeared in the journal *Century* in February 1916. This article had alarmed Sir Matthew Nathan.[92] In the article, 'A forgotten small nationality', Sheehy Skeffington had questioned the sincerity of England's war aims, asking 'must Irish freedom be gained in blood, or will the comity of nations, led by the United States, shame a weakened England into putting into practice at home the principles which are so loudly trumpeted for the benefit of Germany?'[93] After a court martial trial which found Colthurst 'guilty but insane' on 7 June 1916 – a trial of which Tim Healy commented that 'never since the trial of Christ was there a greater travesty of justice' – a royal commission was appointed with Sir John Simon presiding. This commission, whose report was published on 16 October 1916, condemned not only the conduct of Colthurst but also that of the British military command. The report stated unequivocally that 'the shooting of unarmed and unresisting civilians without trial constitutes the offence of murder, whether martial law has been proclaimed or not.'[94]

John Dillon played a significant part in securing this small consolation for the Sheehy Skeffington family. On 11 June 1916 he had written to Lloyd George complaining, in particular, of the conduct of Major Price and, in general, of the policy of martial law. Dillon maintained that:

> the horrible irony of the situation is, that by giving soldiers and Price (Major I.H. Price, director of military intelligence and widely detested in Dublin as Maxwell's right-hand man) a free hand you are making yourselves the instruments of your own worst enemies to defeat your own policy.[95]

Dillon then spelled out how British policy after the Rising was destroying not only the Irish party but also Irish ties of loyalty to the British empire and to the war effort. 'When the fighting was over and the insurrection crushed,' Dillon declared:

> if there had been no executions, the country would have been solid behind us, and we could have done what we liked with it. The tragedy of the situation – and it is one of the greatest tragedies of all history – is that but for the blunders of your government Ireland would be today as loyal to your government as Canada, and you would have had easily double the number of Irish soldiers fighting at the front.[96]

The impact of the British military policy and of Major Price, in particular, upon Ireland and the Irish party could not be better illustrated.

Major Price was also involved in censoring the press at the time of the Rising. His actions against the *Catholic Bulletin*, one of the few journals of advanced nationalism to escape a total ban, were especially revealing. The May 1916 issue had not been published and, on 8 June 1916, Patrick Keohane of Gill's wrote to Price concerning the next issue. He stated that: 'I send herewith the May–June number of the *Catholic Bulletin*, which, to our and our readers' disappointment, has had to be issued with many blank spaces owing to your refusal, at the last moment, to read, as promised, the proofs submitted to you.' Keohane also complained of a recent visit from a detective and an earlier encounter with Price on 25 May.[97] The material that Price saw fit to suppress made the case that the actions taken by the unionists, in their opposition to home rule, had contributed to an armed rebellion. 'Profitless, too, must it seem now,' the editorial declared:

> to reflect on the degree to which the rebellion was due to the example of 'Ulster'; its threat to seek the aid of the greatest Protestant power in Europe against the enactment of home rule; its armed demonstrations and parading of machine guns, glorified by the 'Curragh revolt'; its provisional government, graced by the most favoured officers of State; its Covenant under which 'the loyal minority' pledged themselves to resist – if necessary, by force of arms – the British crown and constitution; its landing at Larne of a ship-load of German rifles, 'patronised', as a correspondent puts it, 'by the Duke of Abercorn and the late Marquis of Londonderry, and blessed by his lordship, Dr Crozier.'

J.J. O'Kelly, the editor, prefaced these remarks with a protest that he was 'writing under direct military censorship'.[98]

The *Bulletin* then made the point that, until these actions by the unionists had prevented the introduction of home rule, the vast majority of Irish nationalists were committed to a constitutional settlement. The editorial reflected on the relationship that Pearse and MacNeill had once enjoyed with Redmond and the Irish party and concluded that:

> it is to be remembered that Mr John MacNeill and the late Mr P.H. Pearse were among the prominent speakers, who, four years ago, assisted at Mr Redmond's monster home rule demonstration in the beautiful Dublin thoroughfare now bounded by red ruin. Previously Mr Pearse, as editor of the Gaelic League's official organ, was one of the few men in Ireland to urge the acceptance of the doomed Councils bill, as a step in the direction of Irish liberty.

'We recall these circumstances,' O'Kelly declared, 'to show how men of proven constitutional instincts may be driven from the constitutional path, and to sound a warning of which our public men seem in urgent need.'[99]

The censorship of these paragraphs by Price reflected the approach adopted by the report of the commission on the Rising, which simply noted that 'arms were entering the province of Ulster from foreign countries, including Germany', and that 'large quantities of arms were surreptitiously imported by night at Larne'.[100] It was not stated, as Joseph Brennan, the finance official in Dublin Castle observed, 'by whom this illegality was committed.'[101] Neither Price nor the royal commission, it would appear, wanted the charge of unionist responsibility for the Rising to be publicised.

One other small, but significant, item was suppressed in the May–June issue of the *Catholic Bulletin*: a poem entitled *Dublin – May 1916*. The title was clearly printed; the poem, however, was not published. The name of the author appeared in small print and was written in Irish as Gobnait ní Bruadhair. The author was, in fact, Albinia Brodrick, the sister of the Earl of Midleton, the leading southern unionist. Brodrick, a Protestant of the wealthy land-owning class, had embraced the social and political ideals of the emerging Irish republic. The last verse of the banned poem read:

> Silent we stand. The iron hand baptises
> Éire, afresh, with blood and tears thy sod!
> Martyrs! One holy place is ours, Unconquered,
> Our souls are safe with God.[102]

Other poets of Protestant background commemorated the Easter Rising in verse. Indeed, it might be said that if the Easter Rising was a rebellion by Catholic poets, it was hailed in verse by their Protestant counterparts. W.B. Yeats was joined by Dora Sigerson Shorter, Alice Milligan, Eva Gore Booth, Dorothy Macardle, and George Russell ('AE') in expressing sympathy with those who had died in the Rising. This was finely expressed in the verse of George Russell in his poem *Salutation*:

> Their dream had left me numb and cold,
> But yet my spirit rose in pride,
> Refashioning in burnished gold
> The images of those who died
> Or were shut in the penal cell.
> Here's to you, Pearse, your dream not mine,
> But yet the thought for this you fell
> Has turned life's waters into wine.[103]

Press censorship not only silenced a significant Protestant voice in favour of the Rising but also forced O'Kelly to tell the story of those who fought and died with an emphasis on their Catholic background. Writing in the July 1916 number of the *Bulletin*, O'Kelly stated that:

> under existing circumstances a magazine like this, in describing the recent insurrection, has little option but to overlook the political and controversial features of the upheaval, and confine comment almost entirely to the Catholic and social aspects of the lives and last moments of those who died either in action or as a result of trial by court martial.[104]

Some historians have suggested that his approach indicated a sectarian dimension to the Rising. It was, in fact, a course forced upon him by the constraints of the press censor.

Within the context of these restraints O'Kelly began, in the July 1916 number, a new feature article entitled 'Events of Easter Week', which ran until March 1919. That particular feature, which was typical of others to follow, ran to some fifteen pages and contained some twenty photographs of those who had participated in the Rising. Brief biographical details of their lives were given, which were often accompanied by poems.[105] The December 1916 issue, which featured over twenty poignant photographs of the widows and children of those whose husbands had died in the Rising, was particularly striking.

Major Price and the Dublin Castle authorities were not happy with the expression of sentiments such as these and action was taken on 21–2 February 1917. J.J. O'Kelly and some twenty other nationalists, all involved in creating a political movement to embody the ideals of the Rising, were arrested and deported without trial. They were charged under the terms of section 14 of the DORR. Among others deported with him were Darrell Figgis, Seán T. O'Kelly, Terence MacSwiney, Tomás MacCurtain and Dr Patrick McCartan.[106]

The identity of the CMA had changed (General Bryan Mahon now filled the office) but the system was the same. The army, however, could only act on the information from the police and John Dillon, speaking in the House of Commons, was in no doubt from where that intelligence had come. The person responsible, he declared, was Major Price, the 'chief spy and controller of the secret service in Ireland'.[107] The centrality of Price to the administration of DORA was also recognised by Hannah Sheehy Skeffington. Reflecting, in 1917, on all the events since the death of her husband, she commented bitterly that 'Major Price still rules in Dublin Castle'.[108]

Price retained his position of prominence until 1 February 1919, when he re-joined the ranks of the RIC and became assistant inspector general on 1 October 1920. Having been warned in January 1922 that his life might be at risk in the new post-Treaty Ireland, he immediately left his office and Ireland. He died in England in November 1931.[109]

EASTER 1916 IN CORK – ORDER, COUNTER-ORDER, AND DISORDER

Gerry White and Brendan O'Shea

INTRODUCTION

The failure of the Cork Brigade of Irish Volunteers to fully participate in the Easter Rising generated considerable resentment amongst those who did, and subsequently resulted in two formal inquiries. Notwithstanding that the leadership was twice exonerated some officers were destined to carry a burden of guilt all the way to their graves.[1] Why was this the case? What happened in Cork to cause such angst? How did the military chain of command disintegrate at the very moment it was most needed?

This paper examines events in Cork before, during, and after the Easter Rising. It uncovers the operation of parallel chains of command; identifies the mobilisation of over 1,000 Volunteers; examines the legality of the arrest and court martial of Thomas Kent; and evaluates the leadership of the brigade commander, Tomás MacCurtain.

PLANNING AND PREPARATION

On Sunday, 9 April 1916 Tomás MacCurtain chaired a meeting of the Brigade Council at his headquarters in the Volunteer Hall on Sheares Street in Cork city. Assembled before him were his second in command, Terence MacSwiney, his brigade staff officers, and many of his battalion and company commanders.[2] MacCurtain's primary task was to finalise plans for his unit's participation in the forthcoming 'Mobilisation' and 'Easter Concentration' which were to be held in accordance with a General Order for 'Manoeuvres' issued six days previously by Pádraig Pearse, the Volunteers' director of operations. Under the terms of this order Volunteer units in the south and west of the country would mobilise in order to secure a shipment of German arms and ammunition that was due to arrive off the Kerry coast. Florence O'Donoghue later wrote that:

The Cork Brigade was to occupy positions on a north-south line from New-market to the Boggeragh mountains and thence westward to the Cork-Kerry border, contacting some units of the Kerry Brigade extending eastwards from Tralee. Limerick was to maintain contact with the northern end of the Cork position and extend northwards to the Shannon, [and the] Clare and Galway Brigades were to hold the line of the Shannon to Athlone.[3]

Seán Murphy, the brigade quartermaster, also recalled that as part of this operation the Volunteers were planning to obstruct and delay the British army at Millstreet and Rathmore by cutting the railway line. However, the written agenda for the meeting on 9 April, which survives in MacSwiney's handwriting, clearly indicates that the Cork Brigade were planning for an 'Easter Concentration', not widespread offensive action, and that matters pertaining to the organisation of companies and battalions, together with the compilation of inventories of arms, equipment, field kit and communications, were of primary concern.

During the course of the meeting MacCurtain outlined each officer's respective tasks and nominated the eight different concentration points to which each company would march two weeks hence. He also stressed the importance of carrying out their orders and notified them that there was a distinct possibility that Crown forces might attempt to interfere with their operations. With this in mind he ordered that all available arms and ammunition were to be carried and each Volunteer should bring his over-coat, some blankets, and two days supply of food.[4]

There had long been expectation within the Cork Brigade that some form of military action might be in the offing, especially if the British authorities attempted to forcibly disarm the Volunteers, if conscription was introduced, or if a shipment of arms arrived from Germany. Seán Murphy later recalled that, during the preceding twelve months:

Officers from Volunteer headquarters [in Dublin] frequently visited [Cork] and informed the brigade staff that Roger Casement had recruited an Irish Brigade in Germany from Irishmen who were prisoners of war there, that the Volunteers would be officered by these men upon their arrival in Ireland, and that ample supplies of arms, ammunition, and light artillery would be made available from Germany.[5]

Therefore, on 9 April, as far as the Cork Brigade were concerned the pur-pose of the 'Easter Concentration' was to provide security for a German arms landing. What weapons the Volunteers already possessed were to be used only to fulfil that mission and to prevent themselves, if necessary, from being forcibly disarmed. They had neither planned nor discussed mounting any widespread offensive military action because without the arrival of additional equipment there was no prospect whatever of that happening. In fact Murphy later stated that:

> Ammunition was so scarce that not a man [had] fired a round of live ammunition in Cork before Easter 1916. Arms consisted of three different patterns of rifles, with some shotguns. The ammunition varied from ten rounds for some patterns of rifles to thirty rounds for others. Around 75% of the latter ammunition was obtained locally through seizures from British army personnel and such. As the Volunteer headquarters in Dublin were unaware of this list or sources of supply, their estimate of ammunition supplies available in Cork for Easter Sunday was ten rounds per rifles with varying amounts for the shotguns … [therefore] the Cork Volunteers had scarcely enough [ammunition] to last five minutes.[6]

While there appears to be some conflict between the accounts given by Murphy and Florence O'Donoghue in relation to exactly how many weapons the Cork Brigade possessed at this time, it is nonetheless clear that not all Volunteers were armed with firearms. Less than 200 men had good quality rifles. The bulk of the remainder were armed with an assortment of old shotguns and revolvers, and at least 100 Volunteers were armed only with pikes. These statistics indicate the real military capability of the Cork Brigade at this time.[7]

However, unknown to both MacCurtain and the Volunteers' Chief of Staff, Eoin MacNeill, the shipment of German weapons was part of a plan for the establishment of an independent Irish Republic that was already at an advanced stage. Immediately after the outbreak of the First World War the Supreme Council of the Irish Republican Brotherhood (IRB) decided that an armed rebellion should be mounted in Ireland before the end of the conflict. That decision was copper-fastened in May 1915 when, with the British army locked in stalemate on the western front, a secret IRB Military Council was established comprising Pearse, Joseph Plunkett and Éamonn Ceannt.[8]

This small group immediately began working on a plan for rebellion which envisaged mobilisation on Easter Sunday 1916 of over 10,000 Irish Volunteers, armed by Germany and augmented by a German expeditionary force. The Dublin Brigade of Volunteers would seize the General Post Office in Dublin and other strategic buildings and establish a series of outposts in the suburbs. Volunteer units throughout the country would establish a line along the river Shannon in order to cover the landing of the German arms shipment and, once the new weapons had been distributed, the Volunteers and their German allies would then advance on Dublin capturing or destroying Royal Irish Constabulary (RIC) barracks along the way. The essential elements of this outline plan were basically sound. In fact it might well have stood some chance of success if the Volunteers nationally had been adequately trained and properly prepared; if Volunteer brigades when mobilised were in possession of clear military orders and specific objectives; if an adequate quantity of arms and equipment had been supplied: and if an integrated all-arms German expeditionary force had actually materialised.[9]

But none of this happened. The Military Council was so obsessed with secrecy that the essential elements of the plan, and its real objectives, were not communicated to the personnel upon whom the success of the operation would ultimately depend – the brigade commanders – until it was far too late. At brigade level, therefore, no military briefings for an armed uprising were held; no mission was analysed in that context; no offensive courses of action were developed; no contingencies were planned; no reserve was identified; no best and worst case scenarios were either identified, developed or 'war-gamed'; and no higher commander's intent or planning guidance was communicated.

Instead, a small group of people, with virtually no military experience between them, developed an outline plan for rebellion, kept it shrouded in secrecy until literally the very last minute, and then expected the entire Volunteer movement to follow them into what would effectively have amounted to a military coup. It was never going to work and the longer the operational units in the country were kept in the dark the worse the eventual outcome was destined to be.

CONFLICTING ORDERS

As the date for the planned rebellion grew closer it finally became necessary to inform the brigade commanders of the Military Council's true intentions. On Monday 17 April, Brigid Foley, a member of Dublin Cumann na mBan, was tasked by Seán MacDermott with delivering a sealed dispatch to the brigade commander in Cork.[10] While the specific contents of this dispatch remain unknown, it is reasonable to conclude that it contained new information which expanded the role the Cork Brigade would be expected to play during the 'Easter Manoeuvres'. Seán Murphy clearly recalled that upon reading the dispatch MacCurtain became so concerned that he decided to send Eithne MacSwiney to Dublin on Wednesday in order to meet with Thomas Clarke, James Connolly and MacDermott, and to arrange a meeting between them and Terence MacSwiney who was prepared to travel to Dublin the following day.[11] If possible she was also to meet with Eoin MacNeill and give him the same message. She left Cork on the 12.45pm train on Wednesday 19 April, the same day that the 'Castle document' was put into circulation in Dublin.[12]

Purporting to have been drafted by the British authorities in Dublin Castle, this document outlined detailed instructions for suppression of the Volunteer movement, and was received with outrage by the leadership, including its more moderate members such as MacNeill. In reality the document had been forged by members of the Military Council in order to encourage the Volunteer movement to support the rebellion – and initially it achieved its objective. Following a meeting of the Volunteer Executive Council that same day MacNeill sent the following order to all brigade commanders, including MacCurtain:

2 Dawson Street, Dublin

April 19 1916

A plan on the part of the Government for the suppression and disarming of the Irish Volunteers has become known. The date of putting it into operation depends only on Government orders to be given.

In the event of definite information not reaching you from headquarters, you will be on the look out for any attempt to put this plan into operation. Should you be satisfied that such action is imminent you will be prepared with defensive measures.

Your object will be to preserve the arms and the organisation of the Irish Volunteers, and the measures taken by you will be directed to that purpose.

In general you will arrange that your men defend themselves and each other in small groups, so placed that they may best be able to hold out.

Each group must be supplied with sufficient supplies of food or be certain of access to such supplies.

This order is to be passed on to your subordinate officers and to officers of neighbouring commands.

[Signed] Eoin MacNeill, Chief of Staff.[13]

This was the scenario that awaited Eithne MacSwiney when she alighted from the train at Kingsbridge station, although initially she had no idea what was going on. MacDermott was at the station to meet her:

> He did not speak to me, but let me know he had seen me. We travelled on the same tram to O'Connell Bridge, but sat at different ends of the tram and, on alighting, Seán told me to go to Tom Clarke's shop in Parnell Square at 7pm that evening. At the shop, at the hour, I saw Mrs Tom Clarke. She showed me a copy of the 'Castle Document' that was causing such excitement at the time. She told me to go to Ballybough – their home – and there, for the first and last time, I saw Tom Clarke. I gave him the message I had brought. 'Impossible', he said, 'altogether impossible. He must not come to Dublin. Everyone is being watched closely; the first attempt to board a train and he would be arrested; everyone must remain at his post.'[14]

When the meeting with Clarke was finished Eithne MacSwiney sent a telegram to MacCurtain informing him of the outcome. She then proceeded to Volunteer headquarters at Dawson Street where Bulmer Hobson, the quartermaster general, told her that the chief of staff would be available to see her brother if he came to Dublin the following day. MacCurtain quickly decided, however, there was little point risking his deputy and decided to keep him in Cork where events were now beginning to conspire against him.

In the meantime Brigid Foley arrived in Cork with yet another dispatch from MacDermott and the following morning MacNeill's order of 19 April was also received by the brigade commander. The situation was now very confused. MacCurtain's own orders for the Easter 'Manoeuvres' had already been issued on 9 April and were now at variance with MacDermott's dispatches and MacNeill's latest instruction. In short, MacCurtain had been planning for manoeuvres designed to provide security for an arms landing, he was then ordered to prepare for offensive operations, and he now found himself instructed to only take defensive measures.

At national level the Military Council's plan was also beginning to unravel. The previous weekend they deemed it necessary to inform two senior Volunteer officers, Commandant J.J. O'Connell, the chief of inspection, and Seán Fitzgibbon, the director of recruiting, that a supply of arms was then en route to Ireland on board the *Aud*, a German vessel disguised as a Norwegian trawler. Both men were assured that MacNeill was fully briefed on this development and they were then tasked with specific duties in relation to the operation. Due to his previous involvement in landing

German arms at Kilcoole in August 1914 Fitzgibbon was ordered to travel to the south west and liaise with the commanding officers of the Kerry and Limerick Brigades, while O'Connell was ordered to take charge of operations in Leinster.[15]

Fitzgibbon duly set off for Kerry and Limerick but O'Connell had doubts as to the authenticity of his orders, and on Thursday night, 20 April, he went to Volunteer headquarters in order to verify them. There he met with Bulmer Hobson. The quartermaster general had earlier attended an IRB meeting and became alarmed when one Volunteer informed him that he had received orders to sabotage a railway line on Easter Sunday. When O'Connell told him of his orders, both men realised there was something seriously wrong. They immediately drove to MacNeill's home at Woodtown Park in Rathfarnham and informed their chief of staff of what they knew.

Furious at having been deceived, and convinced now that an armed rebellion was indeed planned for Easter Sunday, MacNeill, Hobson and O'Connell went directly to confront Pearse at St Enda's College. When Pearse admitted the truth MacNeill declared that, short of informing the British authorities in Dublin Castle, he would do everything in his power to stop the rebellion. To this end, in the early hours of Friday morning (21 April), he drafted the following order for O'Connell in respect of the Volunteers in Munster:

> Commandant O'Connell will go to Cork by the first available train today. He will instruct Commandant MacCurtain, or, in his absence, will select an officer to accompany him to Kerry. Commandant O'Connell will immediately take chief command of the Irish Volunteers, and will be in complete control over all Volunteers in Munster. Any orders issued by Commandant Pearse, or any person heretofore are hereby cancelled or recalled, and only the orders issued by Commandant O'Connell and under his authority will have force. Commandant O'Connell will have full powers to appoint officers of any rank, to supersede officers of any rank, and to delegate his own authority or any part of it to any person in respect of the Irish Volunteers in Munster.
>
> [Signed] Eoin MacNeill
> Chief of Staff
>
> PS Officers in Munster will report to Commandant O'Connell as required by him on the subject of any special orders they have received and any arrangements made or to be made by them as a consequence.
>
> Chief of Staff.[16]

MacNeill also issued a 'General Order' to all Volunteer units re-affirming his instructions, issued in the wake of the 'Castle document', to take only defensive measures in the event of an attack or an attempted disarmament by Crown forces. He was adamant that this order would:

> take the place of any orders that may have been issued in a different sense. All orders of a special character issued by Commandant Pearse, or by any other person heretofore, with regard to military movements of a definite kind, are hereby recalled or cancelled, and in future all special orders will be issued by me or by my successor as Chief of Staff.[17]

Later that morning, however, as O'Connell was making his way to Cork, Pearse and MacDermott called to MacNeill's home and argued that, with the German arms shipment already en route to Ireland, it was now too late to stop the rebellion. After much debate the chief of staff was eventually prevailed upon to countermand his own previous order. Once this was decided MacDermott immediately contacted Volunteer James Ryan and tasked him to take a dispatch to Cork that evening. Ryan later recalled that:

> I was only too glad to get busy at something; and I was told to report at his [MacDermott's] office in D'Olier Street during the afternoon and prepare to travel on the night train to Cork. When I arrived at the office he asked me if I was armed and I said yes. He then handed me a dispatch which was to be delivered to Tomás MacCurtain in Cork. He said that it was a very important message and that I should prevent it falling into hostile hands even at the cost of my life. This looked serious and I began to think that 'another ordinary parade' on Sunday might definitely be counted out.[18]

In Cork, MacCurtain had been informed that O'Connell was on his way to the city and arranged to meet his train at Mallow station. When he got there, however, the train had already passed through. Returning by road MacCurtain found O'Connell at Terence MacSwiney's home at Grand View Terrace on the Victoria Road; Seán O'Sullivan, the officer commanding the Cork City Battalion, was also present. O'Connell brought all of them up to date on events in Dublin and confirmed MacNeill's order in relation to defensive measures. The meeting went on for a long time and around 7pm they took a break for something to eat. Eithne MacSwiney had prepared the meal with her sister Mary, and later left this impression of the men's demeanour as they ate their food:

Though they endeavoured to speak lightly and make jokes, the feeling of gloom and depression predominated. This was in marked contrast to the spirit of buoyant gaiety in which Terry had worked during the previous months.[19]

When the meeting resumed in the sitting room sometime after 8pm, Alice Cashel, a member of Cumann na mBan, arrived to receive orders from MacCurtain in relation to hiring a number of touring cars – ostensibly to drive groups of tourists around Killarney for the Easter weekend. In actual fact these were to be used to transport the arms that were due to be landed in Kerry. Once she had booked the cars she had been told to report back to MacCurtain in order to receive final instructions for Easter Sunday. When Eithne MacSwiney informed MacCurtain that Cashel was present he asked that she wait. Eventually, at around 11pm, Cashel became impatient and insisted on seeing the brigade commander. When Eithne MacSwiney went into the sitting room she was shocked by what she found:

Terry stood on one side of the fireplace, his elbow on the mantelpiece, his head resting on his hand. Tomás stood in a similar attitude on the other side. Facing him, Seán O'Sullivan sat on a sofa near the window, elbows on his knees, his head bowed between his hands. O'Connell sat on an arm-chair, looking as if he had been defending himself; the rather odd look on his face suggested that he was at variance with his three companions; it was a rather smug 'take-it-or-leave-it' expression. This vivid impression was registered in the one glance I gave from one to the other of the four. Without any knowledge of what they had been discussing, it was clear to me that something was very seriously wrong. Only some matter of the gravest import could have produced that atmosphere of anxiety, strain and heaviness of mind which was reflected on the faces and attitudes of the three, Terry, Tomás and Seán O'Sullivan; and I felt that 'Ginger' O'Connell was the cause of the trouble, whatever it was. I said, 'Miss Cashel can't wait any longer. It is after eleven. She wants you to give her her message.' Tomás spoke: 'Tell her there is no message.' I returned and delivered Tomás' answer. The reaction of Alice Cashel was a great surprise to us. She gasped. 'No message,' she repeated. 'But that's impossible. There MUST be a message. That is an extraordinary thing to say. There MUST be a message.' 'Well,' I replied, 'that is what Tomás said', and my sister added, 'Why not leave it 'till tomorrow?' 'But that's just it,' said Alice. 'I CAN'T leave it 'till tomorrow, I MUST have the message tonight. It is an extraordinary situation to be in. I must get an answer tonight.' 'You had better go yourself and ask,' I said, and she went in, to return in a few seconds, looking most upset and completely dumbfounded … She left us in a considerable state of anxiety and bewilderment. We suggested that one of the Volunteers on duty outside the house should see her home, but she considered it safer to go alone. Most of the Volunteers were being watched and followed everywhere.[20]

Meanwhile, Lieutenant Fred Murray of the Cork City Battalion had been busy delivering copies of MacCurtain's original mobilisation orders to both the Eyeries and Kenmare Companies. On his way back to Cork by train he discovered that Sir Roger Casement, who had returned to Ireland on board the German submarine *U19* in an effort to stop the rebellion, had been arrested and the *Aud* intercepted. When he arrived back in the city in the early hours of Saturday morning he raced to the Volunteer Hall in order to inform MacCurtain of these developments.[21] Aware of the potential for disaster which was now unfolding, MacCurtain immediately decided to go to O'Connell's hotel and brief him. As he and MacSwiney were about to leave their headquarters, however, James Ryan arrived from Dublin with MacDermott's latest dispatch, which confirmed that the rebellion would go ahead as planned. Faced with yet another change in plan, MacCurtain clearly felt that he had no other option but to follow standard military procedure by 'obeying the last order' and he told Ryan: 'Tell Seán we'll blaze away as long as the stuff lasts.'[22]

The following day, Easter Saturday (22 April), the situation changed again when MacNeill was informed of Casement's arrest and the interception of the *Aud*. The chief of staff now had no doubts. Without German support, any armed rebellion was doomed to fail and would inevitably result in heavy loss of life. In order to save the Irish Volunteers from annihilation he immediately issued the following instructions, which cancelled all previous orders for mobilisation on Easter Sunday:

> Volunteers completely deceived. All orders for special action are hereby cancelled and on no account will action be taken.
> [Signed] Eoin MacNeill
> Chief of Staff.[23]

Later that day he issued a more specific order, copies of which were dispatched to units throughout the country and placed in the following morning's *Sunday Independent*:

> Owing to the very critical position, all orders given to the Irish Volunteers for tomorrow, Easter Sunday, are hereby rescinded, and no parades, marches or

other movements of Irish Volunteers, will take place. Each individual Volunteer will obey this order strictly in every particular.

Chief of Staff.[24]

In order to ensure that the Volunteers understood that this order was issued by him as Chief of Staff, MacNeill also issued the following authentication note:

> The order issued to the Irish Volunteers, printed over my signature in today's *Sunday Independent*, is hereby authenticated. Every influence should be used immediately and throughout the day to secure faithful execution of this order, as any failure to obey may result in a very great catastrophe.
>
> Chief of Staff.[25]

In the meantime Ryan had reported back to MacDermott and informed him that his mission to Cork had been successful, whereupon MacDermott appointed him to his personal staff with orders to parade at Liberty Hall the following morning. But at around ten o'clock that night Ryan was summoned to a house on Rathgar Road where he discovered the Volunteer executive in conference:

> After some time the door of the meeting room opened and Eoin MacNeill appeared. He asked me if I had carried a dispatch to Cork the previous day and if I knew where to find the leaders there. I answered yes to both questions. Good! Well, I was now to go to Cork again, this time by motor car. It was urgent and I must deliver these dispatches as soon as possible. In his hand he held five or six slips of paper, each in identical terms and signed by him. They were orders cancelling the Sunday manoeuvres. I was to deliver one to Pierce McCann in Tipperary, one to MacCurtain in Cork, one to the OC Tralee, if possible the remainder to officers of any groups of Volunteers I might see on parade on the journey ... Eoin MacNeill's brother, James, was to come with me driving his own car.[26]

MOBILISATION

Whether the Cork Brigade would mobilise as previously ordered by MacDermott, and face the possibility of an armed conflict with the British army, now depended literally on how soon Ryan could get back to MacCurtain. Time was critical because that very afternoon many Volunteers of the Cork Brigade were already beginning to mobilise. Across the city all arms, ammunition and supplies were moved into the Volunteer Hall, which was under armed guard. The first rural Volunteers to mobilise were fifteen men from the Cobh Company commanded by Captain Michael Leahy. This group made their way to the hall on Saturday evening and took over guard duty from the city Volunteers. They were later joined by twenty seven men from the Dungourney Company under the command of Captain Maurice Ahern, and that night all of them slept on the floor of the hall lying on beds made from straw provided by the brigade quartermaster.

Then, as dawn broke on Easter Sunday, Volunteers from all over the county arose, had breakfast, said farewell to their loved ones, and set out for their designated assembly points. In the Volunteer Hall Seán Murphy spent the morning distributing first aid kits and other items of equipment. Speculation was rife about the precise objectives of the 'Manoeuvres' upon which they were about to embark but when Volunteer Dan Donovan from C Company saw the first-aid kits being distributed, followed by tins of Oxo cubes, he turned to a comrade and remarked: 'This looks like the real thing.'[27]

When all supplies had been issued, 163 Volunteers from the Cork City Battalion, together with those from Cobh and Dungourney, formed up outside their headquarters and, after a final address by MacCurtain, marched off to the Capwell railway station where they boarded a train for Crookstown. MacCurtain had arranged to travel to west Cork by car but just as he was about to leave the Volunteer Hall James Ryan arrived and delivered a copy of McNeill's latest order.

The brigade commander was now in an impossible position. All over the county his men were marching to their concentration points as ordered. He was also acutely aware that, in the absence of a national uprising, any possible confrontation with Crown forces was guaranteed to fail. The situation was now fraught with danger but when he weighed up his options MacCurtain decided his only possible course of action was to permit the men to concentrate as ordered, and once that was complete he would then order them all to 'stand down'. His only consolation was that the plan for rebellion had not been disclosed to his unit and this would at least enable him to justify the day's activity as a 'training exercise'.

Then, as heavy rain began to fall, MacCurtain, accompanied by Terence MacSwiney and Bob Hales, set off by car for west Cork. His first stop was near Crookstown, where he dispatched orders for the column marching to Macroom to stand down upon arrival. He next moved on to Bweeing in north Cork, where he met T.J. Golden, the commander of the Courtbrack Company, who later recalled that:

> Tomás MacCurtain appeared to be in a great hurry. He addressed the whole parade and said that the exercises were cancelled. The men were to return quietly to their homes and keep their arms safely. They may soon be wanted again, he said, and may be called upon in the near future. We were to remain alert and 'stand to arms' until further notice.[28]

MacCurtain then carried on to Inchigeela and stood down the Volunteers concentrated at this location. The officers in charge of the other concentration points had already been told to stand down if no further instructions were forthcoming.

So it was that the Volunteers of the Cork Brigade demobilised and returned home confused, dismayed and soaked to the skin with green dye from their Volunteer hats running down their faces.

According to Seán Murphy 'between 1100 and 1200 men had been mobilised in County Cork for Easter Sunday',[29] but Florence O'Donoghue provided the following, more detailed information regarding the number of Volunteers who assembled at the eight designated concentration points:

Concentration Point	Number
Lauragh	80
Kealkil	29
Inchigeela	55
Macroom	399
Bweeing	222
Millstreet	67
Barley Hill	57
Carriganimma	120
Total	**1029**[30]

By late afternoon MacCurtain was completely frustrated with what had turned out to be a totally wasteful exercise and he decided to go to Ballingeary in an attempt to evaluate the situation with Seán O'Hegarty, the senior IRB officer in the county. The headlights on his car failed, however, and MacCurtain, MacSwiney and Hales were forced to spend Sunday night at Carrigadrohid instead. At first light on Easter Monday morning they finally set off for Ballingeary and spent the day discussing developments with O'Hegarty, who proved no wiser than they were. Eventually, and with nothing resolved, they began the return journey to Cork a little after six o'clock that evening.

At this point MacCurtain and MacSwiney were completely unaware that any rising had started in Dublin. It was only the officers back in the city, Seán Murphy and Seán O'Sullivan, who had heard a variety of unconfirmed reports and received a note delivered by Mary Perolz from the Dublin Cumman na mBan. Written on the fly-leaf of a pocket notebook the words read: 'We start at noon today', and it was signed 'P.H.P.'[31] Unsure what action to take these officers decided their best option was to barricade themselves into the Volunteer Hall. They also posted scouts at several strategic points around the city in order to report the movements of the army and police, and Volunteer Tadhg O'Leary was dispatched on the train to Macroom in an unsuccessful attempt to find their commanding officer and his deputy.

Negotiations

When the brigade commander eventually arrived back in Cork at around 9pm on Easter Monday night the first inkling he received that anything was afoot came by way of information received from Volunteer Denis Breen, whom he encountered on the outskirts of the city. When he finally arrived at the Volunteer Hall he was first amazed at the level of activity that was going on, and then became seriously concerned when handed the note from Mary Perolz. While this clearly did not constitute another order it did indicate that at least some Volunteer elements in Dublin were about to embark on military action.

The more MacCurtain thought about the situation, however, the more difficult it appeared. His men had only just returned home from a gruelling day on Easter Sunday, during which the majority had been soaked to the skin and at least one day's rations had been consumed. The expected German arms had not materialised. He had no effective communications with Dublin. He had no reliable intelligence reports from which to make any deductions. His brigade was now completely dispersed and even if he could manage to mobilise some of them they would provide no opposition whatsoever to the combined firepower of the British army and RIC. A hostile crowd had also gathered in the street outside his headquarters, and with the British army in Victoria Barracks probably preparing to move against him MacCurtain knew he no longer had any room to manoeuvre. In the absence of any clear orders or information from Dublin he decided his best course of action was to concentrate on defending the Volunteer Hall against attack. He later recorded that:

> We decided not to leave the hall, come what may. We were convinced that the soldiers would surround us and that we would die there, but we were satisfied – no one could say that we had run away from the fight, and indeed there was no such thought in our minds.[32]

If nothing else this was at least consistent with his last instructions from MacNeill. However, not all of his men were satisfied with this decision. Second Lieut. Robaird Langford, C Company, Cork City Battalion, later recalled:

> The situation was very tense and strained. The younger officers particularly wanted to fight, and were very resentful of the waiting policy adopted by the leaders. They expressed their views, but the weight of the influence and authority of the older men (as they regarded the brigade officers) was against them.[33]

In the meantime, and unknown to MacCurtain, the lord mayor of Cork, Councillor T.C. Butterfield had already commenced an initiative to prevent an outbreak of hostilities in the city by contacting Brigadier General W.F.H. Stafford, the General Officer Commanding (GOC) in Cork. He suggested that before any military attempt be made to capture the Volunteer Hall he (Butterfield) should first be given an opportunity to persuade the Volunteers to hand over their weapons peacefully and thus avoid any casualties or damage to the city. Stafford agreed and appointed his aide-de-camp, Captain F.W. Dickie, to take charge of negotiations. Butterfield then called on the Auxiliary Bishop of Cork, Dr Daniel Cohalan, to enlist his help. On Monday night they went to the Volunteer Hall and met Mac-Curtain, who assured them that he had no intention of initiating military action but would defend his position if attacked. Satisfied that violence was not about to break out Butterfield and Cohalan then began a sequence of negotiations in an effort to find a peaceful solution to the crisis.

The following morning, Tuesday 25 April, saw an intensification of the fighting in Dublin, but in Cork all remained quiet. Some news of the rebellion, however, was now spreading throughout Cork county, and while some individual company commanders responded and mobilised small numbers, in the absence of any concrete information they too decided to remain in their respective locations and await further orders. For his part, MacCurtain remained fortified within his headquarters awaiting further contact with the lord mayor and the bishop, but none was made. Instead, early on Wednesday morning, he received reports that the British army had deployed artillery on the hill of Gurranebraher and positioned a number of machine guns in the Malt House directly opposite the Volunteer Hall. He then received a visit from the City Coroner, William Murphy, who also asked that no military action be taken until Butterfield and Cohalan returned.

Throughout Wednesday and Thursday Butterfield and Cohalan continued to negotiate with Captain Dickie until an agreement was eventually reached. The Volunteers would hand up their arms to the lord mayor on the following Monday for safekeeping, and in return no action would be taken against them.

On Friday Butterfield and Cohalan returned to the Volunteer Hall and put these terms to MacCurtain, together with a threat from Dickie that the Volunteer Hall would be shelled if he refused to accept them. MacCurtain agreed in principle but sought clarification on the following questions: would the matter be kept out of the newspapers; would the arms handed-in be returned to the Volunteers once the crisis was over; would the RIC cease harassing his men; and would MacCurtain and MacSwiney be permitted to visit Volunteer units in Limerick and Kerry to inform them of the situation in Cork and recommend acceptance of similar terms?

These queries were transmitted to General Stafford and later that night Captain Dickie met with Bishop Cohalan at his residence and informed him that as far as the GOC was concerned the arms would be returned once the crisis had passed – but he couldn't speak for parliament or the civil authority. He also stated that the GOC would use his influence to curb the activities of the RIC and to ensure that the terms of the agreement were kept out of the press. He would also issue the travel permits requested by MacCurtain and if these terms were accepted he would agree to a general amnesty for all the Volunteers in his area other than those found in treasonable correspondence with the enemy.[34]

Satisfied with this news Butterfield, accompanied by Captain Dickie, returned to the Volunteer Hall at around 2am on Saturday morning, and met MacCurtain, MacSwiney, and Seán O'Sullivan. The five of them sat around the fire in deep discussion until 5am, when the following terms were agreed:

1. The military have no idea of confiscation, and as far as the military are concerned the arms will be returned once the crisis is over; but the military cannot speak for Parliament or the civil authority, nor can they give an assurance that a law will not be passed to disarm the Irish Volunteers and all similar associations.

2. Care will be taken that the papers do not mention the handing in of the rifles.

3. The County Inspector of Police will be spoken to in order to check the indiscreet zeal of individual policemen.

4. A permit will be given to the Volunteer leaders to visit Limerick, Tralee and other districts, to submit to the Volunteers of these centres the Cork Agreement, and to counsel acceptance of it.

5. If these terms are accepted, there should be a general amnesty, unless in the case of persons found in treasonable correspondence with the enemy.[35]

Having spent the night without sleep agonising over the decisions they had taken, MacCurtain and MacSwiney departed for Limerick and Kerry on the 8am train, unaware that their comrades in Dublin were on the verge of surrender, or that the *Cork Constitution* was carrying a report which stated: 'The Cork Sinn Féiners have handed up their rifles to the police.'[36] This was a flagrant breach of the terms agreed just hours before and caused considerable unrest amongst the Volunteers in the city. The situation was made worse later on Saturday night when Captain Dickie arrived at Volunteer Hall to see MacCurtain on his return from Limerick, and demanded that all arms now be handed up by midnight on Sunday, rather than on Monday as previously agreed. MacCurtain was incensed by this demand and Dickie's failure to keep the matter out of the newspapers. The following morning (Sunday 30 April), accompanied by MacSwiney, he again met with the bishop and lord mayor, and informed them that under the current circumstances he could not possibly ask his men to hand over their arms. After lengthy debate Cohalan eventually persuaded the brigade commander to put the matter before a general meeting of the Volunteers at 8pm on Monday, at which time both he and the lord mayor would also address them. Butterfield then wrote to Dickie outlining explaining the Volunteer's and suggesting a meeting at noon the following day.

While all of these discussions were taking place the Cork Brigade did actually manage to take some offensive military action – but without either MacCurtain's approval or knowledge. On Sunday, 30 April, a small party of Volunteers apprehended, searched and threatened Sergeant Crean of the RIC barracks at Ballinadee in west Cork. They then moved on and cut the telegraph wires between Clonakilty and the war signal station at Galley Head.[37] Clearly these Volunteers wanted to make some contribution to the Rising, but by then it was far too late.

Unknown to them, however, their very limited action probably did have an impact, because when Captain Dickie met with Butterfield and Cohalan in the City Club at noon the following day (Monday, 1 May), his manner was far from conciliatory. In fact he delivered the following ultimatum:

> The agreement between the Asst. Bishop of Cork, the Lord Mayor of Cork, the Cork City Branch of Irish Volunteers, and the General Commanding in the South of Ireland, has not been complied with as agreed on, and the General can no longer hold himself bound by the concessions agreed on. If however, all arms, ammunition and explosives of any kind in the possession of any member of that body be handed over by them to the custody of the Lord Mayor of Cork, before 8pm, on this date, the General will make every effort to ensure that the concessions agreed on will be carried out. He cannot guarantee this, as the matter now rests with the Commander in Chief, Ireland. In the event of arms not being handed over as agreed, it will be the General's duty to consider all concerned as offering opposition to H.M. Forces and they will be dealt with accordingly as rebels in arms against the Crown.
>
> Signed at Cork at noon, on May 1, 1916, on behalf of the General Officer Commanding the South Irish Area.
>
> F.W. Dickie
>
> Captain, ADC and Intelligence Officer, General Staff.[38]

Later that afternoon Cohalan received a phone call from Dickie confirming that all guarantees previously given by the British authorities were now withdrawn. When the bishop protested vehemently at this development Dickie assured him that although the formal guarantees were withdrawn, the arrangements agreed to would go through and it was on this basis that the bishop and the lord mayor went to speak to the rank and file Volunteers that night.[39]

Some 140 Volunteers had gathered in the hall and they heard Butterfield and Cohalan urge them to accept the terms of the agreement and hand up their weapons. In the subsequent ballot 90 per cent of those present voted in favour of the agreement and once the meeting was over some of these Volunteers immediately marched down to the lord mayor's home at 68 South Mall and handed in their guns. Those who disagreed with this decision were adamant that the British would again renege on their commitments, with Second Lieut. Donal Óg O'Callaghan, B Company, Cork City Battalion, declaring: 'There will be treachery. The leopard does not change his spots.'[40] Accordingly, they either retained their arms at secret locations around the city or, in a final act of defiance, removed the firing pins to render the weapons unserviceable. From MacCurtain's perspective the week-long crisis had now been brought to an end without bloodshed; the Cork Brigade remained intact; he genuinely expected the British authorities to honour the terms of the agreement; and all things considered he was convinced he had taken the correct course of action.

However, the agreement lasted a mere twenty four hours because on the morning of Tuesday, 2 May, the homes of known Volunteers across the city were raided with MacCurtain, his brother Seán, and nine others arrested and incarcerated in the county gaol.[41] The lord mayor later managed to negotiate MacCurtain's release but it was abundantly clear that the agreement was not worth the paper upon which it was written.

Thomas Kent

On that same day the last major incident of the Easter Rising occurred, not in Dublin or in Cork city, but at a farmhouse owned by the Kent family at Bawnard, Castlelyons, County Cork. A party of RIC had been dispatched to arrest the Kent brothers – Thomas, David, Richard, and William – as part of the ongoing nationwide round-up of known Volunteers. They were not expecting any violent resistance but that was precisely what they encountered. When called upon to surrender the brothers refused and a gun battle erupted that lasted three hours and only came to an end when David was wounded and all of their ammunition had been expended.

During the fighting Head Constable Rowe had been shot and killed. In reprisal the RIC now decided to summarily execute all four brothers. This was stopped when a British army officer intervened, but when Richard Kent then attempted to escape he was shot and seriously wounded.

The two wounded brothers were taken to the military hospital in Fermoy, but Thomas and William were moved to Cork and incarcerated in the Military Detention Barracks.[42] When they were court martialled on 4 May William was acquitted, but Thomas was found guilty and sentenced to death. He was executed by firing squad in the exercise yard of the barracks at dawn on 9 May.

The circumstances of that court martial, however, the quality and quantity of the evidence produced, the speed with which the entire proceedings were conducted, and the legality of the sentence imposed raised a number of serious issues. In the first instance, the Defence of the Realm Act (DORA), passed by parliament on 8 August 1914, vested extraordinary powers in the hands of the military. Thus when Kent appeared in Victoria Barracks to be charged he found himself standing not before a judge and jury but rather a field general court martial. He was then charged with contravening the Act:

> In that he took part in an armed rebellion and in waging war against His Majesty the King, such act being prejudicial to the Defence of the Realm and being done with the intention and for the purpose of assisting the enemy.[43]

When proceedings got underway he found himself faced with a raft of evidence presented by the policemen and soldiers who had been involved in the gun battle – none of which, however connected Kent to the death of Head Constable Rowe or proved that he had even fired a single shot. Unrepresented by counsel he asked only nine questions in cross-examination, offered a mere seventy one words in a rebuttal statement, and was not permitted to call witnesses to speak on his behalf.

It was also clear that none of the Kent brothers had been involved in what by any stretch of the imagination could be called an armed rebellion. They had neither heard of nor seen the Proclamation of the Republic, and they were certainly not waging a war or assisting the enemy (in this case Germany). In fact the events of Easter Week had completely passed them by. By the time they were arrested Pearse had surrendered in Dublin and MacCurtain had negotiated the agreement in Cork. Therefore if the Kents were 'guilty' of anything it was nothing more than following MacNeill's order of 19 April (cited above) to prevent themselves from being forcibly disarmed – which in this context might have amounted at most to causing an affray or engaging in violent disorder. Accordingly, the charge as presented against Thomas Kent made no sense whatever, especially given that his brother William was acquitted and both of them had been in the same place at the same time in exactly the same circumstances. This begs the question why one was found guilty and one was not – and the answer is obvious.

In the summer of 1915 Thomas Kent had become closely involved with Terrence MacSwiney in arranging public meetings to attract new Volunteers. He was also well known to the RIC, having disrupted a number of British army recruitment meetings, and by Easter 1916 he had become a commandant in the Galtee Battalion. Aged fifty one, he was sentenced to death on 4 May 1916, not for his actions at Bawnard, because there is no evidence in his court martial documentation to suggest that he did anything except surrender. He was sentenced to death because of who he was and because of the leadership position he held within the Volunteer movement. In Dublin General Maxwell wanted to make an example of the Volunteer leadership and Thomas Kent was another convenient scapegoat.[44] He paid for Maxwell's policy with his life, but the charges against him remain unproven. Thomas Kent was not guilty as charged at his court martial and the documentary evidence that survives leaves this matter in no doubt whatsoever.

INCARCERATION

The death of Thomas Kent was not the end of the matter. While he was being court martialled large numbers of Volunteers were being rounded up and also locked behind bars in the Detention Barracks. In fact most of them were woken from their sleep on the morning of 9 May by the volley of shots that terminated Kent's life. Captain Michael Leahy, the officer commanding the Cobh Company, later recalled that in an effort to find out where he and other officers from his unit had hidden their weapons:

> We were told the same fate [as Kent's] would be ours. Another argument that was used to get us to give up our rifles was telling us that the Cork men had given up theirs and that none of them had been arrested. Why should we hold out? … [However] we continued to refuse to give any information.[45]

In fact Crown forces had been busy arresting Volunteers all over Cork city and county since 2 May, and although MacCurtain remained at large he was powerless to intervene. He later recalled the anguish of seeing his fellow Volunteers being taken into custody and not being able to do anything about it:

It was a wretched business that week to be looking at them and hundreds of boys arrested by them. Often I said to myself that it was a great pity that I myself had not been kept in jail when I was there instead of looking at those fine men tied up by them and being brought from every part of the country.[46]

Eventually MacCurtain was also apprehended when, at 7.15pm on the evening of 11 May, the RIC raided his home at 40 Thomas Davis Street and re-arrested him:

Siobhan, my wife's sister, started to cry when I was leaving the house but Eilís (my wife) did not say a word. She did not want to put any trouble on me along with what I had already and she told me to have courage. This was a great help to me. I kissed Siobhan and Síle and Tomas Óg who was in the cot and went with the peelers ... I was put in the Detention Barracks ... I was searched and everything I had was taken from me except for the copy of the *Imitation of Christ* that I had in English, it was a very small little book and a great comfort to me – I was put into the cell ... Eilís gave me a glass of milk before I left the house and I was not hungry ... After all the work I was very tired ... I put the board on the floor of my cell and went to sleep.[47]

The following morning he got his first real taste of prison life when a bell awoke him at 6am in order that he and the other prisoners could wash themselves before breakfast and commencement of the daily routine:

I was given a mug of some stuff at 8 o'clock and a piece of bread – I think the drink was a mixture of chocolate and cocoa – immediately I had that breakfast eaten a solder came to the door to me and said 'Do not be afraid of anyone here but raise your head and look them between the two eyes.' That encouraged me and lifted the spirit in me and I did so ... We were all let out in the air from 11 to 12 o'clock and a guard of soldiers around us. We would be walking around after one another – about six feet apart and we would not be allowed to say a word to one another. We got a dinner which was not too bad altogether and what we got for breakfast we got again in the evening for supper. We had another 'in the air' between four and five o'clock ... it was in the yard in which we used to walk that Tomás Ceannt was buried after he was shot.[48]

By now 140 members of the Cork Brigade were incarcerated in the Detention Barracks where they remained in complete ignorance of their fate for three weeks.

Then, on the evening of 21 May, they were told to be 'ready for road' the following morning. At 7.30am the Volunteers of the Cork Brigade, together with men from other units who had been locked up in Cork, were all handcuffed together in pairs and marched off under military escort to the Great Southern and Western Railway station on the Lower Glanmire Road. They whistled and sang as they marched down Military Hill, through St Luke's Cross, and down Grattan Hill to the station where a large crowd of terrified relatives and friends had gathered. Amid chaotic scenes of anguish and distress the military escort would not permit any contact between the Volunteers and their families and instead herded the captives on board a train bound for Dublin where they were detained in Richmond Barracks.

At this stage fifteen rebel leaders had been executed and a public outcry had begun to reverberate throughout the country. Afraid of alienating the nationalist population of Ireland and aware of pubic opinion in America, the British government decided to stop the executions and intern the rebels in Britain instead. MacCurtain and many of the men under his command left Richmond Barracks on 1 June and, as a sign of the shift in public opinion that was then taking place, they were cheered as they marched through the streets of Dublin to board a cattle ship at the North Wall that would take them into exile.

Upon arrival in Britain they were divided into two groups – one being sent to Wakefield Detention Barracks and the other to Knutsford prison. Later that month MacCurtain, MacSwiney and a number of other Cork Volunteers from both locations were transferred to an interment camp in north Wales at a place called Frongoch.[49] It was here, in a rat-infested former distillery, which until recently had been used to house German prisoners of war, that the Irish internees established their 'university of revolution', with classes soon commencing in Irish history, language and culture. More importantly, it was here that the Volunteers from the Cork Brigade came together with people like Michael Collins, and began a detailed analysis of the failure of the rebellion.

On 11 July MacCurtain was transferred to Reading gaol, where he remained haunted by what had happened and by the perception of his own personal failure. After many long, lonely hours of deliberation he finally reached a conclusion and confided it to his diary:

it is nearly five months ago now and it is many a turn I have had since, and my judgement in the matter is that we could not have done otherwise than we did.[50]

Nevertheless, the failure of the Cork Brigade of Irish Volunteers to take part in the Easter Rising continued to be the cause of much concern at local and national level. Donal Óg O'Callagahan's statement that the brigade had been led by 'three incompetent men in a state of blue funk' represented the view of a militant minority in Cork, while a general concern remained amongst the surviving leaders of both the IRB and Irish Volunteers.[51] Accordingly, after the Volunteers returned to Ireland in 1917, MacCurtain and other senior brigade officers requested Volunteer headquarters to hold an inquiry into their activities during Easter Week.[52]

A court of inquiry consisting of Cathal Brugha, Diarmuid Lynch and Con Collins convened in Cork and interviewed MacCurtain and other Volunteer officers throughout the city and county. The IRB also held its own inquiry and both found that no blame was attributable to the Cork Brigade, as 'it was impossible for them to do anything in the circumstances'.[53]

EVALUATION OF THE BRIGADE COMMANDER

Taken in the context of the time, cognisant of the conflicting orders he received, and recognising the parallel chains of command within which he was forced to operate, it is our firm view that both MacCurtain's own personal evaluation of his leadership and the findings of the two inquiries are correct. In his capacity as commander of the Cork Brigade of Volunteers, MacCurtain could not, and should not, have done anything other than what he did.

The fact that MacCurtain received nine different and conflicting orders within three weeks was intolerable and a situation within which no competent military commander could have been expected to operate successfully.

Orders issued to the Cork Brigade
of Volunteers during April 1916

Date (1916)	Category	Initiated by	Content	Received in Cork
Mon 3 April	General Order	Pearse	Manoeuvres on	5 April
Sun 9 April	Brigade commander's conference			
Mon 17 April	Dispatch	MacDermott via Brigid Foley	Unknown	16 April
Wed 19 April	Castle document published			
Wed 19 April	Dispatch	MacDermott via Brigid Foley	Unknown	19 April
Wed 19 April	Order	MacNeill	Defence only	20 April
Fri 21 April	Order	MacNeill via J.J. O'Connell	Command and Control	21 April
Fri 21 April	General Order	MacNeill	Defence only	21 April
MacNeill reconsiders				
Fri 21 April	Counter-manding Order	MacNeill via James Ryan	Rising on	22 April
Arms landing fails				
Sat 22 April	General Order	MacNeill via James Ryan	Rising can-celled	23 April
Sun 23 April	*Sunday Independent* – Mobilisation cancelled			23 April
Mon 24 April	Note	Pearse via Mary Perolz	Rising on	24 April
Mon 24 April	Dispatch	MacDermott via Brigid Foley	Unknown	Not delivered

Furthermore, the absence of a formal written military operational order proved critical. MacCurtain had no clear mission statement. There was no definable higher commander's intent and no meaningful planning guidance was offered. There was no clear identifiable concept of operations, no serious logistics planning had been undertaken, and the members of the Cork Brigade did not possess sufficient arms and ammunition to mount any meaningful military operations. Furthermore, there was no reserve of arms, ammunition, or equipment other than what might have been landed from the *Aud*, but there was no advance knowledge of whether these stocks were even compatible with the rifles they already possessed.

Kept in abject ignorance of the IRB's real intentions until the very last moment, had MacCurtain chosen to commit his brigade against a credible, competent and far superior military force it is distinctly possible that neither he nor many of his colleagues would have survived – and those who did would in all probability have been promptly executed. The fate of Thomas Kent, for what would have amounted to a significantly lesser offence, adequately proves this point.

Instead, by making a realistic evaluation of the circumstances within which he found himself, recognising his military limitations, and identifying the capability of his enemy, MacCurtain conducted a proper military estimate of the situation and then made the correct military decision. By having the self-confidence to make that hard choice he displayed solid leadership and sound judgment, and preserved his force intact and available for future operations.

MAIN LESSONS LEARNED

The main lesson that Tomás MacCurtain learned from his experience at Easter 1916 was that secret societies were no longer relevant in the quest for Irish freedom. The IRB had deceived and manipulated the Volunteer movement in order to push that quest in a particular direction, which ultimately had probably more to do with making a valiant blood-sacrifice than waging a competent military campaign with some prospect of success.

He also identified the complex command relationships that existed at April 1916 and the manner in which members of both the Supreme and Military Councils of the IRB were able to operate unhindered within the Volunteer command structure. This effectively gave rise to parallel chains of command which in turn caused widespread confusion and ultimately made the positions of the brigade commanders on the ground untenable.

IRB Influence on the Irish Volunteer chain of command during April 1916

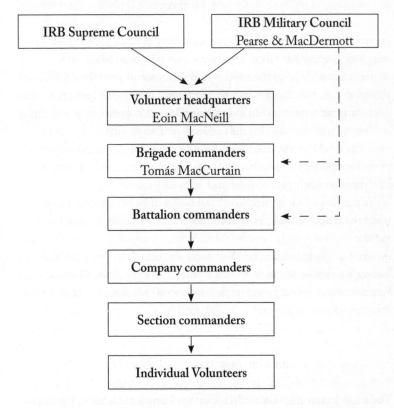

For MacCurtain parallel chains of command were an absurdity and he vowed never to be trapped between them again. At Easter 1916 he was the brigade commander of the Cork Brigade of Irish Volunteers and took his orders in that context directly from the Volunteer Chief of Staff, Eoin MacNeill. However, he was also a member of the IRB, subject to the authority of the Supreme Council, and he found himself taking different instructions from the Military Council. This was never going to work, and on Good Friday Terence MacSwiney described the situation as one of 'order, counterorder and disorder'.[54] Not surprisingly then, MacCurtain resigned from the IRB in 1917, determined instead to regenerate the Cork

Brigade and develop it into a credible military force operating within the parameters of a clearly defined chain of command. Internment did not rid him of his military and political aspirations – it served only to intensify both.

Conclusion

As the process of reorganisation got underway in 1917 not all members of the Cork Brigade had come to the same conclusions as MacCurtain. Some remained convinced of the efficacy and relevance of the IRB, others continued to question his decision to hand over arms to the lord mayor, and a minority were determined to conduct their own operations in the future irrespective of what the brigade commander had to say.

In fact none of the brigade commander's problems had actually disappeared and many of them had in fact become more critical. The difference this time, however, was that he had learned from his experience; he was acutely aware of the difference of opinion within his ranks; and he fully understood the complexity of commanding such a diverse group of individuals.

As the Cork Brigade of Volunteers embarked on the next phase of Ireland's struggle for independence the challenges facing Tomás Mac-Curtain as the brigade commander were immense. It would take a leader of extraordinary talent and huge personal integrity to maintain cohesion within a military unit which was still reeling from the perception of failure at Easter 1916, with many of the more militant Volunteers now intent on amending that situation any way they could. That MacCurtain actually managed to continue operating within the Volunteer chain of command while also keeping his unit intact speaks volumes, and leads to the evaluation that the Volunteers of the Cork Brigade were fortunate to have him as their commanding officer until his murder on 20 March 1920.

Equally it is clear that they were in fact more than fortunate to have had his leadership available to them at Easter 1916, because had any other course of action been taken the outcome would in all probability have been devastating, and the impact unquantifiable. Commandant Tomás Mac-Curtain made the correct military decisions at Easter 1916 – of that there is no doubt whatsoever.

CONSTANCE MARKIEVICZ'S 'THREE GREAT MOVEMENTS' AND THE 1916 RISING

Rosemary Cullen Owens

In 1913 Constance Markievicz told a Dublin meeting that there were three great movements going on in Ireland – the national movement, the women's movement, and the industrial movement, 'all fighting the same fight, for the extension of human liberty'.[1] This article examines the role of Irish women in these movements in the years prior to and following the 1916 Rising. While the equality provisions of the 1916 Proclamation can be seen as reflecting the aspirations of women's groups, what became of those aspirations in the wake of the Rising? In this regard, the implications of legislation passed in the 1920s and 1930s regarding women's employment and public role in the Irish Free State merit examination.

From the early 1900s onwards, Ireland was alive with movements and causes, which included home rule, Sinn Féin, Labour, the Gaelic League, and an active women's movement. Many young women were involved in one or more of these causes. From about 1903 a new generation of Irishwomen became involved in the suffrage campaign. These younger women had benefited from the educational advances obtained during the late nineteenth century by the work of earlier campaigners such as Anna Haslam and Isabella Tod, and many were influenced by contemporary developments in Ireland. In addition, growing awareness of suffrage demands internationally, and the aggressive tactics of Emmeline Pankhurst's Women's Social and Political Union (WSPU) in England from 1903, particularly influenced many such Irish women. The first in a series of new Irish suffrage societies was the Irish Women's Franchise League (IWFL) formed in 1908 by Hanna Sheehy Skeffington and Margaret Cousins. Implicit in its formation was recognition of the quite different political scenario facing suffrage campaigners in Ireland, and their conviction of the need for an independent Irish suffrage society, distinctly separate from any English connection.[2]

From the outset a militant and non-party organisation, the IWFL aimed to obtain votes for women on the same terms as men and decided to work towards having a 'votes for women' clause included in the home rule bill then under consideration. Over the next three to four years a number of other suffrage societies were formed throughout the country, both militant and non-militant, catering for particular regional, religious or political groups. To co-ordinate the work of the emerging smaller associations, the Irish Women's Suffrage Federation (IWSF) was formed in Dublin in August 1911 with Louie Bennett and Helen Chenevix as joint honorary secretaries.[3] By linking together the scattered suffrage groups throughout the country, the IWSF aimed to carry out more effective propaganda and educative work, and form the basis of an organisation to continue after suffrage was attained. The new organisation grew rapidly. By 1913 fifteen groups were affiliated to the IWSF, rising to twenty four by 1916.[4] The diversity of groups within the new federation can be judged by its inclusion of members from a unionist background, including authors Edith Somerville and Violet Martin (Somerville and Ross), and nationalists such as Mary MacSwiney.

Helen Chenevix later wrote that the suffrage movement 'brought women from sheltered homes face to face with the realities of sweated wages and the wretched conditions imposed on women who had to earn their living'.[5] The formation of the Irish Women's Reform League (IWRL) later in 1911, as a Dublin branch of the IWSF by Louie Bennett, was particularly significant in this context. Reflecting her own growing social awareness, Bennett used it to draw attention to the social and economic position of women workers and their families.[6] The IWRL investigated working conditions in Dublin factories, organising public debates and seminars to discuss its findings. Publication of these findings in the *Irish Citizen* ensured that such information was brought to the attention of a broad spectrum of women's groups. The IWRL also initiated a committee to watch legislation affecting women, and established a 'watching the courts committee' to observe and report on cases involving injustice to women and girls. Most of the cases reported concerned marital violence, indecent assault on children, and the seduction of young girls, often by employers. Details of such cases were reported quite frankly; lenient sentencing, early release of those convicted and judicial attitudes were all challenged and criticised. Irish women from quite disparate backgrounds could now choose between the long-established Irish Women's Suffrage and Local Government Association (IWSLGA), the militant IWFL and the middle ground of the IWSF. Activists of the time would have agreed with the comment of Margaret Cousins that 'the era of dumb self-effacing women was over'.[7]

Crucial to the dissemination of information on suffrage activities at home and abroad was the establishment in 1912 of the *Irish Citizen*. This suffrage paper provided feminist activists with an important means of communication, education and propaganda. Circulated throughout the thirty two counties, it acted as an important link between the various societies. The paper continued to be published weekly by Francis Sheehy Skeffington until his murder in 1916. Thereafter, it was published monthly until 1920 with Hanna Sheehy Skeffington and Louie Bennett its main editors. Designed to cater for both militant and non-militant societies, its columns kept women throughout the country informed of suffrage developments. Through its editorials and articles readers were informed of current national developments regarding women's suffrage, as well as being kept up to date on broader aspects of feminism and the struggle for women's rights internationally. By May 1913 there were eighteen suffrage societies in Ireland with an additional eleven affiliated branches nationwide.[8]

POLITICAL DEVELOPMENTS 1910–14

Due to heightened activity on the suffrage issue, a number of attempts were made from 1910 to introduce a women's suffrage bill in the House of Commons. While many individual MPs favoured the principle of female suffrage, party considerations usually determined their attitude if a bill showed any sign of success. Only Labour consistently supported women's suffrage proposals whilst also working towards its goal of full adult suffrage for all citizens regardless of property qualifications.

After the general election of 1910 the Liberals no longer held a majority. An all-party 'Conciliation Committee' was established to promote an agreed suffrage bill amenable to all. Six Irish MPs were on the committee, a number that rose to ten by 1912. The first 'conciliation bill' failed in 1910, but by 1911 the second such bill seemed more likely to succeed. Over 400 MPs had pledged to vote for women's suffrage, and in May 1911 the lord mayor of Dublin presented a petition in favour of the bill at the House of Commons.[9] Although the bill received a majority vote of 167 at its first reading in May 1911, it was defeated on its second reading in March 1912 by fourteen votes. The voting of Irish members was crucial to its defeat. Whereas ten months earlier thirty one Irish members had voted for the bill, in 1912 forty one voted against the bill with ten abstaining. In addition to the known anti-suffrage view of Asquith, John Redmond (also hostile to women's suffrage) was most anxious to avoid any issue that might adversely affect the granting of home rule to Ireland. Indeed, some Irish MPs would have agreed with the sentiments of John Dillon to a suffrage deputation that: 'Women's suffrage will I believe, be the ruin of our western civilisation. It will destroy the home, challenging the headship of man, laid down by God. It may come in your time – I hope not in mine.'[10]

Yet other Irish MPs, like William Redmond (brother of the Irish party leader) and Tom Kettle (married to Mary, a sister of Hanna Sheehy Skeffington), actively supported the cause in parliament. But when home rule manoeuvrings demanded, they stepped into line under their party leader. Fears of endangering home rule, either by precipitating a general election or by triggering the resignation of cabinet ministers, were sufficiently strong to ensure that all women's suffrage measures from this point on would be opposed by all Irish MPs. Feminist reaction to government and Irish party intransigence on the issue of female suffrage resulted in a campaign of militant action from June 1912 to the outbreak of war in 1914. During this time, thirty five women were convicted for militancy in Ireland, twelve of whom went on hunger strike.[11]

WOMEN AND LABOUR

Initial links between the two groups began with the broadening concerns of the new suffrage groups that emerged in the early 1900s, in particular the IWFL and the IWSF. the *Irish Citizen* also regularly published data on women's employment, highlighting problems within particular regional or sectional industries. The paper maintained its active support of Labour throughout the 1913 strike and lockout in Dublin, suffragists from various societies helping strikers in varying ways. Some, like Hanna Sheehy Skeffington and members of the IWFL, worked in the soup kitchens in Liberty Hall organised by Constance Markievicz, pointedly wearing their suffrage badges. Labour journals also increasingly reflected the new alliance, with reports of suffrage meetings and advertisements for suffrage events. That such bonds endured is clear from a note in the

Workers' Republic in 1915 to the effect that: 'Several well known and experienced suffragists have kindly consented to undertake organising work in connection with the union. They are women who showed us their sympathy two years ago.'[12] However not all trade unionists were over-anxious to enfranchise – or indeed unionise – women of their own class, fearing job losses and wage cuts. Craft unions, in particular, still opposed the admission of women. Rather than admit women and guarantee equal pay, many workers preferred to exclude women altogether. *Bean na hÉireann* (the nationalist/feminist paper) reported in 1910 that:

> Some leading members of the Dublin Trades Council have been approached regarding the organising of the women workers of Dublin. So far very little encouragement has been offered on this decidedly urgent question. While generally admitting the needs of the unorganised female workers, the male members of the wage earners look with suspicion on their sister slaves and are seemingly loath to offer any practical help.[13]

From the early 1900s there were a number of significant developments in the organisation of women workers. The Drapers Assistants' Association (DAA), formed in 1901 by Michael O'Lehane, admitted both men and women, the first union to do so since the Irish National Teachers' Organisation (INTO). Dermot Keogh has observed that by recruiting female members, 'O'Lehane showed himself to be most clearly liberated from the prejudices of his trade union colleagues'.[14] By 1914 1,400 of the union's 4,000 members were women.[15]

The formation of the Irish Women Workers Union (IWWU) in 1911 followed a successful strike for better pay by 3,000 women at Jacob's biscuit factory in Dublin in 1911. Delia Larkin was its first secretary, and Jim Larkin its president. During the subsequent Dublin lock-out of 1913, the entire membership of the IWWU came out on strike in support, remaining out for six months. Louie Bennett recalled her clandestine visits to Liberty Hall during that dispute:

> At that time I belonged to the respectable middle class and I did not dare admit to my home circle that I had run with the crowd to hear Jim Larkin, and crept like a culprit into Liberty Hall to see Madame Markievicz in a big overall, with sleeves rolled up, presiding over a cauldron of stew, surrounded by a crowd of gaunt women and children carrying bowls and cans.[16]

In 1915, Helena Molony took over Delia Larkin's role in the IWWU. Molony, feminist, separatist and officer in the Irish Citizen Army, worked closely with James Connolly in promoting the IWWU, and in organising a women's co-op run from Liberty Hall. Shortly before the 1916 Rising Molony sought the help of suffragist Louie Bennett in re-organising the IWWU. Following Molony's request, Bennett had a 'warm discussion' with Connolly during which she argued against his mixing of nationalist and labour ideals. Although anxious to help, Bennett made it clear that as a pacifist she could not support any organisation threatening force.[17] Imprisoned after the Rising of 1916, Molony made a further appeal to Bennett for help with the IWWU. This time Bennett responded positively, and in August 1916 she and Helen Chenevix attended the Trade Union Congress in Sligo. From that time she became identified with the work of the IWWU, an association that would continue for the next forty years. Molony re-joined the union executive following her release from prison. Together Bennett, Chenevix and Molony would form a formidable triumvirate on behalf of women workers.

How did the political wing of the labour movement view feminist ideals and co-operation with the suffrage movement? At the 1912 Irish Trade Union Congress (ITUC) a motion demanding adult suffrage, proposed by Larkin and seconded by William O'Brien, exposed the divisions beneath the surface. One delegate agreed that a woman's status as a wage earner should be raised, but feared that granting the vote would 'tend to take away from the peace of the home' resulting in 'the destruction of that nobility of character for which their women were prized'[18]. Hanna Sheehy Skeffington noted that 'organised labour wanted women to help them press for adult suffrage, ridiculing women's suffrage as "votes for ladies"'.[19] There was some justification for that accusation, as the existing franchise was property based and, if extended, would only benefit middle class women. At the 1914 ITUC there was disagreement on whether a deputation from the IWRL should be admitted to speak on the issue of women's suffrage. James Larkin objected to such a deputation, arguing that 'the suffrage could be used for or against their class'. James Connolly, while noting his preference for the militant wing of suffragism, argued that 'he was out to give women the vote, even if they used it against him as a human right'.[20] Consistently in the pages of the *Irish Citizen* and at meetings of the IWFL and the IWRL the economic position of women was equated with their voteless condition. Connolly continued this theme when he told a meeting of the IWFL:

It was because women workers had no vote that they had not the safeguards even of the laws passed for their protection because these were ignored. They had women working for wages on which a man could not keep a dog. Men's conditions, bad as they were, had been improved because of the vote.[21]

Connolly, described by the *Irish Citizen* as 'the soundest and most thorough going feminist among all the Irish Labour men' was a crucial link between the two movements. At the most difficult time for Irish suffragists – following the 1912 attempts by English suffragettes to attack Prime Minister Asquith during his home rule 'promotional' visit to Dublin – Connolly showed his support for the women's movement by travelling from Belfast to speak at the weekly public meeting of the IWFL, an action long and greatly appreciated by the women. During the following weeks when there was much violence against IWFL public meetings, members of his union, the Irish Transport and General Workers' Union (ITGWU), often protected suffragettes from attack. A regular speaker at suffrage meetings north and south, Connolly told the 1913 ITUC that until women were made equal politically they could only be half free. At a meeting held in the Albert Hall to generate solidarity for the Dublin strikers and to demand the release of the imprisoned Larkin, Connolly was loudly cheered when he declared that he stood for opposition to the domination of nation over nation, class over class, and sex over sex.[22]

In Belfast later, he stressed that agitation for the vote should be accompanied by the more immediate prospect of better working conditions and pay. The *Irish Worker* reported on a series of meetings held to discuss Connolly's ideas, noting that 'labour ideas and ideals are entering in and these meetings will make excellent propaganda'.[23] But propaganda for whom? While individuals within the IWFL and the IWSF brought both groups closer to alliance with Labour, this was due to the beliefs of individual members rather than official policy. Some Belfast suffragists feared that too close an association with Labour might sidetrack their campaign. The question of women's co-operation and involvement with other contemporary movements would prove problematic in Ireland as it had done elsewhere.

In *The re-conquest of Ireland* Connolly wrote that 'the women's cause is felt by all labour men and women as their cause … the labour cause has not more earnest and whole hearted supporters than the militant women'.[24] Certainly, the involvement of young, socialist-oriented feminists in the suffrage campaign from 1908 onwards coincided with a recognition by some labour leaders of common disabilities shared by men and women. As the women's movement organised and radicalised, labour leaders saw its potential as an ally. The most positive influence of both groups can be found in the wording of the 1916 Proclamation, which was addressed to both Irish men and women and guaranteed equal rights and opportunities to all citizens. The other main area of influence between the two groups was the movement of women from the suffrage into the labour movement.

FEMINISM AND NATIONALISM

In states struggling for national self-determination feminists often subordi-
nated their own aims to those of the parent nationalist movement.[25]

By 1913 there were eighteen suffrage societies in Ireland, catering for women of varying political, social and religious backgrounds. Yet, as was pointed out in the *Irish Citizen* that year, there was still no distinct nationalist women's franchise association. Existing suffrage groups had been consistently criticised as being mere branches of English societies. While there were some instances where this was the case, generally the newer groups – particularly the IWFL and the IWSF – recognised the need to assert their Irishness and independence from English groups. In fact, many prominent nationalist women were at some stage involved in the suffrage campaign, particularly in the 1908–14 period. Included in this group were women such as Constance Markievicz, Agnes O'Farrelly, Rosamund Jacob, Dr Kathleen Lynn, Mary MacSwiney and Jenny Wyse Power. Initially two strands of nationalism developed amongst such women:

(1) those that supported home rule for Ireland and fought for the recognition of women as voters within the home rule bill; and (2) those who sought complete independence for Ireland, believing that the suffrage struggle should wait until this was achieved. Hanna Sheehy Skeffington, writing in *Bean na hÉireann* in 1909 on 'Sinn Féin and Irishwomen', addressed both groups when she commented that 'until the parliamentarian and the Sinn Féin woman alike possess the vote, the keystone of citizenship, she will count but little with either party'.[26] The 'parliamentarian' woman, who supported the home rule cause, often deliberately refrained from involvement in the suffrage campaign for fear of damaging the

attainment of home rule. However, with home rule apparently assured in 1914, some women felt more confident in airing suffrage views. One such woman, Elizabeth Bloxham, now appealed to John Redmond to ensure that 'home rule would mean freedom for women as well as men'.[27] Mary Hayden also entered the debate in 1914, and sought an amendment to the bill incorporating women's suffrage on the basis of the local government register. Jenny Wyse Power, re-iterating the stance of nationalist women regarding suffrage during the home rule years, noted that:

> Now the situation has quite changed, and those of us who are Irish national-
> ists can only hope that an appeal at this time of the extension of the suffrage to
> Irishwomen will not fall on unheeding ears [and] that they may be allowed to
> exercise their right to participate in the government of their own country.[28]

A deputation of militant and non-militant suffragists travelled to London to petition for such an amendment, but neither Redmond nor Asquith would receive them.

From this point on, it was the growing separatist movement that most threatened the unity of the women's movement in Ireland. While the *Irish Citizen* argued 'there can be no free nation without free women', the counter argument was made 'neither can there be free women in an enslaved nation'.[29] This argument had been made over the past five years by the second group of 'nationalist' women – those who sought full independence over home rule. Amongst this group, criticism was directed not against the principle of women's suffrage, but against the propriety of Irish women seeking the vote from an English government. Most advocated equality, but believed it would follow automatically on political independence. The 'suffrage first before all else' policy of the *Irish Citizen* led to much conflict with those with different priorities. Agnes O'Farrelly, a member of the Gaelic League and a suffragist, articulated this disagreement from the nationalist side:

> Are we or are we not fighting for the vote before all other things? Some of us
> certainly are not. Keenly anxious as we are for the ordinary rights of citizen-
> ship for ourselves, we give woman suffrage second place to ... some measure
> of freedom – for, at all events, the men of our own country.[30]

Similarly, Rosamund Jacob, another suffragist member of the Gaelic League, and later of Cumann na mBan, wrote:

Political rights conferred on Irishwomen by a foreign government would be a miserable substitute for the same rights won, even three years later, from our own legislative assembly.[31]

Prior to the *Irish Citizen* there had been an earlier Irish women's paper, *Bean na hÉireann*, published between 1909–11 by Inghinidhe na hÉireann (Daughters of Erin), a nationalist women's group with a strong feminist bias. Many issues covered by *Bean na hÉireann* were similar to those later covered by the *Irish Citizen*. That there was concern about the status of women among some nationalist women had been clear from the pages of *Bean na hÉireann*. Its editor, Helena Maloney, stated: 'We wanted it to be "a woman's paper", advocating militancy, separatism and feminism.' In its pages the views of nationalist women on the suffrage issue were made quite clear. An editorial in 1909 declared that:

> We do not refuse to join the women's franchise movement, but we decline to join with parliamentarians and unionists in trying to force a bill through Westminster. We prefer to try and organise a woman's movement on Sinn Féin lines. Freedom for our nation and the complete removal of all disabilities to our sex will be our battlecry.[32]

Correspondence to the journal voiced many similar arguments:

> The women of Irish Ireland have the franchise, and it would be only humiliating themselves and their country to appeal or even demand the endorsement of a hostile parliament. They stand on equal footing with the men in the Gaelic League, in Sinn Féin, and the industrial movement. They are represented on the executives of all these, and under the present circumstances we should be content to regard these as representing Irish government.[33]

Women in the suffrage movement and those represented by *Bean na hÉireann* shared many basic feminist principles on the role and position of women. *Bean na hÉireann* advocated the unionisation of women workers, discussed the migration of Irish women from the farm, and reported progress on the women's suffrage movement abroad. But it was on the precise issue of agitation for parliamentary suffrage from 'an alien government' that sharp differences arose:

> As our country has had her freedom and her nationhood taken from her

by England, so also our sex is denied emancipation and citizenship by the same enemy. So therefore the first step on the road to freedom is to realise ourselves as Irishwomen – not only as Irish or merely as women, but as Irishwomen doubly enslaved, and with a double battle to fight.[34]

Relations between 'separatist nationalists' and sufffage groups became more strained from 1914. The formation of Cumann na mBan in April 1914 crystallised the differences between those who sought national freedom first and equal rights second, and those who sought 'suffrage first before all else'. At the formation of the Irish Volunteers in November 1913 its general secretary had indicated that there would be work for women to do in the organisation. What would be the nature of this work? When the issue of women's role within the Volunteers had been raised with Pádraig Pearse, he had confessed that they had been so busy organising and drilling the men, they had not had time to consider in any detail what work women might do, but he indicated:

First of all there will be ambulance and Red Cross work for them, and then I think a women's rifle club is desirable. I would not like the idea of women drilling and marching in the ordinary way but there is no reason why they should not learn to shoot.[35]

An article in the *Irish Volunteer* early in 1914 suggested that women could do their duty within the movement by forming an ambulance corps, learning first aid, making flags and doing any necessary embroidery work on badges and uniforms, the writer asking: 'To a patriotic Irishwoman could there be any work of more intense delight than this?'[36] Shortly afterwards the organisation of women supporters of the Volunteers emerged in Dublin. The first public meeting of the Irish Women's Council, afterwards known as Cumann na mBan, was held in Wynn's hotel in April 1914, presided over by Agnes O'Farrelly. The first task they set themselves, the initiation of a defence of Ireland fund for arming and equipping the Volunteers, unleashed a torrent of criticism from suffrage campaigners. The pages of the *Irish Citizen* became the scene of a bitter war of words between women activists on both sides. Days after the inaugural meeting of Cumann na mBan, an *Irish Citizen* editorial criticised:

The slavish attitude of a group of women who have just formed an 'Irish Women's Council', not to take any forward action themselves, but to help the men of the Irish Volunteers to raise money for their equipment, in generally toady to them as the Ulster unionist women have done to the Ulster Volunteers.[37]

This latter comment referred to the Ulster Women's Unionist Council (UWUC), which had been formed in 1911 'with the incipient intent of supporting male unionists' opposition to home rule for Ireland'.[38] The *Irish Citizen* editorial continued that 'such women deserve nothing but contempt, and will assuredly earn it'. Such strong criticism engendered counter-criticism. Mary MacSwiney, who had resigned from the suffrage movement in Cork because of the Munster Women's Franchise League (MWFL)'s involvement in war work, wrote to the *Irish Citizen*, accusing the paper of alienating nationalists from the suffrage cause, an argument agreed with by Helena Molony. In the *Freeman's Journal* Hanna Sheehy Skeffington, reporting on a recent Cumann na mBan meeting she had attended, commented:

> Any society of women which proposes to act merely as an 'animated collecting box' for men cannot have the sympathy of any self-respecting woman. The proposed 'Ladies Auxiliary Committee' has apparently no function beyond that of a conduit pipe to pour a stream of gold into the coffers of the male organisation, and to be turned off automatically as soon as it has served this mean and subordinate purpose.[39]

In the *Irish Independent*, Máire Ní Chillín replied to Sheehy Skeffington's arguments, stating:

> The Volunteers have not sought our help. We give it freely and ungrudgingly. There is a large class of Irishwomen who believe that they are represented at the polls and on the battlefields by their husbands, fathers or sons, who want neither vote, nor rifle, nor stone to help them in asserting their rights, who are willing to act as conduit pipes or collecting boxes or armour polishers, or do any other good thing that would help on the cause.[40]

While many key women involved in establishing Cumann na mBan would not have agreed with this statement, the nature of the organisation left it open to charges of passivity. Two of its founders, Mary Colum and Louise Gavan Duffy, attempted to clarify this situation in the *Irish Independent*. Pointing out that their organisation was in no sense a ladies auxiliary society, that it was an entirely distinct organisation from the Irish Volunteers with its own committee and constitution, and its own objects of organising women towards the advancement of Irish liberty, they declared:

> We are a nationalist women's political organisation and we propose to engage in any patriotic work that comes within the scope of our objects and constitution. We consider at the moment that helping to equip the Irish Volunteers is the most necessary national work. We may mention that many of the members of our society are keen suffragists, but as an organisation we must confine ourselves within the four walls of our constitution.[41]

The core disagreement between suffragists and nationalist women in the pre-1916 scenario would appear to have been summed up in a letter to the *Irish Citizen* by Kathleen Connery of the IWFL that stated:

> If there is ignorance of the suffrage to be overcome in Ireland, it is that type of ignorance which has its roots in a false conception of freedom and nationhood, and which is unable to grasp the simple fact that the freedom of Irish womanhood is a vital and indispensable factor in true Irish nationhood, not a mere trifling side issue to be settled anyhow or anytime at the convenience of men.[42]

Post-1916

Later political developments would bring the two groups closer together. The cumulative effect of the 1916 rebellion, the killing of Francis Sheehy Skeffington, and the execution of republican leaders followed by the mass imprisonment of republican activists, all had a profound effect on women's organisations. Although the 1916 Proclamation had been addressed to Irishmen and Irishwomen, and guaranteed equal rights and opportunities to all citizens, events were to prove that some Irish men needed reminding of these points. Neither the Proclamation nor the imminent passage of a British bill giving votes to women over thirty ensured that the way was now clear for women in public life. Following Sinn Féin victories at three by-elections in 1917, a conference held to unite the various groupings identified with Sinn Féin appointed a central steering committee of nine, one of whom was a woman, Josephine Mary Plunkett. Shortly afterwards women delegates to that conference held a meeting of their own. This meeting was attended by women from Inghinidhe na hÉireann, Cumann na mBan, the IWWU, and the Irish Citizen Army.[43]

When the question of suffrage was raised, it was pointed out that Sinn Féin candidates at the recent by-elections had taken their stand on the 1916 Proclamation which granted equal rights to all citizens; therefore, agitation for the vote was not deemed necessary as 'the vote had already been granted to Irishwomen by Irishmen'. However, with the expansion of the original Sinn Féin committee of nine to include released Sinn Féin prisoners, women delegates met with resistance to their request for increased representation. A letter from the women to the Sinn Féin executive stated:

> ... [our claim] to be represented is based mainly on the republican Procla-mation of Easter week 1916, which of course you are determined to uphold, [and] on the risks women took, equally with the men, to have the Irish Republic established.[44]

Their request was refused. The group considered sending a deputation to Sinn Féin, but initially decided against this, believing that 'women have applied to them often enough and the matter should be left for Cumann na mBan for the present to see what they could do'.[45] Cumann na mBan, however, had also been refused representation. Records of the women delegates' group indicate that an article written by Dr Kathleen Lynn at this time, urging women to assert their political rights, had been sent to *Nationality* but not published. Eventually the women did form a deputation to the Sinn Féin executive who agreed to co-opt four women, on condition that none of them represent any organisation and that all be members of a Sinn Féin branch.[46] The four women so co-opted were Jenny Wyse Power, Áine Ceannt, Helena Molony and Mimi Plunkett. A resolution was prepared by the women for consideration at a national convention of Sinn Féin in October 1917. This strongly worded resolution referred unambiguously to the clauses of the republican Proclamation which had guaranteed equal rights and opportunities to all citizens, and equality of women with men in all branches and executive bodies, asking that 'the equality of men and women in this organisation be emphasised in all speeches, leaflets and pamphlets'.[47]

Before the convention the women considered circularising Sinn Féin members already proposed for the new executive regarding their atti-tudes to that paragraph in the Proclamation, but decided not to 'for fear that it would weaken our case to appear to think that there could be any doubt on the point'.[48] After some minor changes the women's resolution was accepted. Four women were elected to the new Sinn Féin executive – Constance Markievicz, Dr Kathleen Lynn, Kathleen Clarke and Grace Plunkett. The *Irish Citizen* congratulated delegates to the convention for 'embodying in their new constitution, in the most unequivocal terms, the democratic principle of the complete equality of men and women in Ireland'.[49] The paper regretted there was so few women delegates, and hoped to see this inequality rectified at future conventions. At this stage the women delegates organised themselves formally into Cumann na dTeachtaire, a society to consist of women delegates to all future conferences held by Irish republicans. Its aims were: to safeguard the political rights of Irishwomen; to ensure adequate representation for them in the republican government; to urge and facilitate the appointment of women to public boards throughout the country; and to educate Irish women in the rights and duties of citizenship.[50]

The formation of this society was most significant. Many of its members had been active in some aspect of the suffrage campaign, and in many ways it appears to have filled a void for committed nationalist feminists. Its formation at this particular time indicates unease amongst such women about their role in the emerging new Ireland. Later events would prove that such unease was not unfounded.

Post-1916 a new co-operative spirit emerged between various women's groups. A number of factors contributed to this. The constitution of Cumann na dTeachtaire noted its preparedness to confer with other women's groups 'whenever it can be accomplished without sacrifice of principle [as] the bringing together of all Irishwomen to discuss matters of common interest on a neutral platform could not but be beneficial to all'.[51] Links between the suffrage and labour movements were strengthened when Louie Bennett took over the running of both the IWWU and the *Irish Citizen*, resulting in increased coverage of labour issues. The IWFL in particular was close to Cumann na dTeachtaire – in many cases women were members of both – and even the more conservative IWSLGA had links with the new nationalist group, again through some joint membership. Increasingly, the pages of the *Irish Citizen* showed a more nationalist bias, supporting the demand for political status for republican prisoners, and condemning forcible feeding. Both Cumann na dTeachtaire and the IWWU adopted St Brigid as their patron, the former declaring that 'such a good suffragist should get recognition'.[52]

A number of significant issues emerged in 1918 that led to much co-operation between women's groups. Chief among these was the attempt to introduce conscription into Ireland that year. Among the many meetings and demonstrations organised against this measure was a mass meeting of women at Dublin's Mansion House, at which women from Cumann na mBan, the IWFL, and other women's organisations pledged resistance.[53] The other major issue on which women's groups co-operated was the campaign against venereal disease and the related implementation of regulation 40d under the Defence of the Realm Act (DORA). In 1907 Arthur Griffith had drawn attention to British army medical reports that confirmed that there was a higher incidence of venereal disease among soldiers in Dublin than elsewhere in the United Kingdom.[54] Concern amongst women's groups about the issue had been evident for some time in the pages of the *Irish Citizen*. In March 1918 Cumann na dTeachtaire organised a conference of women's societies to consider 'this serious menace', which it noted 'was a matter on which women of every shade of political opinion could unite to discuss the best measures to combat this evil'.[55] The implementation of regulation 40d of DORA in August 1918 'to safeguard the health of soldiers' was denounced by the *Irish Citizen* as an attempt to revive the notorious contagious diseases acts which had been repealed in 1886 following strenuous agitation by Irish and English suffragists.[56] Under its terms any woman could be arrested by the police 'on suspicion' and detained until proven innocent by medical examination. A woman could also be held by police on a verbal charge made by a soldier. Some weeks later, the *Irish Citizen* reported the first case taken in Ireland under the Act – that of a Belfast woman given six months hard labour 'for communicating disease' to a Canadian soldier. Deploring the one-sided and discriminatory nature of this regulation, the paper concluded that the real purpose of the Act was 'to make the practice of vice safe for men by degrading and befouling women'.[57] Again, women's groups came together to protest against what the IWFL described as 'the state regulation of vice'. During 1918 co-operation between women's groups was at its highest since 1912. In their emphasis on promoting the political education of women, legislation for the benefit of women, the election of women to government, local boards and councils, all these organisations shared similar objectives.

1918 proved a watershed for the women's movement in Ireland. That year women over thirty years with certain property qualifications obtained the parliamentary vote, thereby achieving the primary aim of suffrage groups while removing the one goal common to all. At the same time the vote was also extended to men of twenty one years. The age provision avoided the immediate establishment of a female majority in the electorate, particularly significant in a population depleted by huge troop losses during the Great War. Despite its limitations, the franchise extension created a demand for more female involvement in national affairs. With a forthcoming general election, the *Irish Citizen* reported that women were much in demand as speakers on party platforms, noting the disappearance of posters such as that formerly published by the Irish party reading 'Public admitted – ladies excluded'.[58] The Labour party was the first to nominate a woman candidate (Louie Bennett) for the election, although she did not run.[59] Sinn Féin also sought the support of the new women voters, asking Irish women to 'vote as Mrs Pearse will vote', promising that 'as in the past, so in the future the womenfolk of the Gael shall have high place in the councils of a freed Gaelic nation'.[60]

This is not quite the way things worked out! Even before the election, there were signs that all was not well. At a 1917 Sinn Féin convention, two resolutions were proposed asking that no candidate be selected for any by-election 'other than a man who took part in the fight of Easter Week'.[61] When the precise question of women candidates in the general election was raised, Sinn Féin's standing committee vacillated as to whether it would be legal. In the event, the party ran only two female candidates – Constance Markievicz in Dublin and Winifred Carney in Belfast – leading the *Irish Citizen* to comment caustically that 'it looks as if Irishmen (even republicans) need teaching in this matter'.[62] Women in fact played a crucial role in this election, both as voters and as party workers, a fact acknowledged by Sinn Féin when they sought 'a woman speaker' for their victory celebrations in Pembroke division. Their request to Hanna Sheehy Skeffington in this regard was made 'in view of the fact that the women voters were the most important factor in our polling district'.[63] In addition to the Sinn Féin landslide victory at that election, there was another particularly sweet victory for Irish women. Although she never took her seat, Constance Markievicz became the first female MP elected to the British House of Commons. Commenting on the 1918 election results, the IWFL noted:

Under the new dispensation the majority sex in Ireland has secured one representative. This is the measure of our boasted sex equality. The lesson the election teaches us is that reaction has not died out with the Irish party – and the IWFL, which has been so faithful to feminist ideals, must continue to fight and expose reaction in the future as in the past.[64]

What was of particular concern to feminists, however, was the fact that, unlike the women of Cumann na dTeachtaire, so few republican women post-1916 held or articulated feminist ideals. In 1917 an article in the *Irish Citizen* highlighted a key weakness in the attitude of many Irish women:

> Many of you stand aloof from feminism because of the political movement. But you have not justified your abstention from the women's struggle by becoming a force within the new movement. You are in revolt against a subjection imposed from without, but you are tacitly acquiescing in a position of inferiority within.

It went on to warn that:

> If in the course of time the new national movement becomes wholly masculine and stereotyped ... you cannot escape your share of responsibility for such a disastrous state of things. If you leave men alone to carry out the task of national creative endeavour, you will have no right to complain later that there are flaws in construction.[65]

To the number of women involved in the nationalist movement before and during the Rising of 1916, many thousands more were added in its wake. From this point up to the bitter political divisions caused by the Treaty in 1921–2, such women played a significant role in the development of the emerging state. Whereas many nationalist women active before 1916 held feminist beliefs, opting to put equality demands 'on hold' until independence was attained, most of those who joined post-1916 did so primarily on nationalist grounds. Although young women now flocked in their thousands to join the organisation, few articulated feminist concerns. Both Rosamund Jacob and Hanna Sheehy Skeffington were concerned at the 'lack of feminism among Sinn Fein women in the provinces'.[66] Cumann na dTeachtaire can be seen as an attempt by some nationalist women to bring feminism within their political remit. In the aftermath of 1916, with large-scale imprisonment of male republicans, Cumann na mBan took on a more active and aggressive role. Its work on behalf of prisoners' dependants, and its determined and focused propaganda campaign to keep the memory and ideals of the executed leaders constantly before the public eye, led Brian Farrell to note that in the year after the Rising 'it was the women who were the national movement'.[67]

As late as 1919 however, the *Irish Citizen* was still critical of Cumann na mBan's status within the republican movement:

> The women are emphatically not a force in the popular movement – they have no status and no influence in its local councils ... and are looked upon rather in the light of an ornamental trimming – useful to give a picturesque touch on occasion and, of course to carry on the traditional role of auxiliaries which so many generations of slave women have been content to accept.[68]

Margaret Ward has pointed out that while Hanna Sheehy Skeffington joined Sinn Féin in 1918, she did not join Cumann na mBan, believing that 'it had not shaken off its auxiliary to the men's status'.[69] In the final issue of the *Irish Citizen* in 1920, Hanna Sheehy Skeffington commented: 'There can be no woman's paper without a woman's movement, without earnest and serious-minded women readers and thinkers – and these in Ireland have dwindled perceptively of late.'[70]

Suffragists had always maintained that possession of the parliamentary vote would give women the power to influence government. That influence – or perhaps fear of that influence – was very real in the early days of the new state. Adult suffrage had been included in the 1916 Proclamation and, in the spirit of that Proclamation, was included in the Irish Free State constitution of 1922, under provisions of which all citizens of twenty one years and upwards were enfranchised. This last phase of franchise extension to women, however, was not attained without a final struggle. During the acrimonious Treaty debates of the Second Dáil in 1921–2, the issue of women's suffrage received heated discussion. Until the provisions of the proposed constitution became law, only women of thirty years could vote. Both pro- and anti-Treaty sides claimed the support of the majority of Irish women, yet it would appear that, as in 1918 when John Redmond's party had feared the effect of a new female electorate, now the pro-Treaty side feared the effect of granting adult suffrage to all citizens over twenty one years. The vociferous anti-Treaty reactions of many women within the nationalist movement, including the majority of Cumann na mBan, did little to reassure them in this regard. Ward has pointed out that 'for feminists, women's issues were firmly back on the agenda'.[71]

In March 1922 pro-Treaty women formed an organisation – Cumann na Saoirse (League of Freedom) – to publicise their position. Keen to play a role in the establishment of the new state, the group included many wives and relatives of Free State government members.[72] The force-ful commitment of women on both sides of the Treaty issue left a bitter legacy for many years. In particular, the role of republican women during the civil war was viewed by Free State supporters as unwomanly, turning them into 'unlovely, destructive minded, arid begetters of violence'.[73] In 1924 P.S. O'Hegarty declared that during the civil war 'Dublin was full of hysterical women [who] became practically unsexed, their mother's milk blackened to make gunpowder, their minds working on nothing save hate and blood'. On the other hand he argued:

> Left to himself, man is comparatively harmless. He will always exchange smokes and drinks and jokes with his enemy, and he will always pity the 'poor devil' and wish that the whole business was over.... It is woman ... with her implacability, her bitterness, her hysteria, that makes a devil of him. The suf-fragettes used to tell us that with women in political power there would be no more war. We know that with women in political power there would be no more peace.[74]

Were women in political power? From the perspective of one writing of a newly born state in which equality of citizenship was included in the constitution, it may indeed have appeared so. It was not long before the issue was put to the test.

WOMEN AND THE IRISH FREE STATE

The equality of rights and opportunities of all citizens guaranteed in the 1916 Proclamation had been endorsed in the Free State constitution of 1922. Yet early hopes that women would play a significant role in the new Ireland were soon quashed as a series of restrictive measures were introduced by government.

The first intimation that was given of such intent came in 1924 when a juries bill was introduced providing for the exemption of women from jury service on application. Women's groups were alarmed at the proposal to exempt women purely on the grounds of sex, arguing that to allow women to evade the duties and responsibilities of citizenship was 'unfair to the men citizens and derogatory to the women'. They denounced this 'retrograde step' which, they feared, 'would open the door a little wider to the forces of reaction'.[75] Their fears were justified. 1925 saw the introduction of the Civil Service Regulation (Amendment) bill, and 1927 a further Juries bill, both designed to curtail the role of women. The former was an attempt to restrict women from entering higher-ranking civil service posts solely on the grounds of sex, while the latter proposed to exempt women completely from jury service.

In the Seanad both Eileen Costello and Jennie Wyse-Power (Cumann na nGaedhael) strongly opposed the Civil Service Regulation (Amendment) bill. In her trenchant opposition to the bill Wyse-Power pointed to the unjustness of this 'sex discrimination [being] made by a male Executive Council and by practically a male Dáil' without any consultation with any women.[76] Drawing on her long involvement in nationalist politics, she noted the changing response to women's participation in public affairs, regretting that such a bill had come 'from the men who were associated in the fight [for freedom] with women when sex and money were not considerations'.

The Juries bill of 1927 provides a keen insight into the attitude of the Free State government towards the participation of women in public life. The Minister for Justice Kevin O'Higgins' view was quite clear in articulating separate spheres for men and women. In the Dáil debate he argued that 'a few words in a constitution do not wipe out the difference between the sexes, either physical or mental or temperamental or emotional'.[77] In the Seánad he described women's reproductive capacity as 'women performing the normal functions of womanhood in the state's economy'.[78] Consistently in both Dáil and Seánad the government saw no contradiction in taking away from women rights which they already enjoyed under the constitution. Inside and outside parliament, women who demanded the right to jury service became increasingly categorised as 'abnormal', with 'normal' women being defined as those who accepted that their primary role was within the home. It was argued in the Dáil that:

> Between the ages of twenty and forty the majority of women … [have] a much more important duty to perform to the state than service on juries, that their functions were motherhood and looking after their families, and they objected to these other women, who have missed these functions, and who wanted to drive to serve on juries those who have something else to do.[79]

As a result of the women's campaign and strong opposition within the Seanad, the government accepted an amendment to the bill which, although exempting women as a class from jury service, allowed individual women to have their names included on jury lists on application. Male ratepayers would be automatically called for jury service, women ratepayers would be eligible but had to volunteer. In this form the bill became law and remained in force until 1976.

These bills did not take place in isolation. Rather, they were introduced against a backdrop of social restrictions implemented during the first fifteen years of the Irish Free State focusing on censorship and control. The legislation of the 1920s regarding women's role in society was but a foretaste of what would follow during the following decade.

The 1930s saw the introduction of significant social and employment legislation that would impinge on Irish women for some forty years. The Criminal Law (Amendment) Act of 1935 dealt with the age of consent, contraception and prostitution. A significant consequence of the debate on the issues contained in the bill – and of unease at the resulting legislation amongst women's groups – was the formation in March 1935 of the Joint Committee of Women's Societies and Social Workers (JCWSSW).[80] Women's employment was the initial focus of legislation during the 1930s. A ban on married female primary school teachers in 1932 was followed six years later with all women teachers being compelled to retire at age sixty rather than sixty five. A similar marriage bar was soon applied to the civil service. Pointing out that this measure was also detrimental to single women, by ruining their promotional prospects, Mary Kettle, a consistent campaigner for the removal or modification of the ban, argued that 'women from their entry [to the service] until they reach the ages of 45 or 50 are looked on as if they were loitering with intent to commit a felony – the felony in this case being marriage'.[81]

Within the labour and trade union movement post-1916 women activists also had to maintain vigilance regarding their status. Louie Bennett was among those whose close identification with Labour did not inhibit criticism where she felt it necessary. During the Irish Convention of 1917, she reported in the *Irish Citizen*:

> When Labour Sunday was celebrated in Dublin a few weeks ago, no woman was invited to stand on the platform by the Labour party. The women of Ireland might have all been free to enjoy the comforts of a home, a fireside, and a cradle to rock for all the interest the Labour party of Ireland manifested in their affairs.[82]

Following the passing of the Representation of the People Act in 1918, which granted the parliamentary vote to women over thirty, Bennett was nominated to stand for the 1918 general election. The *Irish Citizen* congratulated the Irish Labour party on being the first political party to choose a woman candidate. However, reporting on the local elections of the following year, Hanna Sheehy Skeffington noted that 'official Labour has the unenviable distinction of entirely ignoring women on their ticket'.[83] The attitude of the Labour party did little to encourage change. Describing overtures made to the party from the IWWU in 1923, Jones has noted that 'articulate women trade unionists found only a measured welcome'.[84]

Late in 1919 a lively debate took place between Bennett and Cissie Cahalan of the DAA in the pages of the *Irish Citizen* on the issue of single sex unions versus one big union. Advocating separate organisation, Bennett argued that it was futile to deny latent antagonism between the sexes in industry, commenting:

> There is a disposition amongst men workers not only to keep women in inferior and subordinate positions, but to drive them out of industry altogether. So long as women occupy a subordinate position within the trade union movement they will need the safeguard of an independent organisation.[85]

Cissie Cahalan, one of the few examples of working class involvement in the Irish suffrage movement, defended the concept of mixed trade unions. She laid the blame for the under-involvement of women on their own shoulders, arguing that women's reluctance to go forward as candidates for branch or executive committees left the management of trade unions in male hands.[86]

The arguments raised in this debate continued for many years, Bennett's involvement within the trade union movement reinforcing her beliefs. In 1930 she noted that, but for the IWWU, a woman's voice was rarely heard at trades union congress or trades council. Cissie Cahalan, writing in the same journal as Bennett, observed that it was 'deplorable to find men who still think of woman as the enemy – and shut their eyes to the real barrier to a full and complete life for all – the capitalist class'.[87] Helena Molony likewise concluded that working women had made little progress since Connolly's time, pointing out that women were still excluded from certain industries because of their gender, and that a woman's wage was still only 20 to 30 per cent of a man's average wage.[88] Writing in the *Dublin labour year book* of 1930 Bennett, Molony and Cahalan each addressed the issue of women in the political wing of labour. All were unhappy with that role. Molony, referring to the 'sorry travesty of emancipation', advised women and the labour movement to reflect on Connolly's writings and beliefs. Bennett noted that, despite the fact that women made up 50 per cent of the electorate, political parties still treated them as a side issue and women themselves made little use of their political power. She commented that politically the labour movement was completely in the hands of men, and it was evident that working class women did not desire to be so involved. In a similar vein, Cahalan noted that there was not one female labour representative in the Dáil or Seanad. She observed that this reflected the situation of women within the labour movement itself, pointing to the few women delegates appointed to the male dominated Irish Labour Party and Trade Union Congress (ILPTUC).

From 1934 attention focused on Seán Lemass' forthcoming Conditions of Employment bill. The ostensible aim of the 1936 Conditions of Employment Act was to improve working conditions by imposing a maximum forty eight hour working week, guarantee one week's paid holiday, and establish controls regarding overtime.[89] As such, it was in line with international labour office policy. But the Act, which had been drafted by the minister following detailed consultation with male trade union leaders, gave him power under section sixteen to prohibit and/ or control the employment of women in certain industries. The IWWU sought and was refused consultative status in its framing.[90]

The campaign by the IWWU against the implementation of section sixteen of the Act was carried out within the trade union movement, on the political front, and in the public arena through the media and public meetings.[91] Within the trade union and labour movement, the women's case received little if any support. Male trade union leaders supported the proposed legislation, viewing with alarm rising male unemployment figures. The IWWU sought the support of male trade unionists in its campaign. Debate on the issue at the ITUC in August 1935 showed the extent of trade union hostility to any amendment. William O'Brien of the ITGWU revealed that section sixteen had been framed in response to a request by his union's national executive. In the ensuing debate most speakers argued that the replacement of male workers by lower paid female workers provided justification that men should benefit under the Act.[92] Generally it was felt to be 'a very wrong thing that young girls should be sent into factories and young men kept out'.

The congress secretary argued that while the Labour movement generally was in favour of equality, increasing mechanisation, which facilitated the replacement of male workers with cheaper female workers, posed a dilemma. He, along with the majority of members, believed that the needs of male workers should be prioritised to preserve the greater good of working people generally. Defending the right of man as breadwinner, one speaker enthusiastically declared: 'Woman is the queen of our hearts and of our homes, and for God's sake let us try to keep her there.'[93] Helena Molony, in a scathing reply, deplored 'such reactionary opinions expressed ... by responsible leaders of Labour in support of a capitalist minister'.[94] The Labour leader, William Norton, was adamant in his opposition to the IWWU, citing Molony's assertion of women's right to be carpenters and blacksmiths as proof of a wish by women workers to displace men. A memorandum sent to the Women's Consultative Committee at Geneva by Bennett, regarding Irish women's expectation that a native government would have ensured female equality with men, commented that while initially this appeared to have been achieved, 'more recent legislation shows a violent movement in the opposite direction, depriving women of fundamental liberties'.[95]

Bennett sent a copy of this memorandum to President de Valera, who subsequently met a deputation of women to discuss the status of women in the Free State. The success of this meeting can be gauged from Bennett's report to the IWWU executive that the President 'could not see how men and women could be equal'.[96] In the Dáil none of the three female TDs spoke for or against the proposed bill.[97] On the other hand, as before, female senators were most vocal in their opposition. When it came to an attack on the rights of women old political adversaries such as Jenny Wyse-Power and Kathleen Clarke buried their differences.[98] Wyse-Power recalled the hopes of those young girls who had lost their jobs following the 1916 Rising, but who had faith that 'when our own men are in power, we shall have equal rights'. Clarke, responding to the accusation that 'the feminists have run riot' over the bill, stated that although she was sympathetic to the feminist movement, 'her opposition to section 16 of the bill was based on nationalist grounds, and specifically on the 1916 Proclamation which granted equal rights to all citizens'. Both women criticised Labour party support for the bill, Clarke wondering what Connolly's attitude would be, and pointing out that the proposed 'very dangerous' legislation represented 'the thin end of the wedge against women'.[99]

The 1936 Act had been drafted by Seán Lemass following detailed consultation with male trade union leaders who roundly supported the power given by this Act to the minister to regulate or prohibit women workers. The trade union movement during the years following independence reflected the dominant values, the prevailing ethos of the time, in placing emphasis on the family unit, not on individual rights. Confronted with the power of both a trade union movement and a government that was predominantly male both in membership and leadership, women workers and their organisation were vulnerable and restricted in their options. By 1937 the Irish Free State was placed on a blacklist at the international labour organisation.[100]

Why were the first governments of the independent state so determined to keep women out of the public life of the nation? What economic determination justified the removal of jury rights from women? Was the conservatism of the new state as reflected in these Acts unique to a small predominantly Catholic country recently emerged from civil war? On the contrary, similar conservative attitudes emerged worldwide following the 1914–18 war.[101] In the immediate post-war situation, emphasis hinged on population issues and on the need to reverse the fall in birth rates. Pro-family campaigns were initiated in almost all European countries, emphasis being placed on women's reproductive role. The dominant political ideologies of the decades following the Great War agreed that the role of women was within the family, developing 'the cult of the cradle'.[102] Suffrage activity had ceased in many countries during the war years, with voting rights being granted to most women post-war. The absence of a focused women's movement in the post-war years allied to national governments' emphasis on retrenchment and rebuilding helped the promotion of women's family role. The predominance of conservative values during these years was strengthened by Catholic social thought and emergent fascism, both of which had fixed views regarding the role of women. Within an Irish context, Margaret O'Callaghan has argued that the Irish hierarchy's revulsion against the anarchy and breakdown of social and familial bonds during the civil war was a strong element in determining the shape and ethos of the Irish Free State.[103]

Given the equality of citizenship and opportunity granted by the 1922 constitution, based on principles drawn from the 1916 Proclamation, and taking account of the high profile of women such as Constance Markievicz, Jennie Wyse Power, Mary McSwiney, Dr Kathleen Lynn, Hanna Sheehy Skeffington and Kathleen Clarke, to name but a few, it was not unreasonable to expect that women would continue to play a prominent and meaningful role in the development of the new state. Yet, as time would show, this period was in fact the peak of women's political involvement until the early 1980s. Factors contributing to this development included the strong anti-Treaty stance of many nationalist women, the lack of a cohesive women's movement post-suffrage, and the development of an authoritarian society with traditional views regarding women's place. Contemporary argument from women's groups during the 1920s and 1930s against restrictive legislation regarding women clearly articulated their concerns. As early as three years into the new state, protesting against the implications of the 1925 Civil Service (Amendment) bill, the Irish Women's Citizens Association (IWCA) argued that the question was one of principle, pointing out that the bill created 'a principle of sex disqualification which does not at present exist in our legislation'.[104] In December 1935 Mary Kettle, in an address to the National University Women Graduates Association (NUWGA), urged her audience to have vigilance regarding the constitutional position of women, noting that while equality of citizenship had been conferred on women through the existing constitution and the Proclamation of 1916, 'men had little by little begun to take away what they had conferred'.[105] As noted above, while female Dáil deputies rarely spoke against any of the restrictive measures discussed earlier, and generally voted with the government of the day, 'the erosion of women's rights drew a united response from politically divided women senators', despite the legacy of deeply-rooted civil war differences.[106]

Were these then the steps that brought about what Mary Robinson has described as 'the non-participation of women in the new Irish state'?[107] For many who had been active within labour, nationalist, and feminist circles, the state that emerged from the mid-1920s became a travesty of what they had expected. Independence quickly saw the silencing of radicalism, particularly in regard to social legislation. Political leaders between 1922 and 1937 displayed an attitude towards the role of women in the new state 'which was as remarkable for its consensus as it was for its conservatism'.[108] In particular, the opposition of Kevin O'Higgins and Éamon de Valera to a public role for women was instrumental in the passing of a series of restrictive legislative measures. From the introduction of the first such measures in the mid-1920s, the clear message to Irish feminists was that 'the struggle for women's equality in the Free State was far from over'.[109] The road map for the role and status of women in Ireland during the first fifty years of the state was established by criteria laid down by church and state during these years. Predominantly during these decades, a male voice – clerical or political – laid down the guidelines and rules to be followed by women. Perhaps the answer lies in a comment made by Margaret Connery in the *Irish Citizen* in 1919:

> Women have very little to hope for from political revolutions. Social revolution offered an opportunity for reforms which go nearer to the heart of things and affect the lives of women more closely than mere political revolutions.[110]

'SHOT IN COLD BLOOD': MILITARY LAW AND IRISH PERCEPTIONS IN THE SUPPRESSION OF THE 1916 REBELLION

Adrian Hardiman

The immediate legal responses of the British authorities to the 1916 rebellion are easily summarised. First the lord lieutenant proclaimed a state of martial law in Dublin and, within hours of that, the government separately took the necessary steps to allow courts martial instead of the ordinary courts to try persons on charges of breaching the Defence of the Realm Regulations (DORR). On the Friday of Easter week General Sir John Maxwell arrived in Ireland as 'military governor' with 'plenary powers *under martial law* [emphasis added] over the whole country, the Irish executive having placed themselves at his disposal to carry out his instructions', as Asquith put it.[1]

As we shall see, by these actions the government brought into simultaneous existence two quite inconsistent legal regimes. This basic contradiction bedevilled both soldiers and politicians for months. For certain prisoners the consequences of the confusion were literally fatal. Maxwell and the government that had appointed him were soon at loggerheads, with the government trying awkwardly and very slowly to claw back the powers given him. Maxwell, in turn, compelled to work under the Defence of the Realm regulations, did so in such a way as to approximate to martial law. The British legal establishment were quickly agreed that in doing so he had acted unlawfully, in particular by conducting the trials in secret. Asquith and later Lloyd George suffered considerable embarrassment and concern on this account until, in 1917, a British court was found patriotic enough to relieve their anxiety in a judgment startlingly devoid of legal merit.

The authorities had a deeper, hidden, anxiety as well. In June 1916 both Asquith and Maxwell promised that the transcripts of the May 1916 courts martial would shortly be published, and that it would then be seen that the verdicts in the capital cases were hugely supported by evidence.

These promises were given in an attempt to counter the growing feeling, not least in America, that the executed rebels had been 'shot in cold blood'. But the army would not allow publication of the (generally very brief) notes of the courts martial, since, in the words of two very senior officers quoted below, 'there are one or two cases in which the evidence is extremely thin' and 'the evidence in some of the cases was far from conclusive'.[2] These are startling admissions.

Under Maxwell's regime over 3,400 people were arrested and 1,841 of these were interned. More dramatically, 183 civilians were tried by court martial, 90 of whom were sentenced to death. Fifteen of these were shot between 3 and 12 May 1916. A sixteenth, Sir Roger Casement, who had been captured in Kerry, was tried for treason by a London jury and was hanged in London on 3 August. Martial law had been proclaimed on 26 April by the lord lieutenant and on the same day legal steps, discussed below, were taken to deny the persons charged in connection with the rebellion the right to jury trial. They were thus (apart from Casement) tried by field general court martial in secret and without defence lawyers.

A field general court martial is a summary form of general court martial: the precise differences are discussed below. For present purposes the important distinction is that the summary procedure required no 'judge advocate' or legally qualified member of the court. There is a striking contrast between the trial of Eoin MacNeill by general court martial, with judge advocate and counsel for the defence, and that of two or three of the executed prisoners. In each case the evidence was 'extremely thin' but MacNeill's life was saved in part due to the need for the verdict to withstand legal scrutiny.

Within a very short time, as both contemporary nationalist and unionist commentators, and historians, attest, there was what General Sir John Maxwell described in June as 'a revulsion of feeling' in favour of the rebels.[3] The unionist historian and Trinity College Dublin Professor W. Alison Phillips, in his *History of the revolution in Ireland*, quotes a confidential police report from Tyrone on the effect of this: 'The Sinn Féiners, from being objects of contempt, became heroes.'[4] There is much debate amongst historians as to the precise reasons for this: Phillips himself ascribed pride of place to Asquith's visit to Ireland in mid-May 1916 and his promise to take steps to allow the home rule Act to be brought into early operation, so that 'the rebellion was thus advertised to the world as the most successful failure in history'.[5] But no one, including Phillips, doubted the effects of the executions. True it is that the *Irish Times* proclaimed to its readers that: 'Martial law has come as a blessing to us all.'[6] But even the official view, privately expressed by Duke (the new chief secretary) in September 1916, was that 'the reaction in popular feeling upon the repression of the rebellion has altered the relations of the extremists to the general population'.[7] W.B. Yeats' poetic expression of the same view is too well known to require quotation.

My purpose is simply to consider the legal framework under which these things, and especially the executions, took place. We will see how prior events shaped that framework, which was quite different to the ordinary legal system of either Britain or Ireland. Unlike previous (1798) and subsequent (1920–1 and 1922–3) executions in time of martial law, no attempt was made at the time to challenge the legality of the 1916 executions and the process which led to them, but I will nonetheless consider their legality in contemporary, as opposed to present day, terms. We will see that the imposition, by proclamation, of martial law was regarded by British politicians principally as an exercise in 'shock and awe' which rebounded badly and from which the government itself was soon in full retreat. But the military men took it seriously and could not understand the increasing dilutions of it that the 'frocks' (as the soldiers contemptuously called the politicians) forced on them. The resulting confusion and ambiguity was literally fatal in some cases.

A number of contemporary sources, notably certain British papers in the de Valera collection deposited in University College Dublin (UCD) Archives, throw fascinating light on the tension between a martial law approach to the suppression of the Rising, favoured by Maxwell and proclaimed by the government, and the approach under the Defence of the Realm Acts which was, for the most part, actually if imperfectly followed.

DEFENCE OF THE REALM ACTS

The 1916 rebellion broke out in the middle of the First World War. At the very beginning of that conflict, in August 1914, the British government had introduced the first of its Defence of the Realm Acts. These constituted as comprehensive a code of extraordinary legislation, including provision for the trial of offences by military courts, as any war leader could desire. But it emphatically was not martial law and in 1914–15 British lawyers and parliamentarians showed themselves surprisingly alive to its civil liberties implications. In the latter year, indeed, an amending Act expressly preserved the right to jury trial, but this provision itself could be dispensed with in certain circumstances. The central provision of the Defence of the Realm Act (DORA) laws as they were known, permitted the making by ministers of a truly enormous number of Defence of the Realm regulations which allowed the government (without recourse to parliament) to control a huge number of aspects of ordinary life 'for securing the public safety and the defence of the realm', as the second amending Act put it.[8] This permitted the creation of a great number of offences which, if committed 'with the intention of assisting the enemy', carried the death penalty. These covered everything from entering prohibited areas or spreading discouraging reports to failing to answer official question and (in the case of a woman who had a social disease) having intercourse with a member of the armed services. More relevant to Ireland, it allowed for banishment from particular areas and the suppression of newspapers. It might be thought that this comprehensive code contained every power necessary for dealing with the 1916 Rising, and indeed it did.

All the 1916 prisoners relevant for our purposes were charged under the regulations that they had 'taken part in an armed rebellion and in the waging of war against His Majesty the King, such act being of such a nature as to be calculated to be prejudicial to the Defence of the Realm and being done with the intention of and for the purpose of assisting the enemy'.[9] There were also less serious charges not immediately relevant for present purposes.

ASPECTS OF THE DORA REGIME

These Acts were not uncontroversial in Britain. On 8 August 1914, just as the war began, the first Defence of the Realm Act was passed. It is barely half a page long in the statute book and relatively modest in the power conferred. It permitted the making of regulations in effect to prevent espionage and sabotage. The amending Act, introduced on 27 November 1914 was much more general in its effect and permitted regulations to be made 'for securing the Public Safety and the Defence of the Realm' and in particular to ensure the success of the war.[10] It was immediately seen that this power was very wide indeed and open to abuse.[11] It was to attempt to conciliate these civil liberties concerns that in the Defence of the Realm (Consolidation) Act, 1915 it was provided in section 1 that:

Any offence against any regulation made under the Defence of the Realm Consolidation Act, 1914, which is triable by court martial may, instead of being tried by court martial, be tried by a civil court with a jury.

However, section 1(7) provided:

In the event of invasion or other special military emergency arising out of the present war, his Majesty may by proclamation forthwith suspend the operation of this section, either generally or as respects any area specified in the proclamation …

It was this section that was operated by proclamation on 26 April 1916, as regards Ireland. The effect of this step was to permit the trial of the prisoners who were charged with breach of regulations by a field general court martial.

A REMARKABLE SOURCE

In considering how these provisions were implemented in Ireland in 1916, we are very fortunate to have a remarkable source in the form of a private memoir, written for his daughter, by W.E. Wylie, who in 1916 was a king's counsel in Dublin and a member of the Trinity College officers' training corps. Wylie prosecuted at many, but not all, of the major courts martial in 1916. He was subsequently appointed law adviser to the Irish government and became a member of the remarkable group of Dublin Castle public servants who in 1920–1, while serving the Crown, took every opportunity to advise and negotiate a settlement. Unlike many persons closely associated with the British regime, Wylie stayed in Ireland after 1922. He had been appointed a judge of the old High Court of Ireland in November 1920 and in 1924 was appointed a judge of the High Court of the Irish Free State. He was also well known for his association with the Royal Dublin Society (RDS) and the equine industry generally, and with the Irish Red Cross. He died in Dublin in 1964.[12]

Wylie, though merely a lieutenant in the military order, was eagerly seized upon by the British military as an experienced and reliable lawyer. He was not, however, a criminal lawyer but rather an expert in local government law. But he had a sound grasp of principle and his courage and fair-mindedness saved the lives of several prisoners, including W.T.

Cosgrave. He was summoned on 1 May 1916 by General Joseph Aloysius Byrne, assistant adjutant general of the forces in Ireland. Their interview took place at midnight and he was told to start the courts martial the following morning at 9am in Richmond Barracks. He asked what charge he was prosecuting and was told, according to his later recollection: 'That's for you. Make out your charge sheet, notify the accused. General Blackadder will act as president of the court. Carry on.' Wylie wryly commented: 'Not much sleep for me that night.'[13]

From this anecdote there emerges clearly the first unusual feature of the courts martial: their extreme rapidity. The first prisoners at any rate (Pearse, MacDonagh and Clarke) must have had virtually no notice of the charge. There was, of course, considerable evidence against these prisoners. Pearse made a speech which constituted not so much an admission as a proud claim to have done what was alleged. MacDonagh and Clarke, according to Wylie, took no part in the proceedings at all.[14]

But the main consequence of the rapidity of the trials was that for the entire week 2–9 May Maxwell was in sole charge of who was tried and what sentences were confirmed. This, literally, was a power of life and death. Asquith expressed surprise at the speed of the first court martial and the three consequent executions but he did not intervene to prevent more executions until 9 May.[15] Even then he did not prevent the executions of those (Connolly and MacDermott) convicted on that day. When on 9 May the government effectively prevented further executions without reference being made to the political authority, Maxwell sought wriggle room. He wrote on that day: 'As far as I can state these will be the last to suffer capital punishment unless of course any cases of proven murder of soldiers or police.'[16]

By now, however, the government was terribly alarmed and replied on the same day. Its position was a somewhat difficult one. It was convinced that the ongoing executions were counter productive, especially in terms of American opinion; but it was unwilling to be seen to give a direct order to a man who less than a fortnight before it had proclaimed as military governor of Ireland with plenary powers under martial law. Accordingly, it wrote on the same day that the ' … cabinet assume that by "proven murder" you mean special cases other than death in the ordinary course of fighting. In all such cases the charge should be, in terms, one of murder'.[17]

This cabinet instruction – for such indeed it was, in reality if not in form – highlights two other aspects of the legal regime generally and of the decision to try the main prisoners under the DORR. Firstly, the powers conferred on the courts martial, and made effective in Ireland by the suspension of the right to jury trial, were very extensive, but only in relation to offences against DORR. 'Ordinary' crimes such as murder, rape, robbery or burglary were not within the scope of the regulations. This, indeed, was dramatically highlighted in the case of Captain Bowen Colthurst, a British officer who murdered Francis Sheehy Skeffington and two others in Portobello Barracks. It was impossible to contemplate a civil trial for him, because he would almost certainly have been convicted of murder. But the lord chief justice of England, the attorney general and solicitor general of England, the judge advocate general and the Irish law officers all opined that he could not be charged by court martial with murder, because it was a civil offence even when committed by a military officer on duty.[18] Accordingly, it would have been quite impossible to charge any rebel prisoner with murder before a court martial whose sole jurisdiction arose from DORA. Bowen Colthurst was eventually court martialled only after Attorney General Campbell had decided to take a chance on the proposition that no-one would challenge it.

The second, even more dramatic, matter revealed by the cabinet's communication of 9 May is that they did not know of this grave limitation on what offences could be tried by court martial under DORA.

Wylie, according to his later memoir, was not in agreement with the shooting of leaders as a general policy. More specifically, he did not agree with the idea of what he called 'drum head' (i.e. summary) courts martial and was further disturbed by the fact that no defence lawyers had been permitted, and by the speed and secrecy of the trials. These factors were to emerge as vital in the political reaction to the Rising and its suppression.

Late on the day of the first courts martial (2 May 1916) Wylie went to see James Campbell KC, the Irish attorney general. Campbell had been an associate of Carson and Birkenhead in the Ulster troubles and had been appointed attorney general (and later lord chancellor) of Ireland as a sop to unionist opinion. Wylie invited him to have the courts martial heard in public and to allow the prisoners to be defended. According to Wylie: 'Campbell would not hear of it. He would give the prisoners no public advertising and would not be satisfied unless forty of them were shot.'[19] In view of these opinions, and of his history in general, it is ironic that Campbell too remained in Ireland after independence, even though his nationalist predecessor as lord chancellor, Ignatius O'Brien, Lord Shandon, departed to England. Wylie's memoir, written at the beginning of the Second World War, comments: 'It amuses me and is illustrative of politics to remember that Campbell, Lord Glenavy as he became, was within a few years to be the chairman of the Irish Free State senate.'[20]

Wylie, I believe, was right in all the reservations he expressed about the court martial procedures. The speed and secrecy of the trials and the failure to allow any account of the evidence to be published gave rise, as Maxwell himself admitted, to a widespread belief that the prisoners had been shot in cold blood. This phrase was used in Maxwell's report to the Prime Minister of 24 June 1916, and independently in the famous denunciation of Maxwell by Dr O'Dwyer, Bishop of Limerick, on 17 May.[21]

Before considering the legal propriety of this aspect of the courts martial, it is important to recall the atmosphere of the time. Even before the rebellion ended there were rumours of summary executions. Mary Louisa Norway, an Englishwoman and wife of the secretary to the Irish Post Office, chronicled these on the Friday of Easter week in a long diary type letter to her sister in England:

> On Wednesday three of the ring leaders were caught and it is said that they were shot immediately! ... We also hear that Sir R. Casement has been shot in London, but you probably know a great deal more about that than I do, as we see no papers and are completely cut off from all news.[22]

Mrs Norway, however, was constantly in the company of officials and officers and was much better informed than ordinary people. By contrast, the general public's susceptibility to rumour is easy to imagine. Ordinary Dubliners first heard of the proclamation of martial law and then, for nine terrible and enervated days, the curt announcement of executions, without any account of court martial proceedings or the evidence heard at them. On the nationalist side Eoin MacNeill recorded a rumour the following week that a huge grave had been dug in Arbour Hill, to receive the bodies of several hundred rebels.[23] The journalist Warre B. Wells, addressing an English audience, invited them to set aside all question of the propriety or expediency of the courts martial. But he said: 'I am simply inviting you to endeavour to understand their effect on that Irish public which read of them with something of the feeling of helpless rage with which one would watch a stream of blood dripping from under a closed door.'[24]

By reason of the provisions of DORA, it was undoubtedly legal in British law for the prisoners to be tried by field general court martial in certain circumstances. In the words of the first 1914 Act they were liable to be so tried 'in like manner as if such persons were subject to military law and had on active service committed an offence under s. 5 of the Army Act'. This, however, was subject to the right to opt for jury trial, preserved by the 1915 Act, until its suspension in Ireland by proclamation on 26 April 1916. But this was a provision with little comfort for the Crown on the question of closed door proceedings. The 'Act' referred to in DORA 1914 was the Army Act of 1881. The procedures at courts martial were governed by the 1907 rules of procedure, made under that Act. Rule 119 (c) provided that '... Proceedings shall be held in open court, in the presence of the accused, except on any deliberation amongst the members, when the court may be closed.' This seems an unambiguous provision. Moreover, a lawyer construing it would apply the canon or rule of construction described in Latin as *expressio unius exclusio alterius*. This means that where a particular thing is permitted in one, specified, circumstance, that is to be construed as excluding it in any other circumstance. Thus the provision that the court could be closed while the members were deliberating implies that it could not be closed in any other circumstance.

A LEGAL CHALLENGE

We have already seen that no contemporary legal challenge was taken to the proceedings by court martial in May, 1916. The speed with which they were convened, and with which execution followed sentence, may have influenced this, but it is hard to see any of the executed leaders wishing to seek relief in a British court. Certain aspects of the legality of the court martial regime did, however, come before the courts of England in February 1917.[25] Gerald Doyle was a man who had been tried by court martial, sentenced to death, but recommended to mercy on the grounds that he was 'a dupe'. The sentence was commuted to three years' penal servitude. He was serving that sentence in Lewes gaol in England when he sought habeas corpus. His solicitor was George Gavan Duffy who had earlier acted in the defence of Sir Roger Casement. He was later, briefly, minister for foreign affairs in the Free State government but resigned in protest at the abolition of the Sinn Féin courts. He then practised as a barrister in Ireland until appointed president of the high court by de Valera's government in the 1930s. He was, according to Professor John M. Kelly, the judge to whom most of the creative interpretation of the constitution in the first fifteen years of its existence is to be attributed.

Although several points were taken in Doyle's case, there was only one of real legal substance. This was that the trial and conviction were invalid because there had been no legal power to hold the court martial behind closed doors, excluding the public and, perhaps more relevantly, the press. This claim was unsuccessful. The legal approach of the seven judges of the divisional court who considered it was, either by our contemporary standards or even by the standards of the time, crude in the extreme. Their attitude emerges clearly from the judgment of Mr Justice Darling, later Lord Darling, a peer but not a law lord:

> It appears to me to be incongruous that, before the echoes of this rebellion have died away, we should meet here solemnly to consider such points as have been argued before us … The trial took place in barracks when the rebellion in Ireland was still going on. The ruins in Dublin were still hot cinders, and the whole place was in the condition in which it is described by the fact that certain military precautions were taken, and the general in command of his Majesty's Forces came to the conclusion that it would not be possible to administer justice if the public of Dublin were to be invited to attend at an open trial of persons with whom, no doubt, a great many of them sympathised.[26]

In none of the judgments, and particularly not in the leading judgment of Lord Reading CJ (formerly Sir Rufus Isaacs), was there a more sophisticated level of analysis. The judges did reject the Crown's contention (advanced by the attorney general, Sir F.E. Smith KC, later Lord Birkenhead) that the word 'open court' simply meant that the prisoner and his counsel if any were entitled to be present: this is an interpretation for which there is absolutely no legal warrant. But they upheld the secret proceedings on the basis of an affidavit of General Maxwell, which they summarised as saying:

> Being clearly of opinion that, in the existing local conditions, it was necessary for the public safety and for the defence of the realm that neither the public nor the press should be admitted to the trial, he gave orders accordingly and the trial took place in camera.[27]

The divisional court upheld the secrecy of the trial by referring to an earlier case, which found that there was an inherent jurisdiction in every court to exclude the public 'if it becomes necessary for the administration of justice'.[28] Even assuming that to be true, the judgments evade the apparently insuperable obstacle that neither Doyle's court martial, nor any other field general court martial in Dublin in 1916, had itself even purported to exercise this jurisdiction. In a remarkably threadbare argument Lord Reading overcame this difficulty as follows: he cited the opinion of Maxwell as the military authority convening the court martial and continued:

> The commander-in-chief having come to that conclusion and having stated it, *we must assume* [emphasis added] that the field general court martial convened by him, which he was the proper person to convene, and which sat in consequence, held the same view.… . I think he means that if there had been a trial in open court – that is, with the public admitted – in the existing local conditions it would have been unsafe; and in my judgment if it is unsafe for justice to be administered it is equivalent to saying that justice could not in those circumstances be properly administered. In the existence of such a state of circumstances it is quite possible to conceive a number of persons coming into court, if the public had been admitted, who might have terrorised, possibly even shot, witnesses. Having regard to those conditions, it seems to me abundantly plain that this case was well within the principle as stated in *Scott v. Scott* and consequently that there was jurisdiction to try it in camera.[29]

This passage is almost risible. It is the work of judges showing themselves 'more executive minded than the executive', to use the phrase of the great British jurist Lord Atkin in his remarkable dissent in a later wartime case.[30] The courts martial took place in the Richmond Barracks, Dublin, or another absolutely secure location. There was every opportunity for adequate security measures. But quite apart from that the reasoning provides no basis whatever for the exclusion of the press, as opposed to the public. Had they been present it is quite possible that the perception of the executions, or at least some of them, would have been different; certainly, it is less likely that the impression of prisoners being 'shot in cold blood' would have taken hold. But is also likely that, at a public trial, some at least of those executed would not have been convicted of a capital charge.

Reading was one of the most political judges of modern times. Attorney general at the time of his appointment as lord chief justice in 1913, the advent of the war saw him virtually abandon judicial for political work. He was first the unofficial and later the official broker between England and

America in the vital period before the latter joined the war. Equally, he was the chief go-between when relations between Asquith and Lloyd George collapsed at the end of 1916. He disliked judicial work and left it for long periods, once to serve as ambassador to the United States. He eventually resigned to become viceroy of India in the 1920s and lived to hold cabinet office, including that of foreign secretary in the 1930s. He is the subject of Rudyard Kipling's extraordinary anti-semitic hate poem *Gehazi*, written on his appointment as lord chief justice immediately after his involvement in the Marconi share scandal.

A GUILTY OFFICIAL CONSCIENCE: EVIDENCE 'EXTREMELY THIN'

In June 1916, and on at least two other occasions, Prime Minister Asquith, under pressure, promised to publish the court martial proceedings. In fact they were to be suppressed until the 1990s. Asquith's promise horrified and galvanised the military authorities and led to gross obstruction from army lawyers. The reason for this is a startling one: the military and legal authorities did not believe that some of the verdicts could withstand legal scrutiny. Maxwell himself may not have been told of the legal difficulties – it would have been very embarrassing to broach the subject with him. At any event, on 3 June 1916 he was persuaded to give an interview to Associated Press, in order to counter the unfortunate effect that the executions had had on American opinion. He told the correspondent that: 'Every trial was absolutely fair as will be seen from the reports when they are published.'[31] But he was the only significant player on the British side not to be privy to a major legal difficulty that had emerged.

The law officers advised in January 1917 that: 'There does not seem to be any legal justification for the holding of a court martial in camera.'[32] Even more strikingly, the secretary to the Army Council, Sir Reginald Brade, agreed, noting that: 'There appears to be nothing in the Army Act, or the rules of procedure, to justify the holding of a court martial in camera.'[33] I have no doubt that this is correct in law, at least to the extent that the Dublin courts martial had failed even to consider the question of excluding the public and the press; they had simply taken their orders from Maxwell.

Though the army chiefs believed Maxwell had been wrong, they still opposed publication on two grounds, both significant to the historian.

Firstly, they said to publish would imply that Maxwell had been wrong in holding the trial in camera. His life might have been in danger and so might the lives of witnesses. This latter point is nonsense. In the case of all executed prisoners all the witnesses without exception were servants of the Crown; they were nearly all English soldiers, with very few policemen and one prison warden. Nor would publication necessarily involve disclosing names.

The second point urging against publication is still more fundamental and startling. Brade wrote: 'while I can safely say that the evidence taken as a whole is conclusive of their guilt, there are one or two cases in which the evidence is extremely thin'[34]. Sir Neville Macready, the then adjutant general (and later commander in chief in Ireland 1920–21), went further:

> As I have reason to believe that in certain cases the evidence was not too strong, the inevitable results of publication would be that a certain section of the Irish community will urge that the sole reason for the trials in camera was that the authorities intended to execute certain Sinn Féiners whether there was evidence or not. This is an argument which in my humble judgement would be extremely difficult to meet successfully if as I think the evidence in some of the cases was far from conclusive.[35]

MARTIAL LAW

Despite the existence of a comprehensive code of extraordinary legislation in DORA, the legal reaction to the outbreak of the Rising on Easter Monday 24 April 1916 was, from the first, blustering and confused. This was partly because the Rising found the Irish executive both unprepared and physically separated. The chief secretary, Augustine Birrell, was in London, the under secretary Sir Matthew Nathan was at first isolated in Dublin castle and the lord lieutenant, Lord Winborne, was in the vice regal lodge in the Phoenix Park. From here he frantically telegraphed for military assistance. He then issued a proclamation of martial law for the city and county of Dublin. Winborne told Maxwell on 3 May 1916 that this had been drafted by the 'law officers', i.e. James Campbell as attorney general.[36]

Martial law had not been in force in Ireland since the early years of the nineteenth century. Exactly what it meant seems to have been little understood even by those who called for it and continued it. There is ample evidence, some of which will be discussed below, that it was interpreted by some British officers as entitling them to shoot or imprison anyone they liked, without recourse to any other authority.

Winborne's gesture in proclaiming martial law on his own authority may be explained in terms of his own position. Isolated and without advice in the immediate aftermath of the outbreak, he had for some months been in conflict with the chief secretary and other members of the Irish executive over his own lack of power in governing Ireland. He had also been the only member of the Irish government who had issued warnings of unrest and demands for action in the period immediately before 24 April. On that day these warnings of disaster were borne out and he found himself in a position to take decisive action, or at least to make a dramatic, not to say melodramatic, gesture.

His action may also owe something to the fact that, according to what his private secretary later told Lady Cynthia Asquith, in the isolation of the vice regal lodge: 'His Ex. simply swilled brandy the whole time' and was in 'superlatively theatrical form'.[37]

Whatever about Winborne's personal circumstances, his gesture was enthusiastically taken up by the government in London. General Sir John Maxwell was dispatched to Ireland as military governor. As we have seen Maxwell was 'given plenary powers under martial law over the whole country, the Irish executive having placed themselves at his disposal to carry out his instructions'.[38] As those words implied, the government under its own authority extended martial law to the whole of Ireland on 29 April. These two separate proclamations were, and were meant to be, a plangent assertion of British authority in the form of martial law. To government supporters, this was extremely welcome. On 8 May, after the rebellion had been suppressed and the executions were well under way, the *Irish Times* was probably representative of unionist opinion in saying that 'much nonsense is likely to be written in newspapers and talked in parliament about the restrictions of martial law in Ireland. The fact is martial law has come as a blessing to us all.'[39] Several hundred business men petitioned the prime minister against 'any interference in the discretion of the commander-in-chief during the operation of martial law'.[40]

Much more sinisterly, the notorious Captain J.C. Bowen-Colthurst, explaining on 9 May his decision to shoot three entirely innocent men who were prisoners in Portobello Barracks, said: 'I felt I must act quickly, *and believing I had the power under martial law* [emphasis added], I felt under the circumstances that it was clearly my duty to have the three ring leaders shot.'[41] Bowen-Colthurst was certainly eccentric, and was found insane at his court martial. But neither his commanding officer, nor the younger officers from whose custody he took the prisoners nor any more senior officer but one (Major Sir Francis Vane) to whose attention the executions, carried out openly in the main yard of the barracks, came, disputed his power to act as he did. A later report on this incident by Sir John Simon, subsequently lord chancellor, attributed this inaction to a misconception of martial law powers.[42]

In fact, the risks inherent in giving the military a free hand by proclaiming martial law, dramatically illustrated by the Bowen-Colthurst case, was present to the minds of several British politicians and soldiers in the period from 1916 onwards. Lloyd George warned the government that there might be drastic political consequences from 'the unconsidered action of some subordinate officer' if martial law were extended.[43] In 1920, by which time martial law had been re-imposed in certain areas, Macready himself warned a subordinate that one of his divisional commanders, Brigadier General Prescott-Decies 'will think that martial law means he can kill anybody he sees walking the road whose appearance may be distasteful to him'.[44] At the time of the original proclamation of martial law in 1916 there was still actual fighting in progress and the possibility, however vague, of a German landing. Within days, however, the government was taking embarrassed, and for some time inconclusive, steps to claw back the total discretion accorded to the military, and Maxwell in particular, by the proclamation. But for a complex array of reasons, as we shall see, it was unwilling to withdraw it.

The retreat from martial law

On 27 May martial law was proclaimed over the whole country for an indefinite period. References to it as being in force were made by government ministers and other high office holders until the end of the summer. But the government rapidly began to distance itself from the concept. Asquith said privately on 19 May that there had been 'no single case in which it has been or is likely to be necessary to resort to what is called "martial law" and accordingly there is no adequate ground for its continuance'.[45] On 31 July he told the House of Commons that:

> There is no proceeding which has been taken by Sir John Maxwell or the military authorities in Ireland which is not taken under and which could not be

justified by the Defence of the Realm Act. Martial law has never been put in force for any practical or effective purpose in Ireland.[46]

Why then, one might ask, was it proclaimed and continued? The answer appears to be to placate the soldiers and for 'shock and awe' purposes. The Irish law officers led by the Attorney General James Campbell wrote an opinion on the topic that was transmitted by Maxwell to the British government on 20 May 1916. This remarkable document agreed that, in point of law, martial law was unnecessary because the government had, during the rebellion, suspended the provision of the Defence of the Realm Act, 1915 that permitted a defendant to opt for jury trial. But they thought that martial law could nevertheless be extended 'without any risk of serious complaint'. Furthermore, they suggested, there might be some purpose in doing so because:

> undoubtedly the average citizen has an extraordinary belief in the magic term 'martial law', and its continuance would bring home to loyal and law abiding people a great sense of security and safety whereas the very indefinite knowledge of its powers spread terror amongst the disaffected.[47]

Still more remarkably, General Sir John Maxwell himself, the person in whom the plenitude of martial law power (and, according to Asquith's public statement of the effect of martial law, the power to give instructions to the Irish government) was vested, complained bitterly of it. In a report to Asquith dated 24 June 1916 he sadly reported the 'revulsion of feeling' that had set in in favour of the rebels. This was the result, he believed, of suggestions that 'the leaders were murdered or executed in cold blood without trial … that the military had been harsh unjust and oppressive etc.'. This he attributed in part to the fact that: 'A grievance is manufactured because martial law has been declared. All public bodies spend their time in passing resolutions protesting against it.' He pointed out, almost certainly correctly, that there was what he called 'confusion of thought' leading to people thinking that the Defence of the Realm regulations and martial law were one and the same thing. He concluded dramatically that: 'The fact remains that no-one in Ireland has been hurt by martial law because it has not been enforced.'[48]

Despite this Maxwell had campaigned vigorously for martial law to be retained after the second proclamation ran out on 28 May. In a letter of 20 May to Asquith's secretary, Bonham Carter (the two were still in Dublin at the time of the letter), Maxwell said he wished it extended 'for many reasons not least legal difficulties constantly cropping up'.[49] He had still not finished the letter when he received the opinion of the Irish law officers, which has just been quoted. He said he was disappointed with the attorney general's views:

> To my mind he ignores the powers that I might put into force, if the necessity arose, under martial law. It is precisely because the Defence of the Realm Acts and regulations do not fit all cases that martial law being in force may be useful.[50]

The reference to 'legal difficulties' is almost certainly inspired by the facts that the police and the law officers were beginning to assert their right to decide who should be charged with an offence, and in what court he was to be tried, to the exclusion of the military forces. The custom of holding people, perhaps for several weeks, simply to await the decision of the military authorities as to whether they were to be charged had caused a great deal of difficulty and had no obvious legal basis either at common law or under DORA. Maxwell got his wish to the extent that martial law was extended, but he was precluded from taking any particular steps under it.

Accordingly, it would seem that the imposition of martial law was, at first, the ill-considered brain child of the isolated, apprehensive and possibly drunken Winborne. But it was eagerly seized on by the government who not merely extended it to the whole country, and continued it indefinitely a month later, but used language in public debate in the House of Commons which suggested that the consequence of martial law was that Maxwell had taken over the government of the country with 'plenary powers under martial law' and with the ordinary government of Ireland 'at his disposal to carry out his instructions'. How false this was can be seen from a consideration of what actually occurred under the DORA regime. But the impression was quite deliberately created to bolster the standing of the government in the eyes of its supporters, especially in Ireland, and to strike terror into its enemies.

Having gone down that road it is scarcely surprising that one of the first symptoms of the 'revulsion of feeling' of which Maxwell complained was his being described, on 17 May, by the bishop of Limerick, Dr O'Dwyer, as a 'military dictator' who had shot 'the poor fellows who surrendered to you in Dublin ... in cold blood [thereby] outraging the conscience of the country'.[51]

Against such a public indictment it was in vain for Maxwell to complain, as he did privately to the British government, that his powers had been exaggerated. He had been positively portrayed as a sort of archangel of vengeance with plenary powers over all, including the Irish executive, and neither he nor the government could resile from that image, especially after the executions.

Nature of martial law

The term 'martial law' connotes one of the most elusive concepts in law, firstly because it has changed dramatically over time and is probably still changing; secondly, because it is popularly used to connote procedures such as trial by military court which do not amount to martial law; thirdly, because the very fraught circumstances in which martial law arises anywhere in the world do not lend themselves to careful jurisprudential analysis. Accordingly, a full examination of the meaning of the term would involve an extended discourse in law that I do not think is called for here. Fortunately, it is also quite unnecessary since the topic has already been subject to magisterial scrutiny by former Chief Justice Ronan Keane.[52] This article is a remarkable feat of both legal and historical erudition, which traces the concept of martial law from medieval origins up to the foundation of the state. The highlights of this eventful history are the 1628 'Petition of Right' grudgingly conceded by Charles I, against the use of martial law in peace time; and the dramatic issue of a writ of habeas corpus by the lord chief justice of Ireland, Arthur Wolfe, Lord Kilwarden, in favour of Wolfe Tone in 1798. This was on the basis that martial law could not exist while the ordinary courts were open and functioning. When the military refused to act on the writ Kilwarden courageously ordered the military commander and the provost marshal to be taken into custody: further developments were arrested by the death of Tone. It is sad to reflect that Kilwarden was piked to death during Emmet's rebellion in 1803.

What emerges most clearly from Chief Justice Keane's long and detailed account is that the term 'martial law' is a great misnomer. What it actually describes is the absence of law, a state of affairs in which the law of the land is incapable of operating or being enforced so that the only form of authority left is the military power. The common law does not endorse this state of affairs, but it acknowledges it. The duke of Wellington is not usually cited as a legal authority but one may endorse what he said about martial law at the very end of his life: 'Martial law was neither more nor less than the will of the general who commands the army. In fact, martial law means no law at all.'[53] In the more figurative language of Chief Justice Keane:

> Martial law is the lawyer's equivalent of the physicist's anti-matter, a kind of juristic black hole, to shift the metaphor, into which are sucked all the cherished principles which normally guarantee life and liberty. It is only when all else has failed, including the law itself, that it becomes society's last line of defence: *salus populi suprema lex.*[54]

Under martial law, then, military impositions of all kinds (including detentions and executions with or without 'drum head' courts martial, and the destruction of property) may occur. In law it is military necessity, and not a proclamation, which brings this condition about and it exists only where, as long as, and to the extent that, such necessity endures. This state of affairs is acknowledged by the common law, rather than approved by it. Periods of martial law are invariably followed by the passage of an Indemnity Act after it is completed: otherwise those who exercise the military power might well be liable to an action at law for things done under it. This procedure was always followed under English rule. It is a sobering reflection that it was also followed under a native government when an Act of Indemnity for the military forces was passed in 1923. In no other way could many of the military actions of 1922 and early 1923 be defended at law.

A period of so-called martial law, then, is a period when the army reigns supreme and 'the will of the general' is substituted for the law. It is the antithesis of the common law's concept of the rule of law and objectionable to it. It must clearly be distinguished from a period (such as we have had both in the days of the old United Kingdom and after independence) where laws were enforced by military courts. This was the position under the Defence of the Realm Act in 1916 and later, in respect of certain offences, in Cosgrave's and de Valera's Ireland. But military courts do not make martial law: in 1916 the law they were acting under was that providing for the trial of offences against the Defence of the Realm regulations by military courts. There was thus a profound contradiction in the action of the British authorities, on the very same day, in proclaiming martial law and almost simultaneously suspending the grounds of section 1 of the Defence of the Realm Act, 1915, as regards Ireland. The first permitted the trial of offences under the extraordinary wartime legislation to take place in military courts: this was in itself an enormous step. But the second was in effect an assertion that law itself had ceased to operate. This was unreal at the time it was first proclaimed by Lord Winborne, still more so when it was extended to the country as a whole by the government a week later, and it was utterly unrealistic when it was proclaimed permanently at the end of May 1916. To a lawyer's eye, the second and still more surely the third proclamation of martial law appear wholly unlawful, and the first at least otiose.

Martial law and DORA

The papers in UCD Archives, already referred to, throw an interesting light on the co-existence of martial law and the Defence of the Realms Acts. On 2 May, 1916, the day Pearse, Clarke and MacDonagh were tried, Maxwell wrote to Lord Kitchener the following fascinating letter:

> I hope to get through with the courts martial. I have been advised to deal with them under DORA, *I rather wanted to do so under martial law*. Today the presidents of the courts sitting today have begun *to raise legal difficulties*, but I hope to get over these. I will have three courts sitting and ought to be through with this part in a week or ten days.[55] [Emphasis added in both places]

Maxwell's prediction was exactly correct: the last of the relevant courts martial in Dublin took place on 9 May and the last of the executions, those of Connolly and MacDermott, on 12 May. For our purposes, however, attention must focus on the emphasised parts: why was Maxwell persuaded, against his own wishes, to hold the courts martial under DORA and not under martial law? And what were the 'legal difficulties' which General Blackadder and his colleagues raised?

Some light is thrown on the first issue in a letter from Brigadier General Byrne to the Home Office, quoted in Professor Townshend's recent book: 'Sir John was very keen to try everybody "under military courts" held under martial law but I persuaded him against this.'[56] Byrne gave this advice on the basis that the DORA regulations were adequate and 'will not raise any difficulties afterwards'.[57] It is possible to be reasonably sure of the sort of 'difficulties' he had in mind. Most senior soldiers would have been aware that the difficulty with martial law was that acts done under it were regarded as beyond the reach of the ordinary law only during the time and in the place where the operation of the ordinary law had collapsed. There had been well-known cases both in England and in Ireland where acts done under cover of martial law in the colonies had been challenged in the ordinary courts on the grounds of an absence of proven military necessity. The leading such case was *R. v. Nelson and Brand* [1867]. One such case, however, had been tried in Ireland only a few years before 1916, *Rainsford v. Browne*.[58] From these cases it was clear that a civil tribunal, whether exercising criminal or civil jurisdiction, could be very demanding in requiring proof that the ordinary law had in fact collapsed, leaving the military authorities with a free hand.

This, probably, is what Byrne meant by his reference to avoiding later difficulties. It is not possible, at this distance in time, to be definitive about the nature of the legal difficulties raised by the presidents of the courts martial. These men were soldiers and not lawyers: the most senior of them, General Blackadder, is described by W.E. Wylie as 'a rather unimaginative major general'.[59] It is unlikely that they would have devised a legal difficulty of any great sophistication. On the other hand, the work of presiding over mass courts martial of civilians was unusual work for soldiers, and Blackadder himself was observed by the countess of Fingal to be upset after the first court martial: improbably, he had been impressed by the character of the prisoners and in particular Pádraig Pearse.[60] One may speculate, and that is all one can do, that their difficulties related to the holding of the trials in secret, which might have struck a soldier as unusual. If that is so, they received no comfort from Maxwell. Alternatively, the court presidents may have felt that such momentous cases should have merited a general court martial with a full court of thirteen members and a professional judge advocate to instruct them on the law. To judge by Wylie's later account, the presidents of the courts martial before which he appeared gave him every latitude to bring out facts favourable to the defendants and on occasion asked him, privately, if he considered a particular prisoner to be a dupe. He seems always to have replied in the affirmative and the officers then recommended commutation of the sentence.[61]

The notes or transcripts of the field general courts martial in relation to the fifteen persons executed have recently been published with extensive commentary by Brian Barton.[62] From these it appears that the proceedings were perfunctory in the extreme. The evidence typically consisted of that of an officer who had been present at the time the prisoner surrendered or was captured, or sometimes of an officer who had himself been a prisoner of the rebels. In all such cases the evidence was directed at establishing that the prisoner was not merely involved in the rebellion but exercised a position of some authority. In a number of cases, notably those of William Pearse and Michael O'Hanrahan, the evidence on the latter point was virtually non-existent.

Still more significantly, it will be remembered that the death penalty was available under DORR in respect of acts done with intent to assist the enemy. Only in the case of Pádraig Pearse was there express evidence of this, and that evidence came from his own speech. Another court martial president, Brigadier Maconchey, said that he simply refused to write down some things certain prisoners had said on the basis that it simply made their position worse: he may have been thinking of some reference to German allies. Maconchey also, incidentally, had asked to be relieved of the duty of presiding at courts martial on the basis that he was an Irishman, but Maxwell had refused to excuse him.[63]

DID IT MATTER?

After ninety years it is apt to raise the question as to whether the secrecy, the informality of proceedings and the absence of defence counsel made any real difference. Most certainly it made no difference in certain cases: Pearse supplied all the evidence that was needed both to convict him and to expose him to the death penalty. Others, like Clarke and MacDermott, remained absolutely silent and it is difficult to imagine that their attitude would have been different even if counsel had been available to them. But other prisoners such as Éamonn Ceannt and Michael Mallin made strenuous efforts to defend themselves. The former very cleverly cross-examined the officer who took his surrender into admitting that he was not really sure whether or not Ceannt had been armed. Mallin challenged whether he had in fact been in a commanding position and specifically challenged any intention to help Germany.[64]

There is surviving evidence that relations of some of the prisoners attempted to get legal assistance for them. The half-yearly general meeting of the Law Society of Ireland took place on Tuesday 16 May. At that event a number of solicitors led by Mr James Brady complained that they had been retained by relatives of various prisoners but were not permitted to see their putative clients. Mr Brady described how he went to the Richmond Barracks to interview the persons for whom he had been retained, and 'got a point blank refusal of admission'.[65] A solicitor of unionist leanings, Mr Seddall, said that the ordinary court martial rules did not apply since 'under martial law the procedure was entirely different'.[66] From this it can be seen that even some lawyers were confused as to the effect of DORA as opposed to martial law. The Law Society records indicate that this problem was resolved after dealings between the president of the society and Major General Sandbach – but that was too late for many.[67]

A SUGGESTIVE COMPARISON

The fate of the men who were executed may be compared with that of Eoin MacNeill. The question of what to do with MacNeill troubled the authorities greatly since they knew that he was the founder and formerly the head of the Irish Volunteers but also knew that he had taken no part in the rebellion and had attempted to countermand the mobilisation orders on the basis that there was no realistic hope of success and that they lacked a mandate to embark on armed revolution.

In the event, MacNeill was tried by general court martial, as opposed to field general court martial and this may have had a significant role in saving his life. A general court martial consists of a president and twelve officers, as opposed to a president and two officers for field general court martial. Still more significantly, a general court martial required the presence of a 'judge advocate', normally a deputy judge advocate general, invariably a military officer who was a qualified lawyer and who was required to assist the members of the court martial on matters of law in much the same way that a judge assists a jury at a civil trial. This aspect, naturally, ensures a much more sophisticated hearing on legal issues.

MacNeill had taken some steps himself to bring this situation about. In a memoir written in the 1930s he records:

> I certainly had no desire to be executed, and knowing well the frame of mind of Dublin castle and the British military command, I determined to use what means I could to delay the court martial proceedings, calculating that executions, if they took place would be a cause of public horror, and that the British government itself would be forced to put a stop to them.[68]

This, of course, is precisely what occurred. MacNeill then retained solicitor and counsel, his leading counsel being James Chambers KC, a unionist member of parliament. His lawyers then applied to be allowed to appear for him and received a reply from Maxwell of 12 May:

> Sir John has carefully considered the points raised by you and has come to the conclusion that [MacNeill's] case does present more difficult questions of law and of the admissibility of evidence than those which have up to now been tried before field general courts martial. He has therefore decided that the case of Mr MacNeill will be brought to trial before a general court martial and not before a field general court martial.[69]

On the same day MacNeill wrote to his solicitor saying that on the previous evening he had been handed a charge sheet by an officer who did not speak to him other than to confirm his name. It was in the following form:

> Charge.
> Did an act, to wit did take part in an armed rebellion and in the waging of war against his Majesty the King, such act being of such a nature as to be calculated to be prejudicial to the Defence of the Realm and being done with the intention and for the purpose of assisting the enemy. Alternative 2 Did attempt to cause disaffection among the civilian population to his Majesty.

MacNeill recorded that the second charge was written in pencil.[70]

This, as MacNeill's son in law and biographer Michael Tierney points out, 'looks very much as if by some extraordinary blunder the accused had been momentarily admitted to the deliberations of his accusers.'[71] The 'alternative' charge clearly demonstrates that they despaired of convicting him of the graver charge at an open and professionally conducted trial.

The first charge, of course, is that of which all the executed prisoners were convicted. It was an extremely ambitious charge to bring against a man who had attempted to countermand the orders leading to the rebellion: to judge from the later court martials it may have been hoped to support it on the basis that MacNeill would clearly have tolerated or even led some rebellion, and perhaps the Easter week events were that rebellion. Alternatively, said the Crown, his own correspondence showed that he would have led a rebellion in the event of an attempt to disarm the Volunteers and that, they hoped, would be enough.[72]

This charge, however, was difficult to bring home in a legal proceeding with a professionally qualified judge advocate and defence lawyers including a unionist MP, whose verdict was subject to review on legal grounds. Significantly, the military prosecutors did not in the end attempt to do so. On 16 May they brought forward a new charge sheet with twelve counts. Eight were for 'attempting to cause disaffection amongst the civilian population', two were for committing an act to the prejudice of recruitment, one for making statements likely to prejudice recruitment and the twelfth was for possession of documents, including a newspaper and Volunteer documents, 'the publication of such documents being a contravention of the provisions of regulation 27 of the Defence of the Realm regulations'.[73]

These charges were in large part simply an embarrassment. MacNeill had certainly been a sustained, provocative and coherent opponent of the government and anyone who paid attention to him would not have been encouraged to join the Crown forces. But he had never done anything directly or indirectly in relation to recruitment and the alleged attempts to cause disaffection had been an embarrassingly long time before his arrest and trial in May 1916. Although Maxwell hated MacNeill and considered that the fact that he had not been actually involved in the rebellion to be pure happenstance, the military lawyers did not even charge him with an offence remotely likely to carry the death penalty. There is evidence that the members of the court martial may have resented this, because in convicting him on all counts they added the unnecessary finding that 'the accused committed all the offences with the intention of assisting the enemy'.[74] But the game was over before it began. Indeed, the most interesting part of MacNeill's memoir is of his post-arrest interrogation by a Major Price who attempted without success to get MacNeill to implicate the parliamentarians Dillon and Devlin in the rebellion.[75]

MacNeill's circumstances made it particularly difficult to convict him on the gravest charge. But his determined defence also contributed to his survival. His most important tactical victory, however, was to procure an open trial. It is difficult to think that this would not also have benefited some of the executed prisoners, specifically those in whose cases, in General Macready's words 'the evidence ... was far from conclusive'.[76]

THE CATHOLIC CHURCH, THE HOLY SEE AND THE 1916 RISING

Dermot Keogh

INTRODUCTION

What role did the Catholic church in Ireland play in the lead up to the 1916 Rising, and what was its reaction to the armed uprising? There are no simple answers to these two questions. Professor John Whyte set out his view of the response of the church to the event in an essay published in 1967.[1] Based almost entirely on secondary sources, the late Professor Whyte provided a very perceptive account that has stood the test of time. But his work has been added to by a new generation of historians privileged with access to primary sources in different ecclesiastical archives. I refer in particular here to the work of Brian P. Murphy, Thomas J. Morrissey and Jérôme aan de Wiel.[2] The last-named has worked extensively in ecclesiastical archives in Ireland, London, Rome, the Holy See and Paris. He has found a number of very important sources and has helped to provide a new interpretation of the role of the Catholic church in Ireland during the First World War.

My essay will build on that published work. In the past two years I have returned, in particular, to the archives of the Irish College in Rome, where I have consulted the O'Riordan, Hagan and Curran papers. By re-reading those sources, I will attempt to provide another interpretation of the role of the church during the period of the Rising and beyond. Episcopal and clerical reaction to the Rising, and in particular to the subsequent repression and deportations, helped to formalise an already implicit understanding in Irish politics between the hierarchy and the emerging Sinn Féin movement, which led ultimately to the signing of the Anglo-Irish Agreement on 6 December 1921 and the establishment of the Irish Free State. I am uneasy about using the term 'alliance'. It implies too formal a relationship. What existed was both a shared hostility to the British government's mishandling of Irish affairs over three decades and a strongly held belief that self-determination was the way forward for Ireland – a self-determination that for the Catholic hierarchy did not include partition. As the latter became an inescapable aspect of British policy in Ireland, feelings within the church hardened in favour of going beyond home rule and devolved local government.

The British reaction to the 1916 Rising resulted in a style of repression that had not been visited upon the country even during the land wars of the 1880s. It was brutal and draconian and showed scant respect for the rule of law or for the rights of the accused rebel leaders. Mass deportations intensified that sense of public outrage. The Catholic hierarchy and clergy were exposed throughout the conflict to the feelings of their communities. This article seeks to show the contradictions, tensions and complexities of a church caught in a revolutionary situation. Without any initial support for the act of revolution, leading churchmen and women appeared to ascribe the Rising to the work of the left and of the Irish Republican Brotherhood (IRB). The reaction was hostile, if appreciative of the ideals and courage of the participants. That initial hostility and ambivalence, however, changed in a short time to a marked hostility to the British authorities and a shift in allegiance to an emerging coalition clustered around the name Sinn Féin. David Miller put the process in the following way:

> It is a remarkable story in which the church protected, and indeed augmented, her interests – the fervent devotion of her people and the institutional conditions which, she believed, fostered that devotion – up to the last hours of the old order and yet entered the new order with those interests intact for the future as well.[3]

This article provides a partial explanation as to why and how this situation came about.

THE FOUR ARCHBISHOPS, THE BRITISH GOVERNMENT AND IRISH POLITICS

It is best to begin by describing the leading personalities in the Catholic church in Ireland at the time of the 1916 Rising. Archbishop William Walsh of Dublin was born in 1841. He taught on the staff of St Patrick's

College, Maynooth, before being made archbishop in 1885. Although seventy five years old and in very poor health, he was the *de facto* leader of the Irish hierarchy when the violence broke out on Easter Monday, 24 April 1916. He was confined to his bedroom on doctor's orders with instructions that he should not be disturbed for April, May and June, before being sent to Wicklow to recuperate. The Archbishop's house in Drumcondra was relatively close to the city centre. It was a port of call for many people in the weeks leading up to the Rising. Walsh, therefore, through his secretaries, was kept well informed about political developments and plans for a rising. His intellectual faculties were as sharp as his disillusionment with the Irish party was profound. That attitude of outright hostility to the Irish party and its leadership became more pronounced in the aftermath of the Rising. He remained in charge and in control.

His position on Irish politics was shared by many of the bishops. He was very well served by his secretary, Michael Curran, a strong nationalist with close ties to radical cultural nationalists such as the future President of Ireland, Seán T. O'Kelly. Curran was an eye witness to most of the major events of 1916 and he has left a very valuable testimony with the Bureau of Military History. Based on his diary, his memoir chronicles his experiences during the critical months from April to December 1916.[4] (His account should be read in parallel with the testimony of O'Kelly, also contained in the Bureau of Military History.)[5] Curran also corresponded extensively during the Rising with the rector of the Irish College in Rome, Michael O'Riordan, and with its vice rector, John Hagan.[6] There is now thus a wealth of new primary source material, which sheds new light on the changing attitude of leading churchmen during those days of revolution and repression.[7]

Walsh's counterpart in Armagh, Cardinal Michael Logue, was a year older. Born in 1840 he had succeeded to the primacy in 1887. Like Walsh, he had been a professor in St Patrick's College, Maynooth. In contrast to Walsh, however, Logue held on to his faith in the Irish party for much longer. He was a strong critic of direct British rule in Ireland and supported home rule. His mistrust of the ruling Liberal party was summed up in the following quotation, delivered after the publication of 'the people's budget' of 1909: 'England had not only robbed us but continued to rob us and the heaviest hand laid for years was laid on us at present and by a party about which we were all so enthusiastic – the grand old Liberal party of England.'[8] The First World War introduced further tensions into the relationship between the leadership of the Irish Catholic church and the British government. Returning from the conclave that had elected Pope

Benedict XV in 1915, Logue had denounced the 'barbarism of the Germans [in September 1914] in burning Rheims Cathedral', but was quick to counter propaganda claims in London that he had declared himself a supporter of the British.[9]

The Archbishop of Cashel, John Harty, was born in 1867. Between 1895 and 1913 he was on the staff of Maynooth where he held the chair of dogmatic theology and was senior professor of moral theology. He helped found the *Irish Theological Quarterly* in 1906. He was a strong supporter of the Gaelic Athletic Association (GAA). Healy had a keen interest in economic and social matters. Made an archbishop in 1913, he died in 1946 having played a very prominent role in the political life of a country striving for independence.[10] John Healy (born in 1841) was archbishop of Tuam from 1903 until 1918. A professor at Maynooth from 1879 to 1884, he was a prolific writer and editor for several years of the *Irish Ecclesiastical Record*. He was a strong advocate of land reform and was open to political change.[11] He said on the occasion of his episcopal jubilee in 1909:

> There are some people now disposed to regard me as a West Briton, if not something worse, because I cannot fit myself into the very rigid mould they have been kind enough to cast for us all; but I do not heed them because I am sure that thinking men, both now and hereafter, will judge me by my acts and writings rather than by these wild statements and I am prepared to abide by that test.

Although strongly opposed to unconstitutional agitation, he was in 1914 a supporter of the Irish Volunteers.[12]

On the eve of 1916, the four Irish archbishops were very different in style and in temperament. All were independent-minded, but strongly disillusioned by the failure of London to introduce home rule. They shared a deepening suspicion of the *bona fides* of the Liberal government and of their commitment to bring about home rule for the island of Ireland. The other three archbishops usually deferred to William Walsh of Dublin to provide political leadership for the church as a whole. Their disillusionment with the Irish party, and with the leadership of John Redmond, intensified during the early war years. There was a growing admiration for the Irish Volunteers led by Professor Eoin MacNeill and for a progressive nationalist coalition. This point will be developed later.

There were still a number of strong admirers of Redmond and the Irish party on the bench of bishops, even in the wake of the 1916 Rising. Patrick

O'Donnell had been bishop of Raphoe since 1888. He was translated to Armagh in 1922 as coadjutor with right of succession, a position he took over in November 1924. He was made a cardinal in 1925 and died in October 1927. An academic, he had spent his early professional priestly life as professor of dogmatic and moral theology at Maynooth. O'Donnell was the theologian in residence for the hierarchy at the time the Rising broke out. He was supported in his commitment to the Irish party by the Bishop of Ross, Denis Kelly. Both O'Donnell and Kelly remained staunch supporters of the Irish party until 1919. Despite their great integrity, they did not represent the political views of the bulk of the Irish bishops at the outbreak of the Rising.

The Irish College, the Irish in Rome and the 'Irish Question'

The actions and archives of the rector of the Irish College in Rome, Mgr Michael O'Riordan, and the vice rector, Fr John Hagan, are central to this study. O'Riordan held his post from 1904 until his death in 1919. Hagan, vice rector since 1904, succeeded him.[13] Both men were very strong nationalists and saw it as part of their duty to represent Irish interests (of both church and nation) in Rome.

Under both O'Riordan and Hagan, the Irish College was known as a centre of strong nationalist views. O'Riordan had come to prominence in the early years of the twentieth century when he published *Catholicity and progress in Ireland*.[14] This first appeared in article format and later as a volume. It was a response to Horace Plunkett's *Ireland in the New Century*, which was published first in 1904 and had gone into four editions by 1905. O'Riordan took exception to the thesis that Irish Catholicism was the enemy of modernity. His rejoinder ran to over 500 pages. He retained a strong intellectual interest in the development of Irish politics. He was responsible for producing a number of pamphlets in Italian on that subject.

John Hagan was also well known in Ireland. He was the author of the long-running series in the *Catholic Bulletin*, 'Wine from the royal pope', a series of historical articles based on his work in the archives of the Holy See.[15] He also wrote the 'Letter from Rome' in the *Bulletin* under the pen name 'Scottus', and contributed articles on a variety of other topics under a series of different pen names to the same publication. He furthermore produced a four volume *Compendium of catechetical instruction*. Upon his death in 1930 the *Catholic Bulletin* devoted a substantial part of one edition to his memory.[16] Hagan, more so than O'Riordan, developed very strong and active political interests. His correspondence contains letters from leading political figures of the struggle for Irish independence, including Seán T. O'Kelly and Éamon de Valera. His friendship with O'Kelly dated to the 1916 period, while his friendship with Curran went back to the period when they were seminarians in Clonliffe College, Dublin.

The two leaders of the Irish College had, by 1916, come to share the scepticism of a number of the most prominent of the Irish bishops about the reliability of Irish nationalist MPs. The judgment was that they appeared to have spent so long in Westminster that they had failed to retain their independence. John Redmond's commitment to the war effort had ended, in Hagan's view, the era of independent opposition by the Irish party at Westminster.

The Irish College served as the conduit between Rome and the bishops at home. O'Riordan was the agent of the Irish bishops in Rome. He also acted in that capacity for the bishops of Australia and New Zealand. The Irish College, therefore, handled the most sensitive of business for dozens of bishops from all over the world. That meant that the rector was the recipient of a large volume of correspondence, which provided a commentary on events in Australia, New Zealand, the United States and Ireland. The letters frequently contained the unpublished thoughts on politics of bishops too cautious to express such views in public. The vice rector was also in receipt of a wide range of correspondence. In this way, their combined correspondence is a very valuable source for the study of the period leading up to and after the 1916 Rising.

It is important to stress that the rector was far less politically engaged than the vice rector. Nevertheless, both men shared a sense of mutual disappointment with the performance of the Irish party and with the failure of the British government to put home rule for Ireland into practice. The Irish College had the reputation in Rome for being strongly nationalistic. That may also have held true for many of the seminarians. But politics divided the large Irish community in Rome even prior to the Rising. There were many Irish religious houses in Rome. The Dominicans had a community in San Clemente and the Franciscans in St Isadore's. There were Irish Augustinians, Capuchins and Pallotines in the city. The Irish Christian Brothers had a house at Marc Antonio Colonna. There were many Irish living as members of the Jesuits, Benedictines etc. in Rome, where there were also many houses of Irish women religious. Within that extended Irish diaspora there were many people who had been out of Ireland for a long time. Support for the Irish party and John Redmond was strong. That was not the case in the Irish College.

With the outbreak of the First World War in August 1914 the official British presence in Rome had increased. Besides the mission to the Italian state, London had reached the conclusion that the Holy See was also a priority. Without wishing to have formal diplomatic relations with the Vatican, Sir Henry Howard established a 'mission' there. Sent originally in 1914 to represent the king of England at the enthronement of Pope Benedict XV, he had remained in Rome on 'mission' to the Vatican. Initial British concern was less with Ireland than with the perceived need to counter the increase in German and Austrian influence over the pope after the outbreak of war.

O'Riordan and Hagan were aware that the British government had a number of senior curial officials sympathetic to its cause. Cardinal Gasquet, a Benedictine monk, was a staunch British nationalist and an influential member of the curia. Cardinal Merry del Val was in the same camp. An Anglo-Spaniard, he had been decisively defeated in the conclave that followed the death in 1914 of his staunch patron, Pius X.[17] Despite being far less of a force than under the previous pope, he continued to wield influence. He was no admirer of Irish nationalism and was perceived by the Irish College leadership to be hostile to Ireland and its political cause.

There were also a number of English clerical and religious houses in Rome that supported the policies of the government in London on the Irish question. The English College was one such institution. Relations between the English and Irish Colleges were somewhat distant during the war years. Overall, both Hagan and O'Riordan were very much aware of having to confront a formidable pro-British force inside the Holy See, in Rome, and even within a number of Irish religious foundations in the city.

THE CATHOLIC CHURCH AND THE EVOLUTION OF IRISH POLITICS, 1914–16

The 1916 Rising was not the catalyst for a rupture between the Catholic church and the Irish party.[18] This is confirmed by Fr P.J. Walsh, a relative and early biographer of Archbishop William Walsh. He argues that the archbishop, while in favour of the 1912 home rule settlement, disapproved of Redmond's statement that he was prepared to accept the bill as a 'full and complete settlement of Ireland's claim'. Walsh disliked Redmond's speech in the House of Commons at the outbreak of war. He also viewed with great suspicion the negotiations for the temporary exclusion of a portion of Ireland from the operations of the bill.[19] Michael Curran followed the same line of argument in his memoir.[20] Thomas J Morrissey's biography of the archbishop has made extensive use of that source, as will I in the following pages.[21]

When compiling his account of events, Curran drew extensively on his own personal experience during those difficult years. While close to Walsh he was a man of strong personal political views. His interpretation of Walsh's political development, therefore, must be qualified and become the subject of wider research. It would not be prudent to rely upon Curran in an uncritical way as a guide to the political outlook of Archbishop Walsh. In my view, however, he is reliable in broad outline. Curran was in a privileged position to witness at first hand the process of Walsh's disillusionment with the Irish party and the British government. Although overstating the case, he wrote that Walsh had 'thoroughly realised that constitutional methods to active reform were utterly useless'. That was the position he had adopted, wrote his secretary, 'long before the Larne gun-running and the formation of the Ulster Volunteers'. They had failed 'through the subservience of the Irish party to the English Liberals, aggravated by place hunting for their supporters'.[22] The 'final blow' came from the downright treasonable speeches and activities of the highest-placed and more aristocratic members of the Tory governing classes of England and their unqualified support of the Ulster Volunteers. Among those were numbered members of parliament and 'the highest serving officers and former members of Conservative governments'. At first disapproving of the Irish Volunteers, he came to accept that there was 'full justification for their formation since the arms of the Ulster Volunteers frightened and coerced the weak English government'. His opinion of the Irish Volunteers fluctuated, 'but he never believed that the movement would succeed in its objects'. The archbishop always feared 'that some wild irresponsible element would force matters to extremes and ruin the entire national cause'. He became more and more pessimistic 'as much in respect of the helplessness for the time being of Irish efforts as of the strength of the anti-Irish campaign in England'.[23] Indeed, the views attributed here to Archbishop Walsh are very much an accurate reflection of the opinions of Michael Curran.

The alternative to the Irish party during the early war years was a new political coalition of radical and revolutionaries who were associated with the cultural nationalist movement, the Gaelic League and the GAA. At the political level, opposition to Redmond's party centred on the ideas of Arthur Griffith and Sinn Féin on one side, and Pádraig Pearse and the new radicals on the other. The latter was a member of the IRB as were the other signatories of the 1916 Proclamation. James Connolly and the Irish Citizen Army were allied to the IRB by the beginning of 1916. Both radical Labour and the IRB were intent upon staging a revolution with the assistance of the Germans who, it was commonly believed in those circles, would win the war.[24]

Curran described the breakdown within Irish nationalism as follows: 'There was the parliamentary party section, the Eoin MacNeill section, the underground IRB section, headed by Pádraig Pearse who supported Eoin MacNeill at council meetings, and lastly a large body of the rank and file who abstained from the dissensions that began to arise after Redmond's coup and who, inspired solely by the Volunteer ideal, avoided factional conflicts.' The archbishop's secretary stated that he had relations with 'the right wing' of the Volunteers.[25]

The chief of staff of the Irish Volunteers, Professor Eoin MacNeill, was oblivious to the IRB plans for a rising. Born in the glens of Antrim, he had attended St Malachy's College, Belfast. He was a founder member of the Gaelic League and the first editor of *An Claidheamh Soluis*. Since 1909 he had been professor of early and medieval Irish history at University College Dublin (UCD). He was married with eight children. As chief of staff of the Irish Volunteers he had consistently opposed participation by Irishmen and women in the First World War. MacNeill did not believe that armed resistance by the Volunteers was justifiable unless in reaction to the imposition of conscription or an attempt by the British to suppress the movement he led by force of arms. He was to be deceived by his closest comrades over the revolution.

Archbishop Walsh, according to Curran, knew the MacNeill family 'fairly well' as an uncle, Dr Charles Macauley, had been a colleague of the archbishop when he was first a professor (1867–80) and then president of Maynooth (1880–5). Walsh first met the MacNeill boys while they were studying under their uncle as private pupils. In Curran's words: 'Highly as the archbishop valued Eoin's work as an Irish scholar and historian and for his outstanding work for the language, he had no faith in his political judgment and regarded him as the least suitable man for revolutionary leadership.' Without being 'openly critical nor in the least way cynical or sarcastic, he was disposed to smile at the scholar turned revolutionary'.[26] These were views also held by the leadership of the IRB.

During the years 1914 to 1916, the archbishop's health was very poor. He was often confined indoors or to his bed. In September 1915 he suffered a long and serious attack of eczema, which affected him for more than twelve months. That did not prevent him, however, from following events from his sick bed and from being ultra-critical of the Irish party leadership for, according to Curran, 'their continued subservience to the Liberals and their deception of their country in respecting the Liberals as trustworthy champions of home rule and unfailing friends of Ireland'. The party's support for recruitment during the First World War, according to Curran, was supported only by 'no more than two or three Irish bishops', who were 'faithful followers of the Irish Parliamentary Party'. Archbishop Walsh was not among them. He refused to allow recruitment posters to be placed on the railings of Catholic churches in Dublin, and went so far as to discountenance war hospital and Red Cross collections.[27]

On 31 March 1915 Curran wrote in his diary that the archbishop had reacted very strongly to a decision of the military authorities to hold a parade on Easter Sunday, with a religious service in the pro-cathedral. Walsh sent a draft letter to the administrator of the pro-cathedral, Fr Mooney, to be forwarded to the military:

> I have, of course, no authority to interfere in arrangements for services in the pro-cathedral. The matter has been brought to the notice of His Grace, the archbishop, who directs me to express his surprise that the military authorities, without having even applied for permission to make use of that church, announce their 'intention' of holding a parade service there, and I am to add that no such service can be held.

There were other examples of terse exchanges with the military authorities during the war years over efforts to involve the archbishop in recruiting.[28]

When a coalition government was formed in London in May 1915 Edward Carson was made attorney general. Redmond refused the position of postmaster general. There was little the Irish party could hope for now from the British government. It was compromised and without benefits to show for its loyalty. Curran recorded in his diary on 26 September 1915 that the *Irish Independent* had a good leading article on that day, which pointed out that the country had been sold, and 'the only thing Ireland has gained during the Liberal period of office is university building. It might have added "and some jobs for the Irish party". The old *Freeman* is spluttering with rage.'[29]

Curran regarded the funeral of O'Donovan Rossa in Dublin on 1 August 1915 as the 'date that publicly revealed that a new political era had begun. It was the prelude to the 1916 Rising'. The assistant commissioner of the Dublin Metropolitan Police, Mr Quinn, lived on Riversdale, Drumcondra Road, near the archbishop's house. Curran first met him when he was approached by Quinn to build a garage on the grounds in Clonliffe. He would visit the premises often. Curran described him as being 'a typical policeman but, at the same time, he was a sound nationalist of the Irish Parliamentary Party stamp and distinctly anti-military'. The priest gathered that there was considerable tension between the military and the police around the time of the funeral.

Quinn had come to see Curran in an 'extremely agitated' state. The news was indeed alarming. He said that the 'military were determined to raise the most serious trouble'. The remains of O'Donovan Rossa had arrived in Dublin on 27 July and were brought to the pro-cathedral. The military, finding that they could not stop the funeral, 'were resolved to fire on the people'. Quinn knew that the Volunteers were determined to fire rifle volleys at the graveside, 'and to resist by arms any interference by police or military'. Quinn was fully convinced that a massacre would take place, 'and that the military would seize control and wreak bloodshed'. After the funeral, which passed off without incident, Curran 'never saw a man so relieved' as Quinn was.[30]

Curran admitted that he misjudged the balance of power within the Irish Volunteers. He felt at the time of the funeral that Pearse and his followers were:

> in a decided minority; that Eoin MacNeill was definitely against Pearse's intransigence; that MacNeill commanded a majority; and, although it was perfectly evident that Pearse was in favour of forcing a Rising, that he would not succeed in bringing a sufficient number with him. That was my attitude and what I represented to the archbishop as the attitude, as far as I could ascertain, of people in Dublin.

He said later that he felt at the time that Pearse, while determined to force a rising at any cost, 'had such a small body of followers that he would not be able to carry out his intentions'.[31] Curran was quite mistaken in that surmise.

During the months leading up to the 1916 Rising, Curran relied for his information on a range of good sources. An old Fenian, James Collins, who died suddenly on 13 January 1916, was one of his informants, as was Eoin MacNeill whom he met occasionally. Curran also relied upon Mr Keohane of Gills, and Seán T. O'Kelly, manager of *An Claidheamh Soluis*, 'who was his principal informant'. But O'Kelly, whom Curran found to be 'extremely prudent and reliable', was the first to 'make it plain to me that matters were becoming very critical'.[32] His list of top informants was impressive. Curran was receiving accurate information from the horse's mouth.

Writing to Hagan on 23 January 1916, Curran noted that:

> The party is still losing ground. The credit of the anti-conscription movement goes elsewhere. The retrenchment of the education grants also reacted against them. There was a wonderfully successful and enthusiastic political meeting in the Mansion House Round on Monday [14 January]. Fr Fulberton [?] made a wonderfully impressive speech. The whole affair was largely pro-German but it will put a stop to Nathan and alarm the party. Every time Redmond and the party were named there was a storm of booing.[33]

The popularity of the Irish party continued to slide as preparations for the Rising continued apace.

The last major public meeting before the Easter Rising took place in the Mansion House on 30 March 1916. The deputy lord mayor, Alderman Corrigan, presided. According to a memoir of the period, written by Geraldine Plunkett Dillon, a sister of Joseph Plunkett, Pearse 'gave a wonderful speech and held the hall full of people completely silent. The time seemed to flash by'. MacNeill also spoke. Fr Michael O'Flanagan, a radical priest from the diocese of Elphin, spoke at the end of the meeting, 'and his fighting speech put [Bulmer] Hobson's out of people's minds'.[34] The latter had his eyes set against a rising as much as Pearse and his co-conspirators were determined to strike on Easter Sunday, which was then only three weeks away.

Joseph Plunkett, Count Plunkett, Berlin, Pope Benedict XV and the Rising

Count George Noble Plunkett, the father of Joseph, Geraldine and Mimi, was a most unlikely, if, perhaps, unwitting, revolutionary. Born in 1851, he had attended a Marist school in Nice for three years until he was twelve, and completed his education with the Oblate Fathers in Dublin and the Jesuits at Clongowes. He was a regular visitor to Italy where he pursued a strong interest in art. He was also a close friend of the Provencal poet, Fréderic Mistral. Plunkett spoke French and Italian quite fluently. His schooling finished, he worked for a time as a journalist. His wealthy father rented a palazzo for him in Venice for the winter of 1869. He transferred to Paris in 1870 and then signed on in Trinity College Dublin (TCD) to study law. In Rome in 1884, Pope Leo XXIII had requested the Little Company of Mary, known as Blue Sisters, to set up a house in the city. Plunkett, who was in Rome at the time the appeal was made, secured and purchased a house for the order. Plunkett's generosity came at a time when the new Italian state was threatening to confiscate church property in Rome. His munificence earned the pope's gratitude and he was made a papal count, a knight commander of the holy sepulchre, on 4 April 1884.[35] His generosity to the Catholic church was well known to the Holy See. That background may explain why he could get a private audience with Benedict XV. As a frequent visitor to Rome and to Italy, he may have been granted requests for a private audience on a frequent basis. The decision to grant him an audience with the pope in April 1916, therefore, may have been a matter of routine for Vatican authorities.

Plunkett was a member of the Royal Irish Academy and the Royal Dublin Society (RDS). He was made a director of the National Museum in 1907.[36] He died in 1948, aged ninety six. In the circumstances of 1916 he was a most unlikely revolutionary.

His son, Joseph, was a poet and man of letters. He was a prime mover in the planning of the Rising. His family, because of his delicate health as a boy, had taken him frequently to the continent and to Algiers. He was later educated at Stonyhurst. His first book of poetry, *Circle and Sword*, was published in 1911. He became editor of The *Irish Review*. His article 'Twenty plain facts for Irishmen' led to the suppression of the *Review* in November 1914. Active in the Volunteers before the split in 1914, he was to develop radical nationalist views and join the IRB.[37] Joe Plunkett, together with his close friend, Thomas MacDonagh, were at the heart of the conspiracy to lead an insurrection at Easter. Those pressing for insurrection also included the veteran Fenian Tom Clarke, Seán MacDermott, Éamonn Ceannt and Pearse. Their plans crystallised in 1915. Using methods of conspiracy, deception and subterfuge, they shut out all those likely to oppose such 'recklessness'. The chief of staff of the Irish Volunteers, Eoin MacNeill, was the main victim of these Machiavellian tactics. Pearse, his director of organisation and nominal subordinate, was among those who helped to keep his superior in the dark about the plans for the Rising. Pearse, of course, was also a member of the IRB.[38]

Joe Plunkett carried out his first important mission for the IRB in 1915. Spreading the rumour that he was going to Jersey, he set out at Easter time for Germany via London, Paris, San Sebastian, Barcelona, Genoa and Florence. He travelled under the code name James Malcolm. Travelling to Lausanne via Milan, he went on to Berne and thence to Berlin. There he met Roger Casement, who was not a member of the IRB. They laid plans for the sending of a consignment of arms to Ireland at a time to be decided. Plunkett had to receive instructions from the IRB before he could return to Ireland.[39]

Diarmuid Lynch, a member of the Supreme Council of the IRB, had arrived back in Ireland that year and reported to two members of the IRB executive, Denis McCullough and Tom Clarke. He was made aware that an 'Advisory Committee' had been appointed for the purpose of drafting a plan for an uprising in the Dublin area.

In late May the IRB executive met. Lynch, then acting secretary, proposed the standing down of the 'Advisory Committee' and the setting up of a 'Military Committee' (later reconstituted as a 'Military Council'.) That was comprised of Pearse, Joseph Plunkett and Ceannt. Clarke gave assistance later on that year as did MacDermott. James Connolly and MacDonagh were co-opted in early 1916.[40] They were substantially responsible for the planning of the Rising. But others were also involved, including leading members of the Irish Volunteers like Éamon de Valera. As the time for the Rising approached, many people found themselves being 'sworn in'. This may not have been to the IRB *per se*, but was rather merely a device to maintain secrecy about the plans afoot. Owen McGee is at pains to point out:

Most historians have described the 1916 revolt as a purely IRB affair, but this could be said to be a misnomer. Clarke and MacDermott may have presented the idea of the Rising to various volunteers, swore some of them into the IRB and formed a 'military council' which was *in theory* [original emphasis] something to do with the IRB organisation, but Patrick Pearse, Thomas McDonagh, Joseph Mary Plunkett, Éamon de Valera, Countess Markievicz, Roger Casement and other figures who were leaders of the Rising never had anything to do with the IRB and were certainly not a product of 'the organisation' and its political traditions.[41]

Without wishing to dispute the issue, according to Diarmuid Lynch Joseph Plunkett *was* a member of the IRB as was Pearse. In such flexible times, membership of the IRB may sometimes have been confused with being sworn into the conspiracy to take part in the Rising. Without disputing every detail of the statement, Dr McGee's general thesis has validity. The leadership and participants in the 1916 Rising represented a much broader tradition in Irish society, one which encompassed devout members of the Catholic church, other Christian churches and the Jewish faith. Paradoxically, there were strong Catholics who were also members of the IRB and believed that they had been automatically excommunicated, cut off from the church and living in a state of mortal sin.

In January 1916 Michael Collins had returned from London to work full-time for the revolution. He was a regular visitor to the Plunkett house at Larkfield. Tommy Dillon, husband of Geraldine Plunkett, was employed as a bomb-maker. He was helped by Rory O'Connor. The house was a virtual headquarters for the revolutionaries who came and went without being noticed.

Mimi Plunkett, another sister, twice went to the USA in 1916, carrying information on the forthcoming uprising. She met John Devoy in February and told him that the date of the Rising was Easter Sunday. That was to be conveyed to the German authorities, together with a request for the despatch of German officers to help in the Rising and a landing of arms not earlier than Easter Saturday. Devoy sent news to Berlin that the arms could be landed between Holy Thursday and Easter Sunday. Mimi was sent straight back to New York. She carried a message that the Germans were to be told that the arms had to be landed before the night of Easter Sunday, 23 April. She succeeded in doing so.[42]

In the spring of 1916 Count Plunkett was invited by the British authorities to become a director of the National Gallery as well as of the National Museum, provided he and his family stayed away from politics. This would have been the realisation of a lifelong ambition, but the count politely refused. He was instead made another offer. He was sworn into the IRB by his son, Joe, in March 1916. It was, to say the least, something of a contradiction for a papal count to have become a member of a revolutionary oath-bound society. Why did Joe Plunkett take this unusual step?

Geraldine Plunkett Dillon wrote in her memoir that Casement had sent reports from Germany that the British were trying to influence the Holy See to act against the Irish revolutionary nationalist movement. That would result in either a direct papal condemnation of Irish radical separatists or an instruction from Rome to the Irish hierarchy to condemn 'as unjustifiable any political action in Ireland which was taken without the authorisation of the Irish party'. Minds were further concentrated on 31 March 1916 when the press carried reports that the British prime minister, Herbert Asquith, was visiting Rome.[43] He was received by Pope Benedict XV on 1 April. Cardinal Gasquet's diary records that Asquith also met Cardinal Sévin on that day, and that the prime minister was 'entirely in favour of continuing the English mission to the Holy See'.[44] Sir Henry Howard's presence in Rome was a continuing source of concern to Irish nationalists in the city.

Those developments, together with the warnings from Casement, caused great anxiety in revolutionary circles in Dublin. Joe Plunkett, in response, gave his father orders to go *post haste* to Bern and thence to Rome. His mission was two-fold. First, Plunkett had his father memorise a letter to Casement which he was to send to Berlin while *en route*. It repeated the message that Mimi Plunkett had taken to Devoy in New York, advising Casement not to allow German arms to be landed before Easter Sunday. There was again a request to have German officers sent to take part in the Rising. Joe Plunkett and the IRB also wanted a submarine sent to Dublin Bay. The second part of the count's mission was to proceed from Bern to Rome for an audience with Pope Benedict XV. His son had obliged him to memorise the contents of a letter in French to be written upon arrival in Rome and delivered to the pope.[45] (The text of this letter is given in an appendix to this paper)

The count set out from Ireland about 29 March 1916.[46] He arrived in Bern about 5 April and sent a letter to Casement in Berlin via the German legation. It gave the date of the Rising as Easter Sunday, sought a large consignment of arms to be landed in Tralee Bay not later than dawn on Easter Monday, said it was imperative to send German officers, and requested a German submarine for 'Dublin harbour'. It ended: 'The time is very short but is necessarily so for we must act of our own choice and delays are dangerous.'[47] It was signed 'a friend of James Malcolm' (Joseph Plunkett's alias) and, at the top, it had the word *Aisling*, his authenticating word. The letter gave Easter Sunday as the date of the Rising, called for arms and German officers and a submarine in Dublin Bay. The letter delivered to Casement the following day in Berlin was an exact copy of the one carried by Mimi to New York. Casement mistakenly thought that it was Joe, rather than his father, who was in Bern.[48] His reply confirmed that 20,000 rifles and 10 machine guns were being sent. The request for a submarine and officers had been turned down. Count Plunkett was only told about the sending of the arms. He was not informed by the German legation about the refusal of the other requests. Replying to Casement on 11 April, Count Plunkett pressed Casement on the sending of German officers and the submarine:

> The effect of the presence of German officers and of a German submarine (which otherwise might not seem too important) in Irish waters assisting us would be very great. I may add that the Supreme Council of the Irish Volunteers desire to associate Germany in this marked way with the liberation of Ireland.

He added: 'If I could I would discuss with you many matters which are difficult for both of us.' He said he had 'to leave Berne today for Rome', 11 April.[49]

There was a marked contrast between Plunkett's two assignments. In Bern, he told the Germans, through Casement, of the willingness of the Irish to become belligerents in the war. He had to keep that side of his mission secret from Pope Benedict XV, who was intent on trying to bring about peace and an end to the hostilities.

What were the diplomatic objectives of Count Plunkett's mission to the Holy See? Firstly, he was seeking to prevent a papal *démarche* condemning the Rising. As a corollary, he wanted to ensure that the Irish hierarchy would not receive a directive to speak out against any such action. Any intervention from the Vatican in Irish politics in April 1916 – direct or indirect – would have been most unwelcome to the leaders of the Rising. That position united leaders who were agnostics, anti-clerics and Marxists with those who were devout and orthodox Catholics. Hard-line revolutionaries of any persuasion did not want any interference by the Vatican in Irish politics at that juncture.

Secondly, the count was to explain to the pope the theological justification for an uprising and the Catholic ideas and values on which it was based. Being confident enough to announce to Benedict XV the actual date of the Rising was a sign that the Irish revolutionaries wished to place their trust in him. They felt confident that the news would not leak to hostile sources.

Thirdly, the count was to seek a papal blessing for those about to go 'out'. That was of significance. Irish Volunteers taking part in the Rising had sworn an oath to the organisation. Yet they were to undermine the authority of their leader, Eoin MacNeill, by refusing to obey his counter-manding order. Members of the IRB, moreover, were in an oath-bound society, which brought with it a penalty of automatic excommunication. Did that place a number of the participants in a state of mortal sin? The answer was almost certainly yes, or so many believed. It might be too much, however, to expect a papal blessing for those about to strike.

This view may be too heavily influenced by hindsight. Very few people would have known about the count's visit to Bern, and still fewer about his journey to meet the pope. The former had to do with Casement and German engagement. That would have had to be the subject of some discussion with an inner circle of conspirators. The primary purpose of his mission to the Holy See might have been covered by a story that he was on a pilgrimage to the Vatican. There is a fundamental contradiction at the heart of this exercise. Benedict XV was known as a pope of peace. Since the outbreak of war he had protested against inhuman methods of warfare and tried to alleviate suffering. The Vatican opened a bureau for reuniting soldiers with their families. Switzerland was persuaded to receive soldiers from both sides suffering from tuberculosis. The pope had pursued a policy of strict neutrality from the outset of the war. The unresolved 'Roman question' left the Holy See in an ambiguous and legal limbo within the Italian state, then at war on the side of the British. There were persistent accusations from the belligerent countries that the Vatican's neutral stance was in fact very one-sided.[50] In particular there were repeated suggestions that the pope was pro-German. Against that background, it would have been most imprudent for the head of the neutral Vatican to hold extensive talks with an emissary whose primary mission was to ensure that German arms and men were landed in Ireland in time for use in a military venture. The only conclusion that can be drawn is that the pope had no prior warning of what the count intended to raise with him. It was a routine private audience, nothing more and nothing less. Even the count, naïve as he most certainly proved to be, must have been sufficiently knowledgeable about the policy of Vatican neutrality to keep any details about German involvement from him.

Plunkett, however, intended to tell the head of a neutral Vatican that rebellion was about to break out in British territory and to give the date of the event as Easter Sunday. Had that become known in London it most certainly would have compromised the Vatican's neutral stance. The Holy See was known to have a large number of actively pro-British members of the curia. Setting the issue of the Vatican's neutrality to one side, was it wise to give the pope the actual date of the Rising? That information might either be deliberately leaked to the British or slip out inadvertently and then fall into the hands of the 'enemy'.

Count Plunkett, who certainly was naïve in the realm of Vatican diplomacy, knew Italy and France very well. I have found no evidence to show that Eoin MacNeill was consulted at any time in the planning of his twin mission to Bern and to the Holy See. He was deliberately kept in the dark because of his opposition to the Rising. Joe Plunkett, and others, usurped the authority of the chief of staff of the Irish Volunteers. Their objective was to make doubly sure that the message sent through New York for the German government would also be sent again from Bern.

Plunkett left Bern no earlier than the late afternoon of 11 April, probably arriving in Rome on the 12th or 13th. Dr aan de Wiel, who has searched the archives of the Holy See, has not located an official Vatican minute detailing what was said when the count and the pope met. There is, however, a relatively full account of the audience in Geraldine Plunkett Dillon's memoirs. Based on her conversations with her father many years after the event, it reveals that the two men spoke in French. Plunkett told the pope of the plans for an insurrection and requested a papal blessing for the participants: 'Pa told me that the pope sent them his blessing while the tears of sympathy poured down his face and he said "Les pauvres hommes, les pauvres hommes."'[51] Dr aan de Wiel's account states that the pope listened carefully, appeared worried and, having become convinced of the inevitability of the Rising, blessed the rebels. Dr aan de Wiel also found a copy of a letter in Plunkett's handwriting in the archives of the Vatican. It, too, was in French. In it the date of the uprising was clearly stated: 'l'insurrection doit commencer le soir de jour de Pâque prochain'.[52] The text set out the theological justification for rebellion and spoke of the Irish being forced to stage an uprising. Plunkett advised the pope that home rule would only be introduced together with an amending bill that would meet the demands of the unionist minority. Irish-Americans had promised a consignment of arms, and aid had also been pledged by the Germans. Eoin MacNeill was given full credit for having authorised and sanctioned

Count Plunkett's mission: the letter stated that the count had been sent as a delegate on behalf of the *'Président et du Conseil Suprême des Volontaires d'Irlande (troupes nationaux), M. le Président (le prof. Jean MacNeill) m'a donné un document adressé a Votre Sainteté, que les exigeances de l'état present m'ont oblige de laisser en Irlande'*. Count Plunkett had handwritten the text and signed it: *'Le comte Georges Plunkett'*.[53]

But did MacNeill know about the mission and authorise the use of his name in a letter to the pope? 'One can hardly imagine devout Catholics such as Pearse, a daily communicant, and Count Plunkett misleading Benedict XV,' concludes Dr aan de Wiel.[54] I am not so certain. Nothing was going to be left to chance by the IRB radicals. There was too much at stake.

Count Plunkett broke his silence on the details of his papal audience in 1933. MacNeill took the opportunity to clarify his position and answer the question posed above. Count Plunkett's statement appeared in the *Irish Press* on the same day that Éamon de Valera, now the president of the Executive Council of the Irish Free State, was in Rome to be received in audience by Pius XI. The paper's front-page headline on 26 May ran across seven columns, and read: 'A pope who blessed the men of Easter Week'. Another headline ran: 'Count Plunkett makes moving disclosure'. The story spoke of 'one of the most stirring disclosures ever given to the Irish people. It is that when the Easter Week Rising was decided upon, the executive of the Irish Volunteers, acting as the Provisional Government of the Irish Republic, sent the count as envoy to the pope – then Benedict XV.' It continued:

> The count revealed to His Holiness the plans of the leaders of the insurrection, and the pope was deeply moved when told that the date had been fixed.' Readers were informed that Count Plunkett had 'pledged the Irish Republic to fidelity to the Holy See and the interests of religion. Thereupon His Holiness … conferred His Apostolic Benediction on the men who were facing death – for Ireland's liberty.

The *Press* carried an editorial on the same day entitled 'Benediction', which spoke of Ireland learning 'for the first time one of the most moving and glorious stories in connection with the Easter Week'. It felt that the disclosure would

> bring warmth and gratitude to all Irish hearts. It is wonderful to learn that when the men of Easter Week went out they knew that across the continent of Europe the head of Catholicism was aware of their bravery and had blessed it. Those leaders of the Rising who in their lives had shown so deep and practical a Chris-

tianity had that secret thought to treasure at the hour of their execution when they must have felt their isolation even at home complete. In the turmoil on the continent, across the bloody lines of war, was the man who held the most exalted office in the world, caring for the liberty of a little nation and sending to its republican soldiers the approval of his benediction – that surely was sweetness amongst such darkness and suffering.

On Saturday 27 May, the following drawing appeared on the front page of the *Press*, beside a lead story reporting de Valera's own papal audience and his being conferred with the order of chavalier of the grand cross of Pius IX:

BENEDICTION

Eoin MacNeill was quick to counter. Writing in the *Press* on 28 May, he said tersely: 'The statement which appears in the *Irish Press* of May 26, that the executive of the Irish Volunteers at any time before Easter 1916 formed a provisional government, or took any action as a provisional government, is not true in any sense.'

MacNeill was obliged to return to the fray when the widow of Éamonn Ceannt, Áine, wrote in the same newspaper on 31 May, noting that Mac-Neill had neither confirmed nor contradicted Plunkett's assertion that the letter of credence which the count bore to the Vatican was signed by Mac-Neill. She observed that MacNeill had merely denied that the Volunteer executive had ever formed a provisional government: 'In that perhaps he is right, but the shadow cabinet had been considered and certain portfolios suggested. The only post which I remember definitely was that which my husband told me had been allocated to himself, viz. minister for war.' She challenged MacNeill to state unequivocally whether he had ever signed a letter of credence to the Vatican, the name of the envoy not having been inserted? On 1 June, MacNeill replied in clear and unequivocal terms: 'I signed no such letter, and if any sort of letter of credence to the Vatican purporting to be signed by me ever existed it was a forgery.' He had 'no cognizance of any such acts, considerations or suggestions. If there has been any attempt to equivocate, it has not been on my part.' Further, he repeated his denial that the national executive of the Irish Volunteers had ever formed a provisional government and had taken action in that capacity. He also denied that portfolios had been allocated or even brought forward for consideration. The suggestion had 'no truth whatever'.

On 2 June Count Plunkett re-published his original statement in the *Irish Press* on the letters page, pointing out, in addition, that the 1916 Proclamation had been signed by seven officers of the Volunteers and Citizen Army on behalf of the Provisional Government, the first intimation of whose existence appeared therein. He wrote a further letter to the same newspaper on 19 June 1933, in answer to the *Irish Independent* which, he claimed, had tried to 'discredit the agent of those heroic men, when he reports that they sent him on a mission to the pope before the Rising, and that they were blessed by His Holiness as they faced death for the liberty of Ireland'. He further stated:

> That the coming Irish Republic should have been pledged to fidelity to 'the prisoner of the Vatican' and His successors is an offence to the hypocrites who would destroy the cause of these leaders – our cause today – by the brutality of the Safety (!) Act, and the poison of defamation.

His letter concluded: 'When the leaders surrendered to save the people of Dublin by his message to the archbishop of Armagh, Pope Benedict XV showed His continued affectionate sympathy for the insurgents, then exposed to English savagery.'

This correspondence, conducted seventeen years after the event, shows that the count continued to believe that he had gone to Rome with instructions from the highest authority within the Irish Volunteers.[55] He could hardly have presented himself to Benedict XV as the spokesperson for the Supreme Council of the oath-bound, anti-clerical, IRB. MacNeill's denial is authoritative and unequivocal. That showed that he was deceived yet again by a number of those who planned the Rising.

I will now return to the narrative. After the papal audience Count Plunkett visited the Irish College at St Agatha's.[56] There are no details in his daughter's memoir of who he met there. He told O'Riordan and Hagan that the Rising was going to occur on Easter Sunday. Curran received a note from the vice rector which he had mislaid when compiling his account of the events surrounding 1916. According to his recollection, Hagan's note said something like the following: "'The visitor, who will call on you, was seen by me. He had an audience with the pope." That was the gist of it.' Hagan also gave Curran verbal confirmation of this either at the time or subsequently when he took over as vice rector when Hagan became rector in 1920.[57]

Plunkett arrived back in Dublin on either Holy Thursday or Good Friday. He mentioned the latter date in the *Irish Press* on 26 May 1933. He filed a report on his trip with his superiors, which included his son, Joe, but not Eoin MacNeill. Instead of going directly to request a meeting with Archbishop Walsh, as the pope had urged, the count set out for the country where he met about five members of the hierarchy, so worried was he about 'what the bishops might do'.[58] No names are given in the Plunkett-Dillon memoir. It is likely that the count's authoritative account of his audience with Benedict XV was recounted to each in turn. According to his daughter's account Count Plunkett 'warned them that if there was trouble in the immediate future they should not take any action and asked them to refrain from condemning what they did not understand'. The memoir recounts that he was so tired he did not remember the names of the bishops he had spoken to at the time but 'he thought none of the bishops he interviewed condemned the Rising'.[59]

News of the count's audience with the pope may have spread quite quickly amongst the other bishops. Time was short to spread the news if it was as late as Good Friday that he visited the bishops. But they had at least twenty four hours to communicate the extraordinary news that he had brought to them. The pope did not bless the Rising. Count Plunkett, in his retelling of the events in 1933, had the imagination to embellish and embroider. Naïve he might have been, but he was sincere and very devout. His report was readily believed and of great importance to Catholics who felt a great sense of unease about the revolutionary course upon which they were about to embark.

Archbishop Walsh, Curran
and the 'Castle document'

The pace of events had quickened during Count Plunkett's absence from the country. The 1916 leaders feared that Dublin Castle might move against the Irish Volunteers before there was an opportunity to strike. In the weeks leading up to Easter Sunday the drilling and manoeuvres continued throughout the country. Whereas Eoin MacNeill regarded this as nothing more than business as usual, Pearse was preparing the men for the Rising whether they were aware of that fact or not. Drilling and manoeuvres had become so ritualised, however, that there may not have been a widespread awareness that the Irish Volunteers were about to take part in the real thing. Because of the danger of imminent repression by British forces, there was a growing anxiety among the radicals that the Rising might be stopped. Those anxieties had grounds in reality.

The Plunkett-Dillon memoir casts new light on the development of events. It reveals that the IRB had a spy in Dublin Castle. Eugene Smith, a civil servant, had got sight of a document which detailed British plans to round up the Irish Volunteers and confiscate their arms. When he had the opportunity Smith memorised sections of the document and wrote them out later in safety. Having almost completed his task of copying he felt he had come under suspicion so he passed what he had on to his IRB contact. It was then put in code and given to Joe Plunkett, who deciphered it and brought it to the Military Council. The document outlined details of measures that were to be taken against the Volunteers on receipt of an order from the chief secretary's office. There were lists of all the organisations and the members to be arrested. There were arrangements for confining citizens to their houses and for the occupation of houses, including those of MacNeill and Count Plunkett. Volunteer headquarters were to be occupied, as was Archbishop Walsh's house, which was listed as 'Ara Coeli' (Cardinal Logue's house in Armagh) in the version of the text smuggled out by Smith.

Joe Plunkett and others took the decision to publish the document. The type-setting was done in Larkfield, the Plunkett family home. It was then circulated to the newspapers but all refused to publish it.

On 8 April 1916 Curran records that Séamus O'Kelly called to see him, and was very anxious about information received regarding the intentions of the government to disarm the Volunteers: 'He said the evidence was incontrovertible and would be available next Saturday.' He wanted the influence of 'neutral personages to intervene to prevent bloodshed, asserting that the Volunteers were not pro-German'. Assistant Commissioner Quinn was 'on tenterhooks', according to Curran, who also noted that the Volunteers had become very evident of late, holding nightly meetings, and marching through the streets of Dublin, a hundred strong, with rifles on shoulders.

On Sunday 9 April Seán T. O'Kelly called to see Curran. He had the same story as the other O'Kelly about a Castle document. It had been seen piecemeal by a clerk in Dublin Castle who had reported its contents to the Volunteers. They would not have the complete document until the following Saturday. But Seán T. was convinced of its authenticity, and that 'immediate military action against the Volunteers was intended'. Curran decided not to tell Archbishop Walsh until he had the text.[60] But on 16 April he wrote to Hagan:

> Peace negotiations seem to be in the air especially since Asquith's visit to you [in Rome] … We had 5 German U boats in the Irish sea last week. The mails were interrupted for a day or two. The *Lady Master* [?] and another was sunk. According to underground talk, things are very serious here and heading for an outburst. The talk is that govt is to disarm the Sinn Féiners and the latter say they will resist … The police made a foolish attack on the Citizen Army at Liberty Hall, but it was like the naval attack on the Dardanelles. They didn't come prepared only warned the 'Citizens', who forthwith fortified themselves and summoned reinforcements. The govt is stupid … How in the world a conflict is to be avoided for long I cannot see. You may have heard more about it before this letter reaches you.[61]

Seán T. O'Kelly visited Curran again on 18 April 1916, the Tuesday of Holy Week, saying 'that there was little or nothing new but that the situation was very serious. Looks as if the document was not intended for immediate use but drawn up in case of invasion'. Although Curran had his suspicions, he was not certain that O'Kelly was a member of the IRB. In fact, as he was to learn later, his friend was part of the inner circle that had been entrusted with a mission in 1915 to tell John Devoy in America of the decision to stage a rising. Prudence dictated that he should not confide in his clerical friend, who would have been duty-bound to report the matter to the archbishop.

On 19 April Alderman J.J. Kelly read the 'Castle document' on to the record of Dublin corporation. By that time it had already appeared in Patrick Little's paper, *New Ireland*. Once it was part of the official record of the corporation, however, the dailies had no alternative but to report it. The news shocked many and increased a sense of public indignation despite the official denials as to its authenticity by Dublin Castle.[62] Curran wrote again to Hagan on 19 April with news of the document:

You will be interested in the enclosed. Naturally it has caused great excitement this evening. The document was to have been printed [in] Ireland today. The printers got alarmed, brought it to the *Irish Times* who advised its suppression and who I am told sent it to the Castle. Meanwhile the printers consulted a solicitor who also advised its suppression. The editor then thought of giving the gist of the document in the form of notes, but the matter was settled by the Castle stepping in suppressing it. Meanwhile some fifty thousand leaflets were printed. It was then brought today to the evening papers who all refused to publish it. During the day Ald. Tom Kelly published it under special circumstances in the corporation. It is said a meeting of the Privy Council was summoned. At any rate the papers published it in the evening with the usual denial from the military authorities.[63]

Curran provided his own theory, which, he said, was based on 'good ground':

Not long ago there was a grave anxiety lest the Huns would pay us a visit in Lough Swilly, if not on the E. coast of England. Great precautions were naturally taken. What would be more prudent for the military authorities to have in readiness [a] precautionary measure to deal with the armed forces of Liberty Hall and Sinn Féin. They must have had some scheme ready, if they are not fools. Liberty Hall and some of the wilder Sinn Féin people would certainly join the Huns. Equally certain it is that neither John MacNeill nor the National Volunteers would do so. But there is no getting over the fact that some of the same extreme people would.

That being so, Curran argued:

What is there to wonder at in the document except the isolation of this house and the Mansion House? I certainly cannot understand the prohibition of communication to this house and the Mansion House. I could understand neighbouring Volunteers seeking to conceal their weapons about the grounds in case of a general search, but I cannot surmise what they mean by prohibiting communication *from* here [original emphasis]. At any rate there is my theory. As the document has got into the evening papers, the Volunteers do not see the necessity of publishing the document in the way they contemplated.[64]

Curran recorded in his diary on 19 April that the archbishop did not accept Dublin Castle's denials that the document was false; he thought that there was 'a lot of substance' in it. Séamus O'Kelly had visited Curran that same day, and confirmed that view. Curran then went to 2 Dawson Street, the headquarters of the Irish Volunteers. On entering the building, one walked on a stone plaque 'recording the shooting of the civilians at Bachelor's Walk'. (The plaque was later seized by the military.) There Curran met Eoin MacNeill, who also believed that the document was genuine. The conversation continued: 'We were discussing bloodshed. Anyway, it was clearly conveyed to me by him that it would result in armed resistance, and certainly by Seán T., to whom I distinctly remember talking either on that evening of 19 April 1916, or next morning.' Curran had not seen the evening papers. As Dublin Castle had sought to suppress publication of the document, the Volunteers had 50,000 copies of it ready to be handed out. As the following day was Holy Thursday, he said that they should be sent to the churches and the priests would see that they were distributed. Publication meant that it was not necessary to act on his suggestion.

On 20 April, Holy Thursday, the German arms consignment on the *Aud* was intercepted in Tralee Bay by the British navy. Its captain scuttled his ship on 21 April. Sir Roger Casement landed the same day from a U boat, stationed off Banna strand, near Tralee. He carried news that the promised German support would not be sufficient to launch an uprising. Shortly afterwards he was arrested.

On 21 April, Good Friday, Bulmer Hobson was 'arrested' by the IRB. He was opposed to the timing of the Rising. That evening, at 7pm, James MacNeill, Eoin's brother, visited Curran and expressed his grave concern that a 'small rash act by a fool on either side would cause a blaze and involve everybody'. He dreaded 'a calamity arising out of what may well be a misunderstanding'. James, who was not on the council of the Volunteers, told Curran that two men, who were not identified, had called to see his brother that morning. They had 'completely upset Eoin' and he was extremely worried, as was James was. James wanted to seek an unofficial assurance that would be given to some responsible person 'that no disarmament was intended'. This was a reference to Archbishop Walsh. Curran replied that he was ill and that nobody was allowed to see him except Dr Cox. Walsh's doctor would learn the archbishop's views by the following day. Cox was a close friend of the MacNeills. He was also a Privy Councillor with access to Dublin Castle. Curran asked MacNeill to accept him as a possible route to the authorities.

That night Curran told the archbishop of the visit. He listened carefully but said nothing. Curran, meanwhile, had also heard a bit of gossip, to the effect that an officer at a dance had told his partner that he had not taken off his clothes for forty eight hours, and that he had 10 other officers and 200 men in barracks under arms ready to attack the Volunteers. At twenty minutes to ten that night, Good Friday, Curran met Quinn. They talked about the dangers of disarmament 'to which he [Quinn] was fully alive'. But the policeman was convinced that 'the Volunteers were lunatics, playing into the hands of the military'. He mentioned that two men had been landed in Kerry, although he probably did not use the name Roger Casement to Curran on that occasion.

Curran met Dr Cox on Easter Saturday, 22 April, telling him that the archbishop would be prepared to discuss the matter raised by James MacNeill with him. Walsh, however, decided not to interfere. That did not prevent Dr Cox taking steps to make representations to the British authorities. But both Cox and Quinn told Curran that the military controlled everything, and that 'not even the highest placed legal or civil authority carried any weight against the military'.

On 22 April Eoin MacNeill issued a countermanding order, cancelling manoeuvres for the following day. This appeared in the *Sunday Independent* the next day. Curran wrote to Hagan on Saturday, 22 April 1916.

Things are even more serious here. Yesterday the leaders of the Volunteers received serious news. I don't know what it was except that they are convinced on what they regard as absolutely reliable authority that preparations to disarm them are in progress. The Volunteers will resist if this is attempted and are taking steps not to be surprised unawares. A rash step by a fool on either side will precipitate an outburst. Frankly I do not see how the thing can end without a blaze sooner or later.[65]

Curran, who was no amateur in the study of Irish politics, added:

Personally I find it hard to believe that the government or police authorities mean to cause trouble. They deny the genuineness of the published document, but many sane people including His Grace (and, I modestly add, myself) simply regard the denial as worthless. I look at the document as a plan agreed upon, or under consideration, for future eventualities, indefinite as regards time.

He identified the extremists, as he described them, within the nationalist ranks:

> But the military people form the dangerous element on one side and Liberty Hall, the secret societies, and some of the more extreme Irish Volunteers form the dangerous elements on the other. I can hardly imagine the military authorities taking such a critical step without consulting the government and I can hardly imagine the government giving consent. It would simply set the whole country on fire …

He read the events as follows: 'Naturally many people see in these supposed arrangements a move to introduce conscription. All is not plain sailing within the Irish party, nor within the National Volunteers.'[66]

Curran had heard alarming news from a priest who had come to his office in an agitated state after having a conversation with a Volunteer officer. He was told that 'Easter Sunday's mobilisation meant a rising'. The identity of the officer was not revealed by Curran other than that he was well known and much esteemed and that he was killed in the Rising. The officer had consulted the priest to 'satisfy his conscience as to what he ought to do'. After the visit of the priest, Curran went to see Seán T. O'Kelly at the offices of the Gaelic League in 25 Parnell Square. According to Curran's diary entry for that day:

> He told me that the Volunteers were to mobilise on the following day [Sunday] at 4pm with arms and three days provisions. Seán felt like James MacNeill and feared the extremists, including those of his own body, would cause a clash. He was particularly apprehensive of the dangerous influence of Liberty Hall and T. C. [Tom Clarke] Among the other extremists were Pearse [and] Fitzgibbon.[67]

At the time Curran supported the position held by Eoin MacNeill: 'I was entirely opposed to anything in the nature of a rising until the Germans could land.' MacNeill's countermanding orders were ignored by the inner core of the IRB led by Clarke, Pearse, MacDermott, MacDonagh, Joseph Plunkett, Ceannt and others. Bulmer Hobson was kidnapped by his fellow members of the IRB and held under house arrest in order to prevent him from trying to stop the Rising.

Curran wrote to Hagan again, on Easter Sunday, 23 April 1916:

> Things passed off quietly here today. John MacNeill issued an order countermanding the mobilisation of the Volunteers. It was published in the *Irish*

[sic] Independent and by messenger. The more extreme party (Liberty Hall and Pearse) tried to suppress it and declare that it was bogus. Result – a new scare. Miss MacNeill [Eoin's sister] came here [archbishop's house] towards 3pm to obtain help to stop the mobilisation and to declare the MacNeill order authentic. According to John MacNeill the carrying out of the mobilisation would end in a catastrophe and bloodshed. The order was obeyed, though there were small gatherings of Volunteers. A crisis has evidently come. I fear today's change of procedure will lead to a split between the moderate and more extreme Volunteers.[68]

After speaking with the archbishop about Miss MacNeill's visit, Curran undertook to go to priests of the nearer mobilisation districts and deliver a letter from Eoin MacNeill authenticating his order. He selected the districts of Fairview, Rutland Square and Camden Row. He went first to Fr John Flanagan of Marlborough Street. The latter went with the future Archbishop of Dublin, Edward Byrne, to Volunteer headquarters in Parnell Square where they found that MacNeill's countermanding order was being carried out. Curran also gave a letter to Fr Walter MacDonald, later parish priest of Fairview. He agreed to 'see after Fr Mathew Park' (a mobilisation centre). Curran then went with Fr Charles Murphy of Harrington Street to Camden Row where the letter was given to a score of Volunteers. He found that they were disbanding when he arrived. Curran recorded that Quinn had spent all of Easter Sunday in Dublin Castle and had not returned at 10pm.[69]

EASTER RISING AND AFTERMATH

A detailed account of Curran's activities during Easter Week appears elsewhere in this volume. Suffice it to note here that he behaved very courageously during those days of revolution. The violence did not keep him indoors. Unfortunately, his fluent and frequent correspondence with Hagan and O'Riordan was interrupted by the unfolding tragedy.

Archbishop Walsh, it might be noted, came under some pressure on Easter Monday night from James O'Connor, a law officer working in Dublin Castle, who was later knighted for his services to the British Crown. He was attending the race meeting at Fairyhouse when he heard of the Rising. Hurrying back to Dublin, he called at archbishop's house at about 6pm. Walsh received him briefly in a room off his bedroom. Fr Patrick Walsh, a secretary to the archbishop and subsequently his biographer, had a brief word with the departing O'Connor as he was driving away. The archbishop talked with his secretary immediately after the interview. He had found O'Connor to be excited and panicky. The lawyer wanted the archbishop to write a letter calling on the insurgents to desist from their mad enterprise. The archbishop refused. He spoke to his secretary of the effrontery of O'Connor and the British government for trying to make a cat's paw of him. In the presence of O'Connor, he had denounced the incompetence of a government that had allowed blood to be spilt. The archbishop spoke to him of the folly of a rising that could only end in defeat. Finally, he called on the government to resign and that, if they did not do so, they ought to be superseded. Walsh did not like the tactics of Dublin Castle. They had sent a Catholic law officer to him to secure his condemnation of the Rising. He refused to do so. But that did not prevent Fr Walsh writing in his book that: 'Dr Walsh, archbishop of Dublin, expressed his detestation of it [the Rising] in an interview I had with him on Easter Monday of 1916.'[70] The archbishop did not, however, break his public silence at this point.

Eoin MacNeill's composure deserted him momentarily in his home at Woodtown on hearing of the uprising. Falling on his knees, he placed his head on his wife's lap as he broke down and wept. 'Everything is ruined,' he said. He recovered quickly. On the Wednesday his home was visited by Arthur Griffith. He had cycled from Clontarf to Woodtown via Lucan and Templeogue. While neither man approved of the Rising, both agreed that something had to be done to try to bring forces to the relief of the men who were besieged in Dublin. But it was decided that effective action was impossible. Realising that the British would attempt to teach the Irish a lesson, MacNeill had sought to prevent further violence by sending a letter, probably on Tuesday 2 May, to General Maxwell, the commander of the British forces. Anxious that the British might provoke further bloodshed, he offered to try to prevent the spread of violence between the Volunteers and the British forces. His son, Niall, was the courier. Maxwell sent a car to MacNeill's house to bring him to headquarters. He did not see Maxwell then, but was promptly arrested and taken to Arbour Hill. He saw Maxwell instead on Wednesday 3 May, but there was no meeting of minds. He had heard the executions taking place in the yard below on both the Tuesday and Wednesday. Taken out for exercise on Thursday morning, he walked between the wall against which the leaders had been shot and firing squads rehearsing for further action with empty rifles.[71]

In the midst of the executions, the Bishop of Down and Connor,

Joseph MacRory, writing to Michael O'Riordan in Rome on 4 May 1916, may have summed up what the archbishop of Dublin was thinking:

> The Dublin affair is a shocking and idiotic tragedy. It was engineered by a few desperate socialists and a few sincere but silly patriots. Of course it had no chance whatever of succeeding. The danger is that it may have succeeded in gravely injuring Ireland's constitutional cause. Peace is restored everywhere. Belfast remained quiet, thank God, throughout all the excitements.[72]

On 8 May Curran wrote a long, descriptive letter to Hagan reviewing what had happened in Dublin:

> We have had a terrible fortnight since and we have tasted of the horrors of war and don't want any more. It is all a nightmare and I can hardly bear to [think] about it. The whole thing was terribly foolish and tragic! I told you in my last letter that the danger of a collision with the police [and] troops seemed to be at an end, as on that day MacNeill ordered the Easter meeting of the Volunteers should not take place. An attempt to nullify the orders by the extremists was met by a second order from MacNeill authenticating his previous orders, and these orders were obeyed.[73]

Curran then described what happened next:

> What was our dismay on Easter Monday to hear about 12.20 that the GPO was taken by the Volunteers and that the Castle was attacked! It was hard to realise that here in the year 1916 we were back in 1798 and that the Rising was at our very doors, largely by people known to every Dublin man. It would appear that the Larkin crowd leader, James Connolly, the secret soc. men headed by T[om] Clarke and an extreme fanatical section of the Volunteers headed by Padraic Pearse, MacDonagh and Kent, determined on Sunday evening to rise! There seems to be all too convincing evidence that they had conspired with the Germans through the Clan na Gael, or directly, for such a rising and that they used the Irish Volunteers for their own purposes. MacNeill was latterly a mere figure-head in their hands. I fancy MacNeill must have got wind of what was on late on Good Friday or on Holy Thursday. Many say he cancelled the orders for the Easter assembly of the Volunteers – probably on hearing of Casement's appearance in Kerry.

He continued:

> The extremists, seeing that the stopping of the Easter demonstration would spoil their plans, circulated the reports that the cancelling of the Easter parades

was a bogus command – a government dodge. John MacNeill thereupon sent out in all directions new commands authenticating his former command. I saw some myself, for his sister came here in a pitiable state about 3pm on Easter Sunday with copies of them, signed by MacNeill. He wanted the Abp [archbishop] to get the priests to stop the assembly.

He explained further:

At any rate the Connolly-Clarke-Pearse section summoned their men. I have no doubt whatever that very few knew what really was on. The rank and file were composed of young men, very many only 15–17, who formed the Volunteers (1) to counteract Carson's, (2) to be prepared against conscription. These did not want rebellion, though they were prepared, as I warned you, to resist disarmament. Some believed that disarmament was immediately at hand and were quite prepared for resistance, but very many only thought that it was one of the usual route marches. You need have no doubt about these facts for we have all met several instances of such cases during the terrible crisis. Rebellion was the last thing they dreamed of.

Curran was convinced that:

It was the strong men of extreme views that stampeded the whole thing and compromised all. MacNeill was no match for such men and the only strong thing he did was resolutely to refuse [to] countenance them and he certainly saved a general rising all over the country. His words were everywhere obeyed, except to a small extent in Cork city. The risings in the country were due to the news from Dublin on Wednesday and Thursday. We were saved the prospect of a German invasion.

He continued:

The Rising was very nearly being a terribly serious one. Had John MacNeill's orders not been sent and obeyed, we would have had a score of Dublins over the country. The Rising would not be over yet and the entire country would have had to be [deployed] with soldiers and starved and burned.

He noted that 'the material damage done in Dublin is immense'. He also described what it was like to live under martial law: 'We must be indoors at 8.30. Houses are searched for arms and papers. Letters are opened and afford abundant material for prosecution and arrests are being made wholesale.'[74]

What was the reaction of other members of the hierarchy to these events? The Bishop of Ardagh and Clonmacnois, Joseph Hoare, called it a 'mad and sinful adventure'. The Bishop of Ross, Denis Kelly, told his congregation in Skibbereen that he could see no justification for it and that 'on those to blame for it was the guilt of murder'.[75] The Archbishop of Cashel, John Harty, admired and supported the Irish Volunteers. But his initial reaction to the Rising was one of criticism. He told a congregation in St Michael's church, Tipperary, on 7 May:

> We all know that the people of Ireland at large do not want any revolutionary measures ... We are perfectly well aware that the people of Ireland believe that by constitutional means they can obtain substantial redress of their grievances. The history of the past has shown that all revolutionary measures are doomed to failure.[76]

Similar comments were made by the Archbishop of Tuam, John Healy.

Professor Whyte has described the spectrum of reaction among the other bishops, placing the Bishop of Killaloe, Michael Fogarty, and the Bishop of Limerick, Edward Thomas O'Dwyer, as being more on the advanced nationalist side.[77] Jumping forward a month, to 14 June, Michael Fogarty gave an address at Quin, Co. Clare, on the Rising. It was harsh in its criticisms of the British authorities. Writing to Michael O'Riordan on 16 June, he described the political situation thus:

> There are Sinn Féin and sinn féin – those on for rebellion, those short of that in pursuit of the preservation of Irish ideals, religion, moral social etc. The former were few, the great body belonged to the latter class. Practically all Irish Ireland has gone over since the rebellion to this latter class. That is: they don't want rebellion. But the brutal shootings and deportations of their young insurgents after surrender has filled the country with indignation and roused such an anti English feeling as I never saw before.[78]

As regards the priests, Bishop Fogarty said that there was only *one* priest in all Ireland who joined the rebels, as far as the bishops' sources showed. Fogarty had about 150 priests and 'not one of them was connected with rebellion'. The same was true of all Munster as far as he knew. But, he claimed, it suited county inspectors to make sweeping statements without precision:

It is quite true that a great many, mainly most of the young priests, were in sympathy with Volunteers, Sinn Féin etc. but not for rebellion. No one knew rebellion was in the air until the thunder broke. They were in these movements because they aid Irish ideals, as opposed to English, American sensualistic materialism, and as a defence against the threatened attack from Carson's Orangemen. For this it was not the priests who [word unclear] these movements: the usual thing happened; this Irish sap rose simultaneously in young Irishmen whether their call was lay or cleric. The priests were merely exponents of a general sentiment which washed all around them, as in the Land League days. So at this moment the whole country has gone Sinn Féin as a result of the stupid brutal shooting of the insurgents – not that they want or mean to have rebellion: they simply have turned deadly sour, and have lost all sympathy with England.

Fogarty wrote that he did not have time to give O'Riordan a more detailed account, as he was away every day on visitations. In summary, however, he concluded that 'the *Freeman* has become rotten' and 'the Irish party (William O'Brien excepted) has fallen into disrepute. The people resent their language and apathy about the insurgents.' He felt that the chances of home rule being accepted 'with part of Ulster cut off are very problematical'. It was a wise man who would say what was wisest. Before signing off, he gave the news 'Bishop of Cork is dead – going to funeral' and 'Limerick is Ireland's one man at present'.[79]

In Cork, meanwhile, Daniel Cohalan, the then auxiliary bishop, along with the Lord Mayor, T.C. Butterfield, and the High Sheriff, William Harte, sent a telegram to the lord lieutenant, John Redmond and the prime minister protesting against further executions.[80] On 16 May Cohalan, along with Butterfield, Harte, and the chairman of Cork City Council, W.M. Murphy, wrote another letter to the lord lieutenant. Published in the *Cork Examiner* on 17 May, the letter deemed 'it our duty to place on record our protest against the continuance of arrests throughout the country and the further detention of a large number of those who, during the panic of the past two weeks, have been placed under arrest, and in many cases deported'. They did not consider that the state of the country warranted the continuance of those measures any longer. On the contrary, they believed that the 'unrest was thereby prolonged'. There were cases of arrested men where charges could not be brought against them and, in other cases, men were detained because they were members of the Irish Volunteers. The latter did not constitute an offence against the law of the realm. The signatories felt it was 'the bounden duty of the authorities to have these cases investigated without delay' and to provide facilities so that they could make their defence.[81] On 2 July 1916 Cohalan wrote to O'Riordan at the Irish College:

> My letter gives in outline a history of the late eventful Easter week in Cork: and as you can see we did not make much history in Cork. I sent my letter to London to be printed; got it censored in London; and then taken by the Press Association. That got it a wide circulation.[82]

Overall, therefore, it can be seen that Cohalan, who succeeded in August to the bishopric of Cork, was cautious in his reaction to the Rising.

The Archbishop of Dublin, meanwhile, had run into difficulties with the British military authorities. Two priests of his archdiocese had been arrested. Fr Paddy Flanagan, a curate at Ringsend, was held and sent to Richmond Barracks. Released on 9 May he gave 'a dreadful account of the treatment of the prisoners'. Fr Mooney was detained in his own house under armed guard from noon until 6.30pm, 'and then only freed on the promise not to leave the place for three days'.[83] Walsh's anger with General Maxwell over the executions, the extra judicial killings and the mass arrests, was palpable. The following exchange of letters was published in the *Cork Examiner*, dated 12 May:

> Noble priests
>
> General Maxwell's appreciation
>
> The following 'correspondence' has passed between General Maxwell, Commanding the Forces in Ireland, and Archbishop Walsh:
>
> Headquarters, Irish Command,
>
> 8 May 1916.
>
> Your Grace, - I shall be glad if you will convey to the clergy of your church my high appreciation of, and thanks for, the services rendered by them during the recent disturbances in Dublin.
>
> I am aware that such services were practically universal, but it is possible that Your Grace may desire to bring to notice individual cases of special gallantry or devotion.
>
> If such is the case, I shall be obliged if you will inform me of the names of the gentlemen in question. I am, Your Grace's obedient servant,
>
> J.G. Maxwell, General,
>
> Commanding in chief the forces in Ireland.

Archbishop's house, Dublin,

11 May 1916

Dear Sir John Maxwell, - In reply to your letter of Monday, I beg to thank you for your gratifying testimony to the fidelity of our clergy in the discharge of their duties during the recent troubles in Dublin.

I have been much struck by your request to be furnished with the names of the clergy in cases of special gallantry, or devotion, that I might desire to bring under your notice. But I quite concur in your view that services deserving of high praise are practically universal. Many such cases have, of course, come to my knowledge – especially amongst the clergy of my own pro-cathedral parish in Marlboro' street and those of the Cappuchin community in Church street. But I feel that it would be invidious to treat those cases as if they were exceptional.

Again, thanking you for your kindly letter, I remain, your faithful servant. William J. Walsh,

Archbishop of Dublin.

While Walsh did not immediately issue a general statement on the Rising, his exchange with Maxwell reveals how icily he regarded the British authorities. His actions spoke louder than words. On 10 May he subscribed £100 to a relief fund that had been set up by the lord mayor of Dublin.[84] On 13 May, the day following the final executions, he signed a petition from the lord mayor requesting that Alderman Tom Kelly should get a fair and immediate trial. On 15 May the archbishop was invited to meet Prime Minister Asquith at the vice regal lodge. He replied that he was still an invalid and was unable to make such a call. On 23 May he received a telegram from the United States and agreed to act as chairman of the executive committee of Cardinal Farley's Irish Distress Fund, later known as the National Aid Fund. On 27 May two members of the royal commission of inquiry into the causes of the rebellion called on him to ask his views. His answer focused on the breakdown of the constitutional movement.

The Bishop of Limerick, Edward O'Dwyer, was seen nationally as the hero of the hour. That is all the more surprising as he had not always been *persona grata* in nationalist circles in Ireland. He was a man of apparent contradictions.[85] His courage and individualism were never in doubt. He showed both in his reaction to the Rising.

He wrote to his fellow countyman, Michael O'Riordan, on 10 May from the parish of Glenroe in south Limerick. While he shared the

MacRory/Curran thesis about the origins of the Rising, his letter was very revealing of his inner and, as yet, unpublished, thoughts:

You know nearly as much about the genesis of the outbreak in Dublin as we do. The censorship has been very rigid; and it is only now that we are coming to know the simple facts as they happened. I have it from one who ought to know that the immediate cause of the outbreak was that one division of the Irish Volunteers got out of hand, and began the fight, and then the others joined rather than leave the others in the lurch. But there is no doubt that there was a really widespread reorganisation of a physical force body, and that it was only a question of time when they would come out. On Easter Saturday an order was ignored by Eoin MacNeill that the Volunteers were not to assemble on Easter Sunday, and this would point to his apprehending what occurred. Anyhow on Easter Monday large bodies of Volunteers with arms suddenly seized important points in Dublin: the post office O'Connell St, the Four Courts, the Broadstone, [word unclear] St, and Westland Row railway station, but failed in a weak attack upon the Castle. Next day troops were poured in from England, and desperate fighting took place. Asquith in H. of Commons said last night that the casualties among the military amounted to over 500. By all accounts the Volunteers fought with great bravery, but were helpless against artillery, which the military used against the [buildings] which were held by the Irish. The post office was set on fire, I believe by incendiary shells, and burned down and both sides of O'Connell st have been reduced to ruins in the same way. We have not heard the number of casualties amongst the Volunteers but it must be very great. Peirse [*sic*], who was the leader, was wounded, and when it became apparent that they could not succeed surrendered with all his forces...2,000 Volunteers have been deported to England, and it is said that they are to be sent to France. Day after day, for the last week the leaders are being tried, condemned and shot. Peirse [*sic*], a son of count Plunkett, a young fellow named McDonagh, a professor in Nat. University, and I think ten others have been shot. Scores have been sentenced to penal servitude, and no one knows where it all will stop. At Limerick, the Volunteers surrendered their arms without resistance, but whether that will save them from arrest is doubtful. In my opinion it has been reaction against the extreme Britishism of Redmond and co. The national spirit of the young men of Ireland revolted against what has been going on for a year and a half and will do the same again and again. This has been by far the most formidable rebellion since '98 and the government may bless its stars that the Volunteers in Dublin had not more patience. In another year, no one could tell what might happen. If I were at home, I could get you more details, but here we have not even a newspaper.[86]

O'Dwyer wrote another letter to O'Riordan, on 18 May:

There is hardly a second opinion in Ireland as to the savagery with which the govt has been acting. But it will do good. The country was being hypnotised by the politicians, but it is being revived these days. Imagine, Sir J.G. Maxwell had the impudence to write to me asking me, in rather peremptory terms, to remove the Revs Mick Hayes and Thos Wall, as being a serous danger to the peace of the realm. I told him to specify his charges against them, and the evidence which he had to support them, and then I would investigate the matter. He then wrote more civilly that he thought I could deal with the case by disciplinary methods. I don't think he will forget the answer which I sent him yesterday.[87]

(Maxwell's first letter had been sent to O'Dwyer on 6 May, and requested that he discipline the two named priests for their part in radical nationalist politics).

O'Dwyer's blistering reply to Maxwell was delayed by the censor but was published on 27 May in the *Cork Examiner*, and in the Dublin *Evening Mail* on 30 May. The bishop referred to Maxwell's appeal for help 'in the furtherance of your work as military dictator of Ireland'. He stated, however: 'The events of the past few weeks would make it impossible for me to have any part in proceedings which I regarded as wantonly cruel and oppressive.' O'Dwyer referred to Maxwell's part in the Jameson raid, describing those who took part as 'buccaneering invaders' who were deserving of the 'supreme punishment'. Turning to those who took part in the Rising, he continued:

> You took care that no plea for mercy should interpose on behalf of the young fellows who surrendered to you in Dublin. The first information which we got of their fate was the announcement that they had been shot in cold blood. Personally I regard your action with horror, and I believe that it has outraged the conscience of the country. Then the deporting by hundreds and even thousands of poor fellows without a trial of any kind seems to me an abuse of power as famous as it is arbitrary, and altogether your regime has been one of the worst and the blackest chapters in the history of the misgovernment of this country.[88]

This was a strong statement from the seventy four year old prelate, who forwarded his reply to Maxwell to Riordan on 31 May.[89]

The bishop was in fine form when he responded in early June to a resolution of support received from the Limerick board of guardians:

> It would be a sorry day for the church in Ireland if her bishops took their orders from agents of the British government. As to the poor fellows who have given

their lives for Ireland, no one will venture to question the purity and nobility of their motives or the splendour of their courage. But many blame them for attempting a hopeless enterprise. Yet we cannot help noticing that since Easter Monday home rule has come with a bound into the sphere of practical politics.[90]

Fr P.J. Roughneen, on holiday in Dublin from his parish in England, wrote to O'Riordan on 9 June, describing the final moments of the leaders of the Rising: 'Major MacBride refused to be blind-folded, saying: "I have looked down your gun-barrels all my life", a rosary beads hung from his hands. Pearse's last words were that Connolly should die in peace with the church; his prayer was efficacious and Connolly died well.'[91] Thus, the new Catholic image of the leaders of the 1916 Rising was already beginning to take shape at a popular level. Fr Roughneen also spoke very positively of the bishop of Limerick: 'Dr O'Dwyer of Limerick is the hero of the day; rumour has it that his opponent was one of the Jameson raiders, sentenced to death and afterwards reprieved.'[92]

O'Dwyer was enjoying his notoriety. Fr J.J. Ryan wrote to O'Riordan on 23 June:

> I was in Limerick Monday and called on the bishop. I never saw him look better – he all energy 'agin the government'. We are passing through troublous times here at home … There is no leader in church or state as in the Land League days ('when we were boys'). The nation is in a dream and asleeping. The government were rudely aroused from lethargy in the afternoon of Easter Monday and both of them have been doing many foolish things since … How will the poor country emerge from the present chaos is the question.[93]

Meanwhile, Eoin MacNeill had to face court martial. Unknown to him a number of advocates lobbied against his being executed. John Dillon and John Redmond both interceded on his behalf, as they also did on behalf of other leaders.[94] But he faced a court martial and a possible death sentence. He sought to enlist the services of the Dublin solicitor John O'Connell, 'a man of independent position and of high standing in his profession'. But MacNeill wrote that 'he was afraid to defend me and positively refused to take up my case…. His conduct would be hard to explain in the history of the legal profession in Ireland.'[95] MacNeill found an alternative. Maxwell ruled that he would be tried before a general court martial and not a field general court martial. The former allowed him to have his own counsel,

James Chambers KC. Fr Michael Curran was one of the defence witnesses called on his behalf. On 24 May MacNeill was given penal servitude for life. On 31 May, on his way to jail in England, he wrote to his wife Taddie:

> We are all in good form and in excellent spirits. We said the rosary last night in Irish…. What I told you about Éamonn Kent fainting is untrue. He did not faint but went to death in full self-possession, RIP. I pray for them all every night. Jas. Connolly died in the true faith. We have reached Taunton. My cash is done, but a fellow-prisoner is standing me an orange.[96]

On 6 June 1916 Archbishop Walsh left for respite care in Co. Wicklow, where he remained until 6 September. In his absence Fr Bowden, administrator of the pro-cathedral, took over his duties as chairman of the National Aid Fund. The archbishop kept himself well informed of political developments, and the shifting pattern of public opinion. On 29 June, for example, he wrote a public letter announcing that he was sending on £1,000 of the amount subscribed in America 'in aid of the sufferings from recent troubles in Dublin'.[97]

In Rome O'Riordan and Hagan were sufficiently concerned about the drift of events in Ireland to fear a possible British-inspired statement being issued from the Holy See. There was evidence that the British had stepped up their efforts to secure such a *démarche*. On 16 June the rector wrote to the cardinal secretary of state, Pietro Gasparri:

> Being the rector of an ecclesiastical college I am generally detached from the day to day politics and also other like questions. I confirm however that some representation has been made, and is to be made, to the Holy See on the part of the British government regarding the revolution in Ireland and in particular regarding the attitude of some members of the clergy in this area. I don't know if this is true. But I feel compelled to turn to you to make you aware that I am able to give you information in this regard in the form of official documents, private letters coming from reliable sources in Ireland. And I will also refer to the personal consequences for the revolutionaries (even though their acts had failed). And from the agents of the military regime of the government who punished them and afterwards, and even up to this moment, the current popular sentiment found among all classes – from this bloody episode an attitude emerges that is completely contrary to what can be traced in newspapers and politicians. I can say this with certainty, that all classes in Ireland resent profoundly the conduct of the agents of government; and amongst whom are Protestants and also a lot of people who did not have sympathy for the rebel-

lion and not even for the ideal of the revolutionaries. The Irish in England from what I can gather and referring to the most popular Catholic newspaper there, the *Catholic Times*, participate in same feeling … I also heard from trustworthy sources that there is more anger at what has happened in America than in Ireland. Things being as they are, I feel an obligation to put myself at your disposal, your eminence, in order to help you in any way I can in these circumstances.[98]

Both Hagan and O'Riordan, well supplied with cuttings from home, set about documenting the events of the Rising from a Catholic perspective. There the matter rested until early September when the fruits of their combined labours were ready for presentation to the Holy See.

Episcopal opinion had been very significantly radicalised, as may be seen by the statement of Cardinal Michael Logue to the Maynooth Union (a gathering of priests) on 22 June, when he referred to 'late lamentable occurrences'. Perhaps a little naïvely, he believed that 'not one in five hundred of their [Irish Volunteers] members ever foresaw what any inner body was driving at – the organisation of a rebellion.' He rejected the false accusations against the clergy put forward by police at the official inquiry, that the Rising was 'to some extent patronised by the younger clergy'. The cardinal believed that to be 'a calumny' on them. He did not think that there was any sympathy amongst the priests as a general body. Such allegations were gathered up by the police from suspicions that had been 'fished up by their subordinates in the different parts of the country, and these suspicions are founded on the most futile and the most absurd grounds'.[99] The usually mild Logue also rejected similar accusations against teachers, and went on to accuse the British authorities of mis-managing the affair. The public authorities had muddled things, he said, adding:

No person would find fault with them for defending the rights of the state or for punishing moderately and within the laws of humanity those who violated the laws of the state; but they sent emissaries through the whole country and picked up every man who belonged to the Irish Volunteers, although it was the firm conviction that the great body of Volunteers knew nothing about it. They picked all these men up as suspects, took them away from their businesses, their families and their friends, and sent them away to England, either to jails or concentration camps. That was the greatest act of folly any government could have been guilty of. They should have let the matter die out like a bad dream – and it was a dream – so painful that it was not likely to be repeated, without going to these extreme measures.[100]

C.S. (Todd) Andrews, a founder member of Fianna Fáil and senior civil servant, was fifteen years old at the time of the Rising. Living at 42 Summerhill, he was very close to the fighting in O'Connell Street, Dublin. A lifelong republican and political activist, he recalled the following in the first volume of his memoirs, published in 1979:

> The first open manifestation of the deep public feeling aroused by the executions was at the month's mind for the dead leaders. A month's mind is the mass celebrated for the soul of a relative or friend a month after his death. It was the first opportunity that sympathisers of the rebels had to come out in the open. I went with my father to the first of the month's minds, which was for the brothers Pearse, at Rathfarnham. We arrived well in time for mass but could not get into the church and the forecourt was packed right out to the road. I was surprised to see so many well dressed and obviously well-to-do people present. The Volunteers I knew were shop assistants, small clerks, labourers or tradesmen. I did not realise that there was, quite apart from the effect of the rebellion and the executions on public opinion, a sizeable section of Irish nationalists, disillusioned with Redmond and the Irish Parliamentary party, who were anxious to find an alternative outlet for their beliefs. In the sub-conscious of every nationalist, there was a sympathetic response to rebellion.[101]

The June issue of the *Catholic Bulletin* reflected the change of public mood. It had its editorial censored. As a consequence the pages were left blank with 'Dublin – May 1916' written on the final page.[102] The section, 'Matters of the Moment' was also left blank, and the diary of current events censored. John Hagan, the Roman correspondent for the *Bulletin*, caustically began his July 'Letter from Rome': 'Lest the censor, in his anxiety that nothing should come between his efforts to found a new reign of peace, harmony, justice, honour, fair-play, truth and charitableness in Ireland,' might object if he wrote on matters of the moment or even the last century, he would confine himself to a tour of Rome in the footsteps of the earls of Tyrone.[103] But between July and the end of the year the magazine ran a series of articles profiling the executed leaders and men of the Rising. The final edition for 1916 carried profiles of the widows and families of those leaders. The event was presented as being very much a Catholic and/ or Christian rebellion. The issue was bold and provocative, and it proved to be a very popular number.

In his diary entry for 22 July Curran recorded details of a meeting with a former internee, Michael Lennon of Longford Terrace, Dublin. He mentioned 'the barbarous treatment of the prisoners in Kilmainham. He himself was half-strangled by soldiers with his own necktie.' Local feeling had been incensed by such experiences. There was also a very negative reaction to General Maxwell's report, including his supplementary report of 26 May, which was published on 22 July. Curran described the supplementary report as 'plainly a political apology for the executions, etc'. It was a 'scandalous and dishonourable calumny on the Volunteers' fighting conduct, accusing them of murder of police, looting, etc'. He also noted that he had attended a meeting in the Phoenix Park against partition, which had attracted a 'crowd of four or five thousand'.

Curran captures the atmosphere of those days in two letters, sent to the rector and vice rector of the Irish College. Curran wrote to O'Riordan on 29 July:

> We are all in a great ferment of mind in this country, though there is no probability of another rising, unless things go to the dogs altogether. There are considerable stores of arms in many districts; there is any amount of young hot blood ready to rise and become martyrs. The country element is largely untrained, but we think ourselves past masters in rifle work and apparently trust to Germans or Americans or some *deus ex machina* for artillery and other luxuries and refinements of warfare. The spirit is certainly willing, but the materials I fear are sadly weak. I need not tell you how bitter feeling is against the party over the attempted partition of Ulster. The north west is ferocious at the attempt of Devlin and co. to hook them in with the selfish motive of bettering their own position in the Northern Pale. The party would not secure twenty seats in Ireland at present. They know that Devlin himself confessed it in private and that is why that one of the essential conditions always is that the existing MPs are to be the members of the new body, and therefore we had all the furore over the 'diminished representation'. Diminished representation anywhere means an election and that means the kicking out of the partitioners. Here in Dublin we are torn between denunciation of the party and an agitation to secure a public inquiry into the military murders. These are more numerous, more cold-blooded and more revolting than even well informed people ever suspected. It is only within the last fortnight or so that all the evidence has been more or less centralised. If the govt still hold out against an inquiry, it is possible that a private commission may be held. As it is, sworn depositions are already made out. The wholesale military looting has now taken a very subordinate place.[104]

He told O'Riordan that the

> American Representatives of Cardinal Farley's Irish Relief Fund have come over and have gone about everywhere gathering information and learning the

extent and nature of the problem before the relief committees. Two came a fortnight ago. Thomas Hughes Kelly, the treasurer, and another arrived at Liverpool about Wed. last, but were forbidden to land and return to the States today with one of the men who arrived here a fortnight ago. They will raise Cain in America. These feelings run up to boiling point. These Americans say that the Americans won't have war. They expect, and I think welcome, the prospect that Hughes will be elected. They say he is very upright and a real, and not a pretended, neutral. They don't expect war in Mexico. But of course you know everything from the American College. I wonder could you get me from some American in Rome 'cuttings' of the Irish-American demonstrations.[105]

On 30 July 1916 Curran wrote to Hagan:

Public feeling in Dublin is getting more and more fierce. Everything seems calculated to embitter it. Home rule, partition and above all the refusal of the govt to enquire into and punish those guilty of the military murders. These are by no means confined to King's street. Half of the deported are already back and it looks as if Frongoch will be broken up. They are being sent back in fifties to avoid demonstrations. Apparently a few hundreds will be retained in England – partly as hostages perhaps, but more particularly to prevent the rise of literary activity of an inconvenient kind. It is very remarkable to note the releases and the detained. The latter are all the literary, journalistic and student characters, even though many of them had nothing at all to do with the Rising and some were actually against it. These men are being sent to Reading prison – also the trades leaders – include Griffith, Darrell Figgis (as innocent as the king) Seán O'Kelly etc and a few university students. The real active fighters, including captains etc., have been sent home but the unfortunate quill-drivers and BAs are kept. There is a family [name blotted out and M. J. C. written over it to indicate erasure made by Curran and not the censor] which had four boys in the Rising. One was a terror altogether, in the middle of the gun-running and gun-buying from soldiers. He and two of his brothers released but a fourth – a quiet student fellow studying for his degree – is detained … They only want to be called out again. I never saw such spirit. Imagine trying to conscript these chaps![106]

The letter to Hagan was much more radical than his missive the previous day to O'Riordan. It continued:

But despite suppression of papers, the censor, deportation, imprisonment and executions, I never saw such literary activity … Have to see specimens of the mosquito press. The *Catholic Bulletin* for July was sold out in a week and thousands are going around begging, borrowing and stealing the copies among their friends. Gill won't reprint it, though pressed to do so. The number of MS poems in circulation is amazing – mostly very good. The latest I saw is one 'Shall Casement die?', a fine but perfervid protest as to what will happen if the inconceivable event takes place. It is thought that Casement will be reprieved. There will be ructions in America if he is executed. I don't know whether you can appreciate American influence in our affairs through the American College. At any rate it predominates everything at present. Wilson knows he will be forced out if Casement is executed and the English don't want Hughes. It is said (we had it from Mrs Green) that Doyle, the American attorney, was an agent of Wilson's. He had an interview with Grey [the British foreign secretary]. Grey asked him: 'Who will be elected president?' 'I'll tell you that,' said Doyle, 'when I know Casement's fate.'

Curran concluded: 'John Redmond and co. are in a hopeless minority in Ireland at present. The party would not carry 20 seats. That is why there are to be no elections or diminution of the present members.'[107]

On 25 July Walsh broke his public silence. In a strong letter to the press he said that he had never had a moment's doubt for years that the cause of home rule for Ireland was being led in parliament along a line that 'could only bring it to disaster'. He lamented that the majority of those who still retained faith in the efficacy of constitutional agitation had become hopelessly possessed of the disastrous idea that the party or its leadership could do no wrong. Fair criticism had come to an end, he wrote, and anyone who ventured to express an opinion at variance with that of the party at once became a 'fair mark for every political adventurer in the country to assail with the easily handled epithets of "factionalist", "wrecker" or "traitor"'. With what the archbishop described as the abandonment of the policy of independent opposition, 'our country is now face to face with a truly awful prospect'. Home rule was still on the statute book but, he asked, would Irish nationalists any longer be fooled by a repetition of the party cries that this fact made them masters of the situation? He did not think so.

On 28 July Walsh motored from Wicklow to meet an American relief delegation led by Archdeacon John Murphy and John Gill. The archbishop considered the meeting very important as it allowed him to be briefed on Irish-American opinion.[108]

Meanwhile the fate of Roger Casement became the focus of nationalist attention in Ireland. This was a further source of radicalisation. The manner in which the government conducted itself appalled many in Ireland. Frantic efforts were made to mobilise international public opinion to prevent him meeting the same fate as other leaders of the Rising. It is worth noting that on 18 July, while convalescing in Wicklow, Walsh motored to Courtown, Co. Wexford, to meet Mrs Alice Stopford Green, who had written to him concerning Casement. Curran did not accompany Walsh on that occasion but surmised that the archbishop 'could only express his sympathy and confess his inability to achieve anything useful'.[109]

Casement's trial lasted three days. He was sentenced to death on 29 July. Strenuous efforts were made to have his sentence commuted to life imprisonment. Members of the clergy and hierarchy, including Walsh and Logue, lent their names to the campaign. In a letter published in the press on 20 July 1916, Cardinal Logue wrote: 'From motives of mercy and charity, and not from any sympathy whatever with the unfortunate course which was taken, I shall be prepared to sign any petition for the reprieve of Roger Casement.' The archbishop of Dublin and several other Irish bishops also signed the doomed appeal.[110] It was to no avail. On 3 August Casement was hanged in Pentonville gaol.

Curran wrote to O'Riordan on 30 August. He noted: 'Things are fairly quiet as compared with Lent and Easter, but the least thing will cause uproar. Some 'loyalists' are terribly anxious for conscription and there is no limit to the blundering and bigotry of govt.' Referring to the murder of Sheehy Skeffington, he was anxious to have inquiries into other extra-judicial killings investigated: 'If we can only get the King's st and other murders examined we will have revelations! Outside the executions, all the murder and tyranny was due to the lower grade officers and Orange and English Tommies.' In a postscript he set out what in his view were the real causes of the Rising. The breakdown of the constitutional movement, he wrote, was due to two things: '(1) Carson and Curragh rebels and the weak govt (2) the abandonment of independent opposition by the Irish party through corruption and jobbery. Old men could stand by calmly, if helplessly, but young blood could not.'[111]

Bishop O'Dwyer was one such 'old man' but his hostility to the British was akin to the feelings felt amongst the younger generation. His antagonism to the Irish party had grown even stronger and he wrote to O'Riordan on 31 August:

It has been good of you to tell me of the Holy Father's most kind remark. It is the approval that is worth something. Our national affairs are in a strange muddle. P. Albion has been true to her name, and the wretched creatures who have got possession of 'the machine' are not men enough to meet the crisis.

They will get nothing, and they know it, but keep on duping the people at home with promises.[112]

O'Dwyer showed compassion on hearing of the death of the Irish MP, Tom Kettle. He wrote to O'Riordan on 21 September 1916: 'Poor Tom Kettle, a very brilliant fellow, was killed last week in the battle of the Somme, in which the slaughter sees to be enormous. Kettle they tell me, was a good fellow, but for the past few years turned on "the bottle", which explains a good deal.'[113]

The topsy-turvy world of Irish politics in the wake of the Rising was perhaps best captured in a letter, dated 5 September, from the radical nationalist Fr Michael O'Flanagan to John Hagan. In it he remarked:

I suppose you have an idea of how the world would look from this camera obscura – everything would end upsidedown, but we are hoping against hope that they will right themselves somehow. As far as the intellectual side of Ireland is concerned, things are better than ever, and I suppose that is the germ out of which everything grows in the long-run.[114]

Bishop O'Dwyer, by now the toast of Limerick and a celebrity in the international Irish Catholic world of the United States, Australia and New Zealand, was to be honoured by his native city. To that end, a decision was taken to make him a Freeman of Limerick. On 14 September a special meeting of the corporation was called. Members of the public were in attendance. O'Dwyer's speech recalled the earlier days of his episcopacy when he had been regarded in a critical light for his condemnation of violent methods used in land agitation. Aware of the fickle nature of public opinion, he said he would remind himself that 'the weather may change at any moment, and the wind blow from another quarter'. Drawn again into public controversy with General Maxwell, O'Dwyer stated Maxwell had had 'the effrontery to give me directions for the government of my diocese but I hardly think he will repeat the experiment'. Maxwell did not 'know much about Irish ecclesiastics, who have a proud tradition and who have shown by our predecessors to stand up to English brutality'. Even if the Rising was not justified theologically, he asked whether he was to join in the condemnation of Pearse, MacDonagh and Colbert, who 'were shot without trial, and of the men and women who, without trial, were deported from this country in thousands'. His speech then became a virtual justification of the actions of the men who rose in 1916. He questioned whether

Prime Minister Asquith, were he an Irishman, would have the patience to accept the 'tantalising perfidy' of the British who put home rule on the statute book, then hung it up and later announced that before it could be put into practice it would have to be amended. He concluded, to rapturous applause: 'Ireland will never be content as a province, God made her a nation, and while grass grows and water runs there will be men in Ireland to dare and die for her.'[115] Despite censorship, the speech was widely circulated and met with enthusiastic approval.

The Irish College and the 'Red Book'

There must have been rumours of a papal peace initiative in late summer 1916, for on 20 August the rector of the Irish College received a letter from Cardinal Logue, which stated: 'As far as I know there is not a word of truth in the report that the pope has sent any message, directly or indirectly, to the Irish bishops. Had any message been sent, it would likely be sent through me.'[116]

The rector and vice rector had worked throughout the summer compiling an authoritative account in Italian of the events surrounding the Rising. Aware that many Irish clergy and religious in Rome were still supportive of the Irish party and hostile to radical change at home, the two men sought to produce a clear factual account of the events in Dublin and elsewhere. This became known as the 'Red Book'.[117]

Entitled *La recente insurrezione in Irlanda*, it was forty three pages in length. It was dated on the final page, 1 September. The text was heavily footnoted. It spoke of the 1916 leaders as being university professors, lawyers and some members of families of elevated rank: 'All were practising Catholics. There was one exception [James Connolly]. The person who was the exception was born in Great Britain of Irish parents and was a type of socialist; he came to Dublin three years ago, and was not a member of the Volunteers at the time of the insurrection.' The book quoted from the letters sent by three of the condemned men, to a mother, a sister and a wife. It spoke of Pearse seeking reconciliation with God and preparing for his death like a good Catholic. It recorded that Countess Markiewicz, who was a Protestant, had asked to be received into the Catholic church. Roger Casement, also a Protestant, had sought to be recognised as a Catholic while in Pentonville, according to the testimony of the Catholic chaplain there. The account also noted that the insurgents had recited the rosary in the various buildings they occupied during the Rising, and that, despite being surrounded by British forces, mass had been celebrated therein.[118]

The work unfavourably compared the disciplined behaviour of the insurgents with unruly and brutal actions by the British forces. Under the heading, '*il clero e il moviemento insurrezional*', the writer spoke about the denunciation by the bishop of Kerry, issued before the Rising, of the practice of opening mail going to convents in his diocese. It instanced two episodes of sacrilege and violation of the eucharist. In the diocese of Clogher a priest who lived a good distance from the church kept the sacred host in a tabernacle in a private oratory in his house. A British military raiding party was ordered by the officer commanding to break into the tabernacle in search of arms. There was another act of desecration at a convent of the Sisters of Mercy in Kinvara, Co. Galway. The book went on to reproduce the correspondence between General Maxwell and Edward O'Dwyer.[119]

The work concluded that the British government, working through its representatives and civil servants in Ireland, never forgave the Irish bishops and clergy, for three reasons: 1) they had managed to keep the Irish people faithful to the Catholic church, despite generations of injustice; 2) they still had the complete trust of the Irish people; 3) in spite of pressure from the civil authorities to take on the role of civil servants or of policemen, they had persisted in acting independently and as priests. The section ended: 'For similar reasons the government has never forgiven the Catholics of Ireland: *Primum humani ingenii est odiesse quem laeseris.*'[120]

The final section of the book set out a simple thesis. The British government had passed home rule into law. The Irish party had accepted this but the government then broke the agreement. This was not the first time, according to the book, that the British had concluded an agreement and then failed to honour it. The last line in the text was a strong indictment of British rule in Ireland: '*Ad ogni modo il 'pezzo di carta' e stato lacerate e la slealtà rimane un fatto.*' ['In any case, the piece of paper has been torn up and the perfidiousness remains a fact.']'[121]

O'Riordan took a copy of the document to the Holy See sometime after 1 September. It is not clear to whom he gave it. It is probable that he gave a copy directly to Pope Benedict. He most probably also gave it to the cardinal secretary of state, Pietro Gasparri. No evidence has yet come to light as to how the document was received. But the argument running throughout the text implicitly warned the Holy See against intervention. It had presented the idea of a Protestant British government seeking unsuccessfully to drive a wedge between the Catholic church and her people. The manner in which the bishops and clergy had acted in the wake of the Rising had ensured that would not happen, just as their actions in the past centuries had prevented such an eventuality.

News of the existence of the book began to circulate in Ireland in early October 1916. The Bishop of Cork, Daniel Cohalan, wrote to O'Riordan on 14 October: 'I got your red pamphlet. It is a great blessing that we have one at Rome so able, and so watchful about the interests of Ireland.'[122] Cardinal Logue wrote to O'Riordan on 28 October: 'I have read the "Red Book" with interest. It is cleverly written, but there are some minor mistakes. The Bank of Ireland was never in the possession of the insurgents.'[123] Bishop O'Dwyer wrote to O'Riordan on 29 September, thanking him for the presentation of 'my case' before the pope. (A defence of O'Dwyer's statements and actions figured very prominently in the pages of the book.) The bishop continued: 'If you were within my mind you could not do it better. I fear, however, that when complaints are formulated against my speech on getting the "freedom" [of Limerick] you will have to supplement my apologia.'[124] O'Dwyer explained that the 'military censored the speech, and I know that many of a certain class resent it, but I spoke, honestly, *ex abundantia cordis*'. He then made his views on the Rising crystal clear:

> The Irish Volunteers were wrong, and I have said so explicitly but while my judgment condemns them, all my sympathy is with them, as strongly as I condemn the government, and despise the party. It is the old story. Time wears away all the circumstances of our rebels, except the fact which survives in the heart of the country, that they died for Ireland.[125]

O'Dwyer thus summed up the ambivalence of many, clerical and lay, towards the Rising.

While the existence of the Red Book was quite widely known about in Irish episcopal circles, it was not widely circulated in Ireland and may have been sent to only a select few of the bishops given the sensitivity of its contents. It is probable that the text was also sent to carefully chosen and wholly reliable bishops in the USA and in Australia and New Zealand. The book had been compiled to inform the decision-makers in the Holy See. The Irish College sought to counter British influence at the Vatican. Neither the rector nor the vice rector wanted Pope Benedict XV to issue a condemnation of the Rising. The real danger had passed. Such a statement might have been issued in May or June. But the policy of executions, the mass arrests, and the hanging of Roger Casement had enflamed Irish public opinion at home and abroad, particularly in the strongholds of the Irish diaspora.

Although the Red Book was submitted in the name of Michael O'Riordan and he was widely acknowledged as being its author, there is little doubt that the Italian text was also the work of John Hagan. It has a directness which is associated with his writing style. The volume of work required to produce it, particularly the amount of translation, indicates that both men were involved, together with a native Italian speaker. Irrespective of who wrote the book, however, its intention was to dispel any idea put about by those who sought to advance British interests at the Holy See that the 1916 Rising was a secular, laic, anti-clerical insurrection. Dr J. MacCaffrey, the vice president of Maynooth, articulated that salient point in a letter to Hagan on 20 December:

> Yesterday I got a copy of *La recente insurrezione in Irlanda*, kindly lent me by one of the bishops, and I am perusing it with great interest. It will certainly show Their Eminences that those 'out' in Easter week, whatever else they might have been, were not *Carbonari*.[126]

In other words, what had happened in Ireland during Easter week 1916 was very distinct in every aspect from the ideas which motivated the revolutionaries of the Risorgimento and of the new Italian state. The Irish men and women who went out in 1916 were driven by Catholic values and ideals. Those who were executed died as Catholics with the last rites of their church. The Red Book argued that thesis very strongly.

The Irish College, already known as a stronghold of Irish nationalism in British circles in Rome, was a source of even deeper suspicion following the Rising. Both Hagan and O'Riordan were seen as highly politicised prelates and advanced nationalists. Count de Salis, a Limerick man, was sent to take up residence in Rome and represent British government interest at the Holy See. What role had the Irish College played in the general reaction of the Irish Catholic church to the Rising and its aftermath? The visit of Count Plunkett to Pope Benedict XV to forewarn him about the pending uprising on Easter Sunday remains an episode yet to be explained satisfactorily. The College may have only played a passive role in that initiative. The British government and its lay and clerical supporters in Rome may have repeatedly exaggerated the radicalism of the rector and vice rector. Their unlearned lesson was that moderates such as O'Riordan and Hagan were being radicalised by draconian tactics of Crown forces in Ireland. The centre had shifted leftwards.

Both Hagan and O'Riordan had been the recipients of very valuable and revealing correspondence which chronicled the shifting emotions and ideas of clergy and hierarchy to events at home. Because both men were stationed in Italy the clerical and episcopal correspondence – despite British censorship – was very forthright and confrontational. The standing of the two men is revealed in the frankness of the correspondence from a variety of Irish clerical sources. The conservation of those records in the archives of the Irish College has helped reveal a side to episcopal and clerical engagement in politics which would have been virtually impossible to find elsewhere. The reaction to 1916 did not end with the issuing of the initial public statements. The clergy and bishops were forced to respond to the changing situation in the country. They were obliged to shift positions as the executions, mass arrests and deportations engaged a much wider circle of people than the Rising itself had encompassed. Thousands of families were politicised by the transporting of their loved ones to camps in Britain. The British government were the architects of their own destruction in Ireland in the wake of 1916.

Much changed within the Catholic church in Ireland in the years between 1914 and 1916. The constitutional solution of home rule, despite its inherent weaknesses, was offered in 1912, and its implementation postponed in 1914. By late summer 1916 it was clear that partition was probable. The Bishop of Raphoe, Patrick O'Donnell, continued to favour the home rule solution, even at the price of partition. He wrote in his usual challenging hand-writing to Michael O'Riordan on 6 November 1916, outlining his ideas. The bishop, who was by then only supported by Bishop Kelly of Ross, argued that:

> On general principles we would say that it was inevitable the Irish party, living so much out of Ireland, would make mistakes. In the English actions of recent times I dare say mistakes were made before the war and since… . I myself should have liked that Sinn Féiners and recruiting had been treated differently. I am not at all clear that considering the strength of 'Ulster' Mr Redmond could have bargained at the beginning of the war as Birrel suggests. But to me it always seemed a sad mistake to refuse the Lloyd George partition scheme. Certainly under that scheme 'Ulster' could stay out as long as it likes: and it is not impossible an 'Ulster' more powerful in population and resources than

an Australian colony would stay out awhile and probably secure a parliament of its own. But the Irish leaders did not think that it would stay out. They had private assurances from the Ulster leaders that they would work for inclusion; and the presence of two of the protagonists (Carson and Campbell) in the Dublin parliament was to be a token of that. What however moved our men more than anything else, so far as I know, was the dread that at the end of the war, if they waited until then, they would find feeling in England very hostile in regard to the home rule settlement, owing to the rebellion and the cessation of recruiting that it brought about.[127]

O'Donnell was of the view that the Irish party leaders

certainly would not agree to the scheme if they thought it was going to be permanent and of course it is not easy for politicians to do their work and at the same time show their hand. I myself could never favour a scheme that included Derry city, Tyrone and Fermanagh against their will; and I felt like one tied to the ground until Mr Redmond said at Waterford that no parts of Ulster would be coerced to stay out. Now I think that we are back to the sound policy of home rule for all Ireland; and I consider the party has seen its worst days.

O'Donnell's optimism was not widely shared on the bench of bishops. No matter how reflective and nuanced his position, the time appeared to have passed for such intellectual refinement. In May 1917 eighteen Catholic and three Protestant bishops were to sign a manifesto protesting against the imminent partitioning of the island.

O'Donnell continued:

I am convinced that the rebellion helped home rule but whether it helped or hindered it, the difficulty about conscription and recruiting in Ireland these days may cause important developments. However, I have seen none of the leaders for many months and I have no special knowledge. Though it may tell against the Irish party, I think it is right to say to you that I am not convinced that there was a breach of faith on the part of the government in respect of the Lloyd George proposals. English politicians are nothing to me more than I[rish] politicians, and I well know how brilliantly leading statesmen can say and unsay. But the whole thing looks to me to have been a concerted arrangement to [force it?] though in some way, with the hope that what was crooked would soon be straightened out.

He concluded by speculating on how the Rising might impact on the quest for home rule:

The remote cause of the Rising which has put us more under the heel of England I take to be want of union between priests and people in certain political work. There was no trouble in Tipperary or in Donegal. As you [recall?] it was the work of a small section, not of the nation. If the nation called, Tipperary would not be backward. Here we have made a parochial collection for those who have suffered by the rebellion, as we did in preceding years for the victims of the war in Belgium and Poland. I have always felt that a ministry, comprising inciters to rebellion, has no equitable right to take the lives of these boys. But I have also felt that the doctrine of the church on the rebellion is the doctrine of liberty. Whatever right of rebellion there is, the cause of liberty requires that it be limited to the nation and not vested in any section or sections of the people, which otherwise might compromise the nation's chances of freedom and push back the hand of the clock.[128]

His theology of revolution, as stated in the last lines of his letter, was very much in accord with stated Catholic teaching. Events had determined otherwise, however. The leadership of the 1916 Rising had been transformed into Catholic martyrs. The brutality of repression had elided discussion on the theology of rebellion.

In the end, Michael Curran, writing to Hagan on 15 October 1916, articulated a position more akin to that held by the majority of Irish bishops than O'Donnell's:

Things are terribly disquieting here and throughout Ireland. This revival of the threat of conscription had done a lot of harm. Most of those engaged in the cry in the country are doing so for purely political nature – to damage home rule and of course they will succeed. But why the government would not see the folly of the other proposal at once and stifle the outcry in England I can't understand. The country bishops say it is only the dead bodies of our boys they could drag over the half-doors. The same is true of thousands in Dublin. There is a very large quantity of arms yet in the country and sufficient for a definite resistance in Dublin. The intensity of the feeling is unparalleled, though not so manifest. The air of suspicion and uncertainty has now become so ingrained that many, including the bishops of certain districts, fear another rising. Until recently I thought we were now safe, if only conscription were not enforced, but [with?] the growing bitterness between the two countries anything is possible. They say the IRB is spreading in the country. It was already strong in Dublin. Absurdly wild stories of landing of arms, seizure of arms, arrests etc. are in circulation despite denial … At any [rate?] things are very disquieting and will continue until the govt formally renounces conscription in Ireland for ever and abandons the idea of partition.[129]

Curran, in his privileged position in archbishop's house, was well situated to interpret the course of events. Ireland faced a period of great political turmoil and an uncertain future where physical force could not be ruled out.

There was an important postscript to the process of multi-faceted alienation which took place during the weeks following the Rising, the executions and the deportations. The Irish party had been very seriously damaged. It had lost credibility as the political leaders of the Irish people. It was no longer even in a position to guarantee the delivery of home rule for all Ireland that was its very *raison d'être*. Lloyd George had all but destroyed that prospect with discussion about opt outs for the north eastern counties. The parliamentary party leadership had to put a good face on things. But many realised that their popular support had evaporated, as would be illustrated at subsequent by-elections and the general election. That in turn made this leadership very bitter towards the British government. A sense of betrayal was felt by those who had gambled all on support for recruitment in Ireland for the British forces in 1914. There was no turning around in 1916 to face a different political direction. The bitterness and resentment provoked by the executions, the deportations and the public misconduct of British troops in Dublin had alienated many members of the public. The Catholic hierarchy, earlier in the century strongly supportive of a reunited parliamentary party under Redmond, were in the majority hostile to it by the late summer of 1916. The policies of the British government in Dublin had galvanised support for an alternative to the Irish party. That was not support for the IRB or for the 1916 leadership, but there was episcopal and clerical support for those who emerged in the wake of the Rising to lead the emerging Sinn Féin movement. The British policy of repression in Ireland had helped to undermine the alliance of the Irish party and the Catholic hierarchy – which, in any event, was never as solid as has been argued, even in the 1880s.

Despite the thesis of the Red Book to 'Catholicise' the Rising, the events of Easter Week 1916 had visited terrible suffering on people. Patrick McKenna, bishop of Clogher, wrote to O'Riordan on 24 November 1916:

There is really no news of any importance. The country is at least on the surface very quiet, but it is in a very suspicious and distrustful mood both as regards the government and our own politicians. It is not in a temper to be trifled with. We are in for a severe winter. The real hardship and sufferings of the war are pressing severely already on people with small fixed incomes and the labour and artisan classes whose wages have not risen in proportion to the rise in prices. But I fear present energies are only a mild foretaste of the trials in store for the poor.[130]

That growing deprivation and sense of social unrest further stoked the widespread political discontent in the country which saw the return of Count Plunkett as a Sinn Féin candidate in a by-election in Roscommon in 1917.

CONCLUSION

This study shows the turmoil into which the leadership of the Irish Catholic church had plummeted after Easter 1916, tracing the growing radicalisation of many members of the clergy and bench of bishops who had first reacted to the Rising as the work of extremists and of the Liberty Hall-led labour left. Many bishops quickly shifted to a more sympathetic position as the groundswell of support for those who had fought honourably and who had behaved in a fashion that distinguished them from the actions of the Crown forces. The dignified behaviour of those who had been executed, dying with the last rites of the church, stood in contrast to the manner in which some sections of the British army had performed.

But why, if it was initially believed by many bishops that the Rising was the work of extremists and of an oath-bound society, was there no joint condemnation of that event by them? If immediate episcopal reaction, as expressed both privately and in public, was overwhelmingly negative, why did that sentiment not take the form of a joint pastoral? The standing committee of the hierarchy met on the Tuesday in the second week after Easter Sunday. It seems that a draft document resulted from that meeting. It was probably sketched out by the Bishop of Raphoe, Patrick O'Donnell, a strong supporter of the Irish party. The draft is lodged in the archives of the Armagh archdiocese. The fact that it was never issued is highly significant. There is a remote chance that Count Plunkett's audience with Benedict XV may have given members of the hierarchy cause for pause. But that would not explain the collective silence of the hierarchy.

The bishops met annually in June and in October. Certainly, episcopal opinion was by the end of May very far from being conciliatory as this article has shown. This radicalisation may be explained by the swiftness of the pace of events in the wake of the Rising, the brutal manner in which justice was meted out, and the executions that followed. The mass round ups of alleged activists touched every parish and diocese in the country. The deportations helped many people move from a position of passivity and political indifference to a deep sense of alienation from and resentment towards the British authorities. In prison in England and Wales, the internees were politicised and organised. At home relatives grew more resentful and angry.

By the time the bishops met in June 1916, the bench was divided. A majority were sympathetic with Bishop O'Dwyer of Limerick. That would not have been the case a month earlier. Archbishop Walsh had become more definite in his actions and in his words. Any effort to press for a joint condemnation of the Rising at that point, as might have been the idea of Bishops O'Donnell and Kelly, could only have resulted in a split. The church was caught up in the emotional reaction to the draconian nature of the British repression and the policy of executions which provided scant opportunities to the defendants to make an objective case against capital punishment. While the bishops confronted the moral question of the legitimacy of the use of violence by nationalists, they also witnessed the disproportionate countervailing violence of the British government. On balance, the Rising brought to a head the ambivalence and contradictory sentiments felt by members of the hierarchy towards Britain. The hierarchy's pact with the Irish party, if there ever was such a thing, was shattered by 1916. Whatever the hierarchy and clergy felt about the morality of revolution, it was obvious that life would never be the same again in Ireland. The Rising, flawed though it may have been, had changed things. Driven as it was perceived to have been by the Irish radical left and the IRB, it had dealt a serous blow to the Irish party, and in the popular trust in the British government to do anything other than procrastinate and temporise. The Irish bishops had a good nose for change. The long revolution was about to enter another, and even more deadly, phase.

Appendix

Count Plunkett's letter to Pope Benedict XV. The original is in French and is located in the Vatican Archives, AAEESS, 111 Periodo, Inghilterra, posizione 217, fasc. 120.

Most Holy Father,
I wish to bring this report to the attention of Your Holiness; I regret my inability to write French very fluently.

I have been sent as a delegate to Your Holiness on behalf of the President and of the Supreme Council of the Irish Volunteers (national troops). The President (Prof. John MacNeill) entrusted me with a document that the particular circumstances of the present moment have forced me to leave in Ireland. Mr John MacNeill comes from an old Ulster family which has suffered a lot because of its loyalty to the Faith. He is a well known scholar and a Professor of the National University of Ireland. Mr MacNeill wishes me to communicate to Your Holiness the expression of his deep devotion to both the Holy See and the person of the Pontiff. On his behalf I am also charged with bringing to Your Holiness the greetings of the Supreme Council, which, by a unanimous vote, has declared its agreement with the principle of the complete liberation of the Holy See and with the restoration of its ancient rights.

I have also been asked, on behalf of the Council, to make Your Holiness aware of the state of affairs in Ireland about which I also can directly testify. Contemporary public events have their origin in the past but (as a Minister said) in Ireland the action of the English Government is marked by continuity.

1. Home Rule has been passed into law but this law will never be applied. The enemies of Irish freedom are in government, they have all political power and they have declared that we will never have a National Parliament.

2. We have proof (confirmed by certain events) that last year the Orangemen were thinking of massacring Nationalists. While the Home Rule Bill was being discussed in Parliament some English members of this Parliament gave arms, and even artillery pieces, to the Orangemen and these parliamentarians incited the Orangemen to attack Catholics. Among these Englishmen figure Mr Bonar Law and Mr Churchill, both members of the present Cabinet. It has been said that Sir Edward Carson who is the leader of the Orange movement could become Prime Minister. He is already a member of the Cabinet

3. Officers of the English army have been given the option to refuse to take part in operations against the Orangemen in the event of the Home Rule law being applied.

4. The Irish Volunteers were founded for the defence of the Irish nation and people. Then the European war began. Initially the English government did not move to prevent the formation of the Volunteer units because it hoped to recruit some of their members into the English army. But this is no longer the case. The Orangemen carry arms and parade without interference. On the other hand the Volunteers are arrested and their arms are confiscated. Their documents are seized in house searches and their newspapers are banned. They are imprisoned without trial, forced out of their jobs and expelled from their country. In Ireland the military authorities are all-powerful – the English Constitution no longer offers any protection to Catholics.

5. Even if, as long as the war lasts, the fear of negative publicity obliges the

English Government to limit its attacks on the people to the above mentioned measures, it is certain that at the end of the war we will face massacre and the suppression of all freedom. The Ministers who planned the previous roundup will still be in power, they will have the Army at their disposal, and it will be free to subjugate our poor country. One example of their spirit of tolerance is the appointment as judge of a lawyer who is a Member of Parliament, Mr Campbell, a fierce Orangeman.

6. It is our opinion that if Ireland remains subject to the English Parliament she will certainly experience another famine. A Royal Commission has revealed the fact that England has collected in Ireland three hundred million pounds sterling more in taxes than was in fact due. Since the outbreak of the war we are paying taxes of seventeen million pounds annually and we are only four million souls.

7. It is certain that we are oppressed and it is clear that we are in danger of being massacred. We are convinced that the war taxes will lead ineluctably to famine. We have no further resources. Thus we have no choice but to rebel. Because of these circumstances there is not a parish in Ireland where there are no Volunteers. We have an effective force of 80,000 trained men and the people, the Catholic nation, is with us. The Irish in America are going to send us a large consignment of arms and the German government has promised to help us. It is during the war that we will have good prospects of success, of obtaining for our Catholic country the freedom of laws and of our religion.

8. The insurrection will commence on the evening of Easter Monday next.

I am confiding this information as a son to his Father who is so attentive to the interests of his children, and humbly prostrate at the feet of Your Holiness I beg his Paternal blessing for myself, my wife, all my family: and I ask for the prayers of the Head of the Church for my ever faithful country.

[signed]
Count George Noble Plunkett.

BUREAU OF MILITARY HISTORY: TESTIMONY OF MICHAEL CURRAN

Michael Curran

Bureau of Military History, 1913–21
Statement by witness: Right Rev. Monsignor M. Curran, PP
Document no. WS687 (section 1)

The following is an extract from the Witness Statement provided by Monsignor Michael Curran (Father Curran as he was in 1916) to the Bureau of Military History. It details his experiences of Easter Week 1916, when he was serving as secretary to Archbishop Walsh of Dublin. The extract consists both of excerpts from the diary he maintained during Easter Week (reproduced in italics) and of comments added when compiling his statement. As far as possible, original punctuation and capitalisation have been preserved.

Michael J. Curran was born in Dublin on 8 May 1880. He attended the Christian Brothers schools at St Mary's Place and North Richmond Street. In September 1897 he entered Holy Cross College, Clonliffe. From there he was sent to the Irish College in Rome for his theological studies. He was ordained in Rome on 15 March 1904. On his return to Dublin his first appointment was as diocesan examiner, and two years later he became secretary to Archbishop Walsh. In December 1919 he was appointed vice rector of the Irish College Rome and succeeded Monsignor Hagan as rector in 1930. He returned to Dublin in 1939 to become parish priest of Greystones. In 1947 he was transferred to Augrim Street and held this appointment until his death on 9 February 1960. The Irish Catholic Directory for 1961 notes that 'for his work at the Irish College, the Holy Father raised him to the dignity of Protonotary Apostolic ad instar, the highest class of Monsignori, while the King of Italy conferred upon him the Order of the Crown of Italy with the title Commendatore'.[1]

Easter Monday – Count Plunkett describes his audience with the Pope

Easter Monday, 1916, was a holiday, everybody taking a sleep. I have a note in my diary that Dr Cox called at a quarter past eleven in the morning.

At half-past eleven on Easter Monday morning, I must have gone down to the garage to meet Mr Quinn, evidently determined to get the latest news. I found him and had a talk with him on the situation. All I have written down in my diary is, *Serious news*. I cannot recollect what it was about. It must have been about disarmament, the Volunteer mobilisation, Eoin MacNeill's countermanding orders and all the news from Kerry. We must have discussed what all this would lead to – disarmament straight away? He would not tell and possibly knew little of military intentions.

Between half-past eleven and noon on Easter Monday, I have noted in my diary that, while I was talking to Mr Quinn down in the garage, a telephone message was brought to me that Seán T. O'Kelly wanted to see me in Rutland Square. I sent word by the messenger that I would be there in half an hour. At that time I had not known that the Rising was going to take place or that it was so desperately close.

Towards noon on Easter Monday I have noted in my diary the page-boy came down again to the garage, where I was still speaking to Mr Quinn, to say that Count Plunkett had called and was waiting to see me. I told the boy I would be there in a minute. I guessed, of course, that there was some new development. At five minutes past twelve I interviewed Count Plunkett. He said he had come to see the Archbishop. I informed him that the Archbishop was ill in bed and that nobody was allowed to see him except the doctor. I gathered, of course, that it was something urgent, obviously on account of the circumstances. 'Well,' he said, 'it is not necessary that I would see him personally but, if you would tell him, it would be alright.'

Count Plunkett then told me that there was going to be a Rising, that he had been to see the Pope and that he had informed Benedict XV of the whole Irish situation and the intended insurrection. He briefly went over the incidents of his audience. (Later the Count's report was confirmed first by letter and then verbally by Monsignor Hagan, Vice Rector of the Irish College at this time.) Count Plunkett informed His Holiness that a rising for national independence was arranged, that the Volunteers would strike in the course of Easter Sunday and that His Holiness should not be shocked or alarmed. Count Plunkett explained that the movement was purely a national one for independence, the same as every nation had a right to. At the end of his discussion, he asked the Pope's Blessing for the Volunteers. According to him, the Pope showed great perturbation and asked was there no peaceful way out of the difficulty; that the news was extremely grave, and asked had he seen the Archbishop of Dublin. Count Plunkett answered every question, making it plain that it was the wish of the leaders of the movement to act entirely with the good-will or approval – I forget which now – of the Pope and to give an assurance that they wished to act as Catholics. It was for that reason they came to inform His Holiness. All the Pope could do was to express his profound anxiety and how much the news disturbed him, and asked could their object not be achieved in any other way, and counselled him to see the Archbishop. Count Plunkett informed the Pope that he intended to see the Archbishop as soon as he arrived home. At this time, he was only just back in Ireland.

I should still have the letter I received from Monsignor Hagan, confirming Count Plunkett's audience with the Pope. I have it somewhere and I shall come across it. I don't know how it got through the post in the following weeks. Of course, there was nothing openly significant in it, and he did not mention Count Plunkett's name. It read something to this effect: 'The visitor, who will call on you, was seen by me. He had an audience with the Pope.' That was the gist of it.

We are informed by telephone that the Rising has begun

I have noted in my diary that, while I was still talking with Count Plunkett on Easter Monday, the telephone bell in the Secretaries' study rang and I was called to answer it. I said to the Count, 'Wait a moment!', and I went to the 'phone. The call came from a Mr Stokes, a jeweller, who rang me up to say that the GPO was seized by the Volunteers and the Castle was attacked, and he asked could the Archbishop stop it. I told him that was impossible but that I would go down town. I returned to Count Plunkett and told him the Rising had already begun. Count Plunkett, although he implied it was to take place immediately, had not told me when. It was then a quarter past twelve. The count came to tell the Archbishop that it was going to take place. Some delay had occurred as I was at the garage in the lower end of the grounds when the Count called. It was noteworthy that he came on the Monday and not on the Sunday.

I had to hasten up and tell the Archbishop all about Count Plunkett's report and the telephone news of the seizure of the GPO. He thought less of the poor count than of Eoin MacNeill. He looked on the Count as a simple soul and could not conceive a man like him being at the head of a revolution as it really was. Never in my life did I tell so much or so grave a report in such a brief time. I told the Archbishop, 'I'll go down town' – I did not say 'and see Seán' – 'to the GPO to see the situation'. I also said I would call in to the Pro-Cathedral.

I visit Seán T. O'Kelly at 25 Parnell Square

I got on my bicycle and went to see Seán T. O'Kelly. By this time I saw a few Volunteers in the streets, evidently going down town to mobilise. They were in uniform. I was amazed. I saw at least two groups, including one of three; and I remember seeing one individual standing in the doorway of the Christian Brothers Past Pupils' Union building.

I found Seán T. O'Kelly in 25 Parnell Square, as cool as you could imagine. I told him that I knew already what he was going to tell me but that, unfortunately, all those delays had occurred. He confirmed the news. He told me what had happened the evening before and that Pearse had determined to go on with the Rising. He did not tell me that he had seen Pearse himself. He gave me a packet to give to Miss Kit Ryan. He told me that, if anything happened to him, I was to give this packet to Kit Ryan. I guessed already what that meant. It was the first hint. I already knew that Seán was not what he used to describe as a 'gun-man'. But the organisation insisted he should be a Captain in the Intelligence department. Then he told me he was going out. Up to that, Seán T. always gave me the impression that he was supporting Mac-Neill rather than the extremists; but he never for a moment spoke formally and definitely regarding his own personal position. I gathered that his views coincided with mine, that there should be no resort to arms before disarmament or a German invasion, or the delivery of German arms. I am not quite sure now. Seán T. then confirmed that the GPO was seized. I was scarcely ten minutes with him.

I visit the GPO and am asked to procure a Priest at the Pro-Cathedral

Leaving Seán T. O'Kelly in his office, I cycled down at once to the GPO. There were several hundred people, perhaps over a thousand, between Abbey Street and Henry Street. I saw Mr Rock, one of the officials in the GPO who described how the Volunteers had marched in and ejected the entire staff out to the street. I asked him to bring my bicycle over to the Pro-Cathedral presbytery. The first person I saw in the portico outside the GPO was James Connolly in uniform with a huge Colt revolver, shouting out orders. Volunteers were battering out window-panes. When James Connolly saw me, he called out, 'All priests may pass!', as the Volunteers were keeping the inquisitive on-lookers at some distance. The crowd then showed comparatively little excitement. I passed in to the building. The newly arranged central hall was a scene of immense activity but nobody was unduly excited. It must have been then shortly after half-past twelve (Easter Monday).

Speaking to one of the first Volunteers I met in the GPO, I gave my name and said I wanted to see Mr Pearse. 'Commandant Pearse?' he corrected. 'Yes', I said. He went off and got Pearse whom, of course, I knew well. He was flushed but calm and authoritative. I at once said that we had just got word by telephone of this attack, that I had informed the Archbishop of the position and told him I was coming down to ascertain the facts and that, if there was anything that could be done, I would do it. 'But,' I said, 'I see now that nothing can be done.' 'No,' he said, 'we are going to see it out.' 'You know my feelings; if there is any possible thing I can do, I will be very glad to do it,' I said. I thought there might possibly be some message or other. 'No,' he said, 'but some of the boys would like to go to Confession and I would be delighted if you would send over word to the Cathedral.' I promised I would do that, left the GPO and went over to the Pro-Cathedral.

I noticed, when I came out of the GPO, a body of about ten or twelve police – DMP – with an Inspector, lined up at the foot of Nelson Pillar, doing nothing but obviously very tense.

I arrived at the Pro-Cathedral and made sure my bicycle was there. I told the priests who were gathered in the Administrator's room that I had been in to the GPO, had seen Pearse, that he had asked me to send over one of the priests and that I had told him I would do all I could. They were anxious about the Archbishop. I gave them an account of what happened to us in the morning – of the Count's visit, of my conveying his report to the Archbishop, partly because I knew one or two of them were not friendly; others of them were. I assured them that the Archbishop was fully informed of the state of affairs up to midday and that we would try and keep in touch with them. I telephoned Archbishop's House, reported all the information I had, saying I would remain on. I took lunch at the Gresham Hotel.

Having spent not more than ten minutes in the Pro-Cathedral, I returned to O'Connell Street. The first incident I observed – and I must say it made an unfavourable impression on me, from a military point of view – was the sight of a number of Volunteers trying to overturn a tram in Earl Street. One Volunteer on his stomach got under the tram, with something like a line of cord, and put a match to a fuse that was apparently to set off a bomb to overturn the tram – and a rapidly increasing number of people all about! Not only that, but he failed even after two or three attempts. That is all they understood about explosives. Later on, before I left, I saw that they had succeeded in overturning the tram. It blocked the thoroughfare and interrupted traffic. It was not a barricade that could be used to fight behind.

It was either during my absence in the Pro-Cathedral or while I was at lunch in the Gresham (I think the latter) that the flags were hoisted on the GPO. As far as I remember, there were only two. My diary notes that one was a green flag with the words '*Irish Freedom*', and the other the then new green, white and orange. I am morally certain that the tricolour was at the Henry Street corner and the other at the Prince's Street corner.

I remained until after 3.30 in O'Connell Street. About 1pm, as I have noted in my diary, *a squadron of 100–150 lancers appeared from the Rotunda. Riding up Upper O'Connell Street in single file, the first two who passed the Pillar were shot in the throat. Either four or six were killed. I attended one, but he was dead. He had a medal.* Such is the note I have in my diary. I saw the cavalry riding up, heard the shots, witnessed the moderate commotion. It was much less than I have seen on occasions of civil or political disturbance. In a few minutes several people ran to me to say that one of the soldiers shot was a Catholic and asked me to attend him. I found him lying dead on the west side of O'Connell Street, half-way between the Henry Street corner and Gill's bookshop (52 Upper O'Connell Street). A 'miraculous medal' about his neck led these simple people to believe he was a Catholic, but at that time hundreds of English Protestant soldiers wore Catholic medals as charms. It transpired that only one soldier was killed but the number got exaggerated from mouth to mouth. The cavalry were at once withdrawn to the space in front of the Rotunda Hospital. There they remained for an hour or two.

Before 2pm the crowds had greatly increased in numbers. Already the first looting had begun; the first victim was Noblett's sweetshop. It soon spread to the neighbouring shops. I was much disgusted and I did my best to try to stop the looting. Except for two or three minutes, it had no effect. I went over and informed the Volunteers about the GPO. Five or six Volunteers did their best and cleared the looters for some five or so minutes, but it began again. At first all the ringleaders were women; then the boys came along. Later, about 3.30pm when the military were withdrawn from the Rotunda, young men arrived and the looting became systematic and general, so that Fr John Flanagan of the Pro-Cathedral, who had joined me, gave up the attempt to repress it and I left too.

After I had attended the soldier, I passed into Lower O'Connell Street. Standing at the corner of Clery's, Sackville Place, I remember seeing a half-drunken British soldier striding along and giving vent to anti-Irish language. As the people were beginning to handle him roughly, I more or less came to his rescue. Immediately opposite, at the corner of the other side of the street, was a chemist standing at the shop door which had a little railing. I asked the chemist to open the railing and hustled him into the shop. I had no sooner got the soldier into the chemist's shop than I noticed a commotion. A Volunteer was being carried along by two men. He seemed seriously wounded and I was told his wounds were due to a bomb exploding accidentally. I gave him Absolution and he was brought off immediately, through Prince's Street, down to Jervis Street hospital.

The hurriedly entered notes in my diary that Easter Monday evening do not quite record the events of the day in their strict sequence, but the next incident I have noted is: *Soldiers – about eight – fired at intervals from the walls that project from the ABC office.* These British soldiers were behind the low walls, three or four feet high, at the ABC office, which is the present Tramway office (60 Upper O'Connell Street) and the Pillar Picture Theatre. They were on their knees, with their rifles propped up against this parapet, and from time to time they sniped at three Henry Street windows of the General Post Office which were facing towards the Rotunda. Volunteers occupied these windows and from time to time interchanged shots with the soldiers. They might as well have been firing at Windsor! By this time, O'Connell Street was crowded, particularly from Pro-Cathedral Street to Abbey Street. As time went on, the crowds grew more and more reckless, passing under the line of fire of the soldiers and Volunteers.

I turned back towards the Rotunda Hospital where I knew I would find these Lancers, in order to make a report about the dead soldier I had attended previously. I saw the officer on horseback and went over to him. The Lancers so drawn up in front of the Rotunda Hospital could not be seen from the vicinity of Nelson Pillar. I informed the officer that I had attended this soldier who had died, as I was under the impression that he was a Catholic, but that I had learned he was a non-Catholic.

While I was reporting to the officer, I took occasion to make a representation. 'Your soldiers,' I said, 'are firing at the corner windows of the Post Office over the heads of the people. They are doing no earthly good, and people will be killed. You ought either to withdraw these men or disperse the people.' Wrong as the soldiers were, I think it was more indefensible on the part of the Volunteers because the former, being low, could have some control of their fire but the men up on high could not. It may have been in the gaiety of their hearts but it looked desperately alarming.

I am sure that eye-witnesses that late afternoon and next day would say that what most impressed them, and impressed them most unfavourably, was the frivolity and recklessness of the crowd, most of all of the women and children. That is the explanation of the Archbishop's letter which I suggested to him to write. I had in the back of my mind the idea that the less people were on the street, the less looting there would be. At the time it occurred to some that the explanation of the Volunteer firing was to frighten off the crowds and looters.

At the time it I went again to the Pro-Cathedral to get my bicycle and had a talk with Fr Flanagan. I think it was Fr John O'Reilly CC, who went over first to the GPO to hear confessions. I think he was on duty that day. He was a rather timid man. I have a record that Fr Bowden who was Administrator was also there. Fr Flanagan was the last to go and he had to remain in the GPO as he could not get back.

It was after my return from the Rotunda that I noticed that the ten or twelve policemen with their inspector, whom I had seen at the foot of Nelson's Pillar some hours previously, had now moved right under and against the wall of the GPO, near the corner of Henry Street. They were very tense. I spoke very strongly to the DMP inspector, saying it was a scandal to leave the police there with the firing going on. There they were almost under fire. I think I added that the situation was one for the military and not for the police. Two or three minutes afterwards they moved off. Quite unhindered they went off towards Store Street. That was some time coming on to three o'clock. Not a hair of these ten or twelve policemen was touched while they stood at the Pillar or while the firing went on. The DMP suffered no interference from the Volunteers. Their fight was against the British. They did not fire at the DMP at the Pillar.

I was also very much struck by the restraint of Volunteers in the case of another drunken soldier who was an Australian. This happened when I first went to the GPO and met Connolly. The soldier was not quite drunk and was standing eating something, in an attitude of bravado, right under where the Volunteers were firing. Yet the Volunteers did not fire or even disturb him. The soldier was not armed, of course.

I reported to the Archbishop when I returned on Monday evening and told him what had taken place. I recall that what was uppermost in my mind and in my report was the amazing recklessness of the civilians, that I was certain many of them would be killed and that the women and children were the worst. I have noted in my diary that everything was quiet from 10pm on Easter Monday until 1am on Easter Tuesday morning when firing recommenced towards Cabra and Glasnevin.

Monday's varied rumours about the Rising

On Easter Monday evening I determined to write down all the reports that came to the Archbishop's, although I knew the reports were bound to be inaccurate and even fantastic. We were in a favourable way of obtaining information. Our telephone was not cut off for a couple of days. Priests were ringing up, giving us news from the different localities. I wrote these reports down simply as they came. They are as follows:

Seizure of two loads of ammunition by the Volunteers from the North Wall. They did not seize it; they attacked it.

A few minutes past twelve, they entered the GPO, and seized the whole place, tearing up telegraph system.

Stephen's Green seized and entrenched, and tram upset and barricade erected at the Shelbourne.

Jacobs seized by Volunteers. Five soldiers and a woman were killed there.

The City Hall was seized. If an attack was made on the Castle, it failed.

The Protestant Synod Hall was seized for a short time and a few windows broken by bullets.

South Dublin Union was seized but, as a small back door was left unguarded, the military got in and both sides entrenched on the grounds. I think that is true.

Three railway stations were seized, Westland Row, Harcourt Street and, perhaps, Broadstone.

The bridge over the railway on the North Circular Road was seized by the Volunteers.

The Mendicity Institute and the Four Courts were also seized.

It is said that 300 Volunteers entrenched at Finglas and that the 5th Lancers were sent out, but returned.

Church Street is barricaded.

Firing recommenced at half-past five with the coming of some machine guns from the Bull at the Sloblands and Wharf A. Some Volunteers fired on them. It did not last long.

It also broke out on the Upper Quays, on the north side. Anywhere from O'Connell Street to Church Street, I suppose, would be the Upper Quay.

The Manure Works at the North Wall were seized by Volunteers.

Between 9 and 10, the City Hall was recaptured by the military after a big fight. Many Volunteers killed by Maxim guns. This would be nine or ten o'clock in the evening.

The Proclamation of the Irish Republic was put up in a few places. It shows that the outbreak does not include the MacNeill section. It is signed by Pearse, Tom Clarke, Connolly, Joe Plunkett (son of Count Plunkett) McDermott, McDonagh, Kent.

Portobello Bridge was captured, but retaken by the military. Many killed.

Bridge over the Midland Railway on the North Circular Road was blown up, and houses on the city side of it occupied by Volunteers.

James O'Connor interviews the Archbishop

For James O'Connor's interview with the Archbishop on the evening of Easter Monday, see appendix to Monsignor Walsh's *Life of Archbishop Walsh*.

The following verbatim transcript from my diary consists partly of my own observations and partly of information received by telephone during the day:

Easter Tuesday 25th April 1916

On Easter Tuesday morning sniping went on irregularly in all quarters, except Glasnevin and Drumcondra. It was most intense towards the Broadstone and in the direction of the GPO. Some machine guns were firing and a few explosions were heard.

At nine o'clock I went to the Pro-Cathedral, from there to St Andrew's, West-land Row, on to Dr Cox (Merrion Square) *then to (visit John H. O'Donnell our respected solicitor who died three weeks later) Leeson Street, to St Vincent's Hospital, and back to O'Connell Street. Lower O'Connell Street is largely looted, particularly from Lawrence's* (in Upper O'Connell Street) *to the Liffey. The Volunteers occupy the Metropole hotel, the Hibernian bank* (12, 13 Lower O'Connell Street – corner of Lower Abbey Street) *and Kelly's at O'Connell Bridge. The military occupy Trinity College. The side streets leading into O'Connell Street are barricaded against traffic. Two attempts to blow up Nelson's Pillar failed.* (This report was untrue. No such attempt was made.) *Boland's and Kennedy's bakeries supply bread. The gas works are cut off, and James Street is cut off from the central city.*

On the whole, everything is much quieter than one would expect. No military or police are to be seen. Sniping was going on between the military in the Shelbourne Hotel and the Volunteers in Stephen's Green. We hear that serious encounters occurred at Beggars' Bush yesterday and there was fighting on the North Wall. It was stated that Sir Roger Casement was shot yesterday in London and that there are German submarines in the Irish Sea. Guinness's (sic) is also occupied by the Volunteers, and the machine-gun mounted on it is firing on the Royal Barracks. The office of the 'Evening Mail' is also occupied with a machine-gun (sic). A platoon of soldiers advancing up Dame Street was dispersed by this gun.

The Castle is surrounded by Volunteers who keep up continuous sniping from Pim's, 'The Mail', etc. Several soldiers were killed and wounded by shots from Pim's. It is said the Mendicity Institution is evacuated.

The only newspaper printed since yesterday appeared to-day at 11.30. It was a stop-press edition of the 'Irish Times' and contained no news of interest except a Gov-ernment Proclamation notifying that stern measures would be taken to put down the insurrection in Dublin, and warning law-abiding citizens not to frequent the streets nor to assemble in crowds. As a result of my reports to His Grace on the recklessness of the people, especially of the women and children crowding the streets in dangerous places, His Grace adopted my suggestion that notice should be sent to the local parish priests and to the churches of religious, asking the Catholic people to observe this caution. With great difficulty, the notice was printed and circulated.

In making this suggestion to the Archbishop, I had also in mind the widespreading looting in and about O'Connell Street.

Dr Cox and Dr O'Brien called at 2.30 – (leaving at) 3.20. As the Archbishop was disappointed and discouraged by the failure of the medical treatment, he asked me to arrange with Dr Cox to invite Dr O'Carroll to be called in for consultation. Dr Cox fell in with this suggestion.

Dr Cox told me of his very unpleasant experience in crossing the city from Merrion Square to Drumcondra and the dangers attending it, although they were dressed, like all the doctors, in white overalls and had come by Butt Bridge and the quieter area of Gardiner Street. He seemed particularly apprehensive of Beresford Place and of danger from Liberty Hall. Although I told him that our information was that Liberty Hall was unoccupied, he still had such misgivings that I volunteered to accompany him on his return to secure greater safety. We took the Mountjoy Square–Gardiner Street route.

There seemed a perfect lull in the firing and we passed Beresford Place in complete quiet. But, as we had crossed the Quay to step on Butt Bridge pathway, three shots were fired, quite obviously at us, from above the portico of the Custom House. We had an alarmingly narrow escape. One bullet sang between me and a civilian, a yard or two behind me. This man had joined us in crossing the street, as he thought, for greater safety. He was quite definite that these shots from the Custom House were fired by the military. We waited a few minutes under shelter of the (great arcs of) metal work which then formed such a prominent feature of Butt Bridge. Dr Cox could not credit that the shots were fired by the military until a young man in Tara Street came across at a signal from Dr Cox, from whom he (Dr Cox) ascertained that it was perfectly true that the Custom House was occupied by the military. It turned out that this young man was a TCD student – known to Dr Cox – who was acting as intelligence officer for the British. This was at 4.45pm.

Later on, I heard of several such intelligence officers, all organised by the military in TCD. They included many of those who were members of the organisation nicknamed 'Gorgeous Wrecks'.

I left Dr Cox and Dr O'Brien at Denzille Street where, at Browne and Nolan's printing works, I had to see after the dispatch of the Archbishop's circulars. I returned by Brunswick Street, O'Connell Bridge and Bachelor's Walk. Owing to the intense sniping in O'Connell Street between the military in TCD and the Volunteers in O'Connell Street, I had to return by Bachelor's Walk, Liffey Street and Dorset Street. There was continuous sniping, sometimes quite close at hand. Several injured people were removed in the city ambulance which seemed constantly employed.

O'Connell Street presented a ruined appearance. Its houses were looted and Lawrence's was on fire. Volunteers occupied Kelly's, the Hibernian bank and the Metropole Hotel.

The Volunteers attempted to blow up the NCR bridge over the MGR at Phibsborough but were driven into the city by shrapnel. The 5th Dublin Fusiliers from Tipperary occupied Phibsborough, the fork of the road at Glasnevin Orphanage and the top of Iona Road. At 5pm several machine guns and ambulances were assembled in Dorset Street and Mountjoy Street. It is said that some hundreds of Volunteers entrenched at Finglas retreated before the soldiers to Knocksedan. It was rumoured that a few Volunteers deserted during the day. On the other hand, some joined them. I saw four.

From 8.30pm to 10pm an utter stranger, armed with a revolver, stationed himself at the Archbishop's House and made people keep on the other side of the road. He even stopped motor cars and cyclists. We failed to find out his identity. (He seemed to be protecting us.)

We were informed that the Volunteers held some of the ND Union building in North Brunswick St. for some time to-day, but left it for other houses in the street. There was some sniping. It was added that they took 4 soldiers prisoner, but released them later and also left the locality themselves. We also heard during the day that the Volunteers were driven out of Stephen's Green by bombs and machine-guns, fired by the military in the Shelbourne Hotel, and that they lost many killed. The survivors fled to and held, the College of Surgeons. They were also driven out of the 'Mail' office or, rather, all were killed.

Such were the reports we received on the telephone from priests in different districts. They were supplying the rumours current in their own districts.

My diary continues:

Wednesday, 26 April 1916

The Archbishop removed to-day to the drawing-room. The doctors were unable to come. This was his first day out of the bedroom since April 1st.

At 7.45am sniping and machine-guns became active towards the lower Quays. At 8 the 'Helga', in front of the Custom House, battered at Liberty Hall for 12 minutes and fired some 6 shots at longer intervals. Everybody had withdrawn from Liberty Hall. Sniping was very general all day, the streets reverberating with sounds of shooting. A large number of civilians were killed and wounded last evening and during the night. There were 90 such cases in Jervis St. hospital alone.

Looting is spreading through Henry St. and Mary St. The fire in Lawrence's is extending.

At 9 o'clock am I went to the Pro-Cathedral. Dorset St. was occupied by military sentries. The streets were crowded, including O'Connell St., despite the danger. There were several deaths and many were wounded. There was sniping at the Mater Hospital corner of the NCR and soldiers, lying on the pavement outside Mountjoy Prison, were sniping at Volunteers in the houses. Some wounded were brought to the Mater Hospital. The Corporation ambulance is working under great difficulties and was fired upon, presumably unintentionally, by both sides. I came back with Mr Séamus Hughes (whom I met in that neighbourhood) and I met Mr Murphy.

The Volunteers are said to have been driven from the South D. Union yester-

day. The military occupy St Mary's, Haddington Road, and are using the tower for military purposes. The Volunteers hold the Four Courts and they have strongly barricaded the Church St. area. They sell there their paper, 'The War News'. (Our milkman met there young Dillon – aged about 14/15 – armed at a barricade.) From the houses on the opposite side of the Liffey at Winetavern Street, the Volunteers snipe the military on the upper side of the quays. The bridges and quays are most dangerous. The Volunteers are also sniping from the houses in Liffey St.

The soldiers guard the bridges over the MG Rly at Cabra Rd, and the NC Rd. About 1pm the soldiers were sniping at Broadstone Station. It is said 5,000 soldiers landed at Kingstown with a gun.

Fifteen soldiers were sniped at at Clanwilliam Place by Volunteers in Mount St. Fr John McMahon attended the wounded.

Jacobs is still held by the Volunteers. There is much firing at the North Wall.

Minnie and Phyllis Ryan call on Archbishop

At 2pm Minnie (Mrs Mulcahy) and Phyllis (Mrs Seán T.) Ryan called on me at Archbishop's House to report that the military were firing on their Red Cross Post at Clery's, and asked me whether the Archbishop could take steps to dissuade the military from doing so. Unfortunately I was unable to give them any hope as the military showed a strong disposition to ignore all requests from any quarter.

Many women like these two are working at First Aid for the Volunteers in the GPO, Stephen's Green, etc. They also procure news and ammunition.

At 2.30 I went home (211 North Circular Road, between Grangegorman and Cattle Market) *by Iona Road and Cabra Road, calling at the Vincentians in Phibsboro'. The district had an exciting time while the Volunteers were being dislodged from the NC Rd. bridge. The place was shaken by gunfire.* (This same bridge was an example of the incompetence of the 'explosives' section of the Volunteers. I had seen them attempting to mine the bridge. Later on – next day? – I saw the results of their efforts, a mere hollow, no bigger than a bowl, in the middle of the road.)

My diary then reads: *Incident of scout sent by bicycle to Cork on Easter Sunday.* I can't recollect the details of this incident. It must have been an account I received from somebody I met and doubtless refers to a courier conveying Volunteer messages from Dublin.

Seán O'Cuiv called. He had just returned from Cork. There is no disturbance in the South except a little in Tralee. In Cork city the Volunteers and military were about to fight when the Bishop and the Lord Mayor intervened and induced the Volunteers to obey John MacNeill's orders.

Mr Hughes told me that the reason why Amiens St. Station was not seized was because that duty was left to the Ulster Volunteers. They arrived in mufti and were to have been armed on arrival. By some mischance, the arms were not at hand and nothing could be done.

Mr Grace, a DMP detective, said the Volunteers very nearly captured the Castle. The gates were actually open for them, on a policeman being shot.

Fearing a trap, the Volunteers did not enter. Had they done so, they would have captured everything, including Nathan and Campbell. They then seized the City Hall.

(Lieut.) Tom Kettle, MP, called on me twice to-day in reference to his brother, Larry (a National Volunteer).

Sniping from houses, especially from roofs, has become a regular feature.

All was quiet at 7pm. Notices were distributed ordering people off the streets at 8pm. The warning was not observed and the streets were crowded.

The fire at Lawrence's (Upper O'Connell St.) is becoming dangerous, not only to the entire block but to the Pro-Cathedral. The fire-brigade was ordered by the military not to go out. Fr Bowden, Adm., and Fr John Flanagan telephoned to ask the Archbishop to procure the intervention of the Viceregal. The Archbishop permitted me to do so. After consultation with General Friend, the Viceregal agreed to do their best (to allow the brigade to save the Pro-Cathedral). But nothing was done about the matter.

During the evening there was a big fight at Ballsbridge – perhaps an attack on the incoming troops from Kingstown. The Volunteers were defeated and 60 taken prisoner.

The Swords Volunteers have occupied the village. It is impossible to settle down to any mental work in this tense atmosphere.

Mr Séamus Hughes, whom I mentioned in my diary as having accompanied me on my way home from the Pro-Cathedral on Wednesday, the 26th April, was in the Volunteers. I wonder was he doing Intelligence work. He was afterwards secretary to Eoin MacNeill. He lived in the neighbourhood of Drumcondra.

Haddington Road Church is used by British Military

My diary referred to the occupation of Haddington Road Church by the military. This incident was reported to me by Dr Donnelly, Archbishop of Canea, Assistant Bishop of Dublin and PP of St Mary's. One of the priests there – Father McKee – was ill and he attended him. How much sniping the military did from the tower, I do not know. They certainly used it for observation purposes. The military had first entered on the excuse that there were Volunteers up in the tower and they insisted upon inspecting it. They were allowed up; and from that on, they used it for their own purposes. It may have been to prevent other people from using it; they pretended they were fired upon from it. They imagined astonishing things and saw strange visions those days. William M. Murphy, Chairman of the Dublin Tram Company in his address (6th February, 1917) on the year's working, related how their traffic manager found the military at the Pro-Cathedral about to bombard their premises in O'Connell Street. They were convinced that snipers were firing on them from its windows. As the manager had only just left it, he was able to persuade the officer that there was not a word of truth in the report he had received.

The 'young Dillon' mentioned on the same date was a son of our local building contractor. He was an apprentice and had been on jobs about the Archbishop's house a few times.

Father John McMahon, who attended the wounded at Clanwilliam Place on the same date, was a brother of Archdeacon McMahon. They were staunch followers of John Redmond and very unfriendly to the Volunteers. I also referred to a visit I received from Tom Kettle on the 26th April, 1916. He wished to enquire had we news about his brother. I think that was only an excuse. He was in a miserable way over the whole situation. I had two talks with him that week.

Thursday, 27th April, 1916

The following are my own observations and reports which I heard and were written by me in my diary for Thursday, the 27th April, 1916:

The night was comparatively quiet except for the usual sniping and some machine gun fire.

The Castle neighbourhood has been cleared and remains quiet.

At 8.30am I went to the Pro-Cathedral.

The military are stationed at Cahill's corner on the North Circular Road (at Dorset Street), *awaiting with machine-guns the Volunteers from Swords.*

A proclamation has been issued ordering the people off the streets between the hours of 7.30pm and 5am.

There are very few in O'Connell Street. There is continual sniping between the military stationed in both the Rotunda and the Ballast Office and the Volunteers in the GPO, Metropole, Hibernian Bank, DBC, other houses and also in Middle Abbey Street as far as Marlborough Street, that is, in Keating's, etc. Volunteers also occupy Henry Street as far as Moore Street. The houses have been linked up. The Four Courts and Church Street are strongly barricaded.

Communication with the South side is most dangerous.

Several civilians and looters have been killed. The foolhardiness of the looters – mostly women and children – is amazing.

The Pro-Cathedral was only saved by a miracle from the fire. A change in the wind caused the fire to shift towards Earl Street. The priests had everything ready in bags for departure, including the parochial records. The girls from Hickey's and other houses (in Pro-Cathedral Street) spent the night in the Sacristy. The Brigade were not allowed out. Priests attending calls are in great danger. Fr John O'Reilly had a narrow escape attending a Volunteer brought into Wynn's Hotel. Fr Richard Bowden and a Dominican heard confessions in the GPO for several hours yesterday (Wednesday).

I noted a young sentry of fifteen in Williams Lane. He was carefully watching the approaches from Abbey Street. I was very much impressed by the courage with which he stuck to his post, all by himself, despite his nervous tension. I walked along Abbey Street from the Capel Street end to see how near I could get to O'Connell Street with safety; and I got as far as Williams lane. Williams lane is the last thoroughfare – only for pedestrians – leading from Abbey Street to Prince's Street. Middle Abbey Street was absolutely deserted.

The dummy sniper on Miss Quinn's nursing home

Returning by Mountjoy Square, I saw (what I thought was) a Volunteer sniper on the roof of what was Miss Quinn's nursing home. (This was near Russell Street.) *Several soldiers were firing at him from the pavement in front of Mountjoy School.* (The soldiers were firing at this target. On the day of the surrender, I passed again along that way and noticed that the 'Volunteer' was still on the roof. It was then I realised it was a 'dummy' rigged up by the Volunteers, with the head only over the roof, while they moved along sniping from other roofs.)

Towards 11am fierce rifle fire took place here (Drumcondra). We counted several bullets singing by the gate lodge and the house. Later on, one struck the house and several sang over it.

It is stated, on good authority, that the Volunteers seized two machine guns and defeated the military at Summerhill last evening.

Rang up the Lord Lieutenant's Secretary to request that priests would be placed on the same footing as medical practitioners who were allowed out between the forbidden hours of 7.30pm and 5am. (Permission never came.)

After 4pm machine-gun firing was particularly severe for some time. There was some cannonading.

A second fire has broken out at Hugh, Moore and Alexander, and another at Linenhall Barracks.

Cannonading was resumed at 5.10pm. It is stated to be the shelling of houses in O'Connell Street and that the military have set on fire the DBC, to burn out the Volunteers. There is fierce sniping and machine-gun fire.

Many more bullets flew about the house. Another struck the house piercing the east window of the billiard room (now the Archbishop's study) and deflected sharply to the left against an open bookcase, smashing the woodwork. I found the bullet. In consequence, we arranged for the Archbishop to sleep on the north side and barricaded the windows with mattresses. Later, however, in the evening shots were fired along Drumcondra Road from Tolka Bridge towards the Canal. Altogether we are very anxious. We ourselves (that is, the secretaries) established ourselves in the lower corridor in the centre of the house.

The city fires are extending and look most alarming at darkness. O'Connell Street is burned from Abbey Street to Eden Quay, including the DBC, etc. A third centre of fire, though small, is the Provincial Hotel, opposite the Four Courts – and houses in Bridgefoot Street.

Birrell returned to the Castle last night or this morning.

Martial law was proclaimed yesterday. Nevertheless, people crowded the streets after 7.30pm. The military had to drive them indoors by discharging rifle shots over their heads. The streets are without light. There is much sniping here at times.

Lusk and Donabate Volunteers who had arms – about sixty – marched and joined the Swords Volunteers yesterday. They occupied the three Post Offices and Police Barracks, got some twelve rifles and marched to Garristown. All Lusk is wild with excitement and, if they had arms, all would rise. (One of the priests there brought this report.)

That concludes the diary entries of Thursday, the 27th April.

Friday, 28th April, 1916

The following are the entries under Friday, the 28th April 1916:

The situation is much the same as yesterday except that the streets are more deserted and more dangerous.

The Volunteers still occupy all their posts of yesterday. They are still apparently in the South Dublin Union and also in Marrowbone Lane Distillery. They occupy Carton's Lane in the North City Markets district. Volunteer snipers occupy Merrion Square houses. (Probably this information was obtained from Dr Cox who telephoned during the day, but could not get over.)

The fires are still burning. Clery's is now on fire.

Many people have taken refuge in the Pro-Cathedral. People entering or leaving are shot at by the military. Under these circumstances, the administrator applied to the military that they should occupy it. This they did, in great force, later in the day. They occupy both Church and Presbytery, with all the passages, rooms and roofs. (The military had already been in possession of Tyrone House, the Model Schools.) *They also stated that they might have to send there the guests in the Hammam and Gresham Hotels.*

The military also occupy St Catherine's Protestant Church.

Father Edward Byrne (later Archbishop) *and Father Joe MacArdle are in Jervis Street Hospital (on duty). It was thought better to leave them there, on account of the danger passing through the streets. Father John Flanagan is in the GPO.*

Whole districts are without provisions – milk, butter, bread or meat. Only for flour, many would be very badly off. Kennedy's bakeries supply the area.

A sniper close at hand in Fitzroy Avenue or at the railway kept up most persistent sniping from noon to night. He did make things hum. (It was when taking aim at him that the bullets hit the Archbishop's house. I forget who he was. This man kept up sniping for long after the surrenders – to the best of my recollection, until Tuesday forenoon. The houses in Fitzroy Avenue were searched for him several times but he ran about from roof to roof and was not discovered. I heard afterwards who he was. He lived in Fitzroy Avenue.)

My diary then lists all the priests who telephoned or called and then continues:

The military occupy the corner of the North Circular Road and Summerhill, the top of North Richmond Street (or Schools), the top of Russell Street, the Malt House of Portland Street. They have barricaded the bottom of ei> (North) Summer Street. They have a machine gun in Fanning's (corner North Circular Road and Jones' Road).

Telegraphic communication is established with Dublin, but communications with the provinces go through London.

The military shot an incendiary (bomb) into the GPO at [word missing] o'clock and set it ablaze.

The sight at night was most impressive. Firing had almost ceased and everything was deadly quiet and black, except the fires in O'Connell Street and Linenhall Barracks. An occasional shot from our neighbouring sniper (Fitzroy avenue) alone disturbed the quietness of a lovely, calm, starry night.

Saturday, 29th April 1916

The following is a transcript (practically verbatim) from my diary:

Saturday, April 29th, 1916. There seems to be no change overnight. We hear the usual sniping and machine-gun fire. There is, however, great distress through scarcity of food.

I paid a visit home – North Circular Road – from 10–12.

While I was out, the military (Major Price) rang up about eleven o'clock to say that the Government were about to issue a proclamation, described to me as offering terms of surrender to the Volunteers and asking whether the Archbishop would ask the clergy to convey this to the Volunteers. The Archbishop replied that it was not necessary for him to ask them. He was sure they would do it themselves if asked by the military. (My recollection to-day is that this, or some similar military telephonic message, made allusion to the danger that churches and civilian property would run if the Volunteers would not lay down arms. I have some doubt as to the objective accuracy of this telephone message. I was not in the house at the time.)

The military are using an armoured motor-car to take houses in the Capel Street area. They charge into the street, back the car into a shop, smashing everything in. The military get out of the back of the car and storm floor by floor. In this way, they have captured sections of streets and pushed in their barricades.

At 4 o'clock I was in the Secretaries' Study when the telephone bell, which had seldom sounded those days, suddenly rang and a girl's voice abruptly told me: 'The Sinn Féiners have surrendered' – and clapped down the telephone immediately and could not be recalled. (I took it that she was an employee in the telephone office, or the Castle, and was anxious that the Archbishop should know as quickly as possible and that she did it without authorisation. I did my best to re-call her but I could not.) I at once informed the Archbishop and it was arranged that I would go down town to the Pro-Cathedral for information and with instructions.

I walked down by Mountjoy Square and North Great George's Street. There were great numbers in the hall-ways, in an atmosphere of expectancy. The cessation of gun-fire for some hours made people speculate in this area whether the fighting was coming to an end, or had already come to an end, and whether the Volunteers had surrendered. But nobody could obtain news and each sought information from his neighbour.

At the Pro-Cathedral I found them similarly without definite news. The sur-

render was only an unconfirmed rumour. Father Bowden, Administrator, was in the Marlborough Street Schools, finding food and bedding for refugees. I left the Archbishop's directions concerning Sunday, namely, that it was to be announced that there was no obligation to hear mass on next day, Sunday, and no bells were to be rung.

The Archbishop was anxious concerning Father John Flanagan, as some said he had been killed, others that he had probably found his way from the GPO to Jervis Street Hospital, where we knew Father Edward Byrne (the late Archbishop) and Father McArdle were stationed, and where rumours said Father Flanagan also was to be found.

Even then I was under the mistaken impression that the Volunteers had been disarmed and had left the GPO area. It was known by this time that the GPO was burned out and that the Volunteers had fallen back towards Henry Street or Jervis Street. (We had heard that the place was on fire and the roof had fallen in and, of course, we speculated on all the possibilities.) I have a vague recollection that we had already been told that the Volunteers were turning the whole area around there into a barricaded area in an attempt to keep-up communications with the Four Courts and Church Street or join the garrisons there.

I left by Cathedral Street, where a dead civilian lay in the doorway of the (then) DUT Co. parcel department. Emerging into O'Connell Street, I witnessed an indescribable sight. There was not a soul but myself in the whole street. The GPO was a mere shell. The left-hand side (i.e. east) of Lower O'Connell Street was a smoking ruin. The right-hand side was little better. Clery's was burned out and the DBC also was a shell. The smell of burning materials pervaded everywhere. Smoke hung low about. (The dead Lancer's horse lay killed at the foot of Nelson's Pillar, as I had seen it on Monday.) *I aimed to go to Jervis St. through Henry St. Moving across, my every foot-step crunched broken glass. The silence was deadly and already I was beginning to have misgivings. Before I was half-way across I saw that Henry Street was blocked, and so I turned towards the Rotunda where, by this time, I saw a group of military at the foot of the Parnell Monument. With much uneasiness, I ventured past the tramway office, on the right hand side, i.e., east, the Hammam and Gresham Hotels. This side of the street is uninjured. Gill's (west) side is considerably injured by fire, shelling and rifle fire, especially the YMCA. People crowded the doorways and windows of the hotels and called out to me for news. It was then that I began to realise that my notion of the surrender was incorrect, for these people facing O'Connell St. knew nothing about it. When I mentioned the surrender, they came out into the street but were sharply ordered in by the military. At the Gresham Hotel I met Mr D'Arcy of ?, Upper O'Connell Street, who was full of fantastic slanders of the Volunteers.* (I cannot remember the number of the house where he lived. Mr D'Arcy had lodgings in a flat in a house very near John Burke's {solicitor} office. He was one of the D'Arcys, the brewery people. He was in the Gresham. He had been driven out of his house and got rooms in the Gresham Hotel.) The military again peremptorily ordered all indoors and I continued towards the Rotunda.

At the Parnell Monument I met Colonel Portal, Commanding Officer, to whom

I explained who I was and my anxiety to reach Jervis Street Hospital. He at once informed me of the surrender, showed me six copies of the order of surrender, signed by Pearse, and asked me to make it known. I asked him for a copy but, as he had only six, he could not give me one. He warned me that I would need a pass and kindly made out one from his note-book. It must have been the first military pass issued. I had no further conversation with him and still I did not know the real position and thought that the surrender and disarmament had already taken place (elsewhere). *Not many military were to be seen in the immediate neighbourhood of the Parnell Monument. But as I passed down Parnell Street, I saw every street, alley and passage barricaded, with soldiers behind sandbags, and rifles pointed toward the smoking ruins in Moore Street and Henry Street. I was told to slip along these barricades quickly, and then, for the first time, I realised that the disarmament had not yet taken place. But there was no superior officer from whom I could obtain news or information. I continued on to Jervis Street amidst the alarmed warnings and prayers of the people in the doorways.*

At Jervis St. Hospital I met the three priests, but was advised not to venture back to Drumcondra. By this time, I saw plainly I could do nothing else and managed to send a telephone message to Archbishop's House (from the hospital).

That ends my direct contacts with the Rising of Easter Week.

EASTER ETHICS

Séamus Murphy

I. 'JUST WAR' THEORY

It is reported that in the first few days of the 1916 Easter Rising, when the heavy fighting had not yet got under way, Pádraig Pearse and Joseph Plunkett discussed the morality of resorting to arms.[1] Given that they had already committed themselves beyond the point of no return, such discussion appears odd. (It probably appeared more than odd to Clarke and Connolly.) No doubt they had discussed it before, and in this instance it was likely to be an attempt to reassure themselves of the moral rectitude of the Rising.

Since discussion of the morality of the insurrection often focuses on the resort to force, let's look briefly at how the just war theory might be applied to it.

1916 and 'just war' theory

Clarification of the 'just war' concept is in order. First, the term 'just war' is a misnomer, since there is nothing good or just about war as such. It causes death, suffering and destruction, and always involves a loss of wellbeing. The misnomer misdirects moral evaluation, as though we are to focus on the state of affairs of war itself, as distinct from the actions of the protagonists. This can be clarified by considering the case of a police officer and a violent criminal engaged in physical combat. They are, so to speak, in a 'state of war', from which injury or killing is a possible outcome. However, moral evaluation, while cognisant of the loss of wellbeing involved in such an outcome, focuses primarily on the respective *actions*. Although the respective physical behaviours may be similar – striking, shooting, physically overpowering the other – the action of the criminal is morally wrong whereas that of the police officer is morally permissible, and possibly even morally required.

Thus, 'just war' theory focuses on the morality of the respective *actions* of the protagonists. The *outcome* (in death, suffering and destruction) is relevant to that evaluation, but it is not the primary focus. Accordingly, it would be better to think of it as a theory laying down the criteria for permissible resort to force or justifiable use of military power.

Second, 'just war' theory is part of a larger theory of good governance, concerning the balance to be struck between keeping the peace and avoiding war on one hand, and resisting armed aggression on the other. In the case of an insurrection, where one of the protagonists is not a recognised government, it is more difficult to see how to connect it to a political theory of governance. It would have to be closely tied to the self-defence of those taking up arms.

The theory is made up of (a) criteria to be met before resorting to war (*ius ad bellum*) and (b) criteria for the conduct of the war (*ius in bello*).

The criteria for being justified in resorting to arms are: (i) just cause; (ii) competent authority; (iii) comparative justice; (iv) right intention; (v) reasonable prospect of success; (vi) last resort; (vii) proportionality. That is also their logical order, so that, if the proposed resort to force doesn't pass the earlier criteria then passing the later criteria will be either impossible or irrelevant. Lack of just cause excludes right intention and ensures the irrelevance of a good prospect of success.

The 1916 Rising doesn't pass the criteria. The insurgents didn't have a just cause. Just cause is constituted by unprovoked armed inter-state aggression, such as Germany's invasion of Belgium in August 1914, or a government committing genocide against some of its own people. Nothing remotely comparable occurred in Ireland in the period prior to 1916. One could accept that Britain's ruling Ireland was the outcome of 'historic injustice' and that the legitimacy of British rule in Ireland was deeply flawed, but that would not suffice to constitute just cause in 1916.

The Rising's leadership did not amount to a competent authority. A group can't constitute itself a government simply by declaring itself to be such: it must have some recognisable legitimacy or *de facto* control. Only the British government and/or the Irish party, representing the majority of Irish people, could have had either in 1916.

Without just cause or competent authority, the Rising's passing any of the other criteria is irrelevant. Even if it had passed both, it couldn't have passed some of the others: it had no reasonable prospect of success (as its leaders knew), and it was not the last resort. Lack of those two alone would mean it failed proportionality as well.

The criteria for just conduct in war are: (i) not targeting non-combatants, and (ii) not causing disproportionate suffering. The first was violated by the shooting out of hand of a number of civilians, such as the unarmed Constable James O'Brien outside Dublin Castle, and the man who wouldn't surrender his cart to be used in a barricade at Stephen's Green. Generally, however, the insurgents did not target civilians. As regards (ii), since starting the insurrection was unjustified, the causing of any casualties (in this instance 'over 250 civilians, 130 members of the Crown forces and over 60 insurgents') can't be proportionate.[2]

II. Ethical frameworks

The role of context

Applying just war criteria is a dry, scholastic exercise. As presented schematically above, it involves a good deal of detaching or abstracting from the wider context. For such a significant historical event, a richer contextualisation is necessary. The rest of this paper will be concerned with contextually-oriented ethical evaluation of the Rising.

It is important not to exaggerate the weight to be placed on context, and to be aware of the problems in explaining by appeal to context. For a start, to say something is to be 'understood in context' is a truism: the challenge is to pick out the *relevant* explanatory elements in the context. Next, excessive emphasis on context is vulnerable to a possible infinite regress or circular reasoning: the explaining contextual features are themselves also presumably to be explained by context. That can be avoided only if one can say something about major events without being very heavily dependent on contextual explanation. Thus, the rather a-contextual application of 'just war' theory to the Easter Rising, even if inadequate, is not to be dismissed out of hand as irrelevant.

Context can be differentiated into synchronic and diachronic sub-contexts. In the case of the former, one explains by appeal to other events more or less contemporary with the event in question. For the Easter Rising, the home rule bill of 1914, the First World War, and the relative political situations of the Irish party, Sinn Féin (SF), the Ulster unionists, the Irish Volunteers and the Irish Republican Brotherhood (IRB) feature in the relevant context. As regards diachronic sub-contexts, we can differentiate between past and future: what led up to the Rising and what followed from it. The first is the previous history of Ireland, particularly (but not exclusively) as interpreted in the nationalist tradition originating in the Young Irelanders of the 1840s, and leading up to the Rising. The second is the history of the effects of the Easter Rising, which have been substantial, emotionally charged, and ambiguous. It may not be relevant for historical explanation of an event, but it is relevant to the ethicist's evaluation of that event.

The elements of ethical analysis

First, as noted, fuller ethical analysis of something like the Easter Rising requires appropriate attention to contexts. It is worth noting that the historian's contextual analysis of a particular event cannot but carry some element of ethical evaluation, however implicit. Thus, though it is not the historian's goal, ethical analysis is not extraneous or alien to historical understanding.

Second, ethical analysis can focus on (a) persons' characters and motives, (b) actions and policies, or (c) consequences and outcomes. As regards (a), evaluation of individuals, including character and motives, is a matter for the biographer, and can't be provided here. Since our focus is the event of the Rising, what I will have to say about individuals will be indirect, arising from ethical analysis of policies or consequences.

Item (b), evaluation of actions and the policies that give the actions their intentionality or meaning is central to the task. The synchronic aspect of context (crudely, what other groups were up to at the time) is directly relevant to that.[3]

Evaluation of consequences (item (c)) also comes into play, since what has flowed from the Easter Rising affects its ethical evaluation. There is a problem here for the ethicist, in that agents can never foresee with certainty all the consequences of their actions. Sometimes agents can be 'morally lucky' or 'morally unlucky', in the sense of the consequences of their actions turning out a lot better or a lot worse than might be expected. Allowing for that, I think that reasonably expectable consequences, rather than actual consequences, should be what we weigh. This will involve a tangential view of people's character, primarily in that good intentions will not excuse folly, nor make up for prudence, foresight and some understanding of others.

Third, ethical context usually involves an ethical-political framework. It involves identifying the values to be sought, and the norms to be observed with respect to the choice of actions in pursuing those values. Such frameworks include (for example) nationalism, pluralist liberal democracy, Marxism, and Christian social theory. I shall ignore Marxism since it is irrelevant here. Whatever about its role in Connolly's earlier work, and even allowing for some suspicion between the Volunteers and the Irish Citizen Army in the General Post Office (GPO) that Easter week, it casts little light on his involvement in the Easter Rising. I shall also have relatively little to say about Christian social theory. I note in passing that its values, particularly as expressed in Catholic moral theory, are closer to liberal democratic than to nationalist values.

The nationalist ethical framework views the IRB, Sinn Féin and the cultural nationalists as pursuing goals oriented to such values as national independence and self-determination, where those values outweighed virtually all others. They understood what they were doing as part of the Irish nation's long struggle, not just to win national independence, but also to come to a kind of collective spiritual self-consciousness as a nation. Everything else was to be evaluated in light of whether it promoted or hindered that goal, and the people competent to make such evaluation were those steeped in the culture, language, and legends of Ireland, those in tune with Ireland's soul.

The ethical framework of liberal democracy is concerned with representative democracy, human rights and the rule of law. It is largely accepted and endorsed by contemporary western and Irish culture, and hence will be important in this paper. Elements of it were mentioned favourably by the men and women of 1916, although in ways that suggest that it did not cross their minds that it could be incompatible with certain interpretations of nationalism. The bulk of the ethical critique of the 1916 Rising comes from that background, particularly since the 1970s. Moral revulsion in the 1970s at the political philosophy of Sinn Féin and the Irish Republican Army (IRA) violence it supported cast Easter 1916 in a morally unfavourable light for those holding liberal democratic values.

The choice of ethical framework

The significance of there being more than one ethical–political framework is that the respective values or priorities may be mutually incompatible. Nationalism and liberal democracy, compatible on many points, diverge, if not as regards the values, at least as regards their relative importance or the appropriate order of priority. Consider the hypothetical questions: 'If 90 per cent of the people of Ireland, north and south, voted in the morning to re-join the United Kingdom and be ruled from Westminster, should that be accepted?' or: 'If you had to choose between living in an independent Ireland under a dictatorship or living in an Ireland ruled democratically and with due respect for human rights as part of a United Kingdom, which would you choose?' The questions are hypothetical in that we actually have both independence and democracy, and no risk of being obliged to choose. In another way, they have not been hypothetical, for IRA campaigns since 1922 have been an attempt to impose one answer, and Irish governments' repression of the IRA was an insistence on the opposite answer.

Questions about what people would do in counterfactual circumstances (circumstances not currently obtaining) are hypothetical; but the values revealed by their answers are not hypothetical. There is nothing hypothetical about values, for values inform moral and political beliefs, beliefs motivate and guide action, and actions have consequences.

There is a question mark over the democratic credentials of the Easter Rising's leaders, as over those of the IRB since its establishment in 1858.[4] This does not mean that the Easter leaders were opposed in principle to democracy. But if democracy as currently experienced was flawed by their standards, or corrupted beyond redemption through being associated with any kind of submission to or involvement with Britain (essentially the IRB view), then it couldn't count as a democracy, certainly not something with any kind of moral or political authority. In a word, the leaders of the Rising were not democrats in practice: they were nationalists first, and their understanding of democracy was subordinate to their understanding of nationalism.

In the spring of 1922, prominent IRA leaders such as Rory O'Connor and Liam Mellows made it clear that they would impose a military dictatorship on behalf of the 1916 republic, if the outcome of Dáil votes or general elections was not satisfactory. Many of the relatives of the signatories of the 1916 Proclamation rejected the legitimacy of the Free State and regarded its democratic credentials as insignificant if not fraudulent, in some cases for decades after the Civil War ended. It is striking how scant in the debates about accepting the Treaty are the references to ascertaining or being governed by the popular will. This applies not just to anti-Treaty figures, but also to pro-Treaty military and IRB figures such as Collins.[5]

There is a problem, then, with 1916 in the liberal democratic ethical–political framework. The position is less clear in the nationalist ethical–political framework, for one could have shared the values of the 1916 leaders but disagreed with them on tactics; perhaps Eoin MacNeill might fit that description. I emphasise that there is no escaping the choice of some ethical–political framework. There is no ethical perspective or standing point that transcends all ethical–political frameworks: one must choose.

I consider the liberal democratic value system ethically superior to the nationalist one for a variety of reasons. First, it places the individual person at the centre of its value system, and places correspondingly great weight on individual freedom. By contrast, the nationalist tradition, strong on the freedom of the nation, has been ambivalent on individual freedom, particularly where such freedom might be used in ways of which nationalists might not approve.

Second, Irish nationalism was heavily influenced by romantic and nineteenth century German metaphysical doctrines about nations as essences, with individuals constituted as persons by being Irish, French, German, or other. Liberal democracy stands free of that view, rejecting the idea that persons are, in any strong sense, 'parts' of a nation, and sceptical about the historical warrant for the romantic idea of the nation. With the same metaphysics of what a nation is, fascism emerged in the post-1918 era from groups with views similar to those of the 1916 insurgents. The strong nationalism of Pearse and the cultural nationalists was anthropologically wishful, politically illiberal, and philosophically questionable.

Christian thought largely endorses the liberal democratic critique of nationalism. While it would be unhappy at liberalism's tendency to take individual persons to be the only locus of moral significance, Christianity rejects the nation as a locus of moral value equal to or exceeding that of the person, and allows only the human race (and humanity's common good) as having comparable (though not superior) moral value. Catholicism in particular also views nationalism as a force with a marked tendency to war.

I turn, then, to evaluating the Easter Rising of 1916 within a larger context than that of 'just war' theory. That context is the ethical–political framework where democracy, human rights, and the rule of law are primary and overriding values.

Finally, note the contemporary contextual factor that ethical evaluation of the Easter Rising is also coloured by one's view of the 1998 Good Friday Agreement concerning the future of Northern Ireland. Support for the agreement implies endorsement of the view that it would be good that power be shared between nationalist and unionist, that political violence should be forsworn and neither community coerced, that the nationalist and unionist communities should each accept that the other has some moral right to a different perspective and different values, and that the Republic should abandon any formal 'claim' to Northern Ireland. One might allow for ignorance, political immaturity, and naïveté on the part of the 1916 leaders, and mitigate criticism accordingly. But one cannot consistently or coherently praise them for doing the very things that we would condemn if done today.

III. 1916 IN ETHICAL REVIEW

I deem the Easter Rising ethically wrong for the following reasons:

1. It started an unnecessary war. Unnecessary wars are unjustifiable. In addition, starting that war sharpened the mentality of partition both north and south, and was counter-productive in that it endangered northern nationalists.

2. It attacked Irish democracy. It inaugurated an era of military dictatorship that lasted until sometime in 1922, and its influence has continued to undermine the culture of liberal democracy to the present day.

3. It greatly strengthened a romantic and gnostic view of Irish well-being, inimical to freedom of speech and to the notion of a legitimate plurality of views, as well as distracting from socio-economic issues.

4. The cult of Easter 1916 has seriously distorted Irish society's sense of itself, giving it a memory that cannot be integrated with its current reality or serve as a model for political life.

5. Arising from its IRB and cultural nationalist roots, it involved and inculcated a rejection of politics.

6. Arising from its IRB roots, it drastically distorted the ideal of the republic into something unrecognisable in modern classical (American and French) republican philosophy, and divorced the ideal of the republic from the actuality of everyday social practice.

1. The unnecessary War of Independence

The 1916 Rising started a chain of events culminating in the War of Independence (1919–21) and the Civil War (1922–3). It was, of course, not the only causal factor leading to those events. But then, the notion of causality in history and the sciences is not that of a necessary or sufficient factor: a cause or causal factor is simply that which raises the probability of a certain outcome. The historian's task is to weigh different factors and apportion responsibility proportionately. Ethical evaluation is not unlike it.

To evaluate the Easter Rising negatively because it was a cause of those events is not to say that its leaders carry sole responsibility for later wars. But they do carry a great deal of responsibility. The 1919–21 War of Independence seems to have been extraordinarily unnecessary, given that what the Treaty achieved was not that different from what the home rule legislation had achieved.[6] (The anti-Treaty faction was convinced that what the Treaty offered was closer to Redmond's home rule than to Pearse's republic.) The claim is supported by the fact that subsequent Irish governments eliminated virtually all of the objectionable provisions of the Treaty without firing a shot, thus vindicating the gradualism of the Irish party. The only thing they could not eliminate was that which was not, *pace* the nationalist myth, in Britain's gift to give, viz. the consent of the northern unionists to be part of a united and independent Ireland.

2. The long civil war

Militarily insignificant, the Rising's political impact has been considerable, so ethical evaluation of the Rising must focus primarily on it.

Pearse, Eoin MacNeill and the other Irish Volunteers had (in contrast to the IRB) initially resorted to arms, not so much to achieve Irish independence as laid out in the Proclamation, but to respond to the arming of the Ulster Protestants in 1912 and the British government's relatively passive response to that event, and Redmond's failure to negotiate away the proposed partition of Ireland in the 1914 home rule bill. Even when one allows for nationalist wishful thinking that Britain was the ultimate cause of northern unionist opposition to home rule and that it could easily have changed northern minds if it had wished to do so, it is still impossible to see how a military uprising in Dublin, directed against British forces, would bring the northern Protestants to heel. If anything, it was more likely to do the opposite.

The 1916 leaders knew precious little about northern Protestants, and didn't take them seriously. It is no answer to point to northern Protestant IRB members like Bulmer Hobson. In the early twentieth century, James Craig was, and Bulmer Hobson was not, representative of northern Protestants. In the 1880s, Parnell had remarked that 1,000 Royal Irish Constabulary (RIC) men would be enough to take care of any Orange mob once home rule arrived, but by 1914 his successor John Redmond had learned the hard lesson that northern Protestants presented too formidable a force, even without the support of Conservatives and Liberal unionists, to be so lightly dismissed.

It was a lesson that the leaders of the Easter Rising, even those like Seán MacDermott who had some northern experience, were unable and unwilling to learn: that's an ethical failure. If they imagined that the Proc-lamation's ideals of equality for all Irish people, regardless of religion, would have removed unionist fears, they were extremely naïve: in matters such as this, naïveté is morally culpable. The Proclamation referred to struggles for independence going back to 1600, as if its authors hadn't a clue about the Ulster unionist view of the seventeenth century struggles, or had no idea of the great and impassable gulf between seventeenth century Irish Jaco-bite values and the post-religious Jacobin values inherent in Wolfe Tone's dream of a union of Protestant, Catholic and dissenter under the common name of Irishman. While it is not the worst moral failure, ignorance is ethically culpable, particularly when it concerns issues for which one is prepared to kill people. To claim today that the 1916 Proclamation was a serious reaching-out to unionists goes beyond naiveté to silliness.

It would be closer to the truth to say that the 1916 leaders were – even if they were in collective denial about it – prepared to coerce the Ulster unionists into a united Ireland, and that they rejected the Irish party because it was not prepared to fight such a war.[7] Today, we accept that a united Ireland can come about only by consent, and appear to accept it not just as a practical necessity but also because it is morally wrong not to accept it. The implication is that Redmond was realistic and prudent and the Easter leaders were neither, which in turn implies that Redmond's actions (in this area) were morally correct and those of the Easter lead-ers were morally wrong. That ethical wrongness is compounded by the fact that they couldn't actually manage to fight such a civil war, yet by their action they and their successors in the War of Independence started a process bound to heighten unionist insecurity with repercussions for northern nationalists.

The actual political effect of the Rising was to undermine the Irish party and its leadership or hegemony in Irish nationalist politics. Whether the 1916 leaders were aware that such was its objective thrust does not matter; in any case it needed no profound political insight to see it at the time. Redmond and Dillon instinctively realised what was happening, but could do little about it. In addition, given a context where the Irish party virtually incarnated Irish democracy, such as it was at the time, a political attack on it by such means was an attack on Irish democracy.[8]

Here, the Easter Rising did succeed in starting a civil war that has con-tinued for nearly a century, between nationalists who believed that work to achieve nationalist goals had to be subject to constraints of democracy and the rule of law, and nationalists who, following the model of 1916, considered that no such values could override or constrain 'the march of the nation'.

That civil war began with the Easter Rising, registering its impact as the Irish parliamentarians felt the tectonic plates shifting under them in the following months.[9] It was fought out in the 1918 general election between the Irish party and Sinn Féin, in the 'formal' civil war struggle between pro- and anti-Treatyites, and in the low-level but ongoing struggle between the governments of the south and the IRA until the 1990s. The struggle has varied as groups of 'true believers' have periodically seen the light and defected to constitutionalism, but it has continued. While its military element has sometimes been important, its political importance has been greater, involving a struggle over the legitimacy of the institutions of the Irish Free State and later the Republic of Ireland.

Thus, the Rising started a new political culture. As it undermined the Irish party and the political culture and *modus operandi* it represented, so the Rising's self-avowed heirs have rejected the compromises and messiness of politics, including any moral imperative to accept the verdict of a popular vote. Britain may have been the avowed enemy in a military sense. But the political enemy was the messy, ambiguous culture of democracy, with its support for political compromise, squeamishness about the rule of law, and respect for constitutionalism.

Occasionally, constitutional politicians have attempted to claim the mantle from 'the republican movement' for the democratic state. It never works, for the reason that the gap between the methods and goals of the insurgents and those of the democratic constitutional Irish state is too great. The gap is highlighted by the fact that such politicians are unable to argue with the IRA/SF supporter who challenges their claim, realising, no doubt, that they can't win the argument.[10]

3. The dictatorship of the voluntariat

As some of Yeats' poems (e.g. *Easter 1916*, *Sixteen Dead Men*, and *The Rose Tree*) suggest, the Rising modeled an approach to achieving independence that led to the outbreak of war in 1919. It moved the dynamic aimed at Irish independence from the democratic parliamentary mode to the elitist military mode. When the shooting started in January 1919, it occurred almost accidentally: not on foot of a mandate from the Dáil whose members were elected in 1918, but simply arising from the private enterprise of local volunteers starting to shoot RIC men. It was inspired by and in line with the model of the Easter Rising: individuals feeling called to kill and be killed for Ireland, without authorisation by any elected body.[11]

The Dáil assumed a *post factum* responsibility for this undeclared war in August 1919. By so doing, it indicated that the individuals who had started the war (or this phase of the war) had authority to do so. For a state to allow such authority to private individuals amounts to acceptance of anarchy. It was the logical consequence of its endorsing the political and military model of the Easter Rising. It thereby accepted that its own authority was subordinate to that of the Volunteers, private individuals and groups willing to kill for Ireland according to their own lights.

In April 1922 prominent anti-Treaty figures announced that they were prepared for military action against the acceptance of the Treaty. One journalist asked Rory O'Connor if that meant he and his associates were imposing a kind of military dictatorship. He reportedly replied: 'You can take it that way if you like.' Had Pearse, after he had read out the Proclamation on Easter Monday morning, been asked the same question, the answer could hardly have been different: the insurgents were already shooting civilians who obstructed them.

As regards the Dáil in 1919, its mentality was not unlike that of people who live under a military dictatorship, albeit willingly. A military dictatorship might have an elected parliament, and the parliament might be supportive of the dictatorship, even voting to legitimate its existence. Yet it is still a military dictatorship and remains so, as long as the military makes major decisions (for instance, about going to war or making peace) in which the parliament acquiesces.[12] Not until the late spring of 1922 was there any attempt to break from the model of military dictatorship, an attempt led by Arthur Griffith, who was determined to insist on the subordination of the military to the civilian government. While he and Collins were at one as regards implementing the Treaty, Collins remained ambivalent about subordinating the military to the civilian government.

4. The romantic revolutionary virus

The Easter Rising's biggest achievement over the ensuing decades was capturing the imagination of young (and many not-so-young) people from the nationalist population. Those of us old enough to remember the 1966 commemoration of the fiftieth anniversary of the Rising will recall the inspiring, stirring music of Seán Ó Riada in his *Mise Éire* and *Saoirse*. As we were taught history in Irish primary and secondary schools, the

Easter Rising had a romance and glow about it that no other event in Irish history could match. The risings of 1848 and 1867 were trifling in comparison, and were mere pale precursors of the Easter apotheosis, a dawn that elevated anyone who had taken part in it.

The romance, of course, was similar to that of other late nineteenth and early twentieth century European nationalisms: far too fond of war, insufficiently fond of democracy, and ignorant of the rule of law. It elevated the idea of giving one's life for one's country, usually in violence.[13]

There was a second romantic element, viz. the romance of millenarian revolution, expressed in the secret underground society, made up of enlightened and utterly dedicated individuals, with a bright vision of a radically transformed future. This group of the enlightened stood in contrast to the great mass of relatively ignorant and materialistic people, who could not be trusted to know what was good for the nation.

It is worth drawing attention to the Catholic church's opposition in the nineteenth century to secret oath-bound revolutionary societies. Its reasons were many, some of them connected to its unpleasant experience of revolution in France and Italy. Of interest here is its opposition to the secret and oath-bound nature of such organisations. Being secret and oath-bound hermetically sealed such societies off from being influenced or 'contaminated' by others, so that the Church – or anybody else – could neither influence nor enter into dialogue with them. This intellectual 'purity' (or closed mentality) of the secret society also appears among the cultural nationalists. It would not be far-fetched to see in both the secret-society IRB and the high-minded 'spirituality of the Irish soul' in Pearse and the other cultural nationalists a kind of gnosticism. Gnosticism was a tendency in early Christianity, found among those who believed that they had received special enlightenment not vouchsafed to others, revealed only to them because they were pure of spirit and high of mind. Any who disagreed with them had thereby shown themselves not to be among the 'Wise Ones', and hence could be ignored. Such cognitive elitism might be relatively harmless but for the fact that the secret revolutionary group aimed at seizing power and imposing its will on society as a whole.

Part of the romance for the Rising's spiritual descendants was the idea that Easter 1916 was not just a model, but a kind of sacred, holy thing. The way the Rising played, following by the executions, gave a sacrificial and hence sacred aura to the event and to its leaders.

Such nationalist romanticism generated hate. A significant amount of hatred was already present due to centuries of past oppression, and it was a causal factor leading to the emergence of the secret revolutionary society. The romanticist glorification of the nation, magnifying its suffering, heightened by the febrile atmosphere of the underground holding to the overriding importance of never compromising with the Other who was seen as the source of all the nation's ills, aggravated the sense of grievance and injustice, and reinforced hate.[14] Hate tends to war, and war encourages hate. From a Christian viewpoint that which encourages hate is seriously unethical; from a pluralist democratic viewpoint, it undermines tolerance, acceptance of the Other, and acceptance that we are not all going to hold the same values. Getting yourself martyred is a great way to arouse the kind of sympathy that can lead to the hatred of those who have been stupid enough to facilitate your martyrdom.

We are still today trying to get the romantic virus out of our system. In early 1923, after having assiduously cultivated the virus in earlier years, de Valera started to moderate it slightly. He had persuaded a reluctant Liam Lynch, the IRA chief of staff, to dump arms and end the armed struggle against the Free State forces. Much later it was reported that Lynch wondered aloud what Tom Clarke (senior IRB figure in the 1916 Rising) would have thought of the decision, and de Valera allegedly replied: 'Tom Clarke is dead. He has not our responsibilities. Nobody will ever know what he would do for this situation did not arise for him.'[15] In other words, the views of Clarke or the spirit of Pearse were not necessarily normative or invariably action-guiding for later nationalist leaders.

Nevertheless, the idea that they were normative for us had become strong and has remained so. During the commemorations of 1916 in 1966, the kind of question school-children were asked to address was 'What would Pearse think of contemporary Ireland?' The underlying message was clear: what Pearse would think ought to count for far more than what anybody else might think.

5. Censoring memory

It is sometimes said, as a reply to critics of the Easter Rising, that it is 'part of what we are' and hence ought not be criticised. It is indeed part of what we are, just as the Nazi period is for Germans 'part of what we are': the fact that some historical event or era has shaped a country's identity indicates nothing at all about its moral quality. If it is morally objectionable, then the fact that it is 'part of what we are' means that we, whoever we are, have all the greater moral obligation to counter its influence among ourselves.

As successive Irish governments since 1922 have found, to maintain their authority they have had to struggle against the glamour and seduction of 'the republican movement'.

However, they have struggled against that seduction only when it led to things like murders and bank robberies within the state, the kind of actions that the electorate doesn't like. For the rest, Irish governments have been keen enough to celebrate the Easter Rising, without examining too closely what it represents.

Last Easter, with much fanfare and stirring music, the 1916 Rising was celebrated by the Irish government, with participation by many people and probably the support of the majority of the indigenous population of the Republic. It is likely that even more laudatory celebration will occur in 2016 for the Rising's centenary. The probability that it will be used by certain political groups for their own purposes constitutes a further *ethical* reason for clear-eyed moral evaluation of the Rising and its contemporary significance.

What is the purpose of such commemoration? It could be merely to remember dead notables of bygone ages. On that interpretation, Pearse and the other 1916 figures are being remembered much as Patrick Sarsfield, Red Hugh O'Donnell, or Brian Boru might be remembered: Irish heroes of another time, but not leaders with contemporary political significance, or models whose goals or methods might be relevant today. Models, by definition, are for imitating.

If we replace Sarsfield and the others with Davitt, O'Connell, Redmond, or Larkin, all of whom can have contemporary political implications, our contemporary political mentality is such that they will not be celebrated in any fashion comparable to that provided for the Easter insurgents. The message is clear: they are not admirable, they are not models, in the way that Pearse and his comrades are. Given all this, I cannot see how one can avoid the conclusion that Pearse and his comrades are being held up as models for imitation with respect to political aspiration and action.

That recent political culture has not regarded the others as models is evidenced in such instances as the following. On Seán T. O'Kelly's becoming President of Ireland in the late 1940s he had the bust of Daniel O'Connell removed from its prominent place in the foyer of Aras an Uachtaráin and consigned to obscurity in the basement. Many years later, when de Valera was asked about the negative attitude of dominant post-independence political circles to O'Connell, he allegedly replied:

You must think, you must consider our feelings at that time. We firmly believed that the Irish people could only be 'jolted' from their lethargy and Irish freedom and liberty achieved by force of arms. How then could we promote the memory of the man who achieved so much by parliamentary means with no loss of life? To praise him would have made it impossible for us to justify armed insurrection.[16]

In this instance, the seductive glamour of the Easter Rising is still so powerful that we are unable as a nation to do what Mr de Valera more or less did in that instance, viz. look at the ethical implications of exalting the Easter Rising, particularly in its distortion of what we should value in our history.

It also suggests an unethical desire to forget what we have learned from experience. The great political achievement of this state has been to maintain itself as a constitutional democracy precisely against those who, in 1922–3, in 1939–45, in 1956–62, and from 1969 to the present day wanted to imitate the 1916 leaders. Ireland did not have independence in 1914, but, unlike other parts of the empire such as India, it had full legislative representation at Westminster, and was governed by the rule of law. Neither meant a thing to the 1916 leaders, certainly not to the IRB men, since they dismissed the first as irrelevant and directly attacked the second. The trauma of the Civil War was all about the pain of discovering that we needed those values after all.

Yet today, we are trying to maintain a view of the Easter Rising as, not merely good, but positively glorious, and the 1916 leaders as models in ways that no others in Irish history could be. Why? There is no rationality in doing so. Some would indignantly reject the idea that the Rising should be judged at all by the canons of rationality, since their appeal is to national feeling. It's as though the 1916 insurgents have guilt-tripped us. They died for us, and we petty mortals couldn't live up to their ideals, so the very least we can do is bend the knee to the ideals.

The ethical implications are striking. Holding up the Easter Rising as a model for political action means rejecting the goals and methods of O'Connell and Redmond. In the light of the ethical–political values of liberal democracy, it can't be justified. Easter 1916 is ethically unacceptable because its acceptance as model commits us to actions incompatible with democracy and requires us to reject other models from Irish history more in tune with democratic values, respect for human rights, and the rule of law. De Valera didn't go so far as to say as much; but it is a conclusion consistent with what he is reported to have said.

6. The rejection of politics

Like France's *soixante-huitards* (the young activists in the Paris upheaval of 1968), Ireland's 'sixteeners' were not elected politicians: hardly any of them, except Connolly, had ever stood for election, and few of them (except MacDermott) had had much involvement in fighting local or parliamentary elections. They didn't seem to think that mattered much. They had no sense of the give-and-take of normal politics as being the substance of the political community's life. While they were all politically active in their own internal debates, they did not involve the general public in these debates. In the case of the IRB, the real driving force behind the Easter Rising, they did not believe in public debates of any kind: in short, they did not believe in politics.

One gets the impression, reading what they wrote in the years 1912–16, that they did not think that there would be any further 'politics' once the millennium of the independent Irish republic had arrived. They thought of politics – arguments, lobbying, having public demonstrations, etc. – as a mere means to an end. In their book it wasn't the only means, since if it failed there was always armed revolt. But politics was still only a means to an end that transcended politics.

It does not seem to have occurred to them that the debates and political activism of the polis might be part of a good, not just as a means, but also as an end in itself, in the sense that normal political life in a democracy functions like that: messy, characterised by divisions and partisan self-interest, always aiming at persuasion, accepting that nobody or no one group has the sum total of human wisdom, and that compromise is inherent in such politics. Pearse and his friends had gradually been drawn towards the IRB way of seeing all that as corrupt, useless, time-wasting, and soul-destroying. The fall of Parnell, the long-drawn out and tortuous process of achieving home rule, and the disappointment at the Ulster obstacle all no doubt contributed to disillusionment with politics in cultural nationalists such as Pearse, MacDonagh and Plunkett. Again, in this they were typical of many of the younger generation of their time: in many central and eastern European countries, the latter years of the Great War and the 1920s witnessed the emergence, on the left and on the right and particularly among nationalists, of the great impatience with the endless talk of politics and the (to-their-eyes) mediocre and tawdry spectacle of parliamentary democracy.

The Easter insurgents wanted a republic, and it is the conventional wisdom that they laid the foundation of today's Irish Republic. Yet their manner of seeking it sharply differentiates them from the founders of the two historical republican revolutions, viz. the American and French revolutions. The American and French revolutionaries, the Jeffersons and Mirabeaus, the Washingtons and Robespierres, worked their way politically, in the full light of day, towards their goals, and towards political leadership of their nations, and were, in some fashion, and allowing for the fact that democracy was only in its infancy in the late eighteenth century, broadly representative of their peoples.

By contrast, the 'sixteeners' were a clandestine group, who, in the same breath that they revealed themselves and their projects, declared themselves a government and made themselves the nation's rulers. Also in contrast to eighteenth century France, they did it against a backdrop of a relatively well-developed democracy, in which Ireland was probably over-represented in the Westminster parliament. This was of no interest to them. They did not offer themselves to the nation for consideration as a possible future government: they simply imposed themselves on the nation on Easter Monday, telling it that they were its new government. They may have had discussions on the morality of taking up arms, but not on their attempted seizure of power. They do not seem to have weighed the morality of suddenly declaring oneself, with a group of one's friends, the government that the rest of the Irish people must obey, on pain of being shot.

The Easter Rising undermined normal political life in 1916, and to some extent continues to do so. Consider the following from Pearse:

> The man who, in the name of Ireland, accepts as 'a final settlement' anything less by one fraction of one iota than separation from England ... is guilty of so immense an infidelity, so immense a crime against the Irish nation ... that it were better for that man ... that he had not been born.[17]

That is the statement of a revolutionary, an idealist or a fanatic, backed by the reference to scripture *(Mark 14:21)*. It is not the language of a statesman or politician who must negotiate and compromise, and give leadership in doing so. Even when allowing for context, in its damning of all possible compromise it is an inherently anti-political, anti-negotiation, anti-compromise, anti-democratic statement. Those who signed the Treaty, de Valera and his followers who entered the Dáil in August 1927, all subsequent Irish governments, and all Irish political parties that accepted the

Good Friday agreement of 1998 are damned by Pearse's statement.

The option for violence, in a context where democratic parliamentary constitutional politics were operative, is an anti-politics option. Politics is about talking and negotiating. Putting it more philosophically, politics is about dialogue and acknowledging the Other. Violence and the seizure of power is its negation. The 1916 option was for dealing with things with the *'lámh láidir'*: no more compromise, no more talk – no more politics, in short. And politics has ethical value: as Aristotle said, humans are political animals, and part of their human fulfilment is to be involved in the discussion and pursuit of the common good. The anti-politics stance is unethical, in a narcissistic kind of way.

It is the opposite of the model of politics implicit in the Good Friday agreement of 1998. To the extent that one holds the latter to be ethically good, owing to its seeking to realise the values of democracy, the rule of law, and respect for diversity, one has little choice but to judge the Easter Rising to be ethically bad.

Further, the 1916 model is ethically objectionable for another reason, in that, whenever people get bored with democratic politics, impatient with the slow process of dialogue, endless listening, and compromise, the attraction to more 'direct methods' becomes stronger. The concern that contemporary western governments often have around low election turn-outs indicates the need to educate people in democracy. It will not be done by praising the 'sixteeners'.

Finally, to seek to justify the Easter Rising by pointing to the ideals of the Proclamation won't work. Many people held those ideals in 1916: we didn't need Pearse and the others to reveal them. Nor is the citing of high ideals as significant as is sometimes made out. Anybody can come up with high ideals. What tells more about the partisans of the ideals is the means they propose for promoting them.

Similarly, trying to justify the Rising by focusing on the personalities of its leaders is question-begging. Most come across as high-minded persons of personal integrity. But that won't make the politics right. To imagine that it might is to invest them with a status far above that of the rest of us: it's aristocratic in spirit, not democratic or egalitarian.

Holding up the ideals of *liberté, egalité, fraternité* in France does not commit French citizens to viewing particular individuals such as the Abbé Sieyès, Mirabeau or Robespierre as heroes. In the USA, Jefferson, author of the Declaration of Independence, comes closest to a hero; yet his tolerance of slavery is neither denied nor defended. Americans are quite prepared to admit that Jefferson, like Hamilton and Franklin and Burr, had feet of clay. The debates that went on among federalists and anti-federalists, the conflicting visions of Jefferson and Hamilton, are seen as part of normal politics. The extent to which we place Pearse on a higher plane of moral being to Redmond is a measure of the corruption of democratic politics by the Easter Rising, in favour of a kind of revolutionary elitism that despises politics as the trivial diversion of lesser mortals. Ethically, it's all wrong.

7. The betrayal of republicanism

Modern republicanism originated in the eighteenth century American and French revolutions. Early Irish republicanism arose in response. Accordingly, allowing for national differences, Irish republicanism can in part be measured against them.

What is striking is how quickly the democratic element in eighteenth century republicanism was lost in nineteenth century Irish republicanism. The Young Irelanders of the 1840s and the Fenians of the 1860s moved away from the public mass-movement, the democratic element of O'Connell's emancipation and repeal movements.[18] From the 1860s onwards, Irish republicanism, as expressed in the IRB, has more in common with the violent, secret society, including the anarchist movements found in Italy and eastern Europe in the mid to late nineteenth century.

Even if they officially wanted a democratic state and society, they were, by their very nature, unable to contribute to its development.[19] The gradual extension of the franchise in the United Kingdom during the nineteenth century, the rise of the home rule movement and the Irish party were treated by them as having no significance. Democratic evolution in the United Kingdom (including Ireland), in the direction where the popular will was politically expressible, was something to which they did not contribute and that they dismissed. Their political thinking failed to evolve in line with contemporary political developments, so that their idea of what an Irish republic should be and how it might come about became stagnant and dated. The development of a democratic or republican political culture happened independently of them, and in some ways despite them.

In light of that, the question arises of whether the IRB of the 1880–1920 period can be said to be a republican movement at all, in the classic American or French sense of republicanism. By 1916, the IRB's republicanism was no more than secret society conspiracy, whose sole goal was independence from Britain, coupled with a confused but emotionally intense anti-monarchicalism.[20]

Today, there are interesting developments in republican thought, particularly exploration in the USA of the idea of civic republicanism, understood as calling for measures to move people towards socially active citizenship. It presents the republican ideal as a participation in the polis, in opposition to the passive individual consumer, whose real life lies outside of the political realm. Politics is not just about goals, since democracies tend to produce a plurality of philosophies about the right goals; politics is also about the dialogue, the debates, and what Hegel would have called the dialectic, the ideological give-and-take, and the evolution of ideals in the light of what is feasible.[21] Irish secret society republicanism cuts in a diametrically opposed direction, since it seeks to remove the zone of significant political action and decision from the public gaze and confine it to the closed, dark room where only the oath-bound may enter.[22] Pearse and Connolly were committed to the public arena until they joined the IRB and entered the zone of secrecy.

Thus, from an international republican point of view, bearing in mind the ethical values of republicanism, 1916 might best be termed 'the great leap backwards'. First, it undermined the ethical project of building the republic, and has fixed in the Irish national imagination the idea of a republican as an anti-democratic conspirator, indifferent to social justice, freedom of speech, and the right to life. Second, it identified the republic solely with being independent from Britain. While obtaining independence from Britain was necessary for creating an Irish republic, it was not the only requirement, nor the most important. For a republic, as Jefferson and Robespierre would have argued, involves a change in the moral culture of the people, moving from being apolitical or politically excluded subjects, to being politically participating citizens. Whatever they might have said, the praxis of the Easter insurgents had nothing to do with creating such a republic, for nothing else mattered to them but getting the British out. The republicanism of the 1916 insurgents, which then was that of the IRB, was degenerate. It's no good pointing to Connolly's social commitments, or Pearse's high-minded idealism. When they marched out in the spring of 1916, they were marching to Clarke's and MacDermott's tune, and they knew it, a fact reflected in their asking Clarke, as the senior IRB man, to be the first to sign the Proclamation.

What generated a proper republican culture in Ireland was the mass political educational process begun by the Liberator, and developed by Parnell, Davitt, Redmond, and Larkin. Decisions to accept limited sovereignty (as with the Treaty in 1921–2), and to yield or share sovereignty as in the EU referenda, are not (contrary to Pearse) a betrayal of republicanism but its expression, since they occurred as part of the democratic development of public policy responsive to the needs of citizens, oriented to human good and social solidarity. The bastard republicanism, dominant since 1916, has to reject all of these, for its sole concern was independence from Britain: it doesn't require citizens. Contrary to the idea of the republic as something hidden and secret in the hearts of men, an ethically authentic notion of the republic would have seen it as something slowly growing in and through the public social practices of citizens and the meanings created by those practices. The IRB thought of the republic as existing independently of and separately from all that, and thought of its emergence and taking flesh as achievable by no more than a declaration of the republic (as happened on Easter Monday), or perhaps with a recognition by Britain of its existence. But such a republic is a thin, insubstantial thing, compared to that built up through the political and social interaction of citizens.

Nor did the Easter Rising's notion of the republic have much in common with the traditional notion of the republican virtue of international solidarity. Consider the behaviour of the Easter insurgents' spiritual descendants towards Nazi Germany, imitating the IRB's earlier relationship with imperial Germany during the First World War. In the Easter tradition, the IRA thought only of 'England's difficulty': they were indifferent to the nature of the Nazi regime. By contrast, the French republic of the 1790s positively thought it had a duty to liberate subjects elsewhere and make them citizens: however misguided tactically, it expressed the right value.

Conclusion

In a framework of liberal democratic values and norms, the consequences of the Easter Rising were largely negative, and on some points extremely so. Insofar as there were some positive consequences, it is probable that the Rising's influence was minor. The choices and actions of the leaders of the 1916 insurgency are unjustifiable, first because they demonstrate a lack of awareness of the impact on democracy of resort to violence or else a relative indifference to democracy owing to immersion in a political culture of secrecy and exclusiveness, and second because they reflect a refusal to accept the political realities of unionist/nationalist division among Irish people. That refusal, given sharp expression in the form of the Easter Rising and its consequences, delayed (as could have been foreseen at the time) and lengthened the rocky and painful path to reconciliation on this island. The leaders of the Rising can be remembered as noble heroes of the Irish past, only if one ignores or brackets out their politics. That might be possible in a feudal era, but not in a republican democracy.

THE GOLDEN JUBILEE OF THE
1916 EASTER RISING

Rory O'Dwyer

The golden jubilee of the Rising marked the apogee of celebrations accorded
to the event since the establishment of the state. According to Declan Kiberd,
the lavish nature of the myriad of organised activities in 1966 represented 'a
last, over-the-top purgation of a debt to the past'. By concentrating solely on
glorifying the past it could be quietly forgotten that the aims of those who had
sacrificed their lives in the Rising had not yet been properly achieved. Leaders
like Pearse and Connolly were promoted only for their military exploits. Their
radical ideas on education and justice, as yet unattained, were not mentioned.
This kind of simplistic approach, largely fostered by politicians and propagandists, did not encourage much critical exchange of ideas and as a result a mood
of disenchantment quickly set in.[1]

The above quotation appears to typify the feelings of many recent commentators on the fiftieth anniversary commemorations of the 1916 Rising, held throughout Ireland in 1966. These celebrations are usually noted
as one of the major public events to have taken place in the Republic of
Ireland during the 1960s. Although this period was generally marked by
a new mood of national self-confidence many commentators have seen
the jubilee commemorations as a negative reminder of how little had
changed. The historian, Enda Staunton, has described the commemorations as 'expensive splurges of triumphalism reflecting the complacency
of a state still unshaken in its Roman Catholic and nationalist verities
and basking in the first glow of material prosperity since its formation'.[2]
The commemorative events that took place in Ireland, particularly those
in Belfast, are frequently cited as a key factor leading to the outbreak of
violent conflict in Northern Ireland in 1969.[3]

Though many historians and commentators have remarked on the
jubilee and often made colourful and sometimes startling comments on
the impact of the events, none have taken on the subject to a satisfactory extent. Conor Cruise O'Brien, for example, has written briefly on the

jubilee on a number of occasions, noting, in one such instance, how 1966 witnessed an 'explosion of nationalist sentiment', which produced 'the greatest orgy ever of the cult of the Rising'.[4] According to Professor Dermot Keogh, 'what the celebrations did was to sensitise the Irish public and allow for a greater uncritical receptivity to the message of physical force nationalism.'[5] This assertion will have to be evaluated. The activities of the Irish Republican Army (IRA) at this time will have to be closely examined, as well as the republican movement's policy and approach towards the commemorations. This will include an analysis of the extent to which the IRA posed a threat in both states in 1966 and will assay the fears of a major new campaign by the organisation, supposedly to be launched during the jubilee.

In terms of the Republic of Ireland, which will be the focus of this essay, were the commemorations really as triumphalist and as damaging as is frequently noted?[6] According to Brian Girvin the commemorations were entirely one dimensional, 'celebrated so unselfconsciously' in an atmosphere where, according to Girvin and many others, 'it would have been unthinkable to question the Rising'.[7] The impression has been created that historical understanding in the Republic largely reflected a simplistic 'monolithic view of Ireland'.[8] Were leaders like Pearse and Connolly only promoted for their military exploits, with their more socially radical ideas suppressed? Girvin has commented on the 'striking paucity of critical material at this time'.[9] In order to properly assess this view it will be necessary to examine the various scholarly publications produced at the time, as well as contemporary newspapers and journals.

The background to the commemorations will have to be explored, as will the motivations behind those who organised the events, with special attention to the then Taoiseach and leader of the Fianna Fáil party, Seán Lemass, who was very involved in organising the state sponsored events. The suggestion that Lemass and his party 'hijacked' the commemorations for their own party-political interests will be examined. The allegation, implied by Paul Bew, Henry Patterson and other respected commentators, that Fianna Fáil merely sought to exploit the events to vindicate the party tradition, while recklessly endangering recently improved north-south relations in the process, will also have to be evaluated.[10] Could Lemass and his colleagues simply not resist the temptation to let the 'old ghosts' walk again?

An analysis of these issues along with a clear outline of the events that actually took place will provide an informed understanding of an often misinterpreted but significant event in modern Irish history.

Plans for the golden jubilee of the 1916 Rising were already being formulated well over a year before the event took place. At a government meeting on 2 February 1965 Seán Lemass stated that it would be appropriate that the fiftieth anniversary of the Rising of 1916 be celebrated on a large scale, maintaining that the public would expect the occasion to be marked by an extensive range of celebrations. He further proposed that a committee be set up, as had already been proposed in a previous memorandum outlining plans for military ceremonies, but that 'its scope be widened to include the participation by voluntary national organisations, particularly the Old IRA association, in planning and carrying out the programme'. This recommendation was agreed by all present at the meeting.[11]

Invitations were sent to a large number of individuals who had been actively involved or closely associated with the 1916 Rising to serve on the committee. The inaugural meeting of Coiste Cuimhneachán, as the committee was titled, took place in the council chamber of government buildings in Dublin on 19 February 1965.[12] At this meeting Lemass, who was appointed chairman of the committee, confirmed that the Rising was going to be celebrated on a grand scale, that there would be nationwide participation and that members of the committee should not feel bound by expenditure when considering proposed events.[13]

On the same day that the Coiste had its inaugural meeting, the *Irish Times* newspaper carried an advertisement for a rival 'Golden Jubilee Commemoration Committee'.[14] This committee was strongly connected with the republican movement; as a Department of Justice document later highlighted, 'of the 10 members of this committee, the chairman, treasurer and four ordinary members are in the IRA.'[15] When the chairman, Éamon Mac Thomáis, was later asked why a separate body was set up to celebrate the Rising he replied that they felt 'nobody who wanted association with Britain had the right to honour these men who paid the supreme sacrifice, since these men who died did not want any association with Britain.'[16]

The Coiste immediately had both rivals and critics. *The Evening Herald* newspaper featured an article by C. Ó Tornóir that expressed strong reservations:

> The committee in question can scarcely be described as national, seeing that it consists of two leading figures in one political party, eight civil servants and a few ex-IRA men, who no matter how untrammelled by party politics they may

be, can be outvoted by the establishment ... there is every reason to fear that the historic national event will be used for political purposes.[17]

In fact Lemass continually increased the number of civilian representatives on the committee as its ambitions continued to grow. At a meeting on 18 November 1965, it was decided that the general public, through their voluntary organisations and public representatives, were going to be given the opportunity to march in the golden jubilee commemoration parades on Easter Sunday.[18] It was agreed also to publicise the event abroad to encourage parties of Irish people to visit the country during the commemorations. Diplomatic and consular offices were instructed to hold functions in honour of the occasion. Bord Fáilte was requested to prepare a leaflet on the upcoming celebrations and 75,000 copies were printed for distribution to Irish embassies, societies and Bord Fáilte offices abroad.[19]

It was also envisaged that the commemorations would incorporate an educational aspect. Lemass was particularly concerned that 'the rising generation should be made fully aware of the significance of the event, so that they could share the pride of the older generation in it.'[20] It was agreed from the outset that a 'Children's day' would form part of the commemorative programme. The committee, having decided to include in the programme a 'cultural and artistic tribute', sponsored a series of competitions in literature, music and art to enable children to participate in the commemoration of a Rising the leaders of which were themselves gifted in learning and art. In the essay competition the titles were '1916–2016' and 'An Easter week veteran tells his story'. Prizes were also offered for an original poem on any event or theme associated with 1916. The eighteen competitions in the adult section, also covering painting and sculpture, included entries from a number of well-respected sculptors and artists such as Oisín Kelly and Edward Delaney.[21]

It is evident that Lemass and his fellow committee members were not seeking a simplistic glorification of 1916 with a convenient omission of the aims of those who had sacrificed their lives in the Rising. In a very interesting speech given to the Incorporated Law Society of Ireland on 18 February 1966 Lemass revealed his very deep and sincere attachment to the ideals of 1916. In one of his most moving speeches, he also went on to pay tribute to Irish soldiers who fought for the British army in the First World War:

In later years it was common – and I also was guilty in this respect – to question the motives of those men who joined the new British armies formed at the outbreak of the war, but it must, in their honour and in fairness to their memory, be said that they were motivated by the highest purpose, and died in their tens of thousands in Flanders and Gallipoli believing they were giving their lives in the cause of human liberty everywhere, not excluding Ireland.[22]

Lemass was thus the first leader of the Fianna Fáil party to pay open tribute to Irish soldiers who fought for the British army. It was testimony to the vastly improved Anglo-Irish relations in this period. A fine example of this on the British side was the gift of a republican flag that had flown over the GPO in 1916. The flag had previously been on display in the Imperial War Museum in London. Lemass had written to the British Prime Minister, Harold Wilson, to request its return to Ireland. Wilson duly approved the request. At a special conference on 31 March, less than two weeks before the commemorations were to begin, the flag was officially presented to the Irish government. With commendable restraint, however, Lemass 'dwelt on the magnanimity of the British in restoring the flag to Ireland rather than the circumstances in which it was taken in the first place'.[23] In a brief speech he commented on the improved relations between the two states and acknowledged the gift as 'a gesture to the Irish people and as a further contribution by them for the building of goodwill and better relations between the two communities'.[24]

While relations with London were very good, it was inevitably going to be more difficult to maintain harmonious relations with members of the Northern Ireland government, more or less all of whom appear to have considered the rebellion of 1916 a distasteful act of sedition, unworthy of commemoration.[25] Lemass realised that it was very important that his government would not be seen by unionists as utilising the commemoration period to promote anti-partition propaganda. Some reference to partition, however, was inevitable over the commemorative period. Rather than speak of the 'evils' of partition and the unionist regime, Lemass focused on the advantages that lay in the pursuit of a conciliatory approach towards their northern neighbours. In an article he contributed to the *Easter commemoration digest*, Lemass wrote:

Partition remains a central problem of Irish life. It is not yet resolved. In recent years, however, Irishmen, north and south, have begun to try to find a new approach to their reconciliation of divided interests and the solution of mutual problems. If we speak of a new realism in this realm of our affairs, we do not imply a change of principles or an avoidance of responsibility. Quite simply we recognise the movement of time, the fresh avenues of agreement which are thus opened up, the increasingly common interests and goals which each day confront us all as brother Irishmen. It is essential that we grasp the importance of this new opportunity. Here, on the personal level as well as, indeed more than, on the official level, we have responsibilities to face with resolve, patience and understanding.[26]

In the same article (written in advance of the formal commemorative ceremonies) Lemass proudly mentioned the 'excellently organised series of events' planned for the jubilee. The plans had indeed been well laid. The week before the commencement of the jubilee ceremonies, a fifteen minute film on the Easter Rising, made by George Morrison and commissioned by the Department of External Affairs on behalf of the Coiste Cuimhneachán, was sent out to eighty television networks and independent stations in north America and western Europe.[27] It confirmed Lemass and his fellow committee members' determination that the jubilee was going to be a major event and one in which many in the country could take pride.

THE STATE-SPONSORED EVENTS

The official commemoration ceremonies began on Good Friday, 8 April 1966, at Banna strand, Co. Kerry, where fifty years earlier Roger Casement landed from a German submarine, the *U19*, before later being arrested and eventually hanged, on 3 August 1916, in Pentonville prison for his involvement in the Rising. Approximately 1,000 people gathered to pay tribute to his memory and applauded when Mrs Florence Monteith Lynch, a daughter of Robert Monteith, who accompanied Casement on the *U19*, turned the first sod on the site of a memorial to her father and his leader.[28] Among those present on the occasion were Raimund Weisbach and Otto Walter of the crew of the *U19*, as well as Hans Dünker, Fred Schmitz and W. Augustin, of the arms ship, the *Aud*, who were arrested by the British royal navy on Holy Saturday 1916 while waiting to land guns and ammunition for the Rising. The ceremony represented a dignified beginning to the jubilee. Just over one year previously the British government had acceded to repeated requests from the Irish government to have the remains of Roger Casement returned to Ireland.[29] In what might be considered the first major event in the commemoration process his remains were re-interred in March 1965 in Glasnevin cemetery, Dublin, and Casement's wish to be buried in Irish soil was fulfilled. The ceremony at Banna strand offered, at last, a certain sense of closure on what had been a bitter issue.

On Easter Sunday, the jubilee events began in earnest when Dublin 'was the scene of one of the greatest gatherings in its history as vast crowds packed its main thoroughfares' for the military parade – the principal commemorative event.[30] Approximately 600 veterans of the Rising were present at the occasion, some of whom had come from Britain and the United States. Among the other groups to parade from St Stephen's Green to O'Connell Street were representatives of national ex-servicemen, together with various sporting and cultural organisations. Approximately 2,000 veterans of the War of Independence were also present.[31]

At noon the 1916 Proclamation was read to the crowd by a member of the defence forces. The tricolour was then hoisted with full ceremonial honours, on the roof of the General Post Office (GPO).[32] After a salute of twenty one guns, the military parade began to march past the GPO, where the President, Éamon de Valera, took the salute. Various military units followed different routes passing most of the buildings in Dublin occupied by the Irish Volunteers in 1916 before converging on O'Connell Street.[33] As the last units in the parade passed the reviewing stand beside the GPO, a flight of Vampire jet aircraft swept overhead. The event concluded with the playing of the national anthem.

Later in the afternoon the next commemorative event took place in Kilmainham gaol where the President laid a wreath, with full military ceremony, in the yard where the 1916 leaders were executed. Among those present were relatives of the executed leaders including Roddy Connolly, Nora Connolly O'Brien, Ronan Ceannt, Father Joseph Mallin and Bridget Colbert. Following the ceremony the President officially opened the new historical exhibition on the 1916 Rising, contained within the east wing of the old prison building. In his address de Valera paid tribute to the voluntary group who had restored the prison as a national monument and place of commemoration.[34]

That evening *An Tine Bheo* (*The Living Flame*), a film commissioned from Gael Linn by the Coiste Cuimhneachán, premiered at the Savoy cinema in Dublin. The film focused on the events of Easter week 1916 and the forces which led to the Rising. As the scenes of the battles of Easter week, in Dublin and elsewhere, were explored by the camera, veterans of the Rising vividly recounted their experiences. The film was very well received and provided a fitting end to the principal day of commemoration in Dublin.[35]

Apart from the events in Dublin, military ceremonies sponsored by the Coiste Cuimhneachán for Easter Sunday were also organised at twelve provincial centres associated with key individuals or events of the Rising. Practically every town (large and small) in the Republic seemed to organise (on many occasions by sub-branches of the Coiste) a parade to mark the anniversary.

The following day, Easter Monday 11 April, religious ceremonies to mark the jubilee were held in churches of all denominations. The Catholic archbishop of Armagh, Cardinal William Conway, presided at solemn high mass in St Patrick's cathedral, Armagh. In Dublin a solemn votive mass took place in the pro-cathedral, Marlborough Street. Among the congregation were the President, the Taoiseach and veterans of the Rising. On the same morning the Church of Ireland archbishop of Dublin, the Most Reverend Doctor Simms, preached at a united service under the auspices of the Dublin Council of Churches in St Patrick's cathedral. A Jewish service of prayer to mark the jubilee in the synagogue at Adelaide Road was led by the Chief Rabbi of Ireland, Doctor Isaac Cohen.[36]

At noon the Garden of Remembrance in Parnell Square was officially opened. It was dedicated to all those who died for Irish freedom. A wreath-laying ceremony then took place involving the President, the Taoiseach, the lord mayor and members of the diplomatic corps.[37] That evening a commemoration concert in the Gaiety theatre, Dublin, featured a composition by the Irish composer, Dr Brian Boydell, performed by the Radio Éireann symphony orchestra. It was the first performance of *A Terrible Beauty is Born*, a cantata based on the poems of Yeats, MacDonagh, Ledwidge, Russell, Dora Sigerson and T.M. Kettle.[38]

The following day, Tuesday 12 April, witnessed the launch of a special 1916 exhibition, which was formally opened in the National Museum by Patrick Hillery, Minister for Industry and Commerce. Among the many exhibits on display were personal weapons belonging to the leading figures in the movement, rifles landed during the Howth gun-running in July 1914, and rifles salvaged from the cargo of the *Aud*. The centrepiece of the exhibition was the aforementioned green flag which flew over the GPO during Easter week, 1916, and which was presented for permanent display at the museum by the Taoiseach on behalf of the government.[39]

On the same day an exhibition of paintings, portraits, and sculpture on themes relating to the 1916 Rising was launched at the Municipal Art Gallery, Dublin. This included the finest entries in the art competitions sponsored by the Coiste Cuimhneachán. The National Gallery also staged an exhibition at this time featuring almost 200 paintings and sculptures depicting virtually every phase of Irish history, but with special emphasis on the 1916 rebellion. This included portraits and busts of personalities involved in the Rising, as well as pictures of some of the key events that formed the background to it. A special section was devoted to the highly regarded drawings of the sixteen executed leaders by Seán O'Sullivan.

That evening there was the first of five performances during Easter week of *Aiséirí-Glóir-réim na Cásca* (*Resurrection, the Easter pageant*) at Croke Park in Dublin. In the words of the official commemorative booklet:

> Before a giant backcloth and mammoth portraits of the sixteen leaders who were executed after the Rising, the players retold in symbols, actions and words, the story of struggle for independence from the 1790s to the declaration of independence by the first Dáil Éireann in 1919.[40]

The production included a cast of almost 800, most of whom were members of the defence forces. Although the weather proved unfavourable on most of the evenings, the pageant was well attended and acclaimed.

Among the various commemoration ceremonies over the next few days, one of the most notable took place on Friday April 15 at Boland's mills, Dublin, where a plaque was unveiled to commemorate the 3rd battalion, Dublin brigade of the Irish Volunteers in 1916, which had been commanded by Éamon de Valera. Present at the unveiling ceremony, and guest of honour of the State, was Edward J. Hitzen, the British officer who accepted de Valera's surrender. Following a brief ceremony marred by pouring rain, the two men happily exchanged jokes and anecdotes together.[41]

On the following day de Valera delivered another address at the GPO during ceremonies to mark the end of the rebellion. Before he spoke, the national flag on the GPO was slowly lowered to the accompaniment of the bugle notes of *Sundown* from army trumpeters. Although de Valera had not referred explicitly to partition in his various other commemorative speeches, in his final speech he referred to his long-held opinion concerning the resolution of the northern situation:

All that is necessary is that the power which is at present retained in the British parliament should be transferred to a representative all-Ireland parliament ... They can still have local autonomy with the powers they possess at present. The question is whether they want to belong to this nation or to the other island. It would be better for Britain, too, that the union of the two parts of Ireland should take place.[42]

When de Valera concluded his address 'the band sounded a fanfare, a firing party of 120 men lining the roof of the Post Office fired a *feu de joie* while a twenty one gun salute was fired in the grounds of Trinity College.'[43]

Although the main events organised by the Coiste Cuimhneachán were now completed, state-sponsored commemorative ceremonies continued over the following week. On Sunday evening, 17 April, the Taoiseach and Mrs Lemass held a state reception in St Patrick's Hall, Dublin Castle to mark the golden jubilee. Approximately 3,000 people were invited to the occasion.[44] Many veterans of the Rising and their relatives were among the large attendance, which included the President, Cardinal Conway, Archbishop McQuaid, the Most Reverend Doctor Simms, and members of the diplomatic corps, judiciary, government, Dáil, Seanad and the Council of State. Also in attendance were representatives of the National Graves Association, the trustees of the Kilmainham Gaol Restoration Committee, representatives from the Gaelic Athletic Association, Gael Linn and other national organisations.[45]

Among the events over the following week, special church services, representing all denominations, were held throughout the Republic on the morning of Friday 22 April, as school children honoured those who lost their lives in the Rising. Many schools were decorated for the occasion and in many cases the national flag was flown. A framed copy of the Proclamation was formally unveiled with appropriate ceremony in every school. At a Church of Ireland ceremony in St Patrick's Cathedral, Dublin, the Most Reverend Doctor Simms told a congregation of approximately 2,000 children that they were right to meet for worship on the occasion of the fiftieth anniversary of the Rising to dedicate themselves to the service of the country:

We dedicate ourselves today to the kind of service that will be rock-like in laying the foundations of a life of truth and honesty in private and in public, of charitableness in outlook and attitude, with understanding that hears the other side in any human story or in any argument.[46]

The very last state commemoration ceremony took place at Arbour Hill on Sunday 24 April, the actual date that the Rising began in 1916. The President, the Taoiseach, the Tánaiste, members of the government and the judiciary, the lord mayor of Dublin, members of the Oireachtas, veterans of Easter week and relatives of the 1916 leaders attended a special memorial mass celebrated in the military church at Arbour Hill.[47] At the memorial plot afterwards:

> the national flag was lowered and regimental colours were dipped as the last post was sounded; the choir sang *De Profundis*; and, as bugles sounded reveille, the national flag was raised again to full mast. At the close of ceremonies a special guard of four sentries was mounted at the graveside, and reliefs were provided every half-hour until sundown.[48]

With this tribute the state ceremonies for the jubilee had come to an end.

The republican movement's events:

> While attempting to ensure a fitting commemoration of the 1916 Rising, and also trying to maintain improved north-south relations, Lemass and his government had to keep close watch on republican activity. The IRA, and associated organisations, had been consistent in their willingness and enthusiasm to commemorate the event. In this respect little had changed in the republican movement. There were, however, important changes in republican policy in this period. By 1966 the organisation was undergoing a remarkable transition. A new radical political perspective was slowly being incorporated into the movement. A republican socialist study group, the Wolfe Tone Society, had been founded in 1963 to discuss not only the republican heritage but also current social and economic issues. The IRA would, nevertheless, always contain some members with an unremitting desire for militancy and the leadership could do little to prevent occasional unauthorised action in this period. The most spectacular example of this took place on 7 March 1966, when a republican splinter group blew up Nelson's pillar on O'Connell Street. One of the dissidents involved later revealed that they regarded the action as their jubilee tribute to the city – the demolition of an imposing colonial symbol.[49]

Alerted to the possibility of a further gesture from fringe elements in the republican movement, the gardaí mounted a security screen, 'Operation Safety', throughout the commemorative period and extra members were drafted into the special branch.[50] Armed guards were posted at the Garden of Remembrance, at all British monuments, at Teilifís Éireann and

Radio Éireann at Montrose as well as at the GPO. Special guards were also posted at embassies and the residences of diplomatic personnel in Dublin.[51] A radio network was being installed on garda barracks along the border in advance of the jubilee but the installation was cancelled on orders from the Department of Defence, which considered garda HQ to be guilty of over-reacting.[52]

Although there were isolated acts of violence carried out by IRA dissidents, it was clear that nothing like an organised campaign was being conducted or even contemplated by the leadership of the republican movement. The IRA repeatedly declared this, and the position was later clarified in a Department of Justice *aide mémoire* on IRA activity in this period:

> A certain amount of drilling with firearms has been going on since 1962 but there is no more reason now than in any of the past four years to conclude that a campaign of violence is imminent or will commence within, say, the next 12 months ... The organisation is not yet in a financial position to maintain an organised campaign for any length of time. Individual acts of terrorism cannot be ruled out altogether but in 1966 the organisation has been evidencing a strong sense of military discipline amongst its members ... There were fairly strong signs during 1966 that a policy of force might be left in abeyance for a period of years while the military organisation and its political arm Sinn Féin would seek public support through the capture of a sufficiency of seats in municipal and Dáil elections. [53]

The memorandum also stated that leaders of the movement had been attending 'education' classes conducted by persons listed by the police as members of communist organisations. The expansion of the IRA's role was also emphasised:

> Since its inception, the Political Education department of IRA headquarters has spearheaded the organisation's agitational, economic, social and political policy through the following groups: the Wolfe Tone Society, Cómhar Linn, Dublin Housing Action Group, the Economic Independence Committee, Civil Liberties League, Republican Clubs.[54]

The republican movement undoubtedly took a very serious interest in the golden jubilee. The Wolfe Tone Society branches in Dublin, Belfast and Cork organised a number of lectures on the rebellion. Amongst the lecturers provided by the society in Dublin were George Gilmore on 'Labour and 1916', Jack Bennett on 'Connolly and Ulster' and Kader Asmal on

'1916 and twentieth century freedom movements'.[55] The republican 'Golden Jubilee Commemoration Committee', under the chairmanship of Éamon Mac Thomáis, also organised a series of lectures as well as a very large number of commemoration ceremonies throughout the island. In all cases the commemorations consisted of:

> religious services, parades to republican memorials, blowing of the last post and reveille, the laying of wreaths, the reading of the Proclamation and the Easter statement from the Army Council and the delivering of an oration. Invariably the platform party included relatives of men who had given their lives in the struggle for independence as well as veterans of that struggle.[56]

A parade was organised for Easter Sunday from the Customs House in Dublin to the republican plot in Glasnevin cemetery, via O'Connell Street and the GPO. Compared to the orderly procession of the official parade two hours earlier the republican parade appeared disorganised as it passed the GPO.[57] The parade included a number of disparate groups including groups from various 'Celtic' separatist groups from Wales, Brittany, Scotland, the Isle of Man and Cornwall.[58] A spokesman for *Pleidiol Wyfin Gwlad*, a Welsh home rule body, stated: 'We came here to join this parade to show our hatred of England.'[59] Approximately 400 people later took part in a wreath-laying ceremony at Glasnevin, where the speakers included Joseph Clarke, an eighty five year old veteran of the Rising and a member of the republican Commemoration Committee. Clarke was very frank in his introduction: 'If the men they killed in '16 were alive today they'd be up here with us. Our parade is much closer to what they fought for than the one down in O'Connell Street.'[60]

Although the state parade and the republican parade did not meet on Easter Sunday the danger of a clash would be much more likely to occur on the following Sunday (17 April) when another republican parade and demonstration in O'Connell Street was planned to begin while the state event would still be taking place. The Coiste Cuimhneachán attempted to alleviate the possibility of a clash by dialogue but the republicans were insistent on their original plan.[61] On the day the state ceremony conveniently ended somewhat earlier than predicted and the republican procession was quietly delayed long enough for any danger of a clash to pass. The republicans were then permitted the use of the podium and sound equipment used in the state display.[62]

State compliance and harmony with the republican ceremonies, however, was not widespread. Mac Thomáis' committee had approached the national transport company, Córas Iompair Éireann (CIÉ), requesting them to put on a special train to take a party of their members from Dublin to Belfast for 17 April. A further, rather brazen, request was made that the tickets issued for the occasion be overprinted with the slogan 'Freedom train 1966'. On receipt of this application, the general manager of CIÉ, Frank Lemass (brother of the Taoiseach) forwarded the details to Erskine Childers, Minister for Transport and Power, for government views on the matter. After the contents of this letter were brought to the attention of the Taoiseach, counsel was sought from the Minister for Justice, Brian Lenihan. Lenihan recommended that, as this committee was 'composed of members of the IRA, Sinn Féin and Cumann na mBan', their request should not be acceded to. As Lenihan's secretary replied:

> In the minister's view the plans of the IRA/Sinn Féin group to hire a special train to Belfast from Dublin on 17 April in order to have a parade in Belfast and an oration in the cemetery is for IRA organisational purposes. Furthermore the committee's suggestion to CIÉ that the rail tickets should be overprinted with the slogan 'Freedom train 1966' appears to be for the purpose of cocking a snook at the six county authorities and it would probably give rise to feelings of resentment in Belfast.[63]

The views of garda authorities were consulted, and the headquarters responded that there would 'be trouble in Belfast if the train runs; opposition is mounting, even if the travellers do not provoke trouble the opposition will; the train should not be provided if at all possible'.[64] The police authorities in Northern Ireland also sent word to Dublin, stating that they had 'grave apprehension' as to what the outcome might be if the freedom trains were allowed to travel.[65] In response, Seán Lemass instructed Childers to inform CIÉ of these circumstances. The taoiseach did not, however, desire that the government's intervention in the matter would become public knowledge. He instructed Childers to advise CIÉ that if they decided against supplying this train, 'request them to do so without giving this as a reason, or indicating that they have sought the government's advice on the matter'.[66]

As it transpired the potential embarrassment over the issue was alleviated when a decision was taken by Terence O'Neill's cabinet security committee not to permit any trains to enter Northern Ireland on the main line from Dublin to Belfast from 9.30pm on Saturday 16 April until 7pm on Sunday 17 April.[67] The border was effectively sealed off for the main jubilee parade in Belfast. The mass turnout from the south, if it was ever a realistic possibility, did not materialise. The Dublin brigades of the IRA instead concentrated on their main parade the following week in Dublin.

On Sunday 24 April the IRA held their main parade from St Stephen's Green to Glasnevin cemetery. The republican movement's commemoration ceremonies in the south had been poorly attended and although nationalist feeling was undoubtedly high in the country at this time, the IRA failed to capitalise on this popular feeling and there were to be no indications afterwards of an increase in support for the IRA. The movement's 1916 ceremonies paled in comparison to the highly impressive state ceremonies. This suggests that, far from opening a Pandora's box, the official ceremonies actually curtailed republican sentiment. The defence forces of the state had been rigidly determined to quell any signs of republicans fomenting trouble.

LITERATURE AND POPULAR REACTION

Although some modern commentators have commented on the one-dimensional nature of 1916 commemoration in 1966, even the most cursory examination of the publications produced for the commemoration demands a different interpretation. The impression that historical understanding in the Republic largely reflected a simplistic monolithic view of Ireland cannot be easily sustained. In fact the golden jubilee year witnessed a raft of new studies on the Rising and related events. What was so striking about this new material was that it was *not* polemical but clearly sparked by a genuine interest in recovering the past. It must be stressed that much of the literature produced at this time remains unsurpassed in historical scholarship on the period. To any student of the 1916 rebellion publications from this time still form the backbone of any research on the Rising.

One of the earliest intentions of the Coiste Cuimhneachán was to produce a work of historical scholarship on the Rising. Kevin Nowlan and nine other highly regarded historians were approached to produce just such a work.[68] The contributors were given no thesis to prove and no official line to follow; this was to be no mere eulogy of the rebels. *The making of 1916: studies in the history of the Rising*, although not actually published until 1969, includes very valuable analysis and criticism of the Rising. The notion that 1916 could only be treated as a sacrosanct national epic by the establishment (academic, political or otherwise) is simply untrue. A mood of questioning was already becoming apparent even before 1966.

The first real question mark against the 'accepted' story about 1916 appeared in March 1961 with the publication in *Irish Historical Studies* of two memoranda by Eoin MacNeill. As the historian F.X. Martin later recorded:

> Rarely if ever has the appearance of an historical record received such attention at a popular level. Two of the principal national daily newspapers, the *Irish Press* and the *Irish Independent*, displayed posters announcing the publications of the documents, and it was included as an item on the 1pm news bulletin from Radio Éireann on the day of publication. The national daily and evening newspapers ran a series of articles analysing and commenting on the memoranda.[69]

It emerged clearly from the documents that MacNeill had been deceived, in particular by Pearse, Plunkett and MacDonagh, and that at least Pearse and Plunkett had undeniably lied to him about their intentions. It certainly highlighted that Pearse was no plaster saint, and given the wide public interest the documents attracted, this point must have filtered down to a popular level.

Even Éamon de Valera, to some the father figure of the Irish nation in 1966, was the subject of serious critical evaluation. Max Caulfield's *The Easter Rebellion* published less than two years before the golden jubilee, raised serious question marks about de Valera's military leadership during the Rising.[70] Caulfield's account of the Rising has been the most widely read version of the rebellion ever written and has been frequently re-printed. His book was the first on the Rising that included interviews with British officers who were fighting against the rebels. The view of these servants of the British Crown in Ireland was explored in more detail in two highly commended studies which appeared in 1966, Leon Ó Broin's *Dublin Castle and the 1916 Rising*, and *Intelligence Notes 1913–16*, edited by Breandán Mac Giolla Choille.[71]

With the release of so much archival material, nearly all of which had been on fifty year hold, it was a very exciting time for all historians with a sincere interest in uncovering something of the reality of 1916. Such historians were not driven by an overly iconoclastic zeal but a sincere interest in trying to discover the complexities of the time. The result was a considerable number of first class critical evaluations of the 1916 rebellion. The suggestion, therefore, that there was a paucity of critical material in 1966 must be seen as a fundamental, but very common, misunderstanding of the jubilee. What was missing in that year, although not entirely absent, was a corrosively cynical form of examination of the Rising.

Roger McHugh's *Dublin 1916*, also published in 1966, included a wide range of contemporary accounts of Easter week, an impressive attempt to recapture the moods and opinions of some of those involved in the drama and others who observed the actions with various different opinions, nationalist, unionist and undecided.[72] One of the great values of McHugh's book is that the reader could peruse and contemplate contrasting and contrary opinions, 'many of them written either while Dublin was reverberating with the sound of gunfire or while Easter week was still a vivid memory'.[73] Another volume of contrasting opinions about the Rising, *Leaders and men of the Easter Rising: Dublin 1916*, although not published until 1967 was the printed record of nineteen essays composed for a radio series in 1966 to commemorate the Easter Rising.[74] The series was part of the Thomas Davis lectures broadcast on Radio Éireann and under the editorship of Professor F.X. Martin. The rebellion was examined in a detached spirit and from multifarious angles by the cream of historians of modern Ireland (who were themselves from diverse backgrounds and traditions) including F.S.L. Lyons, T. Desmond Williams, F.X. Martin, A.T.Q. Stewart, Leon Ó Broin, Kevin Nowlan, Terence de Vere White, David Thornley and J.C. Beckett. Donagh MacDonagh, the son of Tomás MacDonagh, contributed a talk on Plunkett, MacDonagh and the poets and writers of the revolution. A young Brian Farrell discussed Countess Markievicz and the women of the revolution.

All of the contributions were intended to be accessible to as wide a listenership as possible and the programmes were a great success. As George Boyce has written, the series:

> cast the net widely, drawing in themes and topics hitherto hardly associated with the rising at all. For example, it related the Rising to the Ulster crisis of 1912–14, and to other political developments before 1916. Thus the Ulster Volunteer Force, Sir Edward Carson, Dublin Castle, Lloyd George and Asquith, were all woven into the texture of the Rising, and the historiography of the event moved from the narrow (though of course important) focus on conspiracy and martyrdom to the more general question of the Rising as an episode in the history of all Ireland and indeed of the British Isles.[75]

This highly popular series enabled the listening public to achieve a very informed knowledge on this compelling period of Irish history.

A similar co-operative series of essays, '1916: a historical review of the Easter Rising', appeared as a special supplement of the *Irish Times* on 7 April 1966. These essays appeared as a volume two years later, edited by Owen Dudley Edwards and Fergus Pyle.[76] The book formed an excellent complement to *Leaders and men*; while the latter dealt with personalities the former concentrated mainly on themes concerning the Rising and in the process posed many probing questions about the ideals, as well as the actions of the rebels. Although possessing some particularly fine contributions from F.S.L. Lyons, Nicholas Mansergh and Donal McCartney, the most significant contribution was Conor Cruise O'Brien's 'The Embers of Easter', a deeply opinionated, deliberately provocative, but absorbing critique of the performance of the state since 1916.[77] O'Brien, who had resigned in acrimonious circumstances from the Irish diplomatic corps in 1961, now accused all Irish governments since 1922 of betraying the revolutionary tradition of Tone, Pearse and Connolly. In particular, O'Brien used Connolly 'as a knoute to scourge various opponents', not realising then, of course, that there would later be a subsequent *rapprochement* with some of his erstwhile adversaries:[78]

> Connolly's Worker's Republic is as far off as ever. The *Irish Independent*, which in 1916 continued to call for more executions until it got Connolly, remained the paper of the Irish bourgeoisie. No significant Labour movement exists north or south. The Labour party has been dominated by dismal poltroons on the lines of O'Casey's Uncle Payther. The economic progress which has occurred was mainly due to external forces … There is no cause in this anniversary year for self-congratulation.[79]

Although perhaps lacking the bite of O'Brien's protestations, all the other Irish newspapers included supplements containing interesting comment not just on the Rising but on Irish achievement, or lack of, since 1916. The *Irish Press*, in its supplement, included the final part of a series of articles on the performance of the Irish state since independence. It should be noted that at this time Tim Pat Coogan, shortly afterwards to be appointed editor of the paper, published his *Ireland since the Rising*, which was the first attempt to offer such a synthesis of the story of independent Ireland in book form.[80] Journals, such as *Administration*, carried out similar studies. Practically every Irish journal included some reflection on both the Rising and on the country in general since that year. The *Capuchin Annual* included a particularly impressive series of interviews on 1916 for its Easter issue.

The Jesuit journal *Studies* is also worthy of special mention in this regard. The Easter issue of the journal included a valuable article by Garret FitzGerald on the significance of 1916. It should also be noted here that Fr Francis Shaw, SJ, submitted what was later to become a renowned article, in which he strongly challenged traditional nationalist interpretations of 1916. The bulk of Shaw's essay was devoted, in Roy Foster's words, to 'an intemperate attack on Pearse's politics and actions'.[81] Shaw's essay was not actually published by *Studies* until 1972, for, in his own words, 'it was judged, very understandably, that a critical study of this kind might be thought to be untimely and even inappropriate in what was in effect a commemorative issue.'[82] It was unfortunate that the article did not appear in 1966 because it certainly appears that the Irish public were sufficiently mature to have debated this highly interesting contribution to the study of the 1916 rebellion. The very fact that the article was written by a Catholic priest highlights the changes that had been occurring during the period. Indeed, the historian John A. Murphy has commented on how this period in Ireland witnessed 'a new frankness of discussion, a spirit of positive self-criticism, a liberalisation of religious thinking with the pontificate of John XXIII, an increase in intellectual maturity, and a rejection of paternalism'.[83]

The Irish public's appetite for history, particularly relating to 1916, at this time is surely embodied by the success of this multitude of publications. The popularity of the printed word on the subject of 1916 and the extensive coverage on radio of both the original event itself, as well as the commemorative ceremonies, are not, however, the only testimony of public interest in the commemoration. The national broadcasting service, Radio Teilifís Éireann (RTÉ) set up only five years earlier, devoted unprecedented television coverage to the anniversary, adding immensely to its popular impact. Live coverage of all the principal national events was provided by the network. On Easter Sunday the first part of an eight day televised account of the Rising, written by Hugh Leonard, was broadcast. Insurrection told the day-to-day story of the Rising. It incorporated a modern studio current affairs and newsgathering format with dramatised sequences from the main locations of the Rising. The series was transmitted in full by the BBC and was also shown in Scandinavia, Belgium, Canada, Australia, and elsewhere around the world.[84] Another series produced by RTÉ, On behalf of the Provisional Government, consisted of documentaries on each of the seven signatories to the 1916 Proclamation. A number of other programmes relating to the Rising were also aired on RTÉ during Easter week.

The Irish universities also took part in the commemorations. The New Ireland Association in Queens University Belfast organised a series of lectures, and even attempted to lure Seán Lemass to address one of its meetings. Students in Trinity College Dublin (TCD) printed a special journal, *50 Years On*, to commemorate the Rising and managed to attract a number of highly respected contributors including Seán O'Faoláin and Senator Sheehy Sheffington. Most of the articles were highly critical of government policies since independence. As one of the student contributors, Bruce Arnold, commented:

> We like to believe that 1916 was the exclusive vision of men who, because they attempted to translate their vision into reality, were destroyed. Since then we have witnessed the vain and hollow attempts of the nation to enshrine their vision while at every turn the business and practice of politics, commerce, Church and state have been a betrayal of it.[85]

University College Dublin (UCD) also organised a number of events to commemorate the Rising. A series of public lectures provided by UCD was later published as a book, *The Easter Rising, 1916 and University College Dublin*.[86]

The trade unions organised a special exhibition on the Rising in the Royal Dublin Society (RDS) in Ballsbridge. The exhibition highlighted the role of James Connolly in the Rising, reflecting the great interest among the broad labour movement in Connolly during the jubilee. Although he had often been somewhat marginalised in traditional interpretations of the Rising, in 1966 Connolly became the icon of the Irish left (including the evolving republican movement) and was usually used to provide a nationalist slant for socialist social and economic policies. Desmond Greaves, of the Communist Party of Ireland, had, in 1961, written a fine biography of Connolly, and he was now one of the many to lecture on Connolly as part of the jubilee.[87]

The jubilee events, the state-sponsored events in particular, drew great crowds throughout the country. Exhibitions relating to 1916 held in museums and galleries in different parts of Ireland all appear to have been very well attended. The Kilmainham gaol museum, which had its official opening during the jubilee, attracted very large numbers. Seán Lemass' intuition when founding the Coiste Cuimhneachán, that the Irish public would expect a large series of commemorations, had proved correct. The popular appetite for 1916 commemorative fare was remarkable.

CONCLUSION

It is apparent from this study of the golden jubilee of the 1916 Rising that much modern comment on the Rising, of the type illustrated in the introduction, has not always been based on solid research. The description of the commemorations, as expensive splurges of triumphalism replete with Catholic verities, is clearly in need of revision. As has been evidenced, the state-sponsored events were not splurges of triumphalism but generally sombre and respectful. With regard to the cost of the commemorations, the matter was raised in the Dáil in 1969 when it was revealed that the total expenditure was a mere £108,122.[88] Máire Breathnach, who controlled the financial side of the state-sponsored events for the Department of Finance, was notoriously penny-pinching.[89] As regards Catholic verities there was no obvious tone of Catholicism to the events. In fact all of the main churches in the Republic took part enthusiastically in the commemorations. Only the Methodist and the Presbyterian churches did not take part as institutions *per se*, though some individual members did participate in different ways.[90]

The assertion that the jubilee merely witnessed a glorification of the rebellion is not based on a sound awareness of the events in 1966. The claim that leaders like Pearse and Connolly were only promoted for their military exploits represents a gross simplification. As we have seen there was a wealth of material produced in the jubilee year on the ideas and ideals of Pearse and Connolly, including very high quality analysis and criticism. The general public were encouraged to educate themselves on these ideals, which was one of the main functions of the Coiste Cuimhneachán. As has been shown, the literature produced at this time on the ideals of 1916, some of which was sponsored by the government, was extremely impressive. The Irish public had an opportunity to educate themselves on a very important historical event in a way that they never had before. Something of this refreshing outlook was captured in an *Irish Times* article written during the commemorations:

In keeping with these indications of maturity is the run on bookshops where works about Ireland – not necessarily on the Rising – have been in demand. The effect of the ceremonies is to alert or shame those who have not bothered to study history to take a course of it now. And by this everybody benefits. It has been said ever so often that the Irish should forget their history. This is not true. They should reach enough of it to be able to discern truth from propaganda. A well-stocked mind cannot be a narrow and is less likely to be a bitter one than when the mental diet has been a select list of prejudices. It was also encouraging to see so many people in the Museum, which has made a very commendable effort for the occasion. Even to the least sympathetic observer there must be something infinitely touching about many of the relics collected here. The galleries too have put on exhibitions, and everywhere there are signs of intelligent curiosity about the events of a half a century ago, which, to at least one generation, has seemed as remote as the Cromwellian campaign. There were reasonable fears that the celebrations might spark off explosions, but the weekend has come and gone, and such altercations as have reached the public's attention were very minor indeed. On the other side can be claimed now a mood of reappraisal in some cases, in others a desire to know. It has been apparent since the state began that balance and maturity were essential on the vexed question of the state's origins. Perhaps we have reached the stage now. If as the President said yesterday, Emmet's epitaph cannot yet be written, the reason why can at least be discussed without dust and heat. And that is something.[91]

In terms of the ideals of Pearse and Connolly regarding education and justice, it should be borne in mind that the 1960s was a period of enormous importance in both spheres. In education the 1960s was a period of great excitement and change. A series of highly capable ministers held the education portfolio and there were many new initiatives. Indeed just a few months after the commemorations Lemass endorsed Donagh O'Malley's statement of intention to introduce a comprehensive system of free post-primary education – arguably the most important step in the history of education in post-independence Ireland.

Lemass did not use the jubilee as an opportunity to glorify in the Fianna Fáil party tradition, gloating over achievements and successes. At a party gathering in Galway on 9 October 1965, while setting out his hopes for the commemorations, he was prepared to admit that the party had experienced failures and setbacks:

For us in Fianna Fáil, and indeed for all who are sincerely interested in the future of our country, the celebration of the fiftieth anniversary of the 1916

Rising, while signifying primarily our understanding of its historical importance, will also be a time of national stocktaking, and for trying to look ahead into the mists of the future to see the right road leading to the high destiny we desire for our nation. During these past fifty years there have been tremendous changes in Irish circumstances, mostly good. Of course we have had our disappointments and setbacks, in many spheres our achievements have been less than our hopes. But it can be said that the faith of the leaders of 1916, and of all those who in earlier times had inspired our people to continue to strive for freedom, has been justified, and that the Irish people have demonstrated, beyond argument, their capacity in freedom to manage their affairs in calmness and in confidence, and at least as successfully as other nations. It is right that we should now be concentrating our attention on the opportunities of the future and not on the wrongs of the past. It is our hope that the commemoration of the 1916 Uprising will lead to a new birth of patriotism – a constructive patriotism which will be in tune with the needs and circumstances of our times, and capable of being organised and disciplined to meet the ever-changing conditions that will face us in the future.[92]

Fianna Fáil did dominate the anniversary but this was in a large measure due to a lack of initiative on the part of the opposition leaders. Few ideas seem to have come from them other than how to lambaste Fianna Fáil. The Labour party, for example, accused Fianna Fáil of exploiting the commemorations for party-political purposes. Lemass' party did have impressive connections with the Rising but the policy was not to exploit this fact in an overt way. A letter written by Lemass to the Minister for Defence (Aiken) a month before the jubilee events gives a clear indication of the party's stance:

> As a matter of general policy I have been most anxious to prevent any possibility of an allegation that the ceremonies were being exploited by us for party advantage, or for personal advantage of a political kind. For this reason all local committees were discouraged from seeking the attendance of ministers at their parades, and I said I would ask a minister to attend only where the desire to have one was unanimous. In such cases I have nominated ministers who have no connection with the constituency concerned.[93]

In his capacity as President of Ireland, the former leader of Fianna Fáil, Éamon de Valera, carried out his role impressively throughout the ceremonies. As we have seen, his speeches and activities during the jubilee were generally of a conciliatory tone. It was only in his final speech during the last ceremony of the week-long activities, when he referred to his hope for an all-Ireland parliament in the near future, that some controversy was aroused. The *Irish Times* commented mildly afterwards on de Valera's 'over-simplification' of the issue.[94] On the following day Terence O'Neill made a statement reminding unionists that the north and the south were 'poles apart' politically, socially and economically and 'totally rejected' de Valera's proposal.[95] Sinn Féin also quickly issued a statement firmly rejecting his approach on the grounds that 'if it were done it would still be possible for a pro-British regime to operate its vicious system of gerrymandering in elections, discrimination in jobs and housing and the whole elaborate system operated to keep an ascendancy element in control.'[96]

Regardless of such criticisms de Valera had remained clear and consistent in his aspirations to a united Ireland. Similarly, Seán Lemass' views on partition were unambiguous; while accepting the reality of partition he repeatedly stated that unification was a key aspiration of his government. Lemass was also consistent in his aims for the jubilee. He was determined to ensure a fitting commemoration of the 1916 rebellion. Republicans were given no opportunity to monopolise the 1916 legacy within the Irish state. The prospect of such an occurrence could have had dangerous implications. It is interesting to consider what might have happened had Lemass taken a minimalist approach to the commemorations. Nationalist feeling was very evident in this period and republican-dominated events staged by a new and radical organisation could have had a powerful effect on Irish society.

Through careful planning, however, and with an obvious dedication to its job, the events organised by the state-sponsored Coiste Cuimhneachán won popular approval, indeed acclaim. As a result the golden jubilee of the 1916 Rising was not, contra Conor Cruise O'Brien, 'the greatest orgy ever of the cult of the Rising' (though it could have been) but a sincere, meaningful, and well-organised commemoration with considerable educational potential for anyone with an interest in the 1916 Rising – a complex but intriguing and vital event in twentieth century Irish history. The scale of the commemoration in 1966 is unlikely ever to be equalled, nor the level and quality of historical scholarship produced at the time to be exceeded. The high level of nationalist feeling in the period was generally harnessed in a very positive fashion, whereas republican militant sentiment was effectively curtailed. With much state ceremony the 'ghost' of 1916 was laid to rest in a dignified and respectful tribute. It was now time to move on.

THE COMMEMORATION OF
THE NINETIETH ANNIVERSARY OF
THE EASTER RISING

Gabriel Doherty

INTRODUCTION

'Enjoy the conference, and the rows it will surely rise.' Thus concluded the scripted remarks of President Mary McAleese at the end of her opening address, on the evening of Friday 28 January 2006, to the conference 'The long revolution: the 1916 Rising in context'. She then added, in an off-the-cuff remark, 'I think I may have started a few myself.'

She certainly had. The forthright nature of her speech, with its unapologetic defence of the Rising, galvanised a debate on its significance, and the appropriate manner of its commemoration, that had been slowly gathering momentum for some time. Over the following months, up to Easter weekend itself (15–17 April) this debate broadened rapidly to encompass all media forms (real and virtual). In so doing it touched on a wide range of contentious issues, both historiographical and political. It was, without doubt, the most engaged public discussion of modern Irish history for many years – at least since the release of the feature film *Michael Collins* a decade earlier, and possibly since the much discussed (and widely misinterpreted) fiftieth anniversary commemorations of the Rising. Moreover, no sooner had these particular embers of Easter started to cool than the debate flared back into life, inspired by the critical and commercial success of another film, *The Wind that Shakes the Barley*, set in west Cork during the revolutionary period and winner of the Palme d'Or for best film at the Cannes film festival in May.

The aim of this paper is to document and assess this debate. To this end it is organised into three parts. The first considers some of the factors that explain why this ninetieth (and thus rather unorthodox) anniversary was the occasion for such interest; the second seeks to chronicle the varied forms taken by the debate (with particular emphasis on coverage in the national newspapers); while the third contains an assessment of some of the principal historiographical points of this extended 'national conversation' (to borrow a phrase used by Taoiseach Bertie Ahern in the course of a speech, itself controversial, delivered when opening an exhibition on the Rising at the National Museum).[1] Quite clearly such an assessment, undertaken so soon after the event and before the dust of argument has completely settled, labours under the same liabilities that beset all efforts at 'instant history'. By the same token, however, it is hoped that the summation will convey to readers the immediate atmosphere of the debate and provide pointers for more considered assessments in future.

FACTORS BEHIND THE COMMEMORATION

One of the most important, but least discussed, reasons for the protracted public deliberations over 1916 in the year of its ninetieth anniversary was the fact that large quantities of original source material relating to the Rising had only recently been made available to academic researchers and the general public. Without doubt the single most significant example of such material came in the form of the holdings of the Bureau of Military History, housed in the Military Archives, Cathal Brugha Barracks, Dublin (with duplicates of the collection also available at the National Archives). This collection, which was gathered together in the decade following the establishment of the Bureau in 1947 by the Minister for Defence Oscar Traynor, aimed 'to assemble and co-ordinate material to form the basis for the compilation of the history of the movement for independence' from the formation of Volunteers in November 1913 to the ceasefire in the Anglo-Irish war in July 1921.[2] The backbone of the collection was over 1,700 written testimonies ('Witness Statements') from surviving members of the republican movement of the period (from all parts of the country and of varying degrees of seniority), who recounted their experiences of political and military developments of the time. These were augmented by large quantities of contemporary documents and more limited collections of photographs, voice recordings and press cuttings. While individual elements of the collection had previously been made available (primarily to relatives of those interviewed), the decision, announced in 2002, to open the collection to the general public gave a fillip to researchers of the period, the first fruits of whose labours could be seen in many of the academic works that have appeared in the last year or two.[3]

In addition to these historiographical developments, two other long-term factors both facilitated and influenced the debate about the Rising. The first was the phenomenon of the 'Celtic Tiger', that is, the transformation of the Irish economy, from the mid-1990s onwards, into one of the most successful in Europe. Falling levels of unemployment, double digit growth figures, reduced levels of national debt, low inflation, record job creation, and unprecedented levels of inward migration, all contributed to the creation of a sense of confidence, pride even, in the national economy which was unthinkable only a decade before. While there is as yet no consensus on the precise causes, extent, ramifications and distribution of this new-found prosperity, it undoubtedly has helped to ameliorate in the public mind many of the criticisms of the performance of independent Ireland, both economically and otherwise. To the extent that the Easter Rising was a catalyst for this independence, such a benign contemporary economic environment undoubtedly formed a more favourable context for the 2006 commemoration than had been the case, for example, for the seventy fifth anniversary in 1991.[4]

The principal cause of the muted commemoration of the Rising on this latter occasion was not, however, the depressed state of the Irish economy, but the anguish – indeed shame – felt by many regarding the violence in Northern Ireland, which at that time gave little public sign of abating. With the benefit of hindsight it is clear that there were, even then, straws of hope in the political wind that presaged the subsequent peace process. Among the other elements of the 'peace dividend' that flowed from this process (which included the final decommissioning of the weaponry of the Provisional IRA in late 2005) there emerged both an opportunity and a determination to re-assess the Rising more thoroughly in its own right and with less regard to the identification of the event with the Provisional movement.[5] This identification had been championed by revisionist historians from the 1970s onwards and, ironically, was embraced by that movement as part of its rhetorical and ideological arsenal. This re-assessment was interpreted by some merely as a crude and transparent effort by Fianna Fáil to challenge Provisional Sinn Féin for the republican constituency in the upcoming general election.[6] More subtly it offered all political parties the opportunity to re-assess their pedigrees in light of the aims of the revolutionary generation.[7] While this 'northern' dimension certainly had a bearing on the commemorative process (most notably in the days following the riot in Dublin city centre on Saturday 25 February, which prevented the 'Love Ulster' march from proceeding as arranged down O'Connell Street), it failed to eclipse the 2006 event as had been the case fifteen years earlier.[8]

There were two other developments in the winter of 2005–6 that ensured that the ninetieth commemoration of the Rising would be the object of intense public interest. The first was the announcement, by the Taoiseach, Bertie Ahern, in the course of his address to the Fianna Fáil árd fheis on the evening of Friday 21 October 2005, that the anniversary would be marked by a military parade – the first such parade since the early 1970s.[9] In the short-term this announcement was over-shadowed both by the death of the controversial former Fianna Fáil TD Liam Lawlor in a Moscow car crash (news of which began to filter back to Dublin on the morning after Ahern's speech) and by the publication in the week following the árd fheis of the 'Ferns report'.[10] After Christmas, however, and most especially in the run-up to the weekend of the parade itself the decision was the subject of concerted media attention.

Two questions formed the core of this discussion. First, whether the Taoiseach, by announcing the parade at a party political event, had compromised its function as a symbol of national unity and pride; and second, whether a military parade was the most appropriate manner in which this national pride could be expressed. Both points are considered below. One of the more interesting aspects of this latter issue was the explicit manner in which the Taoiseach, in his address, went out of his way to identify the Irish army as 'the only legitimate army of the Irish people', 'the true successors of the Volunteers' who participated in the Rising who thus alone had the right to style themselves Óglaigh na hÉireann – thereby, of course, both repudiating the claim of the Provisional IRA to be the linear descendants of the Volunteer movement in its 1916–21 incarnation, and challenging the broader Provisional movement's proprietorial attitude towards the Rising.

Such developments – the availability of new source material, the impact of economic prosperity, the peace process, and the reinstatement of a military parade – would, on their own, have been sufficient to ensure that the ninetieth anniversary of the Rising would be marked in a manner not seen for some years. As indicated above, however, it was the speech by President McAleese at the end of January, and the wide exposure it received (primarily as a result of being reproduced in full in, and the lead story of, the following morning's *Irish Times*)[11] that transformed what might otherwise have remained a rather elitist debate into a national colloquium that was prolonged, extensive and searching – the principal aspects of which form the remainder of this paper.

THE COMMEMORATIVE PROCESS

The President's speech

Given the centrality of the President in the debate over the Rising it is fitting that her comments be the point of departure for this section.[12] The address, which in keeping with protocol had been cleared with the Department of the Taoiseach,[13] began with a reference to the pitiful plight of many mothers in Ireland in 1916, whose sons were soon to die in appalling numbers 'in some army's uniform, in a formidably unequal country', where women in particular had 'no vote or voice'. The next part of the speech drew more attention, when the President invited her audience 'to ponder the extent to which today's freedoms, values, ambitions and success rest on that perilous and militarily-doomed undertaking of nine decades ago', and on the words of the Proclamation. She suggested that the 'long-term intellectual power' of the Rising – with its promise of a free republic, committed to a 'philosophy of equality and social inclusion in tune with the contemporary spirit of democracy, human rights, equality and anti confessionalism' – had been initially and unfortunately overshadowed by its emotional legacy, but that in recent years this vision had come closer to realisation.

The response to the speech was mixed, albeit there was clear evidence of increased public support as the formal state commemorative ceremony came and went. To her critics the speech was 'misguided' and 'anachronistic', and 'allowed her political enemies to question the sincerity of her reconciliation efforts towards unionists'. More trenchant criticism labelled it 'deeply flawed and quite improper' and 'a surprisingly crude piece of myth-making, breath-taking in its revisionism of recent history'. One commentator invited the nation to be 'ashamed' of the President, while another went so far as to suggest that her words had 'done dire damage to Irish democracy'.

Praise for the speech was expressed in calmer and ultimately rather more convincing tones. For the President's admirers it was 'difficult to overstate the importance, even profundity' of her speech, which was 'measured and constructive' not least in its emphasis upon a 'shared pride' in the valour of those Irishmen who fought in the various theatres of war in 1916. This 'calm and considered objectivity' ensured that 'the inclusiveness she has voiced since her election' had not been abandoned.[14]

Two ideas put forward by the President proved particularly contentious. The first suggested that the administration of the country at the time of the Rising was 'being carried on as a process of continuous conversation around the fire in the Kildare Street Club by past pupils of minor public schools'. 'It was,' she said, 'no way to run a country, even without the glass ceiling for Catholics.' The comment drew a response from several quarters, with the most considered analysis provided in several opinion pieces by Professor Paul Bew of Queen's University Belfast.[15] He argued (within the evidential constraints imposed by the journalistic medium) that, contrary to the President's claim, the British government had been appointing Catholics 'to the most senior positions' in the Irish administration since the 1830s.[16] Further, and taking his cue from a speech by John Dillon in the aftermath of the Rising, he argued that if the concept of government by members of the Kildare Street Club had any real meaning at the time of the Rising it was more as a consequence, rather than cause, of the event.[17] Both points should be read in light of Professor Bew's broader, favourable assessment of the Redmondite tradition – which, he suggested, had simply, ungenerously, and unwisely been ignored by the President. There is much to commend this line of argument – in particular the pertinent observation that it had been the Liberal party that had governed Ireland during the decade prior to the Rising. It was, however, weakened by the absence of any reference to the creeping demoralisation of the Redmondite camp that was evident long before the Rising, or to the equally pertinent observation that, in spite of the claimed long-standing good government intentions, Catholics in 1916 remained excluded from the most senior positions in the Irish administration, the offices of lord lieutenant and chief secretary. Honours, on this point, seem to have been equally shared between the President and her critics.

The other principal focal point of dispute that arose from the President's address was in response to her suggestion that the fact that the vast majority of nationalists were members of 'a universal church' (i.e. Roman Catholics) 'brought them into contact with a vastly wider segment of the world than that open to even the most travelled imperial English gentleman'. This challenge to the paradigm that counter-pointed British cosmopolitanism and Irish Catholic parochialism sufficed to drive several of the President's long-time critics into rhetorical paroxysms.[18] Few, however, addressed the substance of the claim in any sustained manner. Most merely either lamented what they saw as the deleterious consequences of the 'hegemony' of the Roman Catholic church in post-independence Ireland, or mis-interpreted the President's comments to suggest that she had implied that Protestants were, in some respects, less than fully Irish.

An example of the former approach was to be found in a letter from Robin Bury of the Reform movement to the *Irish Examiner*, 13 February 2006. Therein he alleged that Protestants in the south of Ireland 'were cleared out during a campaign of intimidation and persecution' from 1920–24. In his view the legacy of 1916 'was an independent Ireland that was economically, culturally and intellectually stagnant' as a result of the dominant position of the Catholic church, which, in his words, 'controlled social and cultural life' in the state.[19]

The most egregious example of the latter was provided by historian, biographer of Pearse, and *Sunday Independent* columnist Ruth Dudley Edwards, who, quoting a conversation with a friend, suggested that the inference drawn by the latter from such 'dogma' was that 'non-Catholics feel a sense of "not belonging" to Ireland – of being outsiders who can never really belong'.[20] The non-sequitor involved in such a conclusion is apparent.

There were, of course, a large number of other points raised by the President which gave rise to public comment, some of which are examined in a different context later in this paper. In the opinion of this author, the most insightful immediate response to her comments came, not in the national print or broadcast media, but in a thoughtful article in the *Tullamore Tribune* by Conor Brady, former editor of the *Irish Times*.[21] Therein he lauded the President for having the courage to address what he described as a national sense of self-doubt regarding the state's origins, which was as unwarranted as it was debilitating. He also suggested that the speech – 'a timely portrayal of a proud and independent people' – should be interpreted in the context of a possible state visit to Ireland by Queen Elizabeth II, a visit he regarded as imminent. While at the time of writing no such visit has been announced, the observation is an intriguing one.[22]

GOVERNMENT AND OPPOSITION

Even though, as noted above, Taoiseach Ahern's announcement of the reinstatement of the military parade to mark the Rising was overshadowed by contemporary events and by President McAleese's speech, the significance of his address is clear. His speech, of course, was wide-ranging, and the announcement of the reinstatement of the parade but one among many items that drew applause from the audience. The relevant section of the speech spoke of the 'need to reclaim the spirit of 1916' from those who had 'abused and debased the title of republicanism'. To that end, in addition to the reinstatement of the parade in 2006, he also announced the creation of a committee with responsibility for preparations for the centenary of the event.[23]

Inevitably there was speculation amongst political commentators as to the identity of the individual who first came up with the idea. Gene McKenna of the *Irish Independent* subsequently claimed that Rory Brady, the attorney general, was the individual in question,[24] while Matt Cooper, writing in the *Irish Examiner*, suggested that Ahern himself deserved the credit for what Cooper described as 'the main creative vision of his second term of office'.[25]

Minister for Defence Willie O'Dea provided additional information on the background to Ahern's announcement, in response to a Dáil question on 3 November 2005. He informed the chamber that the initial cabinet discussion of the matter had taken place the previous July. This was followed by consultation with the chief of staff of the defence forces, with the parade that marked the army's withdrawal from its UN deployment in the Lebanon utilised as one possible model. Interestingly, he professed that he was 'amazed' that the matter had not leaked into the public domain prior to the árd fheis. He added that while the centenary seemed some years off, preliminary planning for it was not premature.[26]

Reaction to the idea varied. While a small body of opinion remained irrecoverably opposed to the concept, most welcomed the opportunity to mark the Rising and debate its legacy. There was obvious dissatisfaction amongst the opposition parties as to the nature of the announcement, and broader discussion as to the most appropriate form that the commemoration should take. As Easter weekend approached, however, criticisms became more muted, and once the parade itself had taken place a broad consensus emerged that the event had been, in the words of the journalist, Miriam Lord, 'celebratory, yet reverential, good-natured and good-humoured, patriotic but not triumphalist'.[27]

The initial response to the announcement focused primarily on Ahern's motivation, with several suggestions that his goal was simply and cynically to bolster Fianna Fáil's 'green' credentials in its forthcoming electoral contest with Sinn Féin for the state's nationalist vote ('the Ghost of Elections Future' as the *Irish Independent* described it).[28] This discussion quickly gave way to a debate on the commemoration process itself. One correspondent to the *Irish Times* disparaged sentimental attitudes towards the Rising as a 'national toy box' that was better left closed.[29] Writing in the same paper the columnist Kevin Myers, a long-time, vocal critic of the republican tradition, suggested that for the state to officially commemorate the Rising inevitably implied some degree of celebration of what he described as the consequent 'catastrophic six-year fratricidal war' and the 'illegal and unconstitutional means to political ends' that defined it.[30] Eoghan Harris, another critic, also disparaged the parade as a 'bad idea', on the basis that it was merely designed to allow Fianna Fáil 'appropriate for itself an important part of our past history'. He differed from Myers, however, in his support for some form of commemoration of the Rising, but suggested that a public debate on its legacy was more suitable than a military parade.[31]

Others explored this theme. Fintan O'Toole argued against the parade on the basis that such a display of military power had a negative resonance in the aftermath of the conflict in Northern Ireland. Far better, in his view, to give substance to the republican ideals of liberty, equality and solidarity.[32] Robert Ballagh, the prime mover behind the 'unofficial' commemoration of the seventy fifth anniversary of the Rising, also professed himself 'less impressed' with the military aspect of the revival than with the associated historical debate.[33] In an editorial dated 28 March, accompanying an impressive sixteen page colour supplement on the Rising (which produced the largest single day's sales in the history of the paper), the *Irish Times* concluded that the divergence of opinion on the parade suggested that the implied hope that the Rising could 'again be regarded as an uncontroversial focus of national unity' was mis-placed.

Among those who supported the commemoration idea but found the prospect of a military parade unappealing there was support for a civic, community-based approach. Provisional Sinn Féin and Labour were the principal party-political advocates of such an approach, although the two made rather uncomfortable bed-fellows, especially in the aftermath of the 'Love Ulster' riot.[34] Even those, such as Fergus Finlay (former political and communications director for the Labour party), who were keen to acknowledge the army's valuable contribution to the United Nations, avoided the parade on the basis that it excluded other organisations that had also rendered distinguished service in this regard.[35]

Notwithstanding such objections the government persisted with preparations for the parade, details of which were disclosed to the public by degrees from late 2005. The general theme of the parade had been described by Minister O'Dea, in his speech to the Dáil on 3 November, as 'a celebration of Óglaigh na hÉireann'.[36] Some weeks later, in expounding upon the plans, the Taoiseach was keen to stress that the commemoration be 'inclusive'; for him the aim was 'to respectfully acknowledge the achievements and sacrifices of past generations and to inculcate an awareness and appreciation in modern Ireland of the events and issues of those times.'[37]

Three distinct committees assisted in the preparations for the events of Easter weekend. The first was an all-party Oireachtas committee whose task, in the words of O'Dea, was 'to offer advice on the appropriate scope and content of a 1916 centenary commemoration committee'.[38] At its first, and only, meeting prior to the parade, the committee agreed on several points, notably that the 'starry plough' (the flag associated with the labour movement in general and the Irish Citizen Army in particular) be displayed alongside the tricolour; that a brochure containing the names of all those killed during Easter Week be produced; and that a minute's silence be respected for these fatalities. The principal logistical burden, however, fell on the shoulders of administrators in various state agencies. A higher-level committee, chaired by the assistant secretary to the government and charged with the formulation of policy for the parade, involved representatives of assistant secretary level from several government departments (including Foreign Affairs, Defence and Social, Community and Family Affairs, as well as from the Department of the Taoiseach itself), and other agencies (notably the Office of Public Works and the Garda Síochána). The implementation of policy was the responsibility of a larger, more diverse working group, chaired by the head of protocol in the Department of the Taoiseach, with representatives of all the agencies on the higher-level committee along with the defence forces, RTÉ, the Health and Safety Executive, the organising committee of the St Patrick's day parade, Dublin City Council and others as the need arose. The committee met fortnightly in the months leading up to the parade.[39]

The final programme encompassed three principal elements, all of which took place on Easter Sunday, 16 April: an early morning wreath-laying ceremony in Kilmainham gaol (the site of the executions in 1916 and, since its renovation in 1966, a most impressive heritage centre); the military parade itself (from Dublin Castle to Parnell Square), which began at 11.45am and continued until the early afternoon;[40] and, in the evening, a state reception in Dublin Castle, hosted by President McAleese, for the large number of invited guests and others involved in the organisation of the event. Finally, lunch on the day was provided for all invited guests in the Gresham hotel following the conclusion of the parade and before the state reception commenced.

The logistics involved were impressive, all the more so given that the 'Love Ulster' disturbances had unavoidably led to a re-assessment of the threat of disruption to the day's events, and a consequent tightening up of security arrangements. As things transpired no untoward incidents occurred on the day and there was unanimous agreement among the 900-plus invited guests, upwards of 100,000 spectators, and numerous media commentators, that the affair had been dignified and moving, and that the civil servants involved had done a first class job.[41]

There were a small number of aspects of the build-up to the day that gave rise to public comment. The first was the issue of invitations to the event to members of the unionist community in Northern Ireland. Not surprisingly most turned down the offer, some more politely than others.[42] The second point of note was the acceptance by the British ambassador to Ireland of an invitation from the government to attend the parade. His decision was welcomed by some unionists (David Adams saw it as 'an important and welcome gesture' and proof of the normalisation of relations between Ireland and Britain) and criticised by others (with Jeffrey Donaldson labelling it 'bizarre'.)

The aftermath of the event was also noteworthy. One of the more interesting responses – or rather lack thereof – came from within the state's large, and recently settled, Polish community. Notwithstanding that nation's own troubled relations with powerful neighbours and its long struggle for independence, there seems to have been limited engagement with the commemorative activities.[43] The event did, however, receive some coverage in the *Polish Express*, the most popular magazine within the state's Polish community, a colourful photographic element combining with a commentary that, not surprisingly, expressed sympathy with the insurgents.[44]

From a historian's perspective, the most significant legacy of the commemoration may be the further opening up of archival material from the period. Even prior to the parade this had been a matter of discussion in the Dáil, with Catherine Murphy TD prominent in the campaign to ensure improved facilities for those researching the revolutionary era.[45] In the aftermath of the Easter weekend the Taoiseach promised to expedite the digitisation of Old IRA pension records, and to respond to a request by Pat Rabbitte, leader of the Labour party, that a comprehensive list of all those who died (civilians and combatants on both sides) during the campaign for independence be compiled.[46] The interest shown by the members of the centenary commemoration committee in the issue of archival holdings holds out much promise for future researchers.

It is now time to consider some of the more explicitly party-political aspects of the commemoration debate. One of the more stimulating speeches made during the period was given on Sunday 9 April by Taoiseach Ahern, on the occasion of the opening of an official exhibition on the Rising at the National Museum, Collins Barracks, Dublin. During the course of his address he referred to the 'four cornerstones of independent Ireland in the twentieth century', that is, the 1916 Proclamation, the 1937 constitution, the ratification of the Treaty of Rome in 1972, and the Good Friday Agreement of 1998. Not surprisingly, given that the final three events took place during periods when Fianna Fáil were in office, this interpretation of recent history brought to a head complaints from the opposition that the contributions of their parties to the state's development were being ignored.[47] Enda Kenny, leader of Fine Gael, was in the vanguard of such criticism, noting his party's links to the first post-independence government, the state's entry into the United Nations, and the signing of the Anglo-Irish Agreement.[48] It should be noted that in a subsequent article in Cork's *Evening Echo* the Taoiseach qualified his statement, stating that 'no party has a monopoly on Ireland's past' and paying tribute to the efforts of members of other political traditions throughout the years, 'who shared the same ultimate objective of full national freedom' as Fianna Fáil's founding generation.[49]

Other members of government were also active during the period, with Willie O'Dea especially prominent. It was he, not surprisingly, who was foremost in emphasising the role of the defence forces in the commemoration process[50] and, as the overall co-ordinator of that process, it was he who gained most plaudits for the dignified manner in which the event was conducted.[51] For her part, the Minister for Education and Science, Mary Hanafin, part-funded the *Irish Times* supplement on the Rising, announced a Rising-themed scholarship scheme for schools, and arranged for the sending to schools of educational materials relating to the Rising (the emphasis of which was on a 'sensitive' approach to other traditions and 'a broad and inclusive context'.)[52] Perhaps the most wide-ranging of these contributions was made by the Minister for Enterprise, Trade and Employment, Micheál Martin (one of the few participants in the debate with a postgraduate qualification in history) in a speech in University College Cork (UCC) some weeks after the parade had taken place. During the course of his address he spoke of, amongst other things, the unique atmosphere that had attended the parade, the deleterious role of revisionist historiography in alienating the public from the study and writing of history, and the 'generous response' of the Irish people to the government's insistence that the commemoration of the battle of the Somme be fittingly marked (for more on which, see below).[53]

Given their smaller size and the nature of their ministerial portfolios the Progressive Democrats, Fianna Fáil's partners in government, inevitably played a less active role in the commemoration process. Not surprisingly the party member who was most active in this respect was the Minister for Justice, Equality and Law Reform, Michael McDowell, the grandson of Eoin MacNeill.[54]

Fine Gael, for its part, was also engaged at a variety of levels in the commemorative process, albeit that, inevitably and in common with other opposition parties, it had but a marginal role to play in the official state functions.[55] As was to be expected, Enda Kenny used the opportunity to re-affirm the party's roots in the Rising – but, interestingly, he also sought to stake Fine Gael's claim to the mantle of the constitutional nationalist tradition. In a speech in his native Mayo on Friday 7 April he spoke of Fine Gael's view of the Rising 'as the defining moment in the life of modern Ireland' and listed some of its founding members who were 'out' in 1916.[56] He also, however, paid tribute to the Irish party of Parnell and Redmond for the part it had played 'in establishing and shaping our parliamentary democracy'. He lamented 'the unfair way history has forgotten or sidelined their massive and lasting achievements', not least that of John Dillon, whose son, James, was, of course, a former leader of Fine Gael. The following week, in an interview with the *Evening Echo*, he re-iterated his view of the Rising as 'a defining moment in the life of modern Ireland', 'a national, not a partisan or sectarian event ... which belonged to all the Irish people'.[57]

As a consequence of the prominence of James Connolly in the build-up to, and the events of, the Rising, the Labour party, and with it the trades union movement, was enthusiastic in its engagement with the commemoration process. The central plank of this programme was the 'Liberty project', a collaborative venture between Labour and the Services, Industrial, Professional and Technical Union (SIPTU), which sought 'to accomplish some solid initiatives and projects that would add to our contemporary understanding of 1916 as well as commemorate that catalytic event in our modern history'.[58] The project incorporated numerous activities, including readings, discussion forums, lectures, and joint ventures with the Social Democratic and Labour Party (SDLP) in Northern Ireland.[59]

One of the more striking elements of the Labour movement's commemorative programme was the call by Liz McManus for the state ceremonies to afford parity of recognition to the losses incurred by British forces, and civilians during the Rising, rather than focus exclusively on the republican side.[60] The suggestion was criticised by Senator Martin Mansergh, the historian and prominent Fianna Fáil policy advisor (who was one of the more active participants in the general commemoration debate), but in the event the centenary committee, on which Deputy McManus was the Labour party's representative, decided that a minute's silence to mark all those who died during Easter Week should indeed be held, to little or no protest.[61]

The most active contributor to the Labour movement's commemorative programme was Manus O'Riordan, head of research for SIPTU, who delivered a series of lectures on the topic of Labour and the Rising in various parts of the country, as well as being responsible, either individually or in conjunction with others, for the appearance during the year of several informative publications on Connolly's life and achievements.[62]

In a similar fashion to Labour's emphasis upon the relevance of the Rising to contemporary political and social policy, the Green party used the commemoration as an opportunity to take stock of the nation's progress over the intervening period. Elements of this critique included criticism of government across a range of matters – including its perceived willingness to forsake aspects of state sovereignty,[63] its neglect of the Irish language,[64] and its failure to promote equal opportunities[65] – as well as opposition to the military focus of the parade and the absence of an ecumenical aspect to the annual Arbour Hill religious service.[66]

Provisional Sinn Féin's role in, and attitude towards, the commemoration process received a great deal of attention. Not surprisingly, the party organised a range of events to mark the occasion, including talks, recitations, walking tours, films, plays and musical concerts.[67] A more animated aspect, however, related to the public discussion about the relationship between 1916 and the armed campaign of the Provisional IRA from the early 1970s to the mid 1990s. There were two clear camps. On the one side were those who argued that the latter was a logical continuation of the former, and that there was, in the words of the unionist peer Lord Laird, 'no valid distinction' between killings in the two periods.[68] The same idea was expressed somewhat differently by the journalist Mary Raftery, when she suggested that parallels between the two eras were simply too obvious to ignore: 'Both groups were unelected minorities whose lack of democratic mandate did not inhibit their claim to act on behalf of the Irish people.'[69] Similar sentiments were expressed by Robin Bury in the *Irish Examiner*, 13 February, where he suggested that 1916 'inspired and provided justification for the vile sectarian campaign in Northern Ireland in which 3,500 people died'; and, most interestingly, by a grandson of Cathal Brugha, who stated that he did not 'see any real difference between the IRA then and now. They murdered police officers, Protestants, Catholics then, and have been doing exactly that in recent decades too.'[70]

The opposing camp, in contrast, repudiated such a connection, and employed a variety of arguments to reinforce their case. Martin Mansergh contrasted the failure of the Provisional movement, during its armed campaign, to gain anything close to majority support even within the nationalist community of Northern Ireland, let alone south of the border, with the 'legitimate national revolution' of 1916–21, which 'quite rapidly won and retained the democratic support of the people'.[71] Likewise Willie O'Dea was emphatic in his repeated insistence that the only legitimate armed group within the state was the Irish army, which alone had the right to style itself Óglaigh na hÉireann,[72] and Michael McDowell counterpointed the ethical and conventional (and thus, of course, doomed) military tactics of the 1916 insurgents with the terroristic methods of the Provisional IRA.[73]

One of the more interesting contributors in this regard was Professor John A. Murphy, who, in the course of two articles written in the build-up to the parade, highlighted the uncertainties felt by many on this specific question. In the first he stated that he had never subscribed to the view that 1916 was the wellspring for the Provisional IRA's armed campaign, but rather insisted that 'the Rising was such a powerful dynamic that the state should not let the initiative in celebrating it pass into Provo hands'.[74] In the second, however, in the course of a detailed critique of the language used in, and the underlying ideas of, the 1916 Proclamation, he suggested that its most disturbing phrase was 'through us' – i.e. that war would be waged by 'a self-appointed apostolic elite, a "prophetic shock minority", who regarded their idealistic convictions as sufficient justification for their insurrectionary violence in the name of "the people". Essentially, this has always been the position of the IRA.[75]

One aspect of Provisional Sinn Féin's attitude towards the commemoration must be briefly mentioned before moving on, and that was the absence of the party's leader, Gerry Adams, from the reviewing stand of the military parade.[76] During his speech to the party's árd fheis he had (somewhat ironically in the eyes of some) criticised the militaristic nature of the parade, and expressed a preference for an 'inclusive, civic and cultural celebration'.[77] His absence was defended by his party colleague Caoimhghín Ó Caoláin (who was also absent from the ceremony, as was the party's vice president Martin McGuinness) on the grounds of 'prior commitments' – although the Taoiseach somewhat tartly observed that he had given everyone seven months' notice of the event.[78]

The range of activities undertaken by local authorities to mark the Rising was, if anything, even more impressive than those organised by the state, when one bears in mind the more limited resources available to them – albeit, inevitably, the response was by no means evenly spread across the country. The local commemorations also tended to be characterised by less manifest party-political differences than their national equivalents. Dublin City Council was, naturally, one of the more active centres. It organised a series of lunchtime lectures by several experts on such topics as the Irish Citizen Army, the role of Éamonn Ceannt, and the contributions of two female participants, Dr Kathleen Lynn and Helena Molony; produced a directory of locations in the city associated with the Rising and contemporaneous events; erected a commemorative plaque to Ceannt on his workplace at municipal buildings in Castle Street; made available through its website a previously unpublished eye-witness account of Easter Week; and held a minute's silence in commemoration of the Citizen Army garrison in City Hall at noon on Monday 24 April (the precise anniversary of the start of the Rising).[79]

Most county councils also responded in some manner. Cork County Council, for example, arranged for a formal reading of the Proclamation at its meeting on 27 March, and for a letter to be sent to the Department of Education and Science calling on it to distribute copies of both the Proclamation and the national flag to all national schools in the state. Many such authorities – Donegal, Kerry, Westmeath, and Clare, for example – arranged exhibitions of material relating to the Rising and the independence struggle in county libraries and museums, with a pronounced emphasis upon the involvement of locals in the events. Waterford County

Council, amongst others, increased the provision of literature on the Rising for adults and children through its library service.

Many other local authority bodies were also involved, with noteworthy events organised by Ennis, Athy and Carlow Town Councils, and the Co. Kilkenny Vocational Education Committee, amongst many, *many* others.[80]

Academic activities

One of the lasting achievements of the ninetieth anniversary commemorations of the Easter Rising will surely be its historiographical legacy. Both in the build up to 2006, and during the year itself, a plethora of titles – some of lasting value, others of more dubious merit – appeared in bookshops and, by degrees, worked their way into the thinking of the book-buying and reading public. It is no exaggeration to say that in this respect 2006 is second only to 1966 in terms of the quality of the academic studies produced; and by the time the publishing cycle has fully turned, it may be that the year will prove as significant in its impact upon scholarship on the Rising as it has undoubtedly been in terms of public opinion regarding it.[81]

Two full-length academic monographs about the Rising appeared during the period in question. The first, Michael Foy and Brian Barton's, *The Easter Rising*, is an updated version of a text that originally appeared in 1999 and, as such, inevitably does not incorporate the new source material that has come on stream in recent years.[82] The second, Charles Townshend's magisterial *Easter 1916: the Irish rebellion*, made its appearance in 2005, and suffers from no such handicap.[83]

At a more popular level Tim Pat Coogan's illustrated account of the Rising, originally published in 2001, was re-issued in paperback form and sold well,[84] as did the similarly well-illustrated *Irish Times* book of the 1916 Rising, which was an expanded version of the special supplement produced by the paper mentioned above.[85]

The title of Jonathan Githens-Mazer's *Myths and memories of the Easter Rising* was slightly misleading, in that its focus was as much on the First World War as the Rising, although it did have a useful chapter on the concept of the Rising as a 'cultural trigger point'.[86] James Moran's *Staging the Easter Rising* took a rather different slant on the events in Dublin in 1916, by examining the evolution of its theatrical and other representations in the decades following independence.[87]

Rather more grounded in archival material was Annie Ryan's, *Witness: inside the Easter Rising*, which utilised excerpts from a large number of Witness Statements from the Bureau of Military History to provide a detailed chronological narrative of the events of the Rising, with a welcome emphasis on the role of female participants.[88] Owen McGee's *The IRB: the Irish Republican Brotherhood, from the Land League to Sinn Féin* likewise made extensive use of original source material.[89]

A limited number of older titles were reprinted during the year. Garret FitzGerald's edition of his father's memoirs, *Desmond's Rising: memoirs 1913 to Easter 1916*, which had originally appeared in 1968, was issued in revised form by Liberties press.[90] Likewise, L.G. Redmond Howard's eye-witness account of Easter Week, which had been originally published in the immediate aftermath of the Rising, was re-published by the Aubane Historical Society as part of its on-going, and most welcome, programme of re-issuing neglected texts from the revolutionary period;[91] and Seán Cronin's *Our own red blood: the story of the 1916 Rising* was re-issued after a thirty year gap.[92]

Two studies which took the General Post Office (GPO) as their focus also appeared during the year. The first, *GPO staff in 1916*, was published by An Post and examined the impact of the Rising on the workings of the postal system in Ireland, and its staff at all levels. Keith Jeffery's *The GPO and the Easter Rising* traversed similar ground in rather more detail.[93]

Six works examined different aspects of the rebellion from local perspectives. Two, published by Oxford University Press in 2005, supplied invaluable information on the evolution of nationalist politics in provincial Ireland (notably Connacht) in the decades leading up to the Rising, and, in one case, a few years after.[94] The third, Marie Coleman's *County Longford and the Irish revolution 1910–1923*, adopted a similar approach, albeit on this occasion taking a single county as the focus of study.[95] Two more focused primarily on the activities of the Irish Volunteers, in one case in Cork in the years prior to the Rising,[96] and in the other in Roscommon in the years following.[97] The final work, Lyn Ebenezer's *Fron-goch and the birth of the IRA*, was slightly different in that it examined the role of the famed prison camp in creating a disciplined revolutionary cadre, but with a primary focus on its Welsh aspects.[98]

The anniversary also produced a rich crop of biographical studies. The most significant was Donal Nevin's *James Connolly: 'a full life'*, the first full-length study of the man in several decades.[99] The biggest disappointment was that Ruth Dudley Edwards, in reissuing her commanding biography of Pearse, failed to update the text in any meaningful way, on the basis of the rather puzzling observation: 'Little new material has appeared since 1977 [the date of original publication] and subsequent books and articles on Pearse have been tangential.'[100]

Two of the executed leaders of the Rising (Ceannt and MacDermott) were the focus of middling length studies,[101] a third (Casement) the object of an excellent edited volume of essays,[102] while a fourth (Joseph Plunkett) featured prominently in his sister's memoir of the period.[103] There was also a welcome re-appearance of Jack White's autobiography.[104]

One cannot finish this section without reference to the success of *Recollections of 1916 and its Aftermath*, a hybrid publication which incorporated excerpts from dozens of interviews with survivors of the Rising, undertaken over many years, together with the interviews themselves, supplied on compact disc.[105] The full version of the publication (which runs to thirty such compact discs) is a historical source of undoubted value.

Historical, political and religious journals also provided a range of material for the reading public. Pride of place in this respect must go to *History Ireland*, whose March–April 2006 issue was entirely given over to various aspects of the Rising, with articles on Seán McLoughlin, the Citizen Army, the Rising in Galway, the 1966 commemorations and an acerbic critique of the 2006 official commemorations by Professor Paul Bew. Not surprisingly the defence forces' journal *An Cosantóir* also produced a memorial number, a double-sized issue in April–May, which explored various aspects of Easter Week from a military perspective. Both the *BBC History Magazine* and *History Today* also included articles on the Rising in their April numbers, with journals as diverse as *The Word, Village, The Phoenix, Irish Political Review* and *INC News* offering information and opinion on both the Rising and the commemoration from a range of perspectives.

In addition to this remarkable level of written output there were, of course, other academic activities organised to mark the event. The university sector, for example, organised a number of conferences, of varying size and scope (in addition, of course, to the event held in University College Cork which was the wellspring for this volume). Dublin University (Trinity College Dublin), in fact, organised two such events: the first, '1916: then and now', was a joint enterprise between the Ireland Institute and the university's Historical Society and ran over two days; while the second, 'The 1916 Rising: new perspectives and arguments', was held a week later. University College Dublin adopted a more interdisciplinary approach, the topic of its venture being 'The life and after-life of P.H. Pearse', a two day bi-lingual event split between UCD and the Pearse Museum in Rathfarn-ham. The Centre for Human Settlement and Historical Change in the National University of Ireland, Galway (NUIG) adopted a markedly different approach, with its seminar '1916: local dimensions' in May offering a welcome focus on events during Easter Week outside Dublin, while NUI Maynooth also organised an open debate in which both staff and students participated.[106]

The non-university sector was also active in this respect. Two summer schools, respectively the Byrne Perry event in Gorey in June, and the annual Desmond Greaves symposium in Dublin in August, were both given over in their entirety to analysis of the event (indeed this was the second successive year that the Rising was the principal theme of the Byrne Perry school). Lectures on the theme of the Rising – either as part of a series or one-off events – were also thick on the ground, with events organised by, amongst other agencies, the Gaelic Athletic Association, the Church of Ireland's Representative Church Body, Conradh na Gaeilge, the Robert Emmet Association, the Ireland Institute, the James Connolly Education Trust, Coiste Spiorad 1916, the 1916–21 Club and the Liam Mellows Commemoration Committee.[107]

MEDIA COVERAGE AND CULTURAL EVENTS

Given the manifest public interest in the topic of the Rising, it is no surprise to find that the media gave extensive coverage both to the commemoration ceremonies and to aspects of the original event itself. The various television stations naturally gave airtime to the military parade (with RTÉ covering the entire event live), as well as offering a range of programming that both explored the historical aspects of the Rising and analysed the public debate on its commemoration. Among the historical figures that were the subject of documentaries broadcast at this time were Pearse, Casement and Maxwell, with two separate programmes on the role of women during the Rising. Current affairs or light entertainment shows such as *The Week in Politics*, *Questions and Answers*, *Primetime* and *The Late, Late Show* also devoted either sections of or entire shows to the topic.[108]

It was on radio, however, that the political debate on the appropriate manner of commemorating the Rising was investigated most thoroughly, with Vincent Browne's *Tonight* show on RTÉ Radio One particularly noteworthy in this respect. Other archival or current affairs-themed shows also devoted varying amounts of airtime to the topic, including broadcasts by John Bowman, Rodney Rice, *Rattlebag*, *Morning Ireland* and *Five Seven Live*; and during the immediate build-up to, and the aftermath of, the Easter Sunday parade, the day-time discussion shows of Pat Kenny, Marian Finucance and Joe Duffy also facilitated public discussion of the event on the national broadcaster. Other national and local radio stations also devoted dedicated airtime to coverage, as did BBC Northern Ireland and BBC Radio Three.[109]

Newspapers, both national and local, also covered the anniversary in some depth. As is evident, they are one of the principal sources of information for this paper. Many of the nationals were markedly sceptical of the commemoration process in the early months of the year,[110] only to shift position when it became evident that the public response to the event was overwhelmingly positive.[111] During the week prior to the military parade the *Times*, *Independent* and *Examiner* all devoted areas of their 'comment' sections to various analysis pieces, thereby providing a healthy dissensus of opinion, and the letters pages of all three did likewise throughout the spring months.

The local press, by and large, offered less editorial comment and, where this was forthcoming, it tended to be less hostile towards the Rising and its remembrance than the dailies. Rather these papers focussed on reportage of local commemorative events, with nearly all containing notices of same in their Easter week editions. A particularly interesting approach was taken by the *Kildare Nationalist* in its 28 April number, which was accompanied by a replica of its predecessor, *The Nationalist and Leinster Times*, dated 6 May 1916, replete with descriptions of the after-effects of the Rising.

One of the unique features of the 2006 anniversary of the Rising, as compared to previous commemorations, was the use of the internet, both as a means of distributing information relating to state and non-state events and as a vehicle for a completely open public discussion on the significance of the Rising itself. The largely unmoderated nature of the internet is, of course, one of its defining features, and many discussion boards, blogs and similar websites carried numerous, wide-ranging threads relating to the Rising – even if the absence of editorial control inevitably meant that the quality of some submissions was somewhat questionable.

In terms of artistic and cultural activities the winter of 2005–6 was also characterised by a wide variety of events with the Rising as common theme.[112] Two of the principal cultural institutions in the state – the

National Library and the National Museum – organised very different, but mutually complementary, exhibitions: the former ('The Easter Rising: understanding 1916') a conventional but still impressive exhibition of contemporary artefacts and accompanying commentary; the latter ('The 1916 Rising: personalities and perspectives') an online exhibition, consisting for the most part of newspapers, photographs and manuscript material drawn from the Library's own collection.[113]

Two plays, with contrasting approaches to the Rising, were also staged at this time. The first, 'Shooting Gallery', was performed at the Andrews Lane theatre in late 2005, and viewed the events of Easter Week from the perspective of two down-and-outs. An altogether more serious piece of theatre was staged in Kilmainham gaol (the site of the executions that followed the Rising) in April–May 2006. 'Operation Easter', written by Dónal O'Kelly, sought, in the playwright's words, to 'challenge the nationalist glorification and revisionist hammer bashing that still dominates public perceptions' of the Rising by concentrating on the 'complexity, the full human picture' of the event.[114]

Visual artists, too, responded to the public's demand for material with 1916 as its theme, with several galleries and other sites in different parts of the country staging exhibitions and installations of varying descriptions.[115] Those whose interest lay in the area of motion pictures were also catered for by the re-release, by RTÉ in conjunction with the Irish Film Institute, of the 1926 feature film *Irish Destiny*, one of the first films to take the Irish independence struggle as its theme.[116] Gael Linn also took the opportunity to release the landmark documentary *Mise Éire*, along with its equally memorable score by Seán Ó Riada.

MISCELLANEOUS

Before moving on to an assessment of the historiographical themes that accompanied this diverse range of activities, a small number of other events associated with the commemoration process must be briefly mentioned. The first was the campaign to ensure that 16 Moore Street, the final headquarters of the Irish Volunteers following their flight from the burning shell of the GPO, would not be subject to commercial re-development. This campaign predated the 2006 revival of interest but was undoubtedly given added momentum by the enhanced public awareness that flowed from the year's events. The campaign had initially focussed on the addition of the site to Dublin City Council's record of protected structures, but a series of technical and other obstacles delayed such a move. As this article goes to press it appears that this campaign has been superseded by a government decision to designate the site a national monument.[117]

The campaign over 16 Moore Street threw into sharp relief the conflicting pressures of historical conservation and the demands of modern commerce, and the controversy over the auction of artefacts associated with the Rising did likewise. There were two principal sales at which such items were offered as lots. The first was at Whyte's of Dublin, on 9 April; the second, the widely publicised 'Independence' sale, was a joint affair between Adam's of Dublin and Mealy's of Kilkenny, and took place on 12 April. The range of material on offer at both sales – in particular the Tom Clarke collection and the original handwritten manuscript of *Amhrán na bhFiann* – reflected the unprecedented degree of public interest in the Rising, which in turn led to bids well in excess of predictions for most items. It also led to protests, before, after, and indeed *during* the auctions.[118]

Three other commemorative events must be mentioned in closing. The first was a coda to the military parade in Dublin on Easter Sunday. It was hosted by the Southern Brigade of the defence forces in Collins Barracks, Cork, on 9 May 2006, and consisted of a dignified ceremony in memory of Thomas Kent, apart from Casement the only other participant in the Rising who was executed outside Dublin.[119] The second was the controversy over the mass to mark the ninetieth anniversary of the Rising at the Augustinian priory in Drogheda, Co. Louth, on Sunday 16 April. The concelebrated nature of this service – with the participation of a minister of the Church of Ireland and members of his congregation alongside their Roman Catholic counterparts – produced expressions of concern by both the Catholic and Church of Ireland primates of all Ireland that the service may have hindered, rather than facilitated, the process of ecumenism on the island, and a vigorous subsequent correspondence which explored the merits both of the mass itself and the archbishops' response.[120]

The third and final commemorative event – that of the battle of the Somme in June – was more significant, given that it was explicitly linked by the Irish government to the Easter Rising programme two months earlier in the official literature produced by it in conjunction with both events:

The Government is committed to respecting all traditions on this island equally. It also recognises that developing a greater understanding of our shared history, in all of its diversity, is essential to developing greater understanding and building a shared future.[121]

The analysis of the connection between the two events offered therewith is instructive:

> The war was initially promoted by Britain as 'the defence of little Belgium'. It later evolved into one fought for the rights of small nations as expressed by President Wilson, and the principle of self-determination for such nations, especially in the defeated central European empires, formed much of the debate at the subsequent peace talks at Versailles. For some Irish nationalists there was an irony in fighting in the British army for such a cause. Moreover initial public enthusiasm for the war quickly faded as it was felt that there was little recognition for the contribution of those Irishmen who had enlisted. The rising casualty lists, allied to the threat of conscription, further dented such enthusiasm. It was against this backdrop that the 1916 Rising was organised ... When the Bosnian Serb Gavrilo Princip fired the shots that killed the heir to the Austrian crown Archduke Franz Ferdinand and his wife during their state visit to Sarajevo in June 1914, he started a chain of events that would directly affect Irish people in every part of Ireland and some of those living in Britain, Australia, New Zealand, Canada and the United States. The course of Irish history was greatly altered, leading to the emergence of forces that still influence the politics of today. The increased awareness of the Irish aspects of the War have helped to put those forces to positive use by allowing people from the two major traditions to meet on common ground.[122]

The decision to link the two events gave rise to a certain amount of disagreement. Not surprisingly government supporters tended to row in behind the proposal, as did leading members of Fine Gael. Liz McManus for Labour adopted a different approach, arguing that the separate commemoration of the conflict on the Somme 'simply perpetuates a form of commemorative apartheid'. What was needed instead, she argued, was 'that the language of our official commemoration on Easter Sunday, of our speeches and our publications, should be truly inclusive and reconciliatory and thus extend to all the combatants of 1916, as well as to the innocent civilians'.[123] Others went in the opposite direction, and over a number of weeks at this time a correspondence was conducted on the letters page of the *Irish Independent* under the intriguing heading of 'Was the Great War a crime?'[124] If the government had hoped that the gesture would lead to a *rapprochement* with northern unionists they were quickly disabused of the idea,[125] although it undoubtedly was consoled by the fact that there was no widespread or sustained public criticism, north or south of the border, of its action in marking the anniversary of the Somme in such a manner.[126]

Historiographical themes

So much for the events that took place in 2005–6 to mark the ninetieth anniversary of the Easter Rising. What aspects of the Rising as a *historical event* attracted the attention of those who participated in the diverse forums referred to in the second part of this paper?

Many themes were discussed, not least the legacy of the Rising – for women, for north–south relations, and for the conduct of public affairs in Ireland as a whole. None of these were particularly original, having been examined in depth at periodic intervals over preceding decades – albeit that the passage of time and the changed national circumstances within which the 2006 commemoration took place meant that the arguments inevitably found new audiences. For reasons of space, however, attention will be focussed here solely on the one issue that was more widely and deeply analysed than any other: that is, the justification for the Rising. The centrality of this question is best summed up in the words of Professor John A. Murphy when writing in the *Evening Echo*: 'Contrary to a popular misconception, all historians, revisionists or otherwise, are in agreement about the significance of 1916 ... The real difference among historians and the general public is whether the Rising was a GOOD THING [original emphasis].'[127] The analysis of this issue covered several distinct themes: the state of the country in 1916; the impact of the First World War; the issue of a democratic mandate for the Rising; and explicitly moral issues such as the use of violence and the killing of civilians. These points are now considered in more depth.

Ireland in 1916

Those who were critical of the Rising emphasised two points regarding the state of Ireland in 1916: the satisfactory state of British government of the country at that time, and the fact that a home rule bill had been passed at Westminster. Regarding the former, several aspects of Ireland's recent past were emphasised. Robin Bury, for example, referred to the fact that, by 1916, ownership of land had, by and large, been transferred from landlords to tenants, local government had been opened up and was 'in Catholic hands', and Ireland had a disproportionate representation at Westminster;[128] while Diarmuid Ferriter (the most active participant in the national debate from within the historical profession) noted that 'Irish people generally enjoyed the right to free speech, free assembly, free organisation and a varied and (mostly) uncensored media', in a largely crime-free island where the elderly were now in receipt of pensions and the Catholic demand for suitable university facilities had been conceded by the creation of the NUI.[129] The moral of the story was clear: Ireland, being well-governed, had no immediate need to be self-governed. From this perspective, furthermore, to the extent that a demand for limited self-government did exist, it had been satisfied in September 1914 by the enactment of the third home rule bill.[130]

Those who opposed this line of thinking rejected this depiction of British rule in Ireland as a progressive force. They cited, in particular, the events of 1912–14, with its descent into anarchy predicated on the refusal of northern unionists and British Conservatives to accept the rule of law; and 1919–21, which demonstrated the refusal of the British government to accept Ireland's right to self-determination, if necessary by the use of physical force. Thus, for one correspondent to the *Sunday Independent*, 'The period we should look at is 1914–21 in the light of actions and threats of those people whom [Kevin] Myers/ [Ruth Dudley] Edwards seem to feel were all honourable and were ruling us in a utopian type of democracy.'[131] Tim Pat Coogan echoed the sentiment, and argued that the home rule crisis, and the conduct of the unionist/tory alliance during it, had not just influenced the Rising, but (bearing in mind the formation of the Irish Volunteers came in response to the creation of the Ulster Volunteer Force) was, in fact, a precondition for it.[132] Regarding the home rule legislation, several commentators noted that the Act was not, in fact, in force in 1916 (nor was any variant thereof for several years to come), and that the government had insisted (to the discomfiture of the Irish party) that its application to the whole of the island would have to be reconsidered in light of northern unionist opposition.

IRELAND AND THE WAR

Similarly polarised views were evident regarding Ireland's role in World

War One. For critics of the Rising there was an obvious moral. In the words of one correspondent,

> those resorting to arms in the GPO etc. were reporting to a tiny coterie of the secret and unelected Irish Republican Brotherhood (not Sinn Féin, by the way), whereas those tens of thousands of others marching off during the Kaiser War were responding to the legal (if flawed and distracted) government of the day and to the democratic Irish Parliamentary Party ... The IRB insurgents were essentially armed proto-fascists informed by Pearse's ego. Without even consulting the people, they just 'knew' what the people wanted and how it should be achieved ... The other group were honourable and courageous volunteer servicemen, who paid a fearsome price for their noble service to European freedom in Flanders fields and elsewhere.[133]

For another (Tom Carew of the Irish Congress of Trade Unions (ICTU), one of the few members of the labour movement who publicly opposed the Rising's commemoration), the contrast between the mass participation of Irishmen in the British army and the limited numbers involved in the Easter Rising led him to pose the blunt question: 'Where was the real Ireland in 1916?'[134] Others emphasised the links between republicans and the German government ('the imperial butchers of poor Belgium' in Kevin Myers' phrase).[135]

On the other side of the argument was a more sceptical interpretation of the war, and Ireland's involvement in it as part of the United Kingdom. From this perspective Britain, as an imperial super-power, was as guilty as any of the other major European states for the creation of the conditions that led to the outbreak of war in 1914. Furthermore, given that the war was ostensibly fought over the right to self-determination of small nations, Britain's refusal to concede the same claim to Ireland cast a rather different, and more sinister, light on its actions from 1914–18. In the words of one correspondent to the *Irish Independent*, 'Let us not kowtow to the small quasi-band of narrow-minded imperialists who would appear to believe that the First World War, a battle between mighty empires, was a much more noble and worthy affair, compared to the right of a small country to her freedom.'[136] Martin Mansergh also pointed out the hypocrisy of contemporary unionist criticism of the republicans' association with imperial Germany in 1916, bearing in mind their own willingness to do likewise two years earlier.[137]

Of all the issues relating to the justification, or otherwise, for the Rising, the issue of a democratic mandate was the most frequently, and minutely, discussed. Not surprisingly the discussion was again polarised. On the one hand stood those who insisted that the failure of its leaders, prior to the Rising, to put peacefully their programme to the Irish electorate, and respect their verdict, undermined the republican and democratic aspirations of the Proclamation.[138] Thus, in the words of David Adams, the Rising was the work of 'an unelected, unaccountable, elite embarking on armed insurrection against the wishes of the vast majority of its fellow citizens'.[139] More forcefully, Lord Laird suggested that Pearse (and presumably others in the enterprise) 'subscribed to a dangerous and proto-fascist melange of messianic Roman Catholicism, mythical Gaelic history and blood-sacrifice', and could not, in any circumstances, be described as a democrat.[140]

The most aggressive assault on the democratic credentials of those involved in the Rising, however, came from the other side of the Irish sea, in the form of two vitriolic attacks by journalists working for British newspapers. Geoffrey Wheatcroft, writing in the *Guardian* on 9 April, suggested that the Rising was an early example of the European-wide 'reaction against constitutional liberalism and [decline] into irrationalism' that took place in the 1920s and 1930s. He depicted the United Kingdom of the day as 'a democracy with limited representative government and a rule of law' whose flaws were fewer 'than most countries on earth then or many today'. By contrast the 1916 insurgents could only be compared to the participants in the Beer hall putsch.[141] An even more outspoken piece was penned by Richard Ingrams, writing in the London *Independent* on 15 April. Therein he wrote of the similarity between the actions of the 'terrorists' of 1916 'and their modern Muslim equivalents', on the basis that 'they too' (referring to the rank and file of the Rising) 'had a fervent religious faith and some of their leaders had the same kind of suicidal urges as al-Qa'ida', urges which the British authorities 'were happy to oblige' via the programme of executions.[142]

On the other side of the fence were those who suggested that the nature of Ireland's constitutional relationship with the rest of the United Kingdom was the result of a history in which democratic norms had been routinely ignored by the British government, that the flaws in British democracy conceded by Wheatcroft were neither incidental nor minor, but endemic and structural, that the postponement of the general election which was due to be held in 1916 was symptomatic of same; and that the 1918 general election served as a democratic validation of the revolutionary act. Barry Andrews TD, writing to the *Irish Times*, referred to the undemocratic origins of the Act of Union itself, 'which was imposed and maintained against the will of the Irish people throughout the nineteenth century'.[143] On the same theme, and writing in the same paper, another correspondent listed some of the flaws that vitiated contemporary British democracy (including religious discrimination, a highly restricted franchise and an incomplete separation of the powers), as well as rejecting the suggestion that Pearse (and the other leaders), by their failure to stand for parliament, had forfeited the right to claim a mandate for independence: 'Quite simply, the parliament at Westminster was precisely the reason that the insurgents were fighting in the first place.'[144] Garret FitzGerald, for his part, noted simply that 'there is much hindsight in what passes for today's conventional wisdom that condemns 1916 as "undemocratic."'[145]

Probably the most adroit contribution came from Stephen Collins, political editor of the *Irish Times* and a distinguished historian in his own right. Noting that the leaders of the Rising were bound to adopt conspiratorial methods, they had, he argued, clearly 'defied democratic norms', not just simply in their repudiation of Redmond, but of MacNeill also. Referring to the home rule crisis, however, he argued that 'it was the failure of politics to deliver the democratic will of the majority of Irish people that created the opportunity for the Rising' in the first instance. In any event, he argued that, contrary to the perception that the forces of constitutional nationalism had been eclipsed by 1916, the tradition of O'Connell, Parnell and Redmond had reasserted itself after independence and became the dominant force in the culture of the state.[146]

MORALITY

In contrast to the two-handed rhetorical battlegrounds discussed above, the issue of the general morality of the Rising was a three-cornered contest. There were, as before, those who argued the toss for and against the Rising; but on this occasion there was a third viewpoint, one that argued that the Rising, as a historical event like any other, was not amenable to moral evaluation. The most cogent exposition of this view came from Minister Michael McDowell. He argued, in his customary trenchant manner, that the employment of a moral rhetoric when passing judgement on those involved in the Rising was fundamentally unsound. In his words:

> To say 'Redmond was wrong' and 'Pearse was right' or to claim that history vindicated one and condemned the other is meaningless twaddle. In a complex situation, the motives, values, and perspectives of the actors rarely fit into such childlike moral categories. I prefer to think that the motives and standards of nearly all the main actors were admirable.[147]

Most contributors, however, while they accepted the innate difficulty of employing modern standards to judge past events, accepted the inevitability of doing so in the absence of any viable alternative.

One of the few analyses that explicitly incorporated an assessment of the moral dimensions of Easter Week was provided by Dan O'Brien of the Intelligence Unit of the *Economist* magazine. Writing in the *Irish Times* he applied (in a necessarily brief discussion) what he saw as the two decisive tests of just war theory – proportionality and last resort – and found that the Rising fell down on both counts. He noted that the application of such theories to state formation in other countries was problematic rather than politically significant, but that 'because Ireland's revolutionary ghosts have been uniquely active, the issue has remained live [here]'.[148] An alternative view was provided by Mr Stephen Harrington of Allihies, Co. Cork who, writing in the *Examiner*, suggested that the public's willingness to consider the moral foundations upon which the state was formed indicated a superior civic sense of purpose compared to, for example, the United States, where such national soul searching was conspicuous by its absence.[149]

Two contributions sum up the position of those who expressed doubts about the moral underpinnings of actions undertaken during Easter week. The first came from Senator Brendan Ryan of the Labour party. In a series of rhetorical questions, he implicitly argued that the Rising, while it may have been heroic, was not morally justified:

> Were the conditions of the Irish people so appalling as to justify a resort to violence? Were we denied other routes to achieve our independence? Were we excluded from the media or from politics? Was discrimination against Catholics so deep-rooted and so widespread as to necessitate armed rebellion resulting in the death of large numbers of people?

In common with O'Brien he cautioned against applying retrospective wisdom to the event, on the basis that 'you don't need a degree in moral theology to realise that beneficial outcomes do not confer retrospective morality on an immoral action.'[150]

The second came from Breifne Walker, of the Holy Ghost Fathers in Dublin, who lamented what he saw as the tendency to view the civilian casualties of the Rising as being 'of little moment'. In his eyes both the original Rising itself, and its official commemoration, had 'provided endless legitimacy' for the 'sinister moral calculus' that judged such deaths 'to be of little moment'.[151]

One response to this line of analysis was given by Páraic MacBheatha of Navan, Co. Meath. He argued that, given the inchoate nature of the law of war in 1916, it 'was too ambiguous to either prohibit or permit armed insurrection'; but that the right to national self-determination was internationally recognised.[152] Picking up on this point, a contributor to the *Irish Independent* noted the irony of critics of the Rising having 'no problem in accepting the legitimacy of the Belgian people, with foreign support, resisting by force the German occupiers of their country; but at the same time ... [rejecting] the right of the Irish people to do the same thing'.[153] Finally Barry Andrews noted that the deaths of combatants on both sides 'was a consequence of a quest for national self-determination' – although, it should be noted, such a defence was of limited relevance in the case of civilian casualties.[154]

The most moving contribution to this aspect of the wider debate – indeed, in the view of this author, the single most moving piece of writing to emerge during the entire commemoration – came from a rather surprising source. Rhonda Paisely, daughter of Ian, wrote in plaintive terms, in Cork's *Evening Echo* on the Wednesday prior to the parade, of the immorality of *all* war. While expressing support for the preservation of the GPO, and hostility to both monarchy and partition, she equally clearly expressed her resentment 'that by bloody conflict and through death, destruction and terror I am supposed to submit to those who want to achieve an all-Ireland Republic'. Easter 1916, to her, was 'the woman standing forlorn in the street in Omagh, clothes rent'. 'How dreadful,' she wrote, 'that the sacrifice of the permanent on the altar of the immediate is the ongoing theme of our island's history.'

It was a most dignified conclusion.

CONCLUSION

The rows anticipated – nay, started – by President Mary McAleese continued well into the year. They will, no doubt, flare up again sooner rather than later – not least, of course, because it is in the interest of journalists and historians that they should do so. But what, if any, are the lessons to be drawn from this extended national 'think-in'? At the height of the commemoration debate Martin Mansergh laid down a marker on this point that bears consideration: 'The ninetieth commemoration [of the Rising] sets about the long overdue task of separating out what is valuable, noble and enduring in the Irish republican tradition, and what can by any international standard be regarded as legitimate.'[155] Based on the foregoing discussion it is abundantly clear that, as far as the overwhelming majority of the public were concerned, the 'valuable, noble and enduring' elements of that historic tradition were widely, and passionately, cherished, the rhetorical assaults it had endured for over three decades notwithstanding.

The post-revisionists had indeed won the argument, as Diarmuid Ferriter concluded.[156] That victory was not based, as some would claim, on a triumph of sentiment over reason, but on the triumph of one form of reasoned sentiment over another. It was the revisionists who were found to be guilty of living in the past – the same intellectual crime that had, of course, formed part of their indictment of unreconstructed nationalist historiography. It was they who were shown to be incapable of moving with the times. And it was they who were forced to rely on stale arguments that fell on increasingly unreceptive ears.

They faced a superior enemy on the battlefield of public opinion, and lost without much of a fight.

Few mourned their defeat.

NOTES

Preface:

1   This point is more fully developed in chapter 2, 'Irish independence: rationale and timing', of my book, *Reflections on the Irish state*, IAP, Dublin, 2003.

2   Ó Broin, Leon, *Revolutionary underground: the story of the Irish Republican Brotherhood 1858–1924*, Gill & Macmillan, Dublin, 1976, pp. 165–66.

3   FitzGerald, Garret (ed.), *Desmond's Rising: memoirs 1913 to Easter 1916*, Liberties, Dublin, 2006, p. 143.

4   McGee, Owen, *The IRB: the Irish Republican Brotherhood, from the Land League to Sinn Féin*, Four Courts, Dublin, 2005, p. 356.

5   *Irish Times*, 4 December 1981.

6   Keogh, Dermot, *Twentieth century Ireland: nation and state*, Gill & Macmillan, Dublin, 1994, p. 289.

7   *Irish Times*, 8 April 1966.

Introduction:

1   Useful commentaries on the phenomenon are contained in Bort, Eberhard, 'Commemorating Ireland: towards an inclusive culture of commemoration? An introduction' in Bort, Eberhard (ed.), *Commemorating Ireland: history, politics, culture*, IAP, Dublin, 2004, pp. 1–11; and MacBride, Ian, 'Introduction: memory and national identity in modern Ireland' in MacBride, Ian (ed.), *History and memory in modern Ireland*, CUP, Cambridge, 2001, pp. 1–42. See also Walker, Brian, *Dancing to history's tune: history, myth and politics in Ireland*, IIS, Belfast, 1996; and Dolan, Anne, *Commemorating the Irish civil war: history and memory, 1923–2000*, CUP, Cambridge, 2003.

2   See, for example, Póirtéir, Cathal (ed.), *The Great Irish famine*, Mercier, Cork, 1995; Crawford, E. Margaret (ed.), *The hungry stream: essays on famine and emigration*, IIS, Belfast, 1997; Gribben, Arthur (ed.), *The great famine and the Irish diaspora in America*, UMP, Amherst, 1999; Brown, Michael, Geoghegan, Patrick M., and Kelly, James (eds), *The Irish Act of Union: bicentennial essays*, IAP, Dublin, 2003. The monumental work *1798: a bicentennial celebration*, published by Four Courts, Dublin in 2003 and edited by Thomas Bartlett, David Dickson, Dáire Keogh and Kevin Whelan, stands in a class of its own in this regard.

3   These include Martin, F.X. (ed), *Leaders and men of the Easter Rising: Dublin 1916*, Methuen, London, 1967; Martin, F.X. (ed.), *The Easter Rising, 1916, and University College Dublin*, Browne and Nolan, Dublin 1967;

Dudley Edwards, Owen and Pyle, Fergus (eds), *1916: the Easter Rising*, MacGibbon and Kee, London, 1968; Nowlan, K.B. (ed.), *The making of 1916: studies in the history of the Rising*, Stationery Office, Dublin, 1969; and Ní Dhonnchadha, Máirín and Dorgan, Theo (eds), *Revising the Rising*, Field Day, Derry, 1991.

Europe and the Irish crisis, 1900–17:

1   Keogh, Dermot, *Ireland and Europe, 1919–1948*, Gill & Macmillan, Dublin, 1988, p. 2.

2   Joseph Lee in O'Driscoll, Mervyn, *Ireland, Germany and the Nazis; politics and diplomacy, 1919–1939*, Four Courts, Dublin, 2004, comment on back cover.

3   Murphy, John A., *The French are in the bay: the expedition to Bantry Bay 1796*, Mercier, Cork, 1997.

4   Service historique de l'armée de terre, Vincennes; attachés militaires, 7N1231, chemise 3, report of 27 October 1902. See also Campbell, Christy, *Fenian fire; the British government plot to assassinate Queen Victoria*, HarperCollins, London, 2002, which illustrates Russian interest in Ireland.

5   Milza, Pierre, *Les relations internationales de 1871 à 1914*, Armand Colin, Paris, 2003, pp. 117–24.

6   Herwig, Holger H., *The First World War: Germany and Austria-Hungary, 1914–1918*, Arnold, London, 1997, pp. 46–49.

7   *Ibid.*, pp. 104–5.

8   Geheimes Staatsarchiv, Preußischer Kulturbesitz, Berlin; Hauptabteilung VI, Nachlasse Schiemann, nr 62, Freeman to Schiemann, 10 May 1906.

9   *Ibid.*, Freeman to Schiemann, 31 May 1907 and 9 July 1907.

10 Prill, Felician, *Ireland, Britain and Germany 1870–1914: problems of nationalism and religion in nineteenth century Europe*, Gill & Macmillan, Dublin, 1975, pp. 111–12, 174, endnote 24.

11 Hünseler, Wolgang, *Das Deutsche Kaiserreich und die Irische Frage, 1900–1914*, Peter Lang, Frankfurt, p. 87 and footnote 40.

12 Auswärtiges Amt, Politisches Archiv, Berlin; England no 80, R5866, secret report from Mensdorff to Aehrenthal, 17 November 1908.

13 *Ibid.*, England no 80, 5R866, Freeman to Schiemann, 31 October 1909.

14 Geheimes Staatsarchiv, Preußischer Kulturbesitz, Berlin; Hauptabteilung VI, Nachlasse Schiemann, nr 62, Freeman to Schiemann, 20 July 1915.

15 Stewart, A.T.Q., *The Ulster crisis: resistance to home rule, 1912–1914*, Blackstaff, Belfast, 1997, p. 158.

16 Unfortunately, the old ledgers of the Steyr factory in upper Austria reveal nothing more about the export of the 10,900 Mannlicher and 9,100 Mauser rifles for the UVF. One of the ledgers mentions Benny Spiro's name. Spiro was a German arms dealer who sold the rifles to Major Frederick Crawford of the UVF. The author is grateful to Professor Rudolf Agstner of the Ministry of Foreign Affairs in Vienna for this information.

17   Haus-, Hof- und Staatsarchiv, Politisches Archiv, Vienna; Abteilung VIII, England, box 151, report 18C, 24 April 1914, folio 168–9, 'Aufzeichnungen Baron Franckensteins über Home Rule-Frage', missing.

18   Pethö, Albert, *Agenten für den Doppeladler; Österreich-Ungarns Geheimer Dienst im Weltkrieg*, Leopold Stocker Verlag, Graz, 1998, p. 323.

19   Franckenstein, *Sir George, Facts and features of my life*, Cassells, London, 1939, pp. 127, 131 and 144–45.

20   Stewart, *The Ulster crisis*, pp. 228–29.

21   *Ibid.*, p. 226.

22   Ministère des Affaires Étrangères Belge, Brussels; microfilm P175, correspondance politique: légations, Allemagne, Henri Beyens to Jacques Davignon (Minister of Foreign Affairs), 26 July 1914.

23   Hünseler, Das *Deutsche Kaiserreich und die Irische Frage*, 1900–1914, p. 256.

24   Rauchensteiner, Manfried, *Der Tod des Doppeladlers: Österreich–Ungarn und der Erste Weltkrieg*, Verlag Styria, Graz, 1993, p. 91.

25   Morton, Frederic, *Thunder at twilight; Vienna 1913–1914*, Methuen, London, 2001, p. 306.

26   'Die Österreich-Ungarischen Dokumente zum Kriegsausbruch', Ladislaus Szögyéni to Leopold Berchtold, 12 July 1914, in http://www.lib.byu.edu/~rdh/wwi/1914/austdocs (consulted on 29 June 2002).

27   Brock, Michael and Eleanor (eds), *H.H. Asquith: letters to Venetia Stanley*, OUP, Oxford, 1985, pp. 135–37 and footnote 2.

28   Feldmarschall Conrad, *Aus meiner Dienstzeit, 1906–1918*, Rikola Verlag, Vienna, 1923, vol. iv, p. 172.

29   Hünseler, *Das Deutsche Kaiserreich und die Irische Frage*, 1900–1914, pp. 262–63 and footnote 151.

30   'Die Osterreichisch-Ungarischen zum Kriegsausbruch' Mensdorff to Berchtold 3 August 1914, in http://www.lib.byu.edu/~rdh/wwi/1914/austdocs (consulted on 29 June 2002)

31   Mitchell, Angus, *Casement*, Haus, London, 2003, p. 50.

32   Auswärtiges Amt, Politisches Archiv, Berlin; England no 80, R5869, Bernstorff to Auswärtiges Amt (Ministry of Foreign Affairs), 26 September 1914.

33   Andrew, Christopher, *Secret service; the making of the British intelligence community*, Heinemann, London, 1985, pp. 87, 90–91.

34   Hans-Dieter Kluge, *Irland in der Deutschen Geschichtswissenschaft: Politik und Propaganda vor 1914 und im Ersten Weltkrieg*, Peter Lang, Frankfurt, 1985, p. 180.

35   Wolf, Karin, *Sir Roger Casement und die Deutsch–Irischen Beziehungen*, Duncker, Berlin, 1972, p. 80, footnote 53.

36   Roth, Andreas, '"The German soldier is not tactful": Sir Roger Casement and the Irish brigade in Germany during the First World War' in *The Irish Sword*, vol. xix, no. 78, 1995, p. 318.

37   Wolf, *Sir Roger Casement und die Deutsch–Irischen Beziehungen*, p. 35.

38   Mitchell, *Casement*, pp. 105–6.

39   Kluge, *Irland in der Deutschen Geschichtswissenschaft*, p. 110.

40   *Ibid.*, p. 118.

41 Bundesarchiv-Militärarchiv, Freiburg; Admiral Karl von Truppel papers, N224/13, report of 23 August 1914.

42 Foy, Michael and Barton, Brian, *The Easter Rising*, Sutton, Stroud, 2004, pp. 15, 19–20.

43 Auswärtiges Amt, Politisches Archiv, Berlin; WK nr 11K, Bd. 9, R21161–1 (microfilm), Rudolf Nadolny to Auswärtiges Amt, containing Casement/Plunkett report, 8 June 1915.

44 Doerries, Reinhard (ed.), *Prelude to the Easter Rising: Sir Roger Casement in imperial Germany* Frank Cass, London, 2000, pp. 14–15.

45 Kluge, *Irland in der Deutschen Geschichtswissenschaft*, p. 139.

46 Auswärtiges Amt, Politisches Archiv, Berlin; IA Weltkrieg, WK 11k, Bd. 11, R21163–1 (microfilm), Bernstorff to Auswärtiges Amt, containing Devoy's report, 16 February 1916.

47 Herwig, *The First World War: Germany and Austria-Hungary, 1914–1918*, pp. 180–83.

48 *Ibid.*, pp. 286–88.

49 Spindler, Captain Karl, *The mystery of the Casement ship*, Anvil, Tralee, 1965, pp. 197–98.

50 Herwig, *The First World War; Germany and Austria-Hungary, 1914–1918*, pp. 263–64.

51 Spindler, *The mystery of the Casement ship*, pp. 33–48, 188–89 and 200–1.

52 Doerries (ed.), *Prelude to the Easter Rising*, p. 21.

53 Holmes, Richard, *The little field marshal: a life of Sir John French*, Weidenfeld and Nicolson, London, 2004, pp. 322–23.

54 aan de Wiel, Jérôme, *The Catholic church in Ireland, 1914–1918: war and politics*, IAP, Dublin, 2003, pp. 219–20.

55 *Ibid.*, p. 85.

56 *Ibid.*, pp. 79–87. See also aan de Wiel, Jérôme, 'Easter Rising 1916: Count Plunkett's letter to Pope Benedict XV' in *The Irish Sword*, vol. xxiv, no. 96, winter 2004, pp. 219–32, for the entire letter in French with a translation in English and a commentary.

57 Spindler, *The mystery of the Casement ship*, p. 86.

58 Andrew, *Secret service*, p. 204.

59 O'Halpin, Eunan, 'British intelligence in Ireland, 1914–1921' in Andrew, Christopher and Dilks, David (eds), *The missing dimension: governments and intelligence communities in the twentieth century*, Macmillan, London, 1984, p. 59.

60 Bourne, J.M. *Who's who in World War One*, Routledge, London, 2001, p.99.

61 O'Halpin, *British intelligence in Ireland*, 1914–1921, pp. 57–8.

62 Mitchell, *Casement*, pp. 112–13.

63 Andrew, *Secret service*, p. 247.

64 Herwig, *The First World War: Germany and Austria-Hungary, 1914–1918*, pp. 287–88.

65 Fitzpatrick, David, *The two Irelands, 1912–1939*, OUP, Oxford, 1998, p. 61.

66 Holmes, *The little field marshal*, p. 325.

67 Service historique de l'armée de terre, Vincennes; attachés militaires, 7N1253,

report of de la Panouse, 25 April 1916 and undated report (probably end April 1916).

68   *Ibid.*, grand quartier général, 16N2968, de la Panouse to Joffre, 19 June 1916.

69   Herwig, *The First World War: Germany and Austria-Hungary, 1914–1918*, pp. 230–31, 274 and 277–78.

70   Reichspost, 29 April 1916, ANNO (AustriaN Newspapers Online), Österreichische Nationalbibliothek, Vienna, http://anno.onb.ac.at.

71   *Pester Lloyd*, 5 May 1916, ANNO.

72   Auswärtiges Amt, Politisches Archiv, Berlin; WK nr 11K, Bd. 11, R21163–3 (microfilm), Freyer to Nicolai, reports of 28 and 29 April, and 2, 5 and 7 May 1916.

73   Service historique de l'armée de terre, Vincennes; Grand Quartier Général, 16N2968, fiche no 523, containing report of 29 April 1916.

74   Kluge, *Irland in der Deutschen Geschichtswissenschaft*, pp. 156–57 and 369, footnote 178.

75   Bundesarchiv-Militärarchiv, Freiburg; Admiralstab der Marine 1899–1919, RM5/4757 (microfilm), reports of 9 and 23 December 1916 and 25 January 1917.

76   Kluge, *Irland in der Deutschen Geschichtswissenschaft*, p. 269.

77   Herwig, *The First World War: Germany and Austria-Hungary, 1914–1918*, pp. 315–16.

78   Kluge, *Irland in der Deutschen Geschichtswissenschaft*, p. 160.

79   O'Brien, William and Ryan, Desmond (eds), *Devoy's postbag, 1880–1928*, IAP edition, Dublin, 1979, vol. ii, pp. 512–13.

80   Bundesarchiv-Militärarchiv, Freiburg; Admiralstab der Marine 1899–1919, RM5/4557 (microfilm), Bernstorff to Auswärtiges Amt, 17 January 1917, containing report of Irish revolutionary directory of America, 8 January 1917.

81   CO 904/186, reports of 13 March 1917, containing statement of Irish under secretary (17 February 1917) and under secretary to chief secretary (17 February 1917) and Green to under secretary, 22 February 1917 (containing list), National Archives, Kew.

82   Murphy, Brian P., *Patrick Pearse and the lost republican ideal*, James Duffy, Dublin, 1991, pp. 80–81.

83   O'Halpin, 'British Intelligence in Ireland, 1914–1921', p. 60.

84   CO 904/186, William Patrick Byrne to chief secretary, 17 February 1917 and 'Question and answer in the House of Commons on 21st of March' and Mahon to chief secretary, 18 February 1917, National Archives, Kew.

85   Tuchman, Barbara, *The Zimmermann telegram: how the USA entered the Great War*, Papermac, London, 1988, pp. 155–57.

The Ulster crisis: prelude to 1916?:

1   Tierney, Michael, *Eoin MacNeill: scholar and man of action, 1867–1945*, Clarendon, Oxford, 1980, pp. 108–9.

2   *Ibid.*, pp. 118–19.

3   Jalland, Patricia, *The Liberals and Ireland: the Ulster question in British poli-*

tics to 1914, Harvester, Brighton, 1980, p. 123.

4   *Ibid.*, pp. 63–4; Asquith, H.H., *Home Rule from the Treasury bench: speeches during the first and second reading debates*, Unwin, London, 1912, p. 15.

5   *Ibid.*, pp. 29–30.

6   *Ibid.*, pp. 51–52.

7   For a convenient summary of the bill see Mansergh, Nicholas, *The unresolved question: the Anglo-Irish settlement and its undoing, 1912–72*, YUP, New Haven, 1991, pp. 51–52.

8   Lucy, G., *The great convention: the Ulster Unionist Convention of 1892*, Ulster society, Lurgan, 1995, pp. 79–81.

9   *Ibid.*, p. 105.

10   Jackson, Alvin, 'Unionists and the Empire, 1880–1920' in Jeffery, Keith (ed.), *An Irish empire? Aspects of Ireland in the British empire*, MUP, Manchester, 1996, pp. 132–38.

11   Buckland, Patrick, (ed.), *Irish unionism, 1885–1923: a documentary history*, PRONI, Belfast, 1973, pp. 204–5.

12   Bowman, Tim, 'The Ulster Volunteer Force, 1910–1920: new perspectives', in Boyce, D.G. and O'Day, Alan (eds), *The Ulster crisis 1885–1921*, Palgrave, London, 2005, pp. 247–58, at p. 249. The UVF's peak strength was 110,000 members by July 1914 (*Ibid.*, p. 247).

13   Ring, Jim, *Erskine Childers*, John Murray, London, 1996, p. 59.

14   Boyce, D.G., *Nationalism in Ireland*, Third edition, Routledge, London, 1995, pp. 268, 272.

15   Adams, R.J.Q., *Bonar Law*, SUP, London, 1999, p. 113.

16   Bew, Paul, 'The Ulster crisis: some ideological questions revisited' in Wichert, Sabine (ed.), *From the United Irishmen to twentieth century unionism: a festchrift for A.T.Q. Stewart*, Four Courts, Dublin, 2004, pp. 159–74, at p. 168.

17   Megahey, A.J., *The Irish Protestant churches in the twentieth century*, Palgrave, London, 2000, pp. 105–10.

18   Boyce, *Nationalism in Ireland*, pp. 273–74.

19   Bardon, Jonathan, *A history of Ulster*, Blackstaff, Belfast, 1992, p. 437.

20   Megahey, *Irish Protestant churches*, pp. 24–26.

21   *Ibid.*, p. 30.

22   Lord Milner to Lord Selborne, 18 February 1914, in Boyce, D.G. (ed.), *The crisis of British unionism: the second Earl of Selborne's political papers, 1885–1922*, Historians' press, London, 1987, pp. 102–4.

23   Boyce, D.G., 'Moral force unionism: A.V. Dicey and Ireland, 1885–1922' in Wichert, *From the United Irishmen to twentieth century unionism*, pp. 97–110, at p. 105.

24   Bowman, 'The Ulster Volunteer Force', p. 249.

25   Buckland, *Irish unionism*, p. 261. See also the circular memorandum on the 'Prevention of Arrest of Leaders', 14 May 1914, issued by UVF headquarters, *Ibid.*, pp. 259–60.

26   Lord Selborne to Lord Grey, 3 April 1914, in Boyce (ed.), *Crisis of British unionism*, pp. 105–7.

27   Adams, *Bonar Law*, pp. 107–8.

28   *Ibid.*, p. 154.

29   Beckett, Ian F.W. (ed.), *The army and the Curragh incident, 1914*, Army records society, London, 1986, p. 57.

30   *Ibid.*, pp. 254–55.

31   *Ibid.*, pp. 120–23.

32   *Ibid.*, pp. 246–54.

33   *Ibid.*, p. 21.

34   Adams, *Bonar Law*, p. 106.

35   *Ibid.*, pp. 147–51.

36   Stewart, A.T.Q., 'Craig and the UVF', in Martin, F.X. (ed.), *Leaders and men of the Easter Rising: Dublin 1916*, Methuen, London, 1967, pp. 67–80, at p. 77.

37   Mansergh, *The unresolved question*, pp. 75–76.

38   *Ibid.*, p. 84. Boyce, *Nineteenth century Ireland: the search for stability, second edition*, Gill & Macmillan, Dublin, 2005, pp. 282–83.

39   House of Commons debates, vol. cxvi, cols. 882–93, 15 September 1914.

40   Jeffery, Keith, *Ireland and the Great War*, CUP, Cambridge, 2000, p. 15.

41   *Ibid.*, p. 12.

42   Buckland, *Irish unionism*, pp. 261–63.

43   Boyce, D.G., *Englishmen and Irish troubles: British public opinion and the making of Irish policy, 1918–22*, Gregg Revivals, Aldershot, 1994, p. 107.

44   Laffan, Michael, *The resurrection of Ireland: the Sinn Féin party, 1916–1923*, CUP, Cambridge, 1999, p. 7.

45   Bew, Paul, *Ideology and the Irish question: Ulster unionism and Irish nationalism*, 1912–16, OUP, Oxford, 1994, pp. 110–11.

46   Smith. Jeremy, *The Tories and Ireland, 1910–14: Conservative party politics and the home rule crisis*, IAP, Dublin, 2000, p. 201.

47   Laffan, *Resurrection of Ireland*, p. 8.

48   *Ibid.*, p. 15.

49   Novick, Ben, 'The arming of Ireland: gun-running and the Great War, 1914–16', in Gregory, Adrian and Paseta, Senia (eds), *Ireland and the Great War: 'a war to unite us all?'*, MUP, Manchester, 2002, pp. 94–112, at p. 95.

50   Wheatley, Michael, 'Ireland is out for blood and murder: nationalist opinion and the Ulster crisis in provincial Ireland, 1913–14', in Boyce and O'Day, *The Ulster crisis*, pp. 182–201, at pp. 200–1.

51   Novick, 'Arming of Ireland', p. 108.

52   Lord Grey to Gilbert Murray, 21 September 1920, Gilbert Murray MSS, GM 21, Bodleian Library Oxford.

'Irreconcilable enemies' or 'flesh and blood'?
The Irish party and the Easter rebels, 1914–16:

1   Redmond's cabled statement to the New York paper Ireland, reported in the *Western Nationalist*, 20 May 1916.

2   *Longford Leader*, 19 August 1916.

3   Fitzgibbon speaking to the Castlerea Guardians, as reported in the *Westmeath Independent*, 11 November 1916. Fitzgibbon had also been a strong advocate of recruiting to the British army and had already lost one son

killed in the war, at Gallipoli. A second son would be killed in 1918.

4   Notably by F.S.L. Lyons in *John Dillon: a biography*, Routledge and Kegan Paul, London 1968, pp. 372–83.

5   Wheatley, Michael, *Nationalism and the Irish party: provincial Ireland 1910–1916*, OUP, Oxford 2005.

6   The newspapers studied were as follows: nationalist and pro-party: *Longford Leader, Roscommon Messenger, Sligo Champion, Sligo Nationalist, Strokestown Democrat, Western Nationalist, Westmeath Examiner* and *Westmeath Independent*; nationalist and anti-party: *Leitrim Observer, Midland Reporter, Roscommon Herald* and *Roscommon Journal*; unionist: *Sligo Independent* and *Westmeath Guardian; independent: Leitrim Advertiser* and *Longford Independent.*

7   *Roscommon Journal, Sligo Nationalist, Western Nationalist, Westmeath Examiner*, 29 April 1916.

8   *Westmeath Independent*, 6 May 1916.

9   *Ibid.*, 29 April 1916.

10 *Roscommon Messenger, Sligo Nationalist, Western Nationalist, Westmeath Independent*, 6 May 1916.

11 Redmond's manifesto of 3 May, reported in the *Westmeath Independent*, 6 May 1916.

12 Redmond's statement to the New York paper Ireland, as reported in the *Western Nationalist*, 20 May 1916.

13 Lee, J.J., *Ireland 1912–1985: politics and society*, CUP, Cambridge 1989, p. 21.

14 Hayden speaking to the Mullingar UIL, 21 May 1916, reported in the *Westmeath Examiner*, 27 May 1916.

15 Farrell speaking to the executive of the south Longford UIL, 19 November 1916, reported in the *Longford Leader*, 25 November 1916.

16 Kelly, M.J., *The fenian ideal and Irish nationalism, 1882–1916*, Boydell, Woodbridge, 2006, p. 234.

17 *National Volunteer*, 24 October 1914.

18 *Ibid.*, 17 October 1914. The author of the article under this first set of headlines was Tom Kettle.

19 *Ibid.*, 7 November 1914.

20 Redmond, speaking to the *New York World* from his country home Aughavanagh, as reported in the *Westmeath Independent*, 7 August 1915.

21 *Roscommon Messenger*, 25 December; *Western Nationalist*, 18 December 1915, 25 March 1916.

22 *Sligo Champion*, 15 April 1916. Bradshaw later went on to acquire the *Sligo Nationalist* newspaper, rename it the *Connachtman*, embrace Sinn Féin, become intelligence officer for the Sligo Brigade of the IRA and, during the Civil War, an ardent anti-Treatyite. For details of Bradshaw's later career, see Farry, Michael, *The aftermath of revolution: Sligo 1921–3*, UCDP, Dublin, 2000.

23 Lyons, John Dillon, p. 382.

24 *Western Nationalist*, 24 July 1915.

25 *Roscommon Herald; Westmeath Examiner*, 4, 11 September; *Westmeath Independent*, 2, 9, 16 October; *Midland Reporter*, 4, 11 November, 2 December 1915.

26   *Roscommon Herald*, 13 November 1915; Mac Giolla Choille, Breandán, Intelligence notes 1913–16, Stationery Office, Dublin, 1966, p. 154; *Western Nationalist*, 4 December 1915.

27   *Western Nationalist*, 12 February 1916.

28   See Farry, Michael, *Sligo, 1914–1921: a chronicle of conflict*, Killoran, Trim 1992, p. 57. Reverend O'Grady was president of the Keash UIL branch and later went on to become president of the Keash Sinn Féin club.

29   *Sligo Champion*, 4 December 1915.

30   *Leitrim Observer*, 22 January 1916; *Longford Leader*, 20 November 1915.

31   See also Wheatley, *Nationalism and the Irish party*, pp. 244–47.

32   Monthly report of the RIC inspector general, March 1916, CO 904/99, National Archives, Kew; *Westmeath Independent*, 25 March 1916.

33   For the *Westmeath Independent* the Tullamore affair was local news – King's was a neighbouring county and the paper carried extensive coverage of King's County news.

34   *Midland Reporter*, 6 April; *Westmeath Independent*, 25 March 1916. The ten men still in custody were finally sent to Dublin after the Rising and tried by a court martial. The court martial convicted them of a lesser charge and immediately released them given the length of time they had already been in custody. The *Westmeath Independent* on 24 June praised the court's wisdom.

35   *Longford Leader*, 1 January 1916.

36   *Westmeath Independent*, 5 June 1915.

37   See Wheatley, *Nationalism and the Irish party*, pp. 238–42.

38   *Western Nationalist*, 1 January 1916.

39   *Roscommon Herald*, 1 January 1916.

40   *Westmeath Independent*, 29 April 1916.

41   *Ibid.*, 6 May 1916. De Wet, the leader of the South African rebellion in 1914-15, got a six-year jail sentence (he served less than twelve months) and a £2,000 fine. There was only one execution. 118 prisoners were amnestied within six months.

42   *Sligo Champion*, 6 May 1916.

43   Monthly report of the RIC inspector general, May 1916, CO 904/99, National Archives, Kew.

44   *Roscommon Messenger*, 29 April 1916.

45   *Ibid.*, 13 May; *Roscommon Journal*, 13 May 1916.

46   *Longford Leader*, 20 May 1916.

47   *Ibid.*, 13, 20 May 1916.

48   Mac Giolla Choille, *Intelligence notes*, p. 241.

49   Farrell addressing Longford County Council on 17 May (*Longford Leader*, 20 May); *Sligo Champion*, 27 May; *Sligo Nationalist*, 13 May; *Westmeath Independent*, 13 May 1916.

50   *Westmeath Independent*, 13 May 1916.

51   Lyons, *John Dillon*, pp. 380–83.

52   Jasper Tully addressing Roscommon County Council, 16 May, as reported in the *Westmeath Independent*, 20 May 1916.

53   *Sligo Champion*, 20 May 1916. The paper also stated that Dillon's speech was six days too late.

54 *Western Nationalist*, 10 June 1916.

55 Monthly report of the RIC inspector general, June 1916, CO 904/100, National Archives, Kew.

56 *Ibid.*, August 1916, CO 904/100.

57 *Sligo Champion, Sligo Independent*, 10 June 1916.

58 Keaveny addressing the Knockcroghery, Roscommon UIL branch on 18 June, as reported in the *Western Nationalist*, 1 July 1916; Fitzgibbon addressing the Castlerea Guardians on 13 May and Roscommon County council on 16 May, as reported in the *Westmeath Independent*, 20 May 1916.

59 *Sligo Champion*, 5 August 1916.

60 See *Leitrim Advertiser*, 11 May; *Longford Leader*, 20 May; *Strokestown Democrat*, 13 May 1916.

61 *Westmeath Independent*, 13 May; *Sligo Nationalist, Western Nationalist*, 20 May 1916. *The Westmeath Independent* referred to 'Captain Edward Daly'.

62 See *Sligo Champion*, 27 May, 3 June; *Sligo Nationalist*, 1, 8 and 15 July; *Strokestown Democrat*, 3 June; *Western Nationalist*, 3 June; *Westmeath Examiner*, 10 June; *Westmeath Independent*, 3 June.

63 *Longford Leader*, 5 August 1916.

64 Redmond speaking in Waterford on 6 October, as reported in the *Westmeath Independent*, 14 October, and in Sligo on 29 October, as reported in the *Sligo Champion*, 4 November 1916.

65 Irish party manifesto reported in the *Sligo Champion*, 13 May; leading article in the *Longford Leader*, 13 May 1916.

66 See *Westmeath Examiner*, 27 May, 24 June, 5 August, 1, 30 September, 21, 28 October, 11 November; *Roscommon Messenger*, 11 November 1916.

67 *Longford Leader*, 28 August 1916.

68 *Westmeath Independent*, 20 May 1916.

69 *Sligo Nationalist; Longford Leader*, 12 August 1916.

70 Monthly report of the RIC inspector general, September 1916, CO 904/101, National Archives, Kew.

71 *Westmeath Independent*, 3 June 1916.

72 *Westmeath Examiner*, 22, 29 July; *Sligo Champion*, 28 October 1916.

73 *Longford Leader*, 12 August; *Western Nationalist*, 29 July 1916.

74 *Longford Leader, Roscommon Messenger, Western Nationalist, Westmeath Examiner*, 5 August 1916.

75 *Westmeath Independent*, 9 September 1916.

76 Monthly report of the Leitrim county inspector, August 1916, CO 904/100, National Archives, Kew.

77 Redmond speaking at Waterford on 6 October, as reported in the *Westmeath Independent*, 14 October 1916.

78 *Ibid.*

79 *Sligo Champion*, 6 May 1916.

The First World War and the Rising: mode, moment and memory

1 Jeffery, Keith, *Ireland and the Great War*, CUP, Cambridge, 2000, p. 2.

2   For a more 'microcosmic' exploration of 1916, see my *The GPO and the Easter Rising*, IAP, Dublin, 2006, where I focus not just on the Rising but specifically on the Post Office itself.

3   Arthur Hamilton Norway (secretary to the Irish Post Office), quoted in *Ibid.*, p. 30.

4   See the discussion in Howard, Michael, *Clausewitz*, OUP, Oxford, 1983, chapter 3.

5   Black, Jeremy, *War and the world: military power and the fate of continents, 1450–2000*, YUP, New Haven, 1998, pp. 227–29.

6   The hymn was written for a 'Children's Festival' at Horbury Bridge, York-shire (where Baring-Gould was a curate) in 1864. Watson, Richard and Trickett, Kenneth (eds), *Companion to hymns and psalms*, Methodist publishing house, Peterborough, 1988, p. 407.

7   Springhall, John, *Youth, empire and society: British youth movements, 1883–1940*, Croom Helm, London, 1977.

8   See, for example, his chapter, 'Militarism in Ireland, 1900–1922' in Bartlett, Thomas and Jeffery, Keith (eds), *A military history of Ireland*, CUP, Cambridge, 1996, pp. 379–406.

9   Verhey, Jeffrey, *The spirit of 1914: militarism, myth and mobilisation in Germany*, CUP, Cambridge, 2000, is a salutary corrective to easy generalisations about war enthusiasm.

10 For a discussion of Irish recruitment, upon which I have drawn for this essay, see Jeffery, *Ireland and the Great War*, pp. 5–20.

11 Barry, Tom, *Guerrilla days in Ireland*, Anvil edition, Tralee, 1962, p. 8.

12 A phrase used by Philip Orr in his splendid *The road to the Somme: men of the Ulster division tell their story*, Blackstaff, Belfast, 1987, p. 38.

13 See *Workers' Republic*, 25 December 1915, quoted in Dudley Edwards, Ruth, *Patrick Pearse: the triumph of failure*, Faber edition, London, 1979, p. 245.

14 Jeffery, *Ireland and the Great War*, pp. 14–15.

15 Pearse to Joseph McGarrity, 19 October 1914, quoted in Dudley Edwards, *Patrick Pearse: the triumph of failure*, p. 357.

16 'Peace and the Gael', in Pearse, Patrick H., *Political writings and speeches*, Phoenix, Dublin, 1924, p. 216.

17 See Dudley Edwards, *Patrick Pearse: the triumph of failure*, p. 245.

18 From the *Irish Worker*, 8 August 1914, reprinted in Musgrove, P.J. (ed.), *Connolly, James: a socialist and war, 1914–1916*, Lawrence and Wishart, London, 1941, p. 36.

19 For those who welcomed the war (if, in most cases, only briefly), see Hynes, Samuel, *A war imagined: the First World War and English culture*, Bodley Head, London, 1990, part I.

20 Quoted in Foster, R.H. 'Irish Methodism and war' in McCrea, Alexander (ed.), *Irish Methodism in the twentieth century*, Irish Methodist Publishing Company, Belfast, 1931, p. 76.

21 *Church of Ireland Gazette*, 4 September 1914, quoted in McDowell, R.B., *The Church of Ireland 1869–1969*, Routledge and Kegan Paul, London, 1975, p. 106.

22 Report of diocesan council of Meath for 1914, p. 76.

23 *The Tablet*, 3 April 1915, quoted in aan de Wiel, Jérôme, *The Catholic Church in Ireland 1914–1918: war and politics*, IAP, Dublin, 2003, p. 16.

24 *Irish Catholic*, 25 September 1916, quoted in Privilege, John, 'Michael Logue, the Catholic church and public affairs in Ireland, 1879–1924', unpublished PhD thesis, University of Ulster, 2005, p. 174.

25 Redmond, John, Strong words from Mr Redmond, Joseph Causton, London, 1916, p. 3, quoted in Denman, Terence, *Ireland's unknown soldiers: the 16th (Irish) division in the Great War*, IAP, Dublin, 1992, p. 129.

26 'Anon' [Vivienne Smyly], 'Experiences of a VAD', in *Blackwoods Magazine*, no. 200, July–December 1916, p. 839.

27 Foster, R.F., *Modern Ireland, 1600–1972*, Penguin, London, 1988, p. 483.

28 *Dublin and the 'Sinn Féin Rising'*, Wilson Hartnell, Dublin, 1916.

29 These names have been extracted from Donnelly, Mary, *The last post: Glasnevin cemetery. Being a record of Ireland's heroic dead in Dublin city and county*, National Graves Association, Dublin, n.d. [1932], p. 26, and War Office, *Soldiers died in the Great War, 1914–19*, part 23, The Royal Irish Regiment, HMSO, London, 1921, pp. 19–20.

30 Denman, *Ireland's unknown soldiers*, p. 19.

31 This follows the argument advanced (at greater length) in my 2003–4 Parnell lecture, published as *Ireland and war in the twentieth century*, Magdalene College Cambridge occasional paper no. 33, Cambridge, 2006.

32 A good illustration of this can be found in the activities accompanying the bicentenary of the 1798 Rebellion. Some of the debates can be followed (from a distinct standpoint) in the stimulating work of the distinguished Cork historian, Tom Dunne, including his deservedly prize-winning, *Rebellions: memoir, memory and 1798*, Lilliput, Dublin, 2004.

33 Hill, Judith, *Irish public sculpture*, Four Courts, Dublin, 1998, pp. 71–72.

34 *Irish Builder*, 13 September 1919.

35 Martin, F.X.,'1916 – myth, fact and mystery', *Studia Hibernica*, vol. vii, 1967, p. 68.

36 For the UVF see Timothy Bowman's assessment that 'the UVF certainly did not transform itself en bloc into a division of Kitchener's army' in, 'The Ulster Volunteer Force and the formation of the 36th (Ulster) division', *Irish Historical Studies*, vol. xxxii, no. 128, November 2001, pp. 498–518, at p. 517. For the 'pets' remark see the entry in the diary of Sir Henry Wilson, 31 December 1915, quoted in Jeffery, Keith, *Field Marshal Sir Henry Wilson: a political soldier*, OUP, Oxford, 2006, p. 158. For the 16th (Irish) division generally, see the excellent survey in Denman, *Ireland's unknown soldiers*.

37 Messines ridge was chosen for the site of the 'Island of Ireland peace tower', the location of which is discussed in Jeffery, *Ireland and the Great War*, pp. 138–40.

38 A topic valuably, and thoughtfully, explored in Dolan, Anne, *Commemorating the Irish civil war: history and memory, 1923–2000*, CUP, Cambridge, 2003.

39 I have discussed Irish First World War memorials in *Ireland and the Great War*, chapter 4; and 'The Great War in modern Irish memory' in Fraser,

T.G. and Jeffery, Keith (eds), Men, women and war (Historical Studies XVIII), Lilliput, Dublin, 1993, pp. 136–57. Nationalist and republican memorials are additionally covered in Dolan, *Commemorating the Irish civil war*.

40 See Aalen, F.H.A., 'Homes for Irish heroes: housing under the Irish Land (Provision for Soldiers and Sailors) Act 1919, and the Irish Sailors' and Soldiers' Land Trust' in *Town Planning Review*, vol. lix, no. 3, 1988, pp 305–23; and Fraser, Murray, *John Bull's other homes: state housing and British policy in Ireland, 1883–1922*, LUP, Liverpool, 1996, chapter 7.

41 See Morris, Ewan, *'Our own devices': national symbols and political conflict in twentieth century Ireland*, IAP, Dublin, 2004, for an excellent exploration of the creation and use of 'national' symbols.

42 See Jeffery, *Ireland and the Great War*, pp. 132 (for a photograph of the unveiling of the Longford memorial) and 135.

43 *Cork Weekly Examiner*, 21 November 1925.

44 This starry-eyed attitude attracted some critical comment in reviews of the book. See those by Michael Hopkinson, in *Twentieth Century British History*, vol. xv, no. 2, 2004, p. 205, and Timothy Bowman in *War in History*, vol. xi, no. 3, 2004, pp. 369–71.

45 What Nugent said in August 1923 was: 'The day is not, I hope, far distant when the memory of all those of our country who gave their lives for civilisation as we interpret it and obedience to what they believed to be their duty will be honoured and perpetuated in every town and village in Ireland.' Nugent papers, D.3835/E/7/23, PRONI.

46 Faber, London, 2005.

47 In the discussion following the presentation of this paper in University College Cork on 27 January 2006.

48 Barry, *A long, long way*, p. 157.

49 *Ibid.*, p. 190.

50 Winter, Jay, *Sites of memory, sites of mourning: the Great War in European cultural history*, CUP, Cambridge, 1995.

51 Barry, *A long, long way*, p. 286.

52 *Irish Times*, 14 November 1998.

Who were the 'Fenian dead'?
The IRB and the background to the 1916 Rising

1 O'Hegarty, P.S., *The victory of Sinn Féin*, Talbot, Dublin, 1924, p. 8.

2 Jenkins, Brian, *Fenians and Anglo-American relations during reconstruction*, CUP, London, 1969; Ó Broin, Leon, *Fenian fever: an Anglo-American dilemma*, NYUP, New York, 1971; Quinlivan, Patrick and Rose, Paul, *The Fenians in England, 1865–72: a sense of insecurity*, Calder, London, 1982; Rafferty, O.P., *The church, the state and the Fenian threat, 1861–1875*, Basingstoke, Palgrave, 1999.

3 Campbell, Christy, *Fenian fire: the British government plot to assasinate Queen Victoria*, HarperCollins, London, 2002.

4 Owens, Gary, 'Popular mobilization and the rising of 1848: the clubs of

the Irish Confederation', in Geary, L.M. (ed.), *Rebellion and remembrance in modern Ireland*, Four Courts, Dublin, 2001, pp. 51–63.

5   For the history of the IRB at this time, see McGee, Owen, *The IRB: the Irish Republican Brotherhood, from the Land League to Sinn Féin*, Four Courts, Dublin, 2005.

6   O'Brien, C.C., *Parnell and his party*, OUP, Oxford, 1957, pp. 89–90, 128–30.

7   Ulster Presbyterians, such as J.B. Killen, Rev. Isaac Nelson and Louis Smyth, had been pro-republican leaders of the Land League, while IRB leaders of the 1860s and 1870s included Ulster Presbyterians such as Rev. David Bell and T.N. Underwood. The most well-known champions of republicanism in mid-nineteenth century Ireland, John Mitchel and John Martin, were both Ulster Presbyterians and passive supporters of the IRB.

8   Davitt, Michael, *The fall of feudalism in Ireland*, Harper, New York, 1904, pp. 377–78, 466–67.

9   Thornley, David, *Isaac Butt and home rule*, Macgibbon, London, 1964, pp. 175–77, 227–31, 241; McGee, IRB, pp. 63, 86–87.

10 Price, Roger, *The revolutions of 1848*, Macmillan, London, 1988, pp. 96–100; Taylor, A.J.P., *Revolutions and revolutionaries*, Hamilton, London, 1980, pp. 112–38; Thompson, Dorothy, *The Chartists*, Temple Smith, London, 1984, pp. 335–39.

11 Larkin, Emmet, *The Roman Catholic church and the creation of the modern Irish state 1878–1886*, Gill & Macmillan, Dublin, 1975, p. 396. Several church–state concordats were arranged across Europe during the 1850s to help undo the democratic upheavals of 1848.

12 O'Brien, *Parnell and his party*, pp. 92–103.

13 O'Day, Alan, *Irish home rule 1867–1921*, MUP, Manchester, 1999, pp. 319–24.

14 McGee, IRB, pp. 39, 48, 88; Sullivan, A.M., *New Ireland: political sketches and personal reminiscences of thirty years of Irish public life, Second edition*, Sampson, London, 1882, p. 394.

15 Comerford, R.V., *The Fenians in context (Second edition)*, Wolfhound, Dublin, 1998, p. 30; Paseta, Senia, *Before the revolution: nationalism, social change and Ireland's Catholic elite 1879–1922*, CUP, Cork, 1999.

16 Sullivan, *New Ireland*, pp. 394, 463.

17 Meagher, T.F., 'Catholicism and republicanism', in Lyons, W.F. (ed.), *Brigadier Thomas Francis Meagher*, Burns Oates, London, 1869, pp. 142–47; O'Leary, John, *Recollections of Fenians and Fenianism*, 2 vols, Downey, London, 1896, passim.

18 Clarke was sworn into the IRB by John Daly while working as an assistant teacher in Dungannon. Shortly after taking part in a Land League protest demonstration in late 1880 a warrant was issued for his arrest, and he was forced to emigrate to America. Le Roux, Louis, *Tom Clarke and the Irish freedom movement*, Talbot, Dublin, 1936, pp. 15–16.

19 For the role of freemasonry in inspiring European revolutionary movements, see Billington, James, *Fire in the minds of men: the revolutionary faith*, Basic, New York, 1981 and Zamoyski, Adam, *Holy madness: romantics, patriots and revolutionaries 1776–1871*, Viking, London, 1999.

20   Agulhon, Maurice, *Marianne into battle: republican imagery and symbolism in France 1789–1880*, CUP, Cambridge, 1981, p. 35.

21   McGee, *IRB*, chapter 1; Pilbeam, Pamela, *Republicanism in nineteenth century France*, Palgrave, London, 1995, pp. 1–22.

22   Browne, Fr. P. (ed.), *Collected works of Padraic H. Pearse*, Maunsel, Dublin, 1917, Introduction, pp. xviii–xix.

23   Maume, Patrick, *The long gestation: Irish nationalist life 1891–1918*, Gill & Macmillan, Dublin, 1999, pp. 54–55; McGee, *IRB*, pp. 299–300, 308, 310, 314, 316.

24   British in Ireland microfilm, DMP and RIC précis, report 3–4 May, 2–4 June, 6 July, 2 September 1909, National Archives, Dublin.

25   Denis McCullough papers, P120/24 (9), Denis McCullough statement to Bureau of Military History, UCD Archives.

26   Hobson, Bulmer, *Ireland yesterday and tomorrow*, Anvil, Tralee, 1968, p. 17.

27   Norman, Diana, *Terrible beauty: a life of Constance Markievicz*, Poolbeg, Dublin, 1987, pp. 60–66.

28   The IRB was split during the 1890s after the emergence of a rival 'Irish National Brotherhood' (INB) wing, which was extensively manipulated by the British secret service.

29   O'Brien, William and Ryan, Desmond (eds), *Devoy's post bag*, Fallon, Dublin, 1953, vol. ii, pp. 382, 570; Home Office précis, carton 3, 27742/s, 27804/s, 28377/s, 28429/s, 28634/s, National Archives, Dublin; British in Ireland microfilm collection, DMP and RIC précis, monthly reports for February, April, July and August 1905, and August and September 1908, National Archives, Dublin.

30   Home Office précis, carton 3, 28765/s, 29427/s, 29621/s, National Archives, Dublin.

31   O'Brien and Ryan (eds), *Devoy's post bag*, vol. ii, p. 354.

32   Lynch, Diarmuid, *The IRB and the 1916 insurrection*, Mercier, Cork, 1957, p. 95; O'Brien and Ryan (eds), *Devoy's post bag*, vol. ii, p. 570.

33   Denis McCullough papers, P120/24 (5), statement to Bureau of Military History on IRB personnel, UCD Archives.

34   O'Brien and Ryan (eds), *Devoy's post bag*, vol. ii, pp. 401–2.

35   *Ibid.*, pp. 365–66, 377, 383–84, 390–93.

36   The old (British secret service dominated) INB wing of the Clan, responsible for the 'dynamite war' of the 1880s, still existed as late as 1915, with McGarrity as one of its leaders, *Ibid.*, pp. 480–81 During McGarrity's sole visit to Ireland in late 1904 he advocated a revival of the 'dynamite war'. British in Ireland microfilm collection, DMP and RIC précis, monthly report for Nov. 1904, National Archives, Dublin. Later, McGarrity would finance the institutionalisation of the post-treaty IRA and its dynamite campaign of 1939–40

37   O'Hegarty, P.S., 'Introduction', in Clarke, Tom, *Glimpses of an Irish felon's prison life*, Maunsel, Dublin, 1922; Denis McCullough papers, P120/24 (4), Patrick McCartan statement to Bureau of Military History, UCD Archives.

38   O'Halpin, Eunan, 'The British secret service vote and Ireland, 1868–1922'

in *Irish Historical Studies*, vol. xxii, no 93, 1983, pp. 348–53.

39   Ryan, Mark, *Fenian memories*, Gill, Dublin, 1945, p. 211.

40   McGee, *IRB*, pp. 120–21, 131.

41   Thornley, *Butt*, 240–4; British in Ireland microfilm, CO 904/17/130, National Archives, Dublin; McGee, *IRB*, pp. 191, 294, passim; O'Connor, Frank, *Leinster, Munster and Connaught*, Hale, London, 1950, p. 215.

42   This is clear from the autobiography of Clarke's wife, Kathleen, *Revolutionary woman*, O'Brien, Dublin, 1991, as well as the recent biography, MacAtasney, Gerard, *Seán MacDiarmada: the mind of the revolution*, Drumlin, Manorhamilton, Dublin, 2005.

43   Hobson would in turn dedicate his writings to Clarke, Daly and Devoy. Anon. [Hobson, Bulmer] (ed.), *The voice of freedom*, np, Dublin, 1913.

44   This was particularly true of John Daly and James Egan, who died in 1909. Clarke, *Glimpses of an Irish felon's life*, passim; Le Roux, Tom Clarke, pp. 109–11.

45   Michael McGinn (c.1850–.c1918), native of Omagh. A well-educated man and prosperous baker, he was Tyrone IRB leader from the 1870s until the 1890s, played a prominent role in the Land League agitation and Parnell split controversy and, upon moving to Dublin, worked with Fred Allan in reviving the IRB after 1895. McGee, IRB, passim; British in Ireland microfilm, CO 904/18/752, National Archives, Dublin.

46   Denis McCullough papers, P120/24 (6) & (9), statements of O'Hegarty and McCullough, UCD Archives.

47   Fitzpatrick, David, *Harry Boland's Irish revolution*, CUP, Cork, 2004, p. 34; Hobson, *Ireland yesterday and tomorrow*, p. 42. The 'National Club' at 41 Rutland (later Parnell) Square, founded by Fred Allan in 1887, served as an IRB headquarters for several years, and was also a meeting place of the Wolfe Tone clubs.

48   For a list of the members of the Volunteer executive see O'Brien and Ryan (eds), *Devoy's post bag*, vol. ii, pp. 440–41.

49   Garvin, Tom, 'Introduction', in O'Hegarty, P.S., *The victory of Sinn Féin*, UCDP edition, Dublin, 1998; Coogan, T.P., *Michael Collins*, Hutchinson, London, 1990, pp. 6–10.

50   O'Hegarty, *Victory of Sinn Féin*, pp. 9–10; *Michael Collins, The path to freedom*, Talbot, Dublin, 1922, p. 54.

51   Whyte, John H., '1916 – revolution and religion', in Martin, F.X. (ed.), *Leaders and men of the Easter Rising: Dublin 1916*, Methuen, London, 1967, pp. 215–26.

52   McHugh, Roger, 'Casement and German help' in *Ibid*, pp. 169–70, 181.

53   *Ibid.*, p. 207.

54   O'Brien and Ryan (eds), *Devoy's post bag*, vol. ii, pp. 430–35.

55   Clarke, *Revolutionary woman*, pp. 46–47; O'Brien and Ryan (eds), *Devoy's post bag*, vol. ii, p. 458.

56   Maume, *Long gestation*, p. 166.

57   O'Brien and Ryan (eds), *Devoy's post bag*, vol. ii, pp. 429, 439.

58   McGee, *IRB*, pp. 142, 202, 211.

59   O'Brien and Ryan (eds), *Devoy's post bag*, vol. ii, pp. 445, 448.

60   Devoy, John, 'The story of Clan na Gael', *Gaelic American*, 15 August 1923,

1 September 1923.

61   MacAtasney, *Seán MacDiarmada*, pp. 69, 161.

62   Clarke, *Revolutionary woman*, pp. 51–52

63   O'Brien and Ryan (eds), *Devoy's post bag*, vol. ii, pp. 464–80.

64   The IRB Supreme Council from 1915–16 was as follows. The executive was Denis McCullough (president), Seán MacDermott (secretary) and Tom Clarke (treasurer). The fourth co–opted member was Diarmuid Lynch. The seven district representatives were Seán Tobin (Leinster), Diarmuid Lynch (Munster), Alex McCabe (Connacht), Denis McCullough (Ulster), Patrick McCormick (Scotland), Richard Connolly (southern England) and Joseph Gleeson (northern England), although very few of these had any organisation behind them or experience in directing the IRB. Denis McCullough papers, P120/24 (5), UCD Archives.

65   MacAtasney, *Seán MacDiarmada*, p. 69.

66   Lynch, *The IRB and the 1916 insurrection*, pp. 47, 102, 130–32.

67   *Freeman's Journal*, 24 November 1913, 23 November 1914 Delia Larkin's Irish Women's Workers Union, Cumann na mBan and Fianna Éireann also took part.

68   Rossa had experienced the horrors of the Irish famine first hand, helped found the IRB in the late 1850s, was tortured in prison during the late 1860s, excommunicated and ostracised by the Catholic church in New York during the 1870s (along with all members of John O'Mahony's Fenian Brotherhood), and, having been squeezed out of Irish revolutionary politics (and subject to assassination attempts) by British agents during the mid-1880s had lost all influence by the 1890s.

69   These were Clarke, McGinn, Griffith, James Stritch, Henry Dixon, William O'Leary Curtis, James Connor ('Séamus O'Conchubhair'), John Simmons, James Buggy, Charles Kickham Jnr., and John MacBride. See Diarmuid O'Donovan Rossa, 1831–1915, *Souvenir of public funeral, 1 August 1915*, np, Dublin, 1915.

70   *Ibid.* These were William O'Brien, John Farren and John Lawlor.

71   Edwards, R.D., *Patrick Pearse: the triumph of failure*, Gollancz, London, 1977, pp. 236–37.

72   Lynch, *The IRB and the 1916 insurrection*, pp. 47, 102.

73   Devoy, John, *Recollections of an Irish rebel*, Young, New York, 1929, p. 458.

74   O'Brien and Ryan (eds), *Devoy's post bag*, vol. ii, pp. 504–6.

75   *Ibid.*, p. 504.

76   Lynch, *The IRB and the 1916 insurrection*, pp. 130–32.

77   For the career of James Boland (1856–95), see McGee, *IRB*, pp. 113, 175, 178 and 190–91.

78   Fitzpatrick, *Boland*, p. 34.

79   Ryan, *Fenian memories*, p. 209.

80   Jordan, Anthony, *Major John MacBride*, WHS, Westport, 1991, chapter 15.

81   G.A. Lyons papers, MS 33675/c/2, 'Recollections of IRB', p.11, and article on Peadar Macken, National Library of Ireland.

82   Lyons, G.A., *Some recollections of Griffith and his times*, Talbot, Dublin, 1923, pp. 13–14.

83 Collins, Michael, *The path to freedom*, Talbot, Dublin, 1922, p. 55.

84 This was an apartment above an Irish farm produce shop at 21 Henry Street, run by Jennie (O'Toole) Wyse Power. She was originally a member of the Ladies Land League, who, at an 1881 rally of which, met her future husband, John Wyse Power, a vice president of the IRB's 'Young Ireland Society'. In 1916, Kathleen Clarke was a close friend of Jennie (and a fellow member of Cumann na mBan), and was told by Tom that the Military Council met at 21 Henry Street (Clarke, *Revolutionary woman*, pp. 69–70). It is quite possible that the meeting was held here due to Clarke's older friendship with John, who had been a newspaper editor for thirty five years (most recently for the *Evening Telegraph*, which alone of Irish newspapers published notes regarding the meetings of the Old Guard Union). The *Telegraph* was the paper that the IRB counted on in 1907–8 for publishing appreciative obituaries for old IRB figures like P.N. Fitzgerald and John O'Connor. O'Brien and Ryan (eds), *Devoy's post bag*, vol. ii, pp. 373–74.

85 Clarke, *Revolutionary woman*, pp. 69–70.

86 *Ibid.*

87 This was certainly the case for the IRB constitution of 1873, which reputedly remained in existence until 1917. A copy of the 1873 constitution can be found in Moody, T.W. and O'Broin, Leon (eds), 'Select documents xxxii: The IRB Supreme Council 1868–78', document c, in *Irish Historical Studies*, vol. xix, no. 87, 1974, pp. 286–332.

88 Lynch, *The IRB and the 1916 insurrection*, pp. 83, 142.

89 During the Boer War, the Old Guard Union carried the Irish and French tricolours and marched to La Marseillaise at Manchester martyr and Bodenstown demonstrations. McGee, *IRB*, p. 293. The last occasion the Irish tricolour seems to have been publicly displayed was the 1901 Bodenstown demonstration, chaired by P.N. Fitzgerald.

90 Ryan, Annie (ed.), *Witness: inside the Easter Rising*, Liberties, Dublin, 2005, pp. 156–7.

91 *Ibid.*

92 McGee, *IRB*, pp. 74, 117, 321.

93 *Irish Weekly Independent*, 1 July 1893 (reprint of letter of John Daly from prison to the Limerick IRB leader, John Crowe, the father of M.F. Crowe).

94 Clarke, *Revolutionary woman*, pp. 121–23, 135. John Daly died shortly afterwards, in June 1916, aged seventy one, happy that a rebellion had taken place.

95 Ryan (ed.), *Witness: inside the Easter Rising*, p. 156.

96 O'Hegarty, *The victory of Sinn Féin*, p. 3.

97 Martin (ed.) *Leaders and men of the Easter Rising*, pp. 221–23.

98 O'Brien and Ryan (eds), *Devoy's post bag*, vol. ii, p. 505.

99 Clarke, *Revolutionary woman*, pp. 145, 169.

100 Browne (ed.), *Collected works of Padraic H. Pearse*, Introduction.

101 Diarmuid O'Donovan Rossa, *1831–1915, Souvenir of public funeral, 1 August 1915*, article by Connolly.

102 Clarke, *Revolutionary woman*, pp. 137–38

103 Augusteijn, Joost, *From public defiance to guerrilla warfare*, IAP, Dublin, 1996; Hart, Peter, *The IRA and its enemies: violence and community in Cork 1916–1923*, OUP, Oxford, 1998; Joy, Sinead, *The IRA in Kerry 1916–21*, Collins, Cork, 2005; McGarry, Fearghal (ed.), *Republicanism in modern Ireland*, UCDP, Dublin, 2003, pp. 86–103.

104 See, for example, Pilbeam, *Republicanism in nineteenth century France*, pp. 32–35.

America and the 1916 Rising:

1 Stephens, James, *The insurrection in Dublin*, Barnes & Noble, New York, 1999 [first published 1916], p. 29.

2 See Blessing, Patrick J., 'Irish Emigration to the United States, 1800–1920' in Drudy, P.J. (ed.), *Irish studies 4: The Irish in America: emigration, assimilation, and impact*, CUP, Cambridge, 1985, pp. 11–13; and Fitzpatrick, David, 'Emigration, 1801–70' and Doyle, David Noel, 'The Irish in North America, 1776–1845' in Vaughan, W.E. et al. (eds), *A new history of Ireland V: Ireland under the Union I, 1801–70*, Clarendon Press, Oxford, 1989, pp. 562–622 and 682–725.

3 Foster, R.F., *Modern Ireland*, 1600–1972, Allen Lane, London, 1988, pp. 345–48.

4 Fitzpatrick, David, *Irish emigration, 1801–1922*, Economic and Social History Society of Ireland, Dublin, 1984, p. 5.

5 Department of Commerce, Bureau of the Census, *Thirteenth census of the United States taken in the year 1910*, Government Printing Office, Washington, 1911, vol. i, p. 24.

6 Gywnn, Denis, *The life of John Redmond*, Harrap., London, 1932, pp. 183–88; and Lyons, F.S.L., *John Dillon: a biography*, Routledge and Kegan Paul, London, 1968, p. 320.

7 Patrick Egan to John Redmond, 18 February 1910, Redmond papers, National Library of Ireland; and Gwynn, *The life of John Redmond*, p. 184.

8 Patrick Egan to John Redmond, 1 March 1910, Redmond papers, NLI; and Theodore Roosevelt to John Wynne, 11 April 1910 in Morison, Elting E. et al. (eds), *The letters of Theodore Roosevelt*, HUP, Cambridge, 1954, vol. vii, p. 7.

9 Martin J. Keogh to John Redmond, 29 November 1910, Redmond papers, NLI.

10 Cable to John Redmond, 12 April 1912, box 18, Cockran papers, New York Public Library. Those signing the cable included Congressman W. Bourke Cockran, Judge Martin J. Keogh, Morgan J. O'Brien, John Quinn, and William Gibbs McAdoo. Clan members sent their own cable denouncing home rule as a fraud. See John Devoy to Joseph McGarrity, 17 April 1912, box 16, McGarrity papers, Maloney collection, New York Public Library.

11 Martin J. Keogh to John Redmond, 27 May 1912, Redmond papers, NLI; and Gywnn, The life of John Redmond, p. 202.

12 Theodore Roosevelt to John Redmond, c. June, 1913 in Morison et al.

(eds), *The letters of Theodore Roosevelt*, vol. vii, p. 740; and the *Times*, 11 June 1913. American politicians like Roosevelt were often accused of supporting the Irish cause simply to curry favour with Irish-American voters. Certainly Roosevelt was on record on numerous occasions outlining the benefits to both Britain and the United States of Irish self-government. See, for example, Theodore Roosevelt to Arthur Lee, later Lord Lee of Fareham, 7 July 1913 in Morison et al. (eds), *The letters of Theodore Roosevelt*, vol. vii, p. 740.

13   John T. Keating to John Devoy, 22 January 1910, box J–L, Devoy papers, NLI. Clan leaders found the prestige enjoyed by prominent figures in the United Irish League of America, such as Michael J. Ryan, the City Solicitor of Philadelphia, difficult to stomach. See Dr William Carroll to John Devoy, 7 February 1913 in O'Brien, William and Ryan, Desmond (eds), *Devoy's postbag*, Fallon edition, Dublin, 1958, vol. ii, p. 403.

14   See Petition of the United German-American and United Irish-American Societies of New York to the United States Senate, 2 May 1911, box Larkin, and John T. Ryan to John Devoy, 14 August 1911, box RU-S, Devoy papers, NLI. A Clan circular in 1913 declared that Ireland had the right to complete independence and said: 'We brand as a fraud and a cheat the so-called Home Rule bill, which gives Ireland a legislative body crippled by restraints and prohibitions'. Clan circular, March 1913, Box U.B., *Ibid.*

15   Ó Broin, Leon, *Revolutionary underground: the story of the Irish Republican Brotherhood, 1858–1924*, Gill & Macmillan, Dublin, 1976, p. 140. Also see McCartan, Patrick, *With de Valera in America*, Fitzpatrick, Dublin, 1932; Cronin, Seán, *The McGarrity papers*, Anvil, Tralee, 1972; and Lynch, Diarmuid, *The IRB and the 1916 insurrection*, Mercier, Cork, 1957.

16   Golway, Terry, *Irish rebel: John Devoy and America's fight for Ireland's freedom*, St Martin's, New York, 1998, p. 193.

17   John Devoy to Judge Daniel F. Cohalan, 29 November 1911, cited in Callan Tansill, Charles, *America and the fight for Irish freedom, 1866–1922*, Devin-Adair, New York, 1957, pp. 125–26. Clan leaders eventually broke with the Abbey players over the production of J.M. Synge's *Playboy of the Western World*, although Theodore Roosevelt himself escorted Lady Gregory to a showing of the play in New York. For a description of the relationship between the Irish organisations and the Clan leadership in the USA see Reid, B.L., *The man from New York: John Quinn and his friends*, OUP, New York, 1968; Foster, R.F., *W.B. Yeats: a life, I The apprentice mage, 1865–1914*, OUP, Oxford, 1997; Gonne McBride, Maud, *A servant of the queen: reminiscences*, Gollancz, London, 1974 [first published 1938]; Dunleavy, Janet Egleson and Gareth W., *Douglas Hyde: a maker of modern Ireland*, UCP, Berkeley, 1991; and Kohfeldt, Mary Lou, *Lady Gregory: The woman behind the Irish renaissance*, Atheneum, New York, 1985.

18   The O'Rahilly to John Devoy, 6 April 1914 in O'Brien and Ryan (eds), *Devoy's postbag*, vol. ii, p. 426.

19   Col. Richard O'Sullivan Burke to John Devoy, 6 May 1914, and John T. Ryan to John Devoy, 6 May 1914, *Ibid.*, p. 434; and F. Tobin to James Reidy, 19 May 1914, Box T–Z, Devoy papers, NLI.

20   Circular letter from Joseph McGarrity, Denis A. Spellessy, and Patrick J. Griffin, 2 June 1914, Box 12, and Irish Volunteer Fund Committee Constitution, 1914, Box 13, McGarrity papers, Maloney collection, New York Public Library; and Hobson, Bulmer, *History of the Irish Volunteers*, Candles Press, Dublin, 1918, pp. 130–31; and Tarpey, Marie Veronica, *The role of Joseph McGarrity in the struggle for Irish independence*, Arno, New York, 1976, pp. 61–64.

21   Judge O'Neill Ryan to John Devoy, 30 June 1914 in O'Brien and Ryan (eds), *Devoy's postbag*, vol. ii, p. 453.

22   Eoin MacNeill to Joseph McGarrity, 1 July 1914, box 13, McGarrity papers, Maloney collection, New York Public Library. Also see John Devoy to Joseph McGarrity, 14, 18, 22, and 29 June 1914, *Ibid*. McGarrity, perhaps more than Devoy, was prepared to accept MacNeill's appeal and on 14 June sent a circular letter to Clan members asking for support for the Volunteers. Circular letter from Joseph McGarrity, et al., 14 June 1914, box 12, *Ibid*.

23   Roger Casement to John Devoy, 21 July 1914 in O'Brien and Ryan (eds), *Devoy's postbag*, vol. ii, pp. 460–3. Dr Patrick McCartan was also sent over to the United States in July 1914 to explain the situation to Clan leaders. See 'Extracts from the papers of the late Dr Patrick McCartan. Part Two', *Clogher Record*, vol. v, no. 2, 1964, pp. 184–212.

24   John Devoy, *Recollections of an Irish rebel: a personal narrative,* Chas. D. Young, New York, 1929, p. 393; Cronin, *The McGarrity papers*, pp. 41–45; and Roger Casement to Alice Stopford Green, 26 July 1914, Green papers, NLI. Casement wrote to Mrs Green that if it had not been for the war he could have raised much more money. Roger Casement to Alice Stopford Green, 15 August 1914, Green papers, *Ibid*. Devoy comments that although the Redmond people in the United States claimed that they would raise $100,000 for the Volunteers, they actually sent only $5,000 to Ireland. The Redmond papers indicate that something closer to $10,000 was received.

25   Roger Casement to Alice Stopford Green, 29 July 1914, Green papers, NLI; and Hobson, History of the Irish Volunteers, p. 65.

26   *New York Times*, 27 July 1914.

27   Henry Cabot Lodge to Moreton Frewen, 25 March 1914, box 42, Frewen papers, Library of Congress.

28   W. Bourke Cockran to Moreton Frewen, 25 March 1914, box 16, Cockran papers, New York Public Library.

29   *Irish World*, 26 September and 10 October 1914; and Michael J. Ryan to John Redmond, 2 October 1914, in *Gwynn, The life of John Redmond*, pp. 416–18.

30   For a more extensive account of the decline of support for Redmond and home rule, see, Carroll, F.M., *American opinion and the Irish question, 1910–1923: a study in opinion and policy*, Gill & Macmillan, Dublin, 1978, pp. 36–54.

31   Cronin, *The McGarrity Papers*, p. 52. The best account of Casement in the United States is in Reid, B.L., *The lives of Roger Casement*, YUP, New Haven, 1976, pp. 196–209.

32 *Gaelic American*, 15, 22, and 29 August, and 12 September 1914; and Shaemus O'Sheel to Joseph McGarrity, 18 August 1914, box 14, McGarrity papers, Maloney collection, New York Public Library.

33 German military attaché to Foreign Office, 9 August 1914, cited in Doerries, Reinhard, *Prelude to the Easter Rising: Sir Roger Casement in imperial Germany*, Frank Cass, London, 2000, p. 46. Franz von Papen is now remembered primarily for his role in Hitler's rise to power in Germany.

34 German Embassy, Washington, to Foreign Office, Berlin, 27 September 1914, Documents relative to the Sinn Féin movement, 1921 [cmd.1108] xxlx 429, p. 3.

35 Devoy, *Recollections of an Irish rebel*, pp. 403–6; and Count Johann von Bernsdorff to Foreign Office, 13 and 15 October 1914, cited in Doerries, *Prelude to the Easter Rising*, pp. 50–51.

36 Joseph McGarrity to Tom Clarke, c. August 1914, box 14, McGarrity papers, Maloney collection, New York Public Library; Thompson, William Irwin, *The imagination of an insurrection, Dublin, Easter 1916: a study of an ideological movement*, Harper & Row, New York, 1967, pp. 26–27; and German Embassy, Washington, to Foreign Office, Berlin, 27 September 1914, Documents relative to the Sinn Féin movement, p. 3.

37 Doerries, *Prelude to the Easter Rising*, pp. 6–7; Devoy, Recollections of an Irish rebel, p. 406; and Cronin, *The McGarrity papers*, p. 53.

38 For a good analysis of these efforts by Casement see Doerries, *Prelude to the Easter Rising*, pp. 7–24. Doerries makes the point that the possibility of a German invasion of Ireland was not so preposterous in the light of German operations and plans in the Middle East, Central Asia, Mexico, and Canada. Also see Tarpey, *The role of Joseph McGarrity in the struggle for Irish independence*, pp. 84–85. In his attempt to build the Irish brigade, Casement asked Devoy to have Irish or Irish-American officers sent to Germany. James Larkin was presumably asked by the Germans to go, but suggested his friend Robert Monteith, who did go. See John Devoy to Joseph McGarrity, 13 July 1915, box 16, McGarrity papers, Maloney collection, New York Public Library; and Larkin, Emmet, *James Larkin: Irish labour leader, 1876–1947*, Routledge & Kegan Paul, London, 1965, p. 211. Devoy also arranged with the embassy for Robert Monteith to go to Germany. Monteith, Robert, *Casement's last adventure*, Michael F. Moynihan, Dublin, 1932, p. 63.

39 Hobson, Bulmer, *Ireland yesterday and tomorrow*, Anvil, Tralee, 1968, p. 71.

40 Lynch, *The IRB and the 1916 insurrection*, pp. 24–28.

41 Devoy, Recollections of an Irish rebel, p. 415; Cronin, *The McGarrity papers*, pp. 52–54; Splain, John J., 'The Irish movement in the United States since 1911' in FitzGerald, William G. (ed.), *The voice of Ireland*, John Heywood, Dublin, 1924, p. 226; and financial records, first drawer, Cohalan papers, American Irish Historical Society. As mentioned above, the Clan provided $100,000 in total to the IRB and the Volunteers.

42 John T. Keating to John Devoy, 9 November 1914, Box J–L, Devoy papers, NLI; and John Devoy to Joseph McGarrity, 12 December 1914, Box 16, McGarrity papers, Maloney collection, New York Public Library. The

Clan eventually financed at least part of Casement's defence in his treason trial.

43 See Golway, *Irish rebel*, p. 206; Cronin, *The McGarrity papers*, pp. 66–69; and O'Leary, Jeremiah A., *My political trial and experiences*, Jefferson, New York, 1919, passim.

44 Georg von Skal to W. Pfitzer, 10 February 1916, cited in Coates, Tim (ed.), *The Irish uprising, 1914–1921*, HMSO, London, 2000, pp. 55–56; McGuire, James K., *The King, the Kaiser and Irish freedom*, Devin-Adair, New York, 1915; McGuire, James K., *What could Germany do for Ireland?*, Devin-Adair, New York, 1916; and Carroll, *American opinion and the Irish question*, pp. 50–52 and 130.

45 Larkin, James Larkin, pp. 187–218; von Rintelen, Franz, *The dark invader: wartime reminiscences of a German naval intelligence officer*, Lovat Dickson, London, 1934, pp. 79–186; and Bird, Kai, *The chairman – John J. McCloy: the making of the American establishment*, Simon & Schuster, New York, 1992, pp. 87–89. These German sabotage activities culminated after the von Igel raid in the so-called 'Black Tom' explosion on 30 July 1916, where thousands of tons of explosives and munitions blew up at a shipping terminal on the Jersey side of the New York harbour.

46 John Devoy (David Jones) to Joseph McGarrity (Dear Friend), 19 April 1916, box 16, McGarrity papers, Maloney collection, New York Public Library. Also see Golway, *Irish rebel*, pp. 223–25.

47 The office of Wolf von Igel was not on either embassy or consular property and therefore was deemed not to have diplomatic protection. However, when Ambassador von Bernsdorff asked for the return of the seized papers Secretary of State Robert Lansing agreed. Ambassador Walter Hines Page cabled the State Department on 25 April to say that the Admiralty had asked him to request that photograph copies of any papers acquired in the von Igel raid be shown to the British naval attaché in Washington. Page urged that this be done because the British had previously provided information useful to the Americans about German activity in the US. On 27 April Secretary of State Lansing recorded in his desk diary that the president's secretary had attempted to follow up a rumour that the British had been told about the Rising before it occurred – essentially Devoy's public argument – and presumably Lansing denied any leak of information from the State Department. On 1 May Lansing cabled Page in London to say that the American government had been accused of giving this information to the British. He wrote specifically that 'he did not believe anything of any value has been discovered here', although he would consider the request. This was a week after the Rising. See Robert Lansing to Count J.H. von Bernsdorff, 24 April 1916, American Embassy to Secretary of State, 25 April 1916, and Robert Lansing to American Embassy, 1 May 1916, 701.6211/367, Wolf Von Igel case, State Department Papers, Record Group 59, US National Archives; and Desk Diary, 27 April 1916, Robert Lansing Papers, Library of Congress. F.S.L. Lyons is almost certainly wrong in his assertion that the American government gave the British copies of the von Igel papers, but correct in noting that the British had broken the German diplomatic codes and were reading

all the transatlantic traffic. See Lyons, F.S.L., 'The revolution in train, 1914–16' in Vaughan, W.E. (ed.), *A new history of Ireland V: Ireland under the Union II, 1870–1921*, Clarendon, Oxford, 1996, p. 200.

48 Richard McGinn to John Devoy, 12 October 1915 in O'Brien and Ryan (eds), *Devoy's postbag*, vol. ii, pp. 480–81; John Devoy to Congressman Joseph McLaughlin, 8 December 1915, box Misc., and McLaughlin to Devoy, 21 February 1916, box M, Devoy papers, NLI; John Devoy to Clan brothers, 29 December 1915, and 15 January 1916, box 16, McGarrity papers, Maloney collection, New York Public Library; and Splain, 'The Irish Movement in the United States Since 1911', pp. 226–28.

49 Carroll, *American opinion and the Irish question*, pp. 52–53; Tansill, *America and the fight for Irish freedom*, pp. 188–90; and, for a fuller account, Doorley, Michael, *Irish-American diaspora nationalism: The Friends of Irish Freedom, 1916–1935*, Four Courts Press, Dublin, 2005, pp. 21–61.

50 Devoy, *Recollections of an Irish rebel*, p. 458. Also see Lyons, 'The revolution in train, 1914–16' pp. 201–2.

51 McGarrity sent a message to Clarke that the date for the arms shipment could not be changed, but it proved impossible to deliver it. Cronin, *The McGarrity papers*, pp. 61–62. No one has satisfactorily explained why provisions were not made for receiving the arms shipment over several days.

52 Golway, *Irish rebel*, p. 229.

53 See, for example, 'Ireland fighting for freedom', *Gaelic American*, 29 April 1916, and 'Ireland redeemed by Dublin', *Gaelic American*, 6 May 1916.

54 Theodore Roosevelt to Arthur Hamilton Lee, 7 June 1916 in Morison (ed.), The letters of Theodore Roosevelt, vol. viii, pp. 1,054–55. Interestingly Roosevelt thought Casement to be in an entirely different category. Many other examples, from private correspondence and newspaper editorials, could be given.

55 Cable from C. Spring-Rice to [Sir Edward Grey], 1 August 1916, FO 800/86, National Archives, Kew. Several people with claims to American citizenship who were involved in the Rising may have had their sentences moderated for that reason, among them Éamon (Edward) de Valera and Diarmuid (Jeremiah) A. Lynch. See Dudley Edwards, Owen, 'American Aspects of the Rising' in Dudley Edwards, Owen and Pyle, Fergus (eds), *1916: the Easter Rising*, MacGibbon and Kee, London, 1968, pp. 162–63. For the Casement trial and aftermath, see Ward, Alan J., *Ireland and Anglo-American relations, 1899–1921*, Weidenfeld and Nicolson, London, 1969, pp. 101–24; and Carroll, *American opinion and the Irish question*, pp. 69–77. The White House and the State Department did co-operate with the Philadelphia lawyer, Michael Francis Doyle, who went to London to assist in Casement's defence, and transmitted a message to Casement from his sister. Doyle wrote to the president's secretary, Joseph Tumulty, that he had been told by John Redmond and Lord Northcliffe that a letter from Wilson would save Casement. Michael Francis Doyle to Joseph Tumulty, 6 and 19 July 1916, and Woodrow Wilson to Joseph Tumulty, 20 July 1916, file vi, # 3085, Wilson papers, Library of Congress. Many appeals were made to President Wilson, asking him to intervene personally, which he refused to do.

56   Doorly, Irish-American diaspora nationalism, pp. 51–52; and Carroll, *American opinion and the Irish question*, pp. 78–81. Michael Francis Doyle informed Joseph McGarrity of the probability of these difficulties when he went to London to defend Casement. See Michael Francis Doyle to Joseph McGarrity, June 1916, box 12, McGarrity papers, Maloney collection, New York Public Library. The State Department attempted to intervene, but without success. See Frank K. Polk to the American embassy, London, 25 July 1916, file 133, drawer 77, State Department, Polk papers, Yale University Library.

57   Report of John A. Murphy as delegate in Ireland to the Irish Relief Fund of America, c. 1916, box Misc., Devoy papers, NLI.

58   Woodrow Wilson to Robert Lansing, 10 April 1917, 841d.00/103½, Foreign Relations of the United States, Lansing Papers, vol. ii, pp. 4–5; and cable from Walter Hines Page to Secretary of State, 18 April 1917, marked 'Confidential for the President', 841d.00/106, State Department papers, RG 59, National Archives, Washington. Also see McDowell, R.B., *The Irish Convention, 1917–18*, Routledge & Kegan Paul, London, 1970, passim; and Tansill, *America and the fight for Irish freedom*, pp. 218–50.

59   Carroll, Francis M., 'The American Commission on Irish Independence and the Paris peace conference of 1919' in *Irish Studies in International Affairs*, vol. ii, no. 1, 1985, pp 103–18.

60   Carroll, Francis M., *'Money for Ireland': finance, diplomacy, politics, and the First Dáil Éireann Loans, 1919–1936*, Praeger, Westport, 2002, pp. 13–29.

61   Carroll, Francis M., 'The American committee for relief in Ireland, 1920–22' *Irish Historical Studies*, vol. xxiii, no. 89, May 1983, pp. 30–49.

The Easter Rising in the context of censorship and propaganda with special reference to Major Ivon Price

1   Clery, Arthur, *Dublin essays*, Maunsel, Dublin, 1919, p. 44.

2   Thanks to the research of Eunan O'Halpin and James Herlihy this error has now been corrected. Herlihy, Jim, *Royal Irish Constabulary Officers: a biographical dictionary and genealogical guide, 1816–1922*, Four Courts, Dublin, 2005, p. 258 for detailed account of his life. O'Halpin, Eunan, 'British intelligence in Ireland, 1914–1921,' in Andrew, Christopher and Dilks, David (eds), *The missing dimension: government and intelligence communities in the twentieth century*, Macmillan, London, 1984, p. 55.

3   Ó Broin, Leon, *Revolutionary underground: the story of the Irish Republican Brotherhood 1858–1924*, Gill & Macmillan, Dublin, 1976, pp. 124–25. See Richard Hawkins' review of Ó Broin's book, *Irish Historical Studies*, vol. xx, no. 79, March 1977, p. 365 for clarification of Price's status in the RIC.

4   Herlihy, Jim, *The Royal Irish Constabulary*, Four Courts, Dublin, 1997, p. 217 provides a short outline of his career.

5   Jeffery, Keith (ed.), *The Sinn Féin rebellion as they saw it*, IAP, Dublin, 1998, p. 110; idem, *The GPO and the Easter Rising*, IAP, Dublin, 2006, pp. 40, 129; Herlihy, Royal Irish Constabulary officers, p. 258.

6   Evidence of Major Price in *1916 rebellion handbook*, Mourne, Dublin, 1998 [first published 1916], p. 176.

7   Mackey, Herbert O. (ed.), *The crime against Europe: writings and poems of Roger Casement*, Fallon, Dublin, 1958, p. 112.

8   Gwynne to French, 23 March 1914, Gwynne papers, 19, Bodleian library, Oxford.

9   Wilson, K.M., 'Sir John French's resignation over the Curragh affair: the role of the editor of the Morning Post', *English Historical Review*, vol. xcix, no. 393, October 1984, p. 811; see also Holmes, Richard, *The little field marshal: a life of Sir John French*, Weidenfeld and Nicolson, London, 2004, pp. 166–94 for more on this incident.

10   Jalland, Patricia, *The Liberals and Ireland: the Ulster question in British politics to 1914*, Harvester, Brighton, 1980, p. 247.

11   See Campbell, Colm, *Emergency law in Ireland 1918–1925*, OUP, Oxford, 1994, pp. 9–12 for the origins and development of DORA; see Ewing, K.D. and Gearty, C.A., *The struggle for civil liberties: political freedom and the rule of law in Britain 1914–1945*, OUP, Oxford, 2005, p. 51 et seq. for details of the Defence of the Realm Regulations and chapter 7 for 'Civil liberies: the Irish dimension'. See Murphy, Brian P., *The Catholic Bulletin and republican Ireland*, Athol, Belfast, 2005, p. 228 for the application of DORA in Ireland.

12   *Report of the Royal Commission on the Rebellion in Ireland*, 1916 [cd.8279] xi.171, p. 7.

13   Messinger, Gary S., *British propaganda and the state in the First World War*, MUP, Manchester, 1992, pp. 145–63.

14   The *Times*, 26, 27 November 1914.

15   *Ibid.*, 26 November 1914. Among other publications strongly criticised were George Bernard Shaw's *Common sense about the war*, which was first published on 14 November 1914 as a supplement to the New Statesman. See Kennedy, Thomas C., 'War, patriotism, and the Ulster Unionist Council, 1914–18', Éire-Ireland, vol. xl, nos. 3–4, fall–winter 2005, for more on Long and H.A. Gwynne, mentioned above.

16   As reported in the *Times*, 26 November 1914.

17   The *Times*, 27 November 1914.

18   Carty, James, *Bibliography of Irish history 1912–1921*, Stationery Office, Dublin, 1936, p. xxx. *The Irish Volunteer*, despite attracting attention in the House of Commons, was not suppressed. However, it began a new series on 5 December 1914 (see *Ibid.*, p. 51). I am grateful to Donal Ó Drisceoil for clarifying this point. See also Glandon, Virginia, *Arthur Griffith and the advanced nationalist press: Ireland, 1900–1922*, Peter Lang, New York, 1985; idem, 'The Irish press and revolutionary Irish nationalism', *Éire-Ireland*, vol. xvi, no. 1, 1981, pp. 21–23; Novick, Ben, *Conceiving revolution: Irish nationalist propaganda during the First World War*, Four Courts, Dublin, 2001, pp. 204–7.

19   Novick, *Conceiving revolution*, pp. 20–21; Carty, Bibliography, p. 58. The *National Volunteer*, printed by the *Freeman's Journal*, was published from 17 October 1914 to 22 April 1916. Carty's book has invaluable notes on all the journals of the period.

20   *Irish Freedom*, August 1913; 'Shan Van Vocht' [Roger Casement], 'Ireland, Germany and the next war', *Irish Review*, July 1913; see Mackey (ed.), *The crime Against Europe*, pp. 72–80 for the entire article. See *Irish Freedom*, October 1913 for evidence that the German General von Bernhardi was aware of Casement's writings, and Pollard, H.B.C., *The secret societies of Ireland, Allan*, London, 1922, p. 134 for the claim that Bernhardi actually translated the articles into German. See Clifford, Brendan (ed.), *Roger Casement: the crime against Europe*, Athol, Belfast, 2003 for an important critique of Casement's book.

21   See Mitchell, Angus, *Casement*, Haus, London, 2003, p. 83.

22   'Ardrigh' [Roger Casement], 'Mobilise', *Irish Volunteer*, 28 February 1914. See Mitchell, Angus, 'John Bull's other empire: Roger Casement and the press, 1898–1916', in Potter, Simon J. (ed.), *Newspapers and empire in Ireland and Britain: reporting the British empire, c.1857–1921*, Four Courts, Dublin, 2004, pp. 217–33 for the many pen names used by Casement and invaluable insights on the propaganda context in which he wrote.

23   For a report see *Irish Volunteer*, 25 April 1914.

24   See Nevin, Donal, *James Connolly: a full life*, Gill & Macmillan, Dublin, 2005, chapter 28, 'War', for more on Connolly's writings on the war. For Connolly's differences with Larkin and the IRB at this time see Greaves, Desmond, *The life and times of James Connolly*, Lawrence and Wishart, London, 1961, pp. 292–96.

25   Pearse, P.H., From a hermitage, *Irish Freedom*, Dublin, 1915, pp. 21–22 citing *Irish Freedom*, December 1913. See Lee, J.J., 'In search of Patrick Pearse', in Ní Dhonnchadha, Máirín and Dorgan, Theo (eds), *Revising the Rising*, Field Day, Derry, 1991, pp. 128–29 for a valuable analysis of these words in the context of Pearse and 'blood-sacrifice'.

26   See the editorial 'Recruiting in Ireland' in the *Times*, 31 October 1914.

27   Carty, Bibliography, p. 17. These Notes feature prominently in Phillips, W.A., *The revolution in Ireland 1906–1923*, Longmans, London, 1923.

28   Carty, Bibliography, pp. 52 and 49; see Novick, *Conceiving revolution*, p. 31 for more on the Mahon case.

29   Ginnell, Lawrence, DORA at Westminster, Irish Wheelman, Dublin, 1917, pp. 76–77 for reply of Mr Tennant, under secretary for war, to Ginnell, 12 May 1915. Ginnell became the first director of publicity of Dáil Éireann in April 1919.

30   *Report of the Royal Commission on the Rebellion in Ireland*, p. 5; the date is given as 16 March 1915 on p. 7. See 1916 rebellion handbook, p. 167 for Lord Midleton's evidence on the Parmoor legislation.

31   *Irish Volunteer*, 7 August 1915. See Maume, Patrick, *The long gestation, Irish nationalist life 1891–1918*, Gill & Macmillan, Dublin, 1999, p. 240 and idem, *History Ireland*, March–April 2006, p. 74 for information on this unusual man.

32   *Irish Volunteer*, 7 August 1915.

33   *Report of the Royal Commission on the Rebellion in Ireland*, p. 4.

34   *Ibid.*, p. 4, copy of Joseph Brennan (in the personal possession of the author). See 'Files on Republican and Sinn Féin Suspects, 1899–1921', CO 904, 193–216, National Archives, Kew.

35   A record of the rebellion in Ireland 1920–1921, Jeudwine papers, 72/82/2, Imperial War Museum, vol. ii, Intelligence, p. 4.

36   Ewing and Gearty (eds), *Struggle for civil liberties*, pp. 336–7; *Irish Volunteer*, 7 August 1915; White, Gerry and O'Shea, Brendan, *Baptised in blood*, Mercier, Cork, 2005, p. 56 for P.S. O'Hegarty and J.J. Walsh, and pp. 65–66 for attempted action against Seán O'Hegarty; also Townshend, Charles, *Easter 1916: the Irish rebellion*, Penguin, London, 2005, p. 82.

37   MacAtasney, Gerard, *Seán MacDiarmada: the mind of the revolution*, Drumlin, Manorhamilton, 2004, p. 84.

38   *Irish Citizen*, 22 May 1915. See Dudley Edwards, Owen and Pyle, Fergus (eds), *1916: the Easter Rising*, MacGibbon and Kee, London, 1968, pp. 149–52 for his letter.

39   *Irish Citizen*, 8 August 1914.

40   Sheehy Skeffington, Owen, 'Francis Sheehy Skeffington' in Dudley Edwards and Pyle (eds), *1916: the Easter Rising*, pp. 141–42. He was released under the terms of the 'Cat and Mouse' Act.

41   *Ibid.*, p. 142.

42   *Ibid.*, p. 143. See Millman, Brock, 'HMG and the war against dissent, 1914–1918,' *Journal of Contemporary History*, vol. xl, no. 3, 2005, pp. 413–40 for an invaluable account of DORA in England.

43   Ginnell, *DORA at Westminster*, p. 122.

44   'Historical sketch of the directorate of military intelligence during the Great War, 1914–1919', WO 32/10776, National Archives, Kew, p. 20. See *Ibid.*, pp. 20–22 for details of postal censorship and pp. 17–19 for cable censorship.

45   *Ibid.*, p. 21.

46   Nathan to Postmaster General, 23 November 1914, CO 904/164, National Archives, Kew.

47   Nathan to Postmaster General, 22 July 1915, CO 904/164, National Archives, Kew. See MacAtasney, *Seán MacDiarmada*, facing p. 89 for a reproduction of a suspect list dated 31 December 1915.

48   Novik, Ben, 'Postal censorship in Ireland, 1914–1916,' *Irish Historical Studies*, vol. xxxi, no. 123, May 1999, p. 345 citing CO 904/164/1, National Archives, Kew.

49   Report of G Division, 30 November 1914; report of Sergeant. J. Edwards on John McDermott, 21 December 1914, CO 904/164, National Archives Kew.

50   *Report of the Royal Commission on the Rebellion in Ireland*, p. 8.

51   Evidence of Major Price in *1916 rebellion handbook*, p. 77. There is a discrepancy over the date: in Price's evidence he stated that the letter was a translation from the Irish and was dated 14 April; the Royal Commission report gave the date as 24 March 1916.

52   Ó Broin, Leon, *Dublin Castle and the 1916 Rising*, Helicon, London, 1966, retains its value for elucidating the internal structures of the Castle administration and the role of individuals, especially of Nathan. He has many references to Major Price.

53   *Report of the Royal Commission on the Rebellion in Ireland*, p. 7.

54   *Ibid.*, for evidence of Price; see *1916 rebellion handbook*, p. 167 for Lord

Midleton's warnings; see Jeffery, *The Sinn Féin rebellion as they saw it*, p. 111

55   Evidence of Nathan, in *1916 rebellion handbook*, p. 160.

56   The newspapers were the *Irish Volunteer, Nationality, Hibernian, Spark* and *Workers' Republic*.

57   Nathan to Dillon, 13 November 1915, Dillon papers, Trinity College Dublin; Lyons, F.S.L., *John Dillon: a biography*, Routledge and Kegan Paul, London, 1968, pp. 363–66.

58   Carty, Bibliography, p. 73.

59   Quoted in Redmond-Howard, L.G., *Six days of the Irish republic*, Ponsonby, Dublin, 1916, pp. 116–17. This valuable book, with many references to advanced nationalist journals, has been reprinted this year, with an introduction by Brendan Clifford, by the Aubane historical society.

60   See *Everyman*, War cabinet number, 5 June 1915 for a detailed contemporary view of the new coalition cabinet.

61   Pearse, *From a hermitage*, 'Preface'.

62   Diarmuid O'Donovan Rossa, *1831–1915, Souvenir of public funeral, 1 August 1915*, np, Dublin, 1915. See above fn 28.

63   *Ibid.* p. 40.

64   *Ibid.* p. 36.

65   *Irish Volunteer*, December 1914, supplement. The scheme had been drawn up on 16 December 1914. Pearse was entitled director of military organisation in 1915; *Irish Volunteer*, 6 November 1915. See Martin, F.X. (ed.), *The Irish Volunteers 1913–1915*, Dublin, 1963, for valuable articles and selected extracts from the *Irish Volunteer*.

66   Carty, *Bibliography*, p. 51.

67   See Ó Buachalla, Séamus (ed.), *The letters of P.H. Pearse*, Smythe, Gerrard's Cross, 1980; in particular the foreword, by F.S.L. Lyons, for his opinion that the letters are 'for the most part extremely down-to-earth and as such they are bound to change the traditional view of Pearse.' *Ibid.*, p. vii.

68   Novick, *Conceiving revolution*, p. 58.

69   *Ibid.* p. 60, citing the *Irish Volunteer*, 12 February 1916.

70   Casement, Roger, 'The far-extended baleful power of the lie', *The Continental Times*, 3 November 1915 cited in Mackey, *The crime against Europe*, p. 130, and *Gaelic American*, 4 December 1915; Mitchell, *Casement*, p. 107; Novick, *Conceiving revolution*, pp. 107–9 for Bryce report and chapters 2 and 3 for more on 'atrocity propaganda' including an evaluation of Horne, John and Kramer, Alan, *German atrocities 1914: a history of denial*, YUP, London, 2001. See also de Schaepdrijver, Sophie, 'Champion or still birth? The symbolic uses of Belgium in the Great War', in Barnard, Benno et al. (eds), *How can one not be interested in Belgian history? War, language and consensus in Belgium since 1830*, Academica, Ghent 1995, pp. 55–81. See *The Continental Times War Book, Continental Times*, Berlin, 1915, for a selection of articles.

71   Cited in Mackey, *The crime against Europe*, p. 127.

72   See Messinger, *British propaganda*, for chapters on Masterman, Parker and Bryce.

73   *Gaelic American*, 9 October, 27 November and 18 December 1915; Case-

ment, Roger, *The crime against Ireland and how the war may right it*, np, New York, 1914. The book was composed of previous articles.

74 See Murphy, *Catholic Bulletin*, pp. 210–13 for 'The Catholic Bulletin, Bishop O'Dwyer and the Roman dimension, 1915–1916'; see also Keogh, Dermot, *The Vatican, the bishops and Irish politics 1919–1939*, CUP, Cambridge, 1986 for important background material.

75 Murphy, *Catholic Bulletin*, p. 212.

76 aan de Wiel, Jérôme, 'Easter 1916: Count Plunkett's letter to Pope Benedict XV', *Irish Sword*, vol. xxiv, no. 96, winter 2004, p. 224; also idem, *The Catholic church in Ireland 1914–1918: war and politics*, IAP, Dublin, 2003, for more on the context of the Plunkett mission.

77 Carty, *Bibliography*, pp. 62–3, 'Tracts for the times', number 10 Ghosts, dated 25 December 1915; number 11, The separatist idea, 1 February 1916; number 12, The spiritual nation, 13 February 1916; number 13, The sovereign people, 31 March 1916, Whelan, Dublin, 1916.

78 Pearse, P.H., The sovereign people in Pearse, P.H., *Collected Works of Padraic H. Pearse*, Maunsel, Dublin, 1922, pp. 350 and 342–3 for women's rights.

79 *Ibid.*, p. 372.

80 *Ibid.*, p. 335.

81 Carty, *Bibliography*, p. 71.

82 *Report of the Royal Commission on the Rebellion in Ireland*, p. 9.

83 Letter of Joseph Stanley, Childers, CD 6/8, Bureau of Military History, Military Archives, Cathal Brugha Barracks; Carty, *Bibliography*, p. 70 for the *Spark*, p. 48 for Honesty; and p. 45 for *The Gael*; *Ibid.*, p. 45 citing evidence of Price to the Royal Commission. Also Reilly, Tom, *Joe Stanley: printer to the Rising*, Brandon, Dingle, 2005, pp. 28–30. There is a photo of the raid after p. 96.

84 O'Connor, John, *The 1916 Proclamation*, Anvil, Dublin, 1999, pp. 26–9. All three men submitted Witness Statements to the Bureau of Military History.

85 *Report of the Royal Commission on the Rebellion in Ireland*, p. 10; 1916 rebellion handbook, p. 209; Coates, Tim (ed.), *The Irish uprising 1914–1921*, HMSO, London, 2000, gives the report of the Royal Commission, p. 71 et seq.

86 *Report of the Royal Commission on the Rebellion in Ireland*, p. 13.

87 *Ibid.*

88 *Ibid.* General Friend, however, was asked to explain his absence from Ireland.

89 *Ibid.*

90 *Irish Opinion*, 21 October 1916; *Catholic Bulletin*, November 1916, pp. 594–95; Lyons, John Dillon, pp. 386–87. See Eoin MacNeill papers, NLI, MS 11,437/1 for the original handwritten account by MacNeill.

91 See Sheehy Skeffington, Hanna, *British militarism as I have known it*, Kerryman, Tralee, 1946 [first published 1917], p. 13; also *Ibid.*, pp. 20–2 for a letter, dated 9 April 1917, by Major Vane, giving his account of the events surrounding Sheehy Skeffington's death.

92 *Report of the Royal Commission on the Rebellion in Ireland*, p. 10.

93   Cited in Sheehy Skeffington, Owen, 'Francis Sheehy Skeffington', p. 143.

94   Sheehy Skeffington, Hanna, *British militarism*, pp. 14–15. Colthurst was released from Broadmoor in 1918; *Report of Commission on the arrest and subsequent treatment of Mr Francis Sheehy Skeffington*, 1916 [Cd.8376] xi 311, pp. 11–12; Ginnell, DORA at Westminster, pp. 183–91 for 9 May and 28 June 1916.

95   Dillon to Lloyd George, 11 June 1916, Lloyd George papers, D/4/2/25, quoted in Lyons, John Dillon, p. 392; *Ibid.*, p. 393 for T. P. O'Connor to Lloyd George, 11 June 1916, expressing the same critical opinion of Price.

96   *Ibid.*, p. 392.

97   Keohane to Price, 8 June 1916, chief secretary's office, press censorship records, white cards 1916–17, number 54, National Archives, Dublin; see Murphy, *Catholic Bulletin*, pp. 230–31. The letter was passed on to Lord Decies, press secretary to General Maxwell, who became the official press censor in June 1916. See *The old public school boys who's who*, Eton, np, London, 1933, p. 65.

98   *Catholic Bulletin*, May–June 1916, p. 245.

99   *Ibid.*, p. 246.

100   *Report of the Royal Commission on the Rebellion in Ireland*, p. 5.

101   *Ibid.* Handwritten addition on report by Brennan. See fn. 34.

102   The text of the poem appeared in *Poems and songs of Easter Week*, np, Dublin, nd. See McCoole, Sinead, *No ordinary woman: Irish female activists in the revolutionary years, 1900–1923*, O'Brien, Dublin, 2003, p. 141 for more personal details.

103   FitzHenry, Edna C. (ed.), *Nineteen sixteen: an anthology*, Browne and Nolan, Dublin, 1935, pp. 59–60 and 112. See De Burca rare books, catalogue no. 77, spring 2006, p. 1 for details of the poem's origins. The first edition was limited to twenty five copies.

104   *Catholic Bulletin*, July 1916, p. 393.

105   *Ibid.*, pp. 393–408.

106   *Freeman's Journal*, 23 and 26 February 1917. See Murphy, Brian P., *Patrick Pearse and the lost republican ideal*, James Duffy, Dublin, 1991, pp. 80–81 for the political context of the arrests.

107   Quoted in *Freeman's Journal*, 28 February 1917.

108   Sheehy Skeffington, Hanna, *British militarism*, p. 16.

109   See the *Times*, 17 November 1931 for obituary tribute, wherein Price is described as 'a very gallant gentleman'.

Easter 1916 in Cork – order, counter-order, and disorder:

1   In a letter to Cathal Brugha, sent from Brixton prison on the thirty seventh day of his hunger strike, Terence MacSwiney wrote, 'Ah Cathal, the pain of Easter is properly dead at last'. Cited in Costello, Francis J., *Enduring the most: the life and death of Terence MacSwiney*, Brandon, Dingle, 1995, p. 150.

2   By April 1916 Tomás MacCurtain had succeeded in organsing the Cork

Brigade of Irish Volunteers into forty seven companies. Forty four of these units, with strengths varying from ten men to eighty, formed the Cork brigade under MacCurtain's command while the remaining three (Charleville, Glanworth and Mitchlestown) were attached to the Galtee battalion which was then under the command of Thomas Kent.

3   O'Donoghue, Florence, *Tomás MacCurtain: soldier and patriot*, Anvil, Tralee, 1955, pp. 72–73.

4   O'Donoghue, Florence, 'The Irish Volunteers in Cork 1913–1916' in the *Journal of the Cork Historical and Archaeological Society*, vol. lxxi, nos 213–14, 1966, p. 42.

5   Murphy, Seán, 'Account of Easter Week 1916 in Cork' (unpublished manuscript), p. 2. This document was compiled by Murphy on behalf of the Cork branch of the 1916 Association in November 1956 (authors' collection).

6   *Ibid.*

7   Returns from the twenty companies which still survive, and which are archived at Cork Public Museum, record the statistics as follows: 57 rifles (ammunition 2,776 rounds); 254 shotguns (ammunition 3,075 cartridges); 84 revolvers (ammunition 828 rounds); 131 pikes; and 10lbs gelignite.

8   By Easter 1916 the Military Council also included Thomas Clarke, Thomas MacDonagh, Seán MacDermott and James Connolly.

9   Success was contingent on the successful landing of the German arms. Critical to all IRB planning was the expectation that Germany would send an expeditionary force together with artillery and a large quantity of arms and ammunition. It was also expected that at least one submarine would deploy in the Irish Sea and patrol the east coast in order to prevent the landing of British reinforcements. However, as events unfolded, the German high command were only willing to provide 20,000 old Russian rifles captured at the battle of Tannenburg in 1914, and a relatively small quantity of mixed ammunition.

10   Foley, Brigid, Witness Statement (WS) 1598, Bureau of Military History, Military Archives, Cathal Brugha Barracks, Dublin.

11   Murphy, 'Account of Easter Week 1916 in Cork', p. 3.

12   Brigid Foley returned to Cork on the same day with another dispatch from MacDermott, the contents of which remain unknown.

13   O'Donoghue, *Tomás MacCurtain*, pp. 78–79.

14   MacSwiney, Eithne, WS 119, Bureau of Military History, Military Archives, Cathal Brugha Barracks, Dublin.

15   Foy, Michael and Barton, Brian, *The Easter Rising*, Sutton, Stroud, 1999, pp. 37–38.

16   O'Donoghue, *Tomás MacCurtain*, pp. 78–79.

17   *Ibid.*

18   Ryan, James, 'General Post Office area' in *The Capuchin annual*, 1966, p. 170.

19   MacSwiney, Eithne, WS 119, Bureau of Military History, Military Archives, Cathal Brugha Barracks, Dublin.

20   *Ibid.*

21   The *Aud* was originally due to arrive off the Kerry coast at Tralee Bay and

rendezvous with a contingent of waiting Volunteers on Holy Thursday, 20 April. However the Military Council became concerned that an early landing might alert the British and decided to change the date of the rendezvous to Easter Sunday. This information was transmitted by way of the United States and didn't reach Germany until after the *Aud* had left for Ireland. As wireless was not then fitted to German ships, it never reached its captain, Karl Spindler. The information was, however, intercepted by British naval intelligence but no action was taken at that stage lest it might become clear to Germany that their codes had actually broken. Casement was also at this time trying unsuccessfully to raise an 'Irish brigade' to fight the Allies from Irish soldiers languishing in prisoner of war camps. When he discovered the quantity and quality of the arms being supplied by the Germans he decided to return to Ireland to try and persuade the Military Council to postpone the Rising. Three days after the *Aud* departed Casement left Williamshaven for Ireland, accompanied by Robert Montieth and Daniel Bailey, on board the submarine U19 which was commanded by Lieutenant Weisbach.

22   O'Donoghue, *Tomás MacCurtain*, p. 84.
23   *Ibid.*, p. 87.
24   *Sunday Independent*, 23 April 1916.
25   O'Donoghue, *Tomás MacCurtain*, p. 87.
26   Ryan, 'General Post Office area', pp. 171–72.
27   O'Donoghue, *Tomás MacCurtain*, p. 95.
28   Feeney, P.J., *Glory O, glory O, ye bold Fenian men*, np, Dripsey, 1996, p. 48.
29   Murphy, 'Account of Easter Week 1916 in Cork', p. 4.
30   O'Donoghue, *Tomás MacCurtain*, p. 98.
31   *Ibid.*, p. 108. In his account of events in Cork Seán Murphy states that the order read: 'We go into action at noon today'. Murphy, 'Account of Easter Week 1916 in Cork', p. 7.
32   Transcript of Tomás MacCurtain's diary, L. 1945. 29, Cork Public Museum.
33   Robaird Langford papers, U 156, Cork City and County Archive.
34   Letter from Bishop Cohalan in the *Cork Free Press*, 20 May 1916.
35   *Ibid.*
36   *Cork Constitution*, 29 April 1916.
37   Mac Giolla Ghoille, Breandán (ed.) *Intelligence notes 1913–1916*, Stationery Office, Dublin, 1966, p. 234.
38   Chavasse, Moirin, Terence MacSwiney, Clonmore and Reynolds, Dublin 1961, pp. 73–74.
39   Notwithstanding the rigid stance taken by Captain Dickie during the final stages of the negotiations, in his account of the events in Cork Seán Murphy states that Bishop Cohalan wrote that 'the one bright feature of the events of the past fortnight was our experience of the military gentleman [Dickie] who took part in our peace conferences. He was insistent on securing that there should be no military danger in the city but he wanted no irritating or humiliating conditions. He is a North of Ireland Protestant.' Murphy, 'Account of Easter Week 1916 in Cork', p. 14.
40   Chavasse, *Terence MacSwiney*, p. 76.

41   Cornelius Collins, Dáithí Cotter, Donal Óg O'Callaghan, Christopher O'Gorman, Seán Nolan, Fred Murray, Cornelius Murphy, James Murphy and Patrick Trahey. Mary MacSwiney, the president of Cumann na mBan and Nora O'Brien, its secretary, were also arrested in Cork that Tuesday.

42   Richard Kent died of his wounds two days later.

43   Thomas Kent court martial documentation, p. 5, 'Charge Schedule'. A copy of this documentation can be viewed at the military museum, Collins Barracks, Cork.

44   General Maxwell confirmed the findings of the court martial on 6 May 1916.

45   Leahy, Michael WS 96, Bureau of Military History, Military Archives, Cathal Brugha Barracks, Dublin.

46   MacCurtain diary, L. 1945. 29, Cork Public Museum.

47   *Ibid.*

48   *Ibid.*

49   According to a copy of the 'Frongoch Roll' compiled by Joseph Murray, secretary to the Volunteers' committee of camp management, which is held in the Allen Library, O'Connell school, North Richmond St Dublin, a total of eighty nine Volunteers from Co. Cork were detained in Frogoch.

50   *Ibid.*

51   MacSwiney, Eithne, WS 119, Bureau of Military History, Military Archives, Cathal Brugha Barracks, Dublin.

52   The leadership of the Limerick and Kerry brigades also requested that an inquiry be held into the failure of their units to take part in the Rising.

53   Murphy, 'Account of Easter Week 1916 in Cork', p. 11.

54   Chavasse, *Terence MacSwiney*, p. 82.

Constance Markievicz's 'three great movements' and the 1916 Rising:

1   *Irish Citizen*, 27 September 1913.

2   Sheehy Skeffington, Hanna, 'Reminiscences of an Irish suffragette', in Sheehy Skeffington, A.D. and Owens, Rosemary (eds), *Votes for women: Irish women's struggle for the vote, Attic*, Dublin, 1975, p. 12. Cousins, J.H. and Cousins, M.E., *We two together*, Ganesh, Madras, India, 1950, p.164.

3   *Irish Women's Suffrage Federation annual report 1911–12.*

4   *Irish Citizen*, 7 May 1913. Among societies affiliated in 1913 were the Dublin-based Irish Women's Reform League, Belfast Women's Suffrage Society, six branches of the Munster Women's Franchise League, Connaught Women's Franchise League, Warrenpoint and Rostrevor Suffrage Society, along with societies in Newry, Lisburn, Nenagh, Birr, Armagh, Portrush, Bushmills, Ballymoney and Derry.

5   Chenevix, H., 'Louie Bennett' in *Irish Housewife*, 1959, p. 36.

6   For a comprehensive study of the life and work of Louie Bennett see Cullen Owens, Rosemary, *Louie Bennett*, CUP, Cork, 2001.

7   Cousins and Cousins, *We two together*, p. 185.

8   *Irish Citizen*, 17 May 1913.

9   *Daily Mail,* 13 May 1911.

10 Sheehy Skeffington, 'Reminiscences', p. 18.

11 Twenty two of these incidents took place in Dublin, the remainder in Belfast and Lisburn. For further detail regarding the militant campaign in Ireland, see Cullen Owens, Rosemary, *A social history of women in Ireland 1870–1970,* Gill & Macmillan, Dublin, 2005, pp. 81–107.

12 *Workers' Republic,* 18 December 1915.

13 *Bean na hÉireann,* March 1910.

14 Keogh, Dermot, 'Michael O'Lehane and the organisation of linen drapers' assistants' in *Saothar,* vol. iii, 1977, p. 38.

15 Daly, Mary E., 'Women and Trade Unions' in Nevin, Donal (ed.), *Trade union century,* Mercier, Cork, 1994, p. 107.

16 Fox, R.M., *Louie Bennett: her life and times,* Talbot, Dublin, 1958, p. 42.

17 Cullen Owens, *Louie Bennett,* p. 66.

18 ITUC *Report* 1912, p. 52.

19 Sheehy Skeffington, 'Reminiscences', p. 17.

20 ITUC *Report* 1914, pp. 77–79.

21 *Irish Citizen,* 13 November 1913.

22 *Irish Citizen,* 8 November 1913.

23 *Irish Worker,* 4 April 1914.

24 Connolly, James, *The re-conquest of Ireland,* Maunsel, Dublin, 1917, p. 291.

25 Evans, R.J., *The feminists: women's emancipation movements in Europe, America and Australasia 1840–1920,* Croom & Helm, London, 1977, p. 238.

26 Bean na hÉireann, November 1909, pp. 5–6.

27 *Irish Independent,* 2 June 1914.

28 *Irish Independent,* 28 May 1914.

29 *Irish Citizen,* 2 May 1914.

30 Press cutting of letter from Agnes O'Farrelly in scrapbook in Sheehy Skeffington papers, MS 21,616–56, National Library of Ireland. Neither name of paper or exact date is given, but 1911 is written in pencil in margin.

31 *Irish Citizen,* 30 May 1914.

32 *Bean na hÉireann,* April 1909.

33 *Ibid.*

34 Constance Markievicz writing in *Bean na hÉireann,* July 1909, under her pen-name of Maca.

35 Copy of letter from P.H. Pearse to C. Doyle, 30 November 1913, MS 10,486, National Library of Ireland.

36 *Irish Volunteer,* 4 April 1914.

37 *Irish Citizen,* 11 April 1914. At a meeting of Galway city branch of Cumann na mBan in August 1914, it was regretted that only a hundred men had joined the Volunteers; women present were asked to use their influence to get their brothers and sweethearts to join.

38 Urquhart, Diane, '"The female of the species is more deadly than the male"? The Ulster Women's Unionist Council, 1911–40', in Holmes, Janice, and Urquhart, Diane (eds), *Coming into the light: the work, politics and*

    religion of women in Ulster 1840–1940, IIS, Belfast 1994, p. 94.

39   *Freeman's Journal*, 6 May 1914.

40   *Irish Independent*, 8 May 1914.

41   *Ibid.*

42   *Irish Citizen*, 8 August 1914.

43   Minutes of the conference of women delegates to the all-Ireland conference, 12 May 1917, later known as Cumann na dTeachtaire, Sheehy Skeffington papers, MS 21,194, National Library of Ireland. Among the women in attendance at this or at subsequent meetings were Dr Kathleen Lynn, Áine Ceannt, Madeleine Ffrench-Mullen, Helena Molony, Mabel FitzGerald, Kathleen Clarke, Louise Gavan Duffy, Dulcibella Barton, Winifred Carney, Marie Perolz and Alice Ginnell.

44   Copy of letter sent to Sinn Féin executive, 1 August 1917, *Ibid.* The women proposed by the delegates were Kathleen Clarke, Áine Ceannt, Kathleen Lynn, Jennie Wyse Power, Helena Molony and Mrs Ginnell.

45   *Ibid.*, 17 September 1917.

46   *Ibid.*, 25 September 1917.

47   *Ibid.*, 2 October 1917.

48   *Ibid.*, 16 October 1917.

49   *Irish Citizen*, November 1917.

50   Cumann na dTeachtaire minutes, 2 April 1918, general meeting.

51   *Ibid.*

52   *Ibid.*, 30 January 1919.

53   For details see Cullen Owens, Rosemary, *Smashing times: a history of the Irish women's suffrage movement 1889–1922*, Attic, Dublin 1984, pp. 120–22.

54   *Sinn Féin*, 21 September 1907.

55   Cullen Owens, *Smashing times*, pp. 122–24.

56   *Irish Citizen*, August 1918.

57   *Ibid.*

58   *Ibid.*, December 1918.

59   See Cullen Owens, *Louie Bennett*, p. 76–7. Manoeuvrings between Labour and Sinn Féin as to whether Labour should contest this election may have played a role in Bennett's decision. Ultimately, Labour withdrew from the election.

60   Sinn Féin, *An appeal to the women of Ireland*, Sinn Féin, Dublin 1918.

61   Sinn Fein, *Tenth convention report*, October 1917.

62   *Irish Citizen*, December 1918.

63   Sheehy Skeffington papers, MS 24, 107, National Library of Ireland.

64   *Irish Citizen*, April 1919.

65   *Irish Citizen*, November 1917.

66   Doyle, Damien, 'Rosamund Jacob (1888–1960)', in Cullen, Mary and Luddy, Maria (eds), *Female activists: Irish women and change 1900–1960*, Woodfield, Dublin, 2001, p. 176.

67   Farrell, Brian, 'Markievicz and the women of the revolution', in Martin, F.X. (ed.), *Leaders and men of the 1916 Rising: Dublin 1916*, Methuen, London, 1967, p. 235.

68   *Irish Citizen*, May 1919.

69   Ward, Margaret, *Hanna Sheehy Skeffington: a life*, Attic, Cork, 1997, p. 221, citing minutes of Cumann na dTeachtaire, 20 September 1917, Sheehy Skeffington papers 24,104,National Library of Ireland.

70   *Irish Citizen*, September–December 1920. (The paper had just recently become a quarterly publication).

71   Ward, *Hanna Sheehy Skeffington*, p. 221.

72   O'Callaghan, Margaret, 'Women and politics in independent Ireland, 1921–68', in Bourke, Angela et al. (eds), *The Field Day anthology of Irish writing*, vol. v, CUP, Cork, 2002, p. 122.

73   O'Hegarty, P.S., *The victory of Sinn Féin*, Talbot, Dublin, 1924, p. 58.

74   *Ibid.* pp. 102–5

75   Quoted in Gialanella Valiulis, Maryann, 'Defining their role in the new state: Irishwomen's protest against the Juries Act of 1927' in *Canadian Journal of Irish Studies*, vol. xviii, no. 1, July 1992, p. 44.

76   Clancy, Mary, 'Aspects of women's contribution to the Oireachtas debate in the Irish Free State, 1922–1937', in Luddy, Maria, and Murphy, Cliona (eds), *Women surviving: studies in Irish women's history in the nineteenth and twentieth centuries*, Poolbeg, Dublin 1989, p. 218.

77   Quoted in Gialanella Valiulis, Maryann, 'Power, gender and identity in the Irish Free State', in *Journal of women's history*, vol. vi, no. 4, vol. vii, no. 1, 1995, winter – spring 1995, p. 123.

78   Quoted in Gialanella Valiulis, Maryann, 'Engendering citizenship: women's relationship to the state in Ireland and the United States in the post-suffrage period', in Gialanella Valiulis, Maryann and O'Dowd, Mary (eds), *Women and Irish history*, Wolfhound, Dublin, 1997, p. 164.

79   Quoted in Valiulis, 'Defining their role', p. 54.

80   With changes in membership during the lifetime of the Joint Committee, groups in the early years included the Girls Friendly Society, the Girl Guides, Irish Countrywomen's Association, Irish Matrons' Association, the Irish Save the Children Fund, Irish Women Workers' Union, Irish Schoolmistresses' Association, The Legion of Mary, the Mothers' Union, National Council of Women, Women Graduates Association of Trinity College, Women Citizens' Association, Women's National Health Association, the Holy Child Association, Society for the Prevention of Cruelty to Children, and the University College Dublin Women Graduates' Association.

81   Report of Commission into the civil service 1932–1935, addendum C, p. 185.

82   *Irish Citizen*, July 1917.

83   *Irish Citizen*, February 1920.

84   Jones, Mary, *These obstreperous lassies: a history of the Irish Women Workers' Union*, Gill & Macmillan, Dublin, 1988, p. 59.

85   *Irish Citizen*, November 1919.

86   *Irish Citizen*, December 1919.

87   Cahalan, C., 'Women and the Irish labour movement', in *Dublin labour year book*, Dublin Trades Council, Dublin, 1930, p. 48.

88   Molony, Helena, 'James Connolly and women', *Ibid.*, p. 32.

89   Daly, Mary, 'Women and trade unions', in Nevin, Donal (ed.), *Trade union*

century, Dublin, 1994, pp. 106–16.

90 McLaughlin, Astrid, "'Received with politeness, treated with contempt": The story of women's protests in Ireland against the regressive implications of sections of the Conditions of Employment Act (1936) and Bunreacht na hÉireann, the Irish constitution of 1937', unpublished MA thesis, University College Dublin, 1996, 123.

91 It should be noted that section sixteen of the final Act had been section twelve during most of its drafting stages.

92 ITUC *Report*, 1935.

93 *Ibid.*

94 *Ibid.*

95 The *Irish Times*, 11 July 1935, cited in McLaughlin, "'Received with politeness"', p. 26.

96 IWWU, Executive minutes, 5 September 1935, Irish Women Workers Archive, Irish Labour History Museum, Dublin.

97 The deputies in question were Helena Concannon and Margaret Pearse (Fianna Fáil), and Bridget Redmond (Cumann na nGaedhael).

98 Ward, Margaret, *Unmanageable revolutionaries: women and Irish nationalism*, Pluto, London, 1983, p. 236.

99 Clancy, 'Aspects of women's contribution', p. 220.

100 Beaumont, Catriona A., 'Women and the politics of equality: the Irish women's movement, 1930–1943', in Valiulis and O'Dowd (eds), *Women and Irish history*, p. 8.

101 Whyte, J.H., *Church and state in modern Ireland 1923–1979, 2nd edition*, Gill & Macmillan, Dublin, 1980, pp. 33–34.

102 O'Dowd, Liam, 'Church, state and women: the aftermath of partition', in Curtin, Chris, Jackson, Pauline and O'Connor, Barbara (eds), *Gender in Irish society*, GUP, Galway, 1987, p. 7.

103 Quoted by Margaret MacCurtain in 'Fullness of life: defining female spirituality in twentieth century Ireland', in Luddy and Murphy (eds), *Women surviving*, p. 243.

104 IWCA Report in United Irishwomen, 1925–6, pp. 10–11.

105 McLaughlin, "'Received with politeness"', p. 33.

106 Clancy, 'Aspects of women's contribution', p. 225.

107 Robinson, Mary, 'Women and the new Irish state', in MacCurtain and Ó Corrain (eds), *Women in Irish society*, p. 58.

108 Clancy, 'Aspects of women's contribution', p. 206.

109 Beaumont, 'Women and the politics of equality', p. 175.

110 *Irish Citizen*, May 1919.

'Shot in cold blood': military law and Irish perceptions in the suppression of the 1916 rebellion

1 Asquith to King George V, 27 April 1916, CAB 37 146, National Archives, Kew.

2 Statements by Sir Reginald Brade, secretary of the Army Council, and Sir Neville Macready, adjutant general, as quoted in Barton, Brian, *From behind a closed door: secret court martial records of the 1916 Rising*, Blackstaff,

Belfast, 2002, p. 31.

3   'Report on the state of Ireland since the rebellion', 24 June 1916, CAB 37 150/18, p. 2, National Archives, Kew.

4   Alison Philips, W., *The revolution in Ireland*, Longmans, London, p. 109.

5   *Ibid.*, p. 108.

6   *Irish Times*, 8 May 1916.

7   See Townshend, Charles, *Easter 1916: the Irish rebellion*, Allen Lane, London, 2005, p. 300.

8   Defence of the Realm (Amendment), no. 2, Act 1915.

9   For a facsimile reproduction of the 'Schedule', containing details of charge, plea, verdict and other information in the case of Constance Markiewicz see Barton, *From behind a closed door*, p. 81.

10   Defence of the Realm (No. 2) Act 1914.

11   See chapter 1 of Gearty, Conor and Ewing, Keith, *The struggle for civil liberties: political freedom and the rule of law in Britain, 1914–1945*, OUP, Oxford, 2000.

12   The memoir referred to was the basis of a book by the late Leon Ó Broin, which dealt with Wylie's activities during this period. Ó Bróin, Leon, *W.E. Wylie and Irish revolution*, Gill & Macmillan, Dublin, 1989.

13   *Ibid.*, p. 21.

14   *Ibid.*, pp. 22–23.

15   Barton, *From behind a closed door*, pp. 72–73

16   De Valera papers, 150/512, UCD Archives.

17   *Ibid.*

18   See Townshend, *Easter 1916*, p. 290.

19   Ó Bróin, *W.E. Wylie and Irish revolution*, pp. 23–24.

20   *Ibid.*, p. 24.

21   For O'Dwyer see aan de Wiel, Jérôme, *The Catholic church in Ireland 1914–1918: war and politics*, IAP, Dublin, 2003, p. 106.

22   Jeffery, Keith (ed.), Hamilton Norway, Mary Louisa and Arthur, *The Sinn Féin rebellion as they saw it*, IAP edition, Dublin, 1998, p. 54.

23   Notes by Eoin MacNeill, MacNeill papers, MS 11437, National Library of Ireland, as cited in Martin, F.X. (ed.), Tierney, Michael, *Eoin MacNeill: scholar and man of action, 1867–1945*, Clarendon, Oxford, 1980, p. 224.

24   Wells, Warre B., *An Irish apologia*, Maunsel, Dublin, 1917, p. 66.

25   The case is reported as the R. v. Governor of Lewes Prison, ex parte Doyle [1917] 2 KB 254

26   *Ibid.* at 273.

27   *Ibid.* at 272.

28   Scott v. Scott [1913] AC 417.

29   [1917] 2 KB 254 at 272.

30   Liversidge v. Anderson [1942] AC 206 at 244.

31   De Valera papers, 150/512, UCD Archives.

32   Law officers' opinion, 31 January 1917, WO 141/27, National Archives, Kew.

33   Memorandum by Brade, WO 141/27, National Archives, Kew.

34   *Ibid.*

35   Minute by adjutant general, 10 January 1917, WO 141/27, National

Archives, Kew.

36 Winborne to Maxwell, 3 May, 1916, de Valera papers, 150/512, UCD Archives.

37 Asquith, Lady Cynthia, *Diaries 1915–1918*, Hutchinson, London, 1968, p. 163.

38 See footnote 1.

39 *Irish Times*, 8 May 1916.

40 Memorial by influential persons, Asquith papers, MS 42, Bodleian library, Oxford.

41 Report of the Royal Commission on the arrest on 25th April and subsequent treatment of Mr Francis Sheehy Skeffington, Mr Thomas Dickson and Mr Patrick James McIntyre, 1916 [cd.8376] xi 311, para 42.

42 *Ibid.*, para 55(3).

43 Cabinet minutes 28 April 1916, CAB 42/12, National Archives, Kew.

44 General Macready to Major General Jeudwine, 10 December 1920, Jeudwine papers, Imperial War Museum as cited in Townshend, Charles, *The British campaign in Ireland 1919–1921: the development of political and military policies*, OUP, Oxford, 1975, p. 138.

45 Memorandum by Asquith, 19 May 1916, Bonar Law papers, 63/C/5, House of Lords Record Office.

46 The debate on the condition of Ireland, from which this quote is taken, is to be found in House of Commons debates, vol. lxxxiv, cols 2,106–21.

47 Law officers' opinion contained in de Valera papers, 150/512, UCD Archives.

48 'Report on the state of Ireland since the rebellion', 24 June 1916, CAB 37 150/18, National Archives, Kew.

49 De Valera papers, 150/512, UCD Archives.

50 *Ibid.*

51 Cited in de Wiel, Jérôme, *The Catholic church in Ireland 1914–1918*, p. 106.

52 Keane, Ronan, 'Martial law in Ireland, 1535–1924' in *Irish Jurist*, vols. xv–xvii, 1990–2, pp.150–80.

53 *Ibid.*, p. 161.

54 *Ibid.*, p. 180.

55 De Valera papers, 150/512, UCD Archives.

56 Letter from Byrne dated 28 April 1916, WO 32 4307, National Archives, Kew, quoted in Townshend, Charles, *Easter 1916: the Irish rebellion*, Allen Lane, London, 2005, p. 276.

57 *Ibid.*

58 2 NIJR 185.

59 Ó Broin, *W.E. Wylie and Irish revolution*, p. 26.

60 Fingal, *Countess of, Seventy years young: memories of Elizabeth, countess of Fingal*, Lilliput, Dublin, 1991, p. 376.

61 For the case of W.T. Cosgrave see Ó Broin, *W.E. Wylie and Irish revolution*, pp. 28–9.

62 Barton, *From behind a closed door*.

63 *Ibid.*, pp. 33–34.

64 *Ibid.*, pp. 181–97 (Ceannt), and 267–79 (Mallin).

65 See 50 ILTR, 1916, at 128.

66 *Ibid.*

67 *Ibid.* at 318.

68 Notes by Eoin MacNeill cited in Martin (ed.), *Eoin MacNeill*, p. 225.

69 *Ibid.*, p. 227.

70 *Ibid.*, p. 229.

71 Martin (ed.), *Eoin MacNeill*, p. 229.

72 Notes by Eoin MacNeill cited in Martin (ed.), *Eoin MacNeill*, pp. 232–33.

73 *Ibid.*, p. 228.

74 *Ibid.*, p. 239.

75 *Ibid.*, pp. 223–25.

76 See footnote 2.

The Catholic church, the Holy See and the 1916 Rising

1 Whyte, John J., '1916 – revolution and religion' in Martin, F.X. (ed.), *Leaders and men of the Easter Rising: Dublin 1916*, Methuen, London, 1967, pp. 203–14.

2 See Morrissey, Thomas J., *William J. Walsh, archbishop of Dublin, 1841–1921*, Four Courts, Dublin, 2000; (also Walsh, Patrick J., *William J. Walsh, archbishop of Dublin*, Talbot, Dublin, 1938.) Walsh is very extensively covered in aan de Weil, Jérôme, *The Catholic church in Ireland 1914–1918*, IAP, Dublin, 2003. See also his 'Archbishop Walsh and Mgr Curran's opposition to the British war effort in Dublin, 1914–1916', in *The Irish Sword*, vol. xxii, no. 88, winter 2000, pp. 193–204; and my *The Vatican, the bishops and Irish politics, 1919–1939*, CUP, Cambridge, 1986.

3 Miller, David W., *Church, state and nation in Ireland, 1898–1921*, Gill & Macmillan, Dublin, 1973, p. 14.

4 Statement by Fr Michael Curran, WS 687 (section 1), Bureau of Military History, Military Archives, Cathal Brugha Barracks, Dublin.

5 Statement by Seán T. O'Kelly, WS 1765, Bureau of Military History, Military Archives, Cathal Brugha Barracks, Dublin.

6 Curran became vice rector of the College in 1919 following O'Riordan's death, before succeeding Hagan as rector in 1930.

7 See Michael O'Riordan and John Hagan papers, Irish College Rome. I am most grateful to the archivist, Vera Orschel, who helped greatly in the completion of this research.

8 Canning, Bernard J., *Bishops of Ireland 1870–1987*, Donegal Democrat, Ballyshannon, 1987, p. 42.

9 *Ibid.*

10 *Ibid.*, p. 239.

11 See Joyce, P.J., *John Healy, archbishop of Tuam*, Gill, Dublin, 1931.

12 Canning, *Bishops of Ireland 1870–1987*, pp. 317–18.

13 Hanley, John J., *The Irish College Rome*, Irish heritage series no. 64, Dublin, 1980. See also Silke, John, *Relics, refugees and Rome: an Irish guide*, Irish College, Rome, 1975, p. 82 ff.

14 O'Riordan, Michael, *Catholicity and progress in Ireland*, Kegan Paul, London, 1906.

15 Murphy, Brian P., *The Catholic Bulletin and republican Ireland with special reference to J.J. O'Kelly* ('Sceilg'), Athol, Belfast, 2005.

16 See Magennis, Peter E., 'Monsignor John Hagan' and other articles in The *Catholic Bulletin*, vol. xx, no. 4, April 1936.

17 Leslie, Shane, *Long shadows – memoirs of Shane Leslie*, John Murray, London, 1966, p. 262.

18 See aan de Wiel, Jérôme, 'Archbishop Walsh and Mgr Curran's opposition to the British war effort in Dublin, 1914–1916', passim.

19 Walsh, *William J. Walsh, archbishop of Dublin*, p. 571.

20 Statement by Fr Michael Curran, WS 687 (section 1), Bureau of Military History, Military Archives, Cathal Brugha Barracks, Dublin.

21 Morrissey, *William J. Walsh, archbishop of Dublin*, 1841–1921, p. 272 ff.

22 Statement by Fr Michael Curran, WS 687 (section 1), pp. 8–9, Bureau of Military History, Military Archives, Cathal Brugha Barracks, Dublin.

23 *Ibid.*

24 Ernest Blythe, later a minister in the Irish Free State, was a northern Presbyterian. He was prominent in radical politics and a friend of the IRB man, Bulmer Hobson. In early 1915, Desmond FitzGerald visited Blythe in Dublin. He told him that the decision had already been taken to hold a rising during the war. The same source was convinced that Germany would win the war. See FitzGerald, Garret, (ed.) *Desmond's Rising: memoirs 1913 to Easter 1916*, Liberties, Dublin, 2006, pp. 78–79.

25 Statement by Fr Michael Curran, WS 687 (section 1), pp. 9–10, Bureau of Military History, Military Archives, Cathal Brugha Barracks, Dublin.

26 *Ibid.*

27 *Ibid.*, pp. 11–13.

28 *Ibid.*

29 *Ibid.*, p. 16.

30 *Ibid*, pp. 20–21.

31 *Ibid.*, pp. 18–19.

32 *Ibid.*

33 Curran to Hagan, 23 January 1916, Hagan papers, Irish College Rome.

34 Ó Brolcháin, Honor (ed.), Plunkett Dillon, Geraldine, *All in the blood: a memoir of the Plunkett family, the 1916 Rising and the War of Independence*, Farmar, Dublin, 2006, pp. 208–9.

35 *Ibid.*, pp. 14–22.

36 Murphy, Brian P., *Patrick Pearse and the lost republican ideal*, James Duffy, Dublin, 1991, p. 77 ff.

37 Plunkett Dillon, *All in the blood*, p. 158.

38 Desmond Williams, T., 'Eoin MacNeill and the Irish Volunteers', in Martin (ed.), *Leaders and men of the Easter Rising*, p. 135 ff.

39 Plunkett Dillon, *All in the blood*, p. 176 ff.

40 See Lynch, Diarmuid, *The IRB and the 1916 Rising*, Mercier, Cork, 1957, pp. 102, 131, and footnote on latter page.

41 McGee, Owen, *The IRB: the Irish Republican Brotherhood, from the Land League to Sinn Féin*, Four Courts, Dublin, 2005, p. 356.

42   Plunkett Dillon, *All in the blood*, pp. 201–8.

43   *Ibid.*, pp. 210–11.

44   Leslie, Shane, *Cardinal Gasquet*, Burns Oates, London, 1953, p. 247.

45   Dr Jérôme aan de Wiel has written about this letter in his doctoral thesis, 'The Catholic church in Ireland, 1914–1918', submitted to the University of Caen, France, 1998, pp. 197–205. See also his 'Archbishop Walsh and Mgr Curran's opposition to the British war effort in Dublin, 1914–1916'.

46   In a letter to Casement, dated 11 April 1916, Count Plunkett wrote: 'I do not suppose that any material change has occurred in Irish affairs since I left Dublin on 29 March.' See O'Rahilly, Aodogán, *Winding the clock: O'Rahilly and the 1916 Rising*, Lilliput, Dublin, 1991, pp. 180–81.

47   *Ibid.*, p. 178. Also Murphy, *Patrick Pearse and the lost republican ideal*, pp. 77–78.

48   Plunkett Dillon, *All in the blood*, p. 211.

49   O'Rahilly, *Winding the clock: O'Rahilly and the 1916 Rising*, p. 179.

50   Kelly, J.N.D., 'Benedict XV', in *The Oxford dictionary of popes*, OUP, Oxford, 1986, p. 315.

51   Plunkett Dillon, *All in the blood*, p. 211.

52   'Archbishop Walsh and Mgr Curran's opposition to the British war effort in Dublin, 1914–1916', p. 197, footnote.

53   *Ibid.*

54   *Ibid.*

55   Una McDix, writing from Rathfarnham, continued the exchange in a letter to the *Irish Press* on 9 June 1933. She doubted the veracity of the count's report: 'Surely the ordinary Catholic conception of the pope is as the father of all Christians, even of those who do not recognize his authority. Would a father bless one of his sons for trying to shoot another of his sons, no matter how just his quarrel? I can imagine the pope blessing O'Connell's repeal movement, which certainly would have succeeded without bringing on Ireland the nemesis which inevitably follows war.' She did not 'doubt Count Plunkett's sincerity, but I am convinced there was some misunderstanding. It is so easy to believe what we wish to be true. I am a Catholic and a republican in the sense that I want complete separation; but I no more believe in war than I believe in one man shooting another because he has a quarrel with him. National civil resistance will accomplish much more than force.' In answer to her query, the editor of the Press wrote the following: 'It is history that the popes granted indulgences to those who took part in the Crusades and (see Catholic Encyclopaedia, vol. iv, p. 543) equated service in these wars with the building of churches and monasteries. Pope Gregory XIII met James Fitzmaurice in Rome in 1575 and promised him several ships of munitions and provisions (see Pastor's History of the Popes, vol. xix, p. 407). The Pope sent Rinuccini to Ireland in 1645 "with a good supply of arms, ammunition and money" (*Catholic Encyclopaedia*, vol. xiii, p. 61). In all these cases the defence of religion was either the sole or the main objective, but they answer the point raised by Mrs McDix.'

56   Plunkett Dillon, *All in the blood*, p. 211.

57   Statement by Fr Michael Curran, WS 687 (section 1), pp. 37–9, Bureau of

Military History, Military Archives, Cathal Brugha Barracks, Dublin.

58   Plunkett Dillon, *All in the blood*, p. 211.

59   *Ibid.*

60   Statement by Fr Michael Curran, WS 687 (section 1), pp. 22–25, Bureau of Military History, Military Archives, Cathal Brugha Barracks, Dublin.

61   Curran to Hagan, 16 April 1916, Hagan papers, Irish College Rome.

62   Plunkett Dillon, *All in the blood*, pp. 214–15.

63   Curran to Hagan, 19 April 1916, Hagan papers, Irish College Rome.

64   *Ibid.*

65   *Ibid.*, 22 April 1916.

66   *Ibid.*

67   Statement by Fr Michael Curran, WS 687 (section 1), pp. 28–34, Bureau of Military History, Military Archives, Cathal Brugha Barracks, Dublin.

68   Curran to Hagan, 23 April 1916, Hagan papers, Irish College Rome.

69   Statement by Fr Michael Curran, WS 687 (section 1), pp. 35–37, Bureau of Military History, Military Archives, Cathal Brugha Barracks, Dublin.

70   See O'Connor, Sir James, *History of Ireland 1798–1924*, Arnold, London, 1925, p. 278; this is quoted in Walsh, *William J. Walsh, archbishop of Dublin*, pp. 592–93.

71   Martin, F.X., (ed.), Tierney, Michael, *Eoin MacNeill: scholar and man of action, 1867–1945*, Clarendon, Oxford, 1980, pp. 219–24.

72   MacRory to O'Riordan, 4 May 1916, O'Riordan papers, Irish College Rome.

73   Curran to Hagan, 8 May 1916, Hagan papers, Irish College Rome. Curran had been awoken earlier that morning by stones being thrown up at his window. He was, he wrote, expecting to be arrested himself, 'and I had actually a bag ready, packed, to take with me'. He recognised William Kelly, the archbishop's butler, among a group of three other men. When he went downstairs, he met the brother of Séamus Mallin who was to be shot at 3am. He wanted the archbishop to intervene to seek a reprieve. Curran said it was out of the question owing to Walsh's condition. He inquired who else was to be shot that morning and was told Éamonn Ceannt (who had been in the class below Curran in school), Con Colbert and Seán Heuston. He went on to say mass for all who had been shot later that morning. Ceannt, it might be noted, had been part of an Irish delegation to visit the Holy See in 1908. Seán T. O'Kelly recalled that he had played the bagpipes for Pope Pius X.

74   He added: 'O'Connell Street is a smoking ruin from Cathedral Street to Eden Quay and from Henry Street to Elvery's. Other houses, though standing, are shattered and torn. I suppose 500 civilians and more solders have been killed or wounded. The Volunteers did not lose so many. One redeeming feature was their conduct. They fought courageously against numbers and equipment. They fought cleanly – no drink, no looting, no personal vengeance and no unnecessary destruction of property. The soldiers, too seemed a decent lot – there was no signs of racial hatred and no unnecessary violence.' *Ibid.*

75   Whyte, '1916 – revolution and religion' in Martin (ed.), *Leaders and men of the Easter Rising*, p. 221.

76 Quoted in Canning, *Bishops of Ireland 1870–1987*, pp. 242–44.

77 Whyte, '1916 – revolution and religion' in Martin (ed.), *Leaders and men of the Easter Rising*, pp. 221–24.

78 Fogarty to O'Riordan, 16 June 1916, O'Riordan papers, Irish College Rome.

79 *Ibid.*

80 Statement by Fr Michael Curran, WS 687 (section 1), p. 84, Bureau of Military History, Military Archives, Cathal Brugha Barracks, Dublin.

81 *The Cork Examiner*, 17 May 1916.

82 Cohalan to O'Riordan, 2 July 1916, O'Riordan papers, Irish College Rome.

83 Statement by Fr Michael Curran, WS 687 (section 1), p. 82, Bureau of Military History, Military Archives, Cathal Brugha Barracks, Dublin.

84 *Ibid.*, p. 83.

85 Morrissey, Thomas J., *Bishop Edward O'Dwyer of Limerick, 1842–1917*, Four Courts, Dublin, 2003, pp. 47–288, passim.

86 O'Dwyer to O'Riordan, 4 May 1916, O'Riordan papers, Irish College Rome.

87 *Ibid.*, 18 May 1916.

88 Morrissey, *Bishop Edward O'Dwyer of Limerick, 1842–1917*, p. 378.

89 O'Dwyer to O'Riordan, 31 May 1916, O'Riordan papers, Irish College Rome.

90 Morrissey, *Bishop Edward O'Dwyer of Limerick, 1842–1917*, p. 379.

91 Roughneen to O'Riordan, 9 June 1916, O'Riordan papers, Irish College Rome.

92 *Ibid.*

93 Ryan to O'Riordan, 23 June 1916, O'Riordan papers, Irish College Rome.

94 Douglas Hyde (An Craoibhín) wrote a letter to O'Riordan on 7 August 1916, asking him to sign a petition, drawn up by Denis J. Coffey, the president of UCD, against the possibility of MacNeill's execution. He said that Sir Bertram Windle, president of University College Cork, and Dr Bergin were among those who were willing to sign. Hyde's note pointed out: 1) that MacNeill was a 'scholar of eminence who has specially devoted his attention to certain very important fields of research which on account of their difficulty and obscurity have attracted but few workers'; 2) there was 'at present no one qualified to fill his vacant place in this department of scholarship'; 3) 'in the interest of learning we feel that Mr MacNeill should be placed in a position to continue the work for which he is best qualified, and in which he has already gained a distinguished name.' Hyde wanted MacNeill to have the use of writing materials, and 'at least a small selection of the books bearing on his studies'. O'Riordan papers, Irish College Rome.

95 Martin (ed.), Tierney, *Eoin MacNeill: scholar and man of action, 1867–1945*, p. 225.

96 *Ibid.*, p. 241.

97 *Irish Catholic Directory*, 1917, p. 519.

98 Letter found in the archives of the Vatican by Jérôme aan de Wiel; copy in

O'Riordan papers, Irish College Rome.

99 *Irish Catholic Directory*, 1917, pp. 517–18.

100 *Ibid.*

101 Andrews, C.S., *Dublin made me: an autobiography*, Mercier, Cork, 1979, pp. 89–90.

102 *Catholic Bulletin*, vol. vi, no. 6, June 1916, pp. 249–53.

103 *Catholic Bulletin*, vol. vi, no. 7, July 1916, p. 337.

104 Curran to O'Riordan, 29 July 1916, O'Riordan papers, Irish College Rome.

105 *Ibid.*

106 Curran to Hagan, 30 July 1916, John Hagan papers, Irish College Rome.

107 *Ibid.*

108 Statement by Fr Michael Curran, WS 687 (section 1), pp. 159–63, Bureau of Military History, Military Archives, Cathal Brugha Barracks, Dublin.

109 *Ibid.*, p. 159.

110 See *Irish Catholic Directory*, 1917, pp. 521–52.

111 Curran to O'Riordan, 30 August 1916, O'Riordan papers, Irish College Rome.

112 O'Dwyer to O'Riordan, 31 August 1916, O'Riordan papers, Irish College Rome.

113 *Ibid.*, 21 September 1916.

114 O'Flanagan to Hagan, 5 September 1916, Hagan papers, Irish College Rome.

115 Morrissey, *Bishop Edward Thomas O'Dwyer of Limerick, 1842–1917*, p. 385 ff.

116 Logue to O'Riordan, 20 August 1916, O'Riordan papers, Irish College Rome.

117 No original copy of the 'Red Book' is to be found in the archives of the Irish College, which merely contains, in the O'Riordan papers, a photocopy of a Vatican Archive copy, deposited by Dr aan de Wiel.

118 The 'Red Book', pp. 20–22, O'Riordan papers, Irish College Rome.

119 *Ibid.*, pp. 26–33.

120 *Ibid.*, p. 38.

121 *Ibid.*, pp. 38, 43.

122 Cohalan to O'Riordan, 14 October 1916, O'Riordan papers, Irish College Rome.

123 Logue to O'Riordan, 28 October 1916, O'Riordan papers, Irish College Rome.

124 O'Dwyer to O'Riordan, 29 September 1916, O'Riordan papers, Irish College Rome.

125 *Ibid.*

126 MacCaffrey to Hagan, 20 December 1916, John Hagan papers, Irish College Rome.

127 O'Donnell to O'Riordan, 6 November 1916, Michael O'Riordan papers, Irish College Rome. I am grateful to Professor Matthew MacNamara for deciphering this letter.

128 *Ibid.*

129 Curran to Hagan, 15 October 1916, Hagan papers, Irish College Rome.

130 McKenna to O'Riordan, 24 November 1916, O'Riordan papers, Irish College Rome.

Bureau of Military History: testimony of Michael Curran

1   The editors are grateful to Noelle Dowling, archivist, Dublin Archdiocesan Archives, for the above information, which was taken from the *Irish Catholic Directories* 1907–1961 and Sherry, Richard et al., *Holy Cross College, Clonliffe, Dublin, 1859–1959: College history and centenary*, Irish printers, Dublin, 1962.

Easter ethics

1   Dudley Edwards, Ruth, *Patrick Pearse: the triumph of failure*, Taplinger edition, New York, 1977, pp. 284–85.

2   Cited at the Irish government website on 1916, www.taoiseach.ie (downloaded 11 April 2006).

3   To pick one contextual factor at random: consider the extreme reaction of the Conservative party to the removal of the Lords' veto in 1911 and the home rule bill of 1912. Its relevance to ethical analysis (as distinct from historical explanation) of the Easter Rising is not about whether it excuses the Rising, but about the degree to which the leaders of the Rising properly grasped its political significance and acted accordingly.

4   De Valera noted as much, fifty years later; see Coogan, Tim Pat, *De Valera: long fellow, long shadow*, Hutchinson, London, 1993, p. 680.

5   Nor can we minimise this by pointing to a lack of insight into democracy. Foster, R.F., *Modern Ireland 1600–1972*, Allen Lane, London, 1988 cites the following (pp. 510–11): 'when Kevin O'Higgins declared that a man who killed without a constitutional mandate from the people was a murderer, Liam Mellowes, reasonably enough, interjected: "Easter week?" The ghosts of Pearse's rhetoric were hard to lay.'

6   See Foster, *Modern Ireland 1600–1972*, p. 506. The issue is arguable, and has been vigorously argued. However, the mere fact that the issue is arguable suffices here: it is not obvious that the IRB's war of 1916–21 got more than Redmond's party got in 1914. They certainly didn't get more on the north, and may well have got less than a Redmondite Dublin government might have got. Given the Cumann na nGaedheal government's achievement in transforming the relationship between the British parliament and other dominion parliaments leading to the significant Statute of Westminster 1931, de Valera's use of the 1936 abdication crisis to be rid of the monarchy, and his managing to negotiate the ports out of British hands in 1938, it is hard to believe that armed force had ever been needed.

7   Pearse remarked in November 1913: 'I think the Orangeman with a rifle a much less ridiculous figure than the nationalist without a rifle.' Eoin Mac-Neill's 'The North Began' published some months earlier was a de facto call to arms to prevent the Ulster unionists from opting out of a 'home

rule' Ireland. That the author recognised that it could reasonably be taken to be such is reflected in the 'they started the fight' title, along with the much less credible (but indirectly very revealing) assertion that the Irish Volunteers, founded in response to the unionists' arming themselves, were not meant to coerce the unionists. See Lee, J.J., *Ireland 1912–1985: politics and society*, CUP, Cambridge, 1989, pp. 18–19.

8   To say that there was no such thing as Irish democracy in 1916 because there wasn't an Irish parliament in Dublin is to identify democracy narrowly with the location of parliament, ignoring on-the-ground democratic culture and practice, of which there was quite a lot in nineteenth century Ireland.

9   The following story is illustrative: 'An incident during the Convention [summoned by Lloyd George in 1917 to try to get agreement between Irish political parties on the island's future governance, but boycotted by Sinn Féin] showed how the political tide had turned against Redmond. One day while walking along Westmoreland Street, after leaving the convention, Redmond was confronted by a group of young Sinn Féin members, including Todd Andrews, and physically attacked. Only for the intervention of passers-by who escorted him into the front office of the *Irish Times* he could have been badly injured.' Collins, Stephen, 'Returning home to hostility', the *Irish Times* supplement 'The Somme', 27 June, 2006.

10   Politicians claiming the mantle of 1916 for constitutional republicanism are rarely taken to be serious. Once in a while they are answered. At the 1984 annual Béal na mBláth commemoration of Michael Collins, the then Minister for Justice, Michael Noonan, claimed that Collins' methods in fighting the War of Independence were different from, and morally far superior to, those of the IRA's campaign in the 1970s and 1980s. In a letter published in the *Irish Times*, 17 September 1984, Kevin Burke, then editor of *An Phoblacht*, refuted the minister's claim point by point, in devastating detail. The minister made no public rebuttal of Burke's argument that I know of.

11   See, for instance, Hart, Peter, *The IRA and its enemies: violence and community in Cork 1916–1923*, OUP, Oxford, 1998.

12   Compare Germany, September 1916 until the end of the war, when the generals, Hindenburg and Ludendorff, overrode successive chancellors and cabinets as regards political decisions. In the Dáil, the military's influence was more overt and direct, than in the Reichstag. Note too that political instability does not make 'rule by the soldiers' inevitable: in the contemporary Russian civil war, the civilian Bolsheviks kept tight control of the Red Army.

13   See Greenfield, Liah, *Nationalism: five roads to modernity*, HUP, Boston, 1992, for an interesting study of the variants in nationalism among five of the bigger European nations, and the ways in which its values are often incompatible with those of contemporary liberal democracy.

14   See reference in note 11. On 10 April 1919, de Valera's Dáil motion to ostracise RIC members was seconded by Eoin MacNeill, using what Coogan terms 'inflammatory' language ('The police in Ireland are a force

of traitors'); Coogan, *De Valera*, pp. 132–33. The motion was carried unanimously. Given that the killing of RIC men had already started the previous January, MacNeill must have known well what feeling and consequent action he and the Dáil were inciting. The murders of southern Protestants in 1920–22 are also relevant, as is the reluctance to stop them at the time and refusal in later years to acknowledge them.

15 Bowman, John, *De Valera and the Ulster question 1917–1973*, Clarendon, Oxford, 1982, pp. 330–31, citing Frank Gallagher's draft biography of de Valera. Coogan *De Valera*, p. 351 has interesting comments on the story.

16 Fintan O'Toole, article in the *Irish Times*, 23 May 2006. The same article drew the rather unwelcome conclusion that commemorating the politically significant dead is a zero-sum game. Who is commemorated tells you who will not be commemorated. Commemorating Wolfe Tone requires ignoring Edmund Burke and minimising Daniel O'Connell; if Pearse is a model to follow, then Redmond is not. (O'Toole also noted that, at the time of writing, when there was much fanfare over the ninetieth anniversary of the Easter Rising, the Michael Davitt Memorial Association in Straide, Co. Mayo was having great difficulty in getting any public funding to celebrate the centenary of Davitt's death.)

17 Cited in Bowman, *de Valera and the Ulster question 1917–1973*, p. 3.

18 See Lee, *Ireland 1912–1985*, pp. 86–87 on the mass politicisation of the Irish public (which happened rather earlier in Ireland when compared to other European countries) and which, fairly quickly, developed along party lines, beginning under O'Connell in the early nineteenth century. Lee remarks (referring to a phrase that appeared in the *Freeman's Journal* 17 September 1881): 'There was some truth, even as early as 1881, in the claim that "If ever a country passed through a parliamentary apprenticeship of the fullest term, Ireland is that country."'

19 It is revealing that the involvement of individual Fenians (e.g. Davitt) in such social issues as the tenant–farmers struggle against the landlords was frowned on by the Fenian leadership as a distraction from the transcendent goal of an Irish republic. Their strange idea of a republic was that it transcended crude economic issues and the 'all-politics-is-local' aspect of democracy.

20 Given the uproar over the oath recognising King George V in the Treaty debates, it is curious that some of the 1916 leaders were apparently prepared to contemplate a Hohenzollern monarch for Ireland, as a result of a successful rising and the war being won by Germany, the 'gallant ally' of the Proclamation.

21 For an interesting account of the ethical and political foundations of the concept, see Riordan, Pat, *A politics of the common good*, IPA, Dublin, 1996.

22 It's informative to consider the phrase in the IRB oath, where the oath-taker recognises that the Irish republic is 'virtually established'. The sense is of it established in the hearts of people like a secret, or established like a Hegelian Geist transcending politics. See Foster, *Modern Ireland 1600–1972*, p. 391 for some pithy remarks on the IRB mindset.

The golden jubilee of the 1916 Easter Rising

1   Bhreathnach-Lynch, Sighle, 'The Easter Rising 1916: constructing a canon in art and artefacts', *History Ireland*, vol. v, no. 1, spring 1997, p. 40.

2   Staunton, Enda, *The nationalists of Northern Ireland, 1918–1973*, Dublin, Columba, 2001, p. 247.

3   In his autobiography, Terence O'Neill noted how the improved north–south relations of the period were 'shattered by the insistence of the Belfast Catholics in celebrating the fiftieth anniversary of the Dublin rebellion. It was 1966 which made 1968 inevitable and was bound to put the whole future of Northern Ireland in the melting pot.' David Trimble has also referred to the jubilee events 'starting the slide which became apparent two or three years later'.

4   Cruise O'Brien, Conor, 'From one civil war to the next', *Irish Times*, 4 December 1981.

5   Keogh, Dermot, *Twentieth century Ireland: nation and state*, Dublin, Gill & Macmillan, 1994, p. 289.

6   For a detailed background to the events in Northern Ireland, see O'Dwyer, Rory, 'The Golden Jubilee of the 1916 Rising', unpublished MA thesis, University College Cork, 2003, pp. 44–57.

7   Girvin, Brian, 'Uneasy alliance of traditional and modern', *Cork Examiner*, 2 April 1991.

8   *Ibid.*

9   Idem., 'Changing interpretations', *Cork Examiner*, 6 April 1991.

10 Bew, Paul and Patterson, Henry, *Seán Lemass and the making of modern Ireland, 1945–66*, Gill & Macmillan, Dublin, 1982, p. 184.

11 *Ibid.*

12 Coiste Cuimhneachán, report of first meeting, 19 February 1965, D/T 97/6/57, National Archives, Dublin.

13 *Ibid.*

14 *Irish Times*, 19 February 1965, D/T 97/6/157, National Archives, Dublin.

15 Department of Justice to Taoiseach, 22 February 1966, D/T 96/6/161 S17607E, National Archives, Dublin.

16 *Irish Press*, 9 February 1966.

17 *Evening Herald*, 13 March 1965.

18 Coiste Cuimhneachán, report of meeting, 18 November 1965, D/T 97/6/159 S17607C, National Archives, Dublin.

19 *Ibid.*

20 *Ibid.*

21 Department of External Affairs, Cuimhneachán 1916–1966, *Commemoration: a record of Ireland's commemoration of the 1916 Rising*, Stationery Office, Dublin, 1966.

22 *Irish Times*, 19 February 1966.

23 Boyce, D.G. '"No lack of ghosts": memory, commemoration, and the state in Ireland' in McBride, Ian (ed.), *History and memory in modern Ireland*, CUP, Cambridge, 2001, p. 267.

24   *Irish Times*, 1 April 1966.

25   See O'Dwyer, 'The Golden Jubilee of the 1916 Rising', pp. 44–45.

26   Lemass, Seán, 'The meaning of the commemoration', *Easter commemoration digest*, Graphic, Dublin, 1966.

27   *Irish Independent*, 8 April 1966.

28   Department of External Affairs, *Cuimhneachán 1916–1966*, p. 23.

29   The remains had been buried in a quicklime plot within Pentonville prison.

30   Department of External Affairs, *Cuimhneachán 1916–1966*, p. 24.

31   *Ibid.*

32   The tricolour has been flown from the GPO every day since, following a government decision in 1966; *Ibid.*, p. 28.

33   The Four Courts, the Mendicity Institution, Jacob's factory, Boland's mills, Mount Street bridge and the South Dublin Union were the principal sites in question.

34   The Kilmainham Gaol Restoration Committee was a voluntary group that had commenced the restoration of the historic old building in 1960.

35   Department of External Affairs, *Cuimhneachán 1916–1966*, p. 33.

36   *Ibid.*, p. 43.

37   *Ibid.*, p. 45.

38   *Ibid.*, p. 47.

39   *Ibid.*, p. 48.

40   *Ibid.*, p. 54.

41   The *Times* (London), 16 April 1966.

42   Department of External Affairs, *Cuimhneachán 1916–1966*, p. 64.

43   *Ibid.*

44   Details are to be found in 'Government Reception, Dublin Castle', D/T 97/6/490 S17955 & 97/6/583 S17955 (annex).

45   *Ibid.*

46   Department of External Affairs, *Cuimhneachán 1916–1966*, p. 71.

47   *Ibid.*, p. 72.

48   *Ibid.*

49   This was revealed in an interview with Liam Sutcliff, one of three IRA dissidents responsible for the destruction of the pillar, featured in a television documentary on Nelson's pillar. (Tall Tales: From pillar to spire, Stopwatch productions, 2003.)

50   *Belfast Newsletter*, 9 April 1966.

51   *Irish News*, 7 April 1966.

52   See 'Berry explains his job', *Magill*, vol. ix, no. 3, June 1980.

53   'IRA organisation', 10 December 1966, D/T 98/6/495 S16571H, National Archives, Dublin.

54   *Ibid.*

55   *Tuairisc*, (newsletter of the Wolfe Tone society), p. 5.

56   *United Irishman*, vol. xx, no. 5, May 1966, p. 5.

57   *Irish Times*, 11 April 1966.

58   *Ibid.*

59   *Ibid.*

60   *Ibid.*

61   The correspondence between the two committees is included in D/T 97/6/162 S17607F, National Archives, Dublin.

62   *Ibid.*

63   Department of Justice to Lemass, 22 February 1966, D/T 97/6/161 S17607E, National Archives, Dublin.

64   *Ibid.*

65   *Ibid.*

66   Lemass to Childers, 23 February 1966, D/T 97/6/161, National Archives, Dublin.

67   Lemass to Childers, 23 February 1966, D/T 97/6/161, National Archives, Dublin. For more details on the security committee see O'Dwyer, 'The Golden Jubilee of the 1916 Rising', p. 47.

68   The historians involved were F.S.L. Lyons, F.X. Martin, T. Desmond Williams, R. Dudley Edwards, Maureen Wall, G.A. Hayes McCoy, Donal McCartney, J. Boyle and Brian Ó Cuív.

69   Martin, F.X., '1916: myth, fact and mystery', in *Studia Hibernica*, no. 7, 1967, p. 39.

70   Caulfield, Max, *The Easter rebellion*, Frederick Muller, London, 1964.

71   O'Broin, Leon, *Dublin Castle and the 1916 Rising*, Sedgwick and Jackson, London, 1966; Mac Giolla Choille, Breandán, *Intelligence notes 1913–16*, Stationery Office, Dublin, 1966.

72   McHugh, Roger, *Dublin 1916*, Arlington, London, 1966.

73   Martin, '1916: myth, fact and mystery', p. 48.

74   Martin, F.X. (ed.), *Leaders and men of the Easter Rising: Dublin 1916*, Methuen, London, 1967.

75   Boyce, D.G., '1916: Interpreting the Rising' in Boyce, D.G. and O'Day, A. (eds), *The making of modern Irish history: revisionism and the revisionist controversy*, Routledge, London, 1996, p. 165.

76   Dudley Edwards, Owen and Pyle, Fergus, *1916: the Easter Rising*, MacGibbon and Kee, London, 1968.

77   *Ibid.*, pp. 223–40.

78   Martin, '1916: myth, fact and mystery', p. 50.

79   Cruise O'Brien, Conor, 'The embers of Easter', *Irish Times*, 8 April 1966.

80   Coogan, Tim Pat, *Ireland since the Rising*, Greenwood, Connecticut, 1966.

81   Foster, R.F., 'History and the Irish question', in Brady, Conor (ed.), *Interpreting Irish history: the debate on historical revisionism 1938–1994*, IAP, Dublin, 1994, p. 141.

82   Quoted in Boyce, '1916: Interpreting the Rising', p. 179.

83   Murphy, John A., *Ireland in the twentieth century*, Gill & Macmillan, Dublin, 1975, p. 145.

84   Department of External Affairs, *Cuimhneachán 1916–1966*, p. 74.

85   Arnold, Bruce, 'The arts' in *1916–1966: 50 Years On*, np, Dublin, 1966, pp. 12–14.

86   Martin, F.X., *The Easter Rising, 1916, and University College Dublin*, Browne and Nolan, Dublin, 1966.

87   Greaves, C. Desmond, *The life and times of James Connolly*, Lawrence and Wishart, London, 1961.

88   *Dáil Debates*, vol. 241, 30 October 1969, col. 2281.

89   As recalled in an interview with Pádraig Ó Cuilleanáin, a fellow member of the Coiste Cuimhneachán.

90   *Irish Independent*, 22 March 1966, D/T 96/6/162 S17607F, National Archives, Dublin.

91   'Better than Bunting', *Irish Times*, 14 April 1966.

92   Address by Lemass at dinner arranged by Dublin Comhairle Dáil Cheantair Fianna Fáil in honour of the twenty first anniversary of the election to Dáil Éireann of Patrick Burke, TD, Spa hotel, Lucan, 9 October 1965, D/T 96/6/159 S17607C, National Archives, Dublin.

93   Lemass to Aiken, 7 March 1966, D/T 97/6/162, National Archives, Dublin.

94   *Irish Times*, 18 April 1966.

95   *Belfast Newsletter*, 19 April 1966.

96   *Ibid.*, 21 April 1966.

The commemoration of the ninetieth anniversary of the Easter Rising

1   The full text of the speech can be found on the website of the Department of the Taoiseach (www.taoiseach.gov.ie). Excerpts are contained in reports in the national press on Monday 10 April 2006.

2   Report of the director of the Bureau, 1957, as quoted in Doyle, Jennifer, Clarke, Frances, Connaughton, Éibhlís and Somerville, Orna, *An introduction to the Bureau of Military History, 1913–1921*, Military Archives, Dublin, 2002, p 1. See also Ferriter, Diarmuid, '"In such deadly earnest": the Bureau of Military History', *Dublin Review*, vol. xii, 2003, pp. 36–65.

3   It should also be noted that small quantities of original material for other aspects of the Rising have recently been made available to researchers, with the discovery of a cache of letters from Roger Casement in the archives of Clare County Council in 2003 being but one example. See *Irish Times* 26 April 2005.

4   An interesting exchange of views on the economic legacy of the Rising took place in the columns of the *Irish Times* between Dr Garret FitzGerald and Ian d'Alton of Naas, Co. Kildare. See the original contribution on the topic by Dr FitzGerald (*Ibid.*, 12 April 2006) and the instructive subsequent exchange of letters between the two, beginning with Ian d'Alton's initial reply on 19 April, with further correspondence on 24, 28 and 29 April.

5   See the article '1916: the debate continues' by Professor Dermot Keogh in *The Word*, April 2006, pp. 4–5.

6   See, for example, the article 'Ahern's Rising' in the *Sunday Times*, 5 February 2006.

7   The party-political dimensions of the commemoration are explored in more detail later in the article.

8   See, for example, several references to the riot, and its consequences for the planned parade, in the *Sunday Independent*, 26 February and 5 March, in Fintan O'Toole's column in the *Irish Times*, 28 February, and in the *Belfast Telegraph* on the same day. Details of the security operation under-

taken to protect the parade from any untoward incidents can be found in most national newspapers over the Easter weekend.

9   A marked disagreement between Fintan O'Toole and the Minister for Defence, Willie O'Dea, over the reasons for the suspension of the parade at this time was a central feature of an extended panel discussion on the Rising on the popular Late, Late Show, broadcast by RTÉ on 3 March.

10 This dealt with the mis-handling by members of the Catholic hierarchy of allegations of sexual abuse levelled against certain clergymen in the Ferns diocese.

11 The speech also warranted less extensive coverage in the Independent and Examiner on the same day, with immediate reaction from public representatives aired on RTÉ's The Week in Politics and Questions and Answers shows over the following days.

12 Advance notification of the President's appearance at the conference appeared in various newspapers, including the *Sunday Independent, Irish Examiner, Irish Times* and Cork's *Evening Echo*, during the week prior to her address, with local and national radio reports on the day. See also the reference to the conference by Taoiseach Ahern during a Dáil discussion in December 2005 on arrangements to mark the Rising; *Dáil Debates*, vol. dcxi, 7 December 2005, col. 1446.

13 See Mark Brennock's report in the *Irish Times*, 24 February 2006.

14 These quotations are but a selection of the favourable and critical comments contained in the national press in the weeks and months following the speech.

15 See, for example, the swift, negative response from Senator David Norris, *Seanad Debates*, vol. clxxxii, 1 February 2006, col. 900.

16 *Sunday Independent*, 26 February 2006. See also his insightful article in the *Irish Times* 15 April 2006, wherein he cited Gustave de Beaumont's recently re-published and highly influential study of mid-nineteenth century Ireland, *Ireland: social, political and religious*, HUP, Cambridge, 2006, (most especially from the 'Preface' to the 1863 edition; *Ibid.*, p. 402).

17 *Irish Examiner* 14 April 2006. The same article appeared in *History Ireland*, vol. xiv, no. 2, March – April 2006, pp. 37–39.

18 The worst afflicted was Kevin Myers, long-time columnist for the *Irish Times* (who rather suddenly transferred his allegiances to the *Irish Independent* in the middle of the commemoration debate). See his 'Irishman's diary' columns in the *Irish Times*, 31 January and 1 February 2006. For the response by the editors of this volume see the same newspaper, Saturday 4 February.

19 An interesting response to the charges contained in the letter came from Professor John A. Murphy, who, in the same newspaper on 20 February, referred to Mr Bury's 'sensational assertion' regarding the alleged campaign of intimidation and persecution of southern Protestants, and requested that 'the detailed evidence and the documented statistics' relating to same be furnished forthwith.

20 *Sunday Independent*, 5 February 2006.

21 *Tullamore Tribune*, 8 February 2006.

22 See also the praise for the President's 'pre-emptive success' in deliver-

ing the speech in a letter from Peter Kennedy, Dublin, published in the *Village*, 30 March–5 April 2006. The magazine was one of the principal forums for debate on the commemoration.

23   See the national press on 22 October, and the local press over the following week, for immediate reaction to the announcement.

24   *Irish Independent*, 17 April 2006.

25   *Irish Examiner*, 15 April 2006.

26   *Dáil debates*, vol. dcix, 3 November 2005, cols. 594–96.

27   *Irish Independent*, 17 April 2006. A discordant note was struck by the *Belfast Telegraph*, 19 April 2006, which described the event as 'Kremlinesque'. For a more positive view from the other side of the Atlantic see the *New York Times*, 17 April 2006.

28   *Irish Independent*, 25 October 2005; also Martin Kettle in the *Guardian*, 29 October 2005.

29   Letter from Patrick Goggin, Dun Laoghaire, *Irish Times*, 27 February 2006.

30   *Irish Times*, 20 December 2005.

31   *Sunday Independent*, 12 February 2006.

32   *Irish Times*, 25 October 2006.

33   *Ibid.*, 15 April 2006.

34   See the comments of Labour leader, Pat Rabbitte, in the Dáil on 28 February 2006 (Dail debates, vol. dcxv, col. 1170) and Gerry Adams, president of Provisional Sinn Féin, in his speech to the party's árd fheis, as reported in the *Sunday Independent*, 19 February 2006.

35   *Irish Examiner*, 18 April 2006.

36   In its final form the parade commemorated two distinct elements of the tradition of the defence forces: the spirit of 1916, and the sacrifice of those who had died in the service of the United Nations.

37   *Dáil debates*, vol. dcxi, 7 December 2005, col. 1444.

38   *Ibid.*, vol. dcxv, 23 February 2006, col. 971. The membership of the committee was as follows: Willie O'Dea (Fianna Fáil), Billy Timmins (Fine Gael), Liz MacManus (Labour), Éamonn Ryan (Greens), Aengus Ó Snodaigh (Sinn Féin) and Tony Gregory (Independent, representing the Dáil's 'technical group').

39   I am grateful to Mr Jerry Kelleher of the Department of the Taoiseach for this information. See also the statement made by the Taoiseach, *Dáil debates*, vol. dcxviii, 25 April 2006, col. 9.

40   For more details of the route see the daily press on Saturday and Sunday 16–17 April 2006.

41   The guest list was divided between leading state functionaries and members of the diplomatic corps, relatives of Volunteers killed during the Rising, and members of the defence forces and gardai who had died while on duty with the United Nations.

42   Jeffrey Donaldson, the DUP member of parliament, spoke of the Rising as 'an act of terrorism directed against the British state', *Irish Times* 17 March 2006. Michael Copeland, a spokesman for the UUP, spoke of the event in similar terms: 'It heralded the end of the long and honourable tradition of constitutional Irish nationalism and brought to the fore

the blood-sacrifice ethos of armed republicanism which led directly to the partition of this island and the Irish civil war.' The irony of such a comment, bearing in mind the vituperative contemporary criticism of the Irish party by northern unionists, the formation of the UVF from within their ranks, and their support for partition during the debate over home rule, was apparent to many south of the border. See also the *Irish News*, 7 March 2006.

43 Interview with Anna Pas, of the *Polish Express* magazine, quoted in the *Irish Times*, 15 April 2006.

44 It noted that the 'British fought for the independence of other small European countries but did not recognise the needs of a nation, just across the Irish sea, which had fought for its independence for years already', and 'When the first executions started, when hundreds went to detention camps in Wales and prisons in England, Irish people woke up from the malaise that had lasted for years. The Rising was a spark, which started a fire known later as the War of Independence.' *Polish Express*, April 2006. I am indebted to Ms Bozena Cierlik, of the Department of History, UCC, for her help in translating this piece.

45 *Dáil Debates*, vol. dcxv, 23 February 2006, cols. 970–71. See also the favourable response given by Minister O'Dea at that time, *Ibid*.

46 *Dáil debates*, vol. dcxviii, 25 April 2006, cols. 15–16.

47 Such criticisms had been aired intermittently ever since the original árd fheis announcement. Gay Mitchel, the Fine Gael MEP, equated Ahern's action with the statement by Louis XIV, 'l'état c'est moi' (*Irish Times*, 31 October 2005), while his party colleague Billy Timmins TD denounced the nature of the announcement as amounting to 'bread and circuses' (Dáil Debates, vol. dcix, 3 November 2005, col. 614). Liz McManus TD, deputy leader of the Labour party, was also critical, and suggested that the arrangements amounted to Fianna Fáil 'trying to claim Irish history as their own'. *Irish Times*, 18 February 2006.

48 See the *Irish Times* and *Irish Independent* 14 April 2006.

49 *Evening Echo*, 13 April 2004. The series of articles in the *Echo* during the week prior to the parade are particularly interesting.

50 See, for example, his speech on 6 April at the unveiling at the Curragh camp of a granite stone honouring the signatories of the Proclamation. Therein he re-iterated one of the principal motifs of the commemoration, that is, the role of defence forces, through the United Nations, in assisting other small war-torn nations 'to achieve the peace and freedom which we ourselves long sought'. See the 'Speeches' section of the Department of Defence website, www.defence.ie.

51 See the *Village*, 13–19 April 2006, for an article by Vincent Browne on O'Dea's role.

52 *Irish Times*, 30 March 2006.

53 A brief report of the speech can be found in the *Irish Examiner*, 6 May 2006. In addition to these ministerial level interventions one should also note that numerous Fianna Fáil cumann arranged commemorative events at various locations around the country, as did constituency organisations for the other political parties.

54 See his article in the *Irish Times*, Tuesday 11 April, wherein he described as 'self-indulgent' attempts to 'rubbish' the 'patriotism or sacrifices' of the insurgents. 'In a liberal democracy such as ours,' he wrote, 'there are no mandates from history' – a reference, possibly, to the 'dead generations' cited by the Proclamation as well as the more obvious target, Provisional Sinn Féin.

55 See the insightful article by Pól Ó Muirí in the *Irish Times* 28 October 2005, which noted the discomfiture of the opposition parties in the wake of Ahern's árd fheis speech, and the fact that there existed 'a constituency who are far more comfortable wearing the green than respectable newspapers might have us believe'. Also the article on the same theme by Eoin Ó Murchu in the *Village*, 13–19 April 2006.

56 The speech can be accessed in the 'News' section of the party's website, www.finegael.ie.

57 *Evening Echo*, 14 April 2006. Note should also be made here of the party's decision to mark the centenary of the foundation of Sinn Féin in 1906, as well as the formation in October 2006 by its members of the Collins 22 society, whose function was to preserve the memory of Michael Collins. See the *Irish Times*, 26 November 2005.

58 See the 'Foreword' by Pat Rabbitte in the collection of essays, *Liberty 1916–2006*, edited by Pádraig Yeates and jointly produced by the Labour party and SIPTU, April 2006, p. 5.

59 It is worth noting here that some weeks after the Easter commemoration events, SIPTU announced that it was to assist in the funding of a feature film on the life of James Connolly (*Irish Times*, 13 May 2006 and *Village*, 1–7 June 2006). A full listing of the activities undertaken under the auspices of the Liberty project can be found in the 'Campaigns' section of the Labour party's website, www.labour.ie. The SDLP was the only party with elected representatives in Northern Ireland to send a full delegation, including its party leader, to the parade. Finally, one should note the good-humoured re-enactment of the march of the Irish Citizen Army from Liberty Hall to the GPO, undertaken on Monday 17 April by the Dublin City Pavement Pageants Collective, with the willing participation of Labour TDs Liz McManus and Joe Costello, and the independent TD Tony Gregory.

60 *Irish Times*, 18 February 2006. The call was echoed by the Conservative party in Britain, *Belfast Telegraph*, 3 April 2006.

61 *Irish Independent*, 23 February 2006

62 See, for example, O'Riordan, Manus and Devine, Francis, *James Connolly, Liberty Hall and the 1916 Rising*, ILHS, Studies in Irish labour history no 11, Dublin, 2006, and O'Riordan, Manus, *James Connolly re-assessed: the Irish and European context*, Aubane, Cork, 2006.

63 See the comments by the party's leader, Trevor Sergeant, during his address to the party's annual conference, that the government was a 'disgrace to the men and women of 1916 and the principles of sovereignty and equality for which they died'. *Irish Independent*, 25 March 2006.

64 *Irish Examiner*, 17 April 2006.

65 *Dáil Debates*, vol. dcxv, 23 February 2006, cols. 967–68.

66   *Ibid.*, vol. dcxviii, 25 April 2006, col. 15.

67   During the spring of 2006 *An Phoblacht*, the party's newspaper, noted the activities undertaken to mark the Rising, although more attention was devoted to the party's commemoration of the twenty fifth anniversary of the hunger strikes of 1981.

68   *Irish Times*, 4 February 2006.

69   *Irish Times*, 9 February 2006.

70   *Irish Independent*, 17 March 2006.

71   *Irish Times*, 11 February 2006.

72   *Sunday Independent*, 26 February 2006.

73   *Ibid.*, 16 April 2004.

74   *Evening Echo*, 11 April 2006.

75   *Sunday Independent*, 16 April 2006.

76   The party was represented by 2 MPs, a TD and an MEP.

77   *Sunday Independent*, 19 February 2006.

78   *Dáil Debates*, vol. dcxviii, 25 April 2006, col. 12. A less sympathetic response to the predicament of the provisional movement when faced by the state's ceremonies was articulated by Fine Gael Senator Brian Hayes, who remarked: 'Was it not great to see, for once, the goose stepping black beret brigade put into the second division?' *Seanad Debates*, vol. clxxxiii, 26 April 2006, col. 674.

79   Connell, Joseph, *Where's where in Dublin: a directory of historic locations, 1913–23*, Four Courts, Dublin, 2006.

80   In Carlow, for example, a ceremony was held to honour the memory of Michael O'Hanrahan, one of the executed leaders of 1916 and a native of the town. It consisted of a laying of wreaths, the playing of the national anthem and the last post, and a minute's silence. See *Carlow People*, 30 May 2006 and the *Nationalist*, 2 June 2006.

81   Reviews of the books mentioned here appeared in many different newspapers and journals during the period in question. Among the more noteworthy are those that appeared in the *Guardian*, 24 September 2005; *Irish Independent*, 15 April 2006, *Irish Times*, 13 May 2006, and *History Ireland*, vol. xiv, no. 2, March–April 2006, pp. 63–72.

82   Foy, Michael and Barton, Brian, *The Easter Rising*, Sutton, Stroud, 2004.

83   Townshend, Charles, *Easter 1916: the Irish rebellion*, Allen Lane, London, 2005.

84   Coogan, Tim Pat, *1916: the Easter Rising*, Phoenix, London, 2005.

85   Hegarty, Shane and O'Toole, Fintan, *The Irish Times book of the 1916 Rising*, Gill & Macmillan, Dublin, 2006. It is a pity that the newspaper did not see fit to re-issue its superb 1916 rebellion handbook, which contains enormous amounts of otherwise difficult to obtain source material, including transcripts of the royal commissions into the Rising and the shooting of Francis Sheehy Skeffington. The work initially appeared in 1916, before being re-issued by Mourne River press, with an introduction by Damien Kiberd, in 1998.

86   Githens-Mazer, Jonathan, *Myths and memories of the Easter Rising*, IAP, Dublin, 2006.

87   Moran, James, *Staging the Easter Rising: 1916 as theatre*, CUP, Cork, 2005.

88   Ryan, Annie, *Witness: inside the Easter Rising*, Liberties, Dublin, 2005.

89   McGee, Owen, *The IRB: the Irish Republican Brotherhood, from the Land League to Sinn Féin*, Four Courts, Dublin, 2005.

90   FitzGerald, Garret (ed.), *Desmond's Rising: memoirs 1913 to Easter 1916*, Liberties, Dublin, 2006.

91   Redmond-Howard, L.G., *Six days of the Irish republic*, Aubane, Cork, 2006. Mention might also be made here of the pamphlet, also published by Aubane, *Was 1916 a crime?*, which contains correspondence on many aspects of the Rising culled from the *Village* magazine between July and December 2005.

92   Cronin, Seán, *Our own red blood: the story of the 1916 Rising*, IFP, Dublin, 2006.

93   Ferguson, Stephen, *GPO staff in 1916*, An Post, Dublin, 2006; Jeffery, Keith, *The GPO and the Easter Rising*, IAP, Dublin, 2006. See also the *Irish News*, 6 April 2006.

94   Wheatley, Michael, *Nationalism and the Irish party: provincial Ireland 1910–1916*, OUP, Oxford, 2005; Campbell, Fergus, *Land and revolution: nationalist politics in the west of Ireland 1891–1921*, OUP, Oxford, 1921.

95   Coleman, Marie, *County Longford and the Irish revolution 1910–1923*, IAP, Dublin, 2003.

96   White, Gerry and O'Shea, Brendan, *'Baptised in blood': the formation of the Cork Brigade of the Irish Volunteers 1913–1916*, Mercier, Cork, 2005.

97   Hegarty Thorne, Kathleen, *'They put the flag a-flyin': the Roscommon Volunteers 1916–1923*, Generation, Oregon, 2005.

98   Ebenezer, Lyn, *Fron-goch and the birth of the IRA*, Gwasg Carreg Gwalch, Llanrwst, 2006. Even though it can hardly be said to have been inspired by the anniversary of the Rising, having been many years in gestation, the utmost praise is also due here for Seán McConville's stunning *Irish political prisoners, 1848–1922: theatres of war*, Routledge, London, 2003, which has four chapters (pp. 405–605) dealing with aspects of the prison experiences, in all their varied incarnations, of the Easter insurgents.

99   Nevin, Donal, *James Connolly: 'a full life'*, Gill & Macmillan, Dublin, 2005.

100   Dudley Edwards, Ruth, *Patrick Pearse: the triumph of failure*, IAP, Dublin, 2006.

101   Henry, William, *Supreme sacrifice: the story of Éamonn Ceannt 1881–1916*, Mercier, Cork, 2005; MacAtasney, Gerard, *Seán MacDiarmada: the mind of the revolution*, Drumlin, Manorhamilton, 2004.

102   Daly, Mary E. (ed.), *Roger Casement in Irish and world history*, RIA, Dublin, 2006.

103   Ó Brolchain, Honor (ed.), Plunkett Dillon, Geraldine, *All in the blood: a memoir of the Plunkett family, the 1916 Rising and the War of Independence*, Farmar, Dublin, 2006.

104   White, Captain Jack, *Misfit: a revolutionary life*, Livewire, Dublin, 2005.

105   O'Keeffe, Jane O'Hea and O'Keeffe, Maurice, *Recollections of 1916 and its aftermath: echoes from history, Irish life and lore series*, privately published, Tralee, 2005.

106   It should be noted, also, that Queen's Belfast had, in conjunction with

Humanities Institute in UCD, organised a conference on the theme of the fiftieth anniversary commemoration of the Easter Rising in June 2005. It is understood that the papers will be published as part of a special edition of *Irish Political Studies* during 2007.

107 A large number of schools also organised events to mark the Rising. The author was privileged to address one such occasion, at Ballincollig community school, on 24 April 2006. The dignified tone of the occasion, which incorporated music and poetry readings associated with both the Rising and the First World War, was a tribute to the staff and students involved.

108 RTÉ's website, www.rte.ie, provided extended excerpts from the station's output during the 1966 commemoration. The national broadcaster also released The story of Easter Week, a compact disc containing interviews with participants in the Rising conducted by it over the years.

109 For a review of some of the radio programmes broadcast in the week leading up to the military parade see the *Irish Times*, 15 April 2006.

110 See, for example, the editorials in the *Irish Times*, 11 February 2006, the *Sunday Independent*, 12 February, *Irish Independent*, 15 April, and the hostile tenor of successive numbers of the Irish edition of the *Sunday Times* in February.

111 The glowing editorials in the *Sunday Times*, 16 April, and the *Irish Independent* on Monday 17 April are particularly interesting examples of this change.

112 For an excellent piece on the arts and the Rising see the article by Ian Kilroy in the *Irish Examiner*, 13 April 2006. Also see Liam Ó Muirthile's article in the same edition on the importance of the Irish language in the revolutionary era.

113 The exhibition can be accessed at www.nli.ie/1916.

114 See the interview with the author in the *Irish Times*, 20 April 2006, and the review in the *Guardian*, 29 April 2006.

115 See, for example, the *Irish Independent*, 16 March, for details of portraits by Francis Duffy of leading women of the Rising that were about to be displayed at the Art Ireland exhibition at the RDS; and *Ibid.*, 12 April, for Gerard Mannix Flynn's installation depicting the Proclamation in English, Irish, Polish, Russian, Chinese and Arabic, as displayed on Leeson Street, Dublin. At a slight tangent one should also note the release by An Post of a special commemorative stamp to mark the occasion, designed by Ger Garland and incorporating an image of the GPO.

116 See *Village*, 23–29 March and the *Sunday Times*, 16 April 2006 for more details on the background to the shooting of the film, and its re-release.

117 *Irish Times*, 11 December 2006. It appears likely that, in the build up to the centenary of the Rising, the GPO itself will be converted into a national monument dedicated to the events of 1916.

118 See reports in the press on 13 April 2006.

119 For a report on the event see the *Irish Examiner*, 10 May 2006. See also the expression of hope by Senator Labhrás Ó Murchú that Kent's remains would at some point be re-interred in 'a more appropriate and significant location'. *Seánad Debates*, vol. clxxxiii, 9 May 2006, col. 954. Note might also be made here of the marking, by Conradh na Gaeilge Trá Lí, of the

execution of Sir Roger Casement, on 3 August.

120 *Irish Times*, 19 April 2006.

121 The material can be found by following the '1916 commemorations' link on the website of the Department of the Taoiseach, www.taoiseach.gov.ie. See also the article by the Minister for Foreign Affairs, Dermot Ahern, in the *Irish Times* on Remembrance Day (11 November) 2005. The printed version of the brochure was memorable for many reasons, not the least of which was its judicious use of visual imagery to complement the text.

122 *Ibid.*

123 *Sunday Independent*, 26 February 2006.

124 See, for example, the spirited letter from Pat Muldowney of Derry, *Irish Independent*, 8 March 2006, and the measured response by Gerald Morgan of Trinity College, *Ibid.*, 21 March 2006.

125 See the request for 'reciprocity' from such unionists by Martin Mansergh, *Irish Times*, 11 February 2006, and the response from unionists in the *Irish News*, 7 March 2006.

126 The government's support for the 'Shot at Dawn' campaign, which sought pardons for serving soldiers executed by the British army during the First World War, also attracted commendation in several quarters. For an insightful discussion on the connections between Dublin in Easter Week and events on the western front see Robert Fisk's article in the London *Independent*, 30 April 2006.

127 *Evening Echo*, 11 April 2006.

128 *Irish Examiner*, 13 February 2006.

129 *Irish Examiner*, 10 April 2006.

130 A view articulated, for example, by Kevin Myers in the *Irish Times*, 1 February 2006.

131 Letter from Ernest Crosse, Chapelizod, Dublin, *Sunday Independent*, 12 February 2006. The reference to Ruth Dudley Edwards was to her column in the previous week's edition of the paper, wherein she argued that Ireland was both well, and democratically, governed in 1916.

132 *Evening Echo*, 13 April 2006, and the *Irish Independent*, 15 April 2006.

133 Brian Kennedy, Dublin 2, writing to the *Irish Independent*, 20 February 2006.

134 *Sunday Independent*, 12 February 2006.

135 *Irish Independent*, 10 May 2006.

136 Alan Ó Maonaigh, Co. Meath, writing to the *Irish Independent*, 17 April 2006.

137 *Irish Times*, 11 February 2006.

138 Thus Liz McManus TD wrote in the *Sunday Independent*, 26 February, that the absence of such a mandate was one of the most 'serious and consistent' charges that could be levelled against it.

139 *Ibid.*, 3 February 2006.

140 *Irish Times*, 4 February 2006. See also the reference by Roy Garland to 'fascist elements' within the 1916 revolutionary cohort. *Irish News*, 30 January 2006.

141 *Guardian*, 9 April 2006.

142 London *Independent*, 15 April 2006.

143 *Irish Times*, 3 February 2006.
144 Pádraic MacBheatha, Co. Meath, *Ibid.*, 7 March 2006.
145 *Ibid.*, 12 April 2006.
146 *Ibid.*, 4 February 2006.
147 *Sunday Independent*, 16 April 2006.
148 *Irish Times*, 13 March 2006.
149 *Irish Examiner*, 20 April 2006.
150 *Irish Times*, 21 April 2006
151 *Ibid.*, 4 February 2006.
152 *Ibid.*, 7 March 2006.
153 *Irish Independent*, 18 May 2006.
154 *Irish Times*, 3 February 2006.
155 *Ibid*, 15 April 2006.
156 *Irish Independent*, 18 April 2006.

INDEX